CYBER-RISK INFORMATICS

CYBER-RISK INFORMATICS

Engineering Evaluation with Data Science

MEHMET SAHINOGLU, PH.D.
Auburn University at Montgomery

Published by John Wiley & Sons, Inc., Hoboken, New Jersey
Published simultaneously in Canada

For general information on our other products and services or for technical support, please contact our
Customer Care Department within the United States at (800) 762-2974, outside the United States at
(317) 572-3993 or fax (317) 572-4002.

Wiley also publishes its books in a variety of electronic formats. Some content that appears in print may
not be available in electronic formats. For more information about Wiley products, visit our web site at
www.wiley.com.

Library of Congress Cataloging-in-Publication Data

Names: Sahinoglu, Mehmet, 1951– author.
Title: Cyber-risk informatics : engineering evaluation with data science / Mehmet Sahinoglu.
Description: Hoboken, New Jersey : John Wiley & Sons, 2016. | Includes bibliographical references and
    index. | Description based on print version record and CIP data provided by publisher; resource not viewed.
Identifiers: LCCN 2015036259 (print) | LCCN 2015032749 (ebook) | ISBN 9781119087526 (Adobe PDF) |
    ISBN 9781119087533 (ePub) | ISBN 9781119087519 (cloth)
Subjects: LCSH: Cyber intelligence (Computer security) | Computer systems–Reliability. |
    Computer software–Reliability. | Computer networks–Security measures–Data processing. |
    Risk assessment–Statistical methods.
Classification: LCC QA76.9.A25 (print) | LCC QA76.9.A25 S2497 2016 (ebook) | DDC 005.8–dc23
LC record available at http://lccn.loc.gov/2015036259

Set in 10/12pt Times by SPi Global, Pondicherry, India

Printed in the United States of America

10 9 8 7 6 5 4 3 2 1

ABOUT THE COVER

The multifaceted nature of network security reminds one of the ancient fable, the parable of *The Blind Men and the Elephant*, where the blind men (or security risk researchers today) are touching the elephant (or network security) to understand what it really is or isn't, because they have never encountered an elephant before. One man touches the elephant's tusk, and the other its side, while another touches its tail and yet another its trunk. When they reunite to discuss their findings, they cannot agree what the elephant looks like; such as one thought the trunk was a snake, and the other imagined a tree branch, and so it goes. Much the same happens when it comes to cyber-risk assessment and management. Network security is such a complex, multifaceted topic that cyber-risk specialists are like the veritable blind men grasping at parts and unable to understand the elephant completely. This book's intent is to provide a timely remedy to that symbolic "elephantine" metaphor's puzzle by providing a holistic-theoretical and philosophical as well as practical, user-friendly and useful, and application-oriented within a well-grounded holistic approach to network security risk assessment, such that those *blind men* will no longer be so unfamiliar with the *elephant*! The universal message here is not seeking total "security" (a perfect knowledge of the elephant by seeing it, never to happen for the blind men), however focusing on managing the "insecurity" (understanding the elephant in the best manner that the blind men could), which is what this pioneering textbook is all about.

CONTENTS

PROLOGUE

"A little neglect may breed great mischief…
For want of nail, the shoe was lost;
For want of a shoe, the horse was lost;
And for want of a horse, the rider was lost."

Benjamin Franklin, Poor Richard's Almanac 1758

"A little lack of countermeasure may breed great breach…
For want of firewall, the software was lost;
For want of software, the hardware was lost;
And for want of hardware, the user was lost."

Mehmet Sahinoglu, Cyber-Risk Informatics 2016

REVIEWS

The *Cyber-Risk Informatics* is a sequel to Dr. Sahinoglu's earlier Wiley text of 2007 and is a reinforcement of his popularized risk metric approach to assessing and managing security and reliability of cyber components and networks at large. His Cyber-Risk assurance modeling, employing math statistically sound metric approaches, from Healthcare to Cloud Computing to name a few themes that he has implemented is not to be encountered in today's many case study-based textbooks. I certainly take pride in writing a new foreword this time 8 full years later for his follow-up as I was pleased to personally recommend back in 2011 to prepare a new manuscript to incorporate all of his new findings and journal publications. The inaction of not creating this text otherwise would have left a serious void and waste of resources to reach our new generation of risk (fire) fighters to quench the widely prevalent network (forest) breaches (arsons) as the metaphor goes, if you will.

It is my distinct pleasure to highly recommend this book of multi- and transdisciplinary nature equipped with numerical methods and directly related to software application provided for the readers and students as a gluing medium to synergize all the necessary components of research from Testing to Simulation and from Security Assessment to Cloud Computing and hands-on lab practices. His goal to emphasize the strong link between the academic and corporate worlds that complement one another is well justified. I strongly recommend anyone eager to learn new depths in Cyber-Risk modeling to visit this museum of knowledge that will become a scientific classic to refer to in the decades ahead.

In Memoriam: The academic world with great sadness has lost Professor CV Ramamoorthy on March 9, 2016 to eternity at 90; however his spectacular deeds and unforgettable selfless enlightenments of all scholars around the world will never get lost, and his ever-smiling countenance full of wisdom will always be remembered endlessly at every occasion. A good man and gentleman, who helped many when they were in down times, has proudly made his journey. He was a gentle guide and kind mentor to countless and will be dearly missed. May he rest in peace!

Posthumously To: Dearest Professor Ramamoorthy, This book would have been in your masterful palms adorned and enriched with your natural, humbling observance had you in good health prevailed since the book's prompt delivery was arranged to be sent to you by WILEY. You still will receive it. I would be remiss if I did not quote your timeless and wonderfully crafted e-mail related to the essence of a textbook you encouraged me to compose when you said this project was a must-do. Forever Gratefully!

Dear Prof. Mehmet,
Wonderful information. The topic you are discussing is most important and timely. Please compose an excellent text into an easy to follow sequence of the critical ideas in your presentation—for the layman, to a graduate engineer, and a practicing entrepreneur or financial banker. As I mentioned before, you have the God-given talent in conveying in a very comprehensible form the complex ideas people often find difficult to simplify. I am forwarding this recommendation to John Wiley publisher, Dr. Brett Kurzman of John Wiley to entice you to develop this project. Warmest Regards. Sincerely / RAM

C. V. Ramamoorthy, M.S./Ph.D., Harvard University in EE and Applied Math (Computer Science) Distinguished Professor (Emeritus) of Computer Sciences and Electrical Engineering at the University of California at Berkeley, California. His awards are not limited to IEEE Life Fellow, SDPS Fellow and SR Research Fellow of the ICC Institute at the University of Texas, Austin; Honorary Doctorate in Taiwan and many universities around the world; Editor-in-Chief of *IEEE Transactions on Software Engineering* and *International Journal of Software Engineering and Artificial Intelligence* and *IEEE Transactions on Knowledge and Data Engineering*; Coeditor-in-Chief of the *International Journal of Systems Integration* and of the *Journal of the Society of Design and Process Science*; Distinguished Scholar Award, Society for Design & Process Science, 1995; IEEE Richard E. Merwin Award, 1993; IEEE Computer Society Meritorious Service Award, 1991; IEEE Computer Society Taylor Booth Award, 1990; IEEE Computer Society Outstanding Award, 1987; IEEE Centennial Medal, 1984; Fellow, IEEE, 1978; IEEE Computer Society, Special Education Award, 1978; IEEE Computer Society, Honor Roll Award, 1974; Admiral Grace Hopper Chair, Naval Postgraduate School and others.

The critical status of cybersecurity in today's connected world is self-evident from countless unwanted security breaches in all walks of life. The *Cyber-Risk Informatics* has many interesting discussions and illustrative examples that will present students and other researchers an overview to understand the importance of this area. Furthermore, this book, in addition to examples, presents several computational and intellectual challenges to students and other researchers in this area. The new text on cyber assurance modeling proceeds with a good foundation in mathematics and statistics and culminates to game-theoretic risk computing (including the sensory networks), as well as simulation-based best practices and continues with the popular topic, such as Cloud Computing, in terms of its performance characteristics. This text finally offers the students and researchers a chance to learn enough about the hands-on lab practices to help land a decent cybersecurity job. These building blocks click well with synergy while carefully executed through plenty of examples and screenshots. It is a useful reference text for students and researchers taking courses in search for cybersecurity metrics and risk management methods given the lack of technical resources in this area.

S. S. Iyengar, Ph.D., Director and Ryder Professor, Department of Computer Science FIU School of Computing and Information Sciences, Miami, FL. His awards are not limited to IEEE Fellow, ACM Fellow, AAAS Fellow, and National Academy of Inventors Fellow; Recipient of Florida Innovation Award; The Association of Scientists and Developers and Faculty Award (India); Distinguished Service Award (LSU); Distinguished Research Award (China); IEEE Computer Society Technical Achievement Award; IEEE Computer Society Meritorious Award; IEEE Computer Society Golden Core Membership; LSU Prestigious Distinguished Research Master Award; IEEE Distinguished Visitor, NASA Faculty Fellow; Editor to 16 IEEE and other journals; authored 20 books from sensors to robotics with 5 patents and numerous grants.

In my daily dealings as a director of a cybersecurity center of national importance and as an academician, I have felt the need for a book that gives me foundations and tools to deal with important issues on risk assessment in cybersecurity. Not only I but my many peers across the country have felt the void of a pedagogical resource that combines building blocks of quantitative concepts and practice of risk assessment. This much needed book fills a void in the cybersecurity field. The field of cybersecurity has advanced at a very rapid pace, but the theory and pedagogical components have not kept pace with this advance. This is perhaps the first book that first gives the fundamentals of risk assessment, much needed statistical foundations, network principles, reliability, game-theoretic foundations, etc. and presents it an easy-to-understand manner without compromising the rigor of the field. The book will be very useful to layman and practitioners in the cybersecurity arena, especially in regard to the hands-on lab exercises, as in Chapter 10 and full Java-assisted applets in the Cyber-Risk Solver website with a solution set.

I know that this book will be on my desk within easy reach. I can find no other person better qualified than Professor Mehmet Sahinoglu to address the very important areas of quantitative risk assessment. Professor Sahinoglu brings the best of his academic expertise and 35 years of experience in the field to present a unique balance of theory, practice, and research in this book. The pedagogical components including examples and lab exercises make this book unique and exemplary.

Vir V. Phoha, Ph.D., formerly Director of Center for Secure Cyberspace, College of Engineering, Louisiana Tech University, Ruston, LA; currently Professor of Electrical Engineering and Computer Science, L.C. Smith College of Engineering and Computer Science, Syracuse University, Syracuse, NY.

This may be the first book of its kind in a long time—one that brings real engineering and science back into the world of Cyber-Risk assessments. One of the growing challenges in the world of security today is simply to arrive at a concrete definition of risk. There are literally thousands of books written on or related to the subject of risk in the cybersecurity world. However, finding a book that describes risk in quantitative terms is nearly impossible. The modern practice of determining Cyber-Risk is instead left to the philosophical whims of qualitative deductions and long lists of gadgets and software that will surely make you cyber secure. In a time when computing power is at an all-time high, we find ourselves facing a dearth of knowledge with regard to understanding how much risk we are actually exposed to in our systems. So the question remains, "Does anybody really know what Cyber-Risks we are taking?" Certainly we will never answer that question if we continue merrily down the path of nonquantitative or quasiquantitative methods we are currently pursuing. However, we will also never be able to sleep at night actually knowing the amount of risk we are accepting in our modern and interconnected systems and whether some morning we will all wake up to a world gone mad because of a colossal cyber-attack.

Therefore, it makes sense to once again make an effort to move the Cyber-Risk assessment process back into the world of quantitative methods and concrete conclusions so that we can sleep without anxiety for the morning. Putting the science and rigor back into Cyber-Risk assessments is a great place to start and will directly influence the cyber awareness of both our military and corporate enterprises. Dr. Sahinoglu makes an excellent start at doing just that. Let the quantitative versus qualitative wars begin—again.

Joel Junker, Lt. Col. USAF (Ret.), CISSP, Vice President of Security Systems at DSD Laboratories.

This timely, must-have book provides a rigorous scientific modeling approach for conducting metrics-based quantitative risk assessments in the face of ever-increasing sophistication and ubiquity of cybersecurity threats. This collection of invaluable, thoroughly vetted work not only provides the building blocks for a solid academic foundation that helps students to be better prepared to enter the cybersecurity workforce but also provides a relevant, practical reference for the application of metrics-based quantitative risk assessments in the industry sector. The role of scientific-based quantitative cybersecurity risk assessments in the decision-making process cannot be overstated. Assuredly, while uncertainty exists in any risk assessment process attempting to evaluate a wide breadth of variables associated with threats and the vulnerabilities exposed to those threats, Dr. Sahinoglu's building blocks clearly describe how those uncertainties can be drastically reduced via a disciplined framework that can increase speed, reliability, and accuracy in a cost-effective manner. In an environment where speed, accuracy, and reliability are crucial in determining the risks associated with the vulnerabilities and respective countermeasures, it is crucial for industry to have the tools at their side to counter the threats. Dr. Sahinoglu's book does just that.

Anthony Buenger, Lt. Col. USAF (Ret.), CISSP, Chief, Cybersecurity Assurance Division, Air Force Life Cycle Management Center, Maxwell AFB, Montgomery, AL.

Prof. Sahinoglu has succeeded in authoring a groundbreaking and outstanding book that manages to combine years of fruitful expertise with the explanatory power of a well-structured text. This book stands out as a magnificent source of technical information, artistically visualized and depicted, backed up with a solid structure from beginning to end, promising anyone in the field, whether student, scholar, or analyst, a well-thought-out reading experience that comprehensively addresses every topic required in the cybersecurity field. On examining the book for the first time, we immediately decided to open up courses and workshops in August 2014 at Middle East Technical University (METU) in Ankara, Turkey, to study the topics in detail, so that our staff and students in METU's Cyber Security graduate program and METU Cyber Defense and Security Center (CyDeS) would benefit from his innovative research.

In most courses and textbooks, risk analysis has been approached from a management perspective, which is not the case in this book, which takes, rather aptly, a quantitative matrix-based approach with much concreteness and succinctness in addressing every possible factor involved in the field. As we are all familiar, cybersecurity has a self-evident interdisciplinary nature, which is reflected quite efficiently and clearly in the content and style of this book. Prof. Sahinoglu has internalized the interdisciplinary nature of the field in its all comprehensiveness and presents it to readers together with the most up-to-date information. Without any doubt, the book is destined to fill an immense gap in the cybersecurity field, with its technical resources, quantitative methods, educational extras, structure, and approach.

I am delighted to predict that the book will turn into a reference book for all students as well as the scholars at the METU Informatics Institute Cyber Security graduate program.

Nazife Baykal, Ph.D., Professor and Director of the Informatics Institute, Head of the Cyber Security Department of Informatics Institute of Middle East Technical University (METU), Ankara, Turkey; Director of METU Cyber Defense and Security Center (CyDeS); currently conducting research on Cybersecurity, Health, and Medical Informatics; and author of "Computer Networks."

This is a unique book that covers several related issues in Computer Systems like security, risk management, quality control, and reliability. Since Prof. Sahinoglu has contributed to these topics both as a teacher and a researcher, he manages to convey concepts clearly, precisely, and passionately. One of the main contributions is the quantitative approaches based on metrics analysis. This book can be useful for reference, for research, or as a textbook for advanced graduate or postgraduate courses. It could also inspire new postgraduate or Ph.D. courses on those topics.

Nestor R. Barraza, Ph.D. Professor of Computer Science at the Department of Engineering, Universidad Nacional de Tres de Febrero. He is also with the Electronics Department at the School of Engineering, University of Buenos Aires, Argentina.

In this vastly connected and rapidly moving cyber world, our ability to counter the ever-present security risks has not been able to stem the growing tide of actual cyber breaches. I am very happy to see finally a comprehensive treatment of Cyber-Risks, as contained in this readable book. Dr. Sahinoglu's work over the last 20 years has been focused on ensuring that computing devices are secure enough to be worthy of the trust of users. He has made significant contributions in this brand new area of research. One of his major earlier contributions is the Sahinoglu–Libby probability distribution model, which characterizes the behavior of failure patterns in components/networks and software systems; a set of optimal algorithm-driven stopping rules for terminating software testing; and the concept of security meters to set protective measures for certain required system security levels.

With the Sahinoglu–Libby model as a basis, Dr. Sahinoglu devised a number of surprisingly simple, practical, and yet vigorous data-analytic approaches for the analysis and prioritization of security and privacy risks. His work addresses a long-standing gap in cybersecurity—the ability to accurately measure the risk of compromises, as well as to provide discrete financial impacts of various security and privacy events while a complex system is in operation. By utilizing a multitude of quantitative modeling and estimation techniques, Dr. Sahinoglu provides the needed tools for security analysts/engineers to generate a broad array of scenarios for simulation and analysis. Moreover, his techniques can be utilized across a variety of security disciplines and domains.

I highly recommend this readable book to all people who are involved in the area of cyber-security. Typical to Dr. Sahinoglu's approach, this book, utilizing a data analytical approach, provides comprehensive coverage of the latest applied and quantitative metrics-oriented topics in Security and Reliability Modeling for risk assessment. It is indeed a very impressive work of passion, knowledge, and hard work. It is my expectation that the impact of this well-written book on academia, industry, and our highly connected society will increase greatly in the years to come as new generations of cyber-security analysts, engineers, and managers are being educated in this foundational work.

Raymond T. Yeh is a retired Professor of Computer Science and entrepreneur. He is an IEEE Life Fellow. He was the CDC Distinguished Professor at the University of Minnesota and the Chair of the Department of Computer Science at both the University of Texas at Austin and the University of Maryland at College Park. He was also the founding Editor-in-Chief of *IEEE Transactions on Software Engineering* and founder of *IEEE International Conference on Software Engineering* (ICSE).

This is a unique book on trustworthy computing that continues the series of the books on this timely popular area created by Dr. Sahinoglu. In short, the book can be characterized as the encyclopedia of the state-of-the-art cyber risk techniques and metrics based on the author's approach. Actually the book is one of the world's first and probably the widest scope books on quantitative assessment of cyber security and cyber risk issues. The scope of the book is uniquely large. In particular, it covers quantitative aspects for traditional MTBF and MTTR reliability models; quantitative assessment of network security and risk; game-theoretic approach to cyber risk assessment; modeling and simulation techniques in cyber risk assessment, and many other cutting-edge topics. The most interesting and innovative from my viewpoint is the chapter on quantitative assessment of cyber risk in cloud computing. This chapter is my favorite and is very close to my heart as a cloud computing expert.

Another very attractive aspect of the book is a unique combination of original theoretic methods for quantitative cyber risk assessment with lots of real-life examples of the tasks to be solved by those methods, lots of exercises, hand-on labs, tables and illustrations on each important concepts, methods and topics covered in the book. I do think the book is necessary for each IT student and expert, not just to read, but to very carefully study to grasp this innovative material. The book can be used for any kind of trustworthy computing classes at any university elsewhere, and also for self-education. The book positions the author Dr. Sahinoglu as a worldwide classicist in IT in general and trustworthy computing in particular.

Vladimir O. Safonov is a Professor of Computer Science at St. Petersburg University, one of the leading IT experts in Russia as a Corresponding Member of the Russian Academy of Natural Sciences and a Renowned Contributor to Science and Education at this Academy. His areas of expertise are: cloud computing, trustworthy computing, aspect-oriented programming, knowledge management, programming languages and compiler development, Java and .NET technologies, operating systems, parallel programming, software architectures. He is the author of 17 books, including three Wiley books: "Using aspect-oriented programming for trustworthy software development" (2008), "Trustworthy Compilers" (2010), and "Trustworthy Cloud Computing" (2016), and the author of over 190 articles.

PREFACE

This book is authored out of a dire necessity of merely not finding all SECURITY related core and internship topics in a textbook proper while teaching an advanced cybersecurity graduate course, for example, CSIS 6013, "Network Security and Reliability—Quantitative Metrics," in a recently new graduate degree program founded by the author and accredited in December 2010. The book also relates to CSIS 6912, "Internship: Supervised Practicum with Cyber-Industry Experience," and CSIS 6952, "Security Policy Seminar." See www.aum.edu/csis. These courses have traditionally covered various topics in Cyber-Risk Computing. However, there is no one book that covers the newest applied and quantitative metrics-oriented topics in Security and Reliability Modeling. This book utilizes a data analytical or data scientific approach rather than heuristical and ad hoc methods that most authors employ through individual case studies without scientific modeling that should apply to all cases. Data science is the extraction of knowledge from data where data scientific techniques affect research in many domains, including the biological sciences, medical informatics, healthcare, social sciences, and the humanities. From the business perspective, data science is an integral part of competitive intelligence, a newly emerging field that encompasses a number of activities, such as data mining and data analysis. Data scientists investigate complex problems through expertise in disciplines within the fields of mathematics, statistics, and computer science. Graduate-level exposure as well as a senior class level at an accredited university is a preferable background for the study of this topic. It is anticipated that the audience will be advanced undergraduate and beginning graduate students in the general area of Cybersecurity, Information Technology (a topic that also covers the practitioners), Applied/Computational Statistics, Computer Science/Engineering, or Industrial Engineering Departments for having already been exposed to courses in Security, Reliability, or Dependability. The role of a Cyber-Risk Informatics program graduate is fundamentally similar to an IT graduate, though more possessed with a keen and all-purpose motivation on multifaceted Risk and its repercussions as to how to assess and mitigate the common foe. Cyber-risk Informatics is strictly multi- and transdisciplinary in nature. For example, twenty such roles can be itemized for a Cyber-risk Informatics Scientist and/or Engineer who researches and/or builds as follows:

- Demonstrate an understanding of the technical, management, and policy aspects of cyber systems and information security.
- Identify and respond to information security challenges in distributed and embedded systems.
- Recognize the impact of security issues related to software engineering on distributed information systems.
- Assess information security risks faced by an organization and develop a response plan.
- Demonstrate an understanding of technological and human engineering problems linked to security risks.
- Assess the impact of information security policies and market developments on complex systems and organizational objectives.
- Evaluate and recommend technological tools and protocols to protect against risks.
- Mitigate system vulnerabilities and restore compromised services.
- Manage the development, acquisition, and evolution of a secure information network.
- Construct secure networked and distributed computer systems.
- Troubleshoot large-scale information networks and distributed systems.
- Establish requirements for complex security applications and translate these requirements into design architecture.
- Integrate the use of encryption technology in nonsecure and nonprivate computers and systems.
- Design and conduct research in the area of cyber systems and information security.
- Critically evaluate and apply research and reports of threats to computers and cyber systems.
- Discuss the importance of lifelong learning and professional development in information security disciplines.
- Develop an ability to apply knowledge of statistical computing and mathematics specific to the discipline.
- Develop an understanding of professional, ethical, legal, security, and social issues and responsibilities needed to communicate effectively with a range of audiences and to engage in continuing professional development.
- Develop an ability to identify and analyze user needs and take them into account in the selection, creation, evaluation, and administration of risk-conscious computer-based systems so as to effectively integrate IT-based solutions into the user environment.
- Develop understanding of industry best practices and standards in Cyber-Risk Informatics area and their application.

Primary audience (the people who will find the book a must-have, such as in academia at a graduate or senior college level and similarly CS/MIS/CIS/Cybersecurity researchers):

This is an original and one-of-a-kind metrics approach, based on the author's teaching and research expertise and his previously published books and papers. The author methodically builds from a common understanding based on previous class-tested works to introduce the reader to the current and newly innovative approaches to address the maliciously-by-human-created (rather than by-chance-occurring) threat and related cost-effective management to mitigate such risk. The approach is rational and logical and provides clear entry points for readers of varying skill sets and backgrounds. All students and practitioners (including engineers, applied statisticians, and computer analysts) in the field of Risk Assessment and Management regarding Security and Reliability Modeling are now seriously examining this new-century's popular and notorious topic due to an urgent need to learn more about the common enemy: Indefatigable Risk. How to assess it quantitatively (not only using adjectives) and how to most economically alleviate and assess/manage the risk as the trillion-dollar question as self-evident from the wasted billions of dollars caused by hacking and breach of privacy at an increasing rate? The enriched Java applets provided by the author at the book's website (www. areslimited.com) will enable the reader analyst to utilize the course-related problems with less little effort than normally required. This book aims to fill a gap in current literature by developing a golden thread from classic (and merely descriptive) approaches to risk analysis, and to more demanding rigorous quantitative approaches, and supplying the reader with common implementations and use cases. The organization of the book is planned in mastery, quickly developing a background and base of knowledge before moving into new areas of research and implementation and hands-on lab. The book offers a logical outline that provides to a broad range of readers the ability to pick up anywhere based on their level of competency and working knowledge of similar subject matters. This book aims to fill a significant gap in both lay professional and research texts in the subject area. That is, because of the way the book is developed from background to innovative research, it should reach a much broader target market than traditional academic-only texts. A major strength is that the book was developed while teaching advanced undergraduate and graduate courses by the author. This means the need is perceived from real in-class experience. The author has spent a considerable research effort on this matter evident from his peer-reviewed research and extended writings including a 2007 textbook by John Wiley and Sons, Inc. This book fills a significant gap in titles available vis-à-vis quantitative approaches to risk management and provides a fair mix of theory and application. The book also reserves the flexibility and quality of an online distant educational tool for all continents.

Secondary audience (the people who will find this book a nice-to-have support material such as industrial risk managers in multiple industry verticals dealing with complex graphs and models):

Interested and curious readers belong to this category such as positive scientists and practicing engineers on risk, from the viewpoints of security and risk-related topics or both, such as those from DHS, Mining, Ecology, Safety, etc. whose topics are covered intermittently in the book's wide-ranging applications. The book is robust and, compared to other books on the market, relatively complete given the breadth of content covered. It fills a significant gap in current texts by providing a "one-stop shop" when evaluating

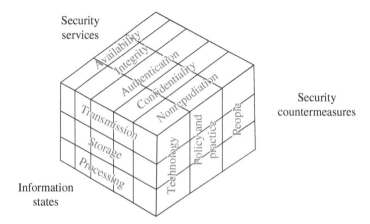

FIGURE 0.1 A summary of concepts as placed on the faces of a die. (Reprinted with courtesy of ACM from "IT 2008: Curriculum Guidelines for Undergraduate Degree Programs in Information Technology.")

strengths and weaknesses in existing approaches to risk assessment and cost management while offering innovative and viable ways to quantitative evaluation. Providing the reader with access to the reliability/security modeling and simulation tools outlined in the text is primary (source code, compiled code, or web-accessible mod/sim tool) and is a noted advantage of the book with plenty of applications.

Why this book is original for academia and cyber industry?

It is anticipated that the followers of this book will be advanced undergraduate (junior/senior) and beginning graduate students in the general area of Cybersecurity, Information Technology (which also covers the practitioners), Applied/Computational Statistics, Computer Science/Engineering, and Industrial Engineering Departments who have been exposed to Security, Reliability or Dependability curriculum. For related programs, one realizes the importance of this book's topics for Computer Assurance or Trustworthiness as well. See http://www.acm.org/education/curricula-recommendations of the Association for Computing Machinery (ACM), which breaks down Computer Science, Computer Engineering, Information Systems, Information Technology, and Software Engineering. See Figure 0.1.

Also p. 27 of http://www.acm.org//education/curricula/IT2008%20Curriculum.pdf explains the draft *Computing Curricula 2008 and Onwards*, which details below the listed concentrations in line with the proposed book's topics for the general topic of Information Technology. Also see Appendix B on pages 129–130 in the same link for descriptions of the IT Fundamentals. The following are the related topics that this book mostly examines related to the ACM curricula studies in the same reference.

IAS, Information Assurance and Security (17 core hours)

1. IAS. Fundamental Aspects (3)
2. IAS. Operational Issues (3)
3. IAS. Policy (3)
4. IAS. Attacks (2)

5. IAS. Security Domains (2)
6. IAS. Forensics (1)
7. IAS. Information States (1)
8. IAS. Security Services (1)
9. IAS. Threat Analysis Model (1)

MS. Math and Statistics for IT (38 core hours)
MS. Basic Logic (10)
MS. Discrete Probability (6)
MS. Functions, Relations, and Sets (6)
MS. Hypothesis Testing (5)
MS. Sampling and Descriptive Statistics (5)
MS. Graphs and Trees (4)
MS. Application of Math & Statistics to IT (2)

The primary purpose therefore is to inform senior undergraduate or beginning graduate students about the newest advances in the second decade of a new century on *Security and Reliability Modeling* with an index-based quantitative approach, in contrast to often encountered verbal or qualitative or subjective case histories that may become obsolete in the next few years when new cases arise. Rather than what this book is about, what is this book not about? This book is not a collection of already available routine chapters that can be found in a multitude of books, therefore avoiding repetitious and readily available encyclopedic information. It is objective and data driven and provides a real-world engagement for practicing statisticians and applied engineers. That said, a healthy comparison with earlier cited methods about how one reaches the new frontiers will be examined. Therefore, there will be a minimal duplication of review text material already encountered, such as the statistical probability distributions, and their simulations in com- pact formats, or reliability models, unless one or two of which are in close association with the innovative topics presented.

There will be a website (www.areslimited.com) that will enable the reader or student to work with hands-on-experience projects, generated in the past decade with a pains- taking, fine-tuned effort and high precision detail. Additionally there are very few books that cover the quantitative metrics-oriented Security and Risk-related topics. This new proposition however is unique as it is purely statistical data oriented, employing computationally intensive techniques such as Monte Carlo simulation, in prestigious journals on assurance sciences. It is also expected that practicing engineers will be able to use the book to benefit their own case studies, examples, and projects by using the meticulously prepared project-website that accompanies the book. A detailed solutions manual and Power point slides will be prepared for both the instructors and students' use at www.wiley.com/go/sahinoglu/informatics. Therefore, there will be an "Exercise Solution Manual", "Power point slides", and JAVA-ready-to-go applications at www. areslimited.com that are different than what other textbooks provide. Moreover, the author has a well-thought-out approach for introducing the topics in the book. This is not a verbal casebook as frequently observed in textbooks that cite "what and how" in a case study with next to none of Engineering and data-scientific modelling.

The book contains a lot of information in the area of quantitative risk assessment that simply does not appear in other books that display none other than scant touches sporadically. Since the topics covered in this book are relatively new, there is much originality contained in this vivid and dynamic book. Many of the topics within the book are cutting-edge research and have applications currently being developed (or already being implemented). A thorough screening of the book media on the web clarified that no other work goes into details as such, other than case histories and general mathematical or statistical theorems without any ready-to-use applications presented before you to be used immediately. In other words, the vast majority of books available on the market do not allow self-inspired creativity because of a lack of scalability, versatility, and programmability into different disciplines. That is, these case-history specialized and one-way-street books lack interdisciplinary patterns. The author believes that the introduction of Chapter 1 needs to be comprehensive but not exhaustive in its review for the book, since there is a good amount of coverage of these standard topics elsewhere in the literature. However through the following chapters, there are many advanced areas discussed throughout the book, requiring more than a hand calculator as in most College Business and Science programs. This aspect should rather be regarded a strength to capture many new emerging concepts and ideas and therefore provides an author-facilitated web access to implement these ideas. The author believes a Cybersecurity curriculum (rather, lack of it in the light of the current fast-paced *cyber cold wars* between the leading cyber powers) is a fast-growing area with many changes and new advancements. The concepts described in this book are relevant and important for individuals interested in computer security and quantitative risk assessment.

Would any supplementary material, for example, a supporting website, be necessary or useful?

Yes, there will be a website to which readers are expected have access so that they could run the applications discussed in the book to solve homework and project problems (www.areslimited.com). It is important for the readers to be able to apply the methodology in the book to really understand the concepts. In addition, the author has the reader follow up with many examples throughout the book as tested while decade-long teaching this material from his notes and a similar-purpose book he published nine years earlier. The book-specific website, www.areslimited.com also will usefully provide the data sets in the examples and any relevant exercises in the "Exercise Solution Manual". To recap, competitive and comparative publications so far in the market generally:

- Approach the problem from roughly estimating with high degrees of error (e.g., qualitative inputs are mapped as quantitative values effectively creating a qualitative model with error rates based on human intuition and judgment call, not supported by statistical sciences-based data analysis).
- Are generally confined to very specific industry segments and use cases, for example, insurance, finance, project management, etc.
- Do not provide the rich flexibility of the author's approach for textbook teaching with Java applications.

Miscellaneous:

Note that IEEE, IEE, Informs, libraries of all academic institutions, IT companies, USAF, and DHS, to name a few, can be inferred as potential readers of this book.

Additionally, the e-book may be popular. Also information can be supplied to the journals that are relevant to the subject matter per Library of Congress. The following short list of library materials (journals, magazines, and the like) on Cybersecurity risk related to the book content of the Cyber-Risk Informatics will be relevant with many more pertinent available:

1. *IEEE Privacy and Security*
2. *IEEE Reliability*
3. *IEEE Transactions on Software Engineering*
4. *IEEE Transactions on Information Forensics and Security*
5. *IEEE Cloud Computing Magazine* and *IEEE Transactions on Cloud Computing*
6. *Network Security*
7. *Infosecurity*
8. *Computer Fraud & Security*
9. *Future Generation Computer Systems*
10. *International Journal of Computers, Information Technology and Engineering*
11. *Cloud Computing Journal*

The Information Technology discipline akin to Cyber-Risk Informatics can be illustrated by http://www.acm.org/education/curricula/IT2008%20Curriculum.pdf diagram as observed on page 19 of the same ACM reference. Overarching the entire foundation and pillars are information assurance and security, and professionalism with which this book deals.

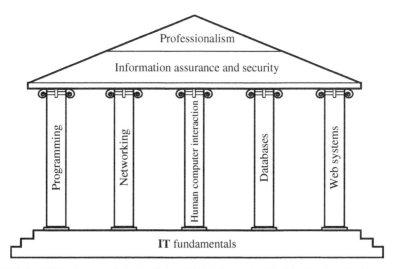

FIGURE 0.2   IT Fundamentals in the Cyber-Risk Informatics World. (Reprinted with courtesy of ACM from "IT 2008: Curriculum Guidelines for Undergraduate Degree Programs in Information Technology.")

While Figure 0.2 does not depict all facets of IT, it helps to describe the relations between the key components. The multifaceted nature of network security recalls an ancient fable about blind men and an elephant where the blind men (security researchers) are touching the elephant to make sense of it and understand since they have never heard of elephants or seen them. Our story resembles that; fortunately we are not that "blind" anymore.

ACKNOWLEDGMENTS AND DEDICATION

I wholeheartedly acknowledge my gratitude to *distinguished experts* who opinionated in the Reviews section. The reviews guide and shine as bright as our indispensable solar SUN!

This challenging and exciting effort in no way could culminate to a mountaintop you are witnessing today without the efforts of the following persons in more than several ways, such as editing, recommending, and also contributing to the chapters' contents:

Robert Barclay, USAF, Ret., CISSP, for his seasoned hands-on expert contributions to Chapter 10; Dr. Susan Simmons, Professor of Statistics and Mathematics at UNCW, Wilmington, NC, for SAS-related contributions to Chapter 3; S. Morton and D. Tyson (M.S. in CS from Troy University); and Preethi Vasudev, Rasika Balasurya, and Sharmila Ashokan (all three with M.S. in CSIS who served as IT employees or graduate student assistants during the writing of this book while at AUM's Informatics Institute for their important contributions at various stages with differing skills). In addition, CSIS graduate students on active duty or retired, originating from US Armed Forces, who toiled the book chapters and the homework problems and exams during 2011 to 2014 by now having graduated, are acknowledged.

Last but not least, I wish to posthumously commemorate the late Professors H. O. Hartley (founder of TAMU Statistics) and A. K. Ayoub (ECE/TAMU), both true gentlemen and my Ph.D. dissertation supervisors from 1977 to 1981 who trusted and encouraged me for Ph.D. (1977 to 1981) studies at Texas A&M, including currently Drs. M. Longnecker and L. Ringer (retired)!

Of course, I desire to honor my own family, to whom I *dedicate* this book, for their undeniably genuine support when I distracted myself at countless occasions, while they warned me promptly "to shape-up and stop worrying, and to go back to book-work!" They are no other than my wife of 33 years, Suna; my falcon-eyed sons, Hakan (20), Efe (28), and Gokturk (31) who always encouraged me to finalize what I started out with, not to leave the baby (i.e., book-to-be) in the cold outside! Thanks to all other colleagues, specifically Distinguished UC Berkeley Professor Ramamoorthy, a North Star to me and other nameless heroes and heroines for helping me convert from a solely stagnant dreamwork to this dynamic book, a "dream-come-true" product. Namely, this book was sleeping giant in my thoughts and dreams for the past 9 years ever since I published my first Wiley textbook in United States in 2007 whereas now an actively working and number-crunching dynamic product to turn your and my learning goals to "reality" on this new territory of Cybersecurity Risk Informatics, or shorter, Cyber-Risk Informatics.

The "selling" point for this book, other than its rich original and unique material as the reviewers graciously noted in a scientific context to their expert opinions, in presenting to the readers will be its usability along with its user-friendliness, and practicality by providing (i) an exercise solution manual (odd problems for the students and all for the instructors' use), (ii) PowerPoint slides to introduce the subject matter, and (iii) Applets' website to help students resolve the project-related assignments. So I may say Godspeed and happy sailing to those who want to visit new fjords of knowledge in the postinformation age when information delivery is no longer a simple routine action, but caught in a deluge; however also no longer smooth but with rocky roadblocks we call security and privacy risks. Last but not the least; the book author, Dr. M. Sahinoglu, candidly thanks Brett Kurzman and Kathleen Pagliaro, and their team from Wiley Inc. at Hoboken, N.J., USA as well as Anumita Gupta and her team at Wiley–India for their professional guidance and hard work.

ABOUT THE AUTHOR

Dr. M. Sahinoglu, Professor Emeritus from DEU and METU, Ankara, Turkey (1999), and formerly the Distinguished Professor of AUM (2008), is the founder of the Informatics Institute (2009) and its SACS-accredited (2010) and National Security Agency (NSA)-certified (2013) Cybersystems and Information Security (CSIS) flagship graduate program (the first such full degree program in Southeastern United States) at Auburn University's metropolitan campus at Montgomery, Alabama. Formerly, he is the founder Dean of Arts and Sciences, the founder Chair of the Department of (Computational) Statistics at DEU/Izmir (1992–1997), the visiting Fulbright and NATO Scholar at Purdue University (1989–1990, 1997–1998) and Case Western Reserve University (1998–1999), and the Eminent Scholar and Computer Science Department's Chair-Professor at the Troy University Montgomery campus (1999–2008); Dr. Sahinoglu has a BSEE from METU/Ankara (1973), MSEE from the University of Manchester, UK (1975), and Ph.D. in ECE and Statistics from Texas A&M University (1981). Dr. Sahinoglu taught at Texas A&M University (1978–1981), METU/Ankara (1982–1992) and DEU/Izmir (1992–1997), Purdue University (1989–1990, 1997–1998), CWRU (1998–1999), Troy University at Montgomery (1999–2008), and AUM (2008–). He is the recipient of Microsoft's Trustworthy Computing Curriculum (TCC) award as one of 14 in the world (2006) and is a fellow member of SDPS (www.sdpsnet.org), IEEE Senior Life member (www.ieee.org), and an elected member of ISI (www.isi-web.org) and 35 year-long member of ASA (www.amstat.org) and its section on Risk Analysis; Dr. Sahinoglu's journal articles titled "Network Reliability Evaluation" and "CLOUD Computing" appearing in Wiley Interdisciplinary Reviews (WIREs) stayed atop the most accessed in 2010–2012. He is the 2015 and 2016 Silver Medal co-recipient of the U.S. Defense Acquisition University (DAU) Hirsch Research Paper Competition Award nationwide regarding Cybersecurity and Digital Forensics topics.

Dr. Sahinoglu has recently established a Cyber-Security Lab at AUM's Informatics Institute (2014). He is the recipient of the "Software Engineering Society Excellence in

Leadership" award presented at the *Twelfth Transdisciplinary Conference Workshop on Integrated Design and Process Science: Informatics and Cyberspace* in Montgomery, Alabama, in November 2009 that he coorganized. He is the author of the textbook titled *Trustworthy Computing* (2007) and a new text titled *Cyber-Risk Informatics* (2016) by John Wiley & Sons, Inc. and more than 60 journal and 130 peer-reviewed proceedings articles and 20 project grants since 1982. He independently cocreated the "Sahinoglu & Libby Probability Distribution (1981)" with Dr. Libby and also derived "Compound Poisson Software Reliability Model & Stopping Rule in Software Testing (1995)" in hardware and software reliability domains and most recently "Security Meter Quantitative Risk Assessment and Management (2000)" algorithms and "CLOURAM (CLOUD Risk Assessor and Manager) 2006."

He authored four memoirs-based social style books: *Wrist-Fight of the Giants: Japan & USA* (1992), *Made in China/Made in Japan* (1993), *Dreaming America* (2004) all three in Turkish, and recently *Raindrops on My Life's Umbrella* (2016) in English with Amazon self-publishing and Kindle. Dr. Sahinoglu has also worked for an extended time as a simultaneous interpreter in national and international conferences as a hobby beside improving his both technical and social written and spoken German, French, Italian and Spanish in addition to his native Turkish and current daily language, English. He has been invited by Turkish State and Private TV in the 1990s and 2000s and NPR in Alabama, United States, locally on educational topics since 1999 including the topics about his textbooks and public-related cybersecurity issues to help the listening area on cybersecurity awareness.

1

METRICS, STATISTICAL QUALITY CONTROL, AND BASIC RELIABILITY IN CYBER-RISK

LEARNING OBJECTIVES

- Operating characteristic curves and Acceptance Sampling in quality control
- User-friendly Pedagogue applications for component and system reliability fundamentals including major software reliability techniques
- Basic reliability concepts and their equations
- Popular statistical distributions used in reliability and their Monte Carlo (MC) simulators

---

1.1 DETERMINISTIC AND STOCHASTIC CYBER-RISK METRICS

Informatics is the study of automation of information, and it is derived from the merging of two concepts, *information* and *automatics*. The first part of Cyber-Risk Informatics, that is, cyber, is derived from the ancient Hellenic word "kybernesis" (or cybernetics, the science of communications and automatic control systems in both machines and living things) to mean to "control skills," later evolving to the Latin word "gubernare," which is "govern" in English. Cyber-Risk Informatics is, therefore, control or governance of information risk in the computing world in an automated way. In today's cyber-risk world, there exist as many metric definitions as there are celestial suns in the universe mainly due to a lack of standardization. We will focus on the software science metrics in this chapter since the hardware metrics will be mostly computer and electrical, and more importantly, traditional semiconductor engineering-oriented metrics that would simply be beyond the scope of this book. There also exist those deterministic metrics, such as Halstead's software science metrics, whose basis was how good a compiler would process the source code to produce an object program. Research has shown that Halstead's primitive measures or metrics were derived from the language constituents that the

Cyber-Risk Informatics: Engineering Evaluation with Data Science, First Edition. Mehmet Sahinoglu.
© 2016 John Wiley & Sons, Inc. Published 2016 by John Wiley & Sons, Inc.
Companion website: www.wiley.com/go/sahinoglu/informatics

compiler would work with so as to transform the program from a higher-level language to the appropriate machine code. In a deterministic world, there are varying measures of program size from line of code (LOC) to the metrics of style and statement, such as lexical metrics and control flow graph metrics. Halstead's software science metrics were divided into two distinct sets: primitive (e.g., cardinality) and derived (e.g., vocabulary or length) metrics. These metrics have never been validated and therefore, not reliable, as Munson states in his book [1]: "We have every reason to believe that Halstead had his heart in the right place but the overwhelming majority of these metrics are not just woven out of whole cloth. There are some real conceptual problems with those metrics...."

Each of the Halstead's metrics theoretically represents a unique program attribute. This being the case, there should be a distinct source of variance contributed by each of the metrics when measuring a program at work. This is simply not the case. The four primitive metrics of operator and operand count account for essentially the variation in all of the rest of the metrics. There are also other deterministic software metrics widely used, such as product defect rate and test defect rate [2]. Recently many different methods have been proposed for software risk assessment combining these deterministic measures [3]. These are much like Halstead's metrics, which do not address product variability within the accepted scientific math–statistical postulates of the new Computer Science, a brainchild of Alan Turing [4].

Therefore the source of variation, as we measure software attributes, is of great concern. This brings us to the source quality issues containing of systematic, intrinsic, and measurement errors. Moreover, other advanced techniques, such as the multivariate principal component analysis, have been proposed [5]. These techniques still use the earlier mentioned deterministic variables as components. This chapter however will examine the statistical tests of hypothesis for comparing one software product's parameter(s) to another or simply testing if the product has stayed within the predefined standardization. However, according to the author of this book, one standard that should stay always fresh and informative is the cross product of producer's risk (alpha: Type I error probability) and consumer's risk (beta: Type II error probability), that is, both posing harm to the producer and consumer wellness, respectively. That is, the lower is the cross product of these two errors, which can be summarized as cyberware software riskiness, the more preferable is the software overall. This leads us to the statistical analyses of hypothesis testing where H_0 = software- or Cyberware-acceptable good versus H_A = software- or Cyberware-unacceptable bad, that is, within both (i) continuous and (ii) discrete domains. We will next take up this popular aspect of acceptance sampling for both cases in the case of cyberware. The following sections will also serve as a useful means of reviewing the basics of statistical hypothesis testing design and additionally lot-by-lot acceptance sampling where the objective is to assure a quality target following a "variables" procedure, not "attributes" [6]. While doing so, the quality of a cyber unit, hardware or software, is the target goal. There will also be basic reliability concepts fully covered.

1.2   STATISTICAL RISK ANALYSIS

1.2.1   Introduction to Statistical Hypotheses

A statistical hypothesis is an assumption about a population parameter. It may or may not be true. The normal way to determine whether a statistical hypothesis is true would be to examine a random sample from the population instead of examining the entire population.

If sample data are not consistent with the statistical hypothesis, the hypothesis is rejected. There are two types of statistical hypotheses as follows:

(i) Null hypothesis—denoted by H_0
(ii) Alternative hypothesis—denoted by H_1 or H_a

1.2.2 Decision Rules

The analysis plan includes decision rules for rejecting the null hypothesis [7].

P-value: The weight of evidence in support of a null hypothesis is measured by the *P*-value. If the *P*-value is less than the significance level, we reject the null hypothesis due to the simple fact when evidential summary statistic lies in the extreme.

Region of acceptance: The region of acceptance is a range of values. If the test statistic falls within the region of acceptance, the null hypothesis is not rejected. The region of acceptance is defined so that the chance of making a Type I error, α (*alpha*), is equal to the significance level.

Region of rejection (critical region): The set of values outside the region of acceptance is called the region of rejection. If the test statistic falls within the region of rejection, the null hypothesis is rejected. In such cases, we say that the hypothesis has been rejected at the level of significance, α.

By "α," we mean the "long-run" relative frequency of making a Type I error when the experiment is repeated many times under identical conditions and using the same decision rule. That is, α is the probability that we will reject a true null hypothesis using the selected test; if so 100α (in percent) is commonly referred to as the significance level. For example, it is the probability of concluding that the coin is biased (i.e., $p \neq 1/2$) when in fact it is unbiased (i.e., $p = 1/2$).

Similarly let *beta* (β) denote the probability of a Type II error; that is, β is the probability of not concluding the coin is biased when in fact it is. The size of α and β will depend on the distribution of the test statistic under the null and alternative hypothesis, respectively. The value of α and β will generally depend upon the sample size.

An important consideration in discussing the probabilities of Type II errors is the "degree of falseness" of a false null hypothesis. In a given experiment, the null hypothesis may be declared false when it is nearly true. However, if the null hypothesis is grossly false (such as hypothesizing that a probability is taken $1/2$ when is actually 1.0), β should be much smaller. For a given experiment testing a specific null hypothesis, the value of "$1 - \beta$" is known as the power of the test. Since the power depends on the difference between the value of the parameter specified by the null hypothesis and the actual value of the parameter where the latter is unknown, $1 - \beta$ should be expressed as a function of the true parameter. Such a function is known as a power function and is expressed as $1 - \beta(\theta)$, where θ represents the true parameter value.

The complementary function, $\beta(\theta)$, is known as the operating characteristic (OC) function. Once we have stated the hypothesis, selected the test statistic, set up the decision rule, and settled on a certain sample size, the values of α and β are determined. On the other hand, it would be preferable to specify the desired values of α and β and then, for a given test statistic and decision rule, determine the sample size necessary to meet the values of α and β. It is more common, however, to ensure that neither of these probabilities is too high by specifying an allowable maximum value for at least one of these probabilities (usually α). Before indicating how a test procedure is established, we plan to first discuss some ideas on selecting allowable values of α and β.

What constitutes suitably small values of α and β? This is not a question that can be answered unequivocally for all situations. Obviously the values of α and β should depend on the consequences of making Type I and II errors, respectively. For example, if we are considering the purchase of a lot of batteries for use in toys, we might hypothesize that a lot is of satisfactory quality. Actually we should state this hypothesis in more precise terms. If this hypothesis is true and we reject it, no great harm has been done since we can always wait for the next lot. Consequently, α can be relatively large (perhaps 0.25 or larger). On the other hand, if the hypothesis is false and we accept it, the result may be a large number of malfunctioning toys. Since this is very undesirable, β should be quite small (may be 0.01 or less). It should be pointed out that the supplier might feel differently about these probabilities.

When establishing a test procedure to investigate statistically the credibility of a stated hypothesis, several factors must be considered. Those factors are as follows, assuming that a clear statement of the problem has been formulated and an associated hypothesis has been stated in mathematical terms: (i) The nature of the experiment that will produce the data must be defined. (ii) The test statistic must be selected. That is, the method of analyzing the data should be specified. (iii) The nature of the critical region must be established. (iv) The size of the critical region must be chosen. (v) A value should be assigned to $\beta(\theta)$ for at least one value of θ other than the value of θ specified by H. This is equivalent to stating what difference between the hypothesized value of the parameter and the true value of the parameter must be detectable and with what probability we must be confident of detecting it. (vi) The size of the sample (i.e., the number of times the experiment will be performed) must be determined [8].

It should be clear that these steps will not always be taken in the order listed. Not all the steps are independent, and frequently it is necessary to reconsider the various steps until a reasonable test procedure is formulated. At any rate, a reference must be made to the OC function to assure that the simple size being considered is adequate.

1.2.3   One-Tailed Tests

A test of a statistical hypothesis, where the region of rejection is on only one side of the sampling distribution, is called a one-tailed test. For example, let null hypothesis state that the mean is less than or equal to 10. The alternative hypothesis would be that the mean is greater than 10:

$$H_0 : \mu \leq 10 \text{ and } H_1 : \mu > 10 \tag{1.1}$$

The region of rejection would consist of a range of numbers located on the right side of a sampling distribution. That is, a set of numbers that are greater than 10.

1.2.4   Two-Tailed Tests

A test of a statistical hypothesis, where the region of rejection is on both sides of the sampling distribution, is called a two-tailed test. For example, let the null hypothesis state that the mean is equal to 10. The alternative hypothesis would be that the mean is less than 10 or greater than 10:

$$H_0 : \mu = 10 \text{ and } H_1 : \mu \neq 10 \tag{1.2}$$

The region of rejection would consist of a range of numbers located on both sides of sampling distribution; that is, the region of rejection would consist partly of numbers that were less than 10 and partly of numbers that were greater than 10.

For the normal distribution test, P-value can be computed as follows:

$$
\begin{aligned}
&2\left[1 - \phi|Z_0|\right] \text{ for a two-tailed test} \rightarrow H_0 : \mu = \mu_0, H_1 : \mu \neq \mu_0 \\
P = &1 - \phi(Z_0) \text{ for an upper-tailed test} \rightarrow H_0 : \mu = \mu_0, H_1 : \mu > \mu_0 \\
&\emptyset(Z_0) \text{ for a lower-tailed test} \rightarrow H_0 : \mu = \mu_0, H_1 : \mu < \mu_0
\end{aligned}
\tag{1.3}
$$

where $\phi(Z)$ is the standard normal cumulative distribution function.

There is a process to determine whether to reject a null hypothesis or not, based on a sample data. This process is called hypothesis testing, and it consists of four steps [8]:

(i) *State the hypotheses.* This involves stating the null and alternative hypotheses. The H_0 and H_1 must be mutually exclusive. That is, if one is true, the other must be false.

(ii) *Formulate an analysis plan.* The analysis plan describes how to use sample data to accept or reject the null hypothesis:

    a. Significance level. Often we can choose significance levels equal to 0.01, 0.05, or 0.10, but any value between 0 and 1 can hypothetically, if not practically, be used.

    b. Test method. Normally, the test method involves a test statistic and a sampling distribution. Given a test statistic and its sampling distribution, we can assess probabilities associated with the test statistic. If the testing statistical probability is less than the significance level, the null hypothesis is rejected.

(iii) *Analyze sample data.* Using sample data do the calculations:

    a. *Test statistic* (Z_0). When the null hypothesis involves a mean or proportion, use either of the following equations to compute the test statistic (Z_0). Let $X \sim N$ (μ, σ^2) and state the hypothesis as follows:

$$H_0 : \mu = \mu_0, H_1 : \mu \neq \mu_0 \tag{1.4}$$

$$Z_0 = \sqrt{n}\left[\left(\bar{X} - \mu\right)\right]/\sigma \tag{1.5}$$

where n is the sample size, $\bar{X}$ is the sample mean, and σ is the standard deviation.

    b. *P-value.* The P-value is the probability of observing a sample statistic as extreme as the test statistic while assuming the null hypothesis true.

(iv) *Interpret the results.* If the sample findings are unlikely given the null hypothesis, we reject the null hypothesis. This involves comparing the probability (P-) value to the significance level and rejecting the null hypothesis when the P-value is less than the given significance level.

1.2.5   Decision Errors

Two types of errors can result from a hypothesis test.

Type I error: A Type I error occurs when the analyst rejects a null hypothesis when it is actually true. The probability of committing a Type I error is called the significance level. This probability is denoted by α. The probability of not committing a Type I error is called the confidence of the test $(1-\alpha)$. This is also known in industrial quality control science as the *producer's risk*. Note if "|" denotes "given that," the *producer's risk* is

$$\alpha = P\{\text{Type I error}\} = P\{\text{reject } H_0 \mid H_0 \text{ is true}\} \qquad (1.6)$$

Type II error: A Type II error occurs when the analyst fails to reject a null hypothesis when it is actually false. The probability of committing a Type II error is denoted by β. This is also known in industrial quality control science as the *consumer's risk* as follows:

$$\beta = P\{\text{Type II error}\} = P\{\text{fail to reject } H_0 \mid H_0 \text{ is false}\} \qquad (1.7)$$

The probability of not committing a Type II error is called the power of the test $(1-\beta)$:

$$(1-\beta) = P\{\text{reject } H_0 \mid H_0 \text{ is false}\} \qquad (1.8)$$

Also the power function is represented as $[1 - \beta(\theta)]$, where θ denotes the true parameter value. The $\beta(\theta)$, the complement of power function, is known as the OC function, popularly used in quality control science and engineering.

Observe Tables 1.1 and 1.2 for types of errors and their cross products.

Cost (opposite of utility) matrix is a function of α, β, and C_{ij} related to the cross product of Type I and II errors. Note if *cost value carries* a negative sign, then it denotes *utility*:

$$\Pi(\alpha,\beta,C_{ij}) = \alpha\beta(C_{11}) + (1-\alpha)\beta(C_{21}) + \alpha(1-\beta)(C_{12})$$
$$+ (1-\alpha)(1-\beta)(C_{22}); \quad 0 < \alpha,\beta < 1 \qquad (1.9)$$

TABLE 1.1   Types of Errors Associated with Hypothesis Tests

	True Situation	
Decision	Hypothesis Is True	Hypothesis Is False
Accept the hypothesis	No error (confidence $= 1 - \alpha$)	Type II error (β)
Reject the hypothesis	Type I error ($\alpha = $ significance)	No error (power $= 1 - \beta$)

TABLE 1.2   Utilities Related to the Cross Products of Types of Errors Associated with Tests of Hypotheses

	$\beta\downarrow$	$(1-\beta)\downarrow$
$\alpha\rightarrow$	C_{11}	C_{12}
$(1-\alpha)\rightarrow$	C_{21}	C_{22}

Let $P_{11}=\alpha\beta$, $P_{12}=\alpha(1-\beta)$, $P_{21}=(1-\alpha)\beta$, and $P_{22}=(1-\alpha)(1-\beta)$ where C_{11}, C_{21}, C_{12}, and C_{22} are per unit costs for accruing 1% (or 0.01 for probability measure), respectively, due to products of error (or nonerror) in Table 1.1 and Table 1.2, which overall imply

$$\alpha = P_{11} + P_{12} \tag{1.10}$$

$$\beta = P_{11} + P_{21} \tag{1.11}$$

1.2.6   Applications to One-Tailed Tests Associated with Both Type I and Type II Errors

1.2.6.1   Example 1 on Cigarette Tar Content Problem   The tar content of a certain type of cigarette has been averaging 11.0 mg per cigarette with a standard deviation of 0.8. A researcher wishes to examine a new filter that s/he suspects will increase the mean tar content beyond 11.0. That is, if μ is the mean tar content of cigarettes with the new filter, s/he claims that $\mu > 11.0\,\text{mg}$. We consider a simplest sample of $n=2$ randomly selected cigarettes having the new filter and find that the average tar content is $\bar{X} = 12.0$. Compute the Type II error probability at $\alpha = 0.10$ significant level. We can approach to the solution for this problem by working through the following steps [9]:

1. State the hypotheses: The first step is to state the null hypothesis and an alternative hypothesis:
   a. Null hypothesis: H_0: $\mu_0 = 11$
   b. Alternative hypothesis: H_1: $\mu_1 = 12 > \mu_0 = 11$
   Note that these hypotheses constitute a one-tailed test.
2. Using Qual-C software (embedded in CyberRiskSolver Java package), we can get the following graphical illustrations, that is, Figures 1.1 and 1.2:

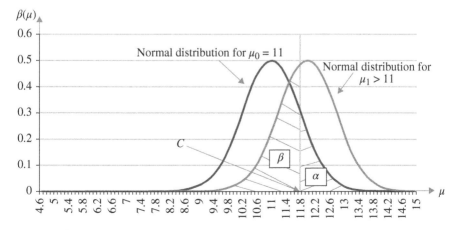

FIGURE 1.1   Illustration of one sample test with Type I and Type II errors.

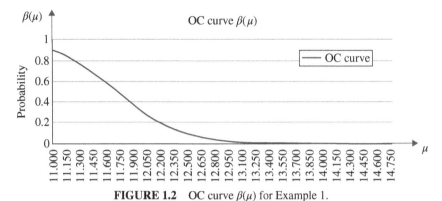

FIGURE 1.2   OC curve $\beta(\mu)$ for Example 1.

TABLE 1.3   Input Parameters and Qual-C (Software) Outcomes for Example 1

significance level	$\alpha =$	0.1
critical value	$Z(\alpha)$	1.28
Sample Size (n) =	2	
standard deviation (σ) =	0.8	
Ho : $\mu =$	$\mu 0 =$	11
	C =	11.7240773
test statistic Z	-0.487767	
β	0.31285746	

H1 : $\mu =$ $\mu 1 > \mu 0$ 12

Therefore given $\alpha = 0.10$, we can compute the $\beta = 0.313$. The probability of the Type I error, denoted by α, is equal to $\alpha = 0.10$ in this example. Also we found the probability of Type II error, when $p = 0.10$, to be $\beta = 0.313$ as illustrated in Table 1.3. The information about the probabilities of Type I and Type II error are summarized in the OC curve for $\alpha = 1 - \beta (\mu_0) = 1 - 0.9 = 0.10$ as in Figure 1.2 [10].

For any given $\mu_1 > 11.0$ we can see the OC function, OC (μ). Let's consider several different values for μ_1 and related β values for a given $\alpha = 0.10$ as follows in Table 1.4 and Table 1.5 respectively.

Also we note that if $\mu_0 = \mu_1$, then $\beta (\mu_1) \sim 0.9$ equal to $(1 - \alpha)$. For larger values of μ_1, $\beta (\mu_1) \to 0$.

1.2.6.2 Example 2 on Cyberware Riskiness, Partial Riskiness, and Nonriskiness

Suppose a cyber (hard- or software) product before release is tested for programming failures. Let $\mu_0 = 11$ (failures) where the software is approved and $\mu > \mu_0 = 11$ where the software is disapproved. If we reject H_0, that is, $\mu > 11$, the error accrued is

$P[\text{reject } H_0 \mid H_0 \text{ is true}] = \alpha$, when α (Type I error) denotes *producer's risk*.

However, if in reality, we release the software product assuming that our null hypothesis was true, while H_1 or H_a is true, then we commit Type II error, β, as follows:

$P[\text{fail to reject } H_0 \mid H_a \text{ is true}] = \beta$; then we can compute:

β (Type II error probability) denotes *consumer's risk*. Now, if we conduct an analysis such that we calculate a range of $\beta = \text{OC}(\mu)$ for H_0: $\mu = \mu_0$ H_a: $\mu > \mu_0$ as follows, that is, for a given $\alpha = 0.10$, we obtain in Table 1.4 and Table 1.5 respectively as follow.

TABLE 1.4 Power and Type II Error for the Differences, $\theta = \mu_1 - \mu_0$

$\theta = \mu_1 - \mu_0$	0	0.5	1	1.5	2	2.5	3
$\beta = OC(\theta)$	0.90	0.65	0.313	0.085	0.012	0.00085	0.00003
Power $= (1 - \beta)$	0.10	0.35	0.6871	0.915	0.988	0.99915	0.99997

TABLE 1.5 Tabulations for Figure 1.2

μ_0	μ_1	$\beta(\mu_1)$	Composite Risk: $\alpha\beta$	Power $= 1 - \beta$
11.0	11.0	0.9000	0.09000	0.10
11.0	11.5	0.6540	0.06540	0.3460
11.0	12.0	0.3129	0.03129	0.6871
11.0	12.5	0.0851	0.00851	0.9149
11.0	13.0	0.0121	0.00121	0.9879
11.0	13.5	0.00085	0.000085	0.99915
11.0	14.0	0.00003	0.000003	0.99997
11.0	14.5	0.0000	0.0	0.0
11.0	15.0	0.0000	0.0	0.0

Then, we can interpret this phenomenon as in the following argument: Given H_0: $\mu = \mu_0$ being tested with a given α (Type I error) versus a given alternative standard H_a: $\mu_1 > \mu_0$, we can estimate the overall (both producer's and consumer's combined) software risk as a combination of the following two metrics, α and β, from the OC curve. Then we define a quasi-Type III error probability as coined by the author, that is, see Table 1.5:

$$\text{Composite cyberware riskiness} = CCR = \alpha * \beta \tag{1.12}$$

In Tables 1.4 and 1.5, $n=2$, $\beta=0.3129$ for $\mu_0=11$ and choosing $\mu_1=12$ for θ, CCR$=\alpha * \beta = 0.1 * 0.3129 = 0.03129$ can be defined as *Composite Cyberware Riskiness* (CCR). Therefore Noncomposite Cyberware Riskiness (*Non-CCR* or *non-composite-cyberware-riskiness*) $= (1 - \alpha) * (1 - \beta) = 1 - \alpha - \beta + \alpha * \beta = (1 - 0.1)$ $(1 - 0.03129) = 0.872$. This leaves *Cyberware Partial Riskiness* (*CPR*) either due to Type I (producer's risk) or Type II (consumer's risk) contributions $=$ significance $*$ (power) $+$ confidence $*$ $(1 - \text{power}) = \{\alpha\,(1 - \beta) + (1 - \alpha)\,\beta\} = 0.0967$. Note, observing also Table 1.1 and Table 1.2, as follows:

$$CCR + \text{Non-CCR} + CPR = 0.03129 + 0.872 + 0.0967 = 0.99999 \approx 1.00 \tag{1.13}$$

Therefore, the lower the product of Type I and Type II error probabilities, the less severe the CCR is. On the other hand, the more the difference between the (μ_0 and μ_1) null and standard that we are testing, that is, $\mu_1 - \mu_0$, the lower will be the $\beta =$ Type II error probability and the higher will be the power ($= 1 - \beta$). If the magnitude of the Type II error probability ($= \beta$) is unacceptably large, then we must resample. If you observe Figure 1.1, then increase the "α" area such that "C" shifts to the left and "β" is reduced; power of the test $(1 - \beta)$ is favorably improved.

1.2.6.3 *Example 3 on a Cyberware Test of Hypothesis to Determine Optimal α and β*
Null hypothesis: H_0: Cyberware is functional (good and operating)
Alternative hypothesis: H_1: Cyberware is dysfunctional (bad or ill operating)

Input sample costs are $C_{11}=+\$800$ (cost loss), $C_{21}=+\$70$ (cost loss), $C_{12}=+\$200$ (cost loss), and $C_{22}=-\$400$ (utility gain) as per unit cost coefficients in order, respectively, for (i) CCR $= \alpha * \beta$, (ii) *Cyberware Partial Riskiness* (CPR_1) due to Type I $(\alpha=$ producer's risk) error $=\alpha(1-\beta)$, (iii) *Cyberware Partial Riskiness* (CPR_2) due to Type II error $(\beta=$ consumer's risk)$=(1-\alpha)\beta$, and (iv) Non-CCR $=(1-\alpha)(1-\beta)$. Solve for the optimal Type I $(\alpha=$ producer's risk) and Type II $(\beta=$ consumer's risk) error probabilities using a Neumann's game-theoretic mixed strategy algorithm examined as follows. See Chapter 5 on game-theoretic risk computing for in-depth details.

Min LOSS, subject to 14 constraints, is as follows:

$$P_{11} \; C_{11}-\text{LOSS}<0, \quad P_{21} \; C_{21}-\text{LOSS}<0, \quad P_{12} \; C_{12}-\text{LOSS}<0, \quad P_{22} \; C_{22}-\text{LOSS}<0;$$
$$P_{22} \geq P_{11}, \quad P_{22} \geq P_{12}, \quad P_{22} \geq P_{21}; \quad P_{11}<1, \quad P_{12}<1, \quad P_{11}<1, \quad P_{12}<1, \quad \text{LOSS}>\text{LOSS}_{min},$$
$P_{11}+P_{12}+P_{21}+P_{22}=1$, and finally the expected cost, $\Pi\,(\alpha, \beta, C_{ij})=P_{11}\,C_{11}+P_{21}\,C_{21}+P_{12}\,C_{12}+P_{22}\,C_{22}<0$ (denoting total \$ cost units accrued shows a positive utility gain or overall profit). If the minimum or at least utility gain assumed for an example is $-$LOSS $\leq -\$5$ or LOSS ≥ 5 (constraints 1–4) per each cell in Table 1.2, then we can set up the Linear Programming (LP) problem given the 14 game-theoretic equations with associated constraints.

The following spreadsheets show the data entry and outputs using various LP programs:

Optimal cost-associated results include utilizing Equations (1.9), (1.10), and (1.11) and solutions to the unknown vector, $[P_{ij}]=[P_{11}, P_{12}, P_{21}, P_{22}]$; $\alpha=P_{11}+P_{12}=0.006249+0.071429=0.077678$ (or 7.77%); and $\beta=P_{11}+P_{21}=0.006249+0.024999=0.031248$ (or 3.13%). Expected cost: $\Sigma P_{ij}C_{ij}=0.006245 * 800+0.07143 * 70+0.0245 * 200+0.897321 * (-400)=-\$343.93$ (Fig. 1.3), which is a favored utility gain for the overall testing plan (Fig. 1.4) by the given hypothesis.

TABLE 1.6   Input Spreadsheet for Example 3 on a Cyberware Test of Hypothesis

Enter/Edit data: Objective function coefficients. For each constraint, enter constraint coefficients, constraint relationship (<, =, >), and constraint right-hand-side value. Do not enter nonnegativity constraints.

Optimization Type: Minimize

Variable Names: [Change if Desired]	P11	P21	P12	P22	LOSS
Objective Function Coefficients:					1

			Coefficients		
Subject To:	P12	P22	LOSS	Relation(<,=,>)	Right-Hand-Side
Constraint 2				<	1
Constraint 3	1			<	1
Constraint 4		1		<	1
Constraint 5	1	1		=	1
Constraint 6		1		>	0
Constraint 7		1		>	0
Constraint 8	-1	1		>	0
Constraint 9			-1	<	0
Constraint 10			-1	<	0
Constraint 11	200		-1	<	0
Constraint 12		-400	-1	<	0
Constraint 13			1	>	5
Constraint 14	200	-400		<	0

Enter/edit data: Objective function coefficients. For each constraint, enter constraint coefficients, constraint relationship (<, =, >), and constraint right-hand side value. Do not enter nonnegativity constraints.

TABLE 1.7   Output Spreadsheet for Example 3 on a Cyberware Test of Hypothesis

```
Objective Function Value =              5.000

        Variable              Value              Reduced Costs
     --------------        --------------        --------------

          P11                0.006                  0.000
          P21                0.071                  0.000
          P12                0.025                  0.000
          P22                0.897                  0.000
          LOSS               5.000                  0.000


        Constraint         Slack/Surplus           Dual Prices
     --------------        --------------        --------------

           1                 0.994                  0.000
           2                 0.929                  0.000
           3                 0.975                  0.000
           4                 0.103                  0.000
           5                 0.000                  0.000
           6                 0.891                  0.000
           7                 0.826                  0.000
           8                 0.872                  0.000
```

TABLE 1.8   Output Spreadsheet for Example 3 Using EXCEL LP Solver Algorithm

					C11	800
MIN	6.000001				C21	70
					C12	200
P11	P21	P12	P22	LOSS	C22	−400
0.00625	0.071428586	0.025	0.897322	5		
P11	0.0062500000		<	1		
P21	0.071428586		<	1		
P12	0.025		<	1		
P22	0.897322414		<	1		
Constraint 1	−343.9289647		<	0		
Constraint 2	1.000001		Equal	1		
Constraint 3	0.897322414		>	0.00625		
Constraint 4	0.897322414		>	0.071429		
Constraint 5	0.897322414		>	0.025		
Constraint 6	0		<	0		
Constraint 7	1E-06		<	0		
Constraint 8	0		<	0		
Constraint 9	−363.9289657		<	0		
Constraint 10	5		>	5		
Constraint 11	5		<	10		

MIN is the objective function; C_{11}, C_{12}, C_{21}, C_{22} are the cost coefficients which are indicated in bold face.

1.2.7   Applications to Two-Tailed Tests (Normal Distribution Assumption)

1.2.7.1   Example 3 on Hardware Testing Scores   Suppose that in the past the built-in self-testing (BIST) hardware testing scores indicated a mean of about 75 points (or failures). Assume that there has been an intervention with the chip development and we really do not

TABLE 1.9   JAVA Input Table for Example 3

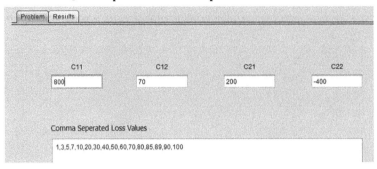

TABLE 1.10   Output Spreadsheet for Example 3 using Java Coding

```
72        float[] c10 = {0.0f,70.0f,0.0f,0.0f,-1.0f};//0 70 -0  0 -1 < 0
73        cons[9] = new Constraint(c10, 0.0f, 0);
74
75        float[] c11  = {0.0f,0.0f,200.0f,0.0f,-1.0f}; //0 0  200 0 -1 < 0
76        cons[10] = new Constraint(c11, 0.0f, 0);
77
78        float[] c12 = {0.0f,0.0f,0.0f,-400.0f,-1.0f}; //0 0  0 -400 -1 < 0
79        cons[11] = new Constraint(c12, 0.0f, 0);
80
81        float[] c13 =  {0.0f,0.0f,0.0f,0.0f,1.0f}; //0 0 0 0 1 > 5
82        cons[12] = new Constraint(c13, 5.0f, 1);
83
84        float[] c14 = {800.0f,70.0f,200.0f,-400.0f,0.0f};//800 70 200 -400 0 < 0
85        cons[13] = new Constraint(c14, 0.0f, 0);
```

Output - security (run)

```
run:
x1 = 0.006249994
x2 = 0.07142854
x3 = 0.024999976
x4 = 0.89732134
x5 = 5.0
BUILD SUCCESSFUL (total time: 2 seconds)
```

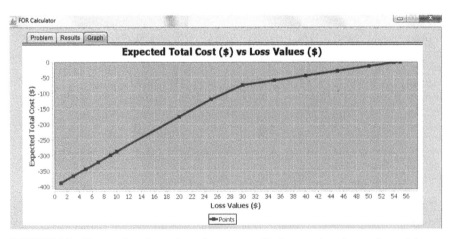

FIGURE 1.3   Expected total cost (negative means utility) versus loss (game-theoretic) cost.

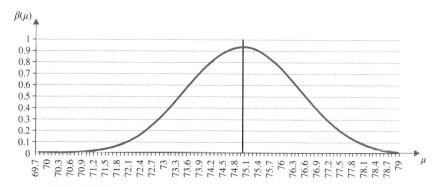

FIGURE 1.4 $\beta(\mu) = OC(\mu)$ illustration with H_0: $\mu = 75$ versus H_1: $\mu \neq 75$.

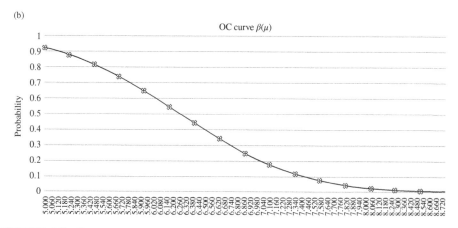

FIGURE 1.5 Type I and II errors for Example 3 using Tables 1.6, 1.7, 1.8, 1.9, and 1.10 and Figure 1.3.

know whether scores will increase, decrease, or stay about the same. Thus we wish to test the null hypothesis H_0: $\mu = 75$ against the two-sided alternative H_1: $\mu \neq 75$. Assume that test scores are normally distributed with mean $\mu = 75$ and variance $\sigma = 1$. Also, the significance level is α. See Figures 1.4 and 1.5.

1. In this example, first, we have to state the null hypothesis and an alternative hypothesis as follows: $H_0: \mu = 75$ and $H_1: \mu \neq 75$.
2. We can observe the OC curve (Fig. 1.4) for any given μ_1 not equal to 75.

Suppose we wish to test a hypothesis about the mean, μ, of a normal population. More specifically, suppose we have a random variable, which can be considered to have a normal distribution, and we want to test the hypothesis $H: \mu = \mu_0$. If the value of σ^2 (variance) is unknown and a random sample is observed from the population, the test statistic "t" is used, where n is the sample size and $\bar{x}$ and s^2 are the sample mean and variance, respectively. Thus the test compares the difference between the sample mean and the hypothesized value μ_0 with the standard deviation of $\bar{x}$ (mean of x). If this difference is large relative to $s_{\bar{x}}$ (standard error), we would want to reject the hypothesis. Otherwise, we have no reason to reject. See Figures 1.6 and 1.7 for an application regarding one- and two-tailed t-tests.

To set up the critical region, we note that if the hypothesis is true, the test statistic t will have a "student's t-distribution" with $v = n - 1$ degrees of freedom and "100α" % significance.

Case 1

$H: \mu = \mu_0; A: \mu \neq \mu_0$

For the simple null hypothesis and the two-sided alternative (A), reject the null (H) if

$$t \leq -t_{(1-\alpha/2)(n-1)} \quad \text{or} \quad t \geq t_{(1-\alpha/2)(n-1)} \tag{1.14}$$

where t_v is the value of a t random variable with v degree of freedom so that $P(t \leq t_v) = \delta$. Otherwise do not reject H.

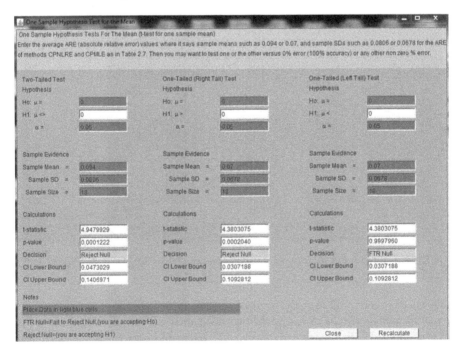

FIGURE 1.6   Case 1, 2, and 3 applications for single sample t-tests of Section 1.2.7.

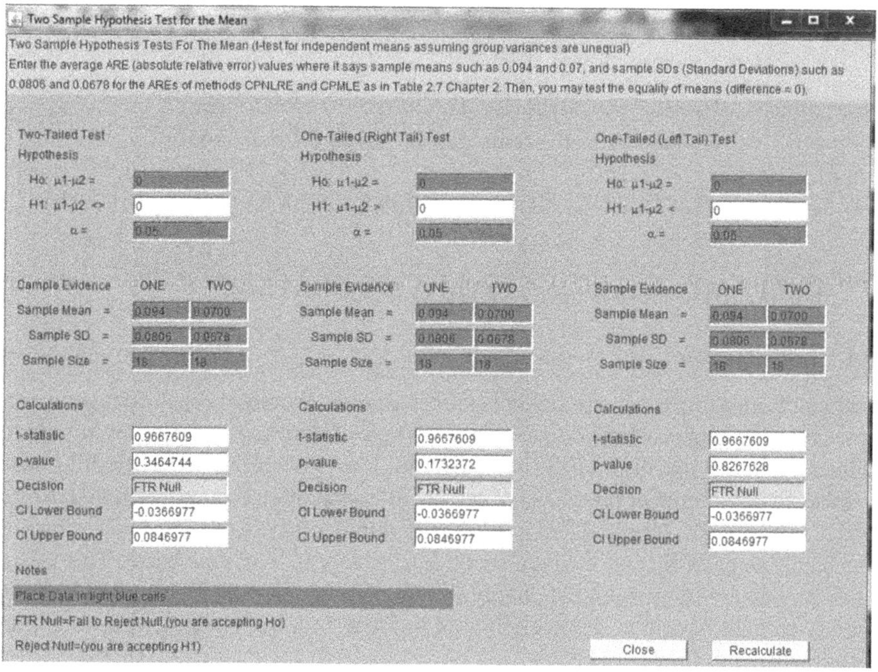

FIGURE 1.7 Case 1, 2, and 3 applications for two sample t-tests of Section 1.2.7.

Case 2
$H: \mu \leq \mu_0$; A: $\mu > \mu_0$

This is the case of a one-sided alternative. For this case, reject H if $t \geq t_{(1-\alpha)(n-1)}$; otherwise, do not reject H.

Case 3
$H: \mu \geq \mu_0$; A: $\mu < \mu_0$

Reject H if $t \leq t_{(1-\alpha)(n-1)}$; otherwise, do not reject H. To recap, when the variance (σ) of the population is not known and only the sample variance (s) is known with a sample size, n, small, the t-test (student's t-distribution) is in effect, not the "z":

$H_0: \mu = \mu_0$ versus $H_1: \mu \neq \mu_0$ and $H_0: \mu_1 - \mu_2 = 0$ versus $H_1: \mu_1 - \mu_2 \neq 0$.

For which, use, respectively, the following tests:

$$t_{n-1} = \frac{\sqrt{n}\left[\left(\bar{X} - \mu\right)\right]}{s} \tag{1.15}$$

$$t_m = \left[\bar{Y} - \left(\mu_1 - \mu_2\right)\right] \bigg/ \sqrt{s^2\left(\frac{1}{n_1} + \frac{1}{n_2}\right)} \tag{1.16}$$

where $n - 1$ denotes the degrees of freedom for one-tailed test. For two-tailed test, $m = n_1 + n_2 - 2$ and $\bar{Y}$ is the difference of two sample means, and both samples have the same shape $\sigma_1^2 = \sigma_2^2$. The following two screenshots illustrate one- and two-sided scenarios where

$$H_0 : \mu = \mu_0 \text{ versus } H_1 : \mu \neq \mu_0 \text{ for } \alpha = 0.05 \text{ and}$$
$$H_0 : \mu_1 - \mu_2 = 0 \text{ versus } H_1 : \mu_1 - \mu_2 \neq 0 \text{ for } \alpha = 0.05. \tag{1.17}$$

Note, for the earlier screenshots, FTR null = fail to reject (or accept) null hypothesis.

1.3   ACCEPTANCE SAMPLING IN QUALITY CONTROL

1.3.1   Introduction

Acceptance sampling is a major field of statistical quality control [11]. A company cannot test every one of its products due to either the fear of destructive testing by ruining the products or the volume of products being exceedingly large. Acceptance sampling solves this by testing a sample of products for defects. It is also more economical due to a lesser amount of inspection error and less handling, therefore less damage. The process involves batch size, sample size, and the number of defects acceptable in the batch. This process allows a company to measure the quality of a batch with a specified degree of statistical certainty without having to test every unit of product. In lot-by-lot acceptance sampling, the following definitions hold true:

Type I error—A Type I error probability (α) is associated with the producer's risk.
Type II error—A Type II error probability (β) is associated with the consumer's risk.

1.3.2   Definition of an Acceptance Sampling Plan

Suppose that a lot of size N has been submitted for inspection. An acceptance sampling plan is defined by the sample size n and the acceptance number "a" when we observe a defective number "d":

1. If d is less than or equal to "a," $(d \leq a) \rightarrow$ the lot will be accepted, where $\rightarrow$ denotes "implies."
2. If d is more than "a," $(d > a) \rightarrow$ the lot will be rejected.

1.3.3   The OC Curve

The important measure of the performance of an acceptance sampling plan similar to continuous sampling plans is the OC curve. Suppose that the lot size N is large. Under this condition, the distribution of the number of defectives, d, in a random sample of n items is binomial with parameter n and p, where p is the fraction of defective items in the entire lot:

$$Y = \sum_{k=1}^{n} X_k \sim \text{Binomial } (n,p) \tag{1.18}$$

$$b(x; n, P) = {}_nC_x * p^x * (1-p)^{n-x} \tag{1.19}$$

TABLE 1.11 Input DATA and Qual-C Outcome for Example 4

Fraction Defective Probability	P[Acceptance]
0.005	0.9965
0.010	0.9483
0.015	0.8165
0.020	0.6288
0.025	0.4383
0.030	0.2810
0.035	0.1681
0.040	0.0950
0.045	0.0512
0.050	0.0264
0.055	0.0132
0.060	0.0064
0.065	0.0030
0.070	0.0014
0.075	0.0006
0.080	0.0003
0.085	0.0001
0.090	0.0000
0.095	0.0000

The probability of accepting a lot, that is, $P[d \leq a]$, can be obtained from this Binomial distribution.

1.3.3.1 Example 4 on Acceptance Sampling This example refers to acceptance sampling in a Cyberware testing environment. Hence, let $N=1000$, $n=200$, and $a=4$. We can create the OC curve with Qual-C software.

Here we can notice that the OC curve starts at 1.00 and ends at 0.0. The OC curve shows the power of the "Acceptance Sampling" plan. For an example, let $n=200$ and $a=4$ where lots are 2% (=4/200) defective and then the probability of acceptance is 0.6288 or 63% (see Table 1.11). That means if 100 lots from a manufacturing process of the same item are tested, the manufacturer submits a 2% "defective" product for the sampling plan. Then, we accept 63 of the lots (63/100) and reject 37 lots (Figs. 1.8 and 1.9).

1.3.3.2 More on Acceptance Sampling Figure 1.10 shows how the OC curve changes as the acceptance number "a" changes when the sample size is fixed. Changing the acceptance number does not severely change the shape of the OC curve.

When $a>4$, OC curve is shifted to the left, and when $a<4$, it shifts to the right. Figure 1.10 shows the shape of the OC curves, when the sample size and the acceptance number both change. If the "a" is decreased, OC curve is shifted to the left. Plans with smaller values of "a" (criterion of acceptance) provide documentation at lower levels of lot fraction (p) defective than do the plans with larger values of "a."

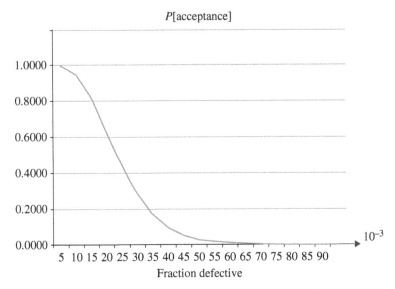

FIGURE 1.8   P[acceptance] versus fraction defective for Example 4.

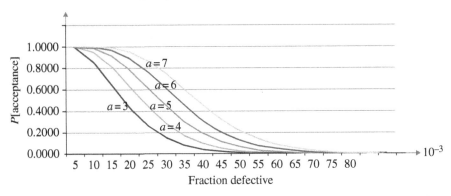

FIGURE 1.9   Comparison of OC curve for different acceptance numbers, $a=3$ to $a=7$ for the same "n."

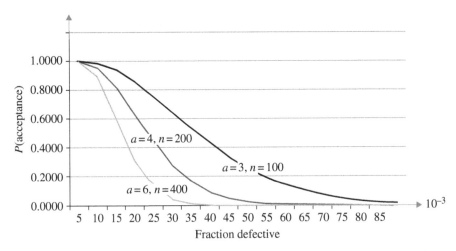

FIGURE 1.10   Comparison of OC curve with different acceptance numbers, $a=3$, 4, 6 for $n=100$, 200, 400.

1.4 POISSON AND NORMAL APPROXIMATION TO BINOMIAL IN QUALITY CONTROL

1.4.1 Approximations to Binomial Distribution

If the sample size is very large, the Binomial tables for large n are not available. In such cases, we use either a Normal or a Poisson approximation to the Binomial probabilities [12].

1.4.2 Approximation of Binomial to Poisson Distribution

When $n \to \infty$ and $p \to 0$, then see as follows:

If $n > 50$ and $p < 0.1$, then assume $\lambda = np$, which leads to the Poisson approximation of the Binomial

$$f(k;\lambda) = \Pr(X = k) = \frac{\lambda^k e^{-\lambda}}{k!} \tag{1.20}$$

1.4.2.1 Example 5 on Poisson Approximation to the Binomial Distribution   A shipment of 2000 portable battery units for microcomputers is about to be inspected by a Malaysian importer. The Korean manufacturer and the importer have set up a sampling plan in which the risk is limited to 5% at an acceptable quality level (AQL) of 2% defective and the risk is set to 10% at a Lot Tolerance Percent Defective (LTPD)=7% defective. We want to construct the OC curve for the plan of $n = 120$ sample size and an acceptance level of $a \leq 3$ defectives. Both firms want to know if this plan will satisfy their quality and risk requirements. To solve the problem, we can use the software whose "a" is set up in terms of the acceptance level C. The rows in Table 1.12 are λ ($= np$), which represents the number of defects we would expect to find in each sample.

TABLE 1.12   The Outcomes for Example 5 of the Poisson Approximation to the Binomial

Fraction Defective Probability (p)	$\lambda = np$ (Poisson Mean Value)	P[Acceptance]
0.010	1.2000	0.9662
0.020	2.4000	0.7787
0.030	3.6000	0.5152
0.040	4.8000	0.2942
0.050	6.0000	0.1512
0.060	7.2000	0.0719
0.070	8.4000	0.0323
0.080	9.6000	0.0138
0.090	10.8000	0.0057
0.100	12.0000	0.0023
0.110	13.2000	0.0009
0.120	14.4000	0.0003
0.130	15.6000	0.0001
0.140	16.8000	0.0000
0.150	18.0000	0.0000
0.160	19.2000	0.0000
0.170	20.4000	0.0000
0.180	21.6000	0.0000
0.190	22.8000	0.0000

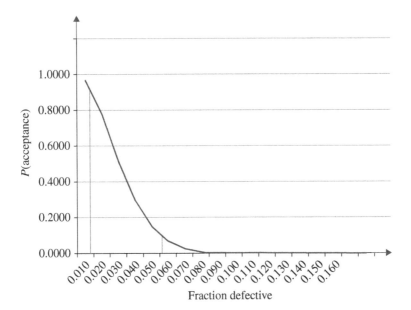

FIGURE 1.11   The outcomes for Example 5 obtained from Table 1.12 with Poisson to Binomial.

By varying the percent defectives (p) from 0.01 (1%) to 0.08 (8%) and holding the sample size constant at $n = 120$, we can compute the probability of acceptance of the lot at each chosen level. The values for P (acceptance) calculated in what follows are then plotted to produce the OC curve shown in Figure 1.11.

Now let us go back to the issue of whether this OC curve satisfies the quality and risk needs of the consumer and producer of the batteries. For the AQL of $p = 0.02 = 2\%$ defects, the P (acceptance) of the lot $= 0.7787$.

This α-risk of $(1 - 0.7787) = 0.2213$, or 22.13%, is one that exceeds the 5% level desired by the producer. The β-risk of 0.0323, or 3.23%, is under the 10% sought by the consumer. It appears that new calculations are necessary with a larger sample size if α level is to be lowered.

1.4.3   Approximation to Normal Distribution

When $n \to \infty$ and $p \to 0.5$, then see as follows:

If $n > 100$ and $p \approx 0.5$ and $npq > 25$, then $\mu = np$, $\sigma = \sqrt{(npq)}$, where $\sqrt{} = $ Sqrt and the Normal approximation to Binomial becomes

$$f(x; \mu, \sigma) = \frac{1}{\sigma\sqrt{2\pi}} e^{-\frac{(x-\mu)^2}{2\sigma^2}} \tag{1.21}$$

$-\infty < x < \infty$, $\mu > 0$, $\sigma_2 > 0$.

We can also calculate the probability using Normal approximation to the binomial probabilities. Since binomial distribution is for discrete random variable and normal distribution is for continuous random variable, we have to make continuity corrections by adding and subtracting 1/2 to approximate a binomial distribution using the normal distribution.

TABLE 1.13   The Outcomes for Example 6 of the Normal Approximation to the Binomial Distribution

Fraction Defective Probability, p	$\mu = np$	Variance	P[Acceptance]
0.010	1.2	1.089954127	0.9507
0.020	2.4	1.533623161	0.6522
0.030	3.6	1.86868938	0.3741
0.040	4.8	2.146625258	0.2009
0.050	6.0 > 5	2.387467277	0.1045
0.060	7.2 > 5	2.601538007	0.0532
0.070	8.4 > 5	2.794995528	0.0267
0.080	9.6	2.971868099	0.0132
0.090	10.8	3.134964115	0.0064
0.100	12.0	3.286335345	0.0031
0.110	13.2	3.427535558	0.0015
0.120	14.4	3.559775274	0.0007
0.130	15.6	3.684019544	0.0003
0.140	16.8	3.801052486	0.0001
0.150	18.0	3.911521443	0.0001

1.4.3.1   Example 6 on Normal Approximation to the Binomial Using Table 1.12 Input

For large n and when $np > 5$ and $nq > 5$, binomial random variable X with $X \sim B(n,p)$ can be approximated by a normal distribution with a mean $= np$ and a variance $= npq$. Let us take the same Example 5 of 1.4.2.1 to compare with the Normal approximation of Table 1.13.

1.4.4   Comparisons of Normal and Poisson Approximations to the Binomial

The following bar chart illustrates the better comparison regarding our two approximating distributions with Binomial Distribution for Example 6.

By varying the percent defectives (p) from 0.01 (1%) to 0.08 (8%) and holding the sample size at $n = 120$, we can see the Normal approximation probability closer to the Binomial probability at $p = 0.07$. At this point, $np = 120*0.07 = 8.4 > 5$. But for $p < 0.07$, that is, $np < 5$, there is a significant difference between Binomial probabilities and Normal approximation values. However, we note that the approximation is close to the exact probability 0.08 and also when the percent defective value, $p > 0.08$, the Normal approximation gives much similar probabilities like Binomial distribution. But the Poisson approximation does much better than Normal approximation when $p < 0.08$. Therefore, Normal approximation is definitely better when both satisfy the conditions of mean $= np > 5$ and variance $= npq > 5$, as stipulated earlier (Figs. 1.12 and 1.13).

1.5   BASIC STATISTICAL RELIABILITY CONCEPTS AND MC SIMULATORS

Some of the most commonly used continuous density functions included are the exponential, normal, rectangular, Weibull, lognormal, and gamma. The characteristics presented are those normally considered important in reliability nomenclature, including

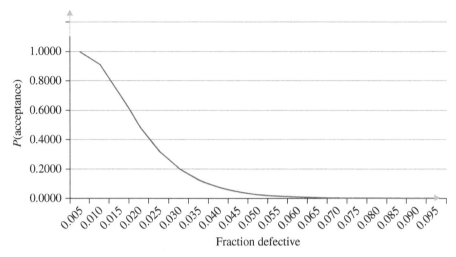

FIGURE 1.12   The outcomes for Example 6 from Table 1.13 with Normal to Binomial.

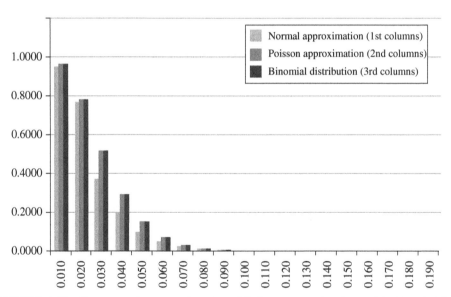

FIGURE 1.13   The comparisons of Normal and Poisson approximations with Binomial for Example 6.

the reliability function $R(t)$, hazard function $h(t)$, mean, variance, mode, and region of definition. The derivations of these characteristics are readily available in statistical texts, and in-depth details are not presented here. However, basics are well outlined. It will be an excellent exercise for the reader to verify these derivations if he or she so desires at his or her own will.

1.5.1 Fundamental Equations for Reliability, Hazard, and Statistical Notions

The following definitions are pertinent for the conceptual reliability derivations. More detail on these definitions is provided throughout, also to be found in other books. See Table 1.14 for common distributions and Tables 1.15 and 1.16 for an extended list of probability distributions supported by their pertinent MC simulators in any order (Fig. 1.14):

1. *The reliability*:

$$R(t) = \int_{t}^{t_u} f(t)\,dt \tag{1.22}$$

    where $f(t)$ is the probability density function and t_u is the upper bound on the region of definition of $f(t)$ with t_1 lower bound 0 or above.

2. *Hazard function*:

$$h(t) = \frac{f(t)}{R(t)} \tag{1.23}$$

    where $h(t)dt = \dfrac{1}{R(t)} dR(t)$

3. *The mean*:

$$\mu = \int_{D} tf(t)\,dt \tag{1.24}$$

    where D (domain) is the region of definition of $f(t)$.

4. *The variance*:

$$\sigma^2 = \int_{D} (t-\mu)^2 f(t)\,dt = \int_{D} t^2 f(t)\,dt - \mu^2 \tag{1.25}$$

5. *The mode*: It is that value of t (if it exists) such that $f(t)$ is a maximum there for densities with a single maximum where solving for $\dfrac{1}{d(t)} df(t) = 0 \rightarrow$ the root, m (mode).

6. *The median*: M is the median or 50th percentile if

$$0.50 = \int_{0}^{M} f(t)\,dt \tag{1.26}$$

7. *Reliability function and reliable life*: The reliability function, $R(t)$, is the probability that failure occurs after time t and is defined as

$$R(t) = \int_{t}^{\infty} f(x)\,dx = 1 - F(t) \tag{1.27}$$

    The reliable life, ρ_R, sometimes called the *minimum life*, is defined for any specified R:

$$R(t) = \int_{\rho_R}^{\infty} f(t)\,dt = R(\rho_R) \tag{1.28}$$

TABLE 1.14 Snapshot for the Common Probability Distributions and Their Reliability and Other Related Functions of 1.5.1

Function→	Negative Exponential	Normal	Erlang	Uniform	Weibull	Lognormal	Gamma
Density, $f(t)$	$\lambda e^{-\lambda t}$	$\dfrac{1}{\sigma\sqrt{2\pi}}\exp\dfrac{-(t-\mu)^2}{2\sigma^2}$	$(x^{k-1}\lambda^k e^{-\lambda x})/k-1!$	$\dfrac{1}{b-a}$	$\dfrac{\beta t^{\beta-1}}{\alpha^\beta}\exp\left\{\dfrac{-t^\beta}{\alpha^\beta}\right\}$	$\dfrac{1}{\sigma\sqrt{2\pi}}\exp\left\{-\dfrac{(\ln t-\mu)^2}{2\sigma^2}\right\}$ where $\mu=\mu_{normal}$ $\sigma^2=\sigma^2_{normal}$	$\dfrac{t^{\alpha-1}e^{-t/\beta}}{\Gamma(\alpha)\beta^\alpha}$
Reliability, $R(t)$	$e^{-\mu}$	$1-\Phi\left(\dfrac{t-\mu}{\sigma}\right)$	$1-[\gamma(k,\lambda x)/k-1!]$	$\dfrac{b-t}{b-a}$	$e^{\frac{-t^\beta}{\alpha^\beta}}$	$0.5-0.5(erf[(\ln t-\mu)/\sigma\sqrt{2}])$	$\displaystyle\int_t^\infty f(t)dt$ or $1/\Gamma(\alpha)\big[\gamma(\alpha,\beta t)\big]$
Hazard, $h(t)=f(t)/R(t)$	Constant, λ	Increasing failure rate (IFR)	$[x^{k-1}\lambda^k e^{-\lambda x}/k-1!]/$ $\{1-[\gamma(k,\lambda x)/k-1!]\}$	IFR	$\beta>1$, IFR; $\beta=1$, constant failure rate (CFR); $\beta<1$, DFR	Depends on the slope of $w=\exp(\sigma^2)$	$\alpha>1$, IFR; $\alpha=1$, CFR; $\alpha<1$, DFR
Mean	$\theta=\lambda^{-1}$	μ	k/λ	$\dfrac{a+b}{2}$	$\alpha\Gamma\left(\dfrac{1}{\beta}+1\right)$	$\mu=\exp\left(\mu_N+\sigma^2/2\right)$	$\alpha\beta$
Mode	0	μ	$(k-1)/\lambda$ for $k>1$	None or any value in $[a,b]$	$\beta\big[(\alpha-1)/\alpha\big]^{1/\alpha}$, $\alpha>1$; 0, $\alpha=1$	$\exp\left(\mu_N-\sigma^2\right)$	$(\alpha-1)/\beta$ for $\alpha>1$
Variance	$\theta^2=\lambda^{-2}$	σ^2	k/λ^2	$\dfrac{(b-a)^2}{12}$	$\alpha^2\left[\Gamma\left(\dfrac{2}{\beta}+1\right)-\Gamma\left(\dfrac{1}{\beta}+1\right)^2\right]$	$\big[\exp(\sigma^2)-1\big]\cdot$ $\big[\exp(2\mu+\sigma^2)\big]$	$\alpha\beta^2$

Median, $\int_0^M f(t)\,dt = 0.5$	μ	No simple closed form	$\dfrac{a+b}{2}$	$\alpha(\ln 2)^{1/\beta}$	$\theta^{\ln 2}$	$\exp(\mu_N)$	$\int_0^M f(t)\,dt = 0.5$ (no simple closed form)
Skewness	0	$2/\sqrt{k}$	0	$\{\Gamma(1+3/\beta)\alpha^3 - 3\mu\sigma^2 - \mu^3\}/\sigma^3$	2	$[\exp(\sigma^2+2)]\sqrt{(\exp(\sigma^2-1)}$	$2/\sqrt{\alpha}$
Excess (kurtosis)	0	$6/k$	$-6/5$	See[a]	6	$\exp(4\sigma^2+2)+2\exp(3\sigma^2)+3\exp(2\sigma^2)^{-6}$	$6/\alpha$
Range	$-\infty \le t \le \infty$	$t>0$	$a \le t \le b$	$0 \le t \le \infty$	$0 \le t \le \infty$	$0 \le t \le \infty$	$0 \le t \le \infty$
Comments	$M = m = \mu$ symmetric	k = shape parameter $\lambda = rate = (1/mean)$	Rectangular	α = scale parameter β = shape parameter	θ = mean $\lambda = rate = (1/mean)$	Normal mean $=\mu_N$ Normal variance $=\sigma^2$ a. If $X \sim$ lognormal, then $Y=\log(x) \sim$ normal b. If $Y \sim$ normal, $\exp(Y) \sim \log n$	β = scale parameter α = shape parameter

[a] Continued from Table 1.14 for Weibull kurtosis: The excess kurtosis is given by

$$\gamma_2 = \frac{-6\Gamma_1^4 + 12\Gamma_1^2\Gamma_2 - 3\Gamma_2^2 - 4\Gamma_1\Gamma_3 + \Gamma_4}{\left[\Gamma_2 - \Gamma_1^2\right]^2}$$

where $\Gamma_i = \Gamma(1+i/k)$. The kurtosis excess may also be written as

$$\gamma_2 = \frac{\lambda^4\Gamma\left(1+\dfrac{4}{k}\right) - 4\gamma_1\sigma^3\mu - 6\mu^2\sigma^2 - \mu^4}{\sigma^4} - 3$$

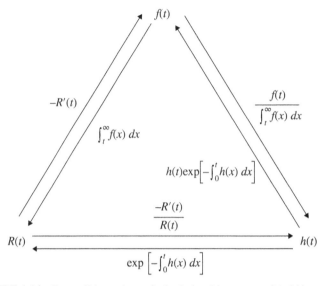

FIGURE 1.14   Reversible mathematical relationships among $f(t)$, $h(t)$, and $R(t)$.

The reliable life, ρ_R, is the same as the qth quantile where $q = 1 - R$. A special case is when $R = 1/2$, which ρ_R becomes the median. Similarly, when $R = 1/4$, ρ_R becomes the first quartile, 25th percentile. When $R = 3/4$, ρ_R becomes the third quartile, 75th percentile.

8. *Moments*: When γ is a finite value, the moments of the failure distribution may be found from $R(t)$. The kth *moment* of t is defined as [13]

$$\mu'_k = \int_{-\infty}^{\infty} t^k f(t)\,dt = \gamma^k + k\int_{\gamma}^{\infty} t^{k-1} R(t)\,dt \tag{1.29}$$

In particular when $k = 1$ and $\gamma = 0$, the *mean time to failure* (MTTF) is given by

$$\text{MTTF} = \mu = \int_{\gamma}^{\infty} tf(t)\,dt = -\int_{\gamma}^{\infty} t\frac{dR}{dt}\,dt = -tR(t)\Big|_0^{\infty} + \int_{\gamma}^{\infty} R(t)\,dt = \int_0^{\infty} R(t)\,dt \tag{1.30}$$

9. *Failure rate, hazard rate, and retired life*: For a period of length δ, the *failure rate*, $G(t,\delta)$, is defined as

$$G(t,\delta) = \frac{1}{\delta}\int_{t}^{t+\delta} \frac{f(x)}{R(t)}\,dx = \frac{F(t+\delta) - F(t)}{\delta R(t)} = \frac{R(t) - R(t+\delta)}{\delta R(t)} \tag{1.31}$$

10. *The hazard rate or instantaneous failure rate*: $h(t)$ is the limit of $G(t,\delta)$ as δ approaches zero:

$$h(t) = \frac{f(t)}{1 - F(t)} \tag{1.32}$$

11. *The retired life or replacement life*: $\xi(ksi)$ is defined for any specified h given by

$$h = \frac{f(\xi)}{R(\xi)} \tag{1.33}$$

12. *Life expectancy*: Suppose that an item has survived until time T. Then the expected additional *life expectancy*, $L(t)$, is given by

$$L(t) = \begin{cases} \mu - T, & T \le \mu \\ \dfrac{1}{R(t)} \displaystyle\int_t^\infty R(t)\,dt, & T > \mu \end{cases} \tag{1.34}$$

13. *Probable life*: The probable life, $B(T)$, is the total expected life of an item with age T:

$$B(T) = L(T) + T \tag{1.35}$$

1.5.2 Fundamentals for Reliability Block Diagramming and Redundancy

Also see the following on redundancy and reliability [13], if R_a is the reliability of a parallel system:

$$R_a = 1 - \prod_{i=1}^n (1 - R_i) = 1 - (1 - R_i)^n \tag{1.36}$$

$$1 - R_a = (1 - R_i)^n \tag{1.37}$$

Reorganizing (1.37) as in (1.38) and taking the natural logarithm of both sides yields

$$n = \frac{\ln(1 - R_a)}{\ln(1 - R_i)} \tag{1.38}$$

If $R_{i=}$ 0.95, then to raise the active parallel system to 99.5% reliability, for example,

$$n = \frac{\ln(1 - 0.995)}{\ln(1 - 0.95)} = \frac{-5.3}{-3.0} \cong 2$$

Series reliability simply assumes that the product of individual reliabilities in a system will result in lower reliability than that of the weakest chain reliability in the system. Such systems are called nonredundant due to this negative effect. The formula depicts this reality

$$R = R_1 R_2 R_3 . R_n \ldots R_N, \; 0 < R_i < 1$$

If $R_i = 0.9$, then $R = R_1 R_2 = 0.81$. If $R_i = 0.99$, then $\displaystyle\prod_{i=1}^{200} R_i = 0.134$ (1.39)

or down to 13.4%

from a 99% for a single component. Simple parallel system is one in which if any individual component is a success and the system input–output or ingress–egress connection is a success. In a simple active (ready to operate without the need of a switch) parallel system, the individual components are positioned in parallel topology, where with n components, each of R_i, the system reliability is given as in Equation (1.36). The series-in-parallel system is composed of k separate series subsystems arranged in active parallel in that if any series branch with n components is a success, the overall system is a success. Such systems are also called high-level redundant (HL). The reliability is

$$R_{HL} = 1 - \left(1 - R^n\right)^k \tag{1.40}$$

For example, given $R_1 = R_2 = R_3 = R_4 = 0.9$ and $k=2$, $n=2$, $R_{HL} = 1 - (1-0.9^2)^2 = 0.9639$. For six identical components this time, $R_{HL} = 1 - (1-R^n)^k = 2R^3 - R^6 = 2(0.9)^3 - 0.9^6 = 0.9266$. The *parallel-in-series system* is one of which maximum reliability can be obtained but in which reliability is hardest to maintain. In this system, an individual component is replaced by k components in an active parallel to increase reliability in a series of n branches. Such systems are also called low-level redundant (LL). This structure is to be used when very high reliability is necessary for a given length of time, as in a missile firing. The reliability is

$$R_{LL} = \left[1 - \left(1 - R\right)^k\right]^n \tag{1.41}$$

For example, given $R_1 = R_2 = R_3 = R_4 = 0.9$ and $k=2$, $n=2$, $R_{LL} = [1-(1-0.9)^2]^2 = 0.9801$. For six identical components this time, $R_{LL} = 1 - (1-R^n)^k = (2R-R^2)^3 = 2(0.9)^3 - 0.9^6 = 0.9703$. We have $R_{LL} - R_{HL} = 6R^3 (1-R)^2 = 0.0437$ for our example of six identical components. Hence, $R_{LL} > R_{HL}$.

Partial parallel topology structure is designated by a group of n components in parallel, out of which any k are required to operate for the system to be successful. A popular example is when of three parallel engines in a jet plane, where $R+Q=1$, at least two $(k=2)$ must work for the jet to operate. If one expands $(R+Q)^3 = R^3 + 3R^2Q + 3RQ^2 + Q^3$, the probability of success is given by $R^3 + 3R^2Q$. In the case of n unlike components, $\prod_{i=1}^{n}(R_i + Q_i) = 1$. We then get rid of those terms that represent failure scenarios for the defined "at least k" statement of system reliability.

Standby redundancy is identical to an active parallel system except that it is termed "standby" redundant when a switch exists to direct the flow of current as desired [3]. Provided that the switch operates perfectly in a more efficient two-component standby system, the second unit is not activated until the first unit fails. The MTTF (reciprocal of λ, which is the rate of failure) of an active two-unit system is 1.5 times higher than that of a single component.

On the other hand, the MTTF of a standby system is twice as high as that of a single unit. However, for $\lambda t \ll 1$, $R(t) = 1 - \exp(-\lambda t) \approx 1 - \lambda t$ for a single component, $R(t) \approx 1 - (\lambda t)^2$ for an active parallel system, and finally, for a standby system, $R(t) \approx 1 - 0.5(\lambda t)^2$. This can be interpreted as follows: For short time intervals where $t \ll 1$, the standby system failure probability, $F = 1 - R$, is only one-half of the reliability of an active parallel system. That is, $F_a \approx (\lambda t)^2$ and $F_{stby} \approx 0.5(\lambda t)^2$. See Equation (1.42) for a general statistical treatment of n components in standby [1–3] as follows:

$$R_{stby}(t) = e^{-\lambda t} \sum_{k=0}^{n-1} \frac{(\lambda t)^k}{k!}, \quad t \geq 0, \ \lambda > 0 \tag{1.42}$$

Then, the reliability of n-unit standby system with imperfect switching reliability [2, 3] is

$$R_{stby}(t) = e^{-\lambda t} R_{ss} \sum_{k=0}^{n-1} \frac{(\lambda t)^k}{k!}, \quad t \geq 0, \ \lambda > 0 \tag{1.43}$$

Common-mode failures occur when common connections or stresses influence the redundant components such that they fail simultaneously. This may be due to a bird destroying a jet engine (recall the Hudson River forced landing), in turn causing a commercial jet liner to land or crash. This would be like installing a component having reliability R' in series with a parallel structure. This displays as follows, if $R = \exp(-\lambda t)$:

$$R'_a = (2R - R^2)R' \tag{1.44}$$

In the example of a twin-engine aircraft, if each engine had probability $p = 10^{-6}$ and the common-mode failure being $p' = 10^{-9}$, the system failure probability, $p'_a \approx 10^{-9}$, is dominated entirely by common-mode failure. If a subscript I denotes independent and C denotes common mode and for $\lambda = \lambda_I + \lambda_C$, we define a factor $\beta = \lambda_C / \lambda$. Then for the active parallel system, it follows

$$R'_a = \left[2\exp(-\lambda_I t) - \exp(-2\lambda_I t) \right] \exp(-\lambda_C t) \tag{1.45}$$

Load sharing limitation is another factor that degrades system reliability in active parallel systems. The failure rate of the second component λ_L will increase due to the stress of the first, which fails with λ resulting in $\lambda_L > \lambda$. With no common-mode failures,

$$R_a = 2\exp(-\lambda_L t) + \exp(-2\lambda_L t) - 2\exp\left[-(\lambda + \lambda_L)t \right] \tag{1.46}$$

Equation (1.46) defaults to the original equation for the active parallel structure if $\lambda_L = \lambda$. Now if $\lambda_L \to \infty$, Equation (1.46) reduces to the reliability of two components placed in series as shown in (1.47). If $\lambda_L > 1.56\lambda$, $MTTF_{system} < MTTF_{single}$. This means if any component causes an instantaneous failure of the second component shared, the parallel system failure rate is as great as that of a single unit [14]:

$$R_a = \exp(-2\lambda t) \tag{1.47}$$

1.5.3   Solving Basic Reliability Questions by Using Student-Friendly Pedagogical Examples

1.5.3.1   Example 7   At the end of 1 year of service, the reliability of a certain software product during its useful life period after the debugging process (assuming a constant failure rate) is 0.7:

(a) What is the failure rate of this software product in hours?

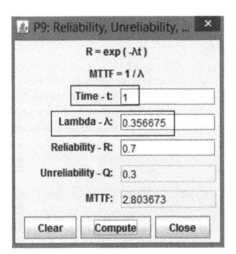
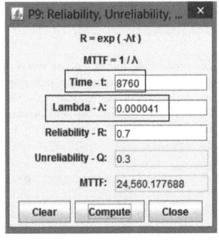

(b) If four of these products are put in series and active parallel independently, what are the annual reliability figures in series and active parallel systems, respectively?

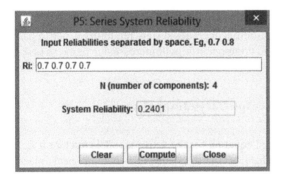
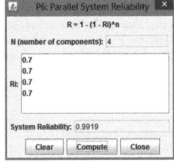

(c) For active parallel, if 30% of the component failure rate may be attributed to common-mode failures, what will the annual reliability become for the two components in parallel?

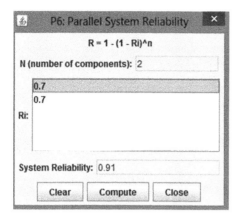

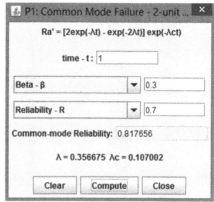

(d) Suppose that the failure rate for a software component is given as 0.08/h. How many components must be placed in active parallel form if a distributed system of modules will have to run for 100 h with a system reliability of no less than 95%?

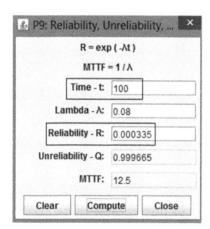

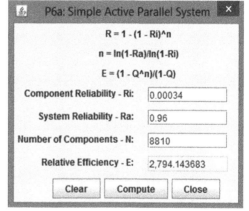

(e) Assuming now that the annual reliability of the software module is improved to 0.8 and a series system of four components is formed. A second set of four components is bought and a redundant system is built. What is the reliability of the new redundant system with?

1. High-level redundancy by drawing the representation in numbered blocks?

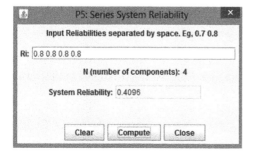

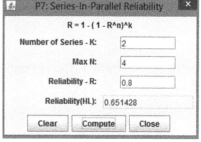

2. Low-level redundancy by drawing the representation in numbered blocks?

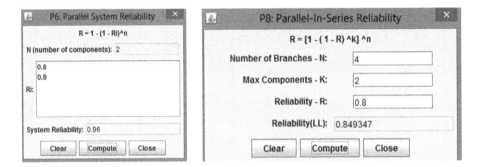

1.5.3.2   Example 8   A constant failure rate device (PC) has an MTTF of 2500 h. The vendor offers a 1-year warranty. What fraction of the PCs will fail during the warm-up period? What if 2-year warranty?

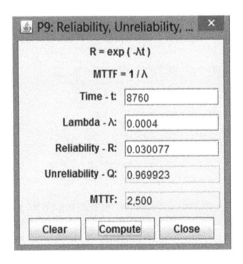
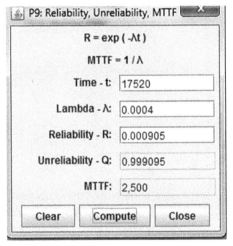

1.5.3.3   Example 9   A software module being marketed is tested for 2 months and found to have a reliability of $R(t)=0.97$ where $\lambda=0.01523$/month; the module is known to have a constant failure rate:

(a) What is the failure rate ($\lambda=0.01523$)? Repeat if $R(t)=0.99$ ($\lambda=0.005025$)?
(b) What is the MTTF (MTTF$=65.66$ month)? Repeat if $R(t)=0.99$ (MTTF$=198.99$ month)?

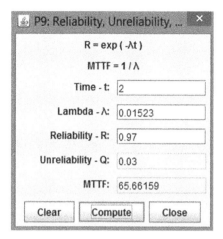

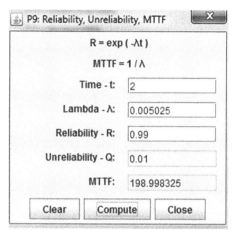

(c) What is the reliability of this product 4 years into its operation if it is in continuous use?

(d) What should the warranty time be to achieve an operational reliability of 96%?

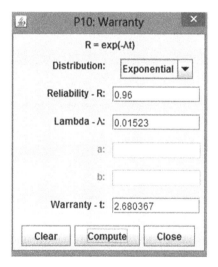

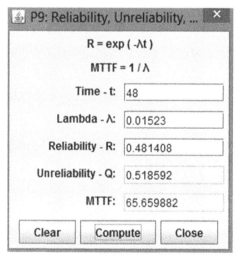

1.5.3.4 Example 10 Calculate the source–target (s–t) reliabilities of the following systems:

(a) Take $s=1$, $t=13$, $R=0.8$ in the figure later either with software or hand calculations.

(b) Take $s=5$, $t=7$ in the figure later either with software or hand calculations.

Solution: 0.72171 using the CD-ROM compression algorithm for simple series–parallel grids [15].

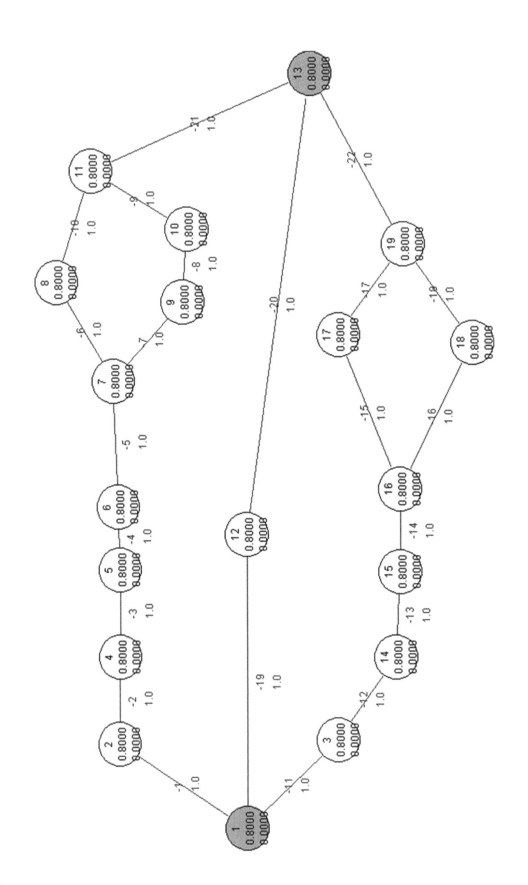

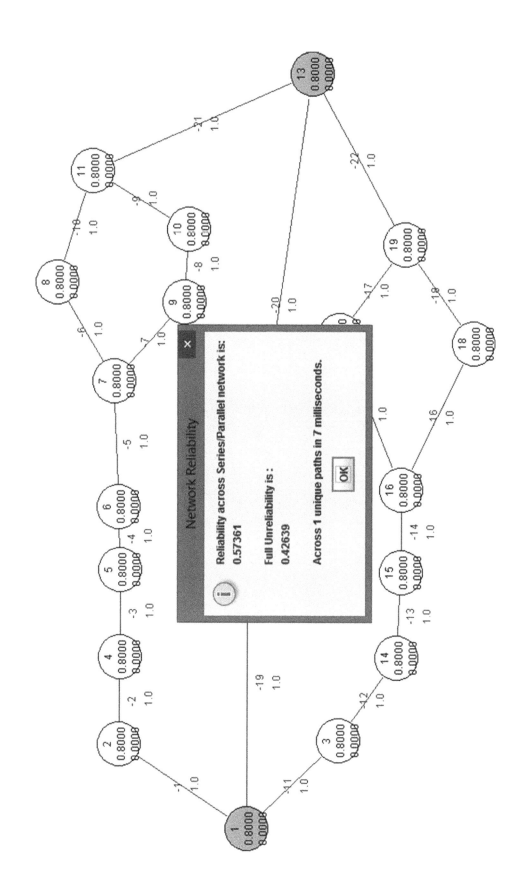

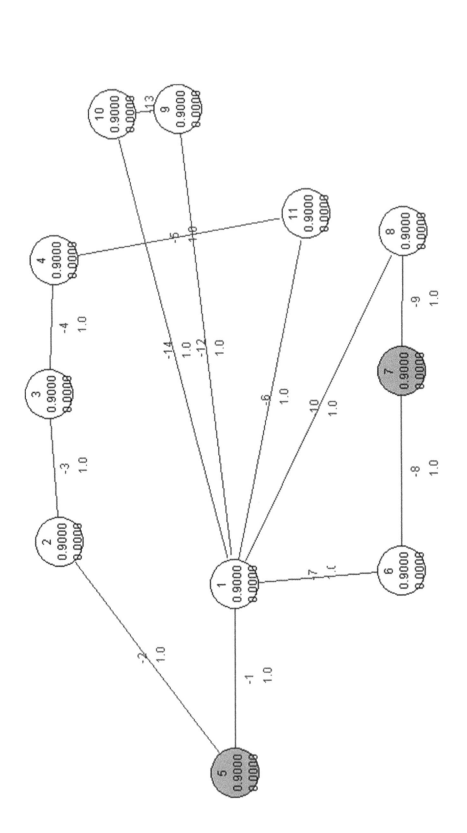

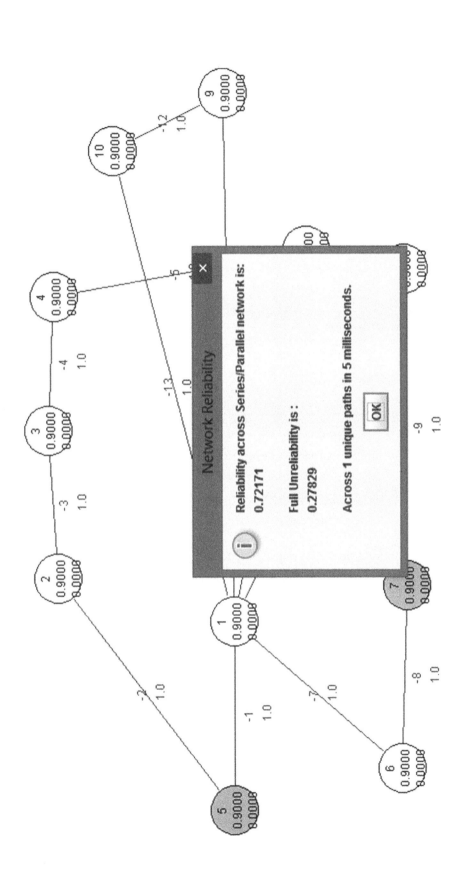

1.5.3.5   *Example 11*   A disk drive has a constant failure rate with an MTTF of 4000 h. What is the probability of failure for 1 year of operation? What is the probability of failure for 1 year of operation if two of the drives are placed in active parallel mode with failures assumed to be independent? What if in series?

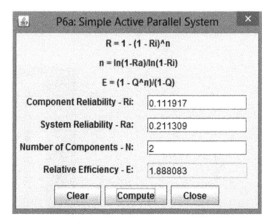

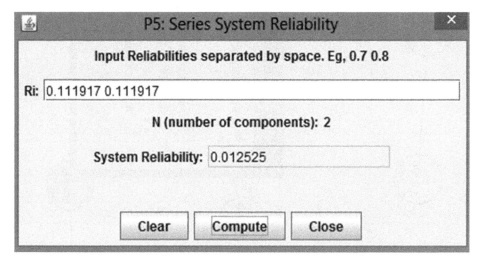

1.5.3.6   *Example 12*   Suppose that a system consists of two components placed in series, independent each with a failure rate = 1.5/year. A redundant system is built consisting of four identical components. Derive and calculate expressions for the system's failure rates after $t = 1$ year of operation:

(a) For high-level redundancy

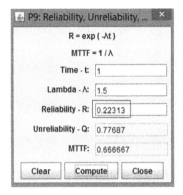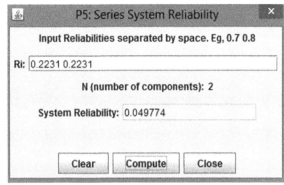

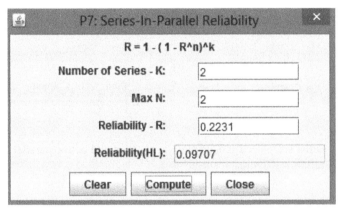

(b) For low-level redundancy

1.5.3.7   Example 13 At the end of 1-year service, the unreliability of a certain brand light bulb, assuming a constant failure rate, is given to be 8%:

(a) What is the failure rate in hours?

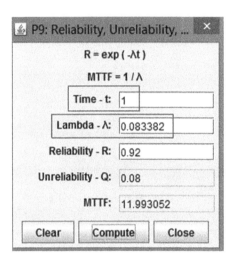
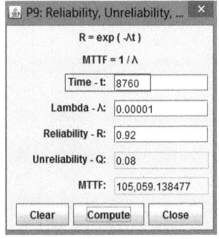

(b) If two bulbs are placed independently in series and active parallel, what are the annual reliability figures, respectively?

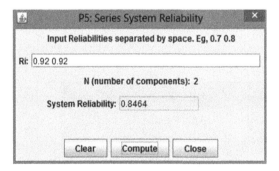
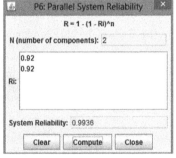

(c) Suppose that the design failure rate for the component is given to be 0.008/h, how many bulbs must be placed in active parallel if a system of lamps will have to run for 100 h with a system reliability of no less than 95%?

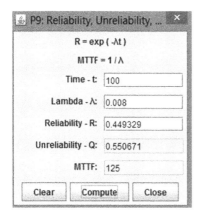

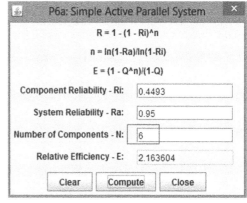

(d) Assuming now that the annual reliability of the bulb is improved to 0.96, a series system of three bulbs is formed. A second set of three components is bought, and a redundant system is built. What is the reliability of the new redundant system with (i) high-level redundancy and (ii) low-level redundancy?

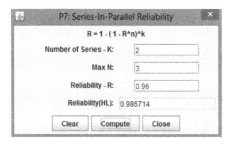

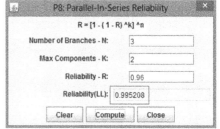

1.5.3.8 Example 14 What is the reliability after 1 year of active parallel operation for $n=2$ where the reliability of a unit is $R=0.8$ if the common mode of failures is 20% of the normal-mode failure rate?

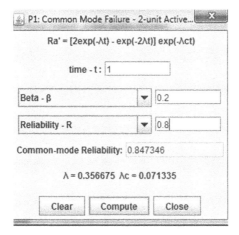

1.5.3.9   Example 15   What is the reliability after 1 year of active parallel operation for $n=2$ where the reliability of a unit is $R=0.8$ and $\lambda=0.223$ and if due to load sharing, the failure rate of the second component is higher than 30% of the normal-mode failure rate, $\lambda_L=1.3(0.223)=0.29$?

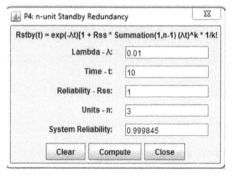

1.5.3.10   Example 16   What is the reliability after 10 h of active parallel operation for $n=2$ where each unit's $\lambda=0.01/h$, but when there is a standby unit with (i) perfect switching reliability $R_{ss}=1$ and (ii) imperfect switching reliability $R_{ss}=0.75$? Recall that the reliability of two identical units in an active parallel system for $R\,(t=10\,h)=\exp(-0.01*10)=\exp(0.1)=0.9048$ is $R_a=1-(1-0.9048)^2=0.99095$. Next $n=3$?

1.5.3.11 Example 17

(a) Suppose that a computer keyboard is life tested and has an MTTF of 68 h and a mean time to repair (MMTR) of 1.5 h. What is the availability with corrective maintenance?

(b) If the MMTR is reduced to 1 h without any extra measures, what MMTF can be tolerated without changing the machine reliability?

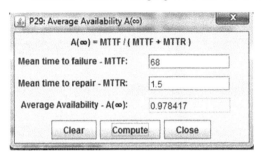
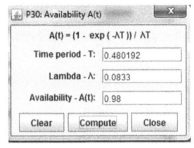

1.5.3.12 Example 18

(a) An annual life test revealed that 92% of computer hard disks were found to be operable. According to these data, what is the reliability (long-term availability) of these disks?

(b) If one is not happy with this availability figure in part A and desires to reach an availability value of 0.98, how often must one perform testing and replacement procedures? $A(T_0) = 0.98 = 1 - (1/2)$ (lambda$*T_0$) $\rightarrow T_0 = 0.48$ year $= 175$ days.

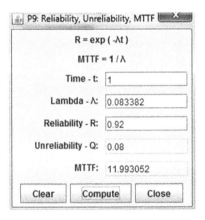
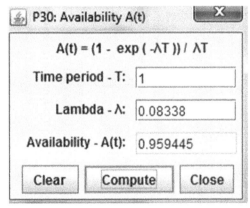

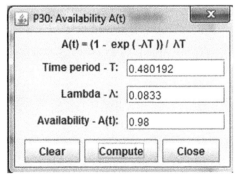

TABLE 1.15 The Commonly Used Probability Distributions and Their Monte Carlo Simulators

#	Distribution Name	Monte Carlo Simulator, Use $U_i \sim$ Standard Uniform ($a=0, b=1$)
1	Negative exponential (λ) = Weibull ($\alpha, \beta=1$), where $\alpha=\lambda^{-1}$	$x_i^* = \lambda^{-1}[\ln(1-u_i)]; i=1,2,\ldots$
2	Weibull (α, β)	$x_i^* = \alpha[\ln(1-u_i)]^{1/\beta}; i=1,2,\ldots$
3	Gamma (α, β)	x_i^* from Johnk's rejection technique [1, p. 18] for $i=1,2,\ldots$ as follows: Let α be a noninteger shape parameter, $\alpha_1 = [\alpha]$, the largest truncated integer of α, and u_i be the ith uniform, $0 \le u_i \le 1$. Then:

1. Let $x = \prod_{i=1}^{\alpha_1} u_i - \ln$
2. Set $A = \alpha - \alpha_1, B = 1-A$
   a. Set $j=1$
   b. Generate random number u_j and set $y_1 = (u_j)^{1/A}$
   c. Generate random number u_{j+1} and set $y_2 = (u_{j+1})^{1/B}$
   d. If $y_1 + y_2 \le 1$, go to f
   e. Set $j = j+2$ and go to b
   f. Let $z = y_1/(y_1+y_2)$, which is a beta random deviate with parameters A and B
3. Generate random number u_N and set $w = -\ln(u_N)$
4. The desired random deviate for gamma pdf is then $G = (x+zw)\beta$

#	Distribution Name	Monte Carlo Simulator
4	Erlang (k, λ)	$x_i^* = \sum_{k=1}^{\alpha} \dfrac{-\ln(1-u_i)}{\lambda}; \quad i=1,2,\ldots$
5	Sahinoglu–Libby ($\alpha=a+c$, $\beta=b+d, L=\beta_1/\beta_2$)	$x_i^* = \dfrac{a'n'}{a'n' + C_1 b'm'}; C_1 = \text{inverse } F_{2m',2n'}(1-u_i); i=1,2,\ldots$
6	Chi-square $\chi_n^2(n)$ = Gamma $\alpha=1/2, \beta=n/2$	$x_i^* = -0.5\ln\left(\prod_{i=1}^{n/2} u_i\right)$ for n even; $x_i^* = -0.5\ln\left(\prod_{i=1}^{(n-1)/2} u_i\right) + \sum_{i=1}^{n}\left[N(0,1)\right]^2$ for n odd
7	Beta(A, B)	$x_i^* = y/(y+z); y \sim$ Gamma $(A,1); z \sim$ Gamma$(B,1); y = -\ln\prod_{i=1}^{A} u_i$ and $z = -\ln\prod_{i=A+1}^{A+B} u_i; j=1,2\ldots$

8	Std normal, $N(0, 1)$	$x_{1i}^* = \sqrt{-2\ln u_2}\{\sin(2\pi u_1)\}; \; x_{2i}^* = \sqrt{-2\ln u_2}\{\cos(2\pi u_1)\}; \; i=1,2,\ldots$
9	Normal (μ, σ)	$z_{1i}^* = \sigma(x_{1i}^*) + \mu, \; z_{2i}^* = \sigma(x_{2i}^*) + \mu; \; z_i^* = \sigma\left(\sum_{i=1}^{12} u_i - 6\right) + \mu; \; i=1,2,\ldots,12$
10	Pareto(c) or Laplace (or double exponential)	$x_i^* = \left(\dfrac{1}{1-u_i}\right)^{1/c}; \; i=1,2,\ldots$
11	Lognormal (μ, σ)	$x_i^* = m\cdot\exp\{\sigma N(0,1)\} = m\exp\left\{\sigma\left(\sum_{i=1}^{12} u_i - 6\right)\right\}, \text{ where } m=e^\mu; \; i=1,2,\ldots,12$
12	Fisher's $F(n_1, n_2)$	$x_{n_1,n_2}^* = \chi_{n_1}^2 n_2 / \chi_{n_2}^2 n_1; \; i=1,2,\ldots$
13	Student's t-distribution (n)	$x_{n-1}^* = \dfrac{N(0,1)}{\sqrt{\chi_n^2/n}}; \; i=1,2,\ldots$
14	Standard Cauchy $(0,1)$	$x^* = \dfrac{\sum_{i=1}^{12} u_i - 6}{\sum_{j=1}^{12} u_j - 6}; \; i,j=1,2,\ldots,12$
15	Power (c)	$x_i^* = (u_i)^{1/c}; \; i=1,2,\ldots$
16	Raleigh=Weibull $(\alpha, \beta=2)$	$x_i^* = \alpha[\ln(1-u_i)]^{1/2}; \; i=1,2,\ldots$
17	Logistic (a, k)	$x_i^* = a - k\ln(1-u_i); \; i=1,2,\ldots$
18	Arc sin=Beta $(A=0.5, B=0.5)$	$x_i^* = y/(y+z); \; y\sim\text{Gamma}(0.5,1) \text{ and } z\sim\text{Gamma}(0.5,1); \; y=-\ln\prod_{i=1}^{0.5}u_i \text{ and } z=-\ln\prod_{i=0.5+1}^{1}u_i; \; i=1,2,\ldots$
19	Gumbel smallest I $(y+\alpha)$	$x_i^* = \alpha + \gamma\ln(\ln u_i), \; i=1,2,\ldots$
20	Gumbel largest I $(y+\alpha)$	$(-) x_i^* = \alpha + \gamma\ln(\ln u_i), \; i=1,2,\ldots$ Note: The sign of x will be reversed
21	Uniform (a,b)	$x_i^* = a + (b-a)u_i; \; i=1,2,\ldots$

(Continued)

TABLE 1.15 (Continued)

#	Distribution Name	Monte Carlo Simulator, Use $U_i \sim$ Standard Uniform ($a=0$, $b=1$)
22	Triangular (a,b,c)	$x_i^* = a + \sqrt{(b-a)(c-a)}u_i$; $i=1,2,\dots$; $0 \le u_i < \dfrac{b-a}{c-a}$ and $x_i^* = c - \sqrt{(c-a)(c-b)}u_i$; $i=1,2,\dots,\dfrac{b-a}{c-a} \le u_i \le 1$
23	Bernoulli (p)	$x_i^* = 1$; $0 < u_i < p$ and $x_i^* = 0$, $p < u_i < 1$; $i=1,2,\dots$
24	Binomial (np)	$x_i^* = \sum_i^n I_i$ if $I_i = 1$, $0 < u_i < p$; $I_i = 0$, $p < u_i < 1$; $i=1,2,\dots$
25	Beta Binomial	$x_i^* = \sum_i^n I_i$ if $I_i = 1$, $0 < u_i < p_j^*$; $I_i = 0$, $p_j^* < u_i < 1$; $i=1,2,\dots; p_j^* = X_j^*$
26	Multinomial ($n, p_1, p_2,\dots,p_m$); $m=3$, trinomial	$x_{i1}^* = \sum_i^n I_{i1}$ if $I_{i1} = 1$, $0 < u_i < p_1$; $x_{i2}^* = \sum_i^n I_{i2}$ if $I_{i2} = 1,2,\dots$ $p_1 < u_i < p_1 + p_2$; $x_{i3}^* = \sum_i^n I_{i3}$ if $I_{i3} = 1$, $p_1 + p_2 < u_i < 1$; $i=1,2,\dots$
27	Poisson (λ)	$x^* = x$ where stop for $\sum_{i=1}^x y_i \le 1 \le \sum_{i=1}^{x+1} y_i$; where $y_i^* = \lambda^{-1}[\ln(1-u_i)]$; $i=1,2,\dots$
28	Geometric (p,q)	$x_i^* = \dfrac{\ln u_i}{\ln q}$; $i=1,2,\dots$
29	Negative Binomial ($k-1,n,p$)	$x_i^* = \sum_{i=1}^k \left(\dfrac{\ln u_i}{\ln q} - 1\right) = \sum_{i=1}^k \dfrac{\ln u_i}{\ln q} - k$
30	Pascal (k,np)	$x_i^* = \sum_{i=1}^k \left(\dfrac{\ln u_i}{\ln q}\right)$ is rounded up to the next larger integer
31	Binomial approximation approximated to hypergeometric (n,M,N)	$x_i^* = \sum_i^n I_i$ if $I_i = 1$, $0 < u_i < p$; $i=1,2,\dots$ where $p = M/N$

1.5.4 MC Simulators for Commonly Used Distributions in Reliability

In modeling real-world events, most of the actions cannot be predicted fully in advance. This is why the analysts resort to probabilistic modeling and digital simulation rather than a traditionally applied and conventionally accepted norm, which we know as determinism. There are many causes of experimental or statistical variation. To the analysts building the model, some statistical models may well describe the process to mimic the scenario at hand. An appropriate stochastic (random) model can be generated by sampling the events studied. The model builder ought to select a known but feasibly fitting probability distribution form, make an estimate of the parameter of the distribution selected, and then test to see how appropriate a goodness of fit has been achieved to continue or not to.

Through a continued effort, a postulated model may be selected at the final stage. This section, illustrated by a summary tabulation in Table 1.15, contains a review of "how to simulate what with which Monte Carlo simulators." This is further is supported by SIM-Moment software for the utilization of these simulators by those who refer to use this book.

The MC simulation technique is widely recognized as a valid method to include complex mathematics such that its results are more likely to be accepted than not. That said, MC Simulation is sometimes criticized as being an approximate and not an exact technique. Even if the quasi-random nature of the uniform, $u_i(0,1)$ random number generation exists, only to be resolved by a satisfactorily excessive number of iterations—at least $i = 1, \ldots, 50,000$ runs due to an empirical Java simulation digital experiment conducted by the author in Chapter 6 should do the job [3]. For a great many problems, these time and space limitations are nowadays irrelevant and inconsistent with the truth of the matter simply because they can be avoided by restructuring the software model into sections easier to master. Last but not least, the commonly used distributions in statistics for reliability analyses in Section 1.5.1 having been tabulated in Table 1.14 are appended with many more in Tables 1.15 and 1.16. The analyst definitely ought to keep the rule of thumb of "positive domain" for the random variable of interest, t (time), or rarely x (distance or operational cycle or epoch) consistently in mind, with $0 < t, x < \infty$ holding true, where $0 < R(t) < 1$. See Table 1.17 for uniform random numbers [3].

TABLE 1.16 Probability Density Functions for the Common Probability Distributions Used in Table 1.15

Order	Distribution Name	Probability Density Function
1	Negative exponential $(\lambda) =$ Weibull $(\alpha, \beta = 1)$	$f(t) = \lambda e^{-\lambda t}$
2	Weibull (α, β)	$f(t) = \dfrac{\beta t^{\beta-1}}{\alpha^{\beta}} e^{-(t/\alpha)^{\beta}}$
3	Gamma(α, β)	$f(x;\alpha;\beta) = \dfrac{x^{\alpha-1} e^{-(x/\beta)}}{\beta^{\alpha} \Gamma(\alpha)}$ for $x > 0$ and $\alpha, \beta > 0$
4	Erlang (k, λ)	$f(x;k;\lambda) = \dfrac{\lambda^{k} x^{k-1} e^{-\lambda x}}{(k-1)!}$ for $x, \lambda \geq 0$
5	Sahinoglu–Libby $(\alpha = a+c, \beta = b+d, L = \beta_1/\beta_2)$	$g(q) = \dfrac{L^{a+c} q^{\alpha+c-1} (1-q)^{b+d-1}}{B(b+d, a+c) \cdot \left[1-(1-L)q\right]^{a+b+c+d}}$

(Continued)

TABLE 1.16   **(Continued)**

Order	Distribution Name	Probability Density Function
6	Chi-square $\chi_n^2(n)$ Gamma($\alpha = 0.5$, $\beta = n/2$)	$f(x;k) = \begin{cases} \dfrac{x^{(k/2)-1}e^{-x/2}}{2^{k/2}\,\Gamma\left(\dfrac{k}{2}\right)} & x \geq 0; \\ 0 & \text{otherwise} \end{cases}$
7	Beta(A, B)	$f(x;\alpha,\beta) = \dfrac{1}{B(\alpha,\beta)}x^{\alpha-1}(1-x)^{\beta-1}$
8	Std normal, $N(0, 1)$	$\varnothing(x) = \dfrac{e^{-\frac{1}{2}x^2}}{\sqrt{2\pi}}$
9	Normal (μ, σ)	$f(x;\mu,\sigma) = \dfrac{1}{\sigma\sqrt{2\pi}}e^{-\frac{(x-\mu)^2}{2\sigma^2}}$
10	Pareto (c) or Laplace (or double exponential)	$f(x;\mu,b) = \dfrac{1}{2b}\begin{cases} \exp\left(-\dfrac{\mu-x}{b}\right) & \text{if } x < \mu \\ \exp\left(-\dfrac{x-\mu}{b}\right) & \text{if } x \geq \mu \end{cases}$
11	Lognormal (μ, σ)	$f(x) = \dfrac{1}{\sigma x\sqrt{2\pi}}e^{-\frac{(\ln x-\mu)^2}{2\sigma^2}}$
12	Fisher's F(n_1, n_2)	$f(x;n_1,n_2) = \dfrac{\sqrt{\dfrac{(n_1x)^{n_1}\,n_2^{n_2}}{(n_1x+n_2)^{n_1+n_2}}}}{x\,\mathrm{Beta}\left(\dfrac{n_1}{2},\dfrac{n_2}{2}\right)}$
13	Student's t-distribution (n)	$f(x) = \dfrac{\Gamma\left(\dfrac{n+1}{2}\right)}{\sqrt{n\pi}\,\Gamma\left(\dfrac{n}{2}\right)}\left(1+\dfrac{x^2}{n}\right)^{-\frac{n+1}{2}}$
14	Standard Cauchy (0,1)	$f(x;0,1) = \dfrac{1}{\pi(1+x^2)}$
15	Power (c)	$f(x) = Cx^{c-1}$
16	Raleigh = Weibull (α, $\beta=2$)	$f(t) = \dfrac{\beta t\beta - 1}{2\alpha}$
17	Logistic (a, k)	$f(x;a,k) = \dfrac{e^{-\frac{x-a}{k}}}{k\left(1+e^{-\frac{x-a}{k}}\right)^2}$
18	Arc sin = Beta ($A=0.5$, $B=0.5$)	$f(x) = \dfrac{1}{\pi\sqrt{x(1-x)}}$ for $0 \leq x \leq 1$
19	Gumbel (smallest extreme) Type I (γ,α)	$f(x) = \dfrac{1}{\gamma}e^{-(z+e^{-z})}$ where $z = -\dfrac{x-\alpha}{\gamma}$
20	Gumbel (largest extreme) Type I (γ,β)	$f(x) = \dfrac{1}{\beta}e^{-(z+e^{-z})}$ where $z = -\dfrac{x-\mu}{\beta}$
21	Uniform (a,b)	$f(t) = \dfrac{1}{(b-a)}$ $a \leq t \leq b$, otherwise $f(t) = 0$

where $y_i^* = \lambda^{-1}[\ln(1-u_i)]$; $i = 1,2,\ldots$

22	Triangular (a,b,c)	$f(x\mid a,b,c)=\begin{cases}0 & \text{for } x<a,\\ \dfrac{2(x-a)}{(b-a)(c-a)} & \text{for } a\le x\le c,\\ \dfrac{2(b-x)}{(b-a)(b-c)} & \text{for } c<x\le b,\\ 0 & \text{for } b<x,\end{cases}$
23	Bernoulli (p)	$f(k;p)=p^k(1-p)^{1-k}$ for $k\in\{0,1\}$
24	Binomial (np)	$f(k;n;p)=\Pr(X=k)=\binom{n}{k}p^k(1-p)^{n-k}$
25	Beta Binomial	$f(x)=\binom{n}{x}\dfrac{\Gamma(\alpha+x)\Gamma(n+\beta-x)\Gamma(\alpha+\beta)}{\Gamma(\alpha+\beta+n)\Gamma(\alpha)\Gamma(\beta)}$
26	Multinomial $(n, p_1, p_2,\dots, p_m)$; $m=3$, trinomial	$f(x)=\dfrac{n!}{x_1!\dots x_k!}p_1^{x_1}\dots p_k^{x_k}$
27	Poisson (λ)	$f(k;\lambda)=\Pr(X=k)=\dfrac{\lambda^k e^{-\lambda}}{k!};\lambda>0$ for $k=0,1,2,\dots$
28	Geometric (p,q)	$\Pr(X=k)=(1-p)^{k-1}p$
29	Negative Binomial $(k-1,n,p)$	$f(k;r;p)=\binom{k+r-1}{k}p^k(1-p)^r$ for $k=0,1,2,\dots$
30	Pascal (k,n,p)	$f(k;n;p)=\binom{k+n-1}{r-1}p^r(1-p)^k$ for $k=0,1,2,\dots$
31	Hypergeometric (n,K,N)	$P(X=k)=\dfrac{\binom{K}{k}\binom{N-K}{n-k}}{\binom{N}{n}}$

TABLE 1.17   500 (50 Rows by 10 Columns) Computer-Generated Random Numbers

0.6953	0.5247	0.1368	0.9850	0.7467	0.3813	0.5827	0.7893	0.7169	0.8166
0.0082	0.9925	0.6874	0.2122	0.6885	0.2159	0.4299	0.3467	0.2186	0.1033
0.6799	0.1241	0.3056	0.5590	0.0423	0.6515	0.2750	0.8156	0.2871	0.4680
0.8898	0.1514	0.1826	0.0004	0.5259	0.2425	0.8421	0.9248	0.9155	0.9518
0.6515	0.5027	0.9290	0.5177	0.3134	0.9177	0.2605	0.6668	0.1167	0.7870
0.3976	0.7790	0.0035	0.0064	0.0441	0.3437	0.1248	0.5442	0.9800	0.1857
0.0642	0.4086	0.6078	0.2044	0.0484	0.4691	0.7058	0.8552	0.5029	0.3288
0.0377	0.5250	0.7774	0.2390	0.9121	0.5345	0.8178	0.8443	0.4154	0.2526
0.5739	0.5181	0.0234	0.7305	0.0376	0.5169	0.5679	0.5495	0.7872	0.5321
0.5827	0.0341	0.7482	0.6351	0.9146	0.4700	0.7869	0.1337	0.0702	0.4219
0.0508	0.7905	0.2932	0.4971	0.0225	0.4466	0.5118	0.1200	0.0200	0.5445
0.4757	0.1399	0.5668	0.9569	0.7255	0.4650	0.4084	0.3701	0.9446	0.8064
0.6805	0.9931	0.4166	0.1091	0.7730	0.0691	0.9411	0.3468	0.0014	0.7379
0.2603	0.7507	0.6414	0.9907	0.2699	0.4571	0.9254	0.2371	0.8664	0.9553
0.8143	0.7625	0.1708	0.1900	0.2781	0.2830	0.6877	0.0488	0.8635	0.3155
0.5681	0.7854	0.5016	0.9403	0.1078	0.5255	0.8727	0.3815	0.5541	0.9833
0.1501	0.9363	0.3858	0.3545	0.5448	0.0643	0.3167	0.6732	0.6283	0.2631
0.8806	0.7989	0.7484	0.8083	0.2701	0.5039	0.9439	0.1027	0.9677	0.4597
0.4582	0.7590	0.4393	0.4704	0.6903	0.3732	0.6587	0.8675	0.2905	0.3058

(Continued)

TABLE 1.17 (Continued)

0.0785	0.1467	0.3880	0.5274	0.8723	0.7517	0.9905	0.8904	0.8177	0.6660
0.1158	0.6635	0.4992	0.9070	0.2975	0.5686	0.8495	0.1652	0.2039	0.2553
0.2762	0.7018	0.6782	0.4013	0.2224	0.4672	0.5753	0.6219	0.6871	0.9255
0.9382	0.6411	0.7984	0.0608	0.5945	0.3977	0.4570	0.9924	0.8398	0.8361
0.5102	0.7021	0.4353	0.3398	0.8038	0.2260	0.1250	0.1884	0.3432	0.1192
0.2354	0.7410	0.7089	0.2579	0.1358	0.8446	0.1648	0.3889	0.5620	0.6555
0.9082	0.7906	0.7589	0.8870	0.1189	0.7125	0.6324	0.1096	0.5155	0.3449
0.6936	0.0702	0.9716	0.0374	0.0683	0.2397	0.7753	0.2029	0.1464	0.8000
0.4042	0.8158	0.3623	0.6614	0.7954	0.7516	0.6518	0.3638	0.3107	0.2718
0.9410	0.2201	0.6348	0.0367	0.0311	0.0688	0.2346	0.3927	0.7327	0.9994
0.0917	0.2504	0.2878	0.1735	0.3872	0.6816	0.2731	0.3846	0.6621	0.8983
0.8532	0.4869	0.2685	0.6349	0.9364	0.3451	0.4998	0.2842	0.0643	0.6656
0.8980	0.0455	0.8314	0.8189	0.6783	0.8086	0.1386	0.4442	0.9941	0.6812
0.8412	0.8792	0.2025	0.9320	0.7656	0.3815	0.5302	0.8744	0.4584	0.3585
0.5688	0.8633	0.5818	0.0692	0.2543	0.5453	0.9955	0.1237	0.7535	0.5993
0.5006	0.1215	0.8102	0.1026	0.9251	0.6851	0.1559	0.1214	0.2628	0.9374
0.5748	0.4164	0.3427	0.2809	0.8064	0.5855	0.2229	0.2805	0.9139	0.9013
0.1100	0.0873	0.9407	0.8747	0.0496	0.4380	0.5847	0.4183	0.5929	0.4863
0.5802	0.7747	0.1285	0.0074	0.6252	0.7747	0.0112	0.3958	0.3285	0.5389
0.1019	0.6628	0.8998	0.1334	0.2798	0.7351	0.7330	0.6723	0.6924	0.3963
0.9909	0.8991	0.2298	0.2603	0.6921	0.5573	0.8191	0.0384	0.2954	0.0636
0.6292	0.4923	1.0276	0.6734	0.6562	0.4231	0.1980	0.6551	0.3716	0.0507
0.9430	0.2579	0.7933	0.0945	0.3192	0.3195	0.7772	0.4672	0.7070	0.5925
0.9938	0.7098	0.7964	0.7952	0.8947	0.1214	0.8454	0.8294	0.5394	0.9413
0.4690	0.1395	0.0930	0.3189	0.6972	0.7291	0.8513	0.9256	0.7478	0.8124
0.2028	0.3774	0.0485	0.7718	0.9656	0.2444	0.0304	0.1395	0.1577	0.8625
0.6141	0.4131	0.2006	0.2329	0.6182	0.5151	0.6300	0.9311	0.3837	0.7828
0.2757	0.8479	0.7880	0.8492	0.6859	0.8947	0.6246	0.1574	0.4936	0.8077
0.0561	0.0126	0.6531	0.0378	0.4975	0.1133	0.3572	0.0071	0.4555	0.7563
0.1419	0.4308	0.8073	0.4681	0.0481	0.2918	0.2975	0.0685	0.6384	0.0812
0.3125	0.0053	0.9209	0.9768	0.3584	0.0390	0.2161	0.6333	0.4391	0.6991

(a)

Weibull(α,β)

α	2
β	1
n	10000

Moment	
E(x)	2.018985
E(x2)	8.192468
E(x3)	50.156295
E(x4)	413.676195
V(x)	4.116169
Std. deviation	2.028834435
Skewness	2.167550
Kurtosis	7.324760

Trials(i)	Random UI	XI=α*(-ln(1-Ui))1/β	X2	X3	X4
1	0.172857301	0.379556097	0.144062831	0.054679926	0.020754099
2	0.057106803	0.117604524	0.013830824	0.001626567	0.000191292
3	0.14643513	0.316667471	0.100278287	0.031754872	0.010055735
4	0.349034889	0.858598464	0.737191322	0.632951336	0.543451045
5	0.641923202	2.05401559	4.218980044	8.665850784	17.79979261
6	0.00901283	0.018107382	0.000327877	5.9376-06	1.07504E-07
7	0.261870829	0.607272882	0.368780353	0.223950308	0.135998949
8	0.143642644	0.310135036	0.096183741	0.029829948	0.009251312
9	0.548072109	1.588465292	2.523221983	4.008050544	6.366649178
10	0.4925764	1.356818244	1.840955746	2.497842342	3.38911806
11	0.138796922	0.298849878	0.089311249	0.026690656	0.007976499
12	0.394033873	1.001862381	1.003728231	1.005597555	1.007470361

FIGURE 1.15 (a) Simulator for Weibull probability distribution from Table 1.15 for $n = 10,000$ simulation runs with $E(x) = 2$. (b) Weibull probability ($\beta = 1 \rightarrow$ Negative Exponential) from Table 1.15 with $E(x) = \alpha = 1$ using Stat-Plot Java software and Pedagogues of Exercise 1.7.49: P31 and P35 shown previously.

(b)

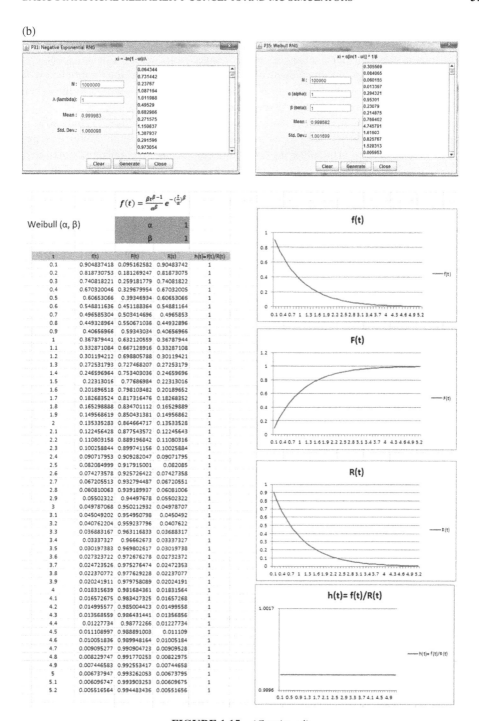

FIGURE 1.15   (*Continued*)

1.6 DISCUSSIONS AND CONCLUSION

This chapter covers five major review sections. It starts with deterministic and stochastic cyber-risk metrics as an introduction pivotal to the book itself and then continues with statistical risk analysis in the context of a feasible and alternative solution to the cyberware metric identification impasse explained through determinism.

Acceptance Sampling in quality control is presented next as a method to study so as to quantify cyberware metrics with certain novel applications through producer's and consumer's risk concepts. The following corrective Poisson and Normal approximation to Binomial distribution in quality control applications follows when input data so allows.

Last section, but not the least, certain analytical details about the basic statistical concepts and commonly used distributions with their MC simulators are presented for completion purposes (an example of which is presented in Figure 1.15).

1.7 EXERCISES

1.7.1 A company uses the following acceptance sampling procedure. A sample equal to 10% of the lot is taken. If 2% or less of the items in the sample are defective, the lot is accepted; otherwise, it is rejected. If submitted lots vary in size from 5,000 to 10,000 units, what can you say about the protection by this plan? If 0.05 is the desired LTPD, does this scheme offer reasonable protection to the consumer?

1.7.2 Suppose that a supplier ships components in lots of size 5000. A single sampling plan with $n=50$ and $c=2$ is being used for receiving inspection. Rejected lots are screened, and all defective items are reworked and returned to the lot:

a. Draw the operating characteristic (OC) curve for this plan.

b. Find the level of lot quality that will be rejected 90% of the time.

c. Management has objected to the use of the above sampling procedure and wants to use a plan with an acceptance number $c=0$, arguing that this is more consistent with their zero defects program. What do you think of this?

d. Design a single sampling plan with $c=0$ that will give a 0.90 probability of rejection of lots having the quality level found in part (b). Note that two plans are now matched at the LTPD point. Draw the OC curve for this plan and compare it to the one for $n=50$, $c=2$ in part (a).

e. Suppose that incoming lots are 0.5% nonconforming. What is the probability of rejecting these lots under both plans? Calculate the average total inspection (ATI) at this point for both plans. Which plan do you prefer? Why?

1.7.3 Let $\bar{x}$ be the mean of a random sample of size $n=36$ from $N(\mu, 9)$. Our decision rule is to reject H_0: $\mu=50$ and to accept H_1: $\mu>50$ if $x \geq 50.8$. Determine the OC (μ) curve and evaluate it at $\mu=50.0, 50.5, 51.0$, and 51.5. What is the significant level of the test?

1.7.4 Consider an $N(\mu, \sigma^2=40)$ distribution. To test H_0: $\mu=32$ against H_1: $\mu>32$, we reject H_0 if the sample mean $\bar{x} \geq c$. Find the sample size n and the constant c such that OC ($\mu=32$)=0.90 and OC ($\mu=35$)=0.15.

1.7.5 Let Y have a binomial distribution with parameters n and p. In a test of $H_0: p=0.25$ against $H_1: p<0.25$, we reject H_0 if $Y/n \leq c$. Find n and c if OC $(p=0.20) = 0.05$. State your assumptions.

1.7.6 Let $\bar{x}$ be the mean of a random sample of size $n=16$ from a normal distribution with mean μ and standard deviation $\sigma=8$. To test $H_0: \mu=35$ against $H_1: \mu>35$, we reject H_0 if $\bar{x} \geq 36.5$:

a. Determine the OC curve at $\mu=35$, 36, and 38.5.

b. What is the probability of a Type I error?

c. What is the probability of a Type II error at $\mu=36$?

1.7.7 Let x and $\bar{y}$ be means of random samples of size $n_1=14$ and $n_2=18$ from the respective normal distributions $N(\mu_1, \sigma_1^2=26)$ and $N(\mu_2, \sigma_2^2=21)$. Let $\theta=\mu_1-\mu_2$. Construct a test of $H_0: \theta=0$ against $H_1: \theta<0$ that has significance level $\alpha=0.025$. Determine the $OC(\theta)$ curve for $\theta=-5, -4, -3, -2, -1, 0$ and graph this function.

1.7.8 The joint probability function (p.f.) of (X,Y) is given by

x	0	1	2
0	1/6	1/6	1/6
1	1/6	0	0
2	1/6	0	0

a. Find VAR(X), VAR(Y), and ρ_{XY}.

b. Determine VAR($X+Y$).

c. Are X and Y independent?

d. Comment on the relation between VAR(X)+VAR(Y) and VAR($X+Y$).

1.7.9 From hospital records collected over several years, it is found that only 2% of cancer patients of a certain type are cured by surgery. A chemotherapist claims that nonsurgical methods may be more successful than surgery. To obtain experimental evidence to support the claims, the nonsurgical technique is tried on 200 patients. Of these, 6 are cured:

a. Formulate the null and alternative hypothesis in terms of the expected number of cures out of 200 patients.

b. If X counts the number of cures in 200 patients:
  (i) What is the distribution of X when H_0 is true?
  (ii) What is the approximate distribution of X when H_0 is true?

c. Determine the P-value.

d. If α is fixed at 0.05, what could we conclude?

1.7.10 Suppose one dead battery has been put into a box with three good ones. If the batteries are tested one at a time until the dead one is found, find the expected number of batteries that have been tested when the defective is found.

1.7.11   Suppose two slot machines are available. Machine A costs $1 to play and, with probability 1/3, returns $2 and, with probability 2/3, returns nothing. Machine B also costs $1 to play but, with probability 1/6, returns $4 and, with probability 5/6, returns nothing. Consider the following two methods of play:

1. Play machine A first, if you win, play A again; otherwise switch to B.
2. Play machine B first, if you win, play B again; otherwise switch to A.

    a. Find the mean and variance of your net gain under the two possible methods of play.

    b. Which of the two methods would you prefer and why?

1.7.12   Let X have the probability mass function (pmf)

$$P(X) = c\left(\frac{1}{4}\right)^{X} \quad x = 0,1,2,....$$

1. Find c so that this is a proper probability function.
2. Determine $E(X)$ and $\mathrm{VAR}(X)$.

1.7.13   The time to service customers at a bank teller's cage is exponentially distributed with a mean of 50 s:

    a. What is the probability that two customers in front of an arriving customer will each take less than 60 s to complete their transactions?

    b. What is the probability that two customers in front will furnish their transactions so that an arriving customer can reach the teller's cage within 2 min?

1.7.14   Lead time is gamma distributed in 100 s of units with a shape parameter of 3 and a scale parameter of 1. What is the probability that the lead time exceeds 2 (hundred) units during an upcoming cycle?

1.7.15   The weekly demand, X, for a slow-moving item has been found to be well approximated by a geometric distribution on the range $\{0,1,2,...\}$ with mean weekly demand of 2.5 items. Generate 10 values of X demand per week, using random numbers from Table 1.17. [Hint: For a geometric distribution on the range $\{q, q+1,...\}$ with parameter p, the mean is $1/p+q-1$.]

1.7.16   Lead times have been found to be exponentially distributed with mean 3.7 days. Generate five random lead times from this distribution.

1.7.17   A machine is taken out of production if it fails or after 5 h, whichever comes first. By running similar machines until failure, it has been found that time to failure, X has the Weibull distribution with $\alpha=8$, $\beta=0.75$, and $\nu=0$. Thus, the time until the machine is taken out of production can be represented as $Y=\min(X,5)$. Develop a step-by-step procedure for generating Y.

1.7.18   Develop a technique for generating a binomial random variable, X, using the convolution technique. [Hint: X can be represented as the number of success in n independent Bernoulli trails, each success having probability p. Thus, $X = \sum_{i=1}^{n} X_{i}$, where $P(X_{i}=1)=P$ and $P(X_{i}=0)=1-P$.]

1.7.19 Write a computer routine to generate gamma variates with shape parameter k and scale parameter θ. Generate 1000 values with $k=2.5$ and $\theta=0.2$ and compare the true mean, $1/\theta=5$, to the sample mean.

1.7.20 If $f(t)=\lambda e^{-\lambda t}$ and $\lambda>0$, $t>0$, what effect does doubling the value of λ have on (a) the MTTF and (b) $R(t)$?

1.7.21 Assume an equipment consists of two components for which the failure rates are $\lambda_1=0.001$ and $\lambda_2=0.002$, respectively. Calculate the equipment reliability for $t=100$ for the following two cases: (a) series connection and (b) parallel connection.

1.7.22 Show that if $n=4$, k out of n binomial equation can be approximated by either $4q$ or $4q-6q^2$. (Note: The reliability analyst makes frequent use of such approximations.)

1.7.23 The failure rate for a television receiver is 0.02 failures/h:

    a. Calculate the mean time between failures.

    b. What is the probability of such a receiver failing in the first 4 h?

1.7.24 The probability distribution function (pdf) for the time to failure of an appliance is $f(t) = \dfrac{32}{(t+4)^3}$, $t>0$, where t is in years:

    a. Find the reliability of $R(t)$.

    b. Find the failure rate $\lambda(t)$.

    c. Find the MTTF.

1.7.25 The reliability of a machine is given by

$$R(t) = \exp\left[-0.041t - 0.008t^2\right] \quad (t \text{ in years})$$

    a. What is the failure rate?

    b. What should the design life be to maintain a reliability of at least 0.90?

1.7.26 An electronic device is tested for 2 months and found to have a reliability of 0.990; the device is also known to have a constant failure rate:

    a. What is the failure rate?

    b. What is the mean time to failure?

    c. What is the design life reliability for a design life of 4 years?

    d. What should the design life be to achieve a reliability of 0.950?

1.7.27 A device has a constant failure rate of 0.7/year:

    a. What is the probability that the device will fail during the second year of operation?

    b. If upon failure the device is immediately replaced, what is the probability that there will be more than one failure in 3 years of operation?

1.7.28 A 1-year guarantee is given based on the assumption that no more than 10% of the items will be returned. Assuming an exponential distribution, what is the maximum failure rate that can be tolerated?

1.7.29 The reliability for the Rayleigh distribution is $R(t)=e^{-(t/\theta)^2}$. Find the MTTF in terms of θ.

1.7.30 A manufacturer determines that average television set is used 1.8 h/day. A 1-year warranty is offered on the picture tube having an MTTF of 2000 h. If the distribution is exponential, what fraction of the tubes will fail during the warranty period?

1.7.31 Night watchmen carry an industrial flashlight 8 h per night and 7 nights per week. It is estimated that on average, the flashlight is turned on about 20 min per 8-h shift. The flashlight is assumed to have a constant failure rate of 0.08/h while it is turned on and off 0.005/h when it is turned off but being carried:

a. In working hours, estimate the MTTF of the flashlight.
b. What is the probability of the flashlight's failing during one 8-h shift?
c. What is the probability of its failing during 1 month (30 days) of 8-h shifts?

1.7.32 The 1-month reliability on an indicator lamp is 0.95 with the failure rate specified as constant. What is the probability that more than two spare bulbs will be needed during the first year of operation? (Ignore replacement time.)

1.7.33 A servomechanism has an MTTF of 2000 h with a constant failure rate:

a. What is the reliability for a 125-h mission?
b. Neglecting repair time, what is probability that more than one failure occur during a 125-h mission?
c. What is the probability that more than two failures will occur during a 125-h mission?

1.7.34 The MTTF for punctures of truck tires is 150,000 miles. A truck with 10 tires carries 1 spare:

a. What is the probability that 1 spare will be used on a 10,000-mile trip?
b. What is the probability that more than the single spare will be required on a 10,000-mile trip?

1.7.35 At the end of 1 year of service, the reliability of a component with a constant failure rate is 0.95:

a. What is the failure rate (include units)?
b. If two of the components are put in active parallel, what is the 1-year reliability? (Assume no dependencies)
c. If 10% of the component failure rate may be attributed to common-mode failures, what will the 1-year reliability be of the two components in active parallel?

1.7.36 A disk drive has a constant failure rate and an MTTF of 5000 h:

a. What will the probability of failure be for 1 year of operation?
b. What will the probability of failure be for 1 year of operation if two of the drives are placed in active parallel and the failures are independent?
c. What will the probability of failure be for 1 year of operation if the common-mode errors are characterized by $\beta = 0.2$?

1.7.37 Suppose that without preventive maintenance, the failure (hazard) rate of a computer hard drive is given by $\lambda(t) = (1.1)(10^{-6})t + (1.0)(10^{-9})t^2$, where t is given in CPU hours and $\lambda(t)$ is per year:

    a. Calculate the design life reliability of the hard drive for a design life of 10,000 CPU hours assuming that no preventive maintenance is performed?

    b. Suppose that by overhaul the hard drive is returned to as-good-as-new condition. How frequently should the PC company perform overhauls to accomplish a design reliability of at least 0.90?

1.7.38 Suppose that a computer keyboard is life tested and has an MTTF$=68$ h and mean time to repair (MTTR)$=1.5$ h. (a) What is the availability with corrective maintenance? (b) If the MTTR is reduced to 1 h with extra measures, what MTTF can be tolerated without altering the machine availability?

    a. An annual life test revealed that 92% of the computer hard disks were found to be operable. (a) According to this data, what is the long-term availability of these disks? (b) If one is not happy with this availability figure and desires to reach an availability of 0.98, how often must one perform testing and replacement procedures?

1.7.39 A component has a 1-year design life reliability of 0.9; two such components are placed in active parallel. What is the 1-year reliability of the resulting system:

    a. In the absence of common-mode failures?

    b. If 20% of the failure are common-mode failures?

1.7.40 In a 1/2 active parallel system, each unit has a failure rate of 0.05 day^{-1}:

    a. What is the system MTTF with no load sharing?

    b. What is the system MTTF if the failure rate increases by 10% as a result of increased load?

    c. What is the system MTTF if one increases both unit failure rates by 10%?

1.7.41 For a 2/3 (k out of n) system:

    a. Express $R(t)$ in terms of the constant failure rates.

    b. Find the system MTTF.

    c. Calculate the reliability y when $\lambda t = 1.0$ and compare the result to a single unit and to a 1/2 system with the same unit failure rate.

1.7.42 The failure rate on a jet engine is $\lambda = 10^{-3}$/h. What is the probability that more than two engines on a four-engine aircraft will fail during a 2-h flight? Assuming that failures are independent?

1.7.43 Calculate the input_output reliabilities of the following systems:

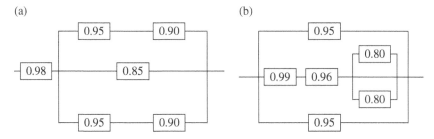

1.7.44   Given 0.90 for all component reliabilities, calculate the reliability of the two systems from Exercise 1.7.43.

1.7.45   An old WWII fighter plane has two constant failure rate ($\lambda=0.223$/year) parallel engines each with a reliability of exp $(-0.223$/year $*1$ year$)=0.8$. What is the probability of failure (downfall of the plane) due to natural causes if it is affected by common-mode errors such as very strong wind turbulence that are characterized by a ratio of $\beta=0.4$ to the independent normal failure mode?

1.7.46   A constant failure rate tablet has a "mean time to failure" (MTTF) of 1500h. The ADPYZ company offers a year warranty. What fraction of these tablets will not fail during the warranty period?

1.7.47   A software product with a constant failure rate to be marketed is being tested for 2 months and found to possess a reliability of 0.95:

   a. What is the failure rate?
   b. What is the MTTF?
   c. What is the reliability of this product 4 years into its operation if it is in continuous use?
   d. What is the warranty time to accomplish an operational reliability of 95%?

1.7.48   Using Table 1.5 from Example 1.2.6.2:

   We define a quasi-Type III error probability, that is, Composite Cyberware Riskiness, CCR $= \alpha*\beta$. Calculate CCR, Non-CCR, and CPR and check if CCR+Non-CCR+CPR$=1.00$?

   Solution: In Table 1.5 of this chapter, $\beta=0.012$ for $\mu_0=11$ and $\mu_1=13$ for $\theta=\mu_1-\mu_0=2$ when $\alpha=0.10$. Then CCR$= \alpha*\beta=0.1*0.012=0.0012$ can be defined as CCR. Therefore *Non-CCR (nonriskiness)*$=(1-\alpha)*(1-\beta)=1-\alpha-\beta+\alpha*\beta=(1-0.1)(1-0.012)=0.8892$.
   This leaves *Cyberware Partial Riskiness (CPR)* either due to Type I (producer's risk) or Type II (consumer's risk) contributions$=$significance $*$ power$+$confidence $*$ $(1-$Power$)=\{\alpha(1-\beta)+(1-\alpha)\beta\}=0.1096$. Note as follows: CCR + Non-CCR +CPR$=0.0012+0.8892+0.1096=1$. Can you derive the probability density functions of the CCR $= \alpha*\beta$, similarly Non-CCR and CPR, using an empirical Bayesian approach to be supported by the MC Simulation [16, 17]?

1.7.49   For the Pedagogues' main menu, make reasonable data available for each of the 61 pedagogical buttons so that one can see the outcome for each of the 61 to a sample input you implemented. See Table 1.18.

1.7.50   Given the following hypothesis test for testing software or hardware product:
   Null hypothesis: H_0: Cyberware is good (functional and operating)
   Alternative hypothesis: H_1: Cyberware is bad (dysfunctional and ill-operating)
   [17–19]

   a. As in Example 3 in Section 1.2.6.3., provided the input sample costs: $C_{11}=+\$800$ (CCR loss), $C_{21}=+\$70$ (CPR$_1$ loss), $C_{12}=+\$200$ (CPR$_2$ loss), $C_{22}=-\$400$ (Non-CCR utility gain) as per unit cost coefficients; this time take the fifth input LOSS$=1,3,5,7,10,20,30,40,50,60,70,80,85,89,90,100$

TABLE 1.18 Pedagogues for Exercise 1.7.49

Pedagogical CSIS 6013		
Main Menu		
○ P1: Common Mode Failure - 2-unit Active Parallel	○ P22: MultiState System Reliability - Simple Parallel	○ P44: Sahinoglu-Libby
○ P2: Load Sharing Reliability - 2-unit Active Parallel	○ P23: MultiState System Reliability - Series-In-Parallel	○ P45: Power(c)
○ P3: 2-unit Standby Redundancy	○ P24: MultiState System Reliability - Parallel-In-Series	○ P46: Geometric(p,q)
○ P4: n-unit Standby Redundancy	○ P25: MultiState System Reliability - Combined System	○ P47: Gumbel Smallest I(y,a)
○ P5: Series System Reliability	○ P26: Goel-Okumoto NHPP	○ P48: Gumbel Largest I(y,a)
○ P6: Parallel System Reliability	○ P27: Musa-Okumoto Logarithmic Poisson Execution	○ P49: Triangular(a,b,c)
○ P6a: Simple Active Parallel System	○ P28: Sahinoglu Poisson^Geometric Model	○ P50: Fisher's F(n1,n2)
○ P7: Series-In-Parallel Reliability	○ P29: Average Availability A(∞)	○ P51: Neg.Binom.(k-1,n,p)
○ P8: Parallel-In-Series Reliability	◉ P30: Availability A(t)	○ P5Z: Pascal(k,n,p)
○ P9: Reliability, Unreliability, MTTF	○ P31: Negative Exponential RNG	◉ P53: Bernoulli(p)
○ P10: Warranty	○ P32: StdNormal RNG	○ P54: Binomial(np)
○ P11: Mean, Variance, Mode, Median, Reliability	○ P33: Normal RNG	○ P55: Standard Cauchy(0,1)
○ P12: Software Testing Stopping Rule 1	○ P34: LogNormal RNG	○ P56: Student's t-distribution(n)
○ P13: Software Testing Stopping Rule 2	○ P35: Weibull RNG	○ P57: Beta(A, B)
○ P14: Cost Profit Analysis - Discrete Time	○ P36: Raleigh RNG	○ P58: Arc Sin = Beta(A = 0.5, B = 0.5)
○ P15: Empirical Bayesian Next Step Stopping Rule	○ P37: Erlang RNG	○ P59: Beta Binomial
○ P16: Empirical Bayesian Stopping Time Rule	○ P38: Gamma RNG	○ P60: Multinomial(n, p1, p2... pm;m=3 trinom
○ P17: Cost Profit Analysis - Continuous Time	○ P39: Uniform RNG	○ P61: Hypergeometric(n,D,M) approx Binomial(np)
○ P18: Weighted Squared-Error Loss Function (q*, r*)	○ P40: Chi-Squared RNG	
○ P19: Weighted Squared-Error Loss Function (q**, r**)	○ P41: Poisson RNG	
○ P20: Maximum Likelihood Estimate (q** (l-s), r** (l-s)	○ P42: Pareto(c) or Laplace	
○ P21: MultiState System Reliability - Simple Series	○ P43: Logistic(a,k)	

(stop when infeasible?) and draw a plot for i) Expected Cost ($\Sigma P_{ij} C_{ij} < 0$), ii) Type-I error (α), iii) Type-II error (β), all vs LOSS.

b. Execute the same as in a) but use $C_{11} = \$800$, $C_{21} = \$70$, $C_{12} = \$200$, $C_{22} = -\$800$.

c. Execute the same as in a) but use $C_{11} = \$800$, $C_{21} = \$70$, $C_{12} = \$200$, $C_{22} = -\$1500$.

d. Execute the same as in a) but use $C_{11} = \$800$, $C_{21} = \$70$, $C_{12} = \$200$, $C_{22} = -\$2000$.

e. Execute the same as in a) but use $C_{11} = -\$2000$, $C_{21} = \$70$, $C_{12} = \$200$, $C_{22} = -\$2000$.

f. Execute the same as in a) but use $C_{11} = -\$2000$, $C_{21} = -\$350$, $C_{12} = \$200$, $C_{22} = -\$2000$.

g. Execute the same as in a) but use $C_{11} = \$2000$, $C_{21} = -\$70$, $C_{12} = -\$1000$, $C_{22} = -\$2000$.

h. Given the following hypothesis test for testing software or hardware product:
Null hypothesis: H_0: Cyberware is good (functional and operating)
Alternative hypothesis: H1: Cyberware is bad (dysfunctional and ill-operating) [17–19]

a) As in Example 3 in Section 1.2.6.3., provided the input sample costs: $C_{11} = +\$800$ (CCR loss), $C_{21} = +\$70$ (CPR$_1$ loss), $C_{12} = +\$200$ (CPR$_2$ loss), $C_{22} = -\$400$ (Non-CCR utility gain) as per unit cost coefficients; this time take the fifth input LOSS = 1,3,5,7,10,20,30,40,50,60,70,80,85,89,90,100 (stop when infeasible?) and draw a plot for i) Expected Cost ($\Sigma P_{ij} C_{ij} < 0$), ii) Type-I error (α), iii) Type-II error (β), all vs LOSS.

b) Execute the same as in a) but use $C_{11} = \$800$, $C_{21} = \$70$, $C_{12} = \$200$, $C_{22} = -\$800$.

c) Execute the same as in a) but use $C_{11} = \$800$, $C_{21} = \$70$, $C_{12} = \$200$, $C_{22} = -\$1500$.

d) Execute the same as in a) but use $C_{11} = \$800$, $C_{21} = \$70$, $C_{12} = \$200$, $C_{22} = -\$2000$.

e) Execute the same as in a) but use $C_{11} = \$2000$, $C_{21} = \$70$, $C_{12} = \$200$, $C_{22} = -\$2000$

   f) Execute the same as in a) but use $C_{11} = \$2000$, $C_{21} = \$350$, $C_{12} = \$200$, $C_{22} = -\$2000$

   g) Execute the same as in a) but use $C_{11} = \$2000$, $C_{21} = \$70$, $C_{12} = \$1000$, $C_{22} = -\$2000$

REFERENCES

[1] Munson, J. C., *Software Engineering Measurement*, Auerbach Publications, CRC Press Company, Boca Raton, FL, 2003.

[2] Kan, S. H., *Metrics and Models in Software Quality Engineering*, Addison Wesley Longman Inc., Boston, MA, 1995.

[3] Sahinoglu, M., *Trustworthy Computing*, John Wiley & Sons, Inc., Hoboken, NJ, 2007.

[4] Halstead, M. H., *Elements of Software Science*, Elsevier, New York, 1977.

[5] Jackson, J. E., *A User's Guide to Principal Components*, John Wiley & Sons, Inc., New York, 1991.

[6] Montgomery, D.C, *Introduction to Statistical Quality Control*, John Wiley & Sons, Inc., Hoboken, NJ, 2005.

[7] Stat Trek. Available at https://www.google.com/webhp?sourceid=chrome-instant&rlz= 1C1CHMO_enUS586US586&ion=1&espv=2&ie=UTF-8#q=Stat+Trek.+Available+at+http %3A%2F%2Fstattrek.com%2F (accessed on 15 September, 2015).

[8] Ostle, B., Mensing, R. W., *Statistics in Research*, The Iowa State University Press, Ames, IA, 1975.

[9] Hogg, R. V., Ledolter, J., *Applied Statistics for Engineers and Physical Scientists*, Macmillan Publishing Company, New York, 1992.

[10] Anirban, D. G., *Statistics 301T, Lecture Notes on Basic Statistical Methods and Statistical Quality Control* Purdue University, West Lafayette, IN, 47907, 1997.

[11] Vose, D., *Risk Analysis*, John Wiley & Sons, Inc., Hoboken, NJ, 2008.

[12] Mendenhall, W., Beaver, R. J., Beaver, B. M., *Introduction to Probability and Statistics*, Brooks Cole publishing Company, Belmont, CA, 1999.

[13] Lewis, E. E., *Introduction to Reliability Engineering*, John Wiley & Sons, Inc., Hoboken, NJ, 1996.

[14] Trivedi, K. S., *Probability and Statistics with Reliability, Queuing and Computer Science Applications*, John Wiley & Sons, Inc., Hoboken, NJ, 2002.

[15] Woltenshome, L. C., *Reliability Modeling a Statistical Approach*, Chapman & Hall, London, 1999.

[16] Kalaylioglu, Z. (2014). Performances of Bayesian model selection criteria generalized for linear models with nonignorably missing covariates, *Journal of Statistical Computation and Simulation*, **84**(8), 1670–1691.

[17] Sahinoglu, M., Balasurya, R., Tyson, D., (2015). *Game-Theoretic Decision Making for Type I and II Errors in Testing Hypotheses*, Proceedings of the JSM 2015, Section on Risk Analysis, 2976–2990, Seattle, WA.

[18] Schlag Karl (2008). Bringing game theory to hypothesis testing; establishing finite sample bounds on inference, http://hdl.handle.net/10230/1232 (accessed on 15 September, 2015).

[19] Grant, J. B. B. (2014). Should have been 8%, not 5%? *ASA, Royal Statistical Society*, **11**(5), 85.

2

COMPLEX NETWORK RELIABILITY EVALUATION AND ESTIMATION IN CYBER-RISK

LEARNING OBJECTIVES

- Examine reliability block diagramming techniques for simple series–parallel and complex systems by studying the "Overlap Algorithm."
- Examine multistate network reliability evaluation when states may operate at derated and degraded above and beyond up and down states.
- Study Weibull distributed components in complex cyber systems.

2.1 INTRODUCTION

Network reliability is the probability that a network with all its subnetworks and constituting components will successfully complete the task it is intended to perform under the conditions encountered for the specified period of time defined between a source and a target. Reliability block diagramming (RBD) has been an active area of research for decades, even more so now with the advent of the embedded systems [1–10]. Rigorous analysis is essential whenever the cost of failure is high [11]. Modeling and simulation allow analysts to determine weak spots in the systems so that the maintenance engineer can inventory a backup list of components. The reliability analysis focuses on the computer network components and the connections between them to determine the overall system reliability as well as the reliabilities between any two individual nodes in the network. Network reliability computations are similar to those developed for industrial applications, but there are a few exceptions. In industrial applications, all of the components in the system are usually considered critical to the overall function of the system. However, in network applications, the target communication between two nodes may select a few components in the system due to redundancy [12, 13].

Cyber-Risk Informatics: Engineering Evaluation with Data Science, First Edition. Mehmet Sahinoglu.
© 2016 John Wiley & Sons, Inc. Published 2016 by John Wiley & Sons, Inc.
Companion website: www.wiley.com/go/sahinoglu/informatics

Currently, most published educational materials cover methods for determining system reliabilities in networks that can be expressed as pure parallel–series systems or reducing a complex topology to a parallel–series one using a conditional "keystone" method. But as experience proves, these ready-to-cook networks with small sizes rarely occur outside textbooks and classrooms. These computations prove impossible or mathematically unwieldy when applied to real complex networks and are therefore useful only to teach basic reliability concepts. The graphical screening ease and convenience of RBD algorithms is advantageous for planners and designers trying to improve system reliability by allowing quick and efficient intervention that may be required at a dispatch center to observe routine operations and identify solution alternatives in case of a crisis. The Boolean decomposition and binary enumeration algorithms [14–16] are outside the practical scope of this chapter due to large networks we normally work with.

The algorithm through a user-friendly and graphical Java applet computes the reliability of any complex parallel–series network. Furthermore, the coded topology can be transmitted remotely and then reverse engineered to reconstruct the original network diagram for purposes of securing classified information and saving space [17–20]. This, too, can be applied to security-related input for wired or wireless systems. All current exact computational algorithms for general networks are based on enumeration of states, minpaths, or mincuts [2, 3]. Network reliability estimation has been used successfully for nontrivial-sized networks using neural networks and heuristic algorithms in Refs. [7, 8] as well as employing a concurrent error detection approach by the coauthor of an earlier research [21]. Other researchers have used efficient Monte Carlo simulation [4, 5]. Bounds such as Jan's upper bound, used to reduce the complexity of computations, are approximate [3]. A thorough analysis is by Colbourn [1]. The next sections demonstrate recent progress in s–t network reliability field with pertinent software tools [22–25].

2.2   OVERLAP TECHNIQUE TO CALCULATE COMPLEX NETWORK RELIABILITY

With the emergence and maturity of reliability engineering over the past few decades, there is a growing need to efficiently produce accurate reliability models for increasingly larger and more complex systems. For purely parallel–series networks, there are simple and widely available algorithms to mathematically determine exact reliabilities between a given ingress and egress node. For complex networks, however, there is very little in the way of freely available algorithms that are simple, accurate, efficient, and scalable. This chapter discusses the discovery and implementation of one such "overlap" algorithm by treating nodes and links in (i) single-state static, (ii) multistate static, and (iii) single-state time-dependent dynamic with a working Weibull probability density function (pdf) [26, 27].

Every network can be represented, in its simplest form, as a binary state chart representing all of the possible states and their respective reliabilities, whose probability sum is always 1. The reliability from one node to another is the sum of all states that constitute at least one path of sequentially connected nodes that form an unbroken link between the source node and the target node. The source and target nodes can be interchanged with no impact on the final result.

2.2.1   Network State Enumeration and Example 1

Consider the five-node sample network in Figure 2.1. Each node has a reliability of 0.9, meaning that 90% of the time it is up (operating, functional, working), while 10% of the time it is down (not operating, dysfunctional, not working). The state diagram would look like the following. The "1–5 Probability" column is only populated in $2^5 = 32$ states that constitute a complete link between node 1 and node 5, where the rest are left out with zero results in Table 2.1.

Note that this returns the same results as standard parallel–series equations as done manually:

$$R_T = R_1 \times \left(1 - \left((1 - R_3) \times (1 - R_2 \times R_4)\right)\right) \times R_5$$
$$= 0.9 \times \left(1 - \left((1 - 0.9) \times (1 - 0.9 \times 0.9)\right)\right) \times 0.9 = 0.79461 \tag{2.1}$$

Using a binary state chart works fine for very small networks, but the exponential nature of the underlying data renders it impossible to use for larger networks. A relatively small 10-node network would require 10 column and 2^{10} (=1,024) rows with 10,240 total cells, while a still small 20-node network would require 20 columns and 2^{20} (=1,048,576) rows with 20,971,520 total cells. This is too much data to handle efficiently in the calculation of small network reliabilities. These state charts can be, however, useful in analyzing how individual paths affect each other while generating reliabilities as a system.

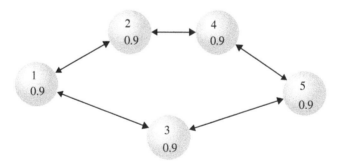

FIGURE 2.1   Example 1's five-node and two-path static network.

TABLE 2.1   Five-Node/Two-Path Static Network State Enumeration Table for "1–5" in Figure 2.1

	Node					
1	2	3	4	5	Probability	1–5 Probability
1	0	1	0	1	0.00729	0.00729
1	0	1	1	1	0.06561	0.06561
1	1	0	1	1	0.06561	0.06561
1	1	1	0	1	0.06561	0.06561
1	1	1	1	1	0.59049	0.59049
Total reliability					1	0.79461

TABLE 2.2   Five-Node and Two-Path Static Network State Probability Table with Useful Paths for Example 1

Node							
1	2	3	4	5	Probability	1, 3, 5	1, 2, 4, 5
1	0	1	0	1	0.00729	0.00729	
1	0	1	1	0	0.00729		
1	0	1	1	1	0.06561	0.06561	
1	1	0	1	1	0.06561		0.06561
1	1	1	0	1	0.06561	0.06561	
1	1	1	1	1	0.59049	0.59049	0.59049
Total reliability					1	0.729	0.6561

For instance, consider the same five-node network in Figure 2.1. We can quickly deduce that the two unique paths through the system from node 1 to node 5 are {1→3→5} and {1→2→4→5}. More on algorithmically determining paths will follow. If all of the nodes in either path are up, there will be a continuous connection between the source and target nodes. If we map the two paths in the state diagram below (all of the states where node 1 is down have been hidden to reduce the size), we find that the sum of two reliabilities (=1.385) is exactly 0.59049 greater than the desired result (Table 2.2).

This is the probability of *overlap* between the two paths. The overlap is found by taking a union of all the nodes in both paths. This union is simply a mathematical state of overlap and does not need to represent a path across.

Unfortunately, reliability calculation for complex networks is not as simple as subtracting the overlaps between unique paths. When there are more than two paths, many states may overlap across multiple paths. When subtracting overlaps, any state that has been subtracted more than once will have to be readded to the final result.

2.2.2   Generating Minimal Paths and Example 2

This practice into the binary nature of reliability networks and the overlapping characteristics of path reliabilities lends itself to the idea of a structured algorithm that could compute a finite set of minimal paths from ingress to egress; thus one considers the individual reliabilities of each path and programmatically adjusts for overlaps. The first step, determining a set of minimal paths, is of utmost importance regarding efficiency and scalability. Theoretically, we could consider the same exact path multiple times, and the algorithm would determine that a duplicate path is a complete overlap. We could then systematically subtract all redundant state reliabilities. However, after brief analysis of the problem pattern, it is apparent that path overlap will have to be computed triangularly. It follows then that any duplication of initial paths can affect the total algorithm time increasing exponentially.

Finding the set of minimal paths across a network from one node to another can be accomplished using a simple stack. As the algorithm will step through node connections in sequence, it is helpful to have the networked nodes uniquely ordered to prevent confusion as to which nodes have already been addressed and which node should come next at any given point along the algorithm. Ordering can either be accomplished by alphabetic sorting, if the nodes have been uniquely named beforehand, or simply assigning an abstract index ($1 \ldots n$) to each node before beginning. The order of the nodes is not important as the set of minimal paths generated will be the same regardless of order. Start by pushing the start node onto the initially empty stack and repeat the following algorithm on the top stack node until the stack is again empty as follows:

1. If the top node connects directly to the target node:
    a. Push the target node onto the stack.
    b. Save the current stack as a new minimal path (the bottom node is the start node and represents the start of the minimal path, while the top node is now the target node representing the end of the path).
    c. Pop the top two nodes (the target node and the node that links directly to it) off of the stack.
2. If the top node does not connect directly to the target node, push the next connecting node onto the stack. The next connecting node can be determined by the following logic:
    a. No node that is already in the stack is a candidate. This would cause a recursion issue as paths could fall into a recurring loop that grows infinitely in size without ever reaching the target node.
    b. If the previous action was a push action (i.e., the current node was newly pushed onto the stack), choose the lowest ordered node connected to the top stack node that is not already in the stack.
    c. If the previous action was a pop action (i.e., one of the nodes connected to the top node had finished its iterations and was removed), choose the next ordered node connected to the top stack node after the previously popped node.
3. If the top node does not connect directly to the target node and no new connecting node was found to push onto the stack, pop the top node off the stack.

Using the simple network depicted in Figure 2.2, it is possible to walk through the minimal path algorithm step by step to find the set of minimal paths across the network starting from node 1 and traversing to node 6.

Step 1: Add the start node to the stack:

$$\boxed{1}$$

Step 2: The top node (1) connect to both nodes 2 and 3, and neither one is already in the stack. As the last action was a push action, push the lowest order node, 2, to the stack.

$$\boxed{1} \, \boxed{2}$$

Step 3: The top node (2) connects to nodes 1 and 4, but 1 is already in the stack, so push node 4 onto the stack.

$$\boxed{1} \, \boxed{2} \, \boxed{4}$$

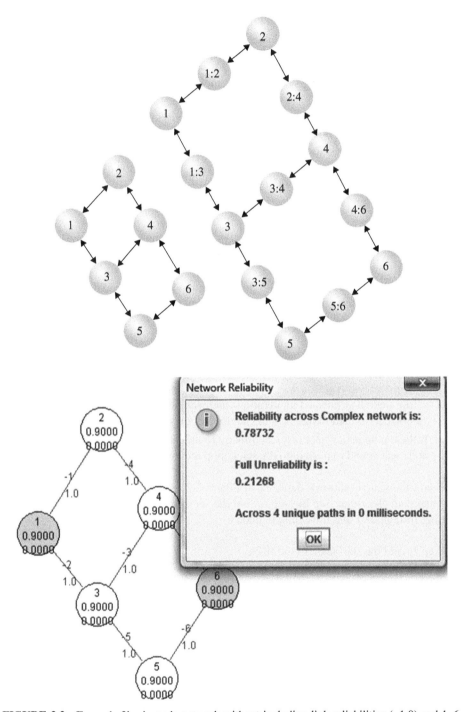

FIGURE 2.2 Example 2's six-node network without including link reliabilities (=1.0) and 1–6 solution.

Step 4: Because the top node (4) links directly to the target node (6), push 6 onto the stack and save the current stack as a minimal path. Then, pop the top two nodes off of the stack. Note, even though there are still possible paths through node 4 (e.g., 1, 2, 4, 3, 5, 6), any such path will be short circuited by 1, 2, 4, and 6 and thus will not need to be considered as a minimal path. Therefore, node 4 can be popped from the stack.

| 1 | 2 | 4 | 6 | Add this to the list of minimal paths.

| 1 | 2 | Pop the last two nodes off the stack.

Step 5: Because node 4 was just popped from the stack and the top node on the stack (2) does not link to any nodes higher than 4, pop node 2 off the stack.

| 1 |

Step 6: Node 2 was just popped off the stack; the next higher node than 2 connected to the top stack node (1) that is not already in the stack is node 3. Push node 3 onto the stack.

| 1 | | 3 |

Step 7: The top node (3) connects to nodes 1, 4, and 5, but 1 is already in the stack, so push the lowest (4) remaining node onto the stack.

| 1 | | 3 | | 4 |

Step 8: The top node (4) connects directly to the target node (6); push 6 on the stack and save the current stack as a minimal path. Then, pop the top two nodes off the stack. Note: At this point, it is clear to see that if node 4 did not link directly to the target node, node 2 would have been the first node to be pushed onto the stack. But from node 2 there would be no way to link to the target node (6) without passing through any nodes already in the stack. In this case, the process would still need to consider node 2 to insure total algorithm inclusion. In small networks such as this example, it is easy to visualize dead ends, but in a very large network, they may not be so clear, and taking shortcuts could result in missed paths and thus incorrect results.

| 1 | 3 | 4 | 6 | Add this to the list of minimal paths.

| 1 | 3 | Pop the last two nodes off the stack.

Step 9: Because node 4 was just popped off the stack, the next highest node connected to the top node (3) that is not already in the stack is node 5. Push node 5 on to the stack.

| 1 | | 3 | | 5 |

Step 10: The top node (5) connects directly to the target node (6); push 6 on the stack and save the current stack as a minimal path. Then, pop the top two nodes off the stack.

| 1 | 3 | 5 | 6 | Add this to the list of minimal paths.

| 1 | 3 | Pop the last two nodes off the stack.

Step 11: Node 5 was just popped off the stack, and there are no higher nodes connected to the top node (3); pop node 3 off of the stack.

$$\boxed{1}$$

Step 12: Node 3 was just popped off the stack, and there are no higher nodes connected to the top node (1); pop node 1 off of the stack.

Step 13: The stack is now empty; the algorithm is complete. The minimum paths generated above are as follows:

1	2	4	6
1	3	4	6
1	3	5	6

The core algorithms presented here never consider link reliabilities. When link reliabilities are required, think of each link as a node itself. Of interesting note is that when considering link reliabilities, steps that would have resulted in an immediate link to the target node (i.e., steps 4, 8, and 10 in the minimal paths example) now have opportunities to venture down additional paths. Networks with link reliability tend to have several more minimal paths than their counterparts without link reliabilities (see Example 2's Fig. 2.2).

2.2.3   Overlap Method Algorithmic Rules and Example 3

Now that the minimal set of paths has been generated, the overlap method can be executed. The overlap method can be implemented with a finite array of stacks. Each stack will be comprised of one or more sets $\{S_1 \ldots S_n\}$. Each set will be comprised of one or more nodes $\{N_1 \ldots N_n\}$. The initial stack will be the set of minimal paths generated across the network from the ingress to the egress nodes. Stacks will create additional stacks recursively per the logic below. A single reliability will be maintained (referred to as the global or working reliability), and each stack will increment or decrement the global reliability accordingly. The initial global reliability is zero. Then proceed as follows:

1. Determine if this stack will be added to or subtracted from the final reliability. If this is the root stack (the set of minimal paths generated for the network), this stack will be added; otherwise the operation will be the opposite of the calling stack.

2. Eliminate any complete overlaps from the stack.
   For each set S_i in $S_1 \ldots S_{(n-1)}$:
   (i)   For each set S_j in $S_{(i+1)} \ldots S_n$;
   (ii) If $S_i\{\} \cap S_j\{\} = S_i\{\}$, remove S_j from the stack.
   (iii) Else if $S_i\{\} \cap S_j\{\} = S_j\{\}$, remove S_i from the stack.

3. If there is only one set remaining in the stack:
   Add or subtract (see step 1) the product of the sole set. The product of a set is the product of the reliabilities of the nodes in the set $(N_1 \times N_2 \times \cdots \times N_n)$. Return to the calling stack. If this is the root stack, the algorithm is complete.

4. For each remaining set in the stack $\{S_1 \ldots S_n\}$, add or subtract (see set 1) the product of the set. The product of a set is the product of the reliabilities of the nodes in the set $(N_1 \times N_2 \times \cdots \times N_n)$.

5. If there are more than one set in the stack:

   For each set S_i in $S_2 \ldots S_n$:

   (i) Create a new empty stack.

   (ii) For each set S_j in $S_1 \ldots S_{(i-1)}$.

   (iii) Add a new set comprised of nodes $S_i\{\} \cup S_j\{\}$ to the new stack. Note: This is a proper union, not a union all. If a given node occurs in both S_i and S_j, it should occur only once in the new set.

   (iv) Perform the overlap algorithm on the new stack.

6. Return to the calling stack. If this is the root stack, the algorithm is complete.

For more details, see Appendix 2.A. To continue with Example 3 for the complex network in Figure 2.3, if all the nodes are 0.9. using "overlap" algorithm

$$
\begin{aligned}
\text{IN-OUT}\{7-8\} = \{7\}\big[& \{1-4\} + \{1-5\} + \{2-5\} + \{3-5\} + \{3-6\} - \{1-4-5\} \\
& -\{1-2-5\} - \{1-2-4-6\} - \{2-5-6\} - \{1-3-4-6\} \\
& -\{1-3-5-6\} - \{2-3-6\} + \{1-2-4-5-6\} + \{1-2-3-4-6\} \\
& -\{1-2-3-4-5-6\}\big]\{8\}
\end{aligned}
\tag{2.2}
$$

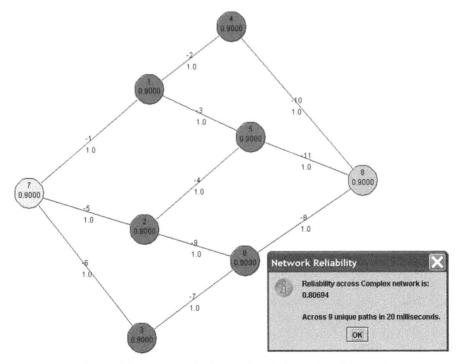

FIGURE 2.3 Example 3's eight-node and nine-path static network.

$$\text{IN-OUT}\{7-8\}=(0.9)\{(5)(0.9^2)-[(4)(0.9^3)+(3)(0.9^4)]+(4)(0.9^5)-(0.9^6)\}(0.9)$$
$$=(0.9)\{(5)(0.81)-(4)(0.729)-3(0.6561)+4(0.59049)-0.531441\}(0.9)$$
$$=(0.9)\{4.05-4.8843+2.36196-0.531441\}(0.9)=(0.996219)(0.81)$$
$$=0.80694$$

$$(2.3)$$

2.3   THE OVERLAP METHOD: MONTE CARLO AND DISCRETE EVENT SIMULATION

The component reliabilities will be simulated using a Bernoulli pdf given the static (time-independent) input data r_i for each component. That is, draw a random deviate, u_i, from the unity uniform $(0,1)$. Lay out a network composed of these r_i. Announce it a passage (success) if $0<u_i<r_i$. If not, component is a failure. Then tally one if there is a working connection between the ingress and egress components for this iteration. In iteration 2, apply the same method as in iteration 1. Tally if there is a connection between the source and target. Once you reiterate this routine, say, with $n=100,000$ runs for the network destination, calculate the ratio of successful arrivals of service from source (ingress) to target (egress). Compute the overall simulation average by dividing the number of service connections by n. The links will also be simulated with respect to a Bernoulli pdf for p (=probability of being operative) taken as a constant. Generate a Bernoulli random deviate; that is, draw a uniform u_i; if $0<u_i<p$, then it is a hit (success) for the link. Therefore, for example, you can advance through the link from 1 to 2. If link reliability is perfect, then do not generate anything, but simply advance to the neighboring component. The number of times out of n trials to advance from s to t with all successful hits will yield the output [24, 26, 28].

For time-dependent discrete event simulation technique, assume the rates for each component, such as $\lambda = $ (mean sojourn time)$^{-1}$. Let us assume that the probability of "up" for a component such as 0.9 denotes 9 time units out of 10 are operating and 1 time unit out of 10 not is operating. The reciprocals of the means yield the rates: λ (failure rate) $= 1/9$ and μ (repair rate) $= 1/1$.

Thus, FOR (forced outage rate or unavailability) $= \lambda/(\lambda+\mu) = (1/9)/[(1/9)+(1/1)] = (1/9)/(10/9) = 0.1$. Using these rates of sojourn to generate times to failure with a negative exponential pdf, one travels from component to component. If both sending and receiving ends operate at the same time, it is a successful connection. How many successes out of how many "n" trials, from $s=1$ to $t=19$ as in Figure 2.4, is the solution.

Slower (due to bookkeeping records of clock time) dynamic simulation result is almost equal to that of the static Monte Carlo, which is easier to program. The overlap method has advantages of being 100% accurate and faster compared to simulation. But when it comes to larger networks with more than 30 nodes and 50 links, the storage and time become a problem. For Examples 4 and 5, see Figures 2.4 and 2.5 for details regarding a 19-node/32-link and a 52-node/72-link complex network, respectively.

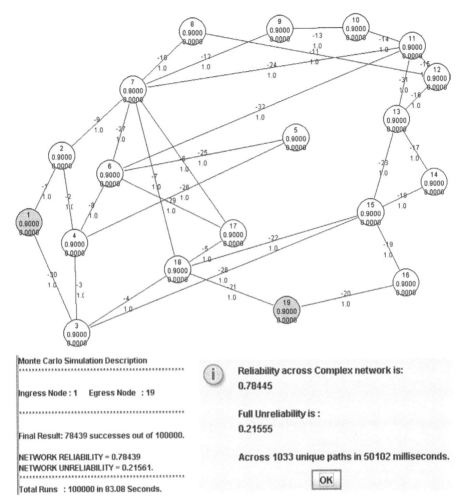

FIGURE 2.4 Example 4: 19-node ($s=1$, $t=19$) complex network with Monte Carlo simulation (83 s) and analytical results (50 s), both 0.784 with simulation taking 33 more seconds.

2.4 MULTISTATE SYSTEM RELIABILITY EVALUATION

When modeling real-life reliability systems, it doesn't always suffice to present an "on or off only" paradigm. Most live systems such as electric power networks contain components that can be not only fully operational or completely nonfunctional but also a range of in-between states of marginal utility such as derated or degraded. It is sometimes inadequate to describe a node's states with only UP (fully operating) and DOWN (fully deficient), but with more states like DERATED (partially operating close to UP) or even DEGRADED (less partially operating close to DOWN) or more downgraded states. Components in these states are functional, but not operating at peak capacity. In computer networks these conditions could be caused by network devices that are currently experiencing

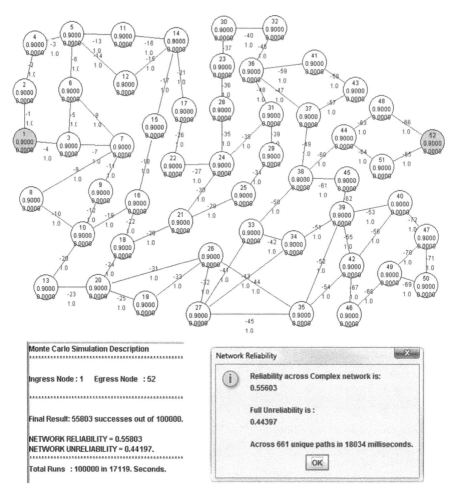

FIGURE 2.5 Example 5's simulation for $(s=1, t=52)$ with 72 links is 0.558 in 17,119 s, and the faster analytical result is 0.556 in 18.034 s in 0.1% of the simulation time. The more simulation runs, the closer results will converge.

extraordinary computing loads. Routers sometimes are capable of trafficking data packets, but only in limited counts. In electric power systems, they are the power plants or turbines with less than full capacity due to lack of water or insufficient fuels such as coal, lignite, or gas. Let's examine briefly a simple multistate network. For this example we will consider a three-state system: UP (fully operational), DER (derated or partially operational), and DN (down and fully nonoperational). Each state has a reliability value between 0 and 1 representing the probability that the component will be in that state at any given time.

The sum of the reliabilities of the states must always equal 1. In this respect, what we referred to as static reliability in the previous sections is really two states, UP and DN. The UP probability was stated, while the DN probability was left unstated and assumed at $\{1-\text{UP}\}$. In the same fashion, when we depict multistate reliabilities, we indicate the UP value first, followed by the remaining functional states in operational order. We omit the DN state, again leaving it assumed. For example, if a component is UP 70% of the time, DER 20% of the

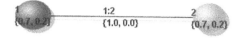

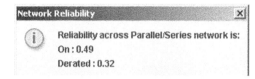

FIGURE 2.6 Example 6's simple series system with a derated state.

time, and DN the remaining 10%, we would write {0.7, 0.2} to indicate the component reliability summary. It is imperative that these states add up to unity 1. Let's take the situation when there are three states, UP, DER, and DN, for simple series and active parallel systems.

2.4.1 Simple Series System with Single Derated States

A simple series system with fully operating and derated states is shown in Figure 2.6 for Example 6.

Our goal is to calculate the simplest series system reliability of a primitive example, where the node has three states, with probabilities $P(\text{UP})=0.7$, $P(\text{DER})=0.2$, and $P(\text{DN})=0.1$ in Figure 2.6. We use two approaches. In this example, there can be $S^N=3^2=9$ combinations, where S is the number of states and N is the number of nodes. $S=3$ and $N=2$; this is the long way. Working on the same two-node simple series system, let's calculate the system up, derated, and down probabilities in Figure 2.6 in a shorter way:

$$P_{\text{sys}}(\text{UP}) = P_1(\text{UP})P_2(\text{UP}) = (0.7)(0.7) = 0.49 \tag{2.4}$$

$$P_{\text{sys}}(\text{DER}) = P_1(\text{UP}+\text{DER})P_2(\text{UP}+\text{DER}) - P_{\text{sys}}(\text{UP}) = (0.7+0.2)^2 - 0.7^2 = 0.32 \tag{2.5}$$

$$P_{\text{sys}}(\text{DN}) = 1 - P_{\text{sys}}(\text{UP}) - P_{\text{sys}}(\text{DER}) = 1 - 0.49 - 0.32 = 0.19 \tag{2.6}$$

2.4.2 Active Parallel System

The system with IN (1) and OUT (4) both perfectly reliable, 2 and 3 DERATED are shown in Figure 2.7 for Example 7.

Working on the same four-node simple parallel–series system, let's calculate the system up, derated, and down probabilities in Figure 2.7 with a shortcut formulation approach:

$$P_{\text{sys}}(\text{UP}) = P_1(\text{UP})\left\{1-\left[1-P_2(\text{UP})\right]\left[1-P_3(\text{UP})\right]\right\}P_4(\text{UP})$$
$$= (1.0)\left[1-(1-0.7)^2\right](1.0) = (1.0)(0.91) = 0.91 \tag{2.7}$$

$$P_{\text{sys}}(\text{DER}) = P_1(\text{UP})P_4(\text{UP}) - \left[1-\left\{1-P_2(\text{UP}+\text{DER})\right\}\left\{1-P_3(\text{UP}+\text{DER})\right\}\right] - P_{\text{sys}}$$
$$(\text{UP}) = 1*(1-0.1^2) - 0.91 = 0.99 - 0.91 = 0.08 \tag{2.8}$$

$$P_{\text{sys}}(\text{DN}) = 1 - P_{\text{sys}}(\text{UP}) - P_{\text{sys}}(\text{DER}) = 1 - 0.91 - 0.08 = 0.01 \tag{2.9}$$

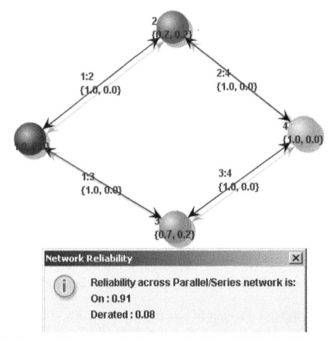

FIGURE 2.7   Example 7's active parallel system with IN and OUT reliability and others derated.

2.4.3 Simple Series–Parallel System

A simple parallel–series system with derated states is shown in Figure 2.8 for Example 8.

The parallel and series topologies merged will contain $3^4 = 81$ combinations, such as UP-UP-UP-UP and DER-UP-UP-UP all the way to DN-DN-DN-DN. This method is cumbersome and time consuming to distinguish the desirable states by enumerating. The shortcut technique is faster as follows:

$$P(\text{UP}) = P_1(\text{UP})P4(\text{UP})\{1 - [1 - P_2(\text{UP})][1 - P_2(\text{UP})]\}$$
$$= (0.7)(0.7)[1 - (1 - 0.7)^2] = (0.49)(0.91) = 0.4459 \tag{2.10}$$

$$P_{\text{sys}}(\text{DER}) = P_1(\text{UP} + \text{DER})P_4(\text{UP} + \text{DER}) - \{1 - [1 - P_2(\text{UP})][1 - P_3(\text{UP})]\} - P_{\text{sys}}(\text{UP})$$
$$= (0.7 + 0.2)^2(1 - 0.1^2) - 0.4459 = (0.81)(0.99) - 0.4459 = 0.356 \tag{2.11}$$

$$P_{\text{sys}}(\text{DN}) = 1 - P_{\text{sys}}(\text{UP}) - P_{\text{sys}}(\text{DER}) = 1 - 0.4459 - 0.356 = 0.19 \tag{2.12}$$

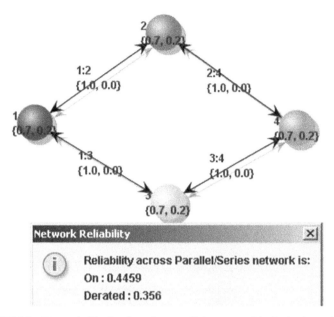

FIGURE 2.8 Example 8's simple series–parallel system with singly derated states.

2.4.4 A Simple Series–Parallel System with Multistate Components

A simple parallel–series system with derated and degraded states is shown in Figure 2.9 for Example 9.

Using the shortcut formulation approach (the state enumeration method requires

$$S^N = 4^4 = 256 \tag{2.13}$$

combinations in general; here, due to 1 and 4 being full states, $4^2 = 16$, and therefore cumbersome to work with), we get, using the same logic as we used earlier,

$$
\begin{aligned}
P(\text{UP}) &= P_1(\text{UP})P_4(\text{UP})\left\{1 - \left[1 - P_2(\text{UP})\right]\left[1 - P_3(\text{UP})\right]\right\} \\
&= (1.0)\left[1 - (1 - 0.4)^2\right] = 1 - 0.36 = 0.64
\end{aligned} \tag{2.14}
$$

$$
\begin{aligned}
P_{\text{sys}}(\text{DER}) &= (1.0)\left\{1 - \left[1 - P_2(\text{UP} + \text{DER})\right]\left[1 - P_3(\text{UP} + \text{DER})\right]\right\} - P_{\text{sys}}(\text{UP}) \\
&= (1.0)\left(1 - 0.3^2\right) - 0.64 = 0.91 - 0.64 = 0.27
\end{aligned} \tag{2.15}
$$

$$
\begin{aligned}
P_{\text{sys}}(\text{DEGR}) &= (1.0) * \left\{1 - \left[1 - P_2(\text{UP} + \text{DER} + \text{DEGR})\right]\left[1 - P_3(\text{UP} + \text{DER} + \text{DEGR})\right]\right\} - P_{\text{sys}}(\text{UP}) \\
&- P_{\text{sys}}(\text{DER}) = (1.0)\left(1 - 0.1^2\right) - 0.64 - 0.27 = 0.99 - 0.64 - 0.27 = 0.08
\end{aligned} \tag{2.16}
$$

$$
P_{\text{sys}}(\text{DN}) = 1 - P_{\text{sys}}(\text{UP}) - P_{\text{sys}}(\text{DER}) - P_{\text{sys}}(\text{DEGR}) = 1 - 0.64 - 0.27 - 0.08 = 0.01 \tag{2.17}
$$

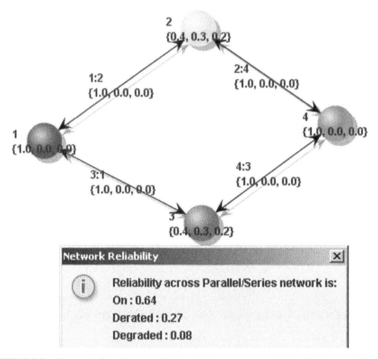

FIGURE 2.9   Example 9 series–parallel multistate system with doubly derated 2 and 3.

2.4.5   A Combined System: Power Plant Example

A hydroelectric power plant in Figure 2.10 can generate 100% (fully operating), 75% (derated 1), 50% (derated 2), 25% (derated 3), or 0% (fully down) of rated electric power capacity depending on the water storage level and thus the amount of steam flow reaching the turbine [24–26]. The corresponding system states are 1, 2, 3, 4, and 5. The power plant consists of four turbines in active parallel and an output transformer in series with the turbines. The available turbine with maximal power is used. For any demand level of $w=1$, 2, 3, 4, 5, the combined system reliability of states takes the recursive form in Example 10:

$$R_{sys}(w) = \left(\sum_{j=1}^{w} R_{5j}\right)\left[1 - \left(1 - \sum_{j=1}^{w} R_{1j}\right)\left(1 - \sum_{j=1}^{w} R_{2j}\right)\left(1 - \sum_{j=1}^{w} R_{3j}\right)\left(1 - \sum_{j=1}^{w} R_{4j}\right)\right]$$
$$- \sum_{j=1}^{w} R_{sys}(j-1) \tag{2.18}$$

where $w=1$, 2, 3, 4, 5 and $R_{sys}(0)=0$.

Multistate system (MSS) elements are statistically independent. If $R_{w1}=0.4$, $R_{w2}=0.3$, $R_{w3}=0.15$, $R_{w4}=0.1$, and $R_{w5}=0.05$, w (state)$=1 \ldots 5$ as shown in Figure 2.10, then the system reliabilities $R_{sys}(w)$ are

$$R_{sys}(1) = 0.4\left[1 - (1-0.4)^4\right] = 0.34816 \tag{2.19}$$

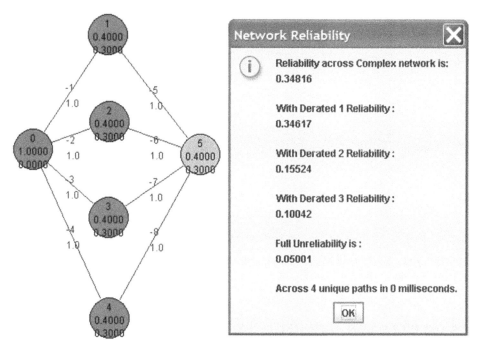

FIGURE 2.10 Example 10's power plant with four derated turbines (nodes 1–4) in parallel and a transformer (egress node 5) in series and node 0 (as an ingress node with full reliability).

$$R_{sys}(2) = (0.4+0.3)\left\{1-\left[1-(0.4+0.3)\right]^4\right\} - R(1) = 0.69433 - 0.34816$$
$$= 0.34617 \tag{2.20}$$

$$R_{sys}(3) = (0.4+0.3+0.15)\left\{1-\left[1-(0.4+0.3+0.15)\right]^4\right\} - R(1) - R(2) = 0.15524 \tag{2.21}$$

$$R_{sys}(4) = (0.4+0.3+0.15+0.1)\left\{1-\left[1-(0.4+0.3+0.15+0.1)\right]^4\right\} - R(1) - R(2) - R(3)$$
$$= 0.10042 \tag{2.22}$$

$$R_{sys}(5) = (0.4+0.3+0.15+0.1+0.05)\left\{1-\left[1-(0.4+0.3+0.15+0.1+0.05)\right]^4\right\}$$
$$- R(1) - R(2) - R(3) - R(4) = 1 - R(1) - R(2) - R(3) - R(4) = 1 - 0.10042$$
$$- 0.15524 - 0.34617 - 0.34816 = 0.05001 \tag{2.23}$$

2.4.6 Large Network Examples Using Multistate Overlap Technique

Using Figure 2.4 for the 19-node large cyber network, we can calculate the ingress–egress overlap reliability using multistate (up=0.7, derated=0.2, down=0.1) as shown in Figure 2.11 for Example 11.

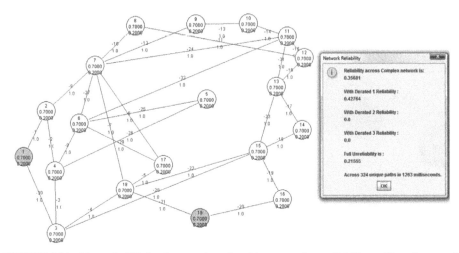

FIGURE 2.11 Example 11's implementation of multistate overlaps reliability to 19-node network in 1.26s. Solution 1–19: full reliability=0.36, derated reliability=0.43, full unreliability=0.21.

2.5 WEIBULL TIME DISTRIBUTED RELIABILITY EVALUATION

2.5.1 Motivation behind Weibull Probability Modeling

When modeling real-life networks, industry engineers have quickly found that static reliabilities do not accurately depict component behaviors because they cannot stay constant at all times. For instance, a 10-year-old fatigued component is much more likely to fail than a brand new component recently commissioned, thus not keeping constant.

Therefore, it is necessary to implement a time-dependent reliability paradigm that can systematically represent a wide range of failure conduct. There are already several industry standard methods capable of modeling sample component heuristics or historical failure data including normal, lognormal, and Weibull. We have chosen Weibull distribution due to the fact that it is currently one of the most widely utilized methods in practical applications and because of the versatile range of characteristics it can model from infancy to useful life and wear-out periods.

The benefit of choosing Weibull distribution is that we can implement the generic mathematical behavior once and satisfy a wide range of component behavior by simply manipulating the shape parameter, β, as run time dictates. As shown in the subsequent graph of Figure 2.12, the entirety of component behavior is spanned.

In recent years, the Weibull distribution has become more popular as a reliability function. It is named after the Swedish scientist Waloddi Weibull, who used it in analysis of the breaking strength of solids. A chief advantage of the Weibull distribution is that as in the bathtub curve, its hazard rate function may be decreasing for $\beta < 1$, constant for $\beta = 1$, or increasing for $\beta > 1$. When $\beta = 2$, the Weibull is called the *Rayleigh* pdf. The Weibull density and reliability functions are given, respectively:

$$f(t) = \frac{\beta t^{\beta-1}}{\alpha^{\beta}} e^{-(t/\alpha)^{\beta}}, \quad t \geq 0, \ \alpha, \beta > 0 \tag{2.24}$$

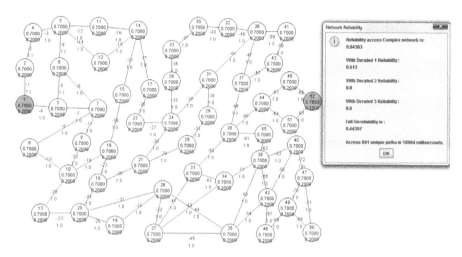

FIGURE 2.12 Example 12's implementation of multistate overlaps reliability to 52-node network in 18 s. Solution 1–52: full reliability = 0.05, derated reliability = 0.51, full unreliability = 0.44.

$$R(t) = e^{-(t/\alpha)^{\beta}}, \quad t \geq 0, \ \alpha, \beta > 0 \tag{2.25}$$

The Weibull family of distributions is a member of the family of extreme value distributions that was discussed earlier. The Weibull distribution is probably the most widely used family of failure (e.g., electronic component, mechanical fatigue, etc.) distributions, mainly because by proper choice of its shape parameter β, it can be used as an increasing failure rate (IFR), decreasing failure rate (DFR), or constant failure rate (CFR, as in the negative exponential case). Often, a third parameter, known as the *threshold* or *location parameter*, t_0, is added to obtain a three-parameter Weibull, where

$$R(t) = e^{-(t-t_0/\alpha)^{\beta}}, \quad t \geq t_0 > 0; \ \alpha, \beta > 0 \tag{2.26}$$

As the graph depicts, when $0 < \beta < 1$, the reliability distribution function represents a failure rate that declines over time. This range of shape values models components where defective units fail early and the reliability of the average unit steadies out at the defective components fall out of the sample set. $\beta = 1$ denotes a CFR.

These components are no more likely to fail at any given time and any other. The failure of constant rate components is generally caused by random events. As β increases from 1, the component fails at an increasing rate over time. These are components whose useful lives are limited by environmental stress in the system. The longer a component is in use, the more likely to fail (Fig. 2.13).

2.5.2 Weibull Parameter Estimation Methodology

Inside the overlap algorithm, there were three types of arithmetic performed on node reliabilities: multiplication, addition, and subtraction. In order to incorporate Weibull reliability directly into the algorithm, we must first find a way to define and implement

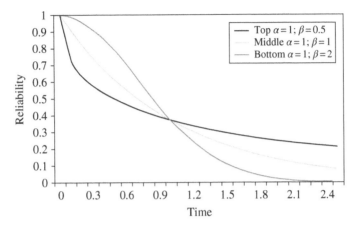

FIGURE 2.13   Weibull reliability distributions.

Weibull math. Unfortunately, due to the nature of the survival (reliability) distribution function, this is not possible. Multiplication is only possible when both components being multiplied share the same shape parameter. When multiplying heterogeneous components, the resultant will not simplify back into cumulative distribution function (cdf) form such as that of a reliability distribution. To compound matters, addition and subtraction will definitely not result in a standard cdf regardless of whether the nodes are homogenous or heterogeneous. Consider the fact that at $t = 0$ a two-parameter Weibull reliability should always be 1; if we were to add two components, the value of $t = 0$ would be $1 + 1$ or 2, directly conflicting with the reliability bounds. Unfortunately, as seen in the past few examples, there is no way of supporting Weibull math in systems containing hybrid shape parameters without incurring a quantitatively large margin of error. The solution lies in breaking the reliability of each component into an array of static reliabilities at evenly distributed points in time. The overlap algorithm is run generating a multitude of reliabilities. Finally, the reliability plot is used to generate a final Weibull goodness of fit.

2.5.3 Overlap Algorithm Applied to Weibull Distributed Components

Before delving into how to estimate a final pair of shape and scale parameters from the solution generated by the overlap algorithm, let's first walk through an example of a slightly more complex network up to this point. Consider Figure 2.14 network [26] from node 1 to node 19 in which each node has both β and α equal to 1 assumed. See Example 13 in Table 2.3 and Figure 2.14.

2.5.4 Estimating Weibull Parameters

Now that we have generated a graphical result, we can use basic axis scale regression and linear least squares to approximate the values for α and β. The goal is to adjust the scale of the x and y axis until the result is a straight line with a slope of m. "Linear least squares"

TABLE 2.3   Nineteen-Node Weibull Overlap Results

Time	Reliability	Time	Reliability	Time	Reliability	Time	Reliability
0.0	1.00000	1.0	0.02736	2.0	0.00041	3.0	0.00001
0.1	0.79467	1.1	0.01801	2.1	0.00027	3.1	0.00000
0.2	0.59842	1.2	0.01184	2.2	0.00018		
0.3	0.43235	1.3	0.00778	2.3	0.00012		
0.4	0.30315	1.4	0.00511	2.4	0.00008		
0.5	0.20812	1.5	0.00336	2.5	0.00005		
0.6	0.14079	1.6	0.00221	2.6	0.00003		
0.7	0.09427	1.7	0.00145	2.7	0.00002		
0.8	0.06268	1.8	0.00096	2.8	0.00002		
0.9	0.04148	1.9	0.00063	2.9	0.00001		

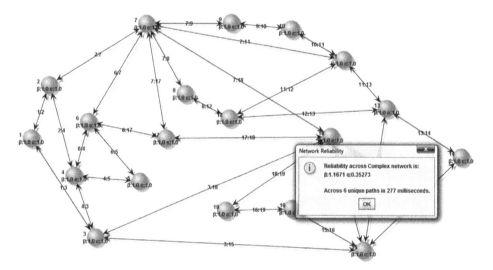

FIGURE 2.14   Example 13's 19-node Weibull network with estimated beta = 1.16 and alpha = 0.35.

will then be used to determine the best fit line through the linear plot points to return the most correct value for m. Recall that the reliability function for a Weibull plot:

$$R(t) = e^{-(t/\alpha)^{\beta}} \qquad (2.27)$$

where from $-\ln(r) = (t/\alpha)^{\beta}$. Graphing the above equation depicts an exponential curve with a power of β (=slope) in Figure 2.15.

To determine the value of β, take the log of both axis and use linear least squares to determine the slope. See Figure 2.16.

The x-coordinates are given by $\log(t)$, while the y-coordinates are $\log(-\ln(r))$ in Table 2.4 and Figure 2.15. The best line's slope function for calculating first-degree polynomials for n number of x and y plot points is given in (2.28) for the standard slope formula "m" and (2.29) for the Weibull slope "β," respectively, as follows:

$$m = \frac{(\Sigma y)(\Sigma x) - n(\Sigma xy)}{(\Sigma x)^{2} - n(\Sigma x^{2})} \qquad (2.28)$$

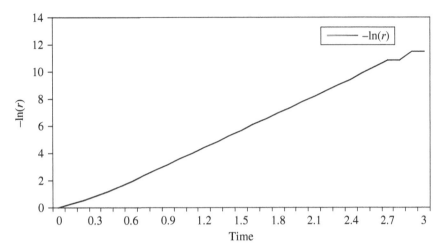

FIGURE 2.15   Negative exponential graph for β.

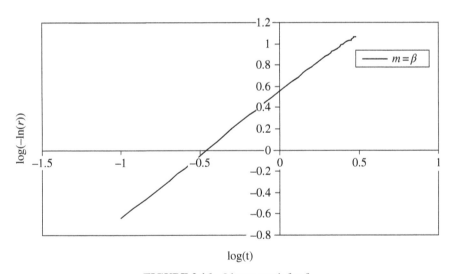

FIGURE 2.16   Linear graph for β.

Substituting the x and y plot functions from above yields the slope to attain the least squares estimation (LSE):

$$\beta = \frac{\left(\sum \log\left(-\ln\left(r\right)\right)\right)\left(\sum \log\left(t\right)\right) - n\left(\sum \log\left(t\right)\log\left(-\ln\left(r\right)\right)\right)}{\left(\sum \log\left(t\right)\right)^2 - n\left(\sum \log\left(t\right)^2\right)} \tag{2.29}$$

Extrapolate the values in the plot table to quickly find the various sums in Table 2.4.

TABLE 2.4   Nineteen-Node Linear Data for β with Least Squares Calculations

t	r	$\log(t)$	$\log(-\ln(r))$	$\log(t)^2$	$\log(t)\log(-\ln(r))$
0	1	—	—	—	—
0.1	0.79467	−1	−0.638596411	1	0.638596411
0.2	0.59842	−0.698970004	−0.289491328	0.488559067	0.202345755
0.3	0.43235	−0.522878745	−0.076486661	0.273402182	0.039993249
0.4	0.30315	−0.397940009	0.076832447	0.158356251	−0.030574705
0.5	0.20812	−0.301029996	0.19580018	0.090619058	−0.058941727
0.6	0.14079	−0.22184875	0.292363714	0.049216868	−0.064860524
0.7	0.09427	−0.15490196	0.373204919	0.023994617	−0.057810173
0.8	0.06268	−0.096910013	0.442434748	0.009391551	−0.042876357
0.9	0.04148	−0.045757491	0.502774402	0.002093748	−0.023005695
1	0.02736	0	0.556142408	0	0
1.1	0.01801	0.041392685	0.603883249	0.001713354	0.024996349
1.2	0.01184	0.079181246	0.647018132	0.00626967	0.051231702
1.3	0.00778	0.113943352	0.68629647	0.012983088	0.07819892
1.4	0.00511	0.146128036	0.722350541	0.021353403	0.105555666
1.5	0.00336	0.176091259	0.755555822	0.031008132	0.133046776
1.6	0.00221	0.204119983	0.786379612	0.041664967	0.160515793
1.7	0.00145	0.230448921	0.815324783	0.053106705	0.187890717
1.8	0.00096	0.255272505	0.841895892	0.065164052	0.214912873
1.9	0.00063	0.278753601	0.867455156	0.07770357	0.241806249
2	0.00041	0.301029996	0.892058599	0.090619058	0.268536396
2.1	0.00027	0.322219295	0.91471797	0.103825274	0.294739779
2.2	0.00018	0.342422681	0.935635908	0.117253292	0.320382956
2.3	0.00012	0.361727836	0.955592456	0.130847027	0.345664391
2.4	0.00008	0.380211242	0.974672114	0.144560588	0.370581295
2.5	0.00005	0.397940009	0.99578816	0.158356251	0.396263949
2.6	0.00003	0.414973348	1.017630634	0.17220288	0.422289591
2.7	0.00002	0.431363764	1.034218361	0.186074697	0.446124325
2.8	0.00002	0.447158031	1.034218361	0.199950305	0.462459046
2.9	0.00001	0.462397998	1.061185693	0.213811908	0.49069014
3	0.00001	0.477121255	1.061185693	0.227644692	0.506314249
Σ(sum)		2.423660075	19.03804202	4.151746254	6.125067395

The number of plot points, n, is 30. The first and last points are omitted as the values of 0 for time and reliability would cause the log functions to return $-\infty$. Solve for $\beta = 1.16$ in (2.30) and α in (2.29) and (2.33), respectively, as supported by the results of Fig. 2.14:

$$\beta = \frac{\left(\Sigma\log(-\ln(r))\right)\left(\Sigma\log(t)\right) - n\left(\Sigma\log(t)\log(-\ln(r))\right)}{\left(\Sigma\log(t)\right)^2 - n\left(\Sigma\log(t)^2\right)} \tag{2.30}$$

$$\beta = \frac{19.03804202 \times 2.423660075 - 30 \times 6.125067395}{2.423660075^2 - 30 \times 4.151746254} = 1.16$$

Use the value of β to estimate for α. Recall the modified exponential equation (2.27) for

$$-\ln(r)^{1/\beta} = \frac{t}{\alpha} \tag{2.31}$$

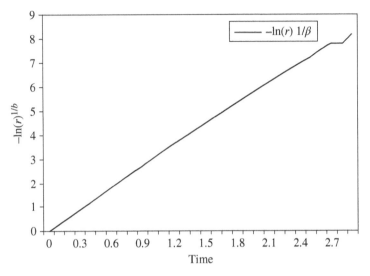

FIGURE 2.17 Linear graph for $1/\alpha$.

$$\alpha = \frac{t}{-\ln(r)^{1/\beta}} = \frac{t}{-\ln(r)^{1/1.159524}} = \frac{t}{-\ln(r)^{0.862423}} \tag{2.32}$$

Plotting t versus $-\ln(r)^{0.862423}$ produces a regression line, the slope of which is $1/\alpha$ (Fig. 2.17). Again, we use the linear LSE principle to approximate the value for α. As the slope of the line is the inverse of the scale parameter, the inverse of the least squares slope formula is used for result interpretation as in Table 2.5:

$$\frac{1}{m} = \frac{\left(\sum x\right)^2 - n\left(\sum x^2\right)}{\left(\sum y\right)\left(\sum x\right) - n\left(\sum xy\right)}$$

Use the equation obtained above to solve for $\alpha=0.354085$ by working the equations below:

$$\alpha = \frac{\left(\sum t\right)^2 - n\left(\sum t^2\right)}{\left(\sum -\ln(r)^{1/\beta}\right)\left(\sum t\right) - n\left(\sum t\left(-\ln(r)^{1/\beta}\right)\right)} \tag{2.33}$$

$$\alpha = \frac{\left(46.5\right)^2 - 30 \times 94.55}{135.4755627 \times 46.5 - 30 \times 273.4606493} = 0.354$$

To verify our results and determine the margin of error, we can chart and graph our original plot points versus the evaluation of the determinate function at each plot point in time. The difference between the generated LSE results and the observed is placed in the final column titled Δ (delta) as in Table 2.6. The sum of the difference is 0.124193; a small margin of error exists in the plots of the two graphs. The sum of the error squares far less will be even more negligible and miniscule (=0.00168). Note the x-axis (Time) has been reduced to a maximum of 1.6. This is the point at which the plotted

TABLE 2.5 Nineteen-Node Linear Data for α with Least Squares Calculations

R	t	$-\ln(r)^{1/\beta}$	t^2	$t(-\ln(r)^{1/\beta})$
1	0	0	0	0
0.79467	0.1	0.281358356	0.01	0.028135836
0.59842	0.2	0.562776615	0.04	0.112555323
0.43235	0.3	0.859085029	0.09	0.257725509
0.30315	0.4	1.164828702	0.16	0.465931481
0.20812	0.5	1.475239606	0.25	0.737619803
0.14079	0.6	1.787068374	0.36	1.072241025
0.09427	0.7	2.098265681	0.49	1.468785977
0.06268	0.8	2.407497631	0.64	1.925998105
0.04148	0.9	2.713964545	0.81	2.442568091
0.02736	1	3.017379678	1	3.017379678
0.01801	1.1	3.317437553	1.21	3.649181308
0.01184	1.2	3.614125826	1.44	4.336950991
0.00778	1.3	3.907309449	1.69	5.079502284
0.00511	1.4	4.197315986	1.96	5.87624238
0.00336	1.5	4.48341211	2.25	6.725118165
0.00221	1.6	4.766414464	2.56	7.626263143
0.00145	1.7	5.048411906	2.89	8.58230024
0.00096	1.8	5.321944188	3.24	9.579499538
0.00063	1.9	5.599035378	3.61	10.63816722
0.00041	2	5.879383438	4	11.75876688
0.00027	2.1	6.149980591	4.41	12.91495924
0.00018	2.2	6.41082401	4.84	14.10381282
0.00012	2.3	6.669984716	5.29	15.34096485
0.00008	2.4	6.927548473	5.76	16.62611633
0.00005	2.5	7.224212891	6.25	18.06053223
0.00003	2.6	7.544456964	6.76	19.61558811
0.00002	2.7	7.797109302	7.29	21.05219512
0.00002	2.8	7.797109302	7.84	21.83190605
0.00001	2.9	8.226040953	8.41	23.85551876
0.00001	3	8.226040953	9	24.67812286
Σ (SUM)	46.5	135.4755627	94.55	273.4606493

reliability function $f(t)$ becomes close enough to the axis to appear as zero to show the similarity of the two lines. See Figure 2.18.

To sum up the past series of calculations, once a set of plot points has been generated by the overlap algorithm for a Weibull network, the two equations for α and β are used in succession to estimate the shape and scale parameters, respectively, of the resulting Weibull solution.

2.5.5 Fifty-Two-Node Weibull Example for Estimating Weibull Parameters

Let's try the overlap algorithm for Weibull networks again, as in Figure 2.19, this time for a substantially more complicated network. In this 52-node 72-link network [24], we will again use unity for both the shape and scale parameters as we generate the reliability block diagram from node 1 to node 52. See Example 14 in Figure 2.19.

TABLE 2.6   Nineteen-Node Weibull Results for Comparison

t	r (Observed)	$r = e^{(-t/0.35)^{1.16}}$	Δ (Difference)
0	1	1	0
0.1	0.79467	0.793872314	0.000797686
0.2	0.59842	0.597116825	0.001303175
0.3	0.43235	0.438171073	0.005821073
0.4	0.30315	0.316047967	0.012897967
0.5	0.20812	0.224921716	0.016801716
0.6	0.14079	0.158303476	0.017513476
0.7	0.09427	.1103625	0.0160925
0.8	0.06268	0.076300916	0.013620916
0.9	0.04148	0.052360252	0.010880252
1	0.02736	0.03568977	0.00832977
1.1	0.01801	0.024177139	0.006167139
1.2	0.01184	0.016285165	0.004445165
1.3	0.00778	0.010911397	0.003131397
1.4	0.00511	0.007274771	0.002164771
1.5	0.00336	0.004827687	0.001467687
1.6	0.00221	0.003189728	0.000979728
1.7	0.00145	0.002098764	0.000648764
1.8	0.00096	0.001375494	0.000415494
1.9	0.00063	0.000898089	0.000268089
2	0.00041	0.000584277	0.000174277
2.1	0.00027	0.000378811	0.000108811
2.2	0.00018	0.000244788	6.4788E−05
2.3	0.00012	0.00015768	3.76803E−05
2.4	0.00008	0.000101259	2.12594E−05
2.5	0.00005	6.4835E−05	1.4835E−05
2.6	0.00003	4.13947E−05	1.13947E−05
2.7	0.00002	2.6356E−05	6.35602E−06
2.8	0.00002	1.6736E−05	3.26395E−06
2.9	0.00001	1.05998E−05	5.99833E−07
3	0.00001	6.69654E−06	3.30346E−06

Note that the more points, the more accurate the plot will be; but more microprocessor run time will be observed. Find the sums of each of the calculated columns and apply the values to the equation for the shape parameter in Table 2.7. Given the newfound value for β in (2.32), compute the values required to estimate the scale parameter α in (2.33). Calculate $-\ln(r)^{1/\beta}$, t^2, and $t\,(-\ln(r)^{1/\beta})$ and their corresponding sums across the plot as shown in Tables 2.8 and 2.9. For each plot point, calculate the values for $\log(t)$, $\log(-\ln(r)$, $\log(t)^2$, and $\log(t)\log(-\ln(r))$ as in Table 2.10:

$$\beta = \frac{\left(\sum\log\left(-\ln\left(r\right)\right)\right)\left(\sum\log\left(t\right)\right) - n\left(\sum\log\left(t\right)\log\left(-\ln\left(r\right)\right)\right)}{\left(\sum\log\left(t\right)\right)^2 - n\left(\sum\log\left(t\right)^2\right)}$$

$$\beta = \frac{6.299380256 \times -3.440236967 - 10 \times -0.939435447}{-3.440236967^2 - 10 \times 2.095633341} \tag{2.34}$$

$$= 1.370000185$$

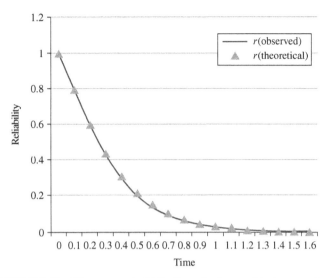

FIGURE 2.18   Nineteen-node Weibull results for graphical comparison.

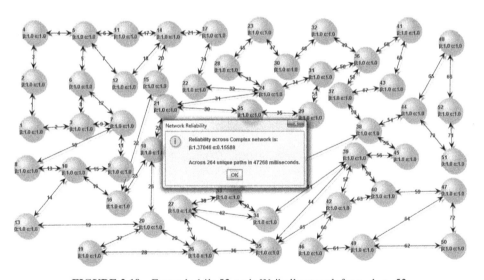

FIGURE 2.19   Example 14's 52-node Weibull network for $s=1$, $t=52$.

TABLE 2.7   Fifty-Two-Node Least Squares Sum for β

Linear Least Squares Sums for β	
$\sum \log(t)$	−3.440236967
$\sum \log(-\ln(r))$	6.299380256
$\sum \log(t)^2$	2.095633341
$\sum \log(t)\log(-\ln(r))$	−0.939435447
# of plot points	10

TABLE 2.8   Fifty-Two-Node Linear Data for α with Least Squares Calculations

T	r	$-\ln(r)^{1/\beta}$	t^2	$t(-\ln(r)^{1/\beta})$
0.0	1.000000	—	—	—
0.1	0.577760	0.640147819	0.01	0.064014782
0.2	0.247430	1.281700255	0.04	0.256340051
0.3	0.084700	1.956920992	0.09	0.587076298
0.4	0.025000	2.637361592	0.16	1.054944637
0.5	0.006710	3.307975147	0.25	1.653987573
0.6	0.001700	3.960862039	0.36	2.376517223
0.7	0.000410	4.599893257	0.49	3.21992528
0.8	0.000100	5.204761729	0.64	4.163809383
0.9	0.000020	5.866299131	0.81	5.279669218
1.0	0.000010	6.14326665	1	6.14326665

TABLE 2.9   Fifty-Two-Node Least Squares Sum for the Intercept Alpha

Linear Least Squares for α for $n=10$	
Σt	5.5
$\Sigma -\ln(r)^{1/\beta}$	35.59918861
Σt^2	3.85
$\Sigma t(-\ln(r)^{1/\beta})$	24.79955109
α	0.1558046057

TABLE 2.10   Fifty-Two-Node Linear Data for β with Least Squares Calculations

T	r	$\log(t)$	$\log(-\ln(r))$	$\log(t)^2$	$\log(t)\log(-\ln(r))$
0.0	1.000000	—	—	—	—
0.1	0.577760	-1	-0.260746792	1	0.260746792
0.2	0.247430	-0.698970004	0.145080609	0.488559067	-0.101406994
0.3	0.084700	-0.522878745	0.392457705	0.273402182	-0.205207792
0.4	0.025000	-0.397940009	0.566894464	0.158356251	-0.225589988
0.5	0.006710	-0.301029996	0.699330868	0.090619058	-0.210519568
0.6	0.001700	-0.22184875	0.804625068	0.049216868	-0.178505065
0.7	0.000410	-0.15490196	0.892058599	0.023994617	-0.138181625
0.8	0.000100	-0.096910013	0.96427568	0.009391551	-0.093447969
0.9	0.000020	-0.045757491	1.034218361	0.002093748	-0.047323237
1.0	0.000010	0	1.061185693	0	0
1.1	0.000000				

$$\alpha = \frac{\left(\Sigma t\right)^2 - n\left(\Sigma t^2\right)}{\left(\Sigma -\ln(r)^{1/\beta}\right)\left(\Sigma t\right) - n\left(\Sigma t\left(-\ln(r)^{1/\beta}\right)\right)}$$

$$\alpha = \frac{5.5^2 - 10 \times 3.85}{24.79955109 \times 5.5 - 10 \times 24.79955109} \qquad (2.35)$$

$$= 0.1558046056966797$$

The final result for the 52-node Weibull system as in Figure 2.19 and Table 2.11 will be given in

$$R(t) = e^{-(t/0.155)^{1.37}}, \ t \geq 0, \ \alpha, \beta > 0 \tag{2.36}$$

The sum of the delta (difference errors) is 0.02849, which is satisfactorily negligible for a large complex network of 52 nodes and 72 links, which would normally take years if calculated manually. The squares sum of errors is even smaller to be 0.00085 (Fig. 2.20).

TABLE 2.11   Fifty-Two-Node Weibull Results for Comparison

t	r (Observed)	$r = e^{-(t/0.155)^{1.37}}$	Δ (Difference)
0.0	1.000000	1.000000	0
0.1	0.577760	0.58272	0.004956812
0.2	0.247430	0.25338	0.005953392
0.3	0.084700	0.09353	0.008834758
0.4	0.025000	0.0305	0.005504651
0.5	0.006710	0.00898	0.002272338
0.6	0.001700	0.00242	0.000721854
0.7	0.000410	0.0006	0.000193922
0.8	0.000100	0.00014	0.0000403337
0.9	0.000020	0.000031	0.0000010568
1.0	0.000010	0.0000063	0.0000037283
1.1	0.000000	0.000000	0

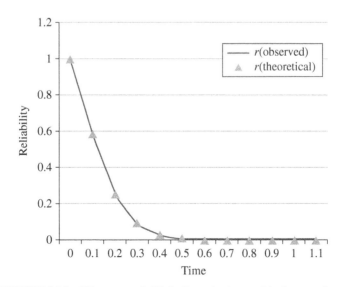

FIGURE 2.20   Fifty-two-node Weibull results for graphical comparison.

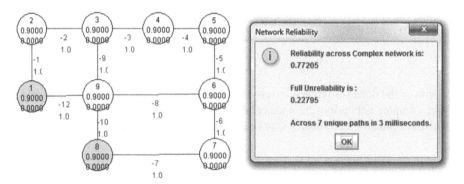

FIGURE 2.21 Analytical input/output reliability for the contour diagram of Figure 2.22; all components have 0.9 reliability including the ground at 9 (in lieu of node 0).

2.5.6   A Weibull Network Example from an Oil Rig System

Given Figure 2.21 diagram for actual oil rig structure of Figure 2.22, with the physical shape and contour, the network reliability ($s = 1$, $t = 8$) is calculated to be 77.2%.

The work illustrated in this chapter on Weibull reliability distributions allows technicians to model and analyze full life-cycle systems inspired from the famous bathtub curve [23, 26]. Using the various behaviors provided by the reliability function, one could model component wear-out or infancy periods and preemptively replace system components before they fail in order to act wisely and proactively [26].

The benefits listed earlier prove that we have documented an algorithm with a true industry application, while the shortcomings really only detail opportunities for growth rather than steadfast barriers. The innovative algorithms documented in this chapter provide a much needed and practically versatile function for both academic and industrial applications. Nondirectional reliability concerns such as in cloud computing with independent units in an additive rather than directional scenario are becoming recently popular and are out of scope in this work suitable in another setting [27]. Last but not the least, the very last example indicates the near equivalence of the overlap and Weibull's LSE outcomes in Figures 2.21, 2.23 for the Figure 2.22 contour [28]. This also empirically proves that the "overlap technique" produces the same outcome as does the "LSE" after painstakingly using a sequence of statistical formulas from (2.27) to (2.35) for both large network examples.

2.6   DISCUSSIONS AND CONCLUSION

The network reliability evaluation algorithm may open many doors into the vast reliability and security engineering field. Of the currently available free resources, most if not all impose strict component or topology limits such as purely series–parallel. The rest of the methods are only commercially available, and no one knows, unless a client purchases it, about what needs to be done and how and why it works [29]. As we have seen in the performance characteristics of complex cyber network reliability generation, due to the

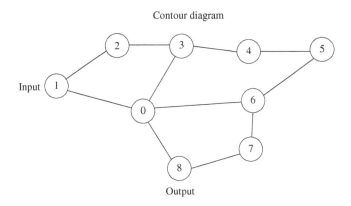

Contour diagram

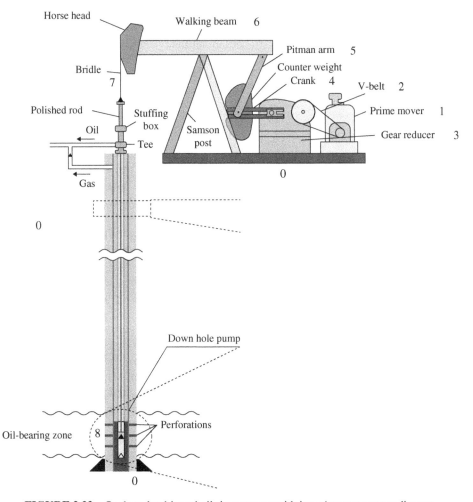

FIGURE 2.22 Onshore land-based oil rig structure with input/output contour diagram.

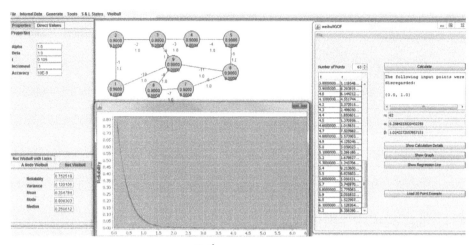

FIGURE 2.23   From (2.25), $R(t) = e^{-(t/\alpha)^{\beta}}$; network reliability $= R(t) = \exp(-0.105/0.3584)^{1.024} = \exp(-0.284) = 0.7525$, after $n = 62$ iterations for $(s = 1, t = 8)$ at $t = 0.105$ covering all units where $R(t = 0.105) = 0.90032$. In the Net (work) Weibull column, see on the lower left when units are assumed to be distributed as Weibull with alpha $= 1$, beta $= 1$ (unity negative exponential) with all units including ground unit at 9 [28].

hardware and time resources required to perform the algorithmic operations; newer algorithms other than for those commercially marketed have not been studied at large. The Overlap Algorithm presented in this chapter, along with the associated performance tuning activities, greatly increases the size and complexity of the networks that are possible [22–25].

This expansion of capability moves the presented set of algorithms from a tool that can only be used in demonstrations and educational activities to an enterprise-level solution, which all then can be used to capably solve real-world scenarios. In addition to static (or constant) node reliability, the inclusion of both multistate and Weibull time-dependent paradigms in this chapter increases the algorithm's practical applicability immensely.

These two additional reliability features build on the power provided by the overlap algorithms to allow modeling of real-world complex network behavior. Multistate networks can be used by engineers to analyze networks in which components can exhibit varying levels of operational effectiveness. In applications such as monitoring a packet-switching network, professionals can plan for situations where traffic controlling hubs may experience heavy systems' loads, and may be operated in a derated state.

The efforts to save time have progressed to a new algorithm for large networks exceeding 20 nodes. However, a novel research project using overlap technique will increase the computation speed for large complex networks on the order of a 50- to 100-fold, from approximately 3000 to nearly 60 s, without sacrificing any accuracy for a network such as with 19 nodes and 32 links.

APPENDIX 2.A   OVERLAP ALGORITHM AND EXAMPLE

2.A.1   Algorithm

Create a list to hold the minimum paths. Create a list of nodes (a working path list). Determine the ingress node for the network. Add the ingress node to the working path list. Include an index in the node to denote the current link. Include an indexed list of links to all other nodes:

```
Current State:     Paths:     Ingress Node:     Egress Node:
Working Path:
Ingress Node (0)
    Links (0) (node-node), (1) (node-node)
    Link Index = -1
```
While there are still nodes present in the working path, continue working.

Step I

1. If no nodes remain in the working path, the process is complete, so go to step II.
2. Increase the link index by 1 for the last node in the work path.
3. If all the links have been processed for the last node in the working path, remove the node and go to step I.
4. Get the node to which the next link points.
5. If it is the egress node, do the following:
   a. Add the egress node to the working nodes.
   b. Add the path contained in the working path to the list of paths.
   c. If the network is currently considered a parallel–series network and there is more than one node in the path, for each node in the path, do the following:
      (i) If the node is not in the assertion list:
         1. Add the node to the assertion list.
         2. Add all the nodes in the path that follow the node to the "always follows" list for the node in the assertion list.
      (ii) If the node is in the assertion list, remove any nodes in the "always follows" list for the node in the assertion list that precedes the node in the path.
      (iii) Set the order number for the node to the highest value it has held in any path.
      (iv) Get the path added to the path list prior to the current path.
      (v) Walk through the paths from the start and determine when the paths diverge.
      (vi) Walk through the paths from the end and determine where they converge.
      (vii) For each node in the current path starting after the divergent node and ending at the node prior to the convergence node:
         1. Add the node to the assertion list if it does not already exist.
         2. Add the divergence node to the "follow nodes" list if it is not in the list.
         3. Add the convergence node to the "lead nodes" list if it is not in the list.

(viii) For each node in the path prior to the current path starting after the divergent node and ending at the node prior to the convergence node:
1. Add the node to the assertion list if it does not already exist.
2. Add the divergence node to the "follow nodes" list if it is not in the list.
3. Add the convergence node to the "lead nodes" list if it is not in the list.

(ix) For each node in the current path, if any node in the "follow nodes" list precedes the node in the current path or any node in the "lead nodes" list follows the node in the current path, mark the network as complex.

   d. Remove the egress node from the working path.

   e. Go to step I.

6. If the node does not short-circuit the path (a node is considered to short-circuit the path if it links to any node already in the working path), add the node to the working path.

7. Go to step I.

Step II
If the network is not parallel–series, go to step IV.

1. Calculate the reliability of the entire network.
2. Get the list of nodes that always follow the ingress node from the assertion list generated in step I.
3. Make this the "always leads" list.
4. If no nodes follow the ingress node, the network reliability is the reliability of the ingress node, so go to step V.
5. Set the target node to the egress node.

Step III

1. If there is only one node in the "always leads" list:
   a. Get the "always leads" list for the node in the current "always lead" list and start step III again.
   b. Recursively call step III with the "always leads" list from item a.
   c. Set the current reliability as the current reliability × the reliability from the recursive call done in item b.
   d. Return the current reliability.
2. If there is more than one node in the "always leads" list:
   a. Find the node in which the all nodes in the "always leads" list eventually reconverge.
   b. Calculate the system reliability as [1.0−(recursively call step III with the node from item a as the target node)].
   c. Get the system reliability of the reconvergence node to the target node.
   d. Calculate the current reliability as the current reliability × (1−system reliability) × reliability from item c.
   e. Return the current reliability.

EXAMPLE 95

Step IV
The network type is a complex network.

1. Remove the paths that overlap:
   a. Test all the paths to determine which paths may be removed due to overlapping another path.
   b. Test each node in the path list against all the nodes that follow it:
      (i) If every node in the path at index *j* is in the path at index *i*, remove it.
      (ii) Else, if every node in the path at index *i* is in the path at index *j*, then remove it.
2. Create a list index and set it to 0.
3. For each node in the list:
   a. Get the current path from the list at the index.
   b. For each path in the "path list" following the current path:
      (i) Get the nodes that are in the path that are not in the current path.
      (ii) Create a new path with these nodes and add it to the "pass on paths" list.
   c. Calculate the reliability as reliability + (path reliability) × [1 − (repeat these steps for the "pass on path list"].

Step V
Algorithm is complete.

2.A.2 Example

See the example as follows employing the algorithmic steps I–V previously explained.

Using the network provided, the following is a simple example of the overlap technique to calculate the reliability by determining the minimal paths for the network. Determine the ingress and egress node for the network. Create a path list, an assertion list, and a working path list. Add the ingress node to the working path list. Include an (link) index in the node to denote the current link with an initial value of −1. Include an indexed list of links to all other nodes. Continue adding nodes until the egress node is reached. Ignore any nodes that are already in the working path [23]:

```
Paths:              Ingress Node          Egress Node
                          1                    5
Working Path:

Node 1       Node 2        Node 4        Node 3        Node 5
Index:0      Index: 1      Index: 1      Index: 2      Index: -1
Links:       Links:        Links:        Links:
0 - 1, 2     0 - 2, 1      0 - 4, 1      0 - 3, 1
1 - 1, 3     1 - 2, 4      1 - 4, 3      1 - 3, 4
2 - 1, 4     2 - 2, 5      2 - 4, 5      2 - 3, 5
```

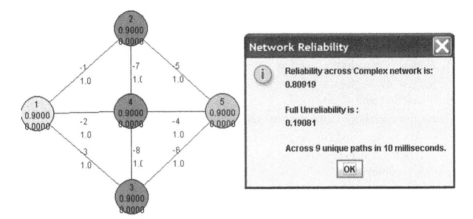

FIGURE 2.24 Five-node network example.

Add the path to the path list and create the assertion list:

```
Assertions:
Network Type: Parallel-Series
               Always                        Lead          Follow
Node           Follows        Order          Nodes         Nodes
1              2, 3, 4, 5                     1
2              3, 4, 5                        2
3              5                              4
4              3, 5                           3
5                                             5
```

Inspect the linked nodes and find the next path:

```
Paths:                        Ingress Node              Egress Node
1, 2, 4, 3, 5                     1                          5

Working Path:

Node 1         Node 2         Node 4         Node 5
Index: 0       Index: 1       Index: 2       Index: -1
Links:         Links:         Links:
0 - 1, 2       0 - 2, 1       0 - 4, 1
1 - 1, 3       1 - 2, 4       1 - 4, 3
2 - 1, 4       2 - 2, 5       2 - 4, 5
```

EXAMPLE   97

Add the path to the path list and update the assertion list:

```
Assertions:
Network Type: Parallel-Series
                Always                        Lead       Follow
Node            Follows           Order       Nodes      Nodes
1               2, 3, 4, 5, 6     1
2               3, 4, 5, 6        2
3               4, 5, 6           3           5          4
4               5, 6              4
5               6                 5
6                                 6
```

The network is still a parallel–series network. Inspect the link nodes and find the next path:

```
Paths:                   Ingress Node          Egress Node
1, 2, 4, 3, 5            1                     5
1, 2, 4, 5

Working Path:

Node 1                   Node 2                Node 5
Index: 0                 Index: 2              Index: -1
Links:                   Links:
0 - 1, 2                 0 - 2, 1
1 - 1, 3                 1 - 2, 4
2 - 1, 4                 2 - 2, 5
```

Add the path to the path list and update the assertion list:

```
Assertions:
Network Type: Parallel-Series
                Always                        Lead       Follow
Node            Follows           Order       Nodes      Nodes
1               2, 3, 4, 5, 6     1
2               3, 4, 5, 6        2
3               4, 5, 6           3           5          4
4               5, 6              4           5          2
5               6                 5
6                                 6
```

The network is still a parallel–series network. Inspect the link nodes and find the next path:

```
Paths:                   Ingress Node          Egress Node
1, 2, 4, 3, 5                 1                     5
1, 2, 4, 5
1, 2, 5
```

Working Path:

Node 1	Node 3	Node 4	Node 2	Node 5
Index: 1	Index: 1	Index: 1	Index: 1	Index: -1
Links:	Links:	Links:	Links:	Links:
0 - 1, 2	0 - 3, 1	0 - 4, 1	0 - 2, 1	
1 - 1, 3	1 - 3, 4	1 - 4, 2	1 - 2, 5	
2 - 1, 4	2 - 3, 5	2 - 4, 5		

Add the path to the path list. Since node 4 precedes node 2 in the current path and node 2 precedes node 4 in the first path in the path list, the network is now considered complex. Inspect the link nodes and find the next path:

Paths:	Ingress Node	Egress Node
1, 2, 4, 3, 5	1	5
1, 2, 4, 5		
1, 2, 5		
1, 3, 4, 2, 5		

Working Path:

Node 1	Node 3	Node 4	Node 5
Index: 1	Index: 1	Index: 2	Index: -1
Links:	Links:	Links:	Links:
0 - 1, 2	0 - 3, 1	0 - 4, 1	
1 - 1, 3	1 - 3, 4	1 - 4, 2	
2 - 1, 4	2 - 3, 5	2 - 4, 5	

Inspect the link nodes and find the next path:

Paths:	Ingress Node	Egress Node
1, 2, 4, 3, 5	1	5
1, 2, 4, 5		
1, 2, 5		
1, 3, 4, 2, 5		
1, 3, 4, 5		

Working Path:

Node 1	Node 3	Node 5
Index: 1	Index: 2	Index: -1
Links:	Links:	Links:
0 - 1, 2	0 - 3, 1	
1 - 1, 3	1 - 3, 4	
2 - 1, 4	2 - 3, 5	

EXAMPLE 99

Inspect the link nodes and find the next path:

```
Paths:                  Ingress Node        Egress Node
1, 2, 4, 3, 5                1                   5
1, 2, 4, 5
1, 2, 5
1, 3, 4, 2, 5
1, 3, 4, 5
1, 3, 5

Working Path:

Node 1          Node 4          Node 3          Node 5
Index: 2        Index: 1        Index: 1        Index: -1
Links:          Links:          Links:
0 - 1, 2        0 - 4, 1        0 - 3, 1
1 - 1, 3        1 - 4, 3        0 - 3, 5
2 - 1, 4        2 - 4, 5
```

Inspect the link nodes and find the next path:

```
Paths:                  Ingress Node        Egress Node
1, 2, 4, 3, 5                1                   5
1, 2, 4, 5
1, 2, 5
1, 3, 4, 2, 5
1, 3, 4, 5
1, 3, 5
1, 4, 3, 5

Working Path:

Node 1          Node 4          Node 5
Index: 2        Index: 2        Index: -1
Links:          Links:
0 - 1, 2        0 - 4, 1
1 - 1, 3        1 - 4, 3
2 - 1, 4        2 - 4, 5
```

Inspect the link nodes and find that all the links have been followed. Thus the following is the path list:

```
Paths:
1, 2, 4, 3, 5
1, 2, 4, 5
1, 2, 5
1, 3, 4, 2, 5
1, 3, 4, 5
1, 3, 5
1, 4, 3, 5
1, 4, 5
```

Calculate the reliability of the network. Remove any paths overlapped by any other path:

```
1, 2, 5
1, 3, 5
1, 4, 5
```

For each path in the path list, calculate the network reliability. Take the first path and compare it to the paths that follow to get the nodes in each path that is not in the first path. Remove any overlapped paths in the "pass on" list. Now repeat the process for each path in the pass on list and any subpass on lists. The following shows the calculations to get system reliability using these steps for the first path in the original list of paths:

```
Path list
1, 2, 5
1, 3, 5
1, 4, 5

Pass on list
3
4

Pass on with the overlapped paths removed
3, 4

Path
3

Pass On list 2
4
```

```
                Path (from the pass on list)
                4
                Pass on list 2 reliability = 0.9
```

$$\text{Reliability} = (\text{current reliability for this level}) + (\text{path reliability})$$
$$(1.0 - \text{Pass on list 2 reliability})$$
$$= 0.0 + (0.9)(1-0.9) = (0.9)(0.1) = 0.09$$

```
Path 4
```

$$\text{Pass on list reliability} = 0.09 + (0.9)(1.0-0.0) = 0.09 + 0.9 = 0.99$$

$$\text{Network reliability} = 0.0 + \left[(0.9)(0.9)(0.9)\right](1.0-0.99) = (0.729)(0.01) = 0.00729$$

```
Original Path list
1   2   5
1,  3,  5
1,  4,  5
Pass on list
4
Pass on with the overlapped paths removed
4
Path
4
```

$$\text{Pass on list reliability} = 0.0 + (0.9)(1.0 - 0.0) = 0.9$$
$$\text{Network reliability} = 0.00729 + \left[(0.9)(0.9)(0.9)\right](1.0 - 0.9)$$
$$= 0.00729 + (0.729)(0.1) = 0.08019$$

```
Original Path list
1   2   5
1,  3,  5
1,  4,  5
```

$$\text{Network reliability} = 0.08019 + \left[(0.9)(0.9)(0.9)\right](1 - 0.0)$$

$= 0.08019 + (0.729)(1.0) = 0.80919$ (Q.E.D., quod erat demonstrandum: thus proof completed)

The network reliability is $0.80919 \approx 80.92\%$ as verified by Figure 2.24. The algorithm has been implemented successfully through hand calculations. For more exercises, see Section 2.7.6.

2.7 EXERCISES

2.7.1 From ERBDC, using the internal data, and overlap reliability Java applet, given the node availabilities are 0.8 and links have perfect (=1.0) and imperfect availability (=0.9), respectively, solve for the ingress (the first node) and egress (the last node) availability for (i) 7-node, (ii) 8-node, (iii) 10-node, (iv) 19-node, and (v) 52-node.

2.7.2 Using MSS reliability principles, supposing that you have fully up (=0.7), fully down (=0.2), and derated (=0.1) states for any node, and with any fastest method you like, calculate $P(\text{UP})$, $P(\text{DER})$, and $P(\text{DOWN})$ for the "newest 6-node topology" in internal data. Repeat this exercise when fully up (=0.6), derated (=0.2), degraded (=0.15), and fully down (=0.05).

2.7.3 Do the same as in 2.7.2 for (i) 7-node, (ii) 8-node, (iii) 10-node, (iv) 19-node, and (v) 52-node, respectively.

2.7.4 Calculate ingress–egress availability for (i) 7-node, (ii) 8-node, (iii) 10-node, (iv) 19-node, and (v) 52-node, respectively, if the node availabilities are nonconstant and stochastic and obey a Weibull ($\alpha=1$, $\beta=1$), which is identical to unity exponential with $\beta=1$. Evaluate at $t=0.1053$ and $t=0.2283$ unit. Compare with 2.7.1's overlap reliability results.

2.7.5 Do the same as in 2.7.2 for (i) 7-node, (ii) 8-node, (iii) 10-node, (iv) 19-node, and (v) 52-node, respectively, if the node availabilities are stochastic, are not deterministic as in 2.7.2 and 2.7.3, and concurrently obey a time-dependent Weibull ($\alpha=1$, $\beta=2$) probability distribution, which is identical to Rayleigh distribution with $\beta=2$. Evaluate reliability for input/output at $t=0.1053$ and $t=0.2283$ units.

2.7.6 For the below three networks in Figures 2.25, 2.26, and 2.27, demonstrate the overlap method by hand calculations following the algorithm in the chapter.

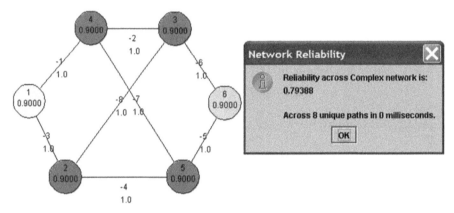

FIGURE 2.25   Six-node complex network.

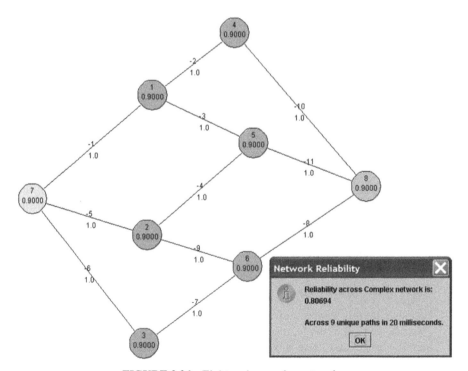

FIGURE 2.26   Eight-node complex networks.

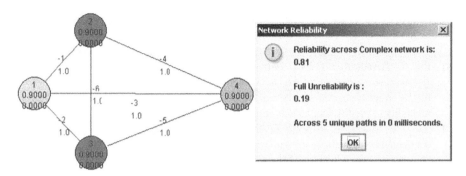

FIGURE 2.27   Four-node complex network.

REFERENCES

[1]   Colbourn, C. J. (1981). Combinatorial aspects of network reliability, *Annals of Operations Research*, R-30, 32–35.

[2]   Aggarwal, K. K., Rai, S. (1981). Reliability evaluation in computer communication networks, *IEEE Transactions on Reliability*, 30(1), 32–35.

[3]   Jan, R. H. (1993). Design of reliable networks, *Computers and Operations Research*, 20(1), 25–34.

[4]   Yeh, M. S., Lin, J. S., Yeh, W. C. (1994). New Monte Carlo method for estimating network reliability, in Proceedings of 16th International Conference on Computers and Industrial Engineering, 723–726.

[5]   Fishman, G. S. A. (1986). Comparison of four Monte Carlo methods for estimating the probability of s-t connectedness, *IEEE Transactions on Reliability*, 35(2), 145–155.

[6]   Sahinoglu, M., Libby, D. (2004). Sahinoglu-Libby (SL) probability density function-component reliability applications in integrated networks, in Proceedings of Annual Reliability and Maintainability Symposium, RAMS03, Tampa, FL, 280–287, 27–30.

[7]   Dengiz, B., Altiparmak, F., Smith, A. E. (1997). Efficient optimization of all-terminal reliable networks using evolutionary approach, *IEEE Transactions on Reliability*, 46(1), 18–26.

[8]   Sahinoglu, M., Libby, D., Das, S. R. (2005). Measuring availability indices with small samples for Component and network reliability using the Sahinoglu-Libby probability model, *IEEE Transactions on Instrumentation and Measurement*, 54(3), 1283–1295.

[9]   Sahinoglu, M. (2000). Reliability index evaluations of an integrated software system for insufficient software failure and recovery data, in Proceedings of ADVIS-2000, Izmir, Turkey, Springer-Verlag, 25–27.

[10] Murphy, K. E., Carter, C. M. (2003). Reliability block diagram construction techniques: Secrets to real-life diagramming woes, in Proceedings of Annual Reliability and Maintainability Symposium—Tutorial Notes RAMS03, Tampa, FL.

[11] Sahinoglu, M., Smith, A., Dengiz, B. (2003). Improved network design method when considering reliability and cost using an exact reliability block diagram calculation (ERBDC) tool in complex systems, ANNIE- Smart Engineering Systems, in Proceedings of the Intelligent Engineering Systems through Artificial Neural Networks, 13, St. Louis, MO, 849–855.

[12] Sahinoglu, M., Ramamoorthy, C. V. (2005). RBD tools using compression and hybrid techniques to code decode and compute s-t reliability in simple and complex networks, *IEEE Transactions on Instrumentation and Measurement*, 54(3), 1789–1799.

[13] Sahinoglu, M., Larson, J., Rice, B. (2003). An exact reliability calculation tool to improve large safety-critical computer networks, in Proceedings DSN2003, San Francisco, CA, IEEE Computer Society, B38–B39.

[14] Luo, T., Trivedi, K. S. (1998). An improved algorithm for coherent system reliability, *IEEE Transactions on Reliability*, 47(1), 73–78.

[15] Rai, S., Veeraraghavan, M., Trivedi, K. S. (1995). A survey on efficient computation of reliability using disjoint products approach, *Networks*, 25(3), 174–163.

[16] Zang, X., Sun, H. R., Trivedi, K. S. (1999). A BDD approach to dependable analysis of distributed computer systems with imperfect coverage, in *Dependable Network Computing*, D. Avresky (ed.), Kluwer Publishers, Amsterdam, 167–190.

[17] Sahinoglu, M., Chow, E. (1999). Empirical Bayesian availability index of safety and time critical software systems with corrective maintenance, in Proceedings of the 1999 Pacific Rim International Symposium on Dependable Computing (PRDC1999), Hong Kong, 84–91.

[18] Sahinoglu, M. (2003). An exact RBD calculation tool to design very complex systems, invited talk, in Proceedings of the 1st ACIS International Conference on Software Engineering Research and Applications, 25–27.

[19] Sahinoglu, M., Munns, W. (2001). Availability indices of a software network, in Proceedings of IX Brazilian Symposium on Fault Tolerant Computing, Florianopolis, Brazil, 123–131.

[20] Sahinoglu, M. (2005). An algorithm to code and decode complex systems, and to compute s-t reliability, in Proceedings of the Annual Reliability and Maintainability Symposium, 24–27.

[21] Ramamoorthy, C. V., Han, Y. W. (1975). Reliability analysis of systems with concurrent error detection, *IEEE Transactions on Computing*, C-24(9), 868–878.

[22] Sahinoglu, M., Rice, B., Tyson, D. (2008). An analytical exact RBD method to calculate s-t reliability in complex networks, *International Journal of Computers, Information Technology and Engineering*, 2(2), 95–104.

[23] Rice, B. (2009). Scalable complex cyber network reliability algorithm, M.S. thesis. Supervisor: M. Sahinoglu (AUM), Troy University Computer Science, Montgomery.

[24] Sahinoglu, M., *Trustworthy Computing: Analytical and Quantitative Engineering Evaluation*, John Wiley & Sons Inc., Hoboken, NJ, 2007.

[25] Sahinoglu M. 2008. Solution manual to trustworthy computing, analytical and quantitative engineering evaluation. Available at: www.areslimited.com (accessed on September 10, 2015).

[26] Lisnianski, A., Levitin, G., *Multi-State System Reliability*, World Scientific Publishing, 2003.

[27] Lewis, E. E., *Introduction to Reliability Engineering*, John Wiley & Sons Inc., Hoboken, NJ, 1996.

[28] Sahinoglu M., Marghitu D., Stockton S., Morton S., Ang D. (2016). Analytical and simulation studies of operational variations for onshore land and offshore oil drilling rigs to forecast, asess and manage security risk, proceedings of the 2016 Taiwan Internatonal Conference on Innovation and Management (ICIM), Taipei, Taiwan, January 13–15.

[29] Reliasoft (1992). BlockSim, Version 6, User's Guide, ReliaSoft Corporation, ReliaSoft Publishing, Tucson, AZ, 1–704.

3

STOPPING RULES FOR RELIABILITY AND SECURITY TESTS IN CYBER-RISK

LEARNING OBJECTIVES

- Describe security and reliability testing, cost-effective metrics for stopping rules.
- Examine time-independent (or effort or grouped) and time-dependent (continuous or time-failure) testing.
- Implement the testing scenarios using automated stopping-rule algorithms.
- Compare and merge with other techniques for cost-effective stopping-rule algorithms.

3.1 INTRODUCTION

The damage or risk inflicted currently by security breaches and unintended software failures in the ubiquitous computer and communication networks as experienced by related businesses or government entities is measured by multiples of billions of dollars. The analysis of such malicious and/or unwanted activities as to when to act to stop testing at the right moment to assure cost efficiency and maximum security and reliability are of a paramount interest to computer scientists and risk analysts, in addition to the business owners and their vulnerable customers. In most situations, corporate testing continues until the time-to-release date or when the testing budget is depleted. These conventionally subjective stopping decision rules inhibit the testers from understanding the extent of potential security breaches and/or chance failures when the product is released. This process can be extremely costly and inefficient. The focus is on determining when given the results of a testing process, whether white box (coverage), or black box (functional) testing, it is most economical to halt testing and release software under the conditions prevailing for a prescribed time period. We are dealing with one progressive way of conducting a quality control analysis of software testing activity with the goal of achieving a defined quality end-product under the given conditions.

Cyber-Risk Informatics: Engineering Evaluation with Data Science, First Edition. Mehmet Sahinoglu.
© 2016 John Wiley & Sons, Inc. Published 2016 by John Wiley & Sons, Inc.
Companion website: www.wiley.com/go/sahinoglu/informatics

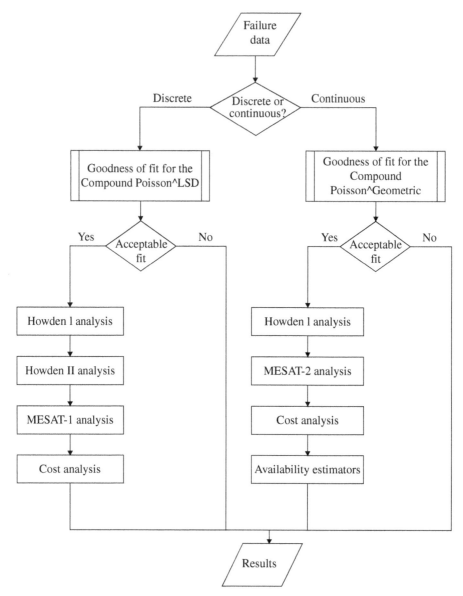

FIGURE 3.1 Flowchart of MESAT-1 and MESAT-2 for discrete and continuous time.

Even though there are many extensive sources in the literature on testing software, there has been no in-depth analysis, specifically on the intricacies and complexities, and more fundamentally, on the science of when to stop most efficiently and economically. Usually, the stopping rule is either a time-to-release date, which is nothing more than a commercial benchmark or a time constraint, or it is a rough percentage of how many bugs detected out of a given total prescribed with no statistical data or trend information. Software testing and product reliability have always been two inseparable issues, but the analysis of stopping rules to render this activity cost-effective has traditionally been ignored. It is now anticipated that 60–75% of software expenses stem from testing [1]. Software testing is a wide topic that has been widely studied, such as by the *Handbook of Software Reliability Engineering* [2] and the *Software Engineering Handbook* [3], as well as references on *Software Testing* [4, 5]. The data examined are one of two types: either stopping at the end of a time period T, such as at an increment of $T_k - T_{k-1}$ for a time-based continuous model, or at the end of a certain amount of testing of the Nth test case, such as stopping at an increment of $N_k - N_{k-1}$ for the test case or synonymously an effort-based discrete model. In this chapter, we deal with the stopping rules in continuous time- and discrete effort-based models and their applications using a programming code compiled under the general title *MESAT*. Namely, *MESAT-1* is an application software for effort-based data and *MESAT-2* is for continuous time-based data. Although this chapter works with empirical data on chance or random failures that cause disruption of the intended service of a hardware or software, the same logic can be utilized for malicious (not chance related or random) attacks that cause security breaches in security testing. Attacks replace test cases, and crashes or penetrations replace the failures herein not countermeasured.

Therefore, we consider two methods defining appropriate stopping rules in security testing; the logistic growth model (*LGM*) and the compound Poisson model (*CPM*). These two methods model failure times based on probabilistic methods and develop criteria-based stopping rules to support each other in synergy. There is another aspect of software security testing, which deals with the functional testing of secure software (as in the metaphor of walking a high wire with a safety net), an entirely different domain and conceptually different than what this chapter addresses. The two common methods for testing whether software has met its security requirements are functional testing [6] and risk-based security testing [7]. The methods proposed herein follow the latter risk-based testing derived from a risk analysis to encompass not only the high-level risks identified during the design process but also low-level risks from the software. Howdens' rule in discrete compared to CPM stopping rule in the effort and time domain will be too covered (Fig. 3.1).

3.2   METHODS

In this section, we define a novel stopping rule that combines two different approaches that have been previously used to determine when to stop testing. One method uses strictly a model-based approach with a stopping rule based on coverage criterion, while the second method uses a probabilistic approach with a stopping rule based on expected cost, coverage, and percent savings. The combination of the two procedures results in a more robust stopping rule than using one approach in isolation. The first stopping rule uses the LGM, which is a model-based approach and was first defined by Verhulst in 1845 to model population growth of species [8]. Over the years, LGM has been used with much regulatory to model growth and decay, including computer software failures [9]. Recently, the LGM has been used to quantitatively determine a coverage-based stopping rule for software testing [10, 11]. The second stopping rule uses a compound Poisson model (CPM), which is a probabilistic-based approach, and it models historic failure times as a Poisson process with clusters modeling logarithmic series distribution (LSD). This model utilizes the following three criteria in its stopping rule: coverage, expected cost of continued testing, and percent savings [12]. We provide more information and greater detail about the LGM and CPM in subsequent sections, respectively. The merger of these two methods (LGM followed up by CPM), otherwise called *Sahinoglu–Simmons* technique by this text's author (or S–S for short, due to authors who used it for the first time in stopping-rule-for-testing-related literature). This approach presents the best of two worlds by leveraging a static stopping rule (by LGM through SAS or SPSS nonlinear regression solution) with the cost parameters using a dynamic follow-up to reach an optimal outcome about when to stop with a favorable cost and benefit structure (by CPM through MESAT-1 software [10, 11]).

3.2.1   LGM by Verhulst

The LGM can easily be fit by many statistical software packages. This approach models the cumulative failures or breaches of a system as a logistic growth curve, which is defined as follows:

$$f(x_i) = \frac{\beta_0}{1 + e^{-\beta_1 - \beta_2 x_i}}; i = 1,2,........ \tag{3.1}$$

In this parameterization of the LGM, the parameter β_0 is the maximum cumulative number of failures or breaches in the system. This method does not require the user to actually reach the maximum cumulative number of failures or breaches in order to estimate the parameter in the model. The parameter β_2 will determine if the LGM is a growth model (i.e., increasing with respect to x) or a decay model (i.e., decreasing with respect to x). In modeling cumulative number of failures, we expect the β_2 parameter to be positive.

To define the stopping criterion, we desire a certain coverage or percent of failures or breaches to be discovered. If we define this percent as q for $0 < q < 1$, we can find the stopping rule as the value of x.

Solving this equation for x, we get

$$x = -\frac{\beta_1 + \ln[(1-q)/q]}{\beta_2} \tag{3.2}$$

We can use this criterion to find the stopping rule for any coverage value; however, we note that the maximum rate at which failures or breaches occur is the inflection point of the curve, which happens when q (coverage) is 0.5, which results in $x = -\beta_1/\beta_2$.

For example, Figure 3.2 illustrates a simulated LGM data set generated with $\beta_0 = 50$, $\beta_1 = -2$, and $\beta_2 = 0.65$ using a simple standard normal error structure. The true maximum failure or breach rate occurs at $x = 3.077$ ($- (-2/0.65)$), and the maximum cumulative number of failures or breaches is 50 ($= \beta_0$).

In the process of testing software, the full curve would not be known unless testing continued until all failures or breaches occur, as in the example mentioned previously; the testing would continue until a total of 50 breaches or failures were found. As a simple example, say the researchers stop at $x = 3.00$ (before the maximum growth rate occurs), it is of interest to estimate where the maximum growth rate occurs and the maximum cumulative number of failures or breaches. Using this truncated data and the SAS PROC

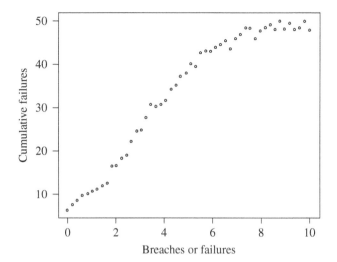

FIGURE 3.2 Simulated software failure (or security breach) cumulative count versus time.

NLIN procedure with initial estimates obtained by using [13], the following estimates were obtained for β_0, β_1, and β_2, where $b_0 = 49.6963 \approx 50$, $b_1 = -1.9794$, and $b_2 = 0.6510$.

These estimates give an approximate maximum growth rate at 3.04 (compared to the truth at 3.077) and an approximate maximum cumulative number of failures of 50 (rounding the β_0 estimate). By the estimated growth curve, we use a stopping rule based on the desired percent of coverage. If a coverage of 0.8 is desired, we need to find the value of x associated with at least 80% coverage or $0.8b_0 = 39.75704$. Using Equation (3.1), this would yield $39.75704 = 49.6963 / (1 + e^{1.9795 - 0.6519x})$, which gives a stopping rule of $x = 5.126$.

To recap, in the LGM by Verhulst, the parameter β_0 is the maximum cumulative number of failures or breaches in the system. The parameters β_1 and β_2 define the rate of cumulative failures (or breaches) and model types respectively. An advantage is that it does not require knowledge of the full test set in order to define the stopping rule. It is possible that the calculated stopping rule will be beyond the cases already observed. However, this method only takes into account the coverage criteria mentioned. Once an LGM is observed fit to the data, the estimated parameters can be used to calculate the stopping rule for approximately $100q\%$ coverage of the failures or breaches, $0 < q < 1$. By defining b_0 as the estimate for β_0 and b_1 and b_2 as the estimate for β_1 and β_2, respectively, the LGM becomes

$$qb_0 = \frac{b_0}{1 + \exp\left(-b_1 - b_2 x\right)} \tag{3.3}$$

Solving Equation (3.3) for x, the stopping rule is given in Equation (3.4)

$$x = \frac{\log\left[(1 - q) / q\right] + b_1}{-b_2} \tag{3.4}$$

3.2.2 Compound Poisson Model

Notation:

CL confidence level; a minimal percentage of branches or failures to cover

NBD Negative binomial distribution

$N(t)$ random variable for the number of Poisson events until and including time t

$X(t)$ total number of failures distributed with respect to Poisson^LSD until time unit t

w_i random variable of failure clump size distributed with LSD at each Poisson event i

$\Theta = \theta$ LSD parameter that denotes the positive correlation

a constant for the LSD random variable of w

k NBD parameter (calculated recursively at each Poisson epoch)

λ Poisson rate or parameter where $\lambda = k\ln(1-\theta)^{-1} = k\ln q$ holds

θ_1 lower limit of θ

θ_2 upper limit of θ

C.f. or $\Phi_{X(t)}$ characteristic function of $X(t)$

dif(θ) range for LSD parameter, the correlation coefficient: $\theta_2 - \theta_1$

q reciprocal of $(1-\theta)$. When $\theta = 0$, no compounding phenomenon, and the process is purely Poisson with $q=1$ (if $q>1$, there is over dispersion)

p related parameter, $p=q-1$; no compounding or pure Poisson when $p=0$

$f(X/\theta)$ discrete negative binomial conditional probability distribution of X

$h(\theta)$ prior distribution of the positive correlation parameter

$h(X)$ marginal distribution of X following the Bayesian analysis

α, β Positive shape and scale parameters of the beta distribution

Beta (α,β) prior beta distribution for the LSD variable

$h(\theta \mid X)$ posterior conditional distribution of θ on X: failure vector

$f(X \mid \theta)$ discrete conditional probability distribution of X given Θ

$E(\theta \mid X)$ Bayes estimator with respect to squared-error loss function, expected value of the conditional posterior random variable θ

$E(X)=kp$ expected value of the conditional $X\sim$NBD whose only parameter is k and based on a single random variable, $\Theta \sim h(\theta \mid X)$, which is a conditional posterior

$S(.)=$s stopping rule S gives the number of failures to stop after (.) discrete time units (days, weeks, etc.) or number of test cases

C combination (n,k) notation denoting how many different unordered combinations of "size k out of a sample of n" as in $\dbinom{n}{k} = \dfrac{n!}{k!(n-k)!}$

$DR1$–$DR8$ effort-based time-independent (test cases) coverage data sets 1–8 in the database

$T1$–$T9$ time-based time-independent (test cases) historical data sets 1–9 in the database

An innovative method incorporating the cost of testing and the discrete nature of the data lies in the CPM [14–16]. In this method, the total number of failures or breaches is assumed to follow a Poisson process with a compounding distribution that describes the failure size. This method assumes that the total number of failures, $X(t)$ follows a Poisson process, where

$$\{X(t), t \geq 0\} = \sum_{i=1}^{N(t)} w_i \tag{3.5}$$

and $N(t) > 1$. The failure size, denoted as w_1, $w_2 \ldots$ are independent, identically distributed LSD with

$$f(w) = a \frac{\theta^w}{w}; \quad 0 < \theta < 1, \; a > 0, \; w = 1, 2, \ldots \tag{3.6}$$

It can be shown that the compound Poisson distribution with LSD as the compounding distribution is equivalent to the negative binomial distribution with $E(X) = kp$ and

$$\lambda = -k \ln(1 - \theta) = k \ln q \tag{3.7}$$

where $q = (1 - \theta)^{-1}$, $p = q - 1$, $\lambda = E(N(t))$, and $N(t) \sim \text{Poisson}(\lambda)$. The parameter θ represents the autocorrelation within each clump or failure size (correlation within each clump size is assumed to be positive). Since the autocorrelation within each clump size is not constant, the parameter θ can be treated as a random variable. Empirical Bayes approach where the θ prior for Beta (α, β) gives $\theta \, |X \sim \text{Beta}(\alpha + X, \beta + k)$ and it follows:

$$E(X) = k \frac{\alpha + X}{\beta - 1 + k} \tag{3.8}$$

Under the assumption of a compound Poisson distribution, three criteria describe when to stop testing. *The first criterion* is the one-step-ahead approach, which stops testing when the ith incremental step at time t has a larger (or equal to) expected cost of stopping than expected cost of continuing, or in other words [12, 14–16],

$$aE(X_{i+1}) < bE(X_i) + c \tag{3.9}$$

where $a = $ cost of fixing a failure once the software has been released, $b = $ cost of fixing software during testing, and $c = $ a fixed value for testing. When $E(X_{i+1}) = E(X_i)$, the above formula simplifies to

$$E(X_{i+1}) - E(X_i) \leq \frac{c}{a - b} = d \tag{3.10}$$

and we can rewrite the above criteria as

$$e(X) = E(X_{i+1}) - E(X_i) < d \tag{3.11}$$

Substituting from Equation (3.8), above (3.11) leads to a stopping criterion of

$$e(X) = k_{i+1} \frac{\alpha + X_{i+1}}{\beta - 1 + k_{i+1}} - k_i \frac{\alpha + X_i}{\beta - 1 + k_i} \leq d \qquad (3.12)$$

However, using the generalized (incomplete) beta prior instead of the standard beta prior can be more reasonable and realistic since the former includes an expert opinion (termed as an "educated guess") about the feasible range of the parameter $0 < \theta < 1$ [12]. Therefore, θ can be entered by the analyst as a range or difference this time in the form dif $(\theta) = \theta_2$ (upper) $- \theta_1$ (lower) to reflect a range of prior belief of positive correlation among the software failures or branches covered in a clump. Finally, we derive a more general equation (3.13) for a generalized beta to replace the earlier equation (3.12) that was derived for the standard beta prior. Equation (3.13) for the generalized beta transforms or defaults into (3.12) if dif$(\theta) = 1$. Therefore, incorporating the generalized beta prior yields the most general equation (3.13):

$$e(X) = k_{i+1} \frac{(\theta_2 - \theta_1)(\alpha + X_{i+1})}{(\alpha + \beta - 1 + X_{i+1} + k_{i+1}) - (\theta_2 - \theta_1)(\alpha + X_{i+1})} -$$
$$k_i \frac{(\theta_2 - \theta_1)(\alpha + X_i)}{(\alpha + \beta - 1 + X_i + k_i) - (\theta_2 - \theta_1)(\alpha + X_i)} \leq d, \quad i = 1, 2, 3 \ldots \qquad (3.13)$$

where, $d = c/(a - b)$ and $\alpha, \beta, k_i, X_i, \theta_2,$ and θ_1 are input values at each discrete step i.

The second criterion is to ensure that a certain level of branch coverage is obtained. In order to ensure that a certain amount of coverage is obtained, the total number of failures or breaches must be prematurely known or estimated. When the total cumulative number of breaches are known, the $100q\%$ coverage is obtained when q^*(total cumulative number of failure or breaches) for $0 < q < 1$ has been reached. *The third and final criterion* used to define when to stop testing is that accrued monetary savings are positive when the testing is halted. The program, **M**ath-**S**tatistical-**C**ost-**E**fficient-**S**topping-Rule-**A**lgorithm-for-**T**esting also dubbed, **MESAT-1** is an easy-to-use software developed to implement the compound Poisson distribution with the above three criteria for stopping [12]. The MESAT-1 software calculates a rule for stopping the testing activity of failure/attack in software/security testing, as contrary to exhaustive testing, given the input parameters including the cost factors, both for effort-based (time independent or discrete) and time-continuous input. The inputs for MESAT-1 software:

1. Values for α and β in the Beta distribution
2. Range of θ
3. Initial value of $k(0)$
4. Coverage criterion
5. Number of coverage
6. Minimum number of test cases

The values for α and β relay the information about the prior distribution for θ, the autocorrelation of failure or breach size. We recommend for starter using a left-skewed distribution indicating a larger autocorrelation ($\alpha=8$ and $\beta=2$). The difference of the θ input (indicating the total range of the autocorrelation values) should remain 1, unless there is good evidence that an improper beta should be used as the prior distribution for θ, which would change the range to a value less than one. The value of d should be derived from the previously stated values of a, b, and c. The value of $k(0)$ is an initial estimate for k as defined in Equation (3.7). The k parameter in the model is not very sensitive to the initial starting value of $k(0)$. We recommend using the value 0.12 for $k(0)$ [12].

The maximum cumulative number of failures or breaches is observed from the provided data. The minimum number of test cases defaults to 0, unless there are a pre-specified number of minimum test cases required. In addition to the previous input, the information for the cost analysis must also be entered. This includes the values of a, b and c, and if there is a budget to the testing, this amount should also be factored into the analysis.

If we were to stop at a discrete interval i, we would assume that the number of failures detected or size of branch coverage (from branch testing) discovered will have to accrue by "a" amount per failure or branch after the fact or following release of the software. Thus, there is an expected cost over the interval $[i, i+1]$ of $aE\{X_{i+1}\}$ for stopping at time $t=t_i$ or test case i. If we continue testing over the interval, we assume that there is a fixed cost of c for testing and a variable cost of b for fixing each failure found during the testing before the fact or preceding release of the software. Note that "a" is almost always larger than "b" since it should be considerably more expensive to fix a failure (or recover an undiscovered branch or defect) once it has been released than fixing it while testing in house. Thus, the expected cost for the continuation of testing for the next time interval or test case is $bE(X_i)+c$. Opportunity or shadow cost is not considered here since such an additional or implied cost may be included within a more expensive and remedial-after-release raised cost coefficient denoted by "a." Some researchers are not content with these fixed costs and argue that these values change as testing continues. However, the MESAT-1 tool employed here can accommodate this problem through a variable costing data-driven approach as needed by the testing analyst. That is, a separate value is entered per choice in the MESAT-1 Java program for "a" or "b" or "c" costs at each test case, if these cost factors are defined to vary from test case to test case. In order to ensure a stopping rule is cost efficient, we recommend considering the following inequalities [11, 12]. That is, letting RF = number of failures remaining after the stopping rule, and RT = number of test cases remaining after the stopping rule, and TF = total failures, and TT = total test cases; a cost-efficient stopping rule is designed as follows:

$$(\text{RF})a \le (\text{RF})b + (\text{RT})c \tag{3.14}$$

From this equation, the following inequality is derived for an optimal "a":

$$a \le \frac{(\text{RF})b + (\text{RT})c}{\text{RF}} \tag{3.15}$$

Test expense (TEXP) = $b*$ no. of failures repaired $+c*$ no. of test cases covered:

$$\text{TEXP} = b*(\text{TF}-\text{RF})+c*(\text{TT}-\text{RT}) \tag{3.16}$$

3.3 EXAMPLES MERGING BOTH STOPPING RULES: LGM AND CPM

3.3.1 The DR5 Data Set Example

We illustrate the synergy of the two methods on a well-studied data set, DR5 [12]. This extensive data set has 2187 time units and 46 attacks. Figure 3.3 illustrates the data with the logistic growth curve overlaid on top of it. Figure 3.4 does the same for data set

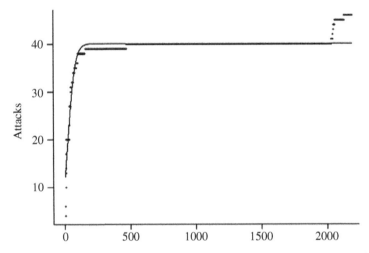

FIGURE 3.3   The DR5 data set (points) with the logistic growth curve overlaid.

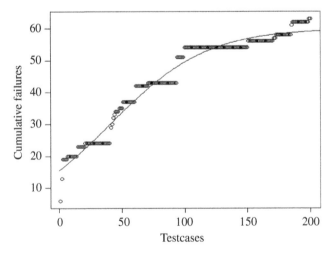

FIGURE 3.4   The DR4 data set with the Verhulst's logistic growth curve overlaid.

DR4. Figure 3.5 performs similarly for XSEDE data set all by LGM. See similarly Figures 3.6 and 3.7 for the DR5 and XSEDE data sets by CPM's MESAT-1 software, respectively. The LGM estimated the parameters as $b_0 = 40.1980$, $b_1 = -0.8643$, and $b_2 = 0.0366$ respectively. Giving the approximate maximum growth rate occurring at $x = -(-0.8643)/0.0366 \approx 23$, with an estimated number of cumulative attacks at this value of $y = 40.1980/(1 + \exp(0.8643 - 0.0366*24)) \approx 20$. Due to the symmetry of LGM, this corresponds to a stopping rule with 50% coverage since $20/40 = 0.5$. In this example, the maximum number of attacks estimated by the model is approximately 40 (instead of the actual 46). This is due to the late negligible lack of increase in the number of attacks toward the end of 2187 test cases or efforts.

We use SAS PROC NLIN (nonlinear procedure) to fit the LGM. In SAS, we need to provide the algorithm with reasonable starting values. To get these values, we make use of some interesting properties of this model. For example, in the LGM, as x goes to infinity, $\{b_0/(1 + \exp(-b_1 - b_2 x))\}$ approaches b_0 (assuming b_2 is positive indicating an increasing curve).

Therefore a reasonable starting value for b_0 is the maximum value for the response, which in the DR5 data set is 46. In order to obtain reasonable starting values for b_1 and b_2, we can apply algebra to our equation to obtain the following table of equations (Table 3.1).

Notice that this is a simple linear equation where $b_1 + b_2 x = y^*$ and where $y^* = \ln(y/(b_0 - y))$. Using the estimate for b_0 as discussed and transforming y, we can fit a simple linear regression and use the y-intercept and slope as estimates for b_1 and b_2, respectively. We illustrate this strategy by applying it to the DR5 data set. Recall that we estimated b_0 as 46 in Section 3.3.1.

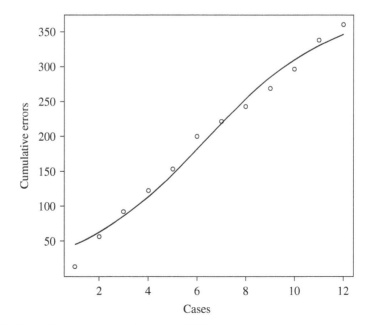

FIGURE 3.5 LGM curve overlaid on the XSEDE; $y =$ cumulative # errors, x-axis $=$ # months.

TABLE 3.1   PROC NLIN (SAS: Statistical Analysis Systems, Procedure Nonlinear)

$y = b_0 / (1 + \exp(-b_1 - b_2 x))$	(3.17)
$1 + \exp(-b_1 - b_2 x) = b_0 / y$	(3.18)
$\exp(-b_1 - b_2 x) = b_0 / y - 1$	(3.19)
$b_1 + b_2 x = -\ln(b_0 - y) / y)$	(3.20)
$b_1 + b_2 x = \ln(y / (b_0 - y))$	(3.21)

```
Inputting data
data dr5;
input testcases    failures cum_fail;
datalines;
1        4    4
2        0    4
3        0    4
.
2184     0    46
2185     0    46
2186     0    46
2187     0    46
...
Create transformed y-values.
data transf;
set dr5;
ynew=log (cum_fail/ (46-cum_fail));
run;
Run linear regression to get point estimates for β₁ and β₂.
proc glm data=transf;
model ynew=testcases;
run;
```

From this output, we see that the b_1 estimate is 1.37 and the b_2 estimate is 0.0004. To run PROC NLIN, we specify the Marquardt nonlinear optimization algorithm. The SAS code for running the LGM for the DR5 data set is shown below. The first statement invokes the nonlinear procedure using the Marquardt optimization algorithm and specifying the DR5 data set (see Table 3.2).

The second statement provides the parameter estimates that were just calculated and the third statement defines the LGM from Equation (3.1).

```
proc nlin method=marquardt data=dr5;
parameters b0 = 46   b1 = 1.37   b2 = .0004;
model cum_fail = b0/(1+exp(-b1-b2*testcases));
run;
```

It is very important that the model converges and there are no issues with model (e.g., with the Hessian matrix containing the partial derivatives), which in this situation rendered the algorithm to converge. There were no issues with the model (Table 3.3).

TABLE 3.2   Output From SAS PROC GLM

The GLM Procedure					
Dependent variable: ynew					
Source	DF	Sum of squares	Mean square	F value	Pr>F
Model	1	170.1109978	170.1109978	863.74	<0.0001
Error	2125	418.5119158	0.1969468		
Corrected total	2126	588.6229136			
R-square	Coeff var	Root MSE	ynew mean		
0.288998	23.8160	0.443787	1.863394		
Source	DF	Type I SS	Mean square	F value	Pr>F
Test cases	1	170.1109978	170.1109978	863.74	<0.0001
Source	DF	Type III SS	Mean square	F value	Pr>F
Test cases	1	170.1109978	170.1109978	863.74	<0.0001
Standard					
Parameter	Estimate	Error	t value	Pr>|t|	
Intercept	1.373336394	0.01925191	71.34	<0.0001	
Test cases	0.000460581	0.00001567	29.39	<0.0001	

Note: y-intercept $= 1.37$, slope $= 0.0004$.

TABLE 3.3   Marquardt Algorithmic Output From PROC NLIN Procedure

Estimation Summary					
Method		Marquardt			
Iterations	b0	b1	b2	Sum of squares	
0	46.0000	1.3700	0.000400	20,265.2	
1	45.5235	1.3261	0.000557	19,605.2	
17	40.1980	−0.8643	0.0366	5,127.5	
18	40.1980	−0.8643	0.0366	5,127.0	
The NLIN Procedure					
Source	DF	Sum of squares	Mean square	F value	Approx Pr>F
Model	3	3,449,841	1,149,947	489,809	<0.0001
Error	2184	5127.5	2.3477		
Uncorrected total	2187	3,454,968			
Approx					
Parameter	Estimate	Std error	Approximate	95% confidence limits	
b0	40.1980	0.0338	40.1317	40.2644	
b1	−0.8643	0.0366	−0.9360	−0.7927	
b2	0.0366	0.000875	0.0348	0.0383	

Therefore, our model is $y = 40.1980/(1 + \exp(0.8643 - 0.0366x)$. Running this data set through MESAT-1 software, with specific set of cost parameters: $c = \$20$, $b = \$10$, and $a = \$50$ and 0.5 ($q = 50\%$) coverage defines a stopping rule at $x(\# \; test \; cases) = 34$ with $S_{CPM}(34) = 23$ attacks where $S_{CPM}(.)$ denotes a CPM stopping rule. Notice that both

TABLE 3.4   Cost Analysis For DR5 With 50% in MESAT-1 For $C=\$20$, $B=\$10$, and $A=\$50$

Item	Dollar Amount
Cost of correcting all 46 errors by exhaustive testing	460.00
Cost of correcting 23 prerelease errors using MESAT-1	230.00
Cost of executing all 2187 test cases by exhaustive testing	43,740.00
Cost of executing 34 test cases by using MESAT-1	680.00
Savings for not correcting the remaining 23 by using MESAT-1	230.00
Savings for not executing the remaining $(2187-34)=2153$ test cases	43,060.00
Total savings using MESAT-1 by stopping test earlier	42,140.00

TABLE 3.5   Marquardt Algorithmic Output From SPSS For LGM For DR1–DR5 With $Q=0.5$

	b_0	b_1	b_2	X	$f(X)$
DR1	177.572	−0.932	0.011	84.727	88.786
DR2	143.652	−1.67	0.013	128.46	71.826
DR3	48.005	−2.227	0.049	45.44	24.002
DR4	60.051	−1.054	0.026	40.53	30.025
DR5	40.198	−0.864	0.037	23.35	20.099

MESAT-1 and the logistic growth curve do stop testing with 20 and 23 attacks or failures, respectively (very close favorably). Compare $S_{LGM}(23)=20$ to $S_{CPM}(34)=23$. $S_{LGM}(.)$ and $S_{CPM}(.)$ denote LGM and CPM stopping rules respectively.

However, the MESAT-1 software also recognizes that it is more cost efficient to stop at 23 attacks or failures after experiencing 34 test cases with the given cost parameters and additionally providing useful financial information as to why this is so. The cost analysis from the MESAT-1 software is in Table 3.4. By merging LGM and CPM, the cost is included.

Table 3.4 illustrates that when using a stopping rule of $x=34$ with 23 identified errors (or failures), the total savings is $42,140.00. Both methods, with a 50% coverage criterion, stopped after 20 and 23 attacks, respectively. However, the CPM realized that stopping at $x=34$ would be the most optimum place to stop whereas the LGM stopped the testing after $x=33$, with 20 attacks visibly clear from the raw columnar input data. Deviation is negligible. See Figures 3.6 and 3.8 in Section 3.3.4. See Table 3.5 for a tabulation of $q=0.5$ for all data sets of DR1 to DR5 utilizing LGM equations from (3.1) to (3.4).

3.3.2   The DR4 Data Set Example

We use the DR4 data set from Sahinoglu [12] as another example of the synergy of the two stopping rules. Figure 3.4 illustrates the data with the fitted logistic growth curve overlaid on the graph. The LGM calculated the following estimates as depicted in Table 3.5:

$$b_0 = 60.0513, \quad b_1 = -1.0545, \quad b_2 = 0.0262 \tag{3.22}$$

This model estimates the maximum cumulative number of failures to be 60.05 (actual maximum is 63). LGM calculates that 50% coverage occurs at approximately 41 test cases by using Equation (3.4) as in Table 1.5. We ran this data set through the MESAT-1 software, which can be found online in CyberRiskSolver software. The MESAT-1 stopping rule reached or exceeded 50% coverage criterion at the 43rd test case with 32 failures accomplishing a failure coverage of 50.79% as in Fig. 3.9; that is, $S_{CPM}(43) = 32$. Based on Table 3.5 whereas the LGM halted the testing activity after $x(\# \ test \ cases) = 41$ with $S_{LGM}(41) = 30$. LGM served as the first-hand initial value or estimator (by hinting $30/63 \approx 48\%$ coverage) and CPM added with the cost optimality details. Therefore $q = 0.48$ or 50% in the CPM for $c = \$20$, $b = \$10$, $a = \$50$ generates $S_{CPM}(43) = 32$ with 50.79% coverage akin to $S_{LGM}(41) = 30$ with savings of $1900. Both stopping rules were very close to each other. Table 3.6 shows the merged cost analysis from MESAT-1.

3.3.3 The Supercomputing CLOUD Historical Failure Data—Case Study

The Extreme Science and Engineering Discovery Environment (XSEDE) is the most advanced, powerful, and robust collection of integrated advanced digital resources and services in the world. It is a single virtual system that scientists can use to interactively share computing resources, data, and expertise. Scientists and engineers around the world use these resources and services—things like supercomputers, collections of data, and new tools—to make our lives healthier, safer, and better. XSEDE, and the experts who lead the program, will make these resources easier to use and help more people use them. The 5-year, $121-million project is supported by the National Science Foundation. It replaces and expands on the NSF TeraGrid project.

More than 10,000 scientists used the TeraGrid to complete thousands of research projects at no cost to the scientists. See https://www.xsede.org/overview for details.

XSEDE lowers technological barriers to the access and use of computing resources. Using XSEDE, researchers can establish private, secure environments that have all the resources, services, and collaboration support they need to be productive. Initially, XSEDE supports 16 supercomputers and high-end visualization and data analysis resources across the country. It also includes other specialized digital resources and services to complement these computers. These resources will be expanded throughout the lifetime of the project.

The XSEDE partnership includes the following: University of Illinois at Urbana–Champaign; Carnegie Mellon University/University of Pittsburgh; University of Texas at Austin; University of Tennessee, Knoxville; University of Virginia; Shodor Education Foundation; Southeastern Universities Research Association; University of Chicago; University of California, San Diego; Indiana University; Jülich Supercomputing Centre; Purdue University; Cornell University; Ohio State University; University of California, Berkeley; Rice University; and the National Center for Atmospheric Research. It is led by the University of Illinois's National Center for Supercomputing Applications (NCSA).

There is a dire need to determine when best to release operations with respect to CLOUD computing to commercial use. CLOUD computing operations centers are multiplying rapidly and offering services to their clientele who believe that they are getting a good deal. However, "devil in the details" is the lack of an assumed reliability where customers soon discover that the services promised or claimed are not offering expected service reliability. This CLOUD reliability testing for assurance purposes opens new avenues in a very critical area of cybersystems and information security defined to be "quantitative stopping rules in reliability and security testing."

This is a new applied research paradigm worth undertaking when compared to the existing and conventionally qualitative or rule-of-thumb rules, which do not lend themselves to probabilistic and cost-effective reasoning. A case study on XSEDE, a continental supercomputing grid to be the world's largest, will be studied and discussed.

We used the historical failure data set obtained from XSEDE (formerly TeraGrid) from March 2009 to March 2010, which is illustrated in Tables 3.7 and 3.8. For example, the first month's (3/2009) 14 recorded failures originated from the XSEDE units: Queenbee (1), ABE (2), Mercury (2), Steele (1), Condor (1), Big Red (1), Pople (1), Ranger and Spur (2), Lonestar (1), NICS (1), and Kraken (1) regardless of how long it lasted before repaired. These were mostly due to network connectivity glitches as reported. The goal of this case study as an demonstrative example is to determine a cost-effective objective (as opposed to subjective) stopping rule on sequential testing when to release a CLOUD operation to a commercial customer use after the beta testing stage such as in Table 3.7 as follows and an extended tabulated data sample in Table 3.8 in Section 3.3.4 [18]. Although not known, CLOUD computing companies such as Amazon, HP, Google, Microsoft, etc. may not have a public policy of quality testing before they release their infrastructures to commercial use by their CLOUD users as media prints their glitches.

Using SAS PROC NLIN as before to fit the LGM to this data set yields the following estimates: $b_0 = 385.5$ (estimate for long-term number of failures which in actuality is 360), $b_1 = -2.4041$, and $b_2 = 0.3823$. Using an 80% coverage criterion, the stopping rule would be $x(\# \, of \, test \, cases \, to \, halt) = 10$ or $S_{LGM}(10) = 296$, using Equation (3.3) with the corresponding

TABLE 3.6   MESAT-1 Cost Analysis For DR4 After LGM With $C = \$20$, $B = \$10$, and $A = \$50$

Item	Dollar Amount
Cost of correcting all 63 errors by exhaustive testing	630.00
Cost of correcting 32 prerelease errors using MESAT-1	320.00
Cost of executing all 200 test cases by exhaustive testing	4000.00
Cost of executing 43 test cases by using MESAT-1	860.00
Savings for not correcting the remaining 31 errors by using MESAT-1	310.00
Savings for not executing the remaining $(200 - 43) = 1576$ test cases	3450.00
Total saving using MESAT-1 by stopping test earlier	1900.00

TABLE 3.7   Historical Failure Data (from 3/9 To 2/10) for the Supercomputer XSEDE

Item	Month and Year	Failures	Cumulative Failures
1	March 2009	14	14
2	April 2009	43	57
3	May 2009	35	92
4	June 2009	30	122
5	July 2009	31	153
6	August 2009	47	200
7	September 2009	21	221
8	October 2009	22	243
9	November 2009	26	269
10	December 2009	27	296
11	January 2010	42	338
12	February 2010	22	360

error count of 296 from Table 3.7 that illustrates the fit of the LGM to the data. Alternatively, running this historical interruption (failure and maintenance) data set of XSEDE (an academic or scientific CLOUD, not a commercial entity), through MESAT-1 software, with $c = \$900$, $b = \$100$, and $a = \$125$ and $0.8(q = 80\%)$ minimal coverage, yields a stopping rule at $x(\# \, of \, test \, cases \, to \, halt) = 10$ with 296 failures or $S_{CPM}(10) = 296$. Two methods here are identical but then the CPM adds the cost-effectiveness notion, which LGM is lacking.

The cost analysis from the MESAT-1 software is shown in Figure 3.10 in Section 3.3.4. Total savings for executing the stopping rule by using MESAT-1 is $200.00 as tabulated in Figures 3.11. The cost parameters $c = \$900$, $b = \$100$, and $a = \$125$ mean every test case or contact protocol with a CLOUD customer costs the operations manager $900 to process the failure, whereas it costs far less, that is, $100 to repair the failure before the release of CLOUD to public, and slightly more, $125, after the release. These are cost factors as valid as any in regard to what the scenario dictates.

3.3.4 Appendix for Section 3.3

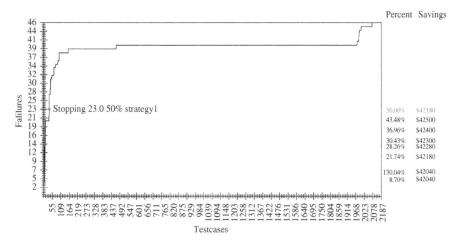

FIGURE 3.6 MESAT-1 algorithm (CPM) results for the DR5 data set in Section 3.3.1.

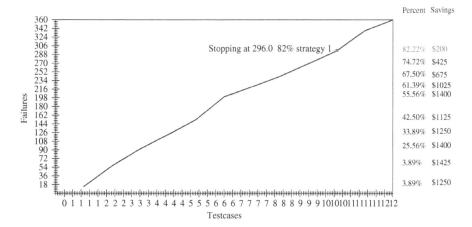

FIGURE 3.7 Graphical display of the stopping-rule algorithm for the CLOUD (XSEDE) sample failure data in Section 3.3.3.

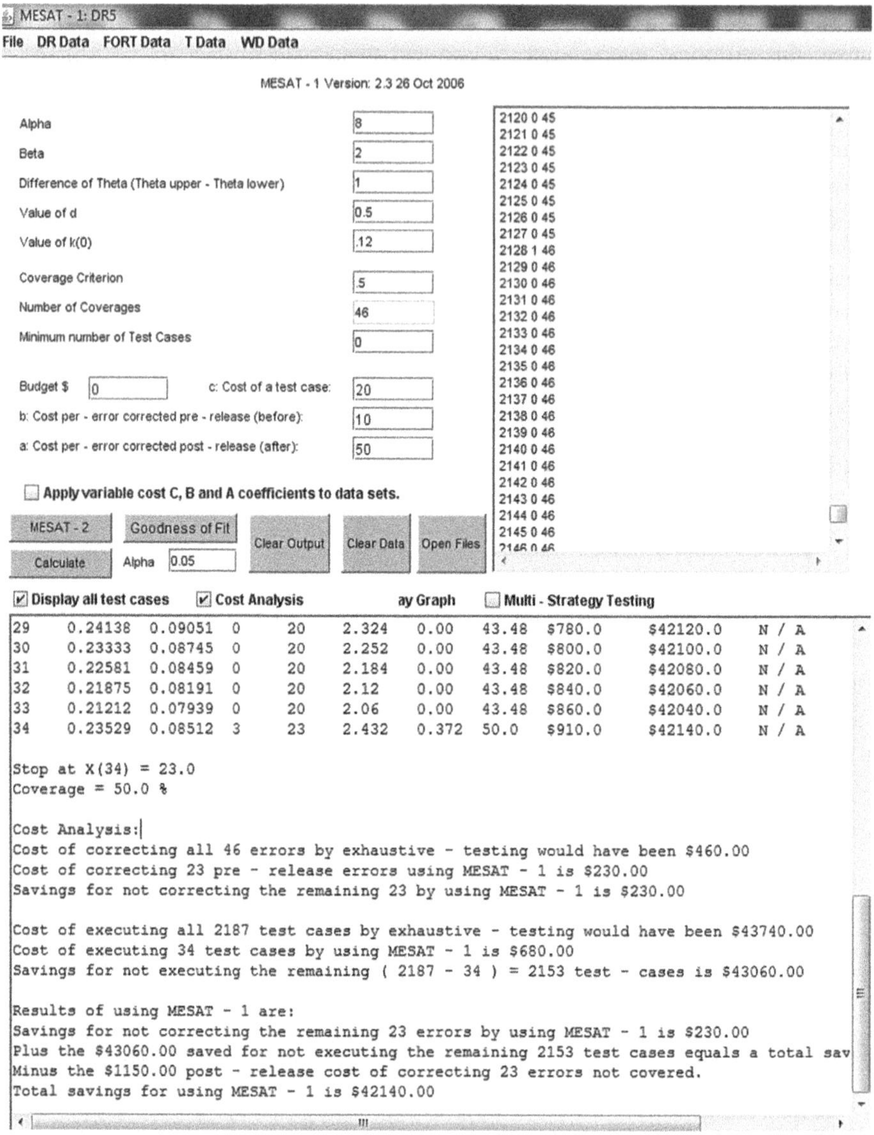

FIGURE 3.8   MESAT-1 algorithm (CPM) results for DR5 data set from Section 3.3.1.

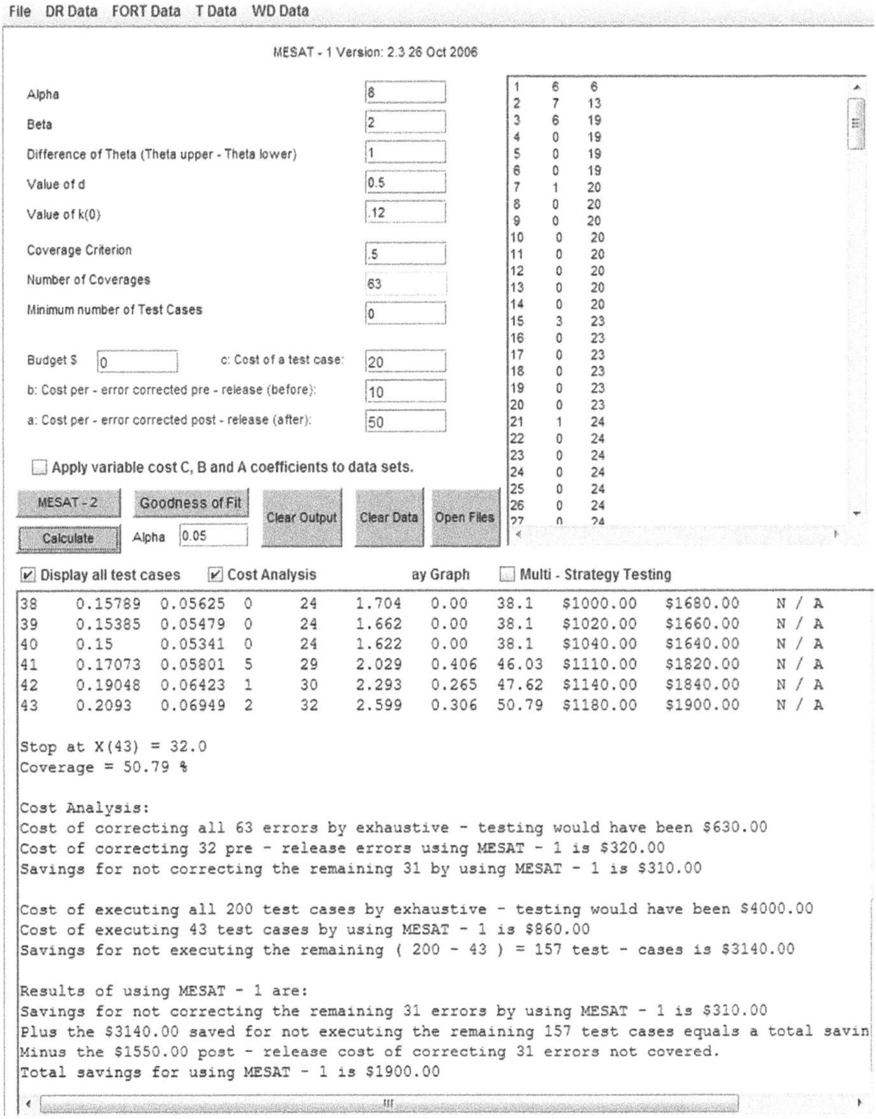

FIGURE 3.9 MESAT-1 algorithm (CPM) results for DR4 data set from Section 3.3.2.

File   DR Data   FORT Data   T Data   WD Data

MESAT - 1 Version: 2.3 26 Oct 2006

Alpha	8	
Beta	2	
Difference of Theta (Theta upper - Theta lower)	1	
Value of d	36.0	
Value of k(0)	.12	
Coverage Criterion	.8	
Number of Coverages	360	
Minimum number of Test Cases	0	

1	14	14
2	43	57
3	35	92
4	30	122
5	31	153
6	47	200
7	21	221
8	22	243
9	26	269
10	27	296
11	42	338
12	22	360

Budget $ 0   c: Cost of a test case: 900

b: Cost per - error corrected pre - release (before):   100

a: Cost per - error corrected post - release (after):   125

☐ Apply variable cost C, B and A coefficients to data sets.

MESAT - 2   Goodness of Fit   Clear Output   Clear Data   Open Files

Calculate   Alpha   0.05

☑ Display all test cases   ☑ Cost Analysis   ☑ Display Graph   ☐ Multi - Strategy Testing

```
4    1.0    0.24533   30    122    25.612   4.827   33.89   $15800.0   $1250.0   N / A
5    1.0    0.233     31    153    30.424   4.813   42.5    $19800.0   $1125.0   N / A
6    1.0    0.21974   47    200    37.472   7.048   55.56   $25400.0   $1400.0   N / A
7    1.0    0.21514   21    221    40.545   3.073   61.39   $28400.0   $1025.0   N / A
8    1.0    0.21093   22    243    43.722   3.177   67.5    $31500.0   $675.0    N / A
9    1.0    0.20659   26    269    47.427   3.705   74.72   $35000.0   $425.0    N / A
10   1.0    0.20265   27    296    51.225   3.798   82.22   $38600.0   $200.0    N / A

Stop at X(10) = 296.0
Coverage = 82.22222222222221 %

Cost Analysis:
Cost of correcting all 360 errors by exhaustive - testing would have been $36000.00
Cost of correcting 296 pre - release errors using MESAT - 1 is $29600.00
Savings for not correcting the remaining 64 by using MESAT - 1 is $6400.00

Cost of executing all 12 test cases by exhaustive - testing would have been $10800.00
Cost of executing 10 test cases by using MESAT - 1 is $9000.00
Savings for not executing the remaining ( 12 - 10 ) = 2 test - cases is $1800.00

Results of using MESAT - 1 are:
Savings for not correcting the remaining 64 errors by using MESAT - 1 is $6400.00
Plus the $1800.00 saved for not executing the remaining 2 test cases equals a total savings
Minus the $8000.00 post - release cost of correcting 64 errors not covered.
Total savings for using MESAT - 1 is $200.00
```

FIGURE 3.10   MESAT-1 algorithm results for XSEDE data from Section 3.3.3.

File   DR Data   FORT Data   T Data   WD Data

MESAT - 1 Version: 2.3 26 Oct 2006

Alpha	8
Beta	2
Difference of Theta (Theta upper - Theta lower)	1
Value of d	11111111111
Value of k(0)	.12
Coverage Criterion	.7
Number of Coverages	63
Minimum number of Test Cases	0

Budget $ [0]   c: Cost of a test case: [100]

b: Cost per - error corrected pre - release (before): [200]

a: Cost per - error corrected post - release (after): [1100]

☐ Apply variable cost C, B and A coefficients to data sets.

[MESAT - 2]   [Goodness of Fit]
                              [Clear Output] [Clear Data] [Open Files]
[Calculate]   Alpha [0.05]

```
1 6 6
2 7 13
3 6 19
4 0 19
5 0 19
6 0 19
7 1 20
8 0 20
9 0 20
10 0 20
11 0 20
12 0 20
13 0 20
14 0 20
15 3 23
16 0 23
17 0 23
18 0 23
19 0 23
20 0 23
21 1 24
22 0 24
23 0 24
24 0 24
25 0 24
26 0 24
27 0 24
```

☑ Display all test cases   ☑ Cost Analysis   ☐ Display Graph   ☐ Multi - Strategy Testing

```
95   0.16842   0.04962   0   51   2.789   0.00   80.95   $19700.00   $-300.00   N / A
96   0.16667   0.0491    0   51   2.761   0.00   80.95   $19800.00   $-400.00   N / A
97   0.16495   0.04859   0   51   2.734   0.00   80.95   $19900.00   $-500.00   N / A
98   0.16327   0.04809   0   51   2.707   0.00   80.95   $20000.00   $-600.00   N / A
99   0.16162   0.0476    0   51   2.681   0.00   80.95   $20100.00   $-700.00   N / A
100  0.17      0.04939   3   54   2.918   0.237  85.71   $20800.00   $1900.00   N / A
101  0.16832   0.0489    0   54   2.89    0.00   85.71   $20900.00   $1800.00   N / A

Stop at X(101) = 54.0
Coverage = 85.71 %


Cost Analysis:
Cost of correcting all 63 errors by exhaustive - testing would have been $12600.00
Cost of correcting 54 pre - release errors using MESAT - 1 is $10800.00
Savings for not correcting the remaining 9 by using MESAT - 1 is $1800.00

Cost of executing all 200 test cases by exhaustive - testing would have been $20000.00
Cost of executing 101 test cases by using MESAT - 1 is $10100.00
Savings for not executing the remaining ( 200 - 101 ) = 99 test - cases is $9900.00

Results of using MESAT - 1 are:
Savings for not correcting the remaining 9 errors by using MESAT - 1 is $1800.00
Plus the $9900.00 saved for not executing the remaining 99 test cases equals a total saving
Minus the $9900.00 post - release cost of correcting 9 errors not covered.
Total savings for using MESAT - 1 is $1800.00
```

FIGURE 3.11   (*Continued*)

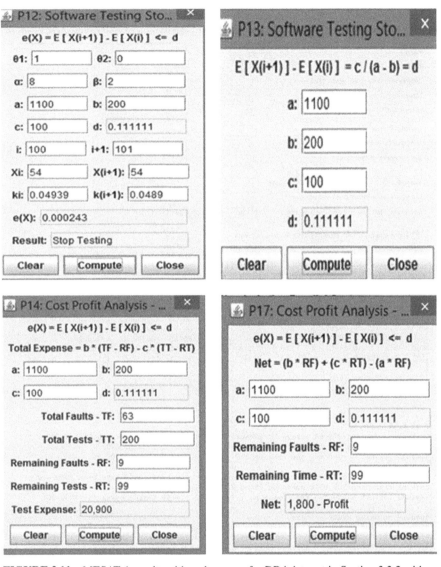

FIGURE 3.11   MESAT-1 results with pedagogues for DR4 data set in Section 3.3.2 with 'a' = $1100 and coverage % = 70, where optimal '$a' cost (below which stopping is profit-able) $\rightarrow a \leq \dfrac{(\text{RF})b + (\text{RT})c}{\text{RF}} = [9(200) + 99(100)]/9 = \$1300.$

TABLE 3.8 Sample of CLOUD (Supercomputer Infrastructure XSEDE) Historical Failure Data from Table 3.7 in Section 3.3.3.

	March 2009	April 2009	May 2009	June 2009	July 2009	August 2009	September 2009
LONI-Queen Bee							
1. Network connectivity problem+I/O and storage problems	1 (18 March-26 h)						
2. InfiniBand switch							
3. Maintenance		1 (8 April-15 h)			1 (10 Jul-2 h)		1 (15 Sep-7.5 h)
4. Storage maintenance					1 (28Jul-h)*		
5. Hardware failure, storage outage					1 (24 Jul-16 h)		
6. File system recovery, software updates							
NCSA-Abe							
1. Scheduler paused/file system problem	1 (18 March)	8 (1 April-3 h, 2 April-1.5 h, 7 April-0.5 h, 13 April-2 h, 14 April-4 h, 21 April-4 h, 22 April-3.5 h, 22 April-3 h)	2 (3 May-0.5 h, 12 May-24 h)	1 (4 Jun-1.5 h)			
2. Maintenance	1 (30 March-27 h)						
3. Power issue			1 (3 May-5.5 h)				
4. Emergency maintenance			2 (4 May-6.5 h, 23 May-6h)				
5. Mass storage issue			1 (13 May-72 h)				
6. Disk failure						1 (14 Aug-118.5h)	

(Continued)

TABLE 3.8 (Continued)

	March 2009	April 2009	May 2009	June 2009	July 2009	August 2009	September 2009
7. Kernel vulnerability							1 (8 Sep-20h)
8. Login nodes unavailable							
NCSA-abe/lincoln							
1. Maintenance		1 (27 April-9h)		1 (24 Jun-6h)			1 (14 Sep-26h)
2. Hardware failure							
3. Power issue			1 (3 May-)	1 (18 Jun-4h)			1 (28 Sep 6h)
4. Scheduler down			1 (12 May-24h)				
5. Mass storage issue			1 (13 May-72h)				
6. Emergency maintenance					1 (8 Jul-7h)	1 (4 Aug-14h)	
7. File system issue			1 (23 May-6h)			1 (28 Aug-1h)	
NCSA-ia64 Mercury							
1. Grid FTP servers problems	1 (25 March-0.5h)						
2. Co-compute node down	1 (28 March-39h)						
3. Scheduler down		1 (30 April-1.5h)	1 (12 May-24h)	1 (13 Jun-1.5)		1 (20 Aug-20h)	
4. Maintenance			1 (7 May-9h)	1 (11 Jun-7h)		2 (12 Aug-9.5h, 26 Aug-12h)	1 (14 Sep-26h)
5. Power issue			1 (3May-4h)				
6. Mass storage issue			1 (13 May-72h)				
7. Emergency maintenance			1 (23 May-6h)				
8. File system issue							
9. Networking issues							
NCSA							
1. System maintenance		1 (8 April-2h)				1 (24 Aug-8h)	
2. 1-wire transport failure		1 (7 April)					
3. Co-compute2 down			1 (19 May-120h)		1 (14 Jul-5.5h)	1 (23 Aug-5.5h)	1 (14 Sep-7.5h)
4. Mass storage maintenance						1 (18 Aug-3h)	

5. Network maintenance

NCSA-cobalt

	April	May	Jun	Jul	Aug	Sep
1. Storage software upgrade	1 (14 April-30h)					
2. Co-compute 1/2/3	1 (11 April)	(12 May-40h)	(7 Jun-0.5h, 11 Jun-15h, 19 Jun-9h, 20 Jun-3h, 26 Jun-7h, 27 Jun-4.5h, 30 Jun-1h)	8 (3 Jul-3h, 9 Jul-4h, 16 Jul-7h, 17 Jul-2h, 18 Jul-2h, 18 Jul-10h, 29 Jul-1.5h, 29 Jul-14.5h)	1 (4 Aug-8h, 5 Aug-h, 13 Aug-3h, 19 Aug-1h, 21 Aug-6h, 30 Aug-1h)	2 (23 Sep-6h, 26 Sep-8h)
3. Fix for X apps	1 (30 April-2h)					
4. Power issue		1 (3 May-5h)				
5. Schedulers, PBS issue		1 (12 May-24h)		1 (5 Jul-8h)	2 (8 Aug-h, 10 Aug-h)	1 (27 Sep-2h)
6. Mass storage issue		1 (13 May-72h)				
7. Emergency maintenance		1 (23 May-6h)	1 (22 Jun-6h)	1 (6 Jul-h)	2 (10 Aug-12h, 31 Aug-6h)	
8. Unavailable				1 (5 Jul-h)		
9. Co-storage2 issue				1 (30 Jul-1.5h)		
10. File system issue					1 (27 Aug-2h)	
11. Maintenance						2 (8 Sep-1h, 13 Sep-5h)
12. Co-login down						1 (23 Sep-11.5h)

(Continued)

TABLE 3.8 (Continued)

	March 2009	April 2009	May 2009	June 2009	July 2009	August 2009	September 2009
Purdue-Steele cluster							
1. PBS job scheduling problem	1 (17 March-81 h)						
2. OS upgrade					1 (14 Jul-58 h)	2 (4 Aug-42 h, 10 Aug-8.5 h)	
3. Emergency maintenance						1 (6 Aug-h)	
4. Maintenance							
5. System updates							
6. Reboot							
Purdue Condor pool							
1. Maintenance	1 (16 March-28 h)						
2. Chilled water problem							
3. System updates							
4. Reboot							

3.4   STOPPING RULE FOR TESTING IN THE TIME DOMAIN

MESAT-2 whereas is a cost-efficient optimal stopping-rule algorithm for the Poisson compounded with geometric distribution (not the LSD as per MESAT-1), that is, Poisson^geometric regarding time domain in contrary to MESAT-1 for the effort domain. It is developed and applied to the problem of sequential testing of computer software. For each checkpoint in time, either the software satisfies a desired economic criterion or the software testing is continued as in the effort domain scenario earlier studied. There are many examples in which events occur according to the Poisson distribution, and furthermore, for each of these Poisson events, one or more other events can occur. For example, automobile accidents on a given highway might follow a Poisson process, but the number of injuries accrued after each accident follows a compound Poisson distribution by Sherbrook [17]. In this chapter, the application is software or hardware testing due to chance or malicious failures. If an interruption that occurs during testing of software program is due to one or more software failures or breaches in a clump, and if the distribution of the number of interruptions is Poisson, the final distribution of the number of clumped failures is compound Poisson [14]. In this section, we present optimal stopping rules using the Poisson^geometric in time-domain software security or reliability testing. Compound Poisson is also used in the modeling of CLOUD computing statistical analysis further to be studied in Chapter 7 [20].

3.4.1   Review of Compound Poisson Process and Stopping Rule

Let $Y(t)$ be the random variable of the number of interruptions, and let $X(t)$ be the random variable of the number of failures that occur up to time t. Then, following Sherbrook, the Poisson with parameter λ compounded with a geometric ρ can be written as follows [19]:

$$P\big(X(t)\big) = \sum \frac{(\lambda t)^y \exp(-\lambda t)}{y!} C_{Y-1}^{X-1} \rho^{x-y}(1-\rho)^y, \quad x = 1,2\ldots, \ \lambda > 0, 0 < \rho < 1 \quad (3.23)$$

where $C_k^n = C(n,k) = \binom{n}{k} = n! / \big[k!(n-k)! \big]$

Using moment-generating functions, Equations (3.9) and (3.10) for the expected value of X yield to a certain rule for determining when to optimally stop software testing. Suppose that we are at time t. It is evident that whenever there is an interruption to the program during the testing interval $[0, t)$, we remove all faults observed. As a result, the values for λ and ρ should be decreasing over time, since there should be fewer and fewer faults in the program. The gradual reduction of ρ is in line with the results of others, such as Musa and Okumoto, who used an exponential function to reduce λ over time [21]. Becker et al. reduced λ by a fixed amount Δ over time [22]. Let X_t be the random variable of the number of failures that occur in $[t, t+1]$, the unit time interval starting at time t, and let λ_t and ρ_t be the values of the parameters at time t. Then the expected number of failures occurring during this unit time interval is:

$$E(X_t) = \frac{\lambda_t}{1-\rho_t} \quad (3.24)$$

If we were to stop at time t, we would assume that the faults that caused these failures would have to be fixed in the field at a cost of "a" per fault. Thus, there is an expected cost over the interval $[t, t+1]$ of $aE(X_t)$ for stopping at time t. On the other hand, if we continue testing over the interval, we assume that there is a fixed cost of "c" for testing and a variable cost "b" of fixing each fault found during the testing. Note that "a" is larger than "b" since it should be considerably more expensive to fix a fault in the field than to observe and fix it while testing. Thus, the cost expected for the continuation of testing for the next time interval is $bE(X_t)+c$. This cost is a similar but simpler than that of Dallal and Mallows but not exactly the same [23]. If for the unit interval beginning at time t, the expected cost of stopping is greater than the expected cost of continuing, that is, if

$$aE(X_t) > bE(X_t)+c \qquad (3.25)$$

It is economical to continue testing through the interval. On the other hand, if the expected cost of stopping is less than the expected cost of continuing, that is, if

$$aE(X_t) < bE(X_t)+c \qquad (3.26)$$

It is more economical to stop. If we let $d = c/(a-b)$, then if the relation so evolves to

$$E(X_t) = \frac{\lambda_t}{1-\rho_t} > d \qquad (3.27)$$

we would continue testing; and if

$$E(X_t) = \frac{\lambda_t}{1-\rho_t} \leq d \qquad (3.28)$$

we would stop testing. With λ_t and ρ_t both being decreasing functions of time,

$$E(X_t) \geq E(X_{t+1}) \qquad (3.29)$$

So that if we should have stopped at time t but did not, we should certainly stop at time $t+1$.

This rule for stopping seems reasonable. It essentially says that if the expected number of faults that can be found in the software unit time is sufficiently small, we stop testing and release the software package to the end user. If the expected number of faults is large, we continue testing.

This stopping rule in the time domain depends on an up-to-date expression for the compound Poisson distribution; that is, we need accurate estimates of λ_t and ρ_t. However, such estimates depend on the history of the testing, which implies the use of the empirical Bayes decision procedures [24].

3.4.2   Empirical Bayes Analysis for the Poisson^Geometric Stopping Rule

We begin with the conjugate prior density function of the initial values of λ and ρ. The conjugate prior density function for the Poisson probability function is the gamma pdf, and the prior density for the geometric is the beta pdf. Thus, the initial prior joint density for λ_t and ρ_t is given by

$$f(\lambda,\rho) = \frac{\beta(\lambda\beta)^{\alpha+1} e^{-\lambda\beta}}{\Gamma(\alpha)} \frac{\Gamma(\mu+\nu)}{\Gamma(\mu)\Gamma(\nu)} \rho^{\mu-1}(1-\rho)^{\nu-1} \qquad (3.30)$$

Note $\alpha > 0$, $\beta > 0$, $\mu > 0$, and $v > 0$ are the parameters of the initial prior density function. Let X and Y be the random variables of the number of failures and interruptions, respectively, that will occur during the first unit time interval. The joint probability function of X and Y, given λ and μ, is the Poisson^geometric:

$$p_{x,y}(x,y \mid \lambda, \rho) = \frac{\lambda^y \exp(-\lambda)}{y!}\binom{x-1}{y-1}\rho^{x-y}(1-\rho)^y \tag{3.31}$$

So that the joint distribution of X, Y, λ, and ρ after observing the process for one unit time period (i.e., when $t=1$) is the product

$$g(x,y,\lambda,\rho) = \frac{\beta^\alpha \lambda^{\alpha+y-1}\exp\left[-(\beta+1)\right]}{\Gamma(\alpha)y!}\binom{x-1}{y-1}\frac{\Gamma(\mu+v)}{\Gamma(\mu)\Gamma(v)}\rho^{x-y+\mu-1}(1-\rho)^{y+v-1} \tag{3.32}$$

The marginal probability function of X and Y is then

$$\begin{aligned} p(x,y) &= \int_0^\infty \int_0^t f(x,y,\lambda,\rho)\,d\rho\,d\lambda \\ &= \frac{\Gamma(\alpha+y)\beta^\alpha \Gamma(\mu+x-y)\Gamma(v+y)\Gamma(\mu)\Gamma(v)}{\Gamma(\mu+v+x)\Gamma(v+\mu)\Gamma(\alpha)(\beta+1)^{\alpha+y}} \end{aligned} \tag{3.33}$$

Therefore, the posterior joint density function of λ and ρ at time $t=1$ is

$$f(\lambda,\rho \mid x,y) = \frac{(\beta+1)[\beta-1)\lambda]^{\alpha+y-1}\exp\left[-\lambda(\beta+1)\right]}{\Gamma(\alpha+y)}\frac{\Gamma(\mu+v+x)\rho^{\mu+x-y-1}(1-\rho)^{v+y-1}}{\Gamma(\mu+v+x)\Gamma(v+y)} \tag{3.34}$$

This is the product of a gamma density with parameters $\alpha + y$ and $\beta + 1$ and a beta density with parameters $\mu + x - y$ and $v + y$. It is well known that the posterior expectation minimizes the mean quadratic loss function so as to use as the Bayes estimators of the parameters λ and μ. We substitute these mean values into $E(X_t)$ for a Bayes estimate on the number of failures in the next unit time period, t, and reach (3.35)

$$E(X) = \frac{\hat{\lambda}}{1-\hat{\rho}} = \frac{(\alpha+y)(\mu+v+x)}{(\beta+1)(v+y)} \tag{3.35}$$

Now suppose that the process is at time t (i.e., the process has been observed for t time periods) with a total of x failures over y, interruptions, where $x_t \geq y_t$. The posterior estimates of λ and ρ at time t are

$$\hat{\lambda}_t = \frac{\alpha_0 + y_t}{\beta_0 + t} = \frac{\alpha_t}{\beta_t} \tag{3.36}$$

$$\hat{\rho}_t = \frac{\mu_0 + x_t - y_t}{\mu_0 + v_0 + x_t} = \frac{\mu_t}{\mu_t + v_t} \tag{3.37}$$

where the zero subscript denotes initial values at time 0. If the unit time period is sufficiently short, such as 1 s, then there will be many time periods with no interruptions, so that y will be less than t, making λ_t a decreasing functions of t. Substituting the values of λ_t and ρ_t into (3.35) for $E(X_t)$ gives

$$E(X_t) = \frac{\lambda_t}{1 - \rho_t} = \frac{(\alpha_o + y_t)(\mu_0 + v_0 + x_t)}{(\beta_0 + t)(v_0 + y_t)} = \frac{\alpha_t(\mu_t + v_t)}{\beta_t v_t} \tag{3.38}$$

Since the Poisson^geometric is memoryless, the posterior expected number of failures at time $t+1$ [i.e., $E(X_t+1)$] can be found as follows. If we denote the number of failures during the interval $[t, t+1]$ as x and the number of interruptions as y, then

$$E(X_{t+1}) = \frac{\lambda_{t+1}}{1 - \rho_{t+1}} = \frac{(\alpha_t + y_t)(\mu_t + v_t + x)}{(\beta_t + t)(v_t + y)} \tag{3.39}$$

Such that the compound Poisson is memoryless, we can assume that the process will be the same starting at time t as starting at time 0 but with different parameters. That is, we need only to observe the process from one time period to the next. Let x_t be the cumulative number of failures to time t and y_t be the cumulative number of interruptions. Thus, the expected value function is as follows:

$$e(t;x_t,y_t) = \frac{(\alpha_t + y_t)(\mu_t + v_t + x_t)}{(\beta_t + t)(v_t + y_t)} \tag{3.40}$$

The empirical Bayesian stopping rule will be:

$$\text{If } e(t;x_t,y_t) = \frac{(\alpha_t + y_t)(\mu_t + v_t + x_t)}{(\beta_t + t)(v_t + y_t)} > d, \text{ continue testing.} \tag{3.41}$$

$$\text{If } e(t;x_t,y_t) = \frac{(\alpha_t + y_t)(\mu_t + v_t + x_t)}{(\beta_t + t)(v_t + y_t)} \le d, \text{ stop testing,}$$

and release the software. Stopping will occur at time t greater than t' where t' is given:

$$t' = \frac{(\alpha_t + y_t)(\mu_t + v_t + x_t)}{(v_t + y_t)d} - \beta \tag{3.42}$$

As software faults are removed, $e(t; x_t, y_t)$ will approach zero, and the testing will stop.

3.4.3 Howden's Model for Stopping Rule

Many models have been proposed assessing the reliability measurements of software systems to help designers evaluate, predict, and improve the quality of their software systems. Unfortunately, all the existing software reliability models assume that failures occur one at a time, except for the MESAT approach proposed, which uses a CP (compound Poisson) that does not assume so. Based on this assumption, expectations of the time between failures are determined. In observing new coverage items in a behavioral model, branches are typically covered in clumps. In the MESAT tools proposed, the positive correlation within a clump is additionally taken into account.

The confidence-based Howden's modeling approach takes advantage of hypothesis testing in determining the saturation of the software failure [12]. A null hypothesis H_0 is performed and later examined experimentally based on an assumed probability distribution for the number of failures in a given software product. Suppose that a failure has a probability of occurring of less than or equal to B, then we are at least $1 - B$ confident that H_0 is true. Similarly, if the failures for the next period of testing time have the same probability of at least B to occur, then for the next N testing cycles, we have a confidence of at least C that no failures will happen, where the following holds:

$$C = 1 - \left(1 - B\right)^{N} \tag{3.43}$$

$$N = \frac{\ln\left(1 - C\right)}{\ln\left(1 - B\right)} \tag{3.44}$$

If $C=0.95$, $B=0.3$, then by using (3.44), $N \approx 100$. This is a single-equation stopping-rule method [12]. To apply Howden's model to the process of HDL verification, we first need to create failures as interruptions, where an interruption is an incident where one or more new parts of the model are exercised. Using branch coverage as a test criterion, an interruption therefore indicates that one or more new branches are covered. We set a probability for the interruption rate B and choose an upper-bound level of confidence C. Time is not involved here. When time is involved, the formula is going to change. Experimentally, we do not examine the hypothesis unless the interruption rate becomes smaller than the preset value B. When so, we calculate the number of test patterns needed to have at least C confidence of not having any new branch in the next N patterns and run them. If an interruption occurs, we continue examining the hypothesis until we prove it and then stop. In this approach we assume that coverage items, or interruptions, are independent and have equal probabilities of being covered. The rate of interruption is decreasing, and we assume that no interruptions will occur in the next N test cases; then the expected probability of interruptions will be [12]

$$B_t = \frac{B}{t + T} \tag{3.45}$$

where T is the last point checked in testing to lead to the reformulation of (3.43) as in (3.46):

$$C = 1 - \prod_{1}^{N}\left(1 - \frac{B}{t + T}\right)^{N} \tag{3.46}$$

In Howden's model, the assumption that failures or interruptions have a given probability B independently is not error free. As we know, branches in an HDL model are strongly dependent of each other. In fact, we can classify some cases where it is impossible to cover the lower-level branches without covering their dominants. Moreover, the clump sizes caused by the interruptions are not modeled in this study, making the decision of continuing or stopping the testing process inaccurate. Finally, this work does not incorporate the cost of testing or releasing the product, and the goal of testing in the first place is not only having a high-quality product but also minimizing the testing cost. The Howden and the modified Howden methods suffer from the problem of not having more than one interruption at a time, which reduces the efficiency of the model when applying it to branch coverage estimation.

3.4.4 Computational Example for Stopping-Rule Algorithm in Time Domain

The stopping rule was applied to data set, named as T4, given of Musa et al. [19]. These data are listed in Table 3.8. The failure times, which are cumulative and in seconds, indicate when failures occur. Note that failures sometimes occur in clumps, as for example at time $t = 4572^{nd}$, 13021st, and 16489th seconds. This clumping is fairly typical in the testing of software, indicating the need for the compound Poisson. Table 3.8 shows the T4 data set of Musa et al. For illustrative purposes it was assumed that $c = \$0.01$, $a = \$6.0$, and $b = \$1.0$; that is, the fixed cost of testing is $0.01 per second, and the cost of fixing each fault while testing is $1.0, and the cost of fixing each fault in the field after release is $6.0. Hence, $d = c/(a-b) = 0.002$. Note that the values of a, b, c are important but it is the ratio $d = c/(a-b)$ used as composite delimiter (Fig. 3.12).

Using T4, the initial estimate of ρ was taken to be 0.056 due to raw data since at the end of the testing time, $\hat{\rho} = 1 - y_t / x_t = 1 - (50/53) = 0.056$. It was assumed that the confidence is equivalent to a sample size of 100 so that $\mu + \nu = 100$. The initial values $\mu = (0.056)(100) = 5.6$ and $\nu = 100 - 5.6 = 95.4$, respectively. μ_t and ν_t will vary for each

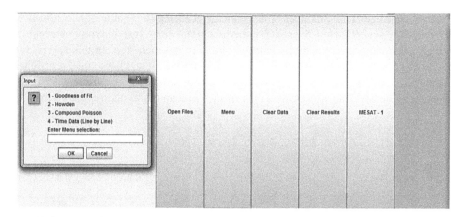

FIGURE 3.12   Click on stopping-rule radio button in cyber-risk solver to use data.

TABLE 3.9 Time-Domain Data Set $T4$, As in Table 3.11 With 47 Singletons and 3 Doubles

n	Δt	Cumulative	n	Δt	Cumulative
1	5	5	27	215	5,784
2	73	78	28	116	5,900
3	141	219	29	283	6,183
4	491	710	30	50	6,233
5	5	715	31	308	6,541
6	5	720	32	279	6,820
7	28	748	33	140	6,960
8	138	886	34	678	7,638
9	478	1364	35	183	7,821
10	325	1689	36	2,462	10,283
11	147	1836	37	104	10,387
12	198	2034	38	2,178	12,565
13	22	2056	39	285	12,850
14	56	2112	40	171	13,021
15	424	2536	41	0	13,021
16	92	2628	42	643	13,664
17	520	3148	43	887	14,551
18	1424	4572	44	149	14,700
19	0	4572	45	469	15,169
20	92	4664	46	716	15,885
21	183	4847	47	604	16,489
22	10	4857	48	0	17,263
23	115	4972	49	774	17,263
24	17	4989	50	256	17,519
25	284	5273	51	14,637	32,156
26	296	5569	52	18,740	50,896
			53	1,526	52,422

(a)

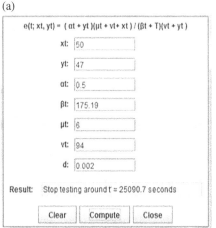

(b)

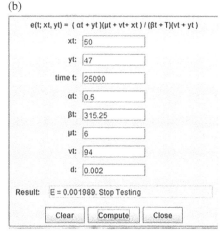

FIGURE 3.13 (a) and (b) Pedagogues (teaching blocks) to solve single equations (3.41) and (3.42) regarding MESAT-2 stopping rule.

varying pair of y_t and x_t. Similarly, the mean time to failure (MTTF) from the data set T4 would be 52,422/53=989.1 s, giving an initial estimate of $\lambda = \text{MTTF}^{-1} = 0.001$. Assuming a randomly selected initial gamma prior parameter, $\alpha = 0.5$, and using (3.36)

$$\lambda = \frac{\alpha}{\beta}, \quad \text{where } \beta = \alpha(\lambda^{-1}) = \alpha(\text{MTTF}) = 0.5(989.1) = 494.5 \tag{3.47}$$

λ is the initial value. At each time t, α_t and β_t will vary. As in Appendix 3.A,

$$t' > \frac{(\alpha_t + y_t)(\mu_t + v_t + x_t)}{(v_t + y_t)d} - \beta \tag{3.48}$$

$$e(t;x_t,y_t) = \frac{(\alpha_t + y_t)(\mu_t + v_t + x_t)}{(\beta_t + t)(v_t + y_t)} \leq d \tag{3.49}$$

where $d = c/(a-b) = 0.01/(6-1) = 0.002$ and $\alpha_t > 0$, $\beta_t > 0$, $\mu_t > 0$, and $v_t > 0$ are all varying throughout the process, testing is stopped and the software is released to the customer at $t' = 24,682s$.

We used Equation (3.42), where $e(t'; x_t, y_t) = 0.001564 < 0.002$. Table 3.9 indicates that testing should be stopped sometime between $t = 17,519$ and $t = 32,156s$ after the 50th failure. At the stopping epoch, $x = 51$, $y = 48$, $\alpha = 0.5$(initial value), $\beta = (\alpha)*$ (MTTF) = 0.5(32,156/51) = 0.5(630.51) = 315.25, but $\beta = \alpha(\text{MTTF}) = 0.5(17,519/50) = 0.5$ (350.38) = 175.19 used in (3.40) to find $t' = 25,090$ a little more than what the software found: 24,682 as illustrated in Table 3.9.

However, $\beta = 315.25$ is used to satisfy the delimiter "d" criterion. The reason is that $t' > 25,090$ can only be $t = 32,156$ where $\beta = 315.25$, and it is definitely a dynamically varying set of values in the MESAT-2 software, which is more precise than the Pedagogue format that are static. See Pedagogues P12, P13, P14 and P17 in Figure 3.13. Now, $\hat{\rho} = 1 - y_t / x_t = 1 - (47/50) = 0.06$. It was assumed that the confidence is equivalent to a sample size of 100 so that $\mu + v = 100$. The values at the stopping epoch are $\mu = (0.06)$ (100) = 6 and $v = 100 - 6 = 94$, respectively. The rest of the analysis is presented at the Figure 3.14 (a) and (b). Savings using stopping rule: $334.03 when the cost parameters are selected as $a = \$6$, $b = \$1$, $c = \$0.01$. However, overall savings using stopping rule: $3475.30 when $a = \$10$, $b = \$5$, $c = \$0.1$ as an alternative set of cost parameters is selected (see Fig. 3.13, 3.14 and 3.15).

TABLE 3.10   Snapshot of the Application of Equation (3.42) For MESAT-2 Example

x	y	Δt	cum t	e
49	46	774	17,263	0.002776
50	47	256	17,519	0.002794
51	48	14,637	32,156	0.001564

3.5 DISCUSSIONS AND CONCLUSION

The magnitude of emerging technologies requires the use of an efficient stopping rule for software development based upon given standards and recent security testing protocols and corporate practices [25]. Whether attacks are random or malicious in nature, an objective decision as to when to halt testing or move onto a new branch or test case is needed [26, 27].

The logistic growth curve, LGM, provides a quick, easy-to-use decision rule that can be found using most statistical software. In this method, the maximum number of attacks does not need to be known; hence decisions about when to stop testing can be made before the maximum number of cumulative errors are found. However, this method does not incorporate any costs associated with testing to render it cost optimal.

Another more comprehensive method is the compound Poisson^LSD method, which incorporates the discrete cost associated with testing as well as the discrete nature of the data. When positive savings and $e(X) < d$ are satisfied before the coverage criterion, then the stopping rules of the two methods demonstrate to be quite similar given a selected cost set.

MESAT-1, which can be found at www.areslimited.com, is a cost-efficient stopping-rule algorithm used to save substantial numbers of test vectors in achieving a given degree of coverage reliability [11, 12]. Through conventional cost-benefit analysis, it is shown how cost-efficient this proposed stopping-rule algorithm performs compared to those employing conventionally exhaustive "shotgun" or "testing-to-death" approaches.

This cost-effective technique is valued for its industrial potential (for automotive, avionics or similar factory quality control purposes) by keeping a tight rein on budgetary constraints as well as using a scientific one-step-ahead formula to optimize incremental resource utilization.

This quantitative evaluation is in sharp contrast to conventional techniques that require the tedious usage of billions of test vectors to guarantee certain reliability. Usually, the stopping rule is either a time-to-release date, which is nothing more than a commercial benchmark or a time constraint, or it is a rough percentage of how many bugs detected out of a given total prescribed with no statistical data or trend modeling merged with cost-effective economic stopping rules. The focus in software testing, for example, is on determining when given the results of a testing process, whether white box (coverage), or black box (functional) testing, it is most economical to halt testing and release software under the conditions prevailing for a prescribed period of time. Moreover, new data sets need to be analyzed from the authentic security world to see the pros and cons of each method proposed. However, these proposed methods are better than none where only descriptive attributes are used conventionally when to stop without actual feeling of cost.

Both LGM and CPM resulted with comparable solutions when using similar coverage criterion, first in the example (DR5) set at 20 and 23 breaches/attacks, respectively. Another data set (DR4) analysis indicated that when using an 50% coverage criterion stopping rule, LGM corresponds to a stop at $x = 43$ test cases and similarly to a stop at $x = 34$ in the CPM. This shows that that the two methods produce comparable stopping rules. However, in situations where test cases are extremely costly to correct, there may be much larger differences in the stopping rules of the two methods.

In other words, the most optimal route to follow is to use first the LGM method and determine the stopping rule (such as stop at 20 breaches in the DR5 example) and then

(a)

Goodness of Fit Analysis:
mttf = 989.0943
lambda = 0.0010
Chi-square sum = 20.2159
Right tailed area = 0.0273
alpha = 0.0100
p-value: 0.0273 >= type -I error: 0.01; Good Fit!

Howden Stopping Rule Analysis:
C value = 0.95
B value = 0.1
Calculated stopping point = 28.4332
Stop at occurrence 29 with elapsed time of 6233,
29 out of 53 total occurrences covered
6233 out of 52422 total-time covered
time coverage = 11.9%
fault coverage = 56.6%

Compound Poisson^Geometric Stopping Rule Analysis Input:
Alpha = 0.5000
d = 0.0100
Coverage Criterion: Yes
Coverage criterion = 50%
Cost per corrected error (post-release), *a* = 6.00
Cost per corrected error (pre-release), *b* = 1.00
Cost per test, *c* = 0.01
Economic criterion, *d* = 0.0020

Compound Poisson^Geometric Stopping Rule Analysis Output:
Calculated stop time = 24682
e = 0.002000
Stop at fault = 50
Fault coverage = 94.34%
Time coverage = 47.08%
Cost analysis 1:
Total faults: tf = 53
Total cycles: tt = 52422

FIGURE 3.14 (a) Alternative to T4 MESAT-2 results where $a=\$6$, $b=\$1$, and $c=\$0.01$, using 70% coverage.

(b)

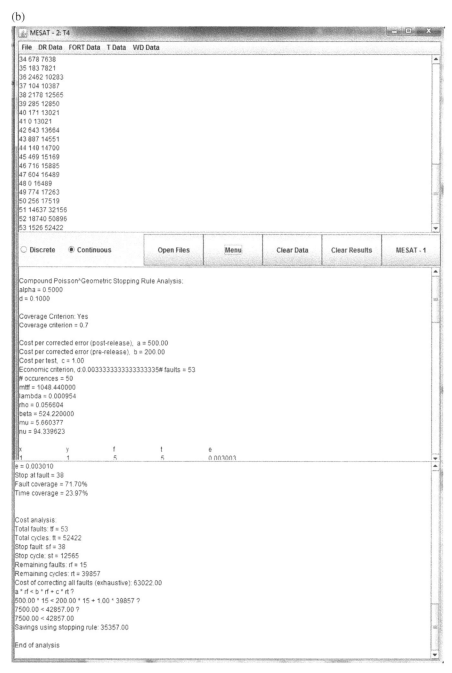

FIGURE 3.14 (*continued*) (b) Alternative to T4 MESAT-2 results using 70% coverage with $a = \$500$, $b = \$200$, and $c = \$1.00$.

```
Stop fault: sf = 50
Stop cycle: st = 17519
Remaining faults: rf = 3
Remaining cycles rt = 34903
Cost of correcting all faults (exhaustive): 577.22
a * rf < b * rf + c * rt?
6.00 * 3 < 1.00 * 3 + 0.01 * 34903?
18.00 < 352.03?
Savings using stopping rule: $334.03
Cost analysis 2:
Cost per corrected error (post-release), a = $10.00
Cost per corrected error (pre-release), b = $5.00
Cost per test, c = $0.10
Economic Criterion:
Cost of correcting all faults (exhaustive): 5507.20
a * rf < b * rf + c * rt?
10.00 * 3 < 5.00 * 3 + 0.10 * 34903?
30.00 < 3505.30?
Savings using stopping rule: 3475.30
```

FIGURE 3.15   The previous Figure 3.14a and b's $T4$ analysis with $a = 10$, $b = 5$, and $c = 0.1$.

employ the CPM method to determine the savings, such as \$42,140.00 that correspond to the said stopping rule for a selected set of cost factors, such as $c = \$20$, $b = \$10$, and $a = \$50$, as in the DR5 data set. Finally, varying experimental data sets are needed for a more rigorous testing in estimating a cost-efficient stopping rule using the both LGM and CPM. The same logic works for DR4.

Additionally, the application for the two synergistic methods applied to a CLOUD computing scenario gave satisfactory results [27]. In an earlier section, the failure and maintenance records causing interruption of the "Supercomputer Infrastructure XSEDE" were tested by the LGM and the CPM. The LGM dictated to stop at 311 failures at the test case of $x = 10$ months to end beta testing if the CLOUD was ready or not to launch commercial operations.

The CPM using the MESAT-1 tool also agreed to stop at $x = 10$ covering 296 (no in-between number of failures can be detected by the CPM method unlike that of the LGM). The LGM does not have any cost-conscious decision making. Therefore the CPM needs to be employed to achieve any cost appreciation. Cost factors c, b, and a were used for cost appreciation and the choice was justified [27, 28].

Last but not least, MESAT-2 for time-dependent continuous data is examined in Section 3.4 with theoretical derivations as supported by numerical examples using T (Time) data. The contribution of Section 3.4 is through an empirical Bayesian approach to determine an economic stopping rule for a compound Poisson process and is a follow-up to previous applied research by Sahinoglu [14–16, 18] on Poisson^geometric as applied to software reliability modeling. The art of software security testing is a vast and open-ended subject under scrutiny [29]. The computational example (see Figs. 3.13, 3.14 and 3.15 for data set T4) illustrates that the rule proposed is practical and valid for software failure data with clumped failures, such as in the data set in Table 3.8 as one of those tabulated in Table 3.11. More such data from T data with clumped software failures exist in the book-specific Java website. Also see Table 3.11 for all T1–T5 for time-data properties.

TABLE 3.11 **A Cross Section of Historical Failure Times of Data Sets** $T1(X,Y)$ **To** $T5(X,Y)$ **in MESAT-2**

$T$1: 21,700 object instructions delivered in 92 calendar days and 24.6 execution CPU hours real tune ($X=136$, $Y=133$): 130 singletons, 3 doubles

3; 33; 146; 227; 342; 351; 353; 444; 556; 571; 709... *5089; 5089*... 11,811; *12,559; 12,559*... 42,188; *42,996; 42,996*... 81,542; 82,702; 85,566; 88,682 (last)

$T$2: 27.700 object instructions delivered in 72 calendar days and 30.2 execution horns real time ($X=54$, $Y=52$): 51 singletons, 1 triplet

191; 413; 693; 983; 1273; 1658; 2228; 2838; 3203; 3593; 3858; 4228; 5028; 6238; 6645... *62,361; 62,361; 62,361*; 62,661; 71,682; 74,201; 81,091; 84,339... 108,708 (last)

$T$3: 23,400 delivered object instructions in 55 calendar days and 18.7 execution hours real time ($X=38$, $Y=37$): 36 singletons, 1 double

115; 115... 198; 376; 570; 706... 36,818; 37,381; 40,151...58,065; 64,789; 67,335 (last)

$T$4: 33,500 delivered object instructions, 71 calendar days, and 14.6 exec. horns real time ($X=53$, $Y=50$): 47 singletons, 3 doubles

5; 78; 219; 710; 715; 720; 748; 886; 1364... 3148; *4572; 4572*... 4664... 12,850; *13,021; 13,021*; 13,664; 14,551... 15,885; *16,489; 16,489*; 17,263... 50,896; 52,422 (last)

$T$5: 2,445,000 object instructions delivered, 173 calendar days, and 1785 exec. hours real time ($X=831$, $Y=810$): 794 singletons, 13 doubles, 2 triplets, 1 quintuple

37,320... 2,712,322; *2,715,360; 2,715,360; 2,715,360*; 2,861,760... *3,014,160; 3,014,160*; 3,104,338... 3,277,760; *3,291,260; 3,291,260; 3,291,260; 3,291,260; 3,291,260*; 3,294,140; 3,296,120; 3,299,960; *3,337,820; 3,337,820*; 3,369,440... 7,108,021; *7,249,520; 7,249,520*; 7,251,320... 7,407,920; *7,488,620; 7,488,620*; 7,493,936... *10,712,788; 10,712,788*; 10,729,436... 15,491,208; *15,566,088; 15,566,088*... 15,573,288... *15,837,888; 15,837,888*; 16,073,188; *16,139,088; 16,139,088*; 16,175,088 ... *16,277,688; 16,277,688*... 16,279,488; *16,502,688; 16,502,688*... 16,750,473; *16,754,343; 16,754,343; 16,754,343*... *16,847,943; 16,847,943*... 18,855,143; 18,696,039; 18,747,761; 18,772,252; 19,608,286... *27,080,924; 27,080,924; 20,901,716; 2,091,716*... 21,120,288 (last)

From Figure 3.14 (a) and (b); additionally find optimal "a" cost above, which the stopping rule is not profitable by (3.14):

$$\text{If } (RF)a < (RF)b + (RT)c \tag{3.50}$$

$15 * a < 15 * 200 + 39,857 * 1$; $a < 2857.133$; so optimal $a = \$ 2857.13$.

3.6 EXERCISES

3.6.1 Clicking MESAT-1 and further DR Data, utilize the discrete effort-based (time-independent) chip design test data: DR1, DR2, DR3, DR4, DR5, DR6. A) Apply MESAT-1 to estimate stopping rules where $a = \$1100$, $b = \$200$ and $c = \$100$ by employing single strategy testing. Choose 80% for your minimal confidence level. B) Show why this CPSRM is not applicable to testing DR7 and DR8 for a stopping rule analysis.

3.6.2 Repeat exercise 3.6.1 where $a = \$1000$, $b = \$200$ and $c = \$100$ but assume that one does not know the total number of test cases before starting. Decide on a minimal number of how many test cases you wish to try and on an initial budget for testing before you release your product following cyber-testing or decide that the product is OK following reliability or security testing. Choose expense dollars at will.

3.6.3 (a) Using MESAT-1 for the data set DR1 to DR5, conduct a single strategy stopping rule study, and tell us using $a = \$700$, $b = \$200$, $c = \$100$ with 80% coverage to show why it is cost-efficient "not to execute exhaustive testing all the way to the end." What are the optimal a $<$, b $>$ and c $>$ when the other two are kept constant with the given above cost values? You need to print out one-page graphical and two-page maximum analytical results, and one-page conclusion stating why it is cost effective? (b) Now this time, use MESAT-2 for the continuous data set T1–T7, and do same as in (a) 80% coverage criteria. c) Now this time, use MESAT-2 for the continuous data set T1-T9, and do same as in (a) with 50% coverage criteria.

3.6.4 (a) Apply MESAT-2 and click on T Data in utilizing the continuous time-based ROME Lab data: T1, T2, T3, T4, T5, T6, T7, T8, T9 to find a stopping rule (alpha=0.5 to initiate the estimation cycle):

    i) Use 80% for coverage criterion where $a = \$6$, $b = \$1$ and $c = \$0.01$

    ii) Use 50% for coverage criterion this time using $a = \$600$, $b = \$200$ and $c = \$1$.

  (b) Compare the results of part A with results using the simplistic Howden method without cost. You are free to choose your new parameters. Hint: Select $C = 0.95$, $B = 0.3$

3.6.5 a) Repeat 3.6.1. this time applying Text Section 3.2.1's LGM (Logistic Growth Model) and then combining with the CPM (Compound Poisson Model) to optimize the cost parameters as applied in Section 3.2. Utilize the discrete effort-based (time-independent) chip design test data: DR1, DR2, DR3, DR4, and DR5. b) By revisiting 3.6.1. to 3.6.5. verify your results usuing the pedagogues provided in Chapter 1's Table 1.7.49. Pedagogues Main Menu.

REFERENCES

[1] Parikh, G., *Handbook of Software Maintenance*, John Wiley & Sons, Inc., New York, 1986.

[2] Farr, W., Lyu, M. R., *Handbook of Software Reliability Engineering*, IEEE Computer Society Press, New York, 1996.

[3] Keys, J., *Software Engineering Handbook*, Auerbach Publications, Boca Raton, FL, 2003.

[4] Marick, B., *Craft of Software Testing*, Prentice Hall, Upper Saddle River, NJ, 1994.

[5] Kaner, C., Falk, J., Nguyen H. Q., *Testing Computer Software*, John Wiley & Sons, Inc., New York, 1999.

[6] Allen, J. H., Barnum, S., Ellison, R. J., McGraw, G., Mead, N. R., *Software Security Engineering: A Guide for Project Managers. SEI-CMU Software Security Series in Software Engineering*, Addison Wesley, Boston, MA, p. 167, 2008

[7] McGraw, G., *Software Security, Building Security*, Addison Wesley, Boston, MA, 2006.

[8] Verhulst, P. F., *Recherches Mathématiques sur la Loi d'accroissement de la Population*. Nouv. mém. de l'Académie Royale des Sci. et Belles-Lettres de Bruxelles, Bruxelles, p. 1–41, 1845.

[9] Yamada, S., Ohba, M., Osaki, S. (1984). S-shaped software reliability growth models and their applications. *IEEE Transactions on Reliability*, **33**, 289–292.

[10] Simmons, S., Sahinoglu, M., Matis, J. (2009). Determining an Efficient Stopping Rule for the Security Testing of Cyber Attacks in Computer and Communication Networks, Invited Risk Session #204120. Quantitative Security and Cyber Systems, Joint Statistical Meetings, Washington, DC.

[11] Simmons, S., Sahinoglu, M., Matis, J., *Efficient Stopping Rules for Quantitative Security Testing of Cyber-Attacks, Invited Session #IPS018*. Trustworthy Computing, ISI (International Statistical Institute), Dublin, Ireland, 2011.

[12] Sahinoglu, M., *Trustworthy Computing: Analytical and Quantitative Engineering Evaluation*, John Wiley & Sons, Inc., Hoboken, NJ, 2007.

[13] Piegorsch, W., Bailer, A. J., *Analyzing Environmental Data*, John Wiley & Sons, Ltd, Chichester, 2005.

[14] Sahinoglu, M. (1992). Compound-poisson software reliability model. *IEEE Transactions on Software Engineering*, **18** (7), 624–630.

[15] Sahinoglu, M., Can, U. (1997). Alternative parameter estimation methods for the compound Poisson software reliability model with clustered failure data, *Software Testing, Verification and Reliability*, **7**(1), 35–57.

[16] Sahinoglu, M., (2003). An empirical Bayesian stopping rule in testing and verification of behavioral models, *IEEE Transactions on Instrumentation and Measurement*, **52**, 1428–1443.

[17] Sherbrooke, C. C., *Discrete Compound Poisson Processes and Tables of the Geometric Poisson Distribution, Memorandum RM-4831-PR*, Rand Cooperation, Santa Monica, CA, 1966.

[18] Randolph, P., Sahinoglu, M. (1995). A stopping-rule for a compound Poisson random variable, *Applied Stochastic Models and Data Analysis*, **11**, 135–143.

[19] Musa, J. D., (1979). *Software Reliability Data*, Bell Telephone Labs, Whippany, New Jersey, 07981, USA.

[20] Sahinoglu, M., Cueva-Parra, L. (2011). CLOUD Computing, *WIREs Computational Statistics*, **139**, 47–68.

[21] Musa, J. D., Okumoto, K. (1984). A logarithmic Poisson execution time model for software reliability measurement, Proceedings of the 7th International Conference on Software Engineering, held at Silver Spring, MD in 1984, IEEE Press, Piscataway NJ, 230–238.

[22] Becker, G., Camarinopoulos, I. (1970). A Bayesian method for the failure rate of a possibly correct program, *Transactions on Software Engineering*, **16**, 1307–1316.

[23] Dallal, S. R., Mallows, C. L. (1988). When should one stop testing software? *Journal of the American Statistical Association*, **83**(403), 872–879.

[24] Maritz, J. S., *Empirical Bayes Methods*, Methuen, London, 1970.

[25] Leung, H. K. N. (1997) Improving the testing process based upon standards, *Software Testing, Verification and Reliability*, **7**(1), 3–18.

[26] Das Sunil, R., Hossain, A., Assaf, M. H., Petriu, E. M., Sahinoglu, M., Jone, W.-B.. (2008). On a new graph theory approach to designing zero-aliasing space compressors for built-in self-testing, *IEEE Transactions on Instrumentation and Measurement*, **57**(10), 2146–2168.

[27] Sahinoglu, M., Simmons, S. J., Matis, J. H. (2011). Cost-effective security testing of cyber systems using combined LGCP: Logistic-growth compound-poisson, *International Journal of Computers, Information Technology and Engineering*, **5**(2), 9–15.

[28] Sahinoglu, M., Cueva-Parra, L., Simmons Susan, J. (2012). Software assurance testing before releasing CLOUD for business - A case study on a supercomputing grid (Xsede), *International Journal of Computers, Information Technology and Engineering*, **6**(2), 73–81.

[29] Wysopal, C., Nelson, L., Zovi Dino, D., Dustin E., *The Art of Software Security Testing: Identifying Software Security Flaws*, Symantec Press, Addison-Wesley, Upper Saddle River, NJ and Boston, MA, 2006.

4

SECURITY ASSESSMENT AND MANAGEMENT IN CYBER-RISK

LEARNING OBJECTIVES

- Describe the three-pronged concept of cyber-security risk (SM: Security-Meter) assessment techniques (quantitative, qualitative, and hybrid or semiquantitative), its advantages and disadvantages, and its relevance to cyber-risk informatics and risk engineering, and further examine nondisjoint vulnerabilities and threats.
- Implement the aforementioned SM triple concepts to actual computational practices to obtain outcomes that are superior to others, not only numerically; making cost-sense.
- Compare the SM probabilistic methods with the theoretical and simulation results.
- Perform risk management following the assessment stage by mitigating the unfavorable risk percentage to a tolerable value through game-theoretic optimization.
- Study privacy risk-meter assessment and management and Polish decoding algorithm.

4.1 INTRODUCTION

An innovative security meter (SM) that provides the convenience of risk measurements in a quantitative manner much required in the security world will be elaborated [1–11]. In pursuit of a practical and accurate statistical design, security breaches will be recorded, and then the model's input probabilities will be estimated using the equations that were developed. Undesirable threats that take advantage of hardware and software weaknesses or vulnerabilities can impact the violation and breakdown of availability (readiness for usage), integrity (accuracy), confidentiality (provision of secrecy), and nonrepudiation (inability to deny), as well as other aspects of software security such as authentication (evidence of identity), privacy (provision of personal information), and encryption (ability to code/decode using a key). There are other methods available. A comparison will be presented further.

Cyber-Risk Informatics: Engineering Evaluation with Data Science, First Edition. Mehmet Sahinoglu.
© 2016 John Wiley & Sons, Inc. Published 2016 by John Wiley & Sons, Inc.
Companion website: www.wiley.com/go/sahinoglu/informatics

4.1.1   What Other Scoring Methods Are Available?

Other qualitative models and methods, such as attack trees and time-to-defeat models, are only deterministic but not quantitative or cost-convertible [2–6]. Recently, various scoring systems have mushroomed on the Internet such as Common Vulnerability Scoring System (CVSS), National Vulnerability Database (NVD), and others.

4.1.1.1   Common Vulnerability Scoring System (CVSS) This is a free and open industry standard for assessing the severity of computer system security vulnerabilities. It is under the custodianship of the Forum of Incident Response and Security Teams (FIRST). It attempts to establish a measure of how much concern a vulnerability warrants, compared to other vulnerabilities, so efforts can be prioritized. The scores are based on a series of measurements (called metrics) based on expert assessment. The scores range within 0–10 (see Fig. 4.1). NVD provides severity rankings of "Low," "Medium," and "High" in addition to the numeric CVSS scores, but these qualitative rankings are simply mapped from the numeric CVSS scores:

1. Vulnerabilities are labeled "Low" severity if they have a CVSS base score of 0.0–3.9.
2. Vulnerabilities are labeled "Medium" severity if they have a CVSS base score of 4.0–6.9.
3. Vulnerabilities are labeled "High" severity if they have a CVSS base score of 7.0–10.0.

Vulnerabilities with a base score in the range of 7.0–10.0 are critical, whereas those in the range of 4.0–6.9 are major and 0–3.9, minor. CVSS provides an open framework for communicating the characteristics and impacts of IT vulnerabilities. Its quantitative model ensures repeatable accurate measurement while enabling users to see the underlying vulnerability characteristics that were used to generate the scores.

Thus, CVSS is well suited as a standard measurement system for industries, organizations, and governments that need accurate and consistent vulnerability impact scores. Two common uses of CVSS are prioritization of vulnerability remediation activities and calculation of the severity of vulnerabilities discovered on one's systems. The NVD

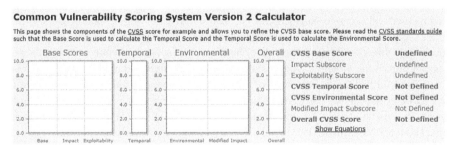

FIGURE 4.1   Vulnerability severity levels based on the NVD/CVSS (USG source https://nvd. nist.gov/cvss.cfm?calculator&version=2).

(a)

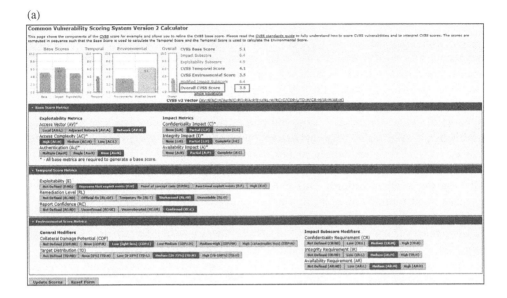

(b)

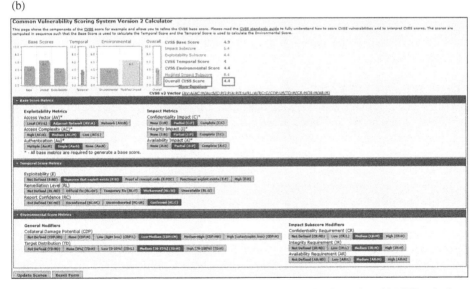

FIGURE 4.2 (a) CVSS calculator example screenshot entered by the author. (b) NVD calculator example screenshot entered by the author.

provides CVSS scores for almost all known vulnerabilities. The specific vulnerabilities can be graded according to the level of risk they pose to the organization. A low rating can be applied to those vulnerabilities that are low in both severity and exposure. Vulnerabilities receive a high rating if the severity and exposure are high. For a CVSS example data entered, see Figure 4.2a.

4.1.1.2   National Vulnerability Database Version 2.2 (NVD)   This is the US government repository of standards-based vulnerability management data presented using the Security Content Automation Protocol (SCAP). This data enables automation of vulnerability management, security measurement, and compliance. NVD includes databases of security checklists, security-related software flaws, misconfigurations, product names, and impact metrics. In particular, NVD supports the CVSS version 2 standards for all CVE vulnerabilities. NVD provides CVSS "base scores," which represent the innate vulnerability characteristics. It does not currently provide "temporal scores" (scores that change over time due to events external to the vulnerability). However, NVD does provide a CVSS score calculator to allow one to add temporal data and to even calculate "environmental scores" (scores customized to reflect the impact of the vulnerability on one's organization). This calculator contains support for US government agencies to customize vulnerability impact scores based on FIPS 199 system ratings (see Fig. 4.2b).

Advantages: The vector facilitates the "open" nature of the framework. It is a text string that contains the values assigned to each metric, and it is used to communicate exactly how the score for vulnerability is derived. Therefore, the vector should always be displayed with the vulnerability score.

Disadvantages: The scores are computed in sequence such that the base score is used to calculate the temporal score and the temporal score is used to calculate the environmental score. The CVSS quantitative model ensures repeatable accurate measurement while enabling users to see the underlying vulnerability characteristics that were used to generate the scores.

4.1.1.3   Bricade CVSS V2.0 Calculator   The authors of CVSS recognize the difficulties in scoring vulnerabilities and assessing their risk. They realize that other scoring systems exist, both commercial and noncommercial. While they are each equally valid, they consider a contrasting and fuzzy set of factors used to determine the final score. CVSS differs by offering an open framework where anyone (and everyone) can use the same model to rank vulnerabilities in a consistent fashion while allowing for personalization within each user environment (Fig. 4.3).

CVSS provides this by identifying and separately scoring the natural vulnerability groupings that combine to determine its overall risk. It offers a common language with which computer application and system vendors and end users can consistently and openly score vulnerabilities. As CVSS matures, these metrics may expand or adjust, making it even more accurate, flexible, and representative of modern vulnerabilities and their risks.

4.1.1.4   JVNRSS: CVSS Version 2.0 (JVN)   JVN provides the "Vendor Status Notes (VN)" and the "Status Tracking Notes (TRnotes)." VN is a service providing information on how to fix vulnerabilities. It is similar to the "CERT Vulnerability Notes" and follows up on the IPA/JPCERT vulnerability reports, US-CERT alerts, US-CERT vulnerability notes, and NISCC advisories. TRnotes is a service providing information on the incidents, specifically what worms do, when the exploit codes were released, and what the countermeasures (CMs) are. Making use of JVNRSS is an essential point in the security information exchange, for this handily encourages the reuse and aggregation of information from vendors (Fig. 4.4).

Bricade CVSS V2.0 Calculator

This page provides a calculator for creating CVSS vulnerability severity scores. The scores are computed in sequence such that the Base Score is used to calculate the Temporal Score and the Temporal Score is used to calculate the Environmental Score.

CVSS Score

CVSS Base Score	5.1
Impact Subscore	6.4
Exploitability Subscore	4.9
CVSS Temporal Score	4.1
CVSS Environmental Score	4.4
Overall CVSS Score	**4.4**

Help Desk

Base Score Metrics

Exploitability Metrics

Attack Vector	Network
Attack Complexity	High
Authentication	None

Impact Metrics

Confidentiality Impact	Partial
Integrity Impact	Partial
Availability Impact	Partial

Temporal Score Metrics

Exploitability	Proof of concept code
Remediation Level	Temporary fix
Report Confidence	Confirmed

Environmental Score Metrics

Collateral Damage Potential	Low-Medium
Target Distribution	Medium (26-75%)

Impact Subscore Modifiers

Confidentiality Requirement	Medium
Integrity Requirement	Medium
Availability Requirement	Medium

Calculate CVSS

FIGURE 4.3 Bricade CVSS V2.0 calculator example screenshot entered by the author.

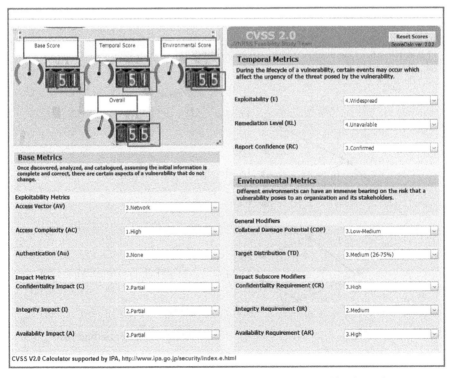

FIGURE 4.4 JVN calculator example screenshot entered by the author.

4.2 SECURITY METER (SM) MODEL DESIGN

Data for malicious attacks that have been prevented or not prevented [8, 9] must be collected. Figure 4.5 shows that the constants are the utility cost (asset) and criticality constant (between 0 and 1), whereas the probabilistic inputs are vulnerability, threat, and lack of countermeasure (LCM) where **LCM** = 1 − **CM** varying between 0 and 1. The residual risk (RR, as in Fig. 4.6) and expected cost of loss (ECL) are the outputs obtained using Equations (4.1)–(4.3). The black box in Figure 4.5 leads to the probabilistic tree diagram in Figure 4.6 to do the calculations. Equations (4.1)–(4.3) summarize Figures 4.5 and 4.6 from input to output. Suppose an attack occurs, and it is recorded. At the very least, we need to come up with a percentage of non-attacks and successful (from the adversary's viewpoint) attacks. Out of every 100 such attempts, the number of successful attacks will yield the estimate for the percentage of LCM. We can then trace the root of the cause to the threat level backward from the outcomes in the tree diagram. Let us imagine that the antivirus (AV) software did not catch it, and a virus attack occurs, which reveals the threat exactly. As a result of this attack, whose root threat is known, the e-mail system may be disabled. Then, the vulnerability comes from the e-mail itself. We have completed the "line of attack" on the tree diagram, as illustrated in Figure 4.6.

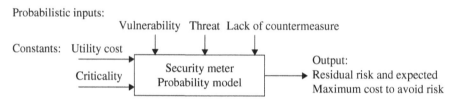

FIGURE 4.5   Quantitative SM model of probabilistic, deterministic inputs and outputs.

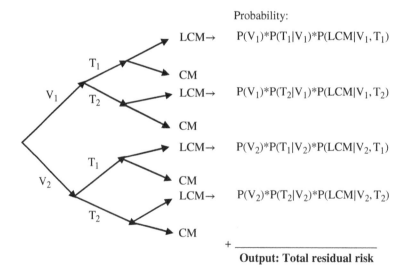

FIGURE 4.6   Simple tree diagram for two threats for each of the two vulnerabilities.

Out of 1000 such cyber-attacks, which maliciously harm the target cyber-operation in some manner, how many of them are not prevented or countermeasured by, for example, smoke detectors or generators, or AV software, or firewalls installed? Out of those that are not prevented by a certain CM device, how many of them are caused by threat 1 or 2, and so on of certain vulnerability? We can then calculate the percentage of vulnerability 1, 2, or 3. The only way to calculate the count of CM preventions is by doing either of the following: (i) guessing a healthy estimator of an attack ratio (e.g., 3% of all attacks are prevented by CM devices) or (ii) using a countermeasuring device to detect a probable attack prematurely. The following equation computes the RRs for each activity in Figure 4.6 for each leg:

$$RR = \text{vulnerability} \times \text{threat} \times LCM \tag{4.1}$$

Covering all legs in a tree diagram, RR's $(0 < RR < 1)$ summed total to total residual risks (TRRs) $(0 < TRR < 1)$ are shown in Figure 4.6.

$$\text{Final risk} = \text{residual risk} * \text{criticality constant}, \left(0 < \text{criticality} < 1\right) \tag{4.2}$$

$$ECL = \text{expected \$cost of loss} \left(\text{after the fact}\right) = \text{final risk} \times \text{capital cost} \left(\$\text{asset}\right), \tag{4.3}$$

The vulnerability (asset becoming weakness under malicious threat conditions) values vary between 0.0 and 1.0 (or 0–100%). In a probabilistic sample space of feasible outcomes of the random variable (rv) for vulnerability, the sum of disjoint probabilities should add up to unity. This is like the probabilities of the faces of a die, such as 1–6, totaling to one, whether the die is fair or not. If a cited vulnerability is not exploited in reality, then it cannot be included in the model or Monte Carlo simulation (MC-SIM) study. Vulnerability has from one to several threats. A threat is defined as the probability of the exploitation of a vulnerability item within a specific time frame under the accepted conditions. Each threat is to be offset by a CM that ranges between 0 and 1 (with respect to the first law of probability) whose complement gives the LCM. The binary CM and LCM values should add up to one, keeping in mind the second law of probability.

The security risk analyst can define, for instance, a network server (v_1) as a vulnerability located in a remotely unoccupied shelter in which a threat (t_{11}), such as persons without proper access, or a fire (t_{12}), could result in the destruction of assets without CMs such as a motion sensor (CM_{111}) or a fire alarm (CM_{121}), respectively. System criticality, which is another constant that indicates the degree of how critical or disruptive the system is in the event of an entire loss, is taken to be a single value that corresponds to all vulnerabilities with a value ranging from 0.0 to 1.0, or from 0 to 100%. Criticality is low if the RR is of little or no significance, such as the malfunctioning of an office printer, but in the case of a nuclear power plant, criticality is close to 100%. Capital (investment) cost is the total expected loss in monetary units (e.g., dollars) for the particular system if it is completely destroyed and can no longer be utilized. This is excluding the shadow or external (or ripple) costs, had the system continued to generate added value for the system.

4.3 VERIFICATION OF THE PROBABILISTIC SECURITY METER (SM) METHOD BY MONTE CARLO SIMULATION AND MATH-STATISTICAL TRIPLE-PRODUCT RULE

An SM's accuracy can be verified by two techniques: (1) MC-SIM [1] using uniformly distributed, U (0, 1), variables of vulnerability, threat, and CM and (2) theoretical math–statistical analytics using triple-product rule [12]. Clarification will be presented in the next sections. Moreover, the problem of nondisjointness and its probabilistically remedial solution (when the sum of available vulnerabilities or their corresponding threats is not a unity) are referred to in an earlier book by the same author who has extensively studied this aspect [13]. A risk analyst conducts MC-SIMs to mimic the relationship among vulnerabilities, threats, and CMs as they exist in real life. That is, a particular vulnerability is threatened by a threat and therefore becomes an attack at the next level if the threat is not countermeasured by a firewall in a computer, or motion sensor in the case of intrusion, or a fire alarm in the case of fire, according to what the actual situation would require.

If fully countermeasured (i.e., CM = 1 or LCM = 0), no attack occurs, as clearly shown in Equation 4.1, where the RR is zero given that one of the factors is zero. The ECL (after the fact, if no action is taken) or the expected cost of repair to avoid the entire risk (if a CM is taken proactively) can be determined using Equation 4.3. Risk analysis has various inputs, such as vulnerabilities, and each threat's CM; criticality and capital cost are constants, so is the number of simulation runs.

From these input values, we determine the expected monetary cost to mitigate the RR. Each risk factor, such as vulnerability (v_i), threat (t_{ij}), and countermeasure (CM_{ijk}), is hypothesized. We assume uniform (or rectangular) density parameters, which can take on values between a lower limit a and an upper limit b. The lower and upper limits are tabulated in Table 4.1 for Figure 4.7 for all risk factors. The average or expected value of a uniformly distributed rv is $\mu = (a + b)/2$. That is, when placed in a decision tree diagram as in Figure 4.6, the expected values will result in an expected output, which should be verified by the MC-SIM, in which 10 thousands of runs are conducted converging to

TABLE 4.1　Probabilistic Input For the Security Meter: Home PC (12 Legs)

Vulnerability		Threat		Lack of Countermeasure	
Lower	Upper	Lower	Upper	Lower	Upper
0.1	0.3	0.1	0.6	0.1	0.5
		0.4	0.9	0.2	0.6
0.0	0.4	0.2	0.6	0.1	0.7
		0.1	0.3	0.0	0.2
		0.1	0.7	0.1	0.4
0.0	0.2	0.1	0.5	0.1	0.4
		0.5	0.9	0.0	0.3
0.0	0.1	0.1	0.4	0.1	0.4
		0.0	0.5	0.2	0.6
		0.1	0.9	0.2	0.6
0.1	0.9	0.1	0.5	0.1	0.3
		0.5	0.9	0.0	0.3

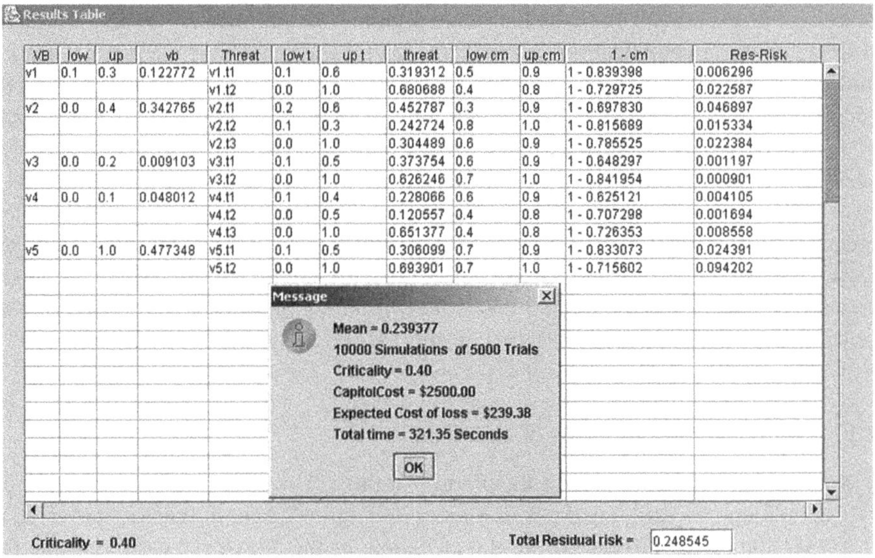

VB	low	up	vb	Threat	low t	up t	threat	low cm	up cm	1 - cm	Res-Risk
v1	0.1	0.3	0.122772	v1.t1	0.1	0.6	0.319312	0.5	0.9	1 - 0.839398	0.006296
				v1.t2	0.0	1.0	0.680688	0.4	0.8	1 - 0.729725	0.022587
v2	0.0	0.4	0.342765	v2.t1	0.2	0.6	0.452787	0.3	0.9	1 - 0.697830	0.046897
				v2.t2	0.1	0.3	0.242724	0.8	1.0	1 - 0.815689	0.015334
				v2.t3	0.0	1.0	0.304489	0.6	0.9	1 - 0.785525	0.022384
v3	0.0	0.2	0.009103	v3.t1	0.1	0.5	0.373754	0.6	0.9	1 - 0.648297	0.001197
				v3.t2	0.0	1.0	0.826246	0.7	1.0	1 - 0.841954	0.000901
v4	0.0	0.1	0.048012	v4.t1	0.1	0.4	0.228066	0.6	0.9	1 - 0.625121	0.004105
				v4.t2	0.0	0.5	0.120557	0.4	0.8	1 - 0.707298	0.001694
				v4.t3	0.0	1.0	0.651377	0.4	0.8	1 - 0.726353	0.008558
v5	0.0	1.0	0.477348	v5.t1	0.1	0.5	0.306099	0.7	0.9	1 - 0.833073	0.024391
				v5.t2	0.0	1.0	0.693901	0.7	1.0	1 - 0.715602	0.094202

Message

Mean = 0.239377

10000 Simulations of 5000 Trials

Criticality = 0.40

CapitolCost = $2500.00

Expected Cost of loss = $239.38

Total time = 321.35 Seconds

OK

Criticality = 0.40   Total Residual risk = 0.248545

FIGURE 4.7   Screenshot of spreadsheets for the residual risk of the security meter simulation runs.

the target output expected. The proposed SM's mathematical accuracy is verified by a Monte Carlo statistical simulation study. A modest 5000 runs, one of which is shown in Figure 4.7, resulting in 24.85% total RR, are conducted by generating rv's from each vulnerability, threat, or CM.

Then the SM method takes effect by multiplying the conditional probabilities at each branch with respect to Equation 4.1 to calculate the RRs and sum them up for the total RR. The average of a selected number of cycles of runs, such as 10,000, will yield the final Monte Carlo result after 50 million runs. Then Equations 4.1 and 4.2 are used to reach the final risk and cost. Figure 4.6 displays the input data for v (a, b), t (a, b), and CM (a, b), which are taken to be uniformly distributed, U (a, b). The budgetary portfolio at the end of such quantitative analyses is an asset. In this hypothetical or educational example, $239.38 is needed for a proactive defense or to repair damage after the fact. Figure 4.7 shows the final MC-SIM result for the final risk and expected monetary damage.

In the SM modeling for quantitative risk assessment, about which a brief description is presented earlier, one is required to take the product of three nonidentical uniforms, U (a, b), which forms one leg of the many that constitute the TRR. The pdf of such a triple product of uniforms is certainly a challenge not encountered in the current literature. We have had a complete agreement of the theoretical mean with the MC-SIM average for large number of simulation runs. Variance from the summation of available legs will converge to simulation variance as the number of legs from TRR increases. However, variance for large number of runs from the simulations compares favorably with the analytical results so as to obtain a complete characterization for the Security Meter Quantitative Risk Probability Model. This work analytically (theoretically) validates the MC-SIM and vice versa. The same concept can be utilized for other applied fields where the triple product of uniforms is vitally needed. The author will further find ways to improve this work by modifying the uniforms with triangular representations for the three rv's of interest. In the SM modeling for quantitative risk assessment, one is required to take the product of three nonidentical uniforms, $U(a, b, c)$, which forms one leg of the many that constitute the TRR as depicted in Figure 4.6. Using the central limit theorem (CLT), we sum the means and variances to find the approximate normal (mean, variance). We have a complete agreement of the theoretical mean with the MC-SIM average for large number of simulation runs as shown by the MAPLE mathematical software. Variance improves as the number of legs increases and compares satisfactorily with the variance for large number of runs from the MC-SIM results, such as $n = 100,000$. Therefore, the simulation mean and variance can be used to model the risk implying that time-consuming and tedious MAPLE software calculations are not necessary every time results are sought [8–10].

4.3.1 The Triple-Product Rule of Uniforms

For determining the distribution of the product of three $U_i(a_i, b_i)$, where $W = xyz$, the pdf of V can be found by applying the well-known Rohatgi result for the case of two rv's [7]. Let us take the "two rv" case before the challenge of the "three rv" case. Assume that the continuous rv X is distributed with $f(x) = U(a, b)$ and rv Y is distributed with $g(y) = U(c, d)$. The pdf of $V = XY$ is therefore given using the transformation of variables, where the proofs are presented in references by Leemis, Glenn, and Drew in 2004 in a reference, which is a 2010 journal publication by Sahinoglu et al. [12]:

$$h(v) = \begin{cases} \int_a^{v/c} g\left(\frac{v}{x}\right) f(x)\frac{1}{x}dx, & ac < v < ad, \quad ad < bc, \\ \int_{v/d}^{v/c} g\left(\frac{v}{x}\right) f(x)\frac{1}{x}dx, & ad < v < bc, \quad ad < bc, \\ \int_{v/d}^{b} g\left(\frac{v}{x}\right) f(x)\frac{1}{x}dx, & bc < v < bd, \quad ad < bc, \end{cases}$$

or

$$h(v) = \begin{cases} \int_a^{v/c} g\left(\frac{v}{x}\right) f(x)\frac{1}{x}dx, & ac < v < ad, \quad ad = bc \\ \int_{v/d}^{b} g\left(\frac{v}{x}\right) f(x)\frac{1}{x}dx, & ad < v < bd, \quad ad < bc, \end{cases}$$

or

$$h(v) = \begin{cases} \int_a^{v/c} g\left(\frac{v}{x}\right) f(x)\frac{1}{x}dx, & ac < v < bc, \quad ad > bc \\ \int_{v/d}^{v/c} g\left(\frac{v}{x}\right) f(x)\frac{1}{x}dx, & bc < v < ad, \quad ad > bc \\ \int_{v/d}^{b} g\left(\frac{v}{x}\right) f(x)\frac{1}{x}dx, & ad < v < bd, \quad ad > bc \end{cases}$$

Take, for example, the rv X with U $(a = 1, b = 2)$ and Y with U $(c = 3, d = 4)$. To determine the distribution of $V = XY$, one can use the MAPLE code, or simply use the previous $h(v)$ derivation, where $ac < bd$:

$$h(v) = \begin{cases} \ln v - \ln 3, 3 < v < 4 \\ \ln 4 - \ln 3, 4 < v < 6 \\ 3\ln 2 - \ln v, 6 < v < 8 \end{cases}$$

Now let us extend this problem under the same theorem with the same working principles to the product of three uniforms such as X with U $(a = 1, b = 2)$ and Y with U $(c = 3, d = 4)$ and a new Z with U $(e = 5, f = 6)$, where $V = XYZ$. There will be $2^3 - 1 = 7$ intervals. We are expecting an overall mean to be $[(1 + 2)/2] [(3 + 4)/2] [(5 + 6)/2] = [1.5][3.5][5.5] = [231/8] = 28.875$. Then, the pdf will be derived as follows:
    S: {(ace = 15 < v <acf = 18), (acf = 18 < v < ade = 20), (ade = 20 < v < adf = 24), (adf = 24< v < bce = 30), (bce = 30 < v < bcf = 36), (bcf = 36 < v < bde = 40), (bde = 40 < v < bdf = 48)} is the useful domain for the following pdf of the rv V. It is zero elsewhere.
    The plot of the pdf of the rv $V = XYZ$, the triple product of the continuous uniforms, and additionally the mean and variance of V is as follows using MAPLE software program:

`> PlotDist (V):`

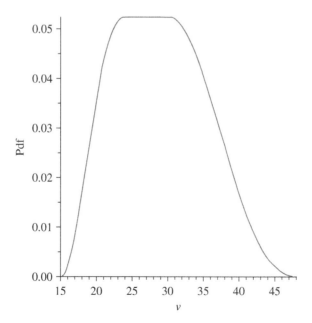

`> Mean (V):` $\dfrac{231}{8}$ `and > Variance (V):` $\dfrac{67669}{1728}$

4.3.2   Data Analysis on the Total Residual Risk of the Security Meter Design

The number of legs such as in the triple product studied earlier will usually be at least 4 or more. A typical SM may have on the average 5 vulnerabilities (V), and if there are 5 threats (T) for each such vulnerability, then there will be $5 \times 5 = 25$ CM actions in a rich but computationally feasible example. By employing the CLT, the approximate normal pdf of the TRR will be the sum of means of each "V-T-CM" triple-product leg, whereas the variance of the TRR will be simply the added sum of the variances for each leg as found in the earlier introduced single leg example. Referring to Table 3.1 on p. 126 by the author in Ref. [13], where lower and upper limits for all parameters are listed, we would like to conduct a statistical analysis for the calculated RR. We will first find each leg's triple uniform product and then add the means and variances to estimate the asymptotic normality (mean, variance) for the TRR to be compared with the simulation results:

4.3.2.1   Security Meter Example for a Home PC   An example inspired from the SM application of a home PC will be studied successively [7–11] (see input in Table 4.1 similar to the JAVA screenshot of Figure 4.7 in Section 4.2).
The leg by leg analysis in MAPLE software can be presented as follows:

Leg 1) *For V1.T1.LCM1*:

```
X1:= UniformRV (0.1, 0.3);
X2:= UniformRV (0.1, 0.6);
X3:= UniformRV (0.1, 0.5);
```

$$X1 := \left[\left[x \to 5.000000000\right], \left[0.1, 0.3\right], \left["\, Continuous, "\, "\, PDF\, "\right]\right]$$
$$X2 := \left[\left[x \to 2.000000000\right], \left[0.1, 0.6\right], \left["\, Continuous, "\, "\, PDF\, "\right]\right]$$
$$X3 := \left[\left[x \to 2.500000000\right], \left[0.1, 0.5\right], \left["\, Continuous, "\, "\, PDF\, "\right]\right]$$

```
> V:= Product(X1, X2, X3);
```

$$:= \left[\left[v \to 596.4635374 + 172.6938820\ln\left(v\right) + 12.50000000\ln\left(v\right)^2,\right.\right.$$
$$v \to 174.6367589 + 27.46530722\ln\left(v\right), v \to -176.2653275$$
$$- 104.9926270\ln\left(v\right) - 12.50000000\ln\left(v\right)^2, v \to -503.4329915$$
$$- 232.8925222\ln\left(v\right) - 25.00000000\ln\left(v\right)^2, v \to -282.9639573$$
$$- 127.8998952\ln\left(v\right) - 12.50000000\ln\left(v\right)^2, v \to -81.22182792$$
$$- 27.46530722\ln\left(v\right), v \to 72.47752567 + 60.19864021\ln\left(v\right)$$
$$\left. + 12.50000000\ln\left(v\right)^2\ \right], \left[\ 0.0010000000000.003000000000\right.$$
$$0.0050000000000.0060000000000.0150000000000.018000000000$$
$$\left. 0.0300000000000.09000000000\ \right], \left["\, Continuous, "\, "\, PDF\, "\right]\right]$$

```
> PlotDist (V):
```

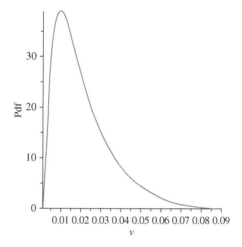

```
> Mean (V): 0.0210000000.
> Variance (V): 0.000200814815
> Total: M:=0.0210000000
> Total: V:=0.000200814815
```

Note: Leg 2 to Leg 11 will be skipped out of similarity and lack of space.

Leg 12) V5.T2.LCM2:

```
X1:= UniformRV(0.1, 0.8);
X2:= UniformRV (0.5, 0.9);
X3:= UniformRV (0.0, 0.3);
```

$$X1 := \left[\left[x \rightarrow 1.428571429\right], \left[0.1, 0.8\right], \left["\,Continuous, ""\,PDF\,"\right]\right]$$

$$X2 := \left[\left[x \rightarrow 2.500000000\right], \left[0.5, 0.9\right], \left["\,Continuous, ""\,PDF\,"\right]\right]$$

$$X3 := \left[\left[x \rightarrow 3.333333333\right], \left[0., 0.3\right], \left["\,Continuous, ""\,PDF\,"\right]\right]$$

```
> V: = Product(X1, X2, X3); similar to Leg1 (intermediate
steps skipped) gives:
> PlotDist (V):
```

```
> Mean (V): 0.0472500000
> Variance (V): 0.00144177082
> Total
```

$M := 0.02100000005 + 0.05199999994 + 0.03200000004$
    $+ 0.004000000040 + 0.02000000006 + 0.007500000046$
    $+ 0.01049999999 + 0.003124999995 + 0.004999999952$
    $+ 0.01000000002 + 0.02699999998 + 0.04725000002$

$M : 0.239375000$
```
> Total
```

$V := 0.0002008148150 + 0.0006259259390 + 0.0007324444470$
    $+ 0.00001481481520 + 0.0003093333350 + 0.00004019444492$
    $+ 0.00009108333300 + 0.000006567708301 + 0.00002314814765$
    $+ 0.00007525926020 + 0.0003605925891 + 0.001441770828$

$V := 0.00392194966$

MAPLE Summary: All 12 legs of the SM to compute the TRR in Table 4.1 are calculated.

From the earlier, we can get:

Mean $= 0.239375 \approx 0.239$ and
Variance $= 0.00392194966 \approx 0.0039$
Approximate normal pdf of V has the following pdf: $N(0.239, 0.062^2)$.

Then, 90% confidence interval estimate of the unknown parameter (where $\sqrt{}$ denotes the square root of the entire expression following the symbol) is given as follows:

$$\mu \text{ of TRR is given by } 0.239 \pm 1.64 * \sqrt{(0.0039)}$$

$= 0.239 \pm 0.102$, which is between 0.137 and 0.341.

Also, 95% confidence interval estimate of the unknown parameter is as follows:

$$\mu = \text{TRR is given } 0.239 \pm 1.96 * \sqrt{(0.0039)} = 0.239 \pm 0.122.$$

We can assert that with 95% confidence, TRR is occurring between 0.117 and 0.361 by the given pdf.

Finally, 99% confidence interval estimate of the unknown parameter is as follows:

$$\mu = \text{TRR is given } 0.239 \pm 2.57 * \sqrt{(0.0039)}$$

$= 0.239 \pm 0.160$, which is between 0.079 and 0.399.

If we wish to know what is the probability of TRR greater than 0.2?

$$\text{Solution: } P\,(\text{TRR} > 0.2) = ?$$
$$P\,[z > (0.2 - 0.239)/\sigma] = P\,(z > (-0.039/\sqrt{(0.0039)}))$$
$$= P\,(z > -0.63) = 1 - 0.2643 = 0.7354$$

Hence, the probability of TRR greater than 0.2 is 0.7354, but the probability of TRR < 0.2 = 0.2646.

Therefore in summary, the statistical analysis of the resultant approximate normal pdf of the TRR will be demonstrated as follows using the MAPLE software:

```
> M:= 0.2393750001;
> V:= 0.00392194966.
```
$X := N\left(M, S\right);$

$$X := \left[\left[x \rightarrow \frac{11.29104126e^{-127.4876128(x-0.2393750001)^2}}{\sqrt{\pi}}\right], [-\infty, \infty]\right]$$

$$\left[\text{" Continuous, "" PDF "}\right]$$

$$\text{PlotDist}\left(\left[\left[x \rightarrow \frac{11.29104126e^{-127.4876128(x-0.2393750001)^2}}{\sqrt{\pi}}\right], [0,1],\right.\right.$$
$$\left.\left.\left[\text{" Continuous, "" PDF "}\right]\right]\right);$$

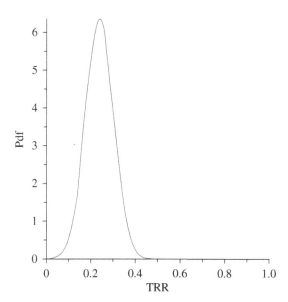

```
> with (Statistics) :
> X := Random Variable (Normal (M, S)):Probability (X < M);
0.500000000
> with (Statistics) :
> X := Random Variable (Normal (M, S)):Probability (X > 0.2);
0.735239631
```

TABLE 4.2   Comparison of Results For the PC Example As in Table 4.1

Monte Carlo Simulation (n = 1,000,000)	MAPLE (Theoretical)
TRR(M) = 0.239685	TRR(M) = 0.239375
TRR(V) = 0.0020756	TRR(V) = 0.0039219
TRR(S) = 0.046	TRR(S) = 0.062

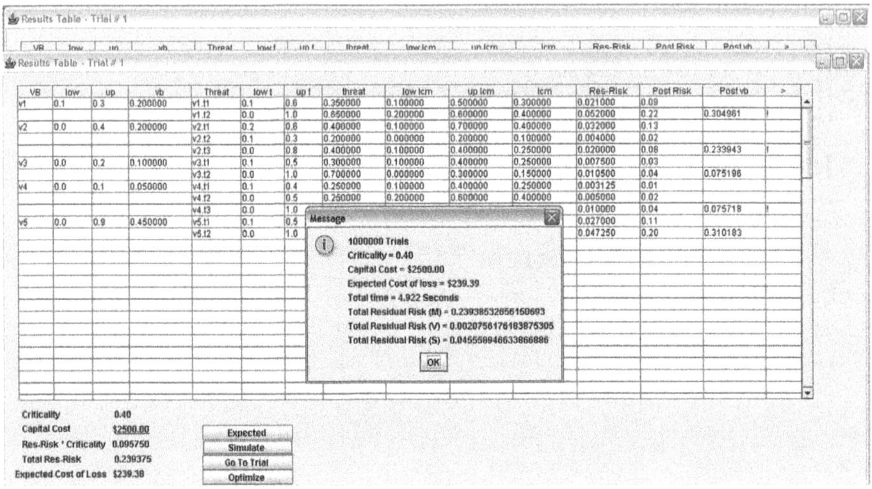

FIGURE 4.8   Monte Carlo simulations for the PC example as in Table 4.1.

When we apply an MC-SIM to the PC example in Table 4.1 following n = 1,000,000 simulation runs, we also get almost an identical expected value, TRR (M) = 0.239385, which is very satisfactorily compared to M = 0.239375 (exact) in the MAPLE solutions earlier (Table 4.2). The MAPLE's variation (V) is 0.0039219 with its $S = \sqrt{(V)} = 0.062$. The Monte Carlo's V = 0.0020756 with its $S = \sqrt{(V)} = 0.046$. The difference is negligible after 1 Million Monte Carlo simulation trials. See Table 4.2. Therefore, approximately N (Mean, Standard Deviation) = $N(\mu = 0.239375, \sigma = 0.0046)$. See Fig. 4.8.

4.3.2.2   Security Meter Example for a University Center Server

The tabulated upper and lower risk values for the parameters in the SM design for the university center server are taken from a real-life example. We will conduct now statistical analysis on the TRR metric for this center employing the same approach explained previously [8]. See input Table 4.3.

The following analyses will follow the same routine as in the previous section except that the TRR will be calculated for all 10 legs for Table 4.3 instead of 12 legs for the previous Table 4.1:

Leg 1) V1.T1.LCM1:

```
X1:= UniformRV (0.34, 0.36);
X2:= UniformRV (0.47, 0.49);
X3:= UniformRV (0.29, 0.31);
```

$X1 := \left[\left[x \rightarrow 50.00000000\right], \left[0.34, 0.36\right], \left["\,Continuous,\,"\,"\,PDF\,"\right]\right]$

$X2 := \left[\left[x \rightarrow 50.00000000\right], \left[0.47, 0.49\right], \left["\,Continuous,\,"\,"\,PDF\,"\right]\right]$

$X3 := \left[\left[x \rightarrow 50.00000000\right], \left[0.29, 0.31\right], \left["\,Continuous,\,"\,"\,PDF\,"\right]\right]$

```
> V:= Product(X1, X2, X3);
> PlotDist (V):
```

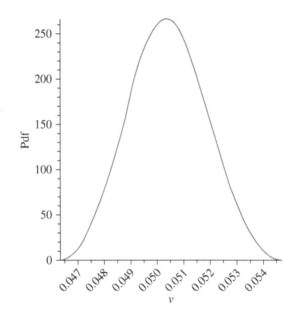

```
> Mean (V): 0.050400047
> Variance (V): 0.00000199763500
> Total M: 0.0504000479
> Total V:= 0.00000199763500
```

TABLE 4.3 Probabilistic Input For the Security Meter: University Center (10 Legs)

Vulnerability		Threat		Lack of Countermeasure	
Upper	Lower	Upper	Lower	Upper	Lower
0.34	0.36	0.47	0.49	0.29	0.31
		0.15	0.17	0.57	0.59
		0.31	0.33	0.02	0.04
		0.03	0.05	0.19	0.21
0.25	0.27	0.21	0.23	0.64	0.66
		0.01	0.03	0.64	0.66
		0.75	0.77	0.03	0.05
0.38	0.40	0.31	0.33	0.27	0.29
		0.58	0.60	0.29	0.31
		0.08	0.10	0.53	0.55

Note, leg 2 to leg 9 will be skipped out of similarity and lack of space.

Leg 10) *V3.T3.LCM3:*

```
X1:= UniformRV(0.38, 0.40);
X2:= UniformRV (0.08, 0.10);
X3:= UniformRV (0.53, 0.55);
```

$$X1 := \left[\left[x \rightarrow 50.00000000\right], \left[0.38, 0.40\right], \left[\text{" Continuous, " " PDF "}\right]\right]$$
$$X2 := \left[\left[x \rightarrow 50.00000000\right], \left[0.08, 0.10\right], \left[\text{" Continuous, " " PDF "}\right]\right]$$
$$X3 := \left[\left[x \rightarrow 50.00000000\right], \left[0.53, 0.55\right], \left[\text{" Continuous, " " PDF "}\right]\right]$$

```
> V:= Product(X1, X2, X3);
```

$$:= \left[\left[v \rightarrow 1.06512252910^6 + 5.16023867910^5 \ln(v) + 62500.ln(v)^2,\right.\right.$$
$$v \rightarrow 19028.42680 + 4630.158960 \ln(v), v \rightarrow -1.01978997510^6$$
$$-5.04982047110^5 \ln(v) - 62500.ln(v)^2, v \rightarrow 237.4961066v \rightarrow$$
$$-9.52849699610^5 - 4.88130924010^5 \ln(v) - 62500.ln(v)^2, v \rightarrow$$
$$-17757.74058 - 4630.158960 \ln(v), v \rightarrow 9.10456049510^5$$
$$+4.77089103210^5 \ln(v) + 62500.ln(v)^2 \left.\right], \left[0.01611200000,\right.$$
$$0.01672000000, 0.01696000000, 0.01760000000, 0.02014000000,$$
$$\left.0.02090000000, 0.02120000000, 0.02200000000, \left[\text{" Continuous, " " PDF "}\right]\right]$$

```
> PlotDist (V):
```

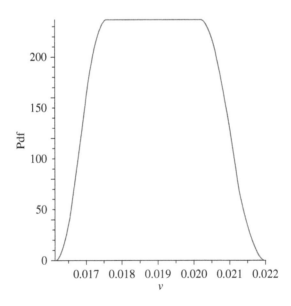

```
> Mean (V): 0.0189540066
> Variance (V): 0.00000159857810
> Total for all 10 legs:
```

$M := 0.05040004790 + 0.03247999996 + 0.003360000913$
$\qquad + 0.002800000577 + 0.03717999068 + 0.003380000475$
$\qquad + 0.007903999736 + 0.03494401504 + 0.06903005201$
$\qquad + 0.01895400665$

$M := 0.260432113$
$V := 0.0000144453852$

MAPLE Summary: All 10 legs of the SM to calculate TRR in Table 4.2 are calculated.

Mean $= 0.2604321138 \approx 0.2604$.
Variance $= 0.00001444538529 \approx 0.000014$.

Probability density function of

$$W = \sum_{1}^{10}\left(W_i\right) = \sum_{1}^{10}\left(\mathrm{RR}_i\right) \approx N\left(\sum_{1}^{10}\mu_i\left(\mathrm{RR}\right), \sqrt{\left(\sum_{1}^{10}\mathrm{Var}_i\left(\mathrm{RR}\right)\right)}\right)$$
$$= N\left(0.2604, 0.0038\right)$$

90% confidence interval estimate of

$$\mu = \mathrm{TRR} \text{ is given } 0.2604 \pm 1.64 * \sqrt{(0.000014)}$$

$= 0.2604 \pm 0.0061$, which is between 0.2543 and 0.2701.
  95% confidence interval estimate of

$$\mu = \mathrm{TRR} \text{ is given } 0.2604 \pm 1.96 * \sqrt{(0.000014)}$$

$$= 0.2604 \pm 0.0073.$$

That is, we can assert 95% TRR occurring between 0.2531 and 0.2677 by the given pdf.
  99% confidence interval estimate of

$$\mu = \mathrm{TRR} \text{ is given } 0.2604 \pm 2.57 * \sqrt{(0.000014)}$$

$= 0.2604 \pm 0.0096$, which is between 0.2508 and 0.2700.
What is the probability of TRR greater than 0.261?

$$\text{Solution: } P\left(\mathrm{TRR} > 0.261\right) =$$

$$P\left(z > (0.261 - 0.2604)/\sigma\right) = P\left(z > 0.0006/0.0037\right)$$

$$= P\left(z > 0.16\right) = 1 - 0.5636 = 0.4364$$

So the probability of TRR greater than 0.261 is 0.4364; in other words, the probability of TRR less than 0.261 is 0.5636. For final results, see the aforementioned MAPLE application:

```
> M:= 0.260432113;
> V:= 0.00001444453852;
> S:= 0.00380070851
> X:= N (M, S);
```

$$X := \left[\left[x \rightarrow \frac{186.0460434e^{-34613.13028(x-0.260432113)^2}}{\sqrt{\pi}}\right], [-\infty, \infty]\right.$$

$$\left[\text{" Continuous, "}\quad \text{" PDF "}\right]\right]$$

```
> PlotDist
```
$$\left(\left[\left[x \rightarrow \frac{186.0460434e^{-34613.13028(x-0.260432113)^2}}{\sqrt{\pi}}\right], [0.2, 0.5],\right.\right.$$
$$\left.\left[\text{" Continuous, "" PDF "}\right]\right]\right);$$

```
> with (Statistics):
> X:= Random Variable (Normal(M, S)) : Probability(X < M);
0.500000000
> X:= Random Variable (Normal(M, S)) : Probability(X < 0.26);
0.454740680
```

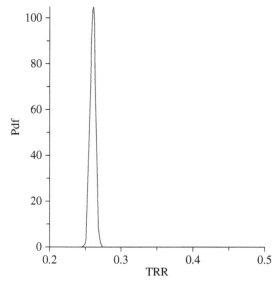

Similarly, when we apply an MC-SIM to the university center server example in Section 3.2 after $n = 1,000,000$ simulation runs, we attempt to get an identical expected value, TRR $(M) = 0.260430$ as very satisfactorily compared to $M = 0.260432$ (exact) in the MAPLE solutions.

TABLE 4.4   Comparison of Results For the University Center Server Example

Monte Carlo Simulation ($n = 1,000,000$)	MAPLE (Theoretical)
TRR(M) = 0.260430	TRR(M) = 0.260432
TRR(V) = 0.0000089	TRR(V) = 0.00001444
TRR(S) = 0.0029	TRR(S) = 0.0038

TABLE 4.5   Probabilistic Input Data For the Security Meter: Privacy Risk (26 Legs)

V. Upper	V. Lower	T. Upper	T. Lower	LCM Upper	LCM Lower
0.05253	0.15761	0.09821	0.29465	0.25	0.75
		0.14285	0.42857	0.3	0.9
		0.08035	0.24107	0.3	0.9
		0.08036	0.24108	0.3	0.9
		0.09821	0.29465	0.225	0.675
0.08879	0.26639	0.19097	0.57293	0.2	0.6
		0.07291	0.21875	0.225	0.675
		0.11805	0.35417	0.125	0.375
		0.11805	0.35417	0.275	0.825
0.06002	0.18008	0.27083	0.81251	0.325	0.975
		0.22917	0.68749	0.275	0.825
0.06002	0.18006	0.09965	0.29895	0.275	0.825
		0.13331	0.39991	0.225	0.675
		0.15253	0.45761	0.3	0.9
		0.11451	0.34353	0.275	0.825
0.08254	0.24764	0.1359	0.4077	0.292857	0.878571
		0.10094	0.30284	0.325	0.975
		0.05451	0.16351	0.25	0.75
		0.07674	0.23024	0.25	0.75
		0.06257	0.18771	0.15	0.45
		0.06933	0.20801	0.5125	0.854166
0.06728	0.20186	0.17246	0.51738	0.275	0.825
		0.18583	0.55749	0.3	0.9
		0.14171	0.42513	0.3125	0.9375
0.08879	0.26639	0.26137	0.78409	0.175	0.525
		0.23863	0.71591	0.25	0.75

The standard deviation due to Monte Carlo is TRR(S) = 0.00299 = 0.003 as compared to MAPLE's TRR(S) = 0.0038 as in Table 4.4, which is the same to one one-thousandth accuracy. Since the number of legs is not around 30 or more as ideally expected from a CLT application, it is recommended to use the TRR(S) value from the MC-SIM runs along with the M to characterize the N (mean, standard deviation) = N (0.260432, 0.003). Simulation variances will always be smaller due to the trimming effect [8] (Table 4.4).

4.3.2.3   Security Meter Example for a Privacy Risk Scenario   This example is taken from the application of a privacy implementation of the SM with 7 vulnerabilities and 26 CMs. See risk input data in Table 4.5. Note: Leg 1 to Leg 25 will be skipped out of "similarity of approach" reasons and lack of space in this section (Fig. 4.9).

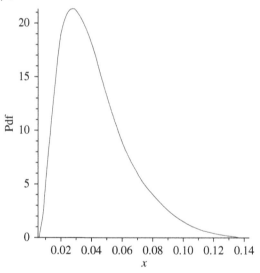

VB	low	up	vb	Threat	low t	up t	threat	low cm	up cm	lcm	Res-Risk	Post Risk	Post vb
v1	0.34	0.36	0.350000	v1.l1	0.47	0.49	0.480000	0.690000	0.710000	0.300000	0.050400	0.19	
				v1.l2	0.15	0.17	0.160000	0.410000	0.430000	0.580000	0.032480	0.12	
				v1.l3	0.31	0.33	0.320000	0.980000	0.980000	0.030000	0.003360	0.01	
				v1.l4	0.0	0.08	0.040000	0.790000	0.810000	0.200000	0.002800	0.01	0.341893
v2	0.25	0.27	0.280000	v2.l1	0.21	0.23	0.220000	0.340000	0.360000	0.850000	0.037180	0.14	
				v2.l2	0.01	0.03	0.020000	0.340000	0.360000	0.850000	0.003360	0.01	
				v2.l3	0.0	1.0	0.760000	0.950000	0.970000	0.040000	0.007904	0.03	0.186091
v3	0.0	0.78	0.390000	v3.l1	0.31	0.33	0.320000	0.710000	0.730000	0.260000	0.034944	0.13	
				v3.l2	0.58	0.6	0.590000	0.690000	0.710000	0.300000	0.089030	0.27	
				v3.l3	0.0	0.18					0.019854	0.07	0.472016

Message

(i) 1000000 Trials
Criticality = 0.40
Capital Cost = $8000.00
Expected Cost of loss = $833.38
Total time = 8.922 Seconds
Total Residual Risk (M) = 0.26043060456877215
Total Residual Risk (V) = 8.945774968541357E-6
Total Residual Risk (S) = 0.0029909488391715025

OK

Criticality 0.40
Capital Cost $8000.00
Res-Risk * Criticality 0.104173
Total Res-Risk 0.260432
Expected Cost of Loss $833.38

Expected
Simulate
Go To Trial
Optimize

FIGURE 4.9 Monte Carlo simulation for the university center as in Table 4.3.

We suffice out of 26 legs to study Leg 26 only due to space limitation. Note: V, T, and LCM denote vulnerability, threat, and LCM, as previously used, respectively.

Leg 26) For V7.T2.LCM2:
```
> PlotDist (V):
```

$$M := 0.01031945010 + 0.01801172978 + 0.01013147975$$
$$+ 0.01013211018 + 0.009287504904 + 0.02713219992$$
$$+ 0.01165398704 + 0.01048262687 + 0.02306192590$$
$$+ 0.04226786436 + 0.03026238413 + 0.01315818478$$
$$+ 0.01440173918 + 0.02197236205 + 0.01512035820$$
$$+ 0.02628184360 + 0.02166451304 + 0.008998230441$$
$$+ 0.01266983202 + 0.006197808706 + 0.01564356303$$
$$+ 0.02552873648 + 0.03000857178 + 0.02383739329$$

```
M:=0.513096656
V:=0.00002890599520 + 0.00008806040890 + 0.00002786275990
    + 0.00002786497740 + 0.00002341385876 + 0.0001998135602
    + 0.00003686753990 + 0.0000298278769 + 0.000144361494
    + 0.000484932804 + 0.0002485733828 + 0.0000469916899
    + 0.00005629207270 + 0.00013103667 + 0.0000620516402
    + 0.0001874820616 + 0.0001273976542 + 0.00002197523793
    + 0.00004356817720 + 0.00001042616040 + 0.0000484757673
    + 0.0001768931411 + 0.0002444235347 + 0.000154230368
    + 0.000286529074 + 0.0004874819850
V:=0.00342573989
```

MAPLE Summary: All 26 legs of the SM to calculate TRR in Table 4.5 are calculated:

Mean = 0.513096656 ≈ 0.5131.
Variance = 0.00342573989 ≈ 0.0034. Standard deviation = $\sqrt{(0.0034)}$ ≈ 0.0583.
Approx. normal pdf of rv V has the pdf = N (0.5131, 0.0583).
90% confidence interval estimate of the unknown parameter μ of TRR is given
0.5131 ± 1.64 * $\sqrt{(0.0034)}$ = 0.5131 ± 0.0956, between 0.4175 and 0.6087.
95% confidence interval estimate of the unknown parameter μ of TRR is given
0.5131 ± 1.96 * $\sqrt{(0.0034)}$ = 0.5131 ± 0.1143.

That is, it can be asserted with 95% confidence that TRR is occurring between 0.3987 and 0.6274 by the given density function. Also 99% confidence interval estimate of the unknown parameter μ of TRR is given 0.5131 ± 2.57 * $\sqrt{(0.0034)}$ = 0.5131 ± 0.1499, between 0.3632 and 0.6630. If we wish to know the probability of TRR greater than 0.48?
    Solution: P (TRR > 0.48) = P (z > (0.48 − 0.5131)/σ) = P (z > −0.0331/0.0583) = P (z > −0.5678) = 1 − 0.2843 = 0.7157. Therefore, the probability of TRR < 0.48 = 0.2843.
    Thirdly, for a very large size privacy risk example (26 legs compared to 10 and 12 legs previously examined) as studied in Section 4.3.2.3, the results are tabulated and compared very satisfactorily (Table 4.6 and Fig. 4.10).

4.3.3   Triple-Product Rule Discussions

From three examples of varying sizes (10, 12, and 26 legs) earlier, we can observe that the means of TRR both from Monte Carlo and MAPLE are almost identical. The simulation variances due to their trimming effect are less than those in MAPLE because each simulation result contains 5000 operations (random number generations) and hence it is the mean of those 5000. When 500,000 or 1,000,000 of each with 5000 runs conducted, one finds roughly the diminished variance of the trimmed means. If available, we recommend to use the total RR standard deviation: TRR(SW) from MAPLE along with the mean to characterize the N (mean, standard deviation). If not, simulation variance is as good an estimate as the other, neither being perfectly accurate but within a very satisfactory margin. A general

TABLE 4.6   Comparison of Results For Privacy Risk Example of Section 4.3.2.3

Monte Carlo Simulation (n = 500,000)	MAPLE (Theoretical)
TRR(M) = 0.5134168	TRR(M) = 0.5130966
TRR(V) = 0.0015	TRR(V) = 0.0034
TRR(S) = 0.0388	TRR(S) = 0.0585

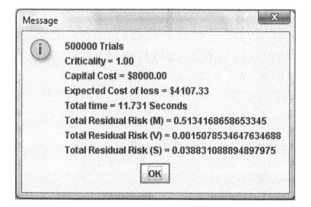

Message

500000 Trials
Criticality = 1.00
Capital Cost = $8000.00
Expected Cost of loss = $4107.33
Total time = 11.731 Seconds
Total Residual Risk (M) = 0.5134168658653345
Total Residual Risk (V) = 0.00150785346476346888
Total Residual Risk (S) = 0.038831088894897975

OK

FIGURE 4.10   Monte Carlo simulation for privacy risk example.

theoretical approach to the determination of the triple product of uniform distributions is studied for validation of the MC-SIM results previously run.

The MAPLE software is used to implement the theory in an SM setup to calculate the mean and variance of the approximate normal distribution. In the end, one can conduct statistical analysis for any given SM design by using the normal (N) approximations as explained. The three examples have given approximate N (μ = 0.239375, σ = 0.062), N (μ = 0.260432, σ = 0.0038), and N (μ = 0.513416, σ = 0.0585) for the home PC, university center server settings, and privacy risk, respectively. These theoretical results are amply simulated and satisfactorily supported by a million simulation runs. This section studies in detail how to conduct a statistical inference by rigorous analysis regarding the total RR metric in the SM design. First, a general theoretical approach to the determination of the triple product of uniform (rectangular) distributions is taken.

Following, the MAPLE software is used to implement the theory in an SM setup to calculate the mean and variance of the approximate normal distribution. Since we do not possess a large number of legs to satisfy the CLT requirement to obtain a measure of variation, we accomplish this through a large number (n = 1,000,000) of MC-SIMs to estimate the variance of the desired metric.

4.4   MODIFYING THE SM QUANTITATIVE MODEL FOR CATEGORICAL, HYBRID, AND NONDISJOINT DATA

Sometimes we do not possess purely quantitative values for each of the attributes in the decision tree diagram in Figure 4.6, and all that are available are qualitative adjectives such as H (high; often), M (medium; occasional), or L (low; occasional) or even W

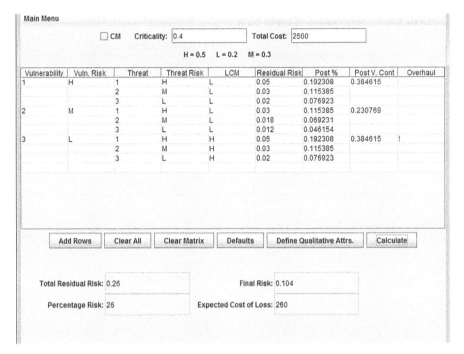

FIGURE 4.11　Qualitative analysis for the security meter.

(rare; unlikely) or more such as Z (very rare; very unlikely), etc., which may extend to all letters of the alphabet as so formulated if necessary. We need to modify our approach as shown in Figure 4.11. We can then, for instance, use the probabilities of H, M, and L, that is, $P(H)$, $P(M)$, and $P(L)$, as long as the addition rule of unity holds for disjoint events (the first three laws of probability). Such outcomes of vulnerability (first branch of the tree diagram) or threat (second branch) may include $H + L = 1$, or $M + L + L = 1$ or $L + L + L + L = 1$, where $H = 0.75$, $M = 0.5$, and $L = 0.25$ hold, where we have dropped the probability symbol P, for simplicity.

Another possibility is when $H + L = 1$, or $M + L + L + L = 1$, or $5L = 1$ to signify five outcomes at most for either vulnerability or a threat variable, where $H = 0.8$, $M = 0.4$, and $L = 0.2$ hold. For up to five vulnerabilities, $H + M = 1$, or $M + L + L + L = 1$, or $5L = 1$, then $H = 0.6$, $M = 0.4$, and $L = 0.2$. If, for example, as shown in Figure 3.4, $H = 0.75$, $M = 0.5$, and $L = 0.25$, the total risk = $HHL + HLL + LMH + LLH + LLH = HHL + 3LLH + LMH = (0.75^2)(0.25) + (3)(0.25^2)(0.75) + (0.25)(0.5)(0.75) = 0.140625 + 0.140625 + 0.09375 = 0.375$ or a 37.5% risk of losing the system's security. Each branch now has letters to signify certain quantities for the vulnerability, threat, and CM where the three fundamental laws of probability hold. The analyst may sometimes have to go an extra step and choose H (high), M (medium), L (low), and W (rare). For example, where $8W = 1$, $M + 3L = 1$, and $H + 2W = 1$, implying that $H = 0.75$, $M = 0.40$, $L = 0.2$, and $W = 0.125$, there may exist at most eight possible outcomes of the vulnerability or threat variable. This scenario is one of many feasible scenarios. Table 4.7 illustrates a simple design. The following are vulnerabilities, threats, and CMs for such a design.

TABLE 4.7   Description of Input Data

Vulnerability	Threat	Countermeasure
Server	System crash	Recover techniques
	Fire	Smoke detectors
	System down	In-house generator
Mailing systems	Virus	Antivirus software
	Hacking	Firewall
	Improper file access	Restrict downloads
Software failure	Coding errors	Prerelease testing
	Configuration errors	Restrict unnecessary connections
	Software down	Upgrade software

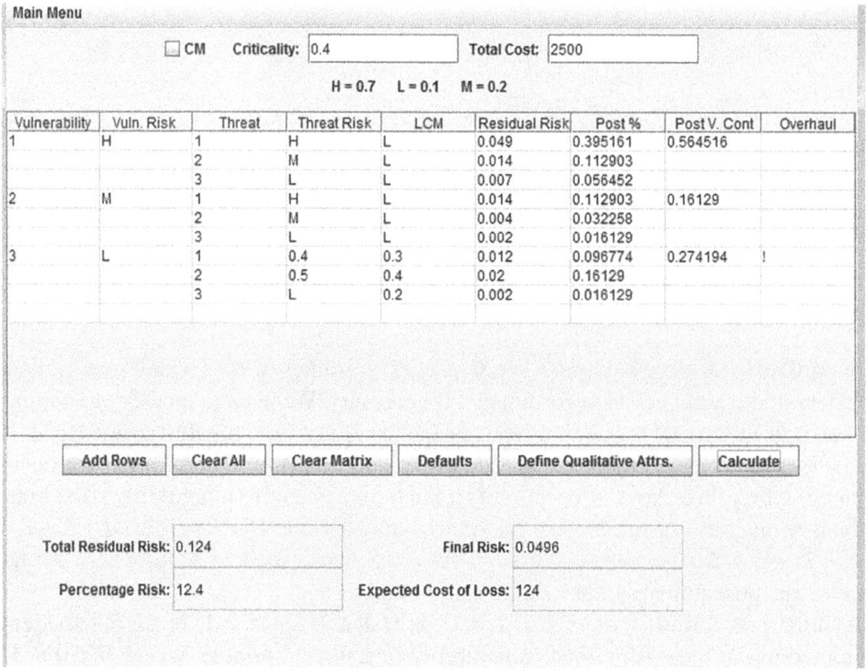

Main Menu

☐ CM   Criticality: 0.4   Total Cost: 2500

H = 0.7   L = 0.1   M = 0.2

Vulnerability	Vuln. Risk	Threat	Threat Risk	LCM	Residual Risk	Post %	Post V. Cont	Overhaul
1	H	1	H	L	0.049	0.395161	0.564516	
		2	M	L	0.014	0.112903		
		3	L	L	0.007	0.056452		
2	M	1	H	L	0.014	0.112903	0.16129	
		2	M	L	0.004	0.032258		
		3	L	L	0.002	0.016129		
3	L	1	0.4	0.3	0.012	0.096774	0.274194	!
		2	0.5	0.4	0.02	0.16129		
		3	L	0.2	0.002	0.016129		

[Add Rows]   [Clear All]   [Clear Matrix]   [Defaults]   [Define Qualitative Attrs.]   [Calculate]

Total Residual Risk: 0.124   Final Risk: 0.0496

Percentage Risk: 12.4   Expected Cost of Loss: 124

FIGURE 4.12   Hybrid analysis for the security meter.

Qualitative and hybrid analyses are presented in Figures 4.11 and 4.12. In a detailed treatment of the SM used as a quantitative risk assessment technique, all the vulnerabilities were assumed to be disjoint and dependent as were the ensuing threats [1, 11, 13]. However, when the vulnerabilities of the quantitative security risk assessment are not perfect (i.e., they are nondisjoint or not mutually exclusive), a new probabilistic approach is needed to replace the special case of disjoint outcomes. The SM's tree diagram has been reformulated in the light of this new reality in Figure 4.13.

The following are the vulnerabilities and threats and countermeasures for the design (Table 4.8):

In a hypothetical example, let $P(V_1) = 0.65$, $P(V_2) = 0.55$, where $P(V_1 \cap V_2) = 0.2$ and $P(V_1 \cap V_2^C) = 0.45$, $P(V_2 \cap V_1^C) = 0.35$, and $P(V_1^C \cap V_1^C) = 0$ in Figure 4.14. In a Venn

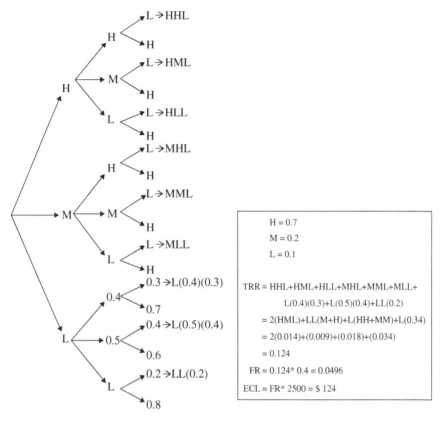

FIGURE 4.13 $2 \times 2 \times 2$ and $3 \times 3 \times 2$ SM designs to accommodate hybrid input data.

TABLE 4.8 Description of Input Data

Vulnerability	Threat	Countermeasure
Software failure	Coding error	Prerelease testing
	Configuration error	Restrict unnecessary connections
Intentional failure	Human error and sabotage	Firewall
	Virus	Install antivirus software

diagram setting, observe the sets solely $V_1 : (V_1 \cap V_2^C)$, solely $V_2 : (V_2 \cap V_1^C)$, and both V_1 and V_2: $(V_1 \cap V_2)$. If none of V_1 and V_2, $(V_1^C \cap V_2^C)$ are all now mutually exclusive or disjoint. Since $P(V_1 \cup V_2) = P(V_1) + P(V_2) - P(V_1 \cap V_2)$, then V_1 and V_2 are not disjoint. Additionally, since $P(V_1 \cap V_2) = 0.2$ is not equal to $P(V_1) P(V_2) = (0.65)(0.55) = 0.3575$, hence V_1 and V_2 cannot be independent.

Sometimes, two nondisjoint events may rarely be independent if this equality holds. Therefore, because V_1 and V_2 are both nondisjoint and nonindependent as vulnerabilities, the classical tree diagram is no longer acceptable. In real life, nondisjoint and dependent vulnerabilities occur frequently in the form of "buckets," where common events intersect. Note that for the independent threats given the vulnerabilities, $P(T_1 \mid V_1) = 0.8$, $P(T_2 \mid V_1) = 0.2$,

$P(T_2 \mid V_1) = 0.5$, and $P(T_2 \mid V_2) = 0.5$. As aforementioned, $P(LCM) = P(CM) = 0.5$ for simplicity. One needs to formulate a similar working table for the threats when they are not disjoint. For a dichotomous threat scenario, one would have disjoint sets such as solely $T_1 : (T_1 \cap T_2^C)$, solely $T_2 : (T_2 \cap T_1^C)$, both T_1 and $T_2 : (T_1 \cap T_2)$, and none of T_1 and $T_2 : (T_1^C \cap T_2^C)$ if applicable. This approach is finally generalized to $n > 2$ for vulnerabilities or threats.

For $n = 3$, such as in Moore and McCabe's coffee, tea, and cola drinkers problem [14, p. 355], the disjoint sets will constitute the following—only $V_1 : (V_1 \cap V_2^C \cap V_3^C)$, only $V_2 : (V_2 \cap V_1^C \cap V_3^C)$, only $V_3 : (V_3 \cap V_1^C \cap V_2^C)$, only V_1 and $V_2 : (V_1 \cap V_2 \cap V_3^C)$, only V_1 and $V_3 : (V_1 \cap V_3 \cap V_2^C)$, only V_2 and $V_3 : (V_2 \cap V_3 \cap V_1^C)$, all V_1, V_2, and $V_3 : (V_1 \cap V_2 \cap V_3)$, and none of V_1, V_2, and $V_3 : (V_1^C \cap V_2^C \cap V_3^C)$. All are now disjoint sets. Thus the 2^n rule (i.e., 4 for $n = 2$, and 8 for $n = 3$) holds for the number of disjoint sets both regarding V and T variables. Note that $P(T_1 \cup T_2) = P(T_1) + P(T_2) - P(T_1 \cap T_2)$, since the threats are no longer disjoint. If there are more than two outcomes, then $P(T_1 \cup T_2 \cup T_3) = P(T_1) + P(T_2) + P(T_3) - P(T_1 \cap T_2) - P(T_1 \cap T_3) - P(T_2 \cap T_3) + P(T_1 \cap T_2 \cap T_3)$. When two or three events are not disjoint, they may or may not be independent. But when disjoint, they are definitely dependent, given no null: $P(\phi) = 0$, or sure: $P(S) = 1$ sets (Figs. 4.14, 4.15, 4.16, 4.17, 4.18, 4.19, 4.20, 4.21, and 4.22).

Let $(n = 2)$ for vulnerabilities in Figure 4.14a and b. Also let

$P(v_1) = 0.65$
$P(v_2) = 0.55$

Then, $P(v_1 \cap v_2) = P(v_1) + P(v_2) - P(v_1 \cap v_2)$

$P(v_1 \cap v_2) = 0.2$ (v_1 and v_2 are nondisjoint)

(a)

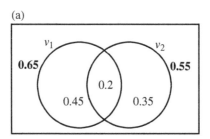

(b)

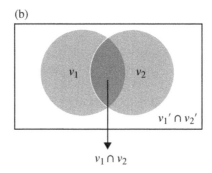

FIGURE 4.14 (a) Venn diagram for $n = 2$ for the given example. (b) General Venn diagram for $n = 2$.

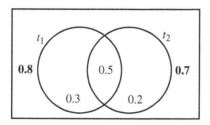

FIGURE 4.15   Venn diagram for $n = 2$ for the given example.

Since $P(v_1)$. $P(v_2) \neq P(v_1 \cap v_2)$, and v_1 and v_2 are dependent:

$$P\left(v_1 \cap v_2^c\right) = 0.45$$
$$P\left(v_2 \cap v_1^c\right) = 0.35$$
$$P\left(v_2 \cap v_1\right) = 0.2$$
$$P\left(v_2^c \cap v_1^c\right) = 0$$

Let $(n = 2)$ for threats in Figure 4.15. Also let

$P(t_1) = 0.8$
$P(t_2) = 0.7$

Then, $P(t_1 \cap t_2) = P(t_1) + P(t_2) - P(t_1 \cap t_2)$
$P(t_1 \cap t_2) = 0.5$ (t_1 and t_2 are nondisjoint)
$P\left(t_1 \cap t_2^c\right) = 0.3$; $P\left(t_2 \cap t_1^c\right) = 0.2$; $P\left(t_1^c \cap t_2^c\right) = 0$; $P(t_1)\ P(t_2) \neq P(t_1 \cap t_2)$, and t_1 and t_2 are dependent.

Let $(n = 3)$ for vulnerabilities in Figure 4.16a and b. Also let

$$P\left(v_1\right) = 0.55$$
$$P\left(v_2\right) = 0.45$$
$$P\left(v_3\right) = 0.45$$
$$P\left(v_1 \cap v_2\right) = 0.15$$
$$P\left(v_1 \cap v_3\right) = 0.25$$
$$P\left(v_3 \cap v_2\right) = 0.10$$
$$P\left(v_1 \cap v_2 \cap v_3\right) = 0.05$$
$$P\left(v_1 \cap v_2 \cap v_3^c\right) = 0.1$$
$$P\left(v_1 \cap v_3 \cap v_2^c\right) = 0.2$$
$$P\left(v_3 \cap v_2 \cap v_1^c\right) = 0.05$$
$$P\left(v_1 \cap v_2^c \cap v_3^c\right) = 0.2$$
$$P\left(v_2 \cap v_1^c \cap v_3^c\right) = 0.25$$
$$P\left(v_3 \cap v_2^c \cap v_1^c\right) = 0.15$$
$$P\left(v_1^c \cap v_2^c \cap v_3^c\right) = 0$$

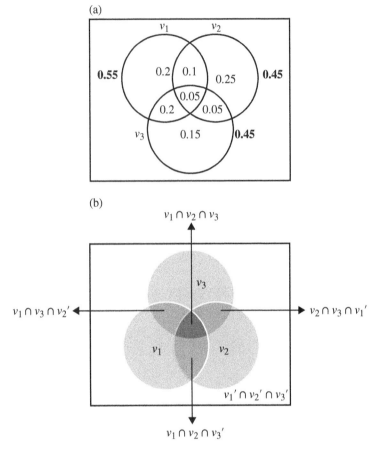

FIGURE 4.16   (a) Specific Venn diagram for the earlier $n = 3$ disjoint problem. (b) General Venn diagram for $n = 3$.

Let ($n = 3$) for threats in Figures 4.17. Also let

$$P(t_1) = 0.36$$
$$P(t_2) = 0.46$$
$$P(t_3) = 0.55$$
$$P(t_1 \cap t_2 \cap t_3^c) = 0.05$$
$$P(t_1 \cap t_3 \cap t_2^c) = 0.1$$
$$P(t_3 \cap t_2 \cap t_1^c) = 0.2$$
$$P(t_1 \cap t_2^c \cap t_3^c) = 0.2$$
$$P(t_2 \cap t_1^c \cap t_3^c) = 0.2$$
$$P(t_3 \cap t_2^c \cap t_1^c) = 0.24$$
$$P(t_1 \cap t_2 \cap t_3) = 0.01$$
$$P(t_1^c \cap t_2^c \cap t_3^c) = 0$$

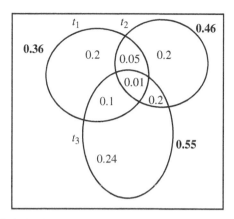

FIGURE 4.17 Specific Venn diagram for $n = 3$ disjoint problem.

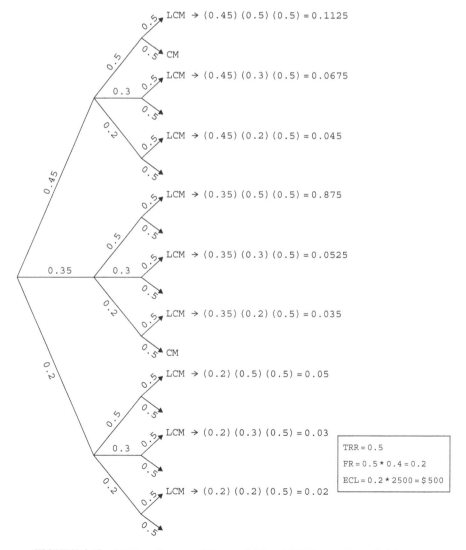

FIGURE 4.18 SM tree diagram of Figures 4.14 and 4.15 for $n = 2$ nondisjoint case.

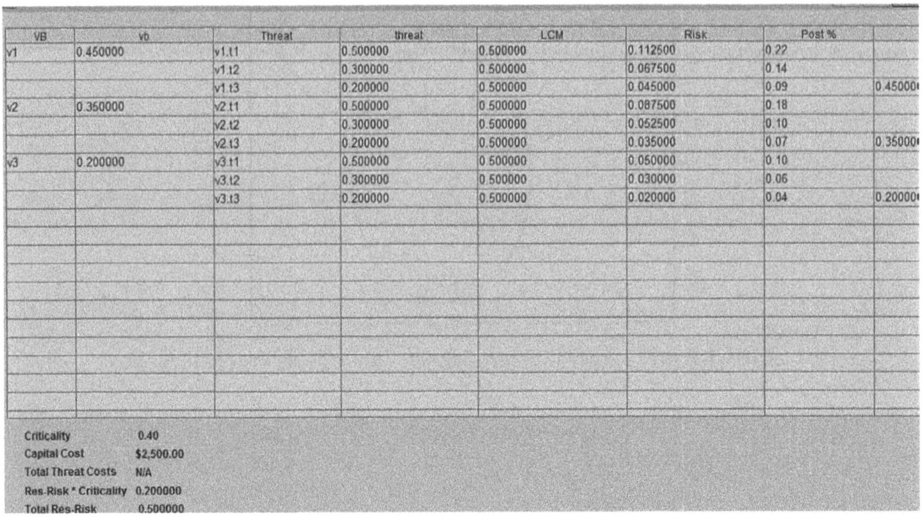

VB	vb	Threat	threat	LCM	Risk	Post %	
v1	0.450000	v1.t1	0.500000	0.500000	0.112500	0.22	
		v1.t2	0.300000	0.500000	0.067500	0.14	
		v1.t3	0.200000	0.500000	0.045000	0.09	0.450000
v2	0.350000	v2.t1	0.500000	0.500000	0.087500	0.18	
		v2.t2	0.300000	0.500000	0.052500	0.10	
		v2.t3	0.200000	0.500000	0.035000	0.07	0.350000
v3	0.200000	v3.t1	0.500000	0.500000	0.050000	0.10	
		v3.t2	0.300000	0.500000	0.030000	0.06	
		v3.t3	0.200000	0.500000	0.020000	0.04	0.200000

Criticality   0.40
Capital Cost $2,500.00
Total Threat Costs   N/A
Res.Risk * Criticality 0.200000
Total Res-Risk   0.500000

FIGURE 4.19 Security meter analysis to represent the tree diagram in Figure 4.18, both TRR = 0.5.

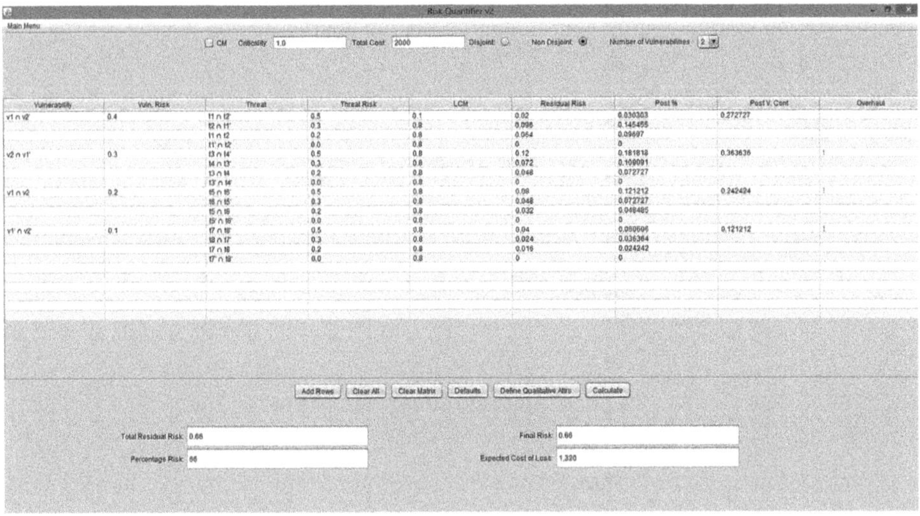

FIGURE 4.20 The Risk Quantifier software for an $n = 2$ nondisjoint converted into disjoint scenario for the following new example: *Input*: $P(v_1) = 0.6$, $P(v_2) = 0.5$, $P(v_1 \cap v_2) = 0.2$; $P(v_1' \cap v_2') = 0.0$. *Output*: $v_1 \cap v_2' = 0.6 - 0.2 = 0.4$; $v_2 \cap v_1' = 0.5 - 0.2 = 0.3$; $v_1 \cap v_2 = 0.2$; $v_1' \cap v_2' = 1 - (0.4 + 0.3 + 0.2) = 0.1$.

4.5 MAINTENANCE PRIORITY DETERMINATION FOR 3 × 3 × 2 SM

Software maintenance, as a general process of making changes to improve a system after its installation can involve (i) the adaptation of software to a new operating environment; (ii) the repair of software faults, ranging from coding errors, which are the cheapest to fix, to design errors, which are more expensive, and finally to requirement

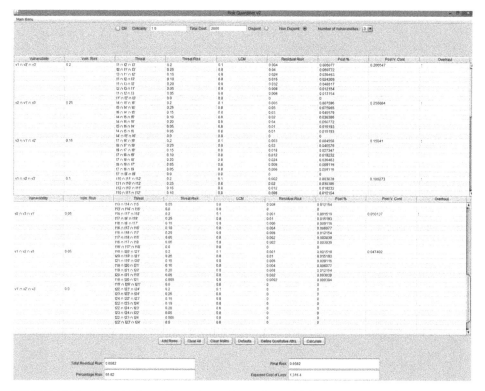

FIGURE 4.21 The Risk Quantifier software for $n = 3$ nondisjoint case converted into a disjoint for the following new *Input*: $P(v_1) = 0.55$; $P(v_2) = 0.45$; $P(v_3) = 0.45$; $P(v_1 \cap v_2 \cap v_3') = 0.15$; $P(v_1 \cap v_3 \cap v_2') = 0.25$; $P(v_2 \cap v_3 \cap v_1') = 0.10$; $P(v_1 \cap v_2 \cap v_3) = 0.05$; $P(v_1' \cap v_2' \cap v_3') = 0.0$. *Output*: $v_1 \cap v_2' \cap v_3' = 0.55 - 0.15 - 0.25 + 0.05 = 0.20$; $v_2 \cap v_1' \cap v_3' = 0.45 - 0.15 - 0.10 + 0.05 = 0.25$; $v_3 \cap v_1' \cap v_2' = 0.45 - 0.25 - 0.10 + 0.05 = 0.15$; $v_1 \cap v_2 \cap v_3' = 0.15 - 0.05 = 0.1$; $v_1 \cap v_3 \cap v_2' = 0.25 - 0.05 = 0.20$; $v_2 \cap v_3 \cap v_1' = 0.10 - 0.05 = 0.05$; $v_1 \cap v_2 \cap v_3 = 0.05$; $v_1' \cap v_2' \cap v_3' = 0.0$.

errors, which are the most expensive; and (iii) the addition or modification of the system's functionality due to internal and external factors such as changing laws and changing markets or business structures.

The method we propose addresses the first two items, corrective and adaptive actions, by providing a quantitatively comparative risk assessment technique. Software maintenance consumes up to 80% of most companies' software budgets and is thus the largest single contributor to high software costs [15]. Therefore research efforts have begun to integrate design and maintenance management policies to reduce unanticipated side effects [16]. *Corrective maintenance* identifies and corrects software performance and application failures, whereas *adaptive maintenance* adjusts the software conform to new data entries (Fig. 4.23).

The SM approach can provide a quantitative comparison and inform the analyst of a budgetary portfolio paving the way for repairing, maintaining, or replacing a module to determine the most cost-effective maintenance strategy [1, 7–11]. Using a single simulation trial, let us apply Bayesian principles to determine the vulnerability that

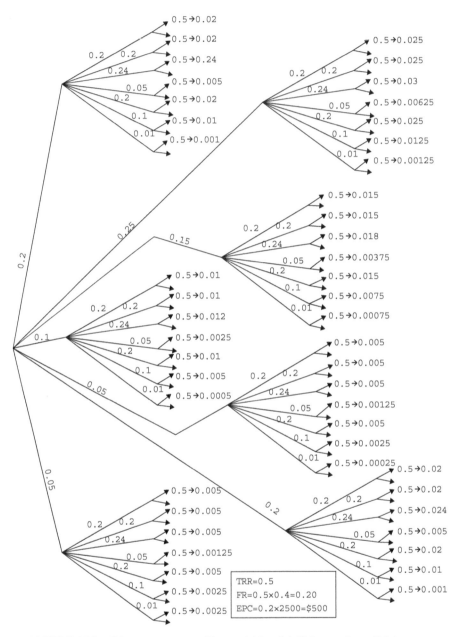

FIGURE 4.22 SM tree to represent Figures 4.16 and 4.17 for $n = 3$ nondisjoint case.

requires the most maintenance. Vulnerabilities that need more surveillance can be ranked from most to least severe through Bayesian analysis (Table 4.9). This is very useful for prioritization purposes saving time and effort in the vast arena of software maintenance [13].

Results Table

VB	vb	Threat	threat	LCM	Risk	Post %	Post vb	>
v1	0.200000	v1.t1	0.200000	0.500000	0.020000	0.04		
		v1.t2	0.200000	0.500000	0.020000	0.04		
		v1.t3	0.240000	0.500000	0.024000	0.05		
		v1.t4	0.050000	0.500000	0.005000	0.01		
		v1.t5	0.200000	0.500000	0.020000	0.04		
		v1.t6	0.100000	0.500000	0.010000	0.02		
		v1.t7	0.010000	0.500000	0.001000	0.00	0.200000	
v2	0.250000	v2.t1	0.200000	0.500000	0.025000	0.05		
		v2.t2	0.200000	0.500000	0.025000	0.05		
		v2.t3	0.240000	0.500000	0.030000	0.06		
		v2.t4	0.050000	0.500000	0.006250	0.01		
		v2.t5	0.200000	0.500000	0.025000	0.05		
		v2.t6	0.100000	0.500000	0.012500	0.02		
		v2.t7	0.010000	0.500000	0.001250	0.00	0.250000	
v3	0.150000	v3.t1	0.200000	0.500000	0.015000	0.03		
		v3.t2	0.200000	0.500000	0.015000	0.03		
		v3.t3	0.240000	0.500000	0.018000	0.04		
		v3.t4	0.050000	0.500000	0.003750	0.01		
		v3.t5	0.200000	0.500000	0.015000	0.03		
		v3.t6	0.100000	0.500000	0.007500	0.01		
		v3.t7	0.010000	0.500000	0.000750	0.00	0.150000	
v4	0.100000	v4.t1	0.200000	0.500000	0.010000	0.02		
		v4.t2	0.200000	0.500000	0.010000	0.02		
		v4.t3	0.240000	0.500000	0.012000	0.02		
		v4.t4	0.050000	0.500000	0.002500	0.00		
		v4.t5	0.200000	0.500000	0.010000	0.02		
		v4.t6	0.100000	0.500000	0.005000	0.01		
		v4.t7	0.010000	0.500000	0.000500	0.00	0.100000	
v5	0.050000	v5.t1	0.200000	0.500000	0.005000	0.01		
		v5.t2	0.200000	0.500000	0.005000	0.01		
		v5.t3	0.240000	0.500000	0.006000	0.01		
		v5.t4	0.050000	0.500000	0.001250	0.00		
		v5.t5	0.200000	0.500000	0.005000	0.01		
		v5.t6	0.100000	0.500000	0.002500	0.00		
		v5.t7	0.010000	0.500000	0.000250	0.00	0.050000	
v6	0.200000	v6.t1	0.200000	0.500000	0.020000	0.04		
		v6.t2	0.200000	0.500000	0.020000	0.04		
		v6.t3	0.240000	0.500000	0.024000	0.05		
		v6.t4	0.050000	0.500000	0.005000	0.01		
		v6.t5	0.200000	0.500000	0.020000	0.04		

VB	vb	Threat	threat	LCM	Risk	Post %	Post vb	>
		v6.t6	0.100000	0.500000	0.002500	0.00		
		v6.t7	0.010000	0.500000	0.000250	0.00	0.050000	
v6	0.200000	v6.t1	0.200000	0.500000	0.020000	0.04		
		v6.t2	0.200000	0.500000	0.020000	0.04		
		v6.t3	0.240000	0.500000	0.024000	0.05		
		v6.t4	0.050000	0.500000	0.005000	0.01		
		v6.t5	0.200000	0.500000	0.020000	0.04		
		v6.t6	0.100000	0.500000	0.010000	0.02		
		v6.t7	0.010000	0.500000	0.001000	0.00	0.200000	
v7	0.050000	v7.t1	0.200000	0.500000	0.005000	0.01		
		v7.t2	0.200000	0.500000	0.005000	0.01		
		v7.t3	0.240000	0.500000	0.006000	0.01		
		v7.t4	0.050000	0.500000	0.001250	0.00		
		v7.t5	0.200000	0.500000	0.005000	0.01		
		v7.t6	0.100000	0.500000	0.002500	0.00		
		v7.t7	0.010000	0.500000	0.000250	0.00	0.050000	

Criticality	0.40
Capital Cost	$2,500.00
Total Threat Costs	N/A
Res-Risk * Criticality	0.200000
Total Res-Risk	0.500000
Expected Cost of Loss	$500.00

Optimize

FIGURE 4.23 Security meter analysis to represent the tree diagram in Figure 4.22.

TABLE 4.9 A Priori Existence and A Posteriori Defective Probabilities of Figure 4.21

| Vulnerability | Contributed to Overall Risk (Percentage) | | Maintenance Priority |
	Initially (prior) (%)	Currently (posterior)	
V_1	50	$P(v_1/v_1^c) = 0.5605$	More (than initially)
V_2	30	$P(v_2/v_2^c) = 0.2556$	Less (than initially)
V_3	20	$P(v_3/v_3^c) = 0.1838$	Less (than initially)

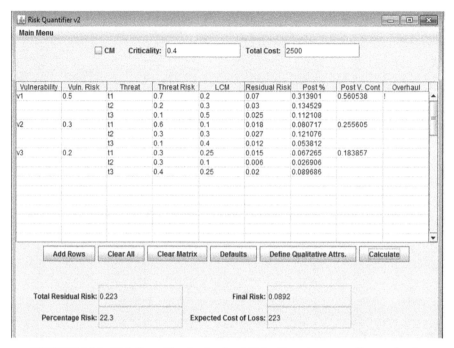

FIGURE 4.24 Risk Quantifier for 3 × 3 × 2 SM with maintenance (! = overhaul).

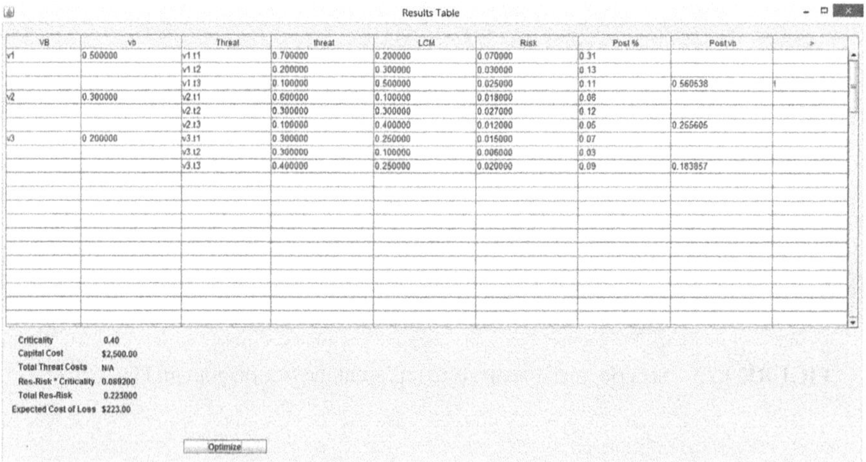

FIGURE 4.25 Security meter analysis for a 3 × 3 × 2 SM as in the Risk Quantifier.

The model proposed is supported by an MC-SIM, which provides a purely quantitative alternative to conventional qualitative models. Let us ask a Bayesian-type question as it relates to our maintenance problem. What is the probability that the office computer software risk is due to chance (e.g., fire, hardware) or is malicious (e.g., virus, hacking)? Another example for the same tree diagram is as follows (Figs. 4.24, 4.25, and 4.26).

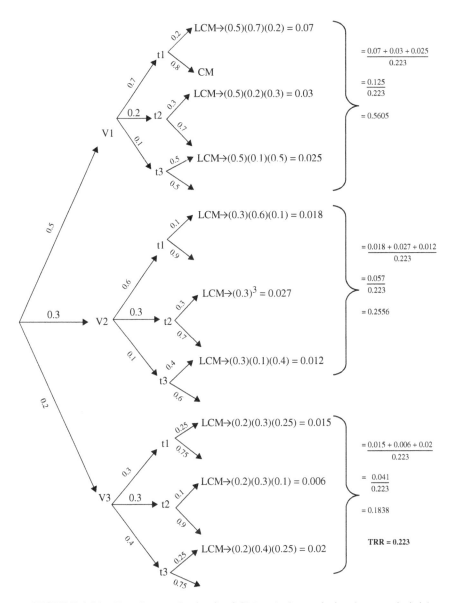

FIGURE 4.26 Tree diagram for 3 × 3 × 2 SM to depict a priori and a posteriori risks.

4.6 PRIVACY METER (PM): HOW TO QUANTIFY PRIVACY BREACH

This section examines the quantification of the lack of privacy similar to quantifying the lack of security. The Privacy Meter (PM) is a math–statistical inferential method through which the likelihood of breach of trust is computed by employing compound Poisson processes. Then, how the privacy risk is managed and mitigated in a quantitative solution through a solid budgetary approach is illustrated. This approach is superior to the conventional descriptive or averaging privacy measures. Some argue that the strong sense of security implies less personal privacy. Others argue that security attacks could not have happened without identity thefts, which point to the lack of privacy [17]. Therefore the consensus is that a sense of security is needed for the privacy of citizen information in daily life [18]. Else put, security is the external shield of the internal world of privacy. Security is tangible, whereas privacy is generally intangible and abstract. So far, quantification of the privacy, or its lack thereof, has only been at the level of spreadsheets and tabulations finding averages and means or percentages [19].

This section outlines a technique to conduct a simple statistical inference to calculate and manage the likelihood of lack of privacy. To quantify and estimate the likelihood of the breach of privacy, one can only be data-specific depending on the source of breach. The breach of privacy can be defined differently at varying locations and conditions including the time and circumstances that dictate the event. Protecting information privacy and fair use of information are complementary where personal data must be protected from unauthorized exposure; this information is used in a fair manner in the economy as a pillar of corporate security [20].

Given a set of data on privacy invasions as in the case of phishing, spoofing, tampering, bots, worms, trojans, and other social engineering sorts of malicious malware, the objective is to estimate the probability (likelihood) of the count of breaches in a given period of time under the conditions encountered [21, 22]. Once the distribution is accomplished, then the cumulative and survival probability functions can be estimated to respond to questions such as the probability of encountering less than or more than a given number of privacy breaches.

Since the rate of breach is not constant throughout the time period, and also the breaches may occur in clusters rather than single outcomes, the nature of the nonhomogeneous Poisson process (NHPP) is a special case. A Java program will illustrate how to calculate the exact probability density and then the cumulative probability and finally the survival (the complement of the cumulative) probability.

4.6.1 Methodology

In repairable systems, repair actions take place in response to the observed failures and the system is returned to the field as good as new. A stochastic model could be experiencing a constant failure rate (CFR), an increasing failure rate (IFR), or a decreasing failure rate (DFR). In a homogeneous Poisson process (HPP), or Poisson, there are no trends and the rate is CFR. The compound Poisson modeling is as follows [23, 24]:

$$\Pr\{N(t)=n\} = \frac{(\lambda t)^n e^{-\lambda t}}{n!}, \quad n = 0,1,2,\ldots,\infty \tag{4.4}$$

$$E(N(t)) = \mathrm{Var}[N(t)] = \lambda t \tag{4.5}$$

If there are no trends in the failure data, it is defined to be a renewal process where the interarrival times may come from any independent identical distributed (i.i.d.) $T_i \sim F(\cdot)$ where $F(\cdot)$ is finite. In the case of NHPPs, there are trends like DFR or IFR where

$$\Pr\{N(t)=n\} = \frac{[\Lambda(t)]^n}{n!} e^{-\Lambda(t)}, \quad n = 0,1,2,\ldots,\infty \tag{4.6}$$

For an interval starting at s and ending at $s + t$,

$$\Pr\{N(t+s) - N(s) = n\} = \frac{\left[\Lambda(t)\right]^n}{n!} e^{-\Lambda(t)} \tag{4.7}$$

where

$$\left[\Lambda(t)\right]^n = \left\{\int_s^{t+s} \mu(x)\,dx\right\}^n \tag{4.8}$$

$$E\left[N(t)\right] = \int_s^{t+s} \mu(x)\,dx \tag{4.9}$$

Further, there may occur more than a single breach at an interval for the NHPP where the size of events at each interval is represented by a compound Poisson process. That is, if the governing process is NHPP, and the size of clusters is geometric with forgetfulness property, the compound Poisson is Poisson^geometric. If, otherwise, the outcomes within a cluster are correlated assuming a compounding probability mass function of logarithmic series, then the CP is defined to be Poisson^logarithmic series or a negative binomial.

4.6.2   Privacy Risk-Meter Assessment and Management Examples

Each financial company or organizational entity can adopt a modified version of this PM model to fit their. In-house running realities are so far that the estimation and mitigation of privacy risk are a key challenge. Due to the practical functionality of the PM software illustrated earlier, the assessment and management of risk in these simple exercises can be extended to more complicated cases given the correct input data to represent the problem accurately at hand. A set of recorded privacy breaches stemming from phishing activity at a government control center in South Korea obtained by the Korean Information Security Agency (Korean CERT) regarding nine different days in May 2006 are as follows: 14, 32, 28, 25, 21, 34, 20, 48, and 28. Note: M (total) = 250, q (variance/mean) = 2.46 [25].

We plan to conduct this experiment by employing a Poisson^LSD (negative binomial), which is a very close alternative to Poisson^geometric where the outcomes in each of nine clusters in the Korean CERT example are assumed to be independent of each other. For when the reverse is assumed to hold true, such that the outcomes are correlated, then the nonhomogeneous compound Poisson^geometric process will not be valid and will not yield an accurate or valid output.

Therefore, that of the Poisson^LSD or NBD (negative binomial) will be used [13] as in the examples below. The following software results are given in Table 4.10. There is a negligible difference between the Poisson^geometric and NBD in terms of software results for large values such as in these examples. Therefore NBD will be used in this example for the conservative scenario of correlated outcomes (Fig. 4.27).

If the company or agency sets a threshold after which the privacy is violated such as $X = 260$ breaches, then the probability of X equal to or exceeding 260, that is,

TABLE 4.10 Probability Tables (Before the Countermeasures Are Taken)

X (# Losses)	Exact Density $f(x)$	Cumulative $P(x)$	Survival $S(x)$
259	0.01255	0.6379	0.3620
260	0.01238	0.6504	0.3496
261	0.01219	0.6625	0.3374

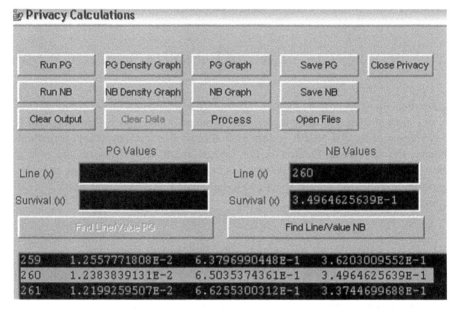

FIGURE 4.27 Privacy Meter (PM) calculations tabulated in Table 4.10.

TABLE 4.11 Probability Table (After the Countermeasures Are Applied)

X (# Losses)	Density $f(x)$	Cumulative $P(x)$	Survival $S(x)$
259	0.000469	0.9954	0.00450
260	0.000428	0.9959	0.00407
261	0.000390	0.9963	0.00368

$P(X \geq 260) = 0.3496 \approx 35\%$. See Table 4.10. Assume now that the company (e.g., bank) or agency wishes to conduct a privacy risk management exercise, through buying certain antiphishing or antipiracy software or else contracting with a software security firm for auditing and probing services to assess and mitigate the privacy risk. For the sake of experimentation, we wish to assess if the said company accomplished its goals a specific time period later. Suppose that the bank has overall spent $0.5 million (or $500,000) to assure successful privacy risk mitigation. Now, after the CMs are taken, the bank collects a new 9-day period data: {14, 32, 28, 25, 19, 24, 22, 22, 04} and runs a new data analysis with $M = 190$, $q = 3.19$. See Table 4.11 for the improved case [23].

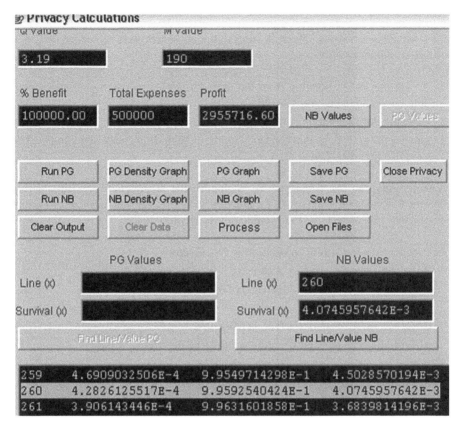

FIGURE 4.28 Privacy Meter (PM) calculations tabulated in Table 4.11.

After the CMs are taken, $P(X \geq 260) = 0.0041 \approx 0.4\%$. The risk defined by the bank has been mitigated by a margin of 34.56% to a low of 0.4% from a high of 34.96%. The risk has been mitigated by a solid 34.56%, amounting to a benefit of $34.56 \times \$100,000 = \$3,456,000$, if each 1% slot on the average signifies a benefit of $100,000 in avoiding identity thefts. Overall, the bank is profiting almost $3.5 million from this transaction, that is, by not losing from future identity thefts and privacy breaches, since the $3.45 million benefit advantages clearly exceed the $500,000 cost for improvement. The subsequent calculations are shown in Table 4.2.

Profit = benefit−cost = $100(0.3496 − 0.004074) × 100,000 (benefit) −$500,000 (cost) = $2,955,716 (or $2,955,716.60 to be exact by the software, which calculates the competing plans as in Fig. 4.28).

4.7 POLISH DECODING (DECOMPRESSION) ALGORITHM

The objective is to generate a reverse-coded reliability block diagram from the Polish notation and recreate the original topology generated by the RBD compression algorithm. The platform used is Java. This diagram helps view complex network paths from an ingress to an egress node, and it ultimately calculates the system reliability for series–parallel reducible networks. The following is the approach taken to recreate the RBD from a given Polish notation:

1. Accept the Polish notation from the user. The Polish notation consists of nodes (numbers) and operators (* or +).
2. Parse the Polish notation to identify the nodes and operations.
3. Identify the node pairs that connect. Use the existing Java components and the node pairs that are identified to draw the RBD.

A stack algorithm was employed to accomplish the aforementioned. The algorithm accepts the Polish notation and parses the notation using Java's StringTokenizer. To identify the node pairs that connect, the following logic was incorporated:

1. Push into the stack until an operator is encountered.
2. If the operator is a * (nodes in series):
   a. Pop the top two elements (nodes) of the stack.
   b. Form a node pair.
   c. Concatenate the nodes and node pairs.
   d. Push the concatenated string onto the top of the stack.
3. If the operator is a + (nodes in parallel):
   a. Pop the top two elements (nodes) of the stack.
   b. Concatenate the operator between the two nodes.
   c. Push the concatenated string on to the top of the stack.
4. Continue performing the foregoing steps until the end of the Polish notation.

After the node pairs are identified, the graphical Java components FC oval (nodes) and FC line (transmissions or connecting links) display the network. Networks utilizing links were deployed using the same algorithmic process. Negative digits, which designate transmission lines, will first be represented as nodes. Once the initial diagram has been generated, a second process will essentially remove the oval object, which represents a node, leaving the negative node name as the transmission line. The smallest node number is the ingress; the largest one is the egress node.

A more complex non-series–parallel commercial telephony network (with 19 nodes and 32 links) whose Polish notation was previously coded is reverse-coded or decoded in Figure 4.29 to reconstruct the original topology. Note that the hard-to-read "Polish notation" box is a page-long Polish notation obtained previously and inserted using the compression algorithm. Although the Polish notation cannot calculate the exact source–target reliability for non-series–parallel networks, it can successfully encode and decode any non-series–parallel or simple network for a secure transport. The Polish notation approach also prepares a base for calculating the exact reliability for any complex system utilizing a hybrid enumeration approach. Figure 4.29 denotes all nodes and links invariably with a sample reliability of 0.99 for place holding and $s = 1$, $t = 19$.

However, these postscripts (Polish notation) do not carry information on the node and link reliabilities. Therefore, converting the topology with all the attached input

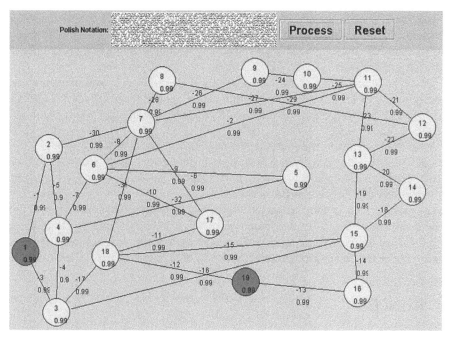

FIGURE 4.29 Decoding (reverse Polish) process for a complex 32-node network.

data into an XML file is an alternative solution and has been done by this author. Exporting and then importing the same XML file as a means for transportation will be efficient but not necessarily secure, as the XML files can be opened. If the topology is of prime interest, decoding algorithm is of value to transport very complex networks safely and discreetly with extremely complicated Polish notations hard to decipher such as in Figure 4.29. Note the unusual length and complexity of the Polish notation box for a 32-node network.

4.8 DISCUSSIONS AND CONCLUSION

The incentives for evaluating security risks are so compelling and indispensable that we should and could, rather than might, be making meaningful estimates [26–28]. In this section, we examined new scientific ways to estimate and infer probabilities: empirically by observing the frequencies of outcomes and by calculating losses associated with security outcomes [13]. In this way, we are kept informed about the extent of the cost of bringing hardware and software systems to a desirable percentage of security. The difficulty in data collection and parameter estimation pose a challenge to practitioners in the testing field.

The author has employed the concept of a simple relative frequency approach, otherwise known as a counting technique [29]. Although we cannot predict the outcome of a random experiment, we can for large values of N (hence the law of large numbers) predict the relative frequency, which is the number of desirable events divided by the sample size, with which the outcome will be included within a desirable set [30]. Different forms of complexity in the SM are studied with plenty of examples.

The PM is a math–statistical inferential method through which the likelihood of a breach of trust is computed using compound Poisson processes. Then, how the privacy risk is managed and mitigated in a quantitative solution through a solid budgetary approach is illustrated.

This approach is superior to the conventional descriptive or averaging privacy or security measures [31]. A similar approach can be applied to security risk assessment. The Java-coded software tools in the CyberRiskSolver website will prove practical and useful.

Aside from calculating the source–target reliability of any complex system, it is shown that the *Polish notation* constructed from a graphical interface using postfixes to describe the topology of any complex network is useful for identifying a given topology. Furthermore, the output can then be transported, for reasons of security or saving storage space, to a remote analyst, who in turn, using this algorithm, can reverse engineer a given Polish notation in a decoding algorithm proposed to reconstruct the topology. Both forward (encoding) and reverse (decoding) algorithms work for both simple series–parallel and non-series–parallel, (i.e., complex) networks. Networks of various complexities are examined.

4.9 EXERCISES

4.9.1 As discussed with the CVSS scoring earlier in the chapter, you need to state two different outcomes and your two inputs. Also, see the supplement to find two other scoring systems on the web. You need to demo how it works with each citing an example screenshot regarding your own desk or laptop's security risk metric. Cite the three advantages and disadvantage of each metric and why? Compare the SM approach with those of the other approaches given in different sources, that is, attack trees, capabilities-based attack trees, etc., in terms of the advantages and disadvantages, studying analytical calculations and economical interpretations if any.

4.9.2 (a) Given the following vulnerabilities, threats, and LCM for a main server, calculate by hand and then using the related software:

1. Power failure: 0.2; threats: 0.35, 0.65; LCM_{11}: 0.3; LCM_{12}: 0.4
2. High speed: 0.2; threats: 0.4, 0.2, 0.4; LCM_{21}: 0.4; LCM_{22}: 0.1; LCM_{23}: 0.25
3. Hardware failure: 0.1; threats: 0.3, 0.7; LCM_{31}: 0.25; LCM_{32}: 0.15
4. Software failure: 0.10; threats: 0.25, 0.25, 0.50; LCM_{41}: 0.25; LCM_{42}: 0.4; LCM_{43}:0.4
5. Other reasons: 0.40; threats: 0.3, 0.7; LCM_{51}: 0.2; LCM_{52}: 0.15

Assume criticality = 1.00; capital cost = $1000.00

Calculate

Residual risk =

Final risk =

Expected cost of loss =

Total residual risk =

Which vulnerability needs to be overhauled with first priority? Show by hand calculations using Bayesian principles (without doing any game-theoretic optimization).

V_1 postcontribution =
V_2 postcontribution =
V_3 postcontribution =
V_4 postcontribution =
V_5 postcontribution =

Using the same topology as earlier, fit as closely as you can qualitatively using $H = 0.7$, $M = 0.5$, $L = 0.3$, and $W = 0.2$, do by hand calculations, and get the RR.

(b) Using the course software (Risk Quantifier in the CyberRiskSolver), verify your solution for (a), by finally mitigating the RR by 10% and attaching your results to your electronic file as well as to your doc file.

4.9.3 Essay Questions (in 4 to 5 ordinary length sentences).

Network security and reliability metrics are useful and crucial for the next generation of cyber-security risk assessment and management in the ever-changing cyber world? Give an example to recap.

Why are digital forensics and cyber-security inseparable and complementary different halves of the same apple? Give an example to recap.

Is safety an inherent software attribute; if not, should it be? Are reliability and safety the same? Give an example where they contradict each other.

Are software security, reliability, and privacy of equal value? What optimal percent would you rather have from each? Show a case where privacy is low and security or reliability is high. Can you think of a combined aggregate metric that encapsulates all for a cybersystem and information system by giving an example?

4.9.4 The following number of breaches has been recorded on ATM machines' software in Montgomery for a regional bank in 2 months (8 weeks):

14, 30, 25, 25, 20, 15, 20, 20

Using the privacy risk software, do the following:

Spend $1M (million) for total investment within the next year and then you get the following new episodes after the investment for another 8 weeks:

10, 25, 25, 25, 10, 15, 10, 15

If each 1% improvement pays back $100,000, does the bank profit or gain at the end of this expenditure? Supported by your hand calculations as well, use the software to verify your results. For the solution below, verify the software results with your hand calculations.

Verify solution as follows (Fig. 4.30):

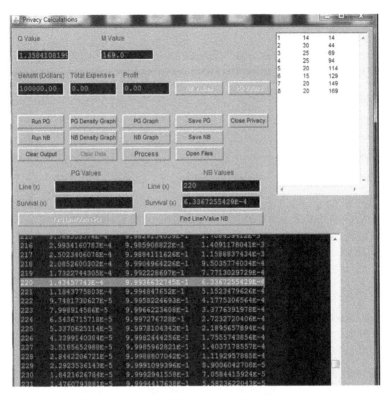

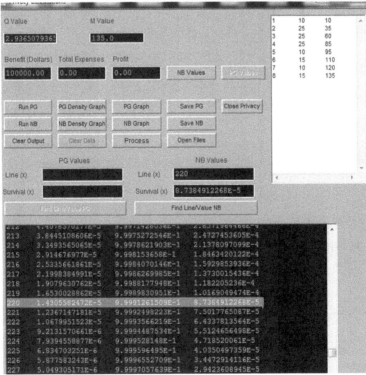

FIGURE 4.30 Three screenshots to be continued for Problem 4.9.4.

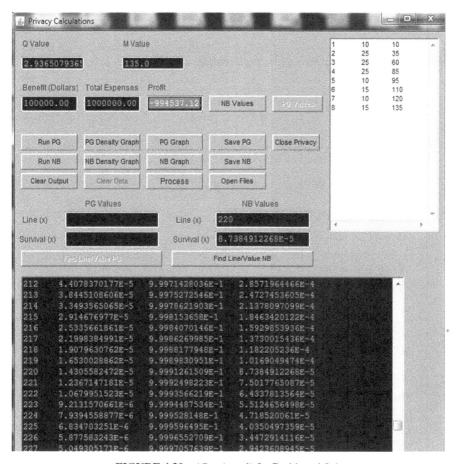

FIGURE 4.30 (*Continued*) for Problem 4.9.4.

4.9.5 SM modified for purely qualitative data: Using Figure 4.6 on a quantitative SM in the chapter, design and calculate a feasible SM design with qualitative data for your PC in a $3 \times 3 \times 2$ setup.

4.9.6 SM modified for hybrid data: Using Figure 4.6, design and calculate a feasible SM design with hybrid data for your PC in a $3 \times 3 \times 2$ setup.

4.9.7 Basic SM for personal and office computers: (a) You are expected to collect for your PC (as in Fig. 4.6) SM design in a two by two SM design or articulate and create data to best estimate your risk. Assuming a criticality of 0.5 and a capital cost of \$2000, calculate the ECL. (b) Proceed as in part (a), but this time, do the same for your office computer and calculate your RR and the ECL.

4.9.8 Modified (for qualitative attributes) SM for your home and office PC: Do the same as in 4.9.7. This time use H (high), M (medium), L (low), and W (rare) making sure that your risk values obey the laws of probability.

4.9.9 SM for your personal and office computers' maintenance planning.

Repeat Exercise 4.9.7, however this time by employing the Bayesian principles. Decide which vulnerabilities need a higher priority, and why?

4.9.10 SM for your personal and office computer-dependent vulnerabilities: Repeat Exercise 4.9.6, however this time employing statistical principles on nondisjointness ($n = 2$) for both vulnerability and threat simultaneously (Fig. 4.6).

4.9.11 General questions about the SM:

(a) If one of the pillars of information security is nonrepudiation, what are the others?

(b) State three of the CMs against hacking and virus at your home office.

(c) Suppose that the following probabilities are given for the vulnerability of loss of e-mail files (0.8) and fire hazard (0.2) at your home computer. Threats against your e-mail system are due to a virus attack (0.6) and hacking (0.4), against both of which an encryption code is equally installed as well as a firewall (0.9). For fire, threats are from the close-by forest (0.3) and old electrical wires of the office (0.7). CM probabilities against both threats are weak at 0.30. The whole setup is in a highly critical scenario (0.95). This office is worth $100,000; how much do you risk losing due to the case study? Use required formulas and be exact. Which vulnerabilities need the highest priority for repair?

4.9.12 More on the SM: Write an Excel program to mimic the SM spreadsheets shown in Table 4.12 and obtain the correct risk results. Assume criticality = 0.3 and capital cost = $2000, and verify total residual risk = 0.28 and ECL = ($2000) (0.28)(0.3) = $168.

4.9.13 SM modified with nondisjoint vulnerabilities and nondisjoint threats: Given Figure 4.6 ($2 \times 2 \times 2$) for both vulnerabilities and threats, use nondisjointness concept when the following risks hold true: (a) $P(V_1) = 0.60$, $P(V_2) = 0.40$, $P(V_1 \cap V_2) = 0.20$, $P(V_1' \cap V_2') = 0.20$; (b) $P(V_1) = 0.55$, $P(V_2) = 0.65$, $P(V_1 \cap V_2) = 0.15$; and (c) $P(V_1) = 0.55$, $P(V_2) = 0.65$, $P(V_1 \cap V_2) = 0.25$. Choose the threat values same as the vulnerabilities and LCM values such as $LCM_1 = 0.2$, $LCM_2 = 0.4$, $LCM_3 = 0.5$, $LCM_4 = 0.3$ (Table 4.13).

TABLE 4.12 Home Computer Network SM Input

Vulnerability	Threat	Countermeasure/Lack of Countermeasure
Power failure: 0.2	1. Loss of data: 0.75	1. Backup generator: 0.6
	2. Hardware failure: 0.25	2. Surge protector: 0.1
Unfavorable high speed: 0.3	1. Virus: 0.5	1. Antivirus software: 0.2
	2. Intrusion: 0.5	2. Firewall: 0.2
Hardware failure: 0.2	1. Loss of data: 0.75	1. Data backup: 0.6
	2. System down: 0.25	2. Alternate laptop: 0.1
Software failure: 0.3	1. Lack of operation: 1.0	1. Software backup: 0.1

TABLE 4.13   Input and Output Table For Exercise 4.9.13

Vulnerability		Threat		LCM	
V1	0.55	t1	0.50	LCM 1	0.45
V2	0.45	t2	0.40	LCM 2	0.30
V3	0.40	t3	0.40	LCM 3	0.20
V1n V2	0.15	t1n t2	0.20	LCM 4	0.50
V1n V3	0.25	t1nt3	0.10	LCM 5	0.40
V2n V3	0.10	t2nt3	0.20	LCM 6	0.50
V1n V2n V3	0.05	t1 t2nt3	0.05	LCM 7	0.25
V1'n V2'nV3'	0.00	t1'n t2'nt3'	0.00	LCM 8	0.40

Non Dis-Joint		Non Dis-Joint		

Continue   Non DisJoint ⇒
Continue   DisJoint ⇒

OUTPUTS

V1n V2n V3	0.05	t1n t2nt3	0.05	LCM 1	0.45
V1n V2nV3'	0.10	t1n t2nt3'	0.15	LCM 2	0.30
V1n V3nV2'	0.20	t1n t3nt2'	0.05	LCM 3	0.20
V3n V2nV1'	0.05	t3n t2nt1'	0.15	LCM 4	0.50
V1n V2'nV3'	0.20	t1n t2'nt3'	0.25	LCM 5	0.40
V2n V1'nV3'	0.25	t2n t1'nt3'	0.05	LCM 6	0.50
V3n V1'nV2'	0.10	t3n t1'nt2'	0.15	LCM 7	0.25
V1'n V2'nV3'	0.05	t1'n t2'nt3'	0.15	LCM 8	0.40

4.9.14   SM modified with dependent vulnerabilities and threats:

(a) Apply the following initial probabilities to your derivations in Exercise 4.9.12 for $n = 3$ $P(V_1) = 0.55$, $P(V_2) = 0.45$, $P(V_3) = 0.40$, $P(V_1 \cap V_2) = 0.15$, $P(V_1 \cap V_3) = 0.25$, $P(V_2 \cap V_3) = 0.10$, and $P(V_1 \cap V_2 \cap V_3) = 0.05$.

(b) Do as in part (a) but replace the Vs by Ts.

(c) Apply to both Vs and Ts at the same time.

(d) Apply this time $P(V_1) = 0.55$, $P(V_2) = 0.25$, $P(V_3) = 0.45$, $P(V_1 \cap V_2) = 0.15$, $P(V_1 \cap V_3) = 0.25$, $P(V_2 \cap V_3) = 0.10$, and $P(V_1 \cap V_2 \cap V_3) = 0.10$. Anything wrong with the input data, why or why not? What changed?

Solution (a, b, c): Left to the student or reader.

The following output will show when the "continue nondisjoint" is clicked (Table 4.14) for Solution (d):

4.9.15   SM risk management:

(a) Verify the earlier mentioned results by using a hand calculator and an Excel program.

(b) Apply a risk management algorithm to mitigate your total RR to lower to (1) 25%, (2) 20%, (3) 15%, (4) 10%, and (5) 5% from 30% RR by determining break-even points when you spend Y per 1% improvement

TABLE 4.14   Input and Output Table For Exercise 4.9.14

Risk Quantifier

Criticality 0.40   Total Cost $2,500.00

Vulnerability	Vuln. Risk	Threat	Threat Risk	LCM	Residual Risk		Post Vulnerability
V1n V2'nV3'	0.20	t1'n t2'n t3'	0.25	0.45	0.0225		
		t2'n t1'n t3'	0.05	0.30	0.0030		
		t3n t1'n t2'	0.15	0.20	0.0060		
		t1'n t2n t3'	0.15	0.50	0.0150		
		t1'n t3n t2'	0.05	0.40	0.0040		
		t3n t2n t1'	0.15	0.50	0.0150		
		t1'n t2n t3	0.05	0.25	0.0025		
		t1'n t2'n t3'	0.15	0.40	0.0120		0.200
V2n V1'nV3'	0.25	t1'n t2'n t3'	0.25	0.45	0.0281		
		t2n t1'n t3'	0.05	0.30	0.0038		
		t3n t1'n t2'	0.15	0.20	0.0075		
		t1'n t2n t3'	0.15	0.50	0.0188		
		t1'n t3n t2'	0.05	0.40	0.0050		
		t3n t2n t1'	0.15	0.50	0.0188		
		t1'n t2n t3	0.05	0.25	0.0031		
		t1'n t2'n t3'	0.15	0.40	0.0150		0.250
V3n V1'nV2'	0.10	t1'n t2'n t3'	0.25	0.45	0.0113		
		t2n t1'n t3'	0.05	0.30	0.0015		
		t3n t1'n t2'	0.15	0.20	0.0030		
		t1'n t2n t3'	0.15	0.50	0.0075		
		t1'n t3n t2'	0.05	0.40	0.0020		
		t3n t2n t1'	0.15	0.50	0.0075		
		t1'n t2n t3	0.05	0.25	0.0013		
		t1'n t2'n t3'	0.15	0.40	0.0060		0.100
V1n V2nV3'	0.10	t1n t2'n t3'	0.25	0.45	0.0113		
		t2n t1'n t3'	0.05	0.30	0.0015		
		t3n t1'n t2'	0.15	0.20	0.0030		
		t1'n t2n t3'	0.15	0.50	0.0075		
		t1'n t3n t2'	0.05	0.40	0.0020		
		t3n t2n t1'	0.15	0.50	0.0075		
		t1'n t2n t3	0.05	0.25	0.0013		
		t1'n t2'n t3'	0.15	0.40	0.0060		0.100
V1n V2n V3	0.05	t1n t2'n t3'	0.25	0.45	0.0056		
		t2n t1'n t3'	0.05	0.30	0.0008		
		t3n t1'n t2'	0.15	0.20	0.0015		
		t1'n t2n t3'	0.15	0.50	0.0038		
		t1'n t3n t2'	0.05	0.40	0.0010		
		t3n t2n t1'	0.15	0.50	0.0038		
		t1'n t2n t3	0.05	0.25	0.0006		
		t1'n t2'n t3'	0.15	0.40	0.0030		0.050
V1'n V2'nV3'	0.05	t1n t2'n t3'	0.25	0.45	0.0056		
		t2n t1'n t3'	0.05	0.30	0.0007		
		t3n t1'n t2'	0.15	0.20	0.0015		
		t1'n t2n t3'	0.15	0.50	0.0038		
		t1'n t3n t2'	0.05	0.40	0.0010		
		t3n t2n t1'	0.15	0.50	0.0038		
		t1'n t2n t3	0.05	0.25	0.0006		
		t1'n t2'n t3'	0.15	0.40	0.0030		0.050

⬅ BACK

Total Residual Risk	0.40
Final Risk	0.16
Expected Cost of Loss	400.00

(Continued)

TABLE 4.14   (Continued)

Risk Quantifier		
Criticality	**0.40**	Total Cost	**$2,500.00**

Vulnerability	Vuln. Risk	Threat	Threat Risk	LCM	Residual Risk		Post Vulnerability
V1n V2'nV3'	0.20	t1n t2'nt3'	0.15	0.45	0.0135		
		t2n t1'nt3'	0.25	0.30	0.0150		
		t3n t1'nt2'	0.10	0.20	0.0040		
		t1'n t2nt3'	0.10	0.50	0.0100		
		t1'n t3nt2'	0.20	0.40	0.0160		
		t3n t2nt1'	0.05	0.50	0.0050		
		t1'n t2nt3	0.05	0.25	0.0025		
		t1'n t2'nt3'	0.10	0.40	0.0080		0.2000
V2n V1'nV3'	0.05	t1'n t2'nt3'	0.15	0.45	0.0034		
		t2n t1'nt3'	0.25	0.30	0.0038		
		t3n t1'nt2'	0.10	0.20	0.0010		
		t1'n t2nt3'	0.10	0.50	0.0025		
		t1'n t3nt2'	0.20	0.40	0.0040		
		t3n t2nt1'	0.05	0.50	0.0013		
		t1'n t2nt3	0.05	0.25	0.0006		
		t1'n t2'nt3'	0.10	0.40	0.0020		0.0500
V3n V1'nV2'	0.15	t1'n t2'nt3'	0.15	0.45	0.0101		
		t2n t1'nt3'	0.25	0.30	0.0113		
		t3n t1'nt2'	0.10	0.20	0.0030		
		t1'n t2nt3'	0.10	0.50	0.0075		
		t1'n t3nt2'	0.20	0.40	0.0120		
		t3n t2nt1'	0.05	0.50	0.0038		
		t1'n t2nt3	0.05	0.25	0.0019		
		t1'n t2'nt3'	0.10	0.40	0.0060		0.1500
V1n V2nV3'	0.10	t1'n t2'nt3'	0.15	0.45	0.0068		
		t2n t1'nt3'	0.25	0.30	0.0075		
		t3n t1'nt2'	0.10	0.20	0.0020		
		t1'n t2nt3'	0.10	0.50	0.0050		
		t1'n t3nt2'	0.20	0.40	0.0080		
		t3n t2nt1'	0.05	0.50	0.0025		
		t1'n t2nt3	0.05	0.25	0.0013		
		t1'n t2'nt3'	0.10	0.40	0.0040		0.1000
V1n V3nV2'	0.20	t1'n t2'nt3'	0.15	0.45	0.0135		
		t2n t1'nt3'	0.25	0.30	0.0150		
		t3n t1'nt2'	0.10	0.20	0.0040		
		t1'n t2nt3'	0.10	0.50	0.0100		
		t1'n t3nt2'	0.20	0.40	0.0160		
		t3n t2nt1'	0.05	0.50	0.0050		
		t1'n t2nt3	0.05	0.25	0.0025		
		t1'n t2'nt3'	0.10	0.40	0.0080		0.2000
V3n V2nV1'	0.05	t1'n t2'nt3'	0.15	0.45	0.0034		
		t2n t1'nt3'	0.25	0.30	0.0038		
		t3n t1'nt2'	0.10	0.20	0.0010		
		t1'n t2nt3'	0.10	0.50	0.0025		
		t1'n t3nt2'	0.20	0.40	0.0040		
		t3n t2nt1'	0.05	0.50	0.0013		
		t1'n t2nt3	0.05	0.25	0.0006		
		t1'n t2'nt3'	0.10	0.40	0.0020		0.0500
V1n V2n V3	0.05	t1'n t2'nt3'	0.15	0.45	0.0034		
		t2n t1'nt3'	0.25	0.30	0.0038		
		t3n t1'nt2'	0.10	0.20	0.0010		
		t1'n t2nt3'	0.10	0.50	0.0025		
		t1'n t3nt2'	0.20	0.40	0.0040		
		t3n t2nt1'	0.05	0.50	0.0013		
		t1'n t2nt3	0.05	0.25	0.0006		
		t1'n t2nt3'	0.10	0.40	0.0020		0.0500
V1'n V2'nV3'	0.20	t1'n t2'nt3'	0.15	0.45	0.0135		
		t2n t1'nt3'	0.25	0.30	0.0150		
		t3n t1'nt2'	0.10	0.20	0.0040		
		t1'n t2nt3'	0.10	0.50	0.0100		
		t1'n t3nt2'	0.20	0.40	0.0160		
		t3n t2nt1'	0.05	0.50	0.0050		
		t1'n t2nt3	0.05	0.25	0.0025		
		t1'n t2'nt3'	0.10	0.40	0.0080		0.2000
					Total Residual Risk	0.37	
					Final Risk	0.15	

⬅ BACK

Vulnerability	Threat	CM LCM	Residual Risk
0.35	0.48	0.7	
		0.3	0.0504
	0.16	0.42	
		0.58	0.03248
	0.32	0.7	
		0.3	0.0336
	0.04	0.8	
		0.2	0.0028
0.14	0.32	0.7	
		0.3	0.01344
	0.02	0.7	
		0.3	0.00084
	0.66	0.97	
		0.03	0.002772
0.51	0.32	0.7	
		0.3	0.04896
	0.59	0.7	
		0.3	0.09027
	0.09	0.46	
		0.54	0.024786

Total Residual Risk	0.300348
Total Residual Risk Percentage	30.03%

Final Risk = Residual Risk x Criticality	
Final Risk = (0.3003) (0.5)	0.150174

ECL = Final Risk x Capital Cost	
ECL= (0.150174) ($8,000.00)	$1,201.39

of the risk by improving CM devices. Calculate the optimal $Y and Δ ECL for b (1) to b (5) to accomplish these objectives.

(c) Repeat (a), using $3 per 1% improvement of the CM devices. What is the new Δ ECL and percentage mitigation achieved in the RR?

4.9.16 See Figure 2.4 in Chapter 2 (19-node network) and verify as in Figure 4.29 by decoding through reverse Polish notation process for a complex network.

4.9.17 Describe in short sentences the following terms: 1) Bot infection, 2) Spam Relay 3) Worm/Virus, 4) Security Incident (Computer Virus, Logic/mail bomb, Denial of Service, Adware/Spyware), 5) Trojan, 6) Phishing Transit Point, 7) Spoofing, 8) Simple Intrusion Attempt, 9) Web-defacement.

4.9.18 Using RSA (Rivest, Shamir and Adelman) and El Gamal Encryption Schemes, devise two examples of encrypting and decrypting a given number (a letter in the alphabet) similar to the examples shown in Appendix 3. **a)** Take H = 8th letter and Q = 17th letters in the English alphabet for RSA to encrypt and decrypt it. **b)** Take P = 16th letter and Q = 17th letters in the English alphabet for El Gamal to encrypt and decrypt it.

4.9.19 Given the following $M = 250$ for incidences of nine separate privacy breaches at a financial center, {14, 32, 28, 25, 21, 34, 20, 48, 28} compute the risk of exceeding 220 breaches using NB method assuming correlated outcomes within a cluster respectively. For the benchmark of 220 breaches, in order to mitigate the risk down to an improved level of approximately 10%, calculate the cost and benefit balance if per 1% mitigation, the bank saves $100,000. NOTE: The bank pays $3,000,000 for an annual contract with a firm to oversee the remedial countermeasures taken. The bank's May 2007 improved anti-phishing activity, {X_i = 14, 32, 28, 25, 21, 34, 20, 48, 28}; q = (Variance/Mean) = 3.463.

REFERENCES

[1] Sahinoglu, M. (2005). Security meter—a practical decision tree model to quantify risk, *IEEE Security and Privacy*, **2005**, 3, 18–24.

[2] Forni, E. (2002). *Certification and Accreditation*, AUM Lecture Notes, DSD (Data Systems Design) Labs, http://www.dsdlabs.com/security.htm.

[3] Gollman, D. (2006). *Computer Security*, 2nd Ed., John Wiley & Sons, Inc., Hoboken.

[4] Schneier, B. (1995). *Applied Cryptography*, 2nd Ed., John Wiley & Sons, Inc., http://www.counter pane.com.

[5] Capabilities-Based Attack Tree Analysis, http://www.attacktrees.com.

[6] Time to Defeat (TTD) Model, www.blackdragonsoftware.com.

[7] Rohatgi, V. K. (1976). *An Introduction to Probability Theory and Mathematical Statistics*, Wiley, New York, 141.

[8] Sahinoglu, M. (2008). An input-output measurable design for the security meter model to quantify and manage software security risk, *IEEE Transactions on Instrumentation and Measurement*, **57**(6), 1251–1260.

[9] Sahinoglu, M. (2005). Security-meter model–a simple probabilistic model to quantify risk, *55th Session of the International Statistical Institute*, Sydney, Australia, Conference Abstract Book, 163.

[10] Sahinoglu, M. (2005). Quantitative risk assessment for software maintenance with Bayesian principles, *International Conference on Software Maintenance*, Budapest, Hungary, ICSM Proc. II, 67–70.

[11] Sahinoglu, M. (2006). Quantitative risk assessment for dependent vulnerabilities, *The International Symposium on Product Quality and Reliability (52nd Year), Proc. RAMS06*, New Port Beach, CA.

[12] Sahinoglu, M., Yuan, Y.-L., Banks, D. (2010). Validation of a security and privacy risk metric using triple uniform product rule, *IJCITAE—International Journal of Computers, Information Technology and Engineering*, **4**(2), 125–135.

[13] Sahinoglu, M. (2007). *Trustworthy Computing: Analytical and Quantitative Engineering Evaluation*, John Wiley & Sons, Inc., Hoboken.

[14] Moore, D. S., Mc Cabe, G. P. (2003). *Introduction to the Practice of Statistics*, 4th Ed., W. H. Freeman Co., New York.

[15] Swanson, E. B., Beath, C. M. (1990). Departmentalization in software development and maintenance. *Communications of the ACM*, **33**(6), 658–667.

[16] Parikh, G. (1986). *Handbook of Software Maintenance*, John Wiley & Sons, Inc., New York.

[17] Rifon, N. J. (2005). Michigan State University. www.ippsr.msu.edu/Documents/Forum Presentations/May05Rifon.pdf.

[18] Singewald, A. J. J. T. (2006). Information privacy in EU, in *Proceedings (in Power Point) of international conference on the digital information industry*, 3–22, Seoul, Korea, November 14–15, 2006.

[19] Lee, J. (2006). Digital Rights Quantification for Digital Rights Management, *Proceedings (in Power Point) of International Conference on the Digital Information Industry*, 575–581, Seoul, Korea, November 14–15, 2006.

[20] Beomsoo, K. (2006). Complementarity between protecting information privacy and the fair use of information, in *Proceedings (in Power Point) of International Conference on the Digital Information Industry*, 311–329, Seoul, Korea, November 14–15, 2006.

[21] Sahinoglu, M. (2006). A universal quantitative risk assessment design to manage and mitigate, in *Proceedings (in Power Point) of International Conference on the Digital Information Industry*, 333–405, Seoul, Korea, November 14–15, 2006.

[22] Sahinoglu, M. (2006). Time-independent security-meter design to quantify risk and time-dependent stochastic model to quantify lack of privacy, Invited Seminar, Department of ECE, University of Massachusetts, Amherst, MA; December 8, 2006.

[23] Sahinoglu, M. (2007). Statistical inference to quantify and manage risk of privacy, in *Proceedings of the 56th Session of the International Statistical Institute (ISI), Session 22 (S80: Risk)*, Lisbon, Portugal; ISI Book of Abstracts, August 2007, 506.

[24] Sahinoglu, M. (2009). Can we quantitatively assess and manage the risk of software privacy breaches, *IJCITAE—International Journal of Computers, Information Technology and Engineering*, **3**(2), 189–191.

[25] Korea Information Security Agency, Seoul, Korea, www.krcert.or.kr

[26] Blakley, B., McDermott, E., Geer, D. (2001). Information Security is Information Risk Management, in *Proceedings of the 2001 Workshop on New Security Paradigms (NSPW'01)*, 97–104.

[27] Cybenko, G. (2006). Why Johnny can't evaluate security risk, *IEEE Security and Privacy*, **4**(5), 5.

[28] Landoll, D. (2006). *The Security Risk Assessment Handbook*, Auerbach Publications, Boca Raton.

[29] Cochran, W. G. (1970). *Sampling Techniques*, 3rd Ed., John Wiley & Sons, Inc., New York.

[30] Hogg, R. V., Craig, A. T. (1970). *Introduction to Mathematical Statistics*, 3rd Ed., Macmillan Pub. Co., New York, Library of Congress Catalog Card No: 74-77968.

[31] Mowbray T. J. (2014). *Cybersecurity*, John Wiley & Sons, Inc., Indianapolis, 46256.

5

GAME-THEORETIC COMPUTING IN CYBER-RISK

> **LEARNING OBJECTIVES**
>
> - Describe the concept of game-theoretic computing with its advantages and disadvantages and its relevance to cyber-risk informatics, engineering, and science.
> - Explore the innovative and newly popular theme of game-theoretic risk computing applications in the cyber-security risk management, citing challenges and advantages.
> - Study a cross section of game-theoretic implementation to a variety of disciplines.
> - Examine cost and benefit scenarios with multidisciplinary-themed risk assessment and management for engineering, business, cyber-security, ecology, healthcare, and others.

5.1 HISTORICAL PERSPECTIVE TO GAME THEORY'S ORIGINS

According to Shubik, the disciplines most heavily involved in the utilization of game theory have been management science and operations research, psychology, education, political science, sociology, engineering, computer science, economics, and the military [1]. The usage of game-theoretic risk computing is steadily increasing in the world of cyber-risk informatics. It is a critical topic because security and privacy, as well as availability and usability, determine the trustworthiness of cybersystems and cyber information.

The origins of game theory, which is the mathematical study of conflict situations as a science of rational conflict, are well known [2]. It was, for all intents and purposes, reborn in 1944 as an established field with the publication of a pioneering book, *Theory of Games and Economic Behavior* by John von Neumann and O. Morgenstern, which proposed that most economic questions could be analyzed as games and first laid out the finite two-person zero-sum game [3].

Cyber-Risk Informatics: Engineering Evaluation with Data Science, First Edition. Mehmet Sahinoglu.
© 2016 John Wiley & Sons, Inc. Published 2016 by John Wiley & Sons, Inc.
Companion website: www.wiley.com/go/sahinoglu/informatics

The 1944 book arrived just about or even a few years before linear programming (LP) methods came upon the scene in 1947 as developed by George Dantzig who worked in close connection with the *Theory of Games and Economic Behavior* authors.

The theoretical underpinnings were originally proposed by the French mathematician Emile Borel about 1921 as noted in Ref. [4]. Borel's theory was successfully analyzed by J. von Neumann who proved its key premise, the minimax theorem in 1928.

Neumann and Morgenstern in 1944 defined the minimax solution and showed that this solution exists in all two-player zero-sum games in which the interests of players are diametrically opposed with no common interest. Therefore, Dantzig's simplex method became an important tool for both practical and theoretical investigations of the theory of matrix games (so-called two-person zero-sum games) in game theory. Six years later in 1950, Nash proposed what became known as the Nash equilibrium (NE) as a means of extending game-theoretic analyses known as no-zero-sum games.

Nash determined a steady-state solution that no other player can outsmart [5]. Even before 1944, the first studies of games in the economics literature were the works by Cournot in 1838 [6], Bertrand in 1883 [7], and Edgeworth in 1897 [8a, b] on the pricing and production of an oligopoly, which is a market or an industry dominated by a small number of sellers.

Game playing is an unlimited topic in scope as old as ancient human history. Although its first seeds were planted in the latter part of the nineteenth century, the popularity of game theory skyrocketed in the twentieth century. This was a period of devastating wars and conflicts that required urgently smart solutions with the advent of transistor-led electronics and further the vast computer storage space and unprecedented computational speed.

In the twenty-first century, cyber hacking, espionage, and terrorism produced a dire necessity to employ gaming solutions to outsmart hostile adversaries, instead of the previous century's invading troops or bombarding warplanes. In retrospect, the first human hunters were involved in game solutions against their enemies, that is, other hunters and carnivorous animals, who played the same game, all of whom and which to satisfy hunger and quench thirst as basic necessities of life itself.

Today, gaming may mean many things to different people, such as gambling or simulation or politics and warfare. The major investments in research, in terms of both time and other resources, have been made through military or business or education support. In the nineteenth century, the models of Cournot and Bertrand viewed the strategies of players as simply their choices of outputs and prices.

One of the insights of von Neumann and Morgenstern in the middle of a new twentieth century was that the strategies of a game could also include more complex plans for contingent reconciliatory actions. For example, "I'll cut my price tomorrow, if you cut yours today." Selten, an Esperantist and the foremost proponent of Esperanto language and the 1994 Nobel laureate awarded for equilibrium notions in dynamic games in 1965 [9a, b], and Harsanyi in 1967 introduced concepts widely used in recent years [10].

Harsanyi proposed a way in which all players know the payoff functions of the other players, to model situations of incomplete information where the players are unsure of one another's payoffs. Harsanyi's Bayesian NE is precisely the NE of the imperfect-information representation of the game and is the cornerstone of game-theoretic analyses as noted in Ref. [11, p. 210].

Nash, Harsanyi, and Selten shared the Nobel Prize in Economics in 1994. According to Osborne and Rubinstein [12a, b], game theory is a bag of analytical tools to help understand the phenomena that we observe when decision makers interact, whereby the models of game theory are highly abstract representations of classes of real-life situations. This means game theory uses mathematics to express its ideas formally, but mathematical results are interesting only if they are confirmed by human intuition.

In short, game theory deals with decisions in conflict situations. Interest in game theory as a science of rational conflict is extremely widespread in our age of competition, strategy, and gamesmanship. "Does Game Theory Work?" asks Binmore and responds that game theory does not work in the laboratory [13].

People don't play NE and they don't use their maximin or minimax strategies in two-person zero-sum games. But who can claim and guarantee that any theory can work in all environments, just as Newton's laws of motion were modified by Einstein's relativity theory in the twentieth century [10]?

Therefore, game theory can't be reasonably expected to work in unfavorable environments in which its tacit assumptions have no chance whatsoever of being true. To the eye of the game theorist, there exist four essential elements, for instance, in a chess or poker game: (i) two players, (ii) opposite interests, (iii) finite game, and (iv) no surprises [14, 15]. However, modern game theory has stretched its limits to new concepts by Aumann (rational expectations) [16], Kadane (subjective probability) [17], and more.

Aumann writes: (i) If the game is not two-person zero-sum, even if there is just one NE, it's not clear what players should expect as payoff in an n-person game. (ii) NE is a solution for strategic games, but rational expectations are more fundamental for the one-shot game if not repeated.

5.2   APPLICATIONS OF GAME THEORY TO CYBER-SECURITY RISK

Cybersystems security that did not exist as a discipline when game theory debuted has recently evolved into a complex and challenging field. The area of cyber network defense mechanism design has been receiving immense attention from the research community for more than two decades ever since the first Internet message was delivered thanks to the Defense Advanced Research Projects Agency (DARPA) research sponsorship, www. darpa.mil. However, the cyber-security problem remains far from solution. Scientists are researching the application of game-theoretic approaches to address security issues, and some of these approaches look promising.

The goal of much ongoing research is to manage cybersystems against malicious cyber-attacks by using game theory and computationally intensive algorithms. The initial papers, among many others, specifically on game-theoretic risk analysis, started appearing a decade ago not long after the tragic events of 9/11 in 2001 [18]. This trend continued in 2002 as applied to information warfare by Hamilton and Saydjari et al. [19a, b].

Concurrently, the role of trust and game strategies as implemented for network security by Lye and Wing [20] appeared. In the following, Cavusoglu et al. [21] and Patcha and Park wrote on IT security and mobile networks, respectively [22]. In 2005, Jormakka and Mölsä published their pioneering paper titled "Modeling information warfare as a game" where they hypothesized a scenario titled "Terrorist Game: Bold Strategy Can Result in Domination" with NE [23].

Sahinoglu also in 2005 pioneered with his quantitative and hybrid security meter (SM) computational model [24] at the risk assessment stage to be followed up by a risk management stage [25]. His findings were followed by other pertinent game-theoretic risk applications [26–30].

After 2004, research on adversarial risk analysis (ARA) has continued until the present time due to a growing interest in countering terrorism [31, 32]. Massive Stackelberg security games [33, 34], decision-theoretic rough sets [35], and attack–defense models, which were oriented to network security risk assessment, are a few of the works in search of a working algorithm to quantify and manage risk [36, 37].

From 2009 to 2011, multiple papers were published by a group of game-theoretic researchers on defense-related game theory [38–45]. Luo et al. in 2010 published a non-cooperative nondynamic game scenario with incomplete information [46]. Recently, problems in counterterrorism and corporate competition have prompted applied research that attempts to combine math–statistical risk analysis with game theory in ways that support practical decision making. Wang and Bank's latest article applies these methods of ARA to the problem of selecting a route through a network, in which an opponent chooses certain vertices for ambush [47].

However, recently well-proposed methods have fallen short of framing and transforming theorems into working expert systems or software programs to generate solid results that are commercially viable and cost-efficient. Game theory, therefore, is a branch of applied mathematics that attempts to analytically model the rational behavior of intelligent agents in strategic situations, in which an individual's success depends on the decisions of others.

While initially developed to analyze competitions in which one individual does better at another's expense, it recently evolved into techniques for modeling a wide class of interactions, characterized by multiple criteria [12a, b].

5.3 INTUITIVE BACKGROUND: CONCEPTS, DEFINITIONS, AND NOMENCLATURE

Game Theory: A branch of mathematics, devoted to the logic of decision making in social or political interactions and concerned with the behavior of decision makers whose decisions affect each other. Note each decision maker has only partial control over the outcome.

Game theory is a generalization of decision theory where two or more decision makers compete by selecting each of the several strategies, while decision theory is essentially a one-person game theory. In general, any game involves the following:

Players: An individual or a group of individuals can be considered a player such as individuals or teams, companies, political candidates, and contract bidders.

Actions (Strategies): The set of moves available to choose from for each player.

Outcomes: An outcome in a game is the act of each player choosing a move from its action set so that numerical payoffs reflecting these preferences can be assigned to all players for all outcomes.

Preferences: Each player prefers some outcome to others based on payoffs or utilities associated with these outcomes. The combination of rivaling strategies establishes the game's worth to the competing players. Game-theoretic computing in the past is implemented, occasionally, heuristically, and inadvertently, to scenarios in which teams (including sports!), companies, political factions, contract bidders and even warring armies, and offender-defender-related cyber-wars, usually in "two-player zero-sum" games that this chapter will suffice to examine. In spite of its name, game theory is not specifically concerned with recreation and pastimes (like children's games), and a less misleading name would have been the theory of interdependent decision making, but it is too late to rename game theory without risking even worse confusion [46].

A simple example will help to provide an intuitive understanding of the kinds of social interactions involving interdependent decision making, which falls within the purview of game theory. We will start with the most popular two-player zero-sum games.

Zero-sum means that the gain (or loss) for one player is equal to the loss (or gain) for the other player with diametrically opposite interests. In other words, what one player wins becomes what the other player loses.

5.3.1 A Price War Example

Two retail companies are each trying to carve out a larger slice of a market for which they compete. Each has to decide on a strategy in ignorance of the other's decisions whether or not to (i) increase advertising for its product, or (ii) provide quantity discounts, or (iii) extend warranty terms.

We will demonstrate a two-player zero-sum game and its solution for the two companies competing for market share. A payoff table showing the percentage gain in the market share for Company A for each combination of strategies is shown in Table 5.1. Any gain in market share for Company A is a loss in market share for Company B because it is a zero-sum game [48, 49]. Minimax strategy exists if maximum (of row minimums)=minimum

TABLE 5.1 Modified Payoff Table Showing the % Gain (Loss) in Market Share for Firm A (B)

A/B	% Increase Advertising: b_1	% Quantity Discounts: b_2	% Extended Warranty: b_3	Row Minimum
% Increase advertising a_1	4	3	2	2 = Maximin
% Quantity discounts a_2	−1	4	1	−1
Extended warranty a_3	5	−2	5(0)	−2
Column maximum	5	4 = Minimax	5(2) = Minimax	*Result*: Solution is for Firm A to raise advertising (a_1) and for Firm B to extend warranty (b_1) by 2%

Firm A's market share will increase by 2%. Firm B's shall decrease by 2%.

Note: 2% ≠ 4%; a pure strategy does not exist initially. It is not optimal for each firm to predict and select a pure strategy regardless of what the other does. By trial and error, optimal solution is a balanced strategy (maximin = minimax = 2).

(of column maximums). The game is said to have a saddle or an equilibrium point. A game has a pure strategy solution when the players cannot improve their payoff by changing to a different strategy. What to do when pure strategy does not exist?

5.3.1.1 Identifying an Optimal Mixed Strategy Solution With a mixed strategy, each player selects its strategy according to a probability distribution. In the market share example in Table 5.1, each company will first determine an optimal probability distribution for selecting whether to increase advertising provide quantity discounts or extend warranty. Then, when the game is played, each company will use its probability distribution to randomly select one of its three strategies. Now consider the game from the point of view of Company B to select one of its strategies based on the following probabilities: PB_1 (to select strategy b_1), PB_2 (to select strategy b_2), and PB3 (to select strategy b_3). Since the objective of Company B is to minimize its expected loss, LOSSB, we have the following LP model. One can guess that the value of the game will be between 2 and 4% in Table 5.1 before solving the mixed strategy problem as follow:

PB_1, PB_2, PB_3, LOSSB ≥ 0, where Min LOSSB, subject to (s.t.):

$$4PB_1 + 3PB_2 + 2PB_3 - LOSSB \Leftarrow 0 \left(\text{strategy } a_1\right)$$
$$-1PB_1 + 4PB_2 + 1PB_3 - LOSSB \Leftarrow 0 \left(\text{strategy } a_2\right)$$
$$5PB_1 - 2PB_2 + 5PB_3 - LOSSB \Leftarrow 0 \left(\text{strategy } a_3\right)$$
$$PB_1 + PB_2 + PB_3 = 1;$$

Solve LP model by using the management scientist by Ref. [48]:

$PB_1 = 0$, $PB_2 = 0.375$, $PB_3 = 0.625$, LOSSB $= 2.375$ (objective function value).

5.3.1.2 Results of the Two-Player Mixed Strategy Game Firm B's optimal mixed strategy is to provide quantity discounts (b_2) with probability 0.375 and extend warranty (b_3) with probability 0.625 and should not increase advertising b_1 with probability 0. Expected loss of market share for Firm B of this mixed strategy is 2.375% or a gain of 2.375% for Firm A. This tableau is in equilibrium. Firm B (or A) cannot improve the game by changing the B's (A's) probabilities. The expected B loss (or A gain) of this mixed strategy is an in-between value of 2.375%, which is better than Firm B's best pure strategy (b_2) with minimax, 4% of share in the payoff table, or A's maximin, 2%.

Other solutions to games exist besides two-player zero-sum strategy for maximin = minimax [48, 50, 55] as follow:

(a) Backward induction (solution concept for extensive form games): Steps similar to Bellman's dynamic programming are as follows: (i) Determine the optimal choices in the final stage K for each history h^K. (ii) Go back to stage $K-1$, and determine the optimal action for the player on the move there, given the optimal choice for stage K. (iii) Roll back until the initial stage is reached [48, Chap. 18; 59, p. 23, 43].

(b) NE (solution concept for normal form games): In summary, the game solution theory we review has two components. First, each player chooses her/his action according to the model of rational choice, given her belief about the other player's actions. Second, every player's belief about the other players' actions is correct. These two components are embodied in the following definitions.

Definition 1

An action profile $a*$ with the property that no player i can do better by choosing an action different from a_i^* given that every other player j adheres to a_j^*. NE of a strategic game is an action profile in which every player's action is optimal given every other player's action [12a, p. 22]. It is a steady state of an idealized situation. Expressed differently, NE embodies a stable social norm: If everyone else adheres to it, no individual wishes to deviate from it. NE provides a powerful solution concept for security games. At NE, the players cannot improve their outcome by altering their decision unilaterally while others play their NE strategy. Using a new notation, we can restate the condition for an action profile $a*$ to be an NE as follows.

Definition 2

The action profile $a*$ in a strategic game with ordinal preferences is an NE if, for every player i and every action a_i of player i, $a*$ is at least as good as according to player i's preferences as the action profile $(a_i, a* - 1)$ [12a, b, p. 23]. Player i chooses a_i; every other player j chooses a_j^*.

Equivalently, for every player i, $U_i(a*) \geq U_i(a_i, a* - 1)$ for every action a_i of player i, where U_i (U for utility) is a payoff function that represents player i's preferences. This definition implies neither that a strategic game necessarily has NE nor that it has at most one. Examples in this section will show that some games have a single NE, some possess none, and others have plenty NE. NE as a much broader concept is achieved if an operation point is reached where each player is giving her best response facing her opponents' strategies. For none of the players, there is a unilateral incentive to change her strategy, given that the strategy chosen by all opponents are fixed. Namely, each player's strategy is a best reply to the strategies of the others [51].

(c) Mixed strategy of probabilities in contrary to two-player zero-sum solution for strategic games: Risk management with a mixed strategy is examined as an alternative to two-player zero-sum solution if one does not exist. A pure strategy provides a complete definition of how a player will play a game as in a two-player zero-sum solution. In particular, it determines the move a player will make for any situation she could face. A player's strategy set is the set of pure strategies available to that player. A mixed strategy is an assignment of a probability to each pure strategy or a probability distribution over the player's actions. This allows for a player to randomly select a pure strategy. Since probabilities are continuous, there are infinitely many mixed strategies available to a player, even if their strategy set is finite. One can regard a pure strategy as a degenerate case of a mixed strategy, in which that particular pure strategy is selected with probability 1 and every other strategy with probability 0. Not all two-player zero-sum games have a saddle point minimax = maximin, as is shown in Table 5.2 where we observe that minimax ≥ maximin i.e. 20 > −10 [1].

Von Neumann extended the concept of both saddle point and strategy by considering probability mixes of strategies called mixed strategies. Von Neumann also argued that the correct play for Person 1 in a game such as shown in Table 5.2 would be to use a random device (such as coin or pair of dice) to generate the appropriate odds. In this case, select strategy 1 with a probability of 3/8 and strategy 2 with a probability of 5/8. For example,

TABLE 5.2   Two-Player Mixed Strategy Game Example

Column →		1	2	Row min
Row ↓		$\beta = 5/8$	$1 - \beta = 3/8$	↓
1	$\alpha = 3/8$	20	−30	−30
2	$1 - \alpha = 5/8$	−10	20	−10
Col max	→	20	20	

in a 2×2 setting against any strategy of Person 2, this gives Person 1 an expected gain in a scenario where right risks are chosen as in Table 5.2 to assure NE proven in Section 5.3:

$$(3/8)(20) + (5/8)(-10) = 5/4 \text{ (against 1 of Person 2)},$$
$$(3/8)(-30) + (5/8)(20) = 5/4 \text{ (against 2 of Person 1)}.$$

We plan to implement a varying range of mixed strategy solutions, including an NE scenario, as a steady state to see the impact so as to compare with a two-player zero-sum solution. A mixed strategy equilibrium predicts that the outcome of a game is stochastic, so that for a single play, its prediction is less precise than that of a pure strategy. How the NE solutions may be derived for several examples as alternatives to the conventional mixed strategy will be illustrated next.

5.4   RANDOM SELECTION FOR NASH MIXED STRATEGY

Defender decides whether to use selection combination or not. Adversary decides whether to game the combination or the single classifier. We will use random probabilistic selection based on random primitive as a defense against gaming of the selector. Let us consider a static game in mixed strategies where both players randomize between the two options by solving the game for optimal randomization probability for each player. Game theory is one of the possible ways to study information warfare with mathematical models. *Modeling Information Warfare as a Game* by Jormakka and Mölsä [24] presents four example games, which illustrate the different requirements for an effective playing strategy in information warfare. These games determine how a bold playing strategy can lead to domination, how a mixed playing strategy can reduce domination, how it can be useful to play a dominating strategy only part of the time, and how excessive domination can lead to rebels where all playing parties lose. If the loss of one player is precisely the same as the gain of the other for each branch of the game, then the game is defined to be zero-sum (otherwise non-zero-sum), often described by a matrix game. A nonzero sum finite two-player game is called a bimatrix game. Each matrix entry represents the cost and gain of the attacker and defender for their respective actions.

5.4.1   Random Probabilistic Selection

The possible NE involving mixed strategies can be found by differentiating payoff functions as follows:

α = the probability of adversary gaming the selector

β = the probability of classifier using the selection combination

Expected cost of the payoff matrix:

$$\Pi_C = \alpha\beta c_{11} + (1-\alpha)\beta c_{12} + \alpha(1-\beta)c_{21} + (1-\alpha)(1-\beta)c_{22}$$

NE (α, β) can be obtained by solving the simultaneous equations $\dfrac{\partial \Pi_C}{\partial \alpha}$ and $\dfrac{\partial \Pi_C}{\partial \beta}$ for continuous variables α and β. The application of differential calculus to Table 5.2 to determine the optimal multipliers for NE:

$$\Pi_C = \alpha\beta(20) + \alpha(1-\beta)(-30) + (1-\alpha)\beta(-10) + (1-\alpha)(1-\beta)20$$

$$\frac{\partial \Pi_C}{\partial \alpha} = \beta(20) + (1-\beta)(-30) + \beta(10) - 20 + \beta(20) = 0 \,(\text{Eq.1})$$

$$\frac{\partial \Pi_C}{\partial \beta} = \alpha(20) + \alpha(30) + (1-\alpha)(-10) - 20 + \alpha(20) = 0 \,(\text{Eq.2})$$

Solution: $\alpha = 3/8$; $\beta = 5/8$, same as the mixed strategy of probabilities selected randomly in Table 5.2.

5.4.2 Does Nash Equilibrium (NE) Exist for the Company A/B Problem in Table 5.1?

No, it does not. The following is a battery of analyses with Nash differential equations:

$$\Pi_C = \alpha_1\beta_1(4) + \alpha_1\beta_2(3) + 2\alpha_1(1-\beta_1-\beta_2) + \alpha_2\beta_1(-1) + \alpha_2\beta_2(4)$$
$$+ \alpha_2(1-\beta_1-\beta_2) + 5\beta_1(1-\alpha_1-\alpha_2) - 2\beta_2(1-\alpha_1-\alpha_2) + 0$$

$$\frac{\partial \Pi_C}{\partial \alpha_1} = \frac{\partial \Pi_C}{\partial \alpha_2} = \frac{\partial \Pi_C}{\partial \beta_1} = \frac{\partial \Pi_C}{\partial \beta_2} = 0$$

$$+2\beta_1 + \beta_2 = -2$$
$$-2\beta_1 + 3\beta_2 = -1$$
$$-3\alpha_1 - 7\alpha_2 = -5$$
$$3\alpha_1 + 5\alpha_2 = 2$$

where $\alpha_1 = \dfrac{-11}{6}$; $\alpha_2 = \dfrac{3}{2}$; $\alpha_3 = \dfrac{4}{3}$ are infeasible; $\beta_2 = \dfrac{3}{4}$ but one of $\beta_1 = \dfrac{-11}{8}$ and $\beta_3 = \dfrac{-13}{8}$ is negative with no feasible solution.

Therefore a Nash mixed strategy equilibrium may not always exist. Not every strategic game has NE by Osborne and Rubinstein, titled *A Course in Game Theory* as the famous game titled matching pennies demonstrates [12a, Chap. 2, p. 19]. The conditions under which the set of NE of a game are nonempty have been investigated by Kakutanis' fixed point theorem of 1941 [12a, chap. 2, p. 20].

5.4.3   An Example: Matching Pennies

If two players choose the same face, player 2 pays person 1 a $1. If different faces, player 1 pays player 2 a penalty of $1 as in Table 5.3.

Note that each person cares about the money he or she receives. Such a game where the players' interests are diametrically opposed is called strictly "competitive." The game "matching pennies" has no NE with none of the cubicles holding equality. That is, NE isolates no steady state as follows. Since the actions can only be discrete (0 or 1), the payoff function is nondifferentiable. The same result of no NE is confirmed in words in Ref. [12a, b] on p. 17. If $\alpha = 1$, $\beta = 1$, $\Pi_1 = 1$, and $\Pi_2 = -1$ as in the payoff matrix for i (first row) = 1, then j (first column) = 1, etc.

5.4.4   Another Game: The Prisoner's Dilemma

The prisoner's dilemma [12, 52] game has two players (the prisoners): George and Dick. Each of them has two possible strategies: to confess the other or not. Each of them should concurrently decide which one of his strategies to follow (without knowing the choice of the other). Their choices determine their gain: If they both confess, each gets 1 year in prison, but if only one confesses, she/he will be freed (zero prison time) and used as a witness against each other, who will receive a sentence of 4 years. Finally, if neither confesses, they both get 3 years' imprisonment for a minor offense (see Table 5.4).

Thus, the action (Confess, Confess) consists of best-response strategies for all players of the game with the least prison time. Whatever one player does, the other prefers Confess to the action of Don't Confess, so that the game has a unique NE (Confess, Confess). This action constitutes an NE of the game. Since all players use a single strategy in this profile, it is called pure profile or strategy. That is, if $\alpha = 0$, $\beta = 0$ to represent (Confess, Confess at $i = 2$, $j = 2$); $\Pi_1 = 1$ and $\Pi_2 = 1$ will yield the least penalty of 1 year prison for each. The differentiation to find other solutions is out of question since the two actions (0 or 1) are discrete; therefore payoff functions are discontinuous and not differentiable. Finding NE in this game seems to be not a difficult task. But in general, there are more than two players involved with much more complicate payoff functions to lead to difficulties to find NE.

TABLE 5.3   Matching Pennies

Player 1↓/Player 2→	Head (β)	Tail ($1-\beta$)
Head (α)	1, −1	−1, 1
Tail ($1-\alpha$)	−1, 1	1, −1

TABLE 5.4   The Prisoner's Dilemma

Player 1↓/Player 2→	Don't Confess (β)	Confess ($1-\beta$)
Don't Confess (α)	3, 3	0, 4
Confess ($1-\alpha$)	4, 0	1, 1

5.4.5 Games with Multiple NE (Terrorist Game: Bold Strategy Result in Domination)

The main contribution of this game is to show that a game with more than one conflicting NE can only end up in domination. In a symmetric warfare, at least one of the players (who are rational) is expected to be in a weaker position than the other players. Terrorist (T) capture hostages and threaten to blow up the hostages if the requirements of the terrorist are not accepted. The government (G) proposes that terrorists should surrender and be put to jail. Both players have strategies or actions, π_1 and π_2. The strategy π_1 means *accepting what the other player suggests: Terrorists surrender or the government accepts the requirements (e.g., pays the ransom)*. The strategy π_2 means *rejecting what the other player suggests: Terrorists kill the hostages or the government rejects to negotiate*. The payoffs are the following by Jormakka and Mölsä [23] (Table 5.5):

Note: *G accepts ransom; T surrenders but goes to jail but gets benefit. Both get −1. **G rejects ransom; T surrenders and goes to jail. T gets −5 and G gets 0. ***G accepts the ransom; hostages are free. T gets free. T gets 1 and G gets −5. ****G rejects ransom; T kills hostages and themselves. Both get −10. Let us assume T plays mixed strategy $(p_T \pi_1,(1-p_T)\pi_2)$ where $0 \le p_T \le 1$. This signifies that T plays π_1 with the probability of p_T and π_2 with the probability of $(1-p_T)$. G plays the mixed strategy $(p_G \pi_1,(1-p_G)\pi_2)$ where $0 \le p_G \le 1$. The expected payoff V_T for the row bound T is given as follows:

$$V_T = -p_T p_G -10(1-p_T)(1-p_G)-5p_T(1-p_G)+(1-p_T)p_G$$
$$= p_T(5-7p_G)-10+11p_G,$$

and the expected payoff V_G for the columnar G is

$$V_G = -p_T p_G -10(1-p_T)(1-p_G)-0p_T(1-p_G)-5(1-p_T)p_G$$
$$= p_G(5-6p_T)-10+10p_T$$

NE points $(p_T p_G)$ for this game are computed by analyzing the best-response correspondences $p_T{}^*(p_G)$, which is the value of p_T that maximizes $V_T(p_G)$, and also analyzing $p_G{}^*(p_T)$, which is the value of p_G that maximizes $V_G(p_T)$. These correspondences describe how the optimal mixed strategy selection probability depends on the opponents' probability. First, we identify the pure strategy NE:

$p_T{}^*(0)=1$ and $p_G{}^*(1)=0$: NE point is $(1,0)$.

$p_T{}^*(1)=0$ and $p_G{}^*(0)=1$: NE point is $(0,1)$.

TABLE 5.5 Terrorist Game Example Between Terrorist (T) and Government (G)

Column (G) →	1	2	Row Min
Row (T) ↓	action π_1 with p_G	action π_2 with $(1-p_G)$	
1 action π_1 with p_T	(-1,-1)*	(-5,0)**	-5
2 action π_2 with $(1-p_T)$	(1,-5)***	(-10, -10)****	-10
Col Max→	1	0	

The possible NE involving mixed strategies can be found by differentiating the payoff functions for the continuous vector $(p_T, p_G)^T$:

$$\frac{\partial V_T}{\partial p_T} = 5 - 7p_G = 0 \rightarrow p_G = \frac{5}{7}$$

$$\frac{\partial V_G}{\partial p_G} = 5 - 6p_T = 0 \rightarrow p_T = \frac{5}{6}$$

The NE are thus the following multiple points: $(1,0)$, $(0,1)$, and $\left(\frac{5}{6}, \frac{5}{7}\right)$. These points reflect the intersection points of the best-response correspondences. The payoffs (V_T, V_G) at the equilibrium points are $(-5,0)$, $(1,-5)$, and $\left(-\frac{15}{7}, -\frac{10}{6}\right)$. The two NE points with pure strategies (π_1, π_2) and (π_2, π_1) give the best and highest amid the available payoffs for V_G and V_T, respectively. Thus the third equilibrium point is not in interest for neither player. As such, however these results do not yet provide any unique solution to this static game.

A bold strategy can however result in a unique solution in the long term when the static terrorist game is repeated. What is a bold strategy? Let us assume that G is bold and always plays π_2 (rejecting the rival so that it will not negotiate with T). Player T may not believe that G will play boldly and T may try π_2 for finitely many times. But if G sticks on to playing π_2, T will eventually finish with a finite negative gain and T will have to start playing π_1 in order to minimize the losses. This familiar real-life game can only end up in domination, where T accepts that G always plays π_2 and will accept losing on this game, or in blowing up hostages and terrorists. Then rational player T must always play π_1. A bold rational player always wins over the less bold rational player in the long term when the terrorist game is repeated. The cause for asymmetric warfare is often the domination in the first place. There exist three other examples such as:

1. Evildoer game (mixed defense strategies can reduce domination) where there are two players (an attacker and a victim) with two possible choices of each and no pure NE [23].
2. Vandal game (domination can have a limited time span) where Jormakka and Mölsä [23] do not consider defense strategy but only the fact that the victim will simply not use the system (say, network) and not suffer from the attack [51].
3. Rebel game (extreme domination can result in rebellions) where the dominating solution is expected to cause extremely high costs to the weaker party, who in turn will eventually start to rebel. This may fire back at the dominator [23]!

In addition, a solution point where none of the players can improve his/her payoff by a unilateral move is known as noncooperative equilibrium. Otherwise it signals cooperative game theory if the players were able to enter into a cooperative agreement so that the selection of decisions is done collectively and with full trust so that all would benefit to the extent possible.

5.5   ADVERSARIAL RISK ANALYSIS MODELS BY BANKS, RIOS, AND RIOS

Applications in counterterrorism and corporate competition have led to the development of new methods for the analysis of decisions when there are *intelligent opponents and uncertain outcomes*. This field represents a combination of statistical risk analysis and game theory and is sometimes called ARA. Prevalent methodologies are based on *game theory, decision analysis, or conventional risk analysis*, emphasizing separate aspects of the analysis. Rios, Rios, and Banks [32] describe a unified framework for the analysis of decisions under uncertainty *in the presence of intelligent adversaries.*

The case of a defend–attack situation, a sequential decision game is presented in which Daphne (defender) chooses a defense in $D = \{d1, d2\}$ and then Apollo (attacker), having observed the defense, chooses an attack in $A = \{a1, a2\}$. The only uncertainty is a binary outcome S representing the success or failure of the attack. Thus, the consequences for both players depend on the success of his attack. Figure 5.1 shows an influence diagram and a decision tree representing this situation. The arcs into a utility node represent functional dependence.

First, the authors describe how standard game theory solves the defend–attack sequential decision game. The game-theoretic approach to ARA requires the probability assessment over S, conditional on (d, a). As Daphne and Apollo may have different assessments for success S, these are $pD(S = 1 \mid d, a)$ and $pA(S = 1 \mid d, a)$, respectively. To compute NE, one needs the expected utilities of the players at node S of the tree in Figure 5.1.

As a simple, realistic, and specific case of ARA, they consider two applications in auctions. The first is nonadversarial but introduces the basic ideas, and another, the adversarial case. Moreover, it applies the ARA framework to a simultaneous decision-making problem in which the assessment of probabilities on the adversary's actions needs to be more elaborate than in the sequential defend–attack decision game.

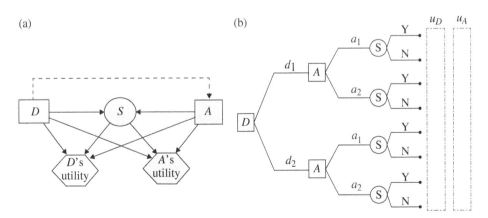

FIGURE 5.1   The defend–attack sequential decision game. (a) Influence diagram, (b) decision tree representations. Figure is taken from Ref. [53] with permission.

Suppose now that Daphne and Apollo are bidding against each other. Each knows her own valuation of the auctioned object but does not know the valuation of the other. Each submits their bid in a sealed envelope without knowing the other's bid, and the winner is the highest bidder. This simultaneous decision-making situation is shown in the influence diagram in Figure 5.2 and elaborated in Figure 5.3.

Harsanyi's approach on the other hand leads to the solution concept of Bayes–NE for games with incomplete information, based on the assumption that players share a common prior, which in this case requires those players disclose, inter alia, their true beliefs about the other player's valuation [10]. Thus, Daphne's probabilistic assessment of Apollo's valuation and Apollo's probabilistic assessment of Daphne's valuation would be common knowledge. Only under this assumption it is possible to compute the solution. See also Rothkopf for a related discussion concerning the role of game theory in auctions [54]. The Rios, Rios, and Banks approach [32] seems to be more realistic than Harsanyi's. Rios, Rios, and Banks have described a Bayesian approach to ARA problems and modified influence diagrams to represent these situations. They have illustrated it with applications in the context of terrorism, with a sketch of the defend–attack model, and bidding

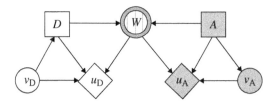

FIGURE 5.2 ID of the sealed bid auction problem. Figure is taken from Ref. [53] with permission.

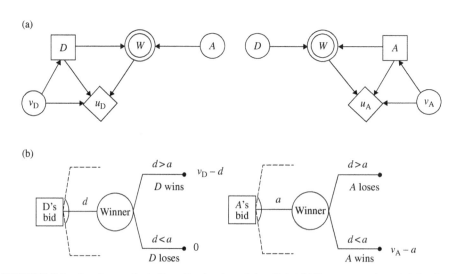

FIGURE 5.3 Auction analysis from Daphne's and Apollo's bidding perspectives. (a) Daphne's bidding decision problem, (b) Apollo's bidding decision problem. Figure is taken from Ref. [53] with permission.

in price-sealed auctions. They have focused on two-person games, but the ideas directly extend to harder and more realistic problems as well as to n-person games. ARA is a new branch of collaborative statistics. Another paper by Banks and Harris [32a, b] contend that the classical game theory focuses upon a single game, but in many situations such as counterterrorism, it is appropriate to plan for a repeated play as Aumann claims [16]. The game problems are numerous and the applications are important. The authors Rios, Rios, and Banks believe that the Bayesian perspective has important contributions to make in this arena and that their formulation is more realistic than the traditional NE analysis in operations research or the ad hoc decisions commonly made in practice by federal agencies and corporate executives.

5.6 AN ALTERNATIVE MODEL: SAHINOGLU'S SECURITY METER FOR NEUMANN AND NASH MIXED STRATEGY

In conventional qualitative risk analyses, assets can be classified on a scale of *crucial–critical* or *very significant*, *significant,* or *not significant.* Vulnerabilities and associated threats can be rated on a scale of *highly likely*, *likely*, *unlikely*, or *highly unlikely*. On the subject of countermeasures (CMs) and risk mitigation, the qualitative approach is from *strong (high) to acceptable (medium) and unacceptable (low)*. If there was a numerical value, such as 90% security, one could tell just how secure we were thought to be, similar to the way one differentiated for temperature (Fahrenheit) readings. The same concept applies to the risk accrued for one's computer or a hospital's patient-centered healthcare system. To quantify risk, the risk-meter (RM or RoM) tool based on a game-theoretic algorithm will be explained by citing examples [24]. The RM method has been theoretically validated by Sahinoglu, Yuan, and Banks [27] through applying MAPLE software and through digital simulation [24, 25]. This automated risk assessment and management algorithm provides a quantitatively strong alternative to the current mostly qualitative and subjective models. The model was explained in Chapter 4.

Following the initial risk assessment, one proceeds with the risk management stage to compute the game-theoretic LP solution vector CM_{ij} to mitigate risk from 26% to 10% for Tables 5.6 as in Figure 5.4. That is, refer to Figure 5.4 for the risk management results regarding surveyed input data of Table 5.6 [25]. After running the RM through the software developed by the principal author, one obtains a break-even cost of $5.67 accrued per 1% CM improvement. See Tables 5.7 and 5.8.

This is the result after the CMs are taken to bring the undesirable security risk (e.g., 26.04%) to a tolerable level (e.g., 10%). The average break-even cost C per 1% must be calculated to procure personnel, hardware, and software costs. On the positive side, the expected cost of loss (ECL) will decrease with a gain of Δ ECL, while the software- and hardware-related CM improvements are added on as fringe benefits or serendipity.

The break-even point is where the benefits and costs are equal, correctly guiding the security manager to follow up on corrective actions. The *base server* of the example in Figure 5.4 (left half of Table 5.7) shows the organizational policy of mitigating the RR from 26.04% down to 10% ($\leq$10%) in the *improved server*. Then for each improvement action, such as increasing from 70% to 100% for $v_1 t_1$ branch, etc., $30 \times \$5.67 = \$170.1$ is spent. The total minimal change of $90.52\% \times \$5.6715$ per

TABLE 5.6 Sample Security Meter Input Chart for Local University Server Center

Vulnerability	Threat	Countermeasure
$V_1 = 0.35$ (internal security breach)	$T_{11} = 0.48$ (internal abuse of network access)	$\text{CM}_{11} = 0.70$ (security awareness training)
		$\text{LCM}_{11} = 0.30$ by subtraction
	$T_{12} = 0.16$ (system penetration)	$\text{CM}_{12} = 0.42$ (smart cards)
		$\text{LCM}_{12} = 0.58$ by subtraction
	$T_{13} = 0.32$ (denial of service)	$\text{CM}_{13} = 0.97$ (firewalls)
		$\text{LCM}_{13} = 0.03$ by subtraction
	$T_{14} = 0.04$ (financial/telecom fraud)	$\text{CM}_{14} = 0.80$ (security audit)
		$\text{LCM}_{14} = 0.20$ by subtraction
$V_2 = 0.26$ (external security breach)	$T_{21} = 0.22$ (abuse of wireless network and website defacement)	$\text{CM}_{21} = 0.35$ (public key infrastructure)
		$\text{LCM}_{21} = 0.65$ by subtraction
	$T_{22} = 0.02$ (sabotage)	$\text{CM}_{22} = 0.35$ (intrusion prevention)
		$\text{LCM}_{22} = 0.65$ by subtraction
	$T_{23} = 0.76$ (virus)	$\text{CM}_{23} = 0.96$ (antivirus)
		$\text{LCM}_{23} = 0.04$ by subtraction
$V_3 = 0.39$ (both internal and external breach)	$T_{31} = 0.32$ (unauthorized info access)	$\text{CM}_{31} = 0.72$ (intrusion detection)
		$\text{LCM}_{31} = 0.28$ by subtraction
	$T_{32} = 0.59$ (malicious code)	$\text{CM}_{32} = 0.70$ (server access)
		$\text{LCM}_{32} = 0.30$ by subtraction
	$T_{33} = 0.09$ (theft of proprietary information)	$\text{CM}_{33} = 0.46$ (encrypted files)
		$\text{LCM}_{33} = 0.54$ by subtraction

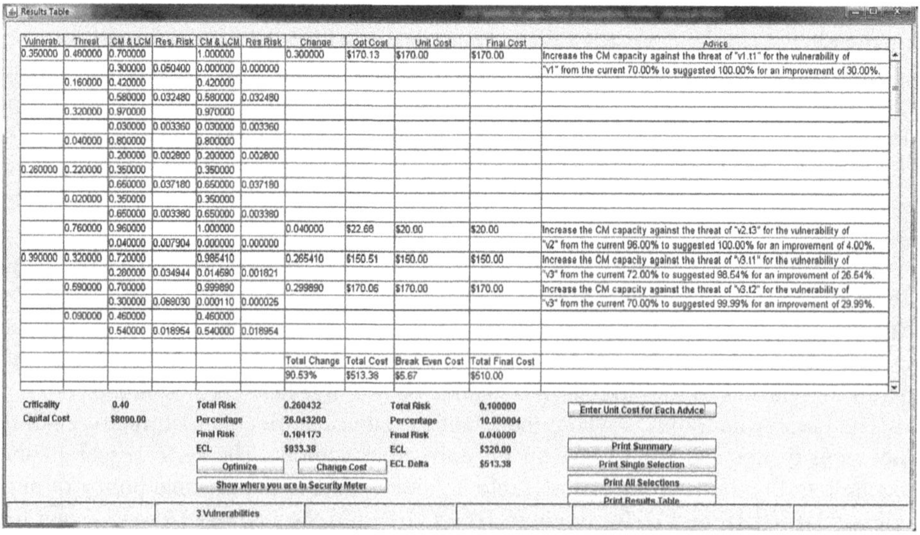

Results Table

Vulnerab.	Threat	CM & LCM	Res. Risk	CM & LCM	Res Risk	Change	Opt Cost	Unit Cost	Final Cost	Advice
0.350000	0.480000	0.700000		1.000000		0.300000	$170.13	$170.00	$170.00	Increase the CM capacity against the threat of "v1.t1" for the vulnerability of
		0.300000	0.050400	0.000000	0.000000					"v1" from the current 70.00% to suggested 100.00% for an improvement of 30.00%.
	0.160000	0.420000		0.420000						
		0.580000	0.032480	0.580000	0.032480					
	0.320000	0.970000		0.970000						
		0.030000	0.003360	0.030000	0.003360					
	0.040000	0.800000		0.800000						
		0.200000	0.002800	0.200000	0.002800					
0.260000	0.220000	0.350000		0.350000						
		0.650000	0.037180	0.650000	0.037180					
	0.020000	0.350000		0.350000						
		0.650000	0.003380	0.650000	0.003380					
	0.760000	0.960000		1.000000		0.040000	$22.68	$20.00	$20.00	Increase the CM capacity against the threat of "v2.t3" for the vulnerability of
		0.040000	0.007904	0.000000	0.000000					"v2" from the current 96.00% to suggested 100.00% for an improvement of 4.00%.
0.390000	0.320000	0.720000		0.985410		0.265410	$150.51	$150.00	$150.00	Increase the CM capacity against the threat of "v3.t1" for the vulnerability of
		0.280000	0.034944	0.014590	0.001821					"v3" from the current 72.00% to suggested 98.54% for an improvement of 26.54%.
	0.590000	0.700000		0.999890		0.299890	$170.06	$170.00	$170.00	Increase the CM capacity against the threat of "v3.t2" for the vulnerability of
		0.300000	0.069030	0.000110	0.000025					"v3" from the current 70.00% to suggested 99.99% for an improvement of 29.99%.
	0.090000	0.460000		0.460000						
		0.540000	0.018954	0.540000	0.018954					
						Total Change	Total Cost	Break Even Cost	Total Final Cost	
						90.53%	$513.38	$5.67	$510.00	

Criticality 0.40
Capital Cost $8000.00
Total Risk 0.260432
Percentage 26.043200
Final Risk 0.104173
ECL $833.38
Total Risk 0.100000
Percentage 10.000004
Final Risk 0.040000
ECL $320.00
ECL Delta $513.38
Optimize
Change Cost
Show where you are in Security Meter
Enter Unit Cost for Each Advice
Print Summary
Print Single Selection
Print All Selections
Print Results Table
3 Vulnerabilities

FIGURE 5.4 Example of a game-theoretic cost-optimal risk management from Table 5.6.

TABLE 5.7 Game-Theoretic Cost-Optimal Risk Management (by Neumann and Nash)

1	2	3	4	5	6	7	8	9	10	11	12	13
Vuln	Threat	CM & LCM	Res. Risk	CM & LCM	Res. Risk	Change	Cost	Beta M	Change	Game	Beta Vector	Game Cost
0.35	0.48	0.7				0.3	$170.14	0.333	0.284	0.98	0.016	$46.88
		0.3	0.050	0	0							
	0.16	0.42		0.42		0	$0.00	1	0.58	1	0.049	$95.78
		0.58	0.032	0.58	0.032							
	0.32	0.97		0.97		0	$0.00	0.5	0.03	1	0.024	$4.95
		0.03	0.003	0.03	0.003							
	0.04	0.8		0.8		0	$0.00	4	0.2	1	0.198	$33.03
		0.2	0.002	0.2	0.002							
0.26	0.22	0.35		0.35		0	$0.00	0.979	0.65	1	0.048	$107.34
		0.65	0.037	0.65	0.037							
	0.02	0.35		0.35		0	$0.00	10.769	0.65	1	0.534	$107.34
		0.65	0.003	0.65	0.003							
	0.76	0.96		1		0.04	$22.69	0.283	-0.124	0.84	0.014	-$20.39
		0.04	0.007	0	0							
0.39	0.32	0.72		0.985		0.26	$150.41	0.448	0.28	1	0.022	$46.24
		0.28	0.034	0.014	0.001							
	0.59	0.7		1		0.3	$170.14	0.243	0.018	0.72	0.012	$3.04
		0.3	0.069	0	0							
	0.09	0.46		0.46		0	$0.00	1.595	0.54	1	0.079	$89.17
		0.54	0.018	0.54	0.018			BetaMSum Total=				CostSum=
	SUMnew	Tot RISK	0.260	Tot RISK	0.1	0.905	$513.38	20.152	3.109		Beta Total=	$513.38
	7.335	Percentage	26.04%	Percentage	10.00%						Beta (2)	1
BASE	SERVER	Final Risk	0.104	Final Risk	0.04	IMPRVL SERVER	0.049				NESolution	NE TotCm$_{ij}$=
Asset= $8000	ECL		$833.38	ECL	$320.00	per%	Total CM$_{ij}$ per%				0.178	3.34
Criticality= 0.40	Total CM$_{ij}$		6.43	Delta ECL	$513.38	$5.67	$1.65				17.87%	

TABLE 5.8 LP Solution of Example of Table 5.7 and Figure 5.4 when ≥ Constraints on CM$_{ij}$ Are Missing in Column 3 of Table 5.7

```
Optimal Solution
Objective Function Value =        0.1653

        Variable            Value         Reduced Costs
        --------            -----         -------------
            X1             0.9839             0.0000
            X2             1.0000             0.0000
            X3             1.0000             0.0000
            X4             1.0000             0.0000
            X5             1.0000             0.0000
            X6             1.0000             0.0000
            X7             0.8365             0.0000
            X8             1.0000             0.0000
            X9             0.7184             0.0000
           X10             1.0000             0.0000
           X11             0.1653             0.0000
```

1% = \$513.38 improvement cost and Δ ECL = \$833.38 (base server) – \$320 (improved server) = \$513.38 for a diminished RR are now identical. Table 5.7 and Figure 5.4 show how the RM is used to manage risk with a game-theoretic algorithm of threats versus CMs as two opposing actions.

See Delta ECL of \$513.38 at the bottom of Table 5.7 and Figure 5.4. If the user can find a provider to improve their PC or system for less than \$5.67 per 1%, they will accrue a profit. Note Figure 5.4 (JAVA) or Table 5.7 (EXCEL) were built from a related security survey of a server at a US University's Computer Center as illustrated in Table 5.6 [25]. Consequently, optimal CMs are generated using a game-theoretic computational algorithm, RM, to optimize mitigation as illustrated under the *change* column. The algorithm brings significant advantages to information warfare [19, 25, 55] on how to optimize the CMs (CM) in an offense versus defense setting in national cybersecurity theme [76]. More details on columns 9 and 12 are in section 5.8.

Using the input chart of Table 5.6 and the results of Table 5.7 and Figure 5.4 and to improve the base risk by mitigating from 26% to 10%, we implement the prioritized and recommended actions from the *advice* column as follows: (i) Increase the CM capacity for the vulnerability of *Internal Security Breach* and its threat *Internal Abuse of Network Access* from the current 70–100%. (ii) Increase the CM capacity for the vulnerability of *External Security Breach* and its threat *Virus* from the current 96% to 100%. (iii) Increase the CM capacity for the vulnerability of *Both Internal and External Breach* and its threat *Unauthorized Info Access* from the current 72% to 98.54%. (iv) Increase the CM capacity for the vulnerability of *Both Internal and External Breach* and its threat *Malicious Code* from the current 70% to 99.99%. A *total improved final cost* of <\$513.38 is advised, each within the limits of optimal costs annotated, staying below the break-even cost of \$5.67 per every %CM improvement.

The next management step may proceed with seeking optimization to a next desirable percentage once these CM services are provided, such as mitigating to 5% from 10% if the budget exists. One can also see under Table 5.7's *Game* column 11 the alternative CM values were obtained through a new LP optimal solution in Table 5.8 where the *improvement* constraint, that is, $\geq$ column 3, is liberated or disabled. Namely, the new CM constraints earlier in column 5 for the sought optimal vector were bound to be greater than or equal ($\geq$) to those previously enabled in column 3 for improvement. The new solution CM vector as in column 11 all may not be $\geq$ those of column 3 as one can see in Table 5.7's *change* column 10 that may contain a negative value. For this alternative in Table 5.8, to provide the same benefits, one has to experience a change of 310% at the bottom of column 10 compared to 90.5% of column 7 in Table 5.7. For a fixed cost of recovery, one has to pay at least three times. The break-even cost per % change is \$1.65. Game Cost (Column 13) is the column 10 value times the break-even cost of \$1.65.

However, columns 8 and 13 of Table 5.7 yield the identical ECL due to differing break-even costs. Therefore, what's in *change* column of Figure 5.4 (JAVA) that is identical to column 7 of Table 5.7 (EXCEL) is the most optimal solution. Column 10 is the difference vector between column 11 (an alternative mixed strategy solution using Table 5.8's LP solution when the greater than or equal to column 3's CMs are omitted for a free-ride solution) and column 3 of CM_{ij} also in Tables 5.6 and 5.7. *Defense* (user) picks the smallest column-wise, while *offense* (attacker) picks the largest row-wise risk. The maximin and minimax equilibrium works as in Table 5.9 illustrating the diagonal loss matrix as in Table 5.7's Column 5 which is the solution vector as the improved CM_{ij}.

TABLE 5.9 Diagonal Loss Matrix (Table 5.7, 5.8, Columns 1–3, 5) of Neumann; β (Column 12) of Nash Mixed Strategy Solution (NE)

Cross-Products	$LCM_{11}=$ $(1-0.7)$ $=0.3$	$LCM_{12}=$ $(1-0.42)$ $=0.58$	$LCM_{13}=$ $(1-0.97)$ $=0.03$	$LCM_{14}=$ $(1-0.80)$ $=0.20$	$LCM_{21}=$ $(1-0.35)$ $=0.65$	$LCM_{22}=$ $(1-0.35)$ $=0.65$	$LCM_{23}=$ $(1-0.96)$ $=0.04$	$LCM_{31}=$ $(1-0.72)$ $=0.28$	$LCM_{32}=$ $(1-0.7)$ $=0.30$	$LCM_{33}=$ $(1-0.46)$ $=0.54$
$V_i\times T_{ij}\times LCM_{ij}$	$\beta_1=0.0165$	$\beta_2=0.0496$	$\beta_3=0.0248$	$\beta_4=0.1985$	$\beta_5=0.0486$	$\beta_6=0.5344$	$\beta_7=0.0141$	$\beta_8=0.0223$	$\beta_9=0.0121$	$\beta_{10}=0.0792$
$V_1\times T_{11}=$ $.168=0.35\times0.48$	0.0504									
$V_1\times T_{12}=$ $.056=0.35\times0.16$		0.0325								
$V_1\times T_{13}=$ $.112=0.35\times0.32$			0.0034							
$V_1\times T_{14}=$ $.014=0.35\times0.04$				0.0028 Minimax						
$V_2\times T_{21}=$ $.0572=0.26\times0.22$					0.03718					
$V_2\times T_{22}=$ $.0052=0.26\times0.02$						0.00338				
$V_2\times T_{23}=$ $.1976=0.26\times0.76$							0.0079			
$V_3\times T_{31}=$ $.1248=0.39\times0.32$								0.0035		
$V_3\times T_{32}=$ $.2301=0.39\times0.59$									0.069 Maximin	
$V_3\times T_{33}=$ $.0351=0.39\times0.09$										0.019

5.7 OTHER INTERDISCIPLINARY APPLICATIONS OF RISK METERS

The RM's risk assessor and manager expert system is capable of implementing this algorithm into diverse themes such as [57–66] and more to come:

1. Computer and network security RM
2. Computer and network (incl. social networks') privacy and security RM
3. Ecological RM
4. Electronic-voting RM
5. Business contracting RM
6. Campus safety and security RM
7. Department of Public Health HIPAA (privacy/security) RM
8. Hospital-based nonambulatory patient-centered healthcare RM
9. Federal (national) and state cyber-security RM
10. National healthcare (overall: ambulatory and nonambulatory) RM
11. Mining safety and security RM
12. Offshore oil-spill wireless sensory network (WSN) RM
13. Usability RM
14. CLOUD RM
15. Airport service RM
16. Banking customer service RM
17. Digital forensics RM
18. Home security RM
19. Software development RM
20. Software application RM

For the sake of a popular example, let us present a case in regard to item 2 (social networks' privacy and security RM) from the listing above, where a number of real people (not simulated) were interviewed and the results were discussed [61]. With the advent and unprecedented popularity of the now ubiquitous social networking sites such as Google+, Facebook, MySpace, and Twitter, etc., in the personal sphere and others such as LinkedIn in business circles, undesirable security and privacy risk issues have come to the forefront as a result of this extraordinary rapid growth. The most salient issues are mainly lack of trustworthiness, namely, those of security and privacy. One can address these issues by employing a quantitative approach to assess security and privacy risks for social networks already under pressure by users and policymakers for breaches in both quality and sustainability. One can also demonstrate, using a cost-optimal game-theoretic solution using RM algorithmic tool, how to assess and manage risk.

The applicability of this applied section material to diverse fields from security to privacy and healthcare, and ecorisk or business is an additional asset. See an example in Section 5.8.2 on the social networks' privacy and security theme along with both Neumann and Nash mixed strategy solutions.

5.8   MIXED STRATEGY FOR RISK ASSESSMENT AND MANAGEMENT-UNIVERSITY SERVER AND SOCIAL NETWORK EXAMPLES

5.8.1   University Server's Security Risk-Meter Example

In the preceding university server's security example of Figure 5.4 and Tables 5.6, 5.7, 5.8 and 5.9 applying RoM, we had a strictly diagonal loss (opposite to utility or payoff full) matrix. The probabilistic action set is not discrete but continuous and differentiable, and all lie between 0 and 1. Note CM_{ij} in the CM and LCM column in Figure 5.4 and Tables 5.7, 5.8, and 5.9. Let's start with differentiating diagonal matrix's *expected loss* in Table 5.9, such as in Section 5.4, to obtain the NE solution vector. See Equations (5.1–5.6):

$$\Pi_C = (1-0.168)\alpha_1\beta_1 + (1-0.056)\alpha_2\beta_2 + (1-0.112)\alpha_3\beta_3 + (1-0.014)\alpha_4\beta_4$$
$$+ (1-0.0572)\alpha_5\beta_5 + (1-0.0052)\alpha_6\beta_6 + (1-0.1976)\alpha_7\beta_7$$
$$+ (1-0.1248)\alpha_8\beta_8 + (1-0.2301)\alpha_9\beta_9$$
$$+ (1-0.0351)\left[\left(1-\sum_1^9 \alpha_i\right)\left(1-\sum_1^9 \beta_i\right)\right]$$

$$(5.1)$$

Note Π_C is the cost equation. Then, the NE of the $(\alpha\beta)^T$ vector can be obtained by solving the simultaneous differentiable equations $\dfrac{\partial \Pi_C}{\partial \alpha}$ and $\dfrac{\partial \Pi_C}{\partial \beta}$ for α and β vectors that are continuous variables defined in (0,1) range [50, 57].

Taking the derivatives and equating to zero,

$$\frac{\partial \Pi_C}{\partial \alpha_1} = 0.168\beta_1 - 0.0351\left(1-\sum_{i=1}^9 \beta_i\right) = 0 \qquad (5.2)$$

$$\frac{\partial \Pi_C}{\partial \alpha_2} = 0.056\beta_2 - 0.0351\left(1-\sum_{i=1}^9 \beta_i\right) = 0 \qquad (5.3)$$

$$\cdots\cdots\cdots\cdots\cdots\cdots\cdots\cdots\cdots\cdots\cdots\cdots$$

$$\frac{\partial \Pi_C}{\partial \alpha_9} = 0.2301\beta_9 - 0.0351\left(1-\sum_{i=1}^9 \beta_i\right) = 0 \qquad (5.4)$$

Therefore, the resultant equations for the NE's differential equations are given as follows:

$$0.168\,\beta_1 = 0.056\beta_2 \rightarrow \beta_1 = 0.333\beta_2$$
$$0.056\beta_2 = 0.112\beta_3 \rightarrow \beta_3 = 0.500\beta_2$$
$$0.112\beta_3 = 0.014\beta_4 \rightarrow \beta_4 = 4\beta_2$$
$$0.014\beta_4 = 0.0572\beta_5 \rightarrow \beta_5 = 0.9792075\beta_2$$
$$0.0572\beta_5 = 0.0052\beta_6 \rightarrow \beta_6 = 10.769229\beta_2$$
$$0.0052\beta_6 = 0.1976\beta_7 \rightarrow \beta_7 = 0.283403\beta_2$$

$$0.1976\beta_7 = 0.1248\beta_8 \rightarrow \beta_8 = 0.448721\beta_2$$
$$0.1248\beta_8 = 0.2301\beta_9 \rightarrow \beta_9 = 0.243374\beta_2$$
$$0.2301\beta_9 = 0.0351\beta_{10} \rightarrow \beta_{10} = 1.595454\beta_2 \qquad (5.5)$$

Also, $\beta_2 = 1.0\beta_2$ is the identity equation. Now add $\Sigma \beta_i = 20.1524$ $\beta_2 = 1.000 \rightarrow \beta_2 = 0.049622$. The final NE solution vector for β_i substituting in (5.5) as tabulated in Table 5.9 is as follows:

$$\beta_1 = 0.0165241$$
$$\beta_2 = 0.0496218$$
$$\beta_3 = 0.0248109$$
$$\beta_4 = 0.1984872$$
$$\beta_5 = 0.0485900$$
$$\beta_6 = 0.5343885 \qquad (5.6)$$
$$\beta_7 = 0.0140629$$
$$\beta_8 = 0.0222663$$
$$\beta_9 = 0.0120766$$
$$\beta_{10} = 0.0791693$$

Now add $\Sigma \beta_i = 1.000$, which checks to unity. Also, $\alpha_i = \beta_i$ for $i = 1, 2, 3, 4, 5, 6, 7, 8, 9, 10$. Therefore, there is no need to solve for $\dfrac{\partial \Pi_C}{\partial \alpha}$.

These beta multipliers of (5.5) are displayed under beta multiplier (M'lier) in column 9 of Table 5.7 where $\beta_2 = 0.049622$. The final NE's beta vector is displayed in column 12 of Table 5.7, as well as Table 5.9's second top row, summing to beta total = 1.00. If this solution vector is unconstrained and used as is, the residual risk will fall to 17.87% worse than 10% by the Neumann's as the column 6 as shown at the bottom of column 12 from an original 26.04% in column 4. However, some of these NE solution vector values are unrealistic since they exceed a probability of 1.00, such as in the case of $\beta_6 = 0.534$, which actually means $CM_{22} = 0.534 \times 6.43$ (CMs summed total CM_{ij} at the bottom of column 4 in Table 5.7) $= 3.43 > 1.0$. This cannot to be allowed since CM_{ij} probabilities cannot exceed 1.0. Therefore the NE solution vector is not valid. We will review a diagonal matrix case as follows in Figure 5.5. NE solution is feasible but engineering-wise not realistic. Note, column 12's sum, $0.1787 = 0.168 \times \beta_1 + \cdots + 0.0351 \times \beta_{10}$, all in Table 5.9.

5.8.2 Social Networks' Privacy and Security Risk-Meter (RM) Example

In another example, see Figure 5.5 for the application of NE solutions on a new RM scenario. In a new example, seeking NE solution vector for the RM tableau in Figure 5.5 for a different example from reference [61], the RM's CM_{ij} solution vector is obtained as follows with respect to Figure 5.5. Solving the differential equations for the NE vector

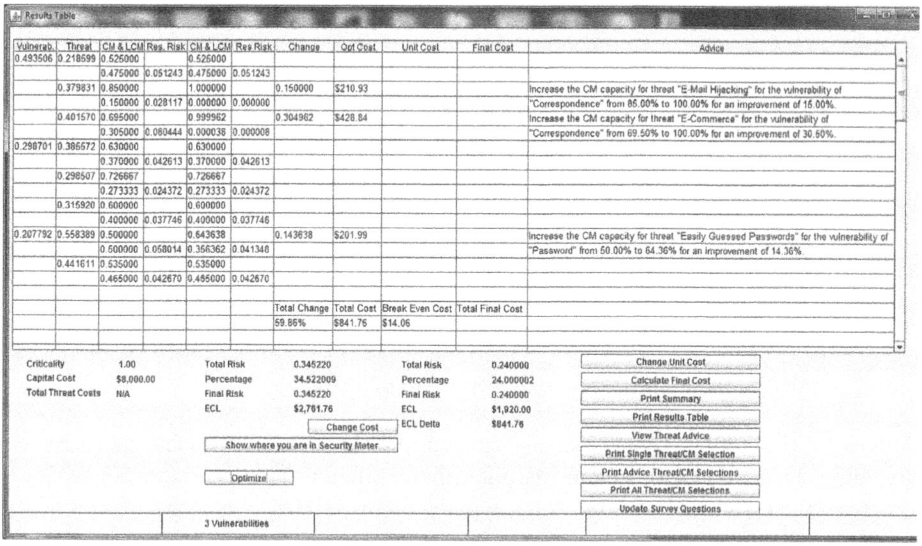

Vulnerab.	Threat	CM & LCM	Res. Risk	CM & LCM	Res Risk	Change	Opt Cost	Unit Cost	Final Cost	Advice
0.493506	0.218599	0.525000		0.526000						
	0.379831	0.850000		1.000000		0.150000	$210.93			Increase the CM capacity for threat "E-Mail Hijacking" for the vulnerability of
		0.150000	0.028117	0.000000	0.000000					"Correspondence" from 85.00% to 100.00% for an improvement of 15.00%.
	0.401570	0.695000		0.999962		0.304982	$428.84			Increase the CM capacity for threat "E-Commerce" for the vulnerability of
		0.305000	0.060444	0.000038	0.000008					"Correspondence" from 69.50% to 100.00% for an improvement of 30.50%.
0.298701	0.386572	0.630000		0.630000						
		0.370000	0.042613	0.370000	0.042613					
	0.298507	0.726667		0.726667						
		0.273333	0.024372	0.273333	0.024372					
	0.315920	0.600000		0.600000						
		0.400000	0.037746	0.400000	0.037746					
0.207792	0.558389	0.500000		0.643638		0.143638	$201.99			Increase the CM capacity for threat "Easily Guessed Passwords" for the vulnerability of
		0.500000	0.058014	0.356362	0.041348					"Password" from 50.00% to 64.36% for an improvement of 14.36%.
	0.441611	0.535000		0.535000						
		0.465000	0.042670	0.465000	0.042670					

Total Change	Total Cost	Break Even Cost	Total Final Cost
59.86%	$841.76	$14.06	

Criticality	1.00		Total Risk	0.345220		Total Risk	0.240000
Capital Cost	$8,000.00		Percentage	34.522009		Percentage	24.000002
Total Threat Costs	N/A		Final Risk	0.345220		Final Risk	0.240000
			ECL	$2,761.76		ECL	$1,920.00
						ECL Delta	$841.76

Change Unit Cost
Calculate Final Cost
Print Summary
Print Results Table
View Threat Advice
Print Single Threat/CM Selection
Print Advice Threat/CM Selections
Print All Threat/CM Selections
Update Survey Questions
Change Cost
Show where you are in Security Meter
Optimize

3 Vulnerabilities

FIGURE 5.5   Social network privacy and security cost-optimal risk analysis.

through (5.7) to (5.8) as we did in the previous example, the NE mixed strategy solution vector will follow:

$$0.1078\beta_1 = 0.1862\beta_2 \rightarrow \beta_1 = 1.727\beta_2$$
$$0.1862\beta_2 = 0.076\beta_3 \rightarrow \beta_3 = 2.45\beta_2$$
$$0.076\beta_3 = 0.117\beta_4 \rightarrow \beta_4 = 1.591\beta_2$$
$$0.117\beta_4 = 0.09\beta_5 \rightarrow \beta_5 = 2.069\beta_2 \tag{5.7}$$
$$0.09\beta_5 = 0.093\beta_6 \rightarrow \beta_6 = 2.002\beta_2$$
$$0.093\beta_6 = 0.1176\beta_7 \rightarrow \beta_7 = 1.582\beta_2$$
$$0.1176\beta_7 = 0.0924\beta_8 \rightarrow \beta_8 = 2.015\beta_2$$

Also, $\beta_2 = 1.0\beta_2$ is the identity equation. Now add $\sum \beta_i = 14.43\beta_2 = 1.000 \rightarrow \beta_2 = 0.069278$. The following is the final NE mixed strategy solution vector for β_i:

$$\beta_1 = 0.119644 \rightarrow \beta_1 \times 5.06 = 0.61 = CM_{11}$$
$$\beta_2 = 0.069278 \rightarrow \beta_2 \times 5.06 = 0.35 = CM_{12}$$
$$\beta_3 = 0.169732 \rightarrow \beta_3 \times 5.06 = 0.86 = CM_{13}$$
$$\beta_4 = 0.110222 \rightarrow \beta_4 \times 5.06 = 0.56 = CM_{21}$$
$$\beta_5 = 0.143337 \rightarrow \beta_5 \times 5.06 = 0.73 = CM_{22} \tag{5.8}$$
$$\beta_6 = 0.138695 \rightarrow \beta_6 \times 5.06 = 0.70 = CM_{23}$$
$$\beta_7 = 0.109598 \rightarrow \beta_7 \times 5.06 = 0.55 = CM_{31}$$
$$\beta_8 = 0.139596 \rightarrow \beta_8 \times 5.06 = 0.71 = CM_{32}$$

Now add $\Sigma \beta_i = 1.000$, which checks. Also $\beta_i = \alpha_i$, for $i = 1,2,3,4,5,6,7,8$.

Also $\alpha_i = \beta_i$, for $i = j$.

CM_{ij} sum $= 0.53 + 0.85 + 0.69 + 0.63 + 0.73 + 0.6 + 0.5 + 0.53 = 5.06$, adding CMs in column 3 of Figure 5.5.

When calculated, although realistic within bounds, NE vector worsened risk level from 34.5% to 37.5% (while a mitigation drop was expected), that is, when these NE vector values are implemented as we did in Table 5.7. From Figure 5.5,

$$\begin{aligned}
TRR &= 1 - V_i T_j CM_{ij} = 1 - 0.493506 \times \left[0.218599 \times 0.61 + 0.379831 \times 0.35 + 0.401570 \times 0.86\right] \\
&\quad - 0.298701 \times \left[0.385572 \times 0.56 + 0.298507 \times 0.73 + 0.315920 \times 0.70\right] - 0.207792 \\
&\quad \times \left[0.558389 \times 0.55 + 0.441611 \times 0.71\right] = 1 - 0.0653 + 0.0651 + 0.1702 + 0.0642 \\
&\quad + 0.0647 + 0.0662 + 0.0644 + 0.0646 = 1 - 0.625 = 0.375.
\end{aligned}$$

Although NE solution computationally worked, it is not practical because new CM_{ij} do not mitigate risk! Whereas, Neumann's algorithmic solution vector in Figure 5.5 using LP generated 0.24 from an initial 0.345 through the improved CM_{ij}.

5.8.3 Clarification of Risk Assessment and Management Algorithm for Social Networks

In order to mitigate a certain survey taker's (representing an undisclosed identity with a median risk value of 34.5% amid nine randomly selected graduate students from social network users at an international university, METU, Ankara, Turkey) social network privacy/security risk from 34.5% to 24%, the following CMs were guided by the RM [61, 69, 70]: (i) Increase the CM capacity for the threat of *E-Mail Hijacking* in the vulnerability of *Correspondence* from 85% to 100% for an improvement of 15% by procuring goods or services for $210.93. (ii) Increase the CM capacity for the threat of *E-Commerce* in the vulnerability of *Correspondence* from 69.5% to 100% for an improvement of 30.50% by procuring goods or services for $428.84. (iii) Increase the CM capacity for the threat of *Easily Guessed Passwords* in the vulnerability of *Password* from 50% to 64.36% for an improvement of 14.36% by procuring goods or services for $201.99. A total cost of $841.76 is allocated to mitigate the risk from 34.5% to 24% for cost-optimal improvement yielding a *total change* of 59.86% as RM results show in Table 5.5 (see Fig. 5.6 for the related tree diagram).

One can recursively continue to mitigate the present risk of 24% (down from an initial 34.5%) to lower target values such as 10% if one has a sufficient budget remaining for further improvement. This is to say that one (median subject) will implement the above clarified CMs by purchasing the services needed to mitigate one's privacy/security risk from a high of 34.5% to a low of 24%. She will do that by simply referring to the CM questions as cited and converting the negative (no) responses to positives (yes) by taking recommended CMs. While doing so, she optimizes her costs by the optimal allocation plan suggested by the RM's game-theoretical solutions, which are with respect to Neumann mixed strategy. The only NE mixed strategy solution, however, did not generate an improvement on 34.5% but, on the contrary, worsening to 37.5%.

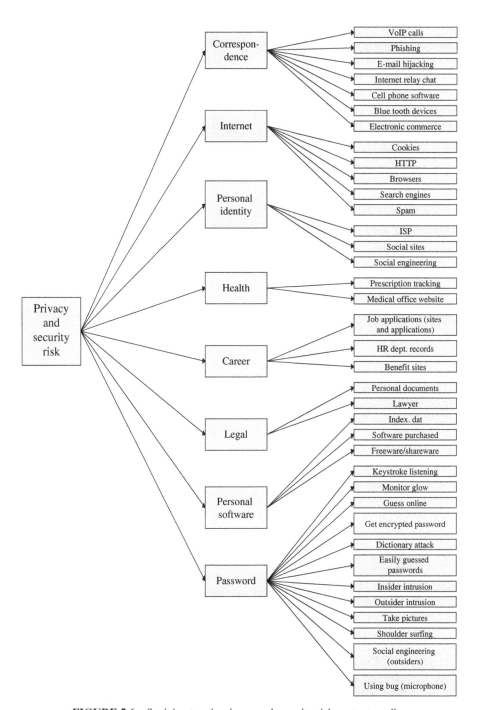

FIGURE 5.6   Social network privacy and security risk-meter tree diagram.

5.9   APPLICATION TO HOSPITAL HEALTHCARE SERVICE RISK

Next we wish to study a hospital healthcare RM theme by studying Figure 5.7 and the following tree diagram in Figure 5.8 [63]. As covered in Chapter 4, on top of providing an assessment of IT resource vulnerabilities, the RM (generically known as SM) provides an objective mitigation advice list in the form of specific recommendations and dollar figures. Maintaining the quality level of patient care at hospitals cannot be accurately accomplished without a risk assessment first and then a risk management. The RM will greatly facilitate conducting an accurate and thorough assessment of threats and vulnerabilities of hospital patient-centered healthcare by the following incomplete list of topics:

1. Admissions, billing, and accounting (ABA)
2. Hospital support services
3. Outpatients and daily visits
4. Inpatients
5. Surgery
6. Emergency room (services)
7. Radiology
8. Central (all-purpose) labs
9. IT resources
10. Physicians and interns
11. Nurses and auxiliary personnel
12. Pharmacy

There are 11 Alabama counties covering public health areas for a futuristic area study. However, in this section, the author collected surveys from 15 participating randomly selected former patients to have visited their area hospitals in the State of Alabama regardless of which clinic or hospital with no specific address in mind [62, 63, 64].

Optimization (Risk Management) Follow-Up Analysis: In Table 5.10, the median score is that of patient 11, thus making patient 11 as our patient base. We went back to patient 11 and cost-optimized risk percentage from 58% to 40%. The initial cost to mitigate this risk (at 57.79%) is $577.90 per patient for $1000 per-unit patient asset base. Bringing it down to 40%, we will mitigate the ECL down to $400.00 (a savings of $177.90 per patient). See Figure 5.7 inspired by the decision-making tree diagram of Figure 5.8. For this output, the following actions need to be taken with due investments:

1. Increase the CM capacity for the vulnerability of "ABA" (Admissions-Billing-Accounting) and its related threat "Insufficient Follow-Up with Patients and Filing Errors" from 45% to 100%. For this an investment of $98.93 is guided to be allocated for every $1000 per unit of the hospital's general assets.

TABLE 5.10 Survey Tabulation of 15 Patients (No. 11: Median Risk Score 58%)

Patient	Location	Risk Estimate	%	Comments
3	Montgomery, AL	0.307	31	Minimum
4	Montgomery, AL	0.3859	39	
2	Montgomery, AL	0.4618	46	
8	Montgomery, AL	0.4838	48	First quartile
1	Montgomery, AL	0.5158	52	
12	Montgomery, AL	0.5202	52	
5	Montgomery, AL	0.5704	57	
11	Montgomery, AL	0.5779	58	Median
14	Montgomery, AL	0.6255	63	
15	Montgomery, AL	0.6268	63	
13	Montgomery, AL	0.6288	63	
7	Montgomery, AL	0.6318	63	Third quartile
6	Montgomery, AL	0.6541	65	
10	Montgomery, AL	0.6664	67	
9	Montgomery, AL	0.7146	71	Maximum

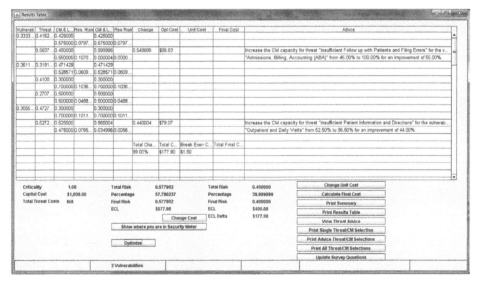

FIGURE 5.7 The risk assessment and management (to mitigate from 58 to 40% for a pilot study) tableau for patient #11 with median score to represent the population subjects sampled.

2. Increase the CM capacity for the vulnerability of "Outpatient and Daily Visits" and its related threat "Insufficient Patient Information and Directions" from 52.5% to 96.5% for a performance improvement of 44%. For this an investment of $79.07 is guided to be allocated for every $1000 per unit of the hospital's general assets.

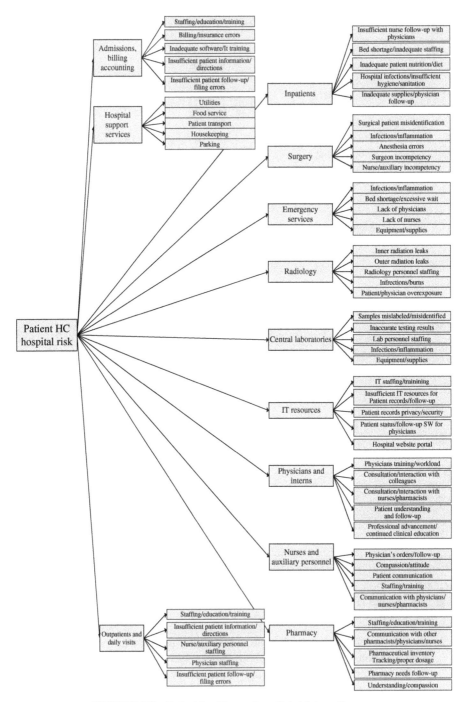

FIGURE 5.8 Patient health care hospital risk tree diagram.

5.10   APPLICATION TO ENVIRONMETRICS AND ECOLOGY RISK

Next we wish to study an environmetrical RM theme by studying the following tree diagram in Figure 5.9 [65].

We used a volunteer group of 15 survey takers, although not in a scientifically designed random sample from the overall population at two different college campuses (i.e., University of North Carolina at Wilmington, NC, and Auburn University at Montgomery, AL) who exercised the Eco-RM guided by Figure 5.9's ecological risk tree diagram. Survey was conducted at different times and in varying geographical regions.

We used a volunteer group of 15 survey takers, although not in a scientifically designed random sample from the overall population at two different college campuses (i.e., University of North Carolina at Wilmington, NC and Auburn University at Montgomery, AL) who exercised the Eco-RoM guided by Figure 5.9's ecological risk tree diagram. Survey was conducted at different times and in varying geographical regions. The 15 survey takers and their geographical locations are listed in Ref. [65] and Table 5.10.

The risk scores produced are summarized in the box plot of Figure 5.10 [66] as follows: average (mean), 0.56; standard deviation, 0.18; range (max–min), 0.47; variance, 0.0324; median (50th percentile), 0.53; first quartile, 0.39; and third quartile, 0.79. A screenshot of the results for the median survey taker, Robert, among the 15 such participants displaying vulnerability, threat, CM, residual risk indices, optimization options, as well as mitigation advice is displayed in Figure 5.11.

As there is no perfectly fitting representative or an artificially constructed person among these 15 subjects, we used the median, #8 ranked subject's risk values as the most representative respondent to demonstrate how the RM program performs game-theoretic optimizations for the risk management stage (Fig. 5.11). The results are displayed after an optimization based on this risk value as performed on this respondent's results. One million dollars, including externalities (shadow costs), is selected as a default value for the entire loss of assets due to ecological damages from vulnerabilities and threats listed in Figure 5.9 with their related CMs studied in this single survey round of the RM software. The initial risk realized by this respondent representing the 15 survey takers and the overall population was 0.5325 or 53.25%. However, after allocating $132,565 (the cost of CMs) to mitigate the threats they perceive, the risk is reduced to 0.4 or 40%.

In order to reduce the risk from an undesirable 53.25% to a more tolerable 40%, we need to perform three CM actions as displayed in Figure 5.11: (i) Increase the CM expenditure or eco-relief capacity for the vulnerability or ecological component of "Climate Change" due to its related threat or stressor "Greenhouse Gases" from the current 29.17% to 99.9% for an improvement of 70.73%. (ii) Increase the CM capacity for the vulnerability or ecological component of "Climate Change" due to its related threat or eco-stressor, "Nonuse of Renewable Energy Sources" from the current 40% to 54.33% for an improvement of 14.33%. (iii) Increase the CM capacity for the vulnerability or ecological component of "Oceanic" and its related threat or eco-stressor "Oil Spills" from the current 50% to 100% for an improvement of 50%.

These measures collectively yield a CM improvement value of 135%. This represents a cost-optimal minimum of all possible percentage increases to realize a planned mitigation of eco-risk from 53.25% to 40%. In taking actions as in Figure 5.11, a total

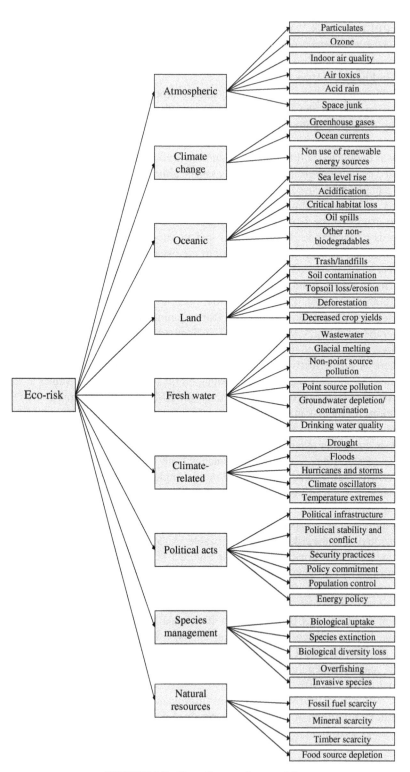

FIGURE 5.9 Tree diagram for eco-risk.

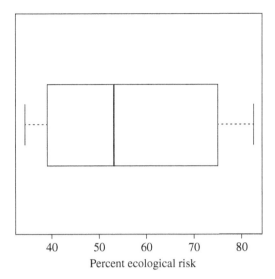

FIGURE 5.10   Box plot of the 15 survey takers as described.

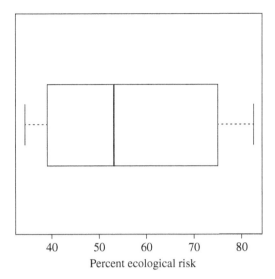

FIGURE 5.11   Game-theoretic cost-optimal eco-risk management analysis.

amount $\leq$ \$132,565 to allocate to (i) greenhouse gases, (ii) nonuse of renewable energy sources, and (iii) oil spills invested within the constraints of optimal costs annotated generates the break-even cost. That is, "investment" ÷ sum of % CM changes = \$132,565 ÷ 13 5% = \$982 is to be invested per 1% improvement in the \$1 million default situation, which is only a reasonable assumption. The investors should not spend more than \$982 per 1% improvement investment to reach the aimed goal. The next step may continue with an optimization study to a next desirable percentage once services or acquisitions are provided as feedback, such as to reduce the risk down to 30% from the earlier target of 40%, provided the budget can be met.

The need for ecological risk assurance is self-evident. The pervasiveness of this critical topic requires primarily risk assessment and management through quantitative means. In order to do an assessment, repeated risk probes, surveys, and input data measurements must be taken and verified toward the goal of risk mitigation. One can evaluate risk using a probabilistically accurate statistical estimation scheme in a quantitative RM model that mimics the events of the breach of ecological assets. The design improves as more ecological and environmental data are collected and updated. Practical aspects of the RM are presented with a real-world example and a risk management scenario. For the RM's risk management stage following the risk assessment stage to implement a game-theoretic algorithm on the above tabulated "results table" outcomes, the following system of linear equations (1)–(32) holds true in Table 5.11. There exist three times the threat number of equations plus two = 3×10 (# of threats) + 2 = 32. See Figure 5.11, columns 3 and 5 for CM and LCM before and after.

Optimal Solution: See column 5 in Figure 5.11 of the improved scenario for the newly obtained solution: $CM_{11} = 0.5$, $CM_{12} = 04833$, $CM_{21} = 0.999$, $CM_{22} = 0.5433$, $CM_{31} = 0.5$, $CM_{32} = 1.00$, $CM_{33} = 0.6166$, $CM_{41} = 0.7$, $CM_{32} = 0.45$, $CM_{33} = 0.35$.

TABLE 5.11   Ecological Risk-Meter Game-Theoretic Linear Programming Equations

Minimize (Min) column loss (COLLOSS), subject to:

$1CM_{11} < 1$ (1), $1CM_{12} < 1$ (2), $1CM_{21} < 1$ (3), $1CM_{22} < 1$ (4), $1CM_{31} < 1$ (5), $1CM_{32} < 1$ (6), $1CM_{33} < 1$ (7), $1CM_{41} < 1$ (8), $1CM_{42} < (9)$, $1CM_{43} < 1$ (10), 1 COLLOSS < 1 (11), for nonnegativity

$1CM_{11} > 0.5$ (12), $1CM_{12} > 0.4833$ (13), $1CM_{21} > 0.2917$ (14), $1CM_{22} > 0.4$ (15), $1CM_{31} > 0.50$ (16), $1CM_{32} > 0.50$ (17), $1CM_{33} > 0.6167$ (18), $1CM_{41} > 0.70$ (19), $1CM_{42} > 0.45$ (20), $1CM_{43} > 0.35$ (21)

For improvement of the countermeasure vector column:

$0.17365 * 0.468627 (= 0.081377) * CM_{11} - 1COLLOSS < 0$,   (22)

$0.17365 * 0.531373 (= 0.092273) * CM_{12} - 1COLLOSS < 0$,   (23)

$0.19539 * 0.518939 (= 0.101395) * CM_{21} - 1COLLOSS < 0$,   (24)

$0.19539 * 0.481061 (= 0.093995) * CM_{22} - 1COLLOSS < 0$,   (25)

$0.22682 * 0.293785 (= 0.066636) * CM_{31} - 1COLLOSS < 0$,   (26)

$0.22682 * 0.417676 (= 0.094737) * CM_{32} - 1COLLOSS < 0$,   (27)

$0.22682 * 0.288539 (= 0.065446) * CM_{33} - 1COLLOSS < 0$,   (28)

$0.125458 * 0.214286 (= 0.026884) * CM_{41} - 1COLLOSS < 0$,   (29)

$0.125458 * 0.464286 (= 0.058248) * CM_{42} - 1COLLOSS < 0$,   (30)

$0.125458 * 0.321429 (= 0.040326) * CM_{43} - 1COLLOSS < 0$,   (31)

For game-theoretic constraints to facilitate risk mitigation to from 53 to 40%:

$0.081377*CM_{11} + 0.092273*CM_{12} + 0.101395*CM_{21} + 0.093995*CM_{22} + 0.066636*CM_{31}$
$+ 0.094737*CM_{32} + 0.065446*CM_{33} + 0.026884*CM_{41} + 0.058248*CM_{42}$
$+ 0.040326*CM_{43} > 0.6$ (32)

The game theory application software stabilized this lack of equilibrium into a desired two-player zero-sum game with mixed strategy. This provides a list of CM probabilities, CM_{21} with probability 0.999, CM_{22} with 0.5433, and CM32 with 1.0 as those marked to improve. This is the optimal mixed strategy for the defense mechanism to minimize its expected loss while the offense mechanism maximizes its gain. There is no better game plan at equilibrium by altering CM_{ij} in any other format; the author also experimented in vain with NE mixed strategy of probabilities [2]. See also Table 5.12 for an alternative feasible solution. Figure 5.11, however, delivers the "most minimum" objective function value among all feasible solutions supported by Table 5.13 [48] survey respondent's outcomes.

TABLE 5.12   An Alternative Optimal Solution Obtained For Eco-Risk Project using LP

```
Optimal Solution
Objective Function Value =        0.0709143

          Variable              Value            Reduced Costs
        --------------       --------------     ----------------
             cm11             0.7225995           0.0000000
             cm12             0.7685266           0.0000000
             cm21             0.6993861           0.0000000
             cm22             0.7544471           0.0000000
             cm31             1.0000000           0.0000000
             cm32             0.7485381           0.0000000
             cm33             1.0000000           0.0000000
             cm41             1.0000000           0.0000000
             cm42             1.0000000           0.0000000
             cm43             1.0000000           0.0000000
          Colloss             0.0709143           0.0000000
```

TABLE 5.13   Ecological Risk-Meter Survey Outcomes

Subject	Location	Eco-Risk Estimate	Comments
A	UNCW, Wilmington, NC	0.3424 or 34.24%	Minimum
B	AUM, Montgomery, AL	0.3581 or 35.81%	
C	AUM, Montgomery, AL	0.3812 or 38.12%	
D	UNCW, Wilmington, NC	0.389 or 38.90%	First quartile
E	UNCW, Wilmington, NC	0.3929 or 39.29%	
F	UNCW, Wilmington, NC	0.4059 or 40.59%	
G	AUM, Montgomery, AL	0.5171 or 51.17%	
H	AUM, Montgomery, AL	0.5325 or 53.25%	**Median** or second quartile
I	UNCW, Wilmington, NC	0.5575 or 55.75%	
J	AUM, Montgomery, AL	0.6308 or 63.08%	
K	UNCW, Wilmington, NC	0.7418 or 74.18%	
L	UNCW, Wilmington, NC	0.7608 or 76.05%	Third quartile
M	UNCW, Wilmington, NC	0.7825 or 78.25%	
N	UNCW, Wilmington, NC	0.7919 or 79.19%	
O	UNCW, Wilmington, NC	0.8260 or 82.60%	Maximum

5.11 APPLICATION TO DIGITAL FORENSICS SECURITY RISK

Next we wish to study a digital forensics RM theme by studying the following tree diagram in Figure 5.12. Computer forensics as a general topic is an after-the fact (post-facto) approach or technique used by investigators to identify the source of attack on cyber data-related systems. Driven by the ubiquity of computers in modern life and the subsequent rise of cybercriminality and cyberterrorism, the topic of digital forensics is an increasingly salient one, and as a new discipline, it deals with the collection, retrieving, and evaluating of electronic data for the purpose of stopping and mitigating if not entirely avoiding computer fraud by compiling and preserving adequate digital evidence to conduct criminal investigation or to salvage data accidentally lost or deleted.

Though primarily located in the law enforcement community, digital forensics is increasingly practiced within the corporate world as a result of legal and regulatory requirements such as Sarbanes–Oxley. Digital forensics risk essentially involves the assessment, acquisition, and examination of digital evidence in such a manner that legal standards of proof and admissibility are met. In this applied section material, we will adopt a model of digital forensics risk that quantifies an investigator's experience with eight crucial aspects of the digital forensics process.

This section adds the novel concept of quantifying the risk involved in the process through a designed algorithm by the principal author to calculate a digital forensics risk index.

To accomplish this task, numerical and/or cognitive data was collected to supply the input parameters to calculate the quantitative risk index for the digital forensics process. This section will not only present a quantitative model but also generate a prototype numerical index study that facilitates appropriate protocols and procedures in ensuring that legal standards of proof and admissibility are met.

Digital forensics risk arises, for example, when personnel lack the proper tools to conduct investigations, fail to process evidentiary data properly, or do not follow accepted protocols and procedures. Assessing and quantifying digital forensics risk is the goal of this section. To do so, a digital forensics RM based on a series of questions designed to assess personnel's perceptions of digital forensics risk will be utilized. Based on the responses, a digital forensics risk index will be calculated.

Where this approach differs from others such as the ones in the US Department of Justice's *Forensic Examination of Digital Evidence: A Guide for Law Enforcement* (general guidelines and worksheets) [67]; *Error, Uncertainty, and Loss in Digital Evidence* (certainty levels); *Cyber Criminal Activity Analysis Models using Markov Chain for Digital Forensics* (suspicion levels); *Two-Dimensional Evidence Reliability Amplification Process Model for Digital Forensics* (evidence reliability); and *Building a Digital Forensic Laboratory: Establishing and Managing a Successful Facility* (checklist) is that those approaches typically provide general guidance in the form of best practices, classification schemes, or at best a checklist for digital forensics procedures and do not provide quantitative tools (based on game theory) for risk management and mitigation.

One approach that does employ quantification, Metrics for Network Forensics Conviction Evidence, is confined to network forensics, mostly measuring severity impact and does not provide mitigation advice [68].

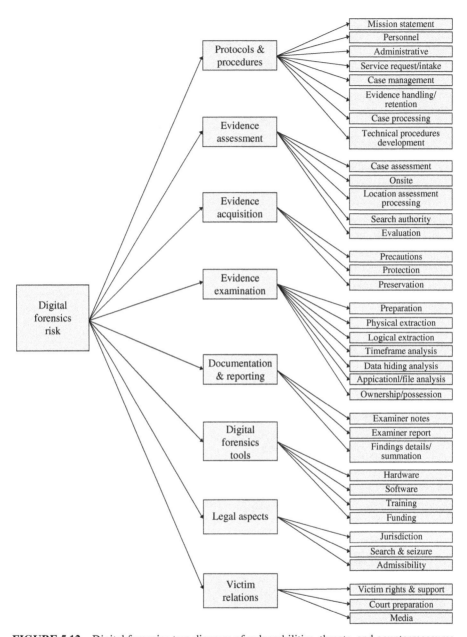

FIGURE 5.12 Digital forensics tree diagram of vulnerabilities, threats, and countermeasures.

The digital forensics RM presented in this chapter will provide objective, automated, dollar-based risk mitigation advice for interested parties such as investigators, administrators, and officers of the court to minimize digital forensics risk (see Fig. 5.13). See Figure 5.14's advice column for sample mitigation advice generated from the respondent's submitted inputs based on industry best practice guidelines, such as the US Department of Justice's *Forensic Examination of Digital Evidence: A Guide for Law*

Digital Forensics Risk Survey

This survey has 8 main categories of vulnerabilities. Please identify the areas below where you have observed vulnerabilities while involved with digital forensics activities within your organization

* A minimum of 2 categories must be chosen:

Vulnerability Area	Reference Page
☐ Protocols & Procedures	Pages 1 & 2
☐ Evidence Assessment	Pages 3 & 4
☐ Evidence Acquisition	Page 5
☐ Evidence Examination	Pages 6 & 7
☐ Documentation & Reporting	Page 8
☐ Digital Forensics Tools	Page 9
☐ Legal Aspects	Page 10
☐ Victim Relations	Page 11

Directions:

This Page:
- Select all vulnerability areas that apply
- Proceed to appropriate pages to complete survey for each vulnerability area.

Survey Page(s):
Vulnerability
- Rate **Vulnerability** (0.1-10) with 10 being *most* vulnerable and 0.1 being *least* vulnerable
- Select all vulnerability statements that apply (*must choose at least one*)
Threat
- Rate **Threat** (0.1-10) with 10 being *greatest* threat and 0.1 being the *least* threat.
- Using square check box, select all threat statements that apply to each threat category chosen. (*must choose at least one*)
Countermeasure
- Rate associated **Countermeasure** for each threat category chosen above (0.1-10) with 0.1 being *least* effective and 10 being the *most* effective countermeasure.
- Using square check box, select all countermeasure statements that apply (*must choose at least one*)

FIGURE 5.13   Digital forensics diagram instructions page for survey subjects.

Enforcement; eight specific vulnerabilities are assessed: Protocols and Procedures, Evidence Assessment, Evidence Acquisition, Evidence Examination, Documentation and Reporting, Digital Forensics Tools, Legal Aspects, and Victim Relations. Within each vulnerability category, questions pertain to specific threats and CMs.

For example, within the Evidence Acquisition vulnerability, respondents are asked questions regarding precautions, protection, and preservation threats and CMs. Within the Evidence Examination vulnerability, respondents are asked questions regarding preparation, physical extraction, logical extraction, timeframe analysis, data hiding analysis,

Vulnerab.	Threat	CM & LCM	Res. Risk	CM & LCM	Res Risk	Change	Opt Cost	Unit Cost	Final Cost	Advice
0.220042	0.415771	0.325000		0.325000						
		0.675000	0.061754	0.675000	0.061754					
	0.237754	0.375000		0.375000						
		0.625000	0.032697	0.625000	0.032697					
	0.346476	0.550000		0.550000						
		0.450000	0.034308	0.450000	0.034308					
0.317111	0.559259	0.450000		0.721705		0.271705	$49.77			Increase the CM capacity for threat "Examiner Notes" for the vulnerability of "Documentation and Reporting" from 45.00% to 72.17% for an improvement of 27.17%
		0.550000	0.097541	0.278296	0.049355					
	0.440741	0.375000		0.375000						
		0.625000	0.087352	0.625000	0.087352					
0.462847	0.408269	0.725000		0.999195		0.274195	$50.23			Increase the CM capacity for threat "Victim Rights and Support" for the vulnerability of "Victim Relations" from 72.50% to 99.92% for an improvement of 27.42%
		0.276000	0.051966	0.000805	0.000162					
	0.250646	0.575000		0.575000						
		0.425000	0.049305	0.425000	0.049305					
	0.341085	0.725000		0.725000						
		0.275000	0.043414	0.275000	0.043414					

Total Change	Total Cost	Break Even Cost	Total Final Cost
54.59%	$100.00	$1.83	

Criticality	1.00	Total Risk	0.458337	Total Risk	0.358337
Capital Cost	$1,000.00	Percentage	45.833670	Percentage	35.833698
Total Threat Costs	N/A	Final Risk	0.458337	Final Risk	0.358337
		ECL	$458.34	ECL	$358.34
				ECL Delta	$100.00

Change Cost · Show where you are in Security Meter · Optimize

Change Unit Cost · Calculate Final Cost · Print Summary · Print Results Table · View Threat Advice · Print Single Threat/CM Selection · Print Advice Threat/CM Selections · Print All Threat/CM Selections · Update Survey Questions

3 Vulnerabilities

FIGURE 5.14 Digital forensics risk-meter game-theoretic risk management results of the median subject.

application/file analysis, and ownership/possession threats and CMs. Within the Digital Forensics Tools vulnerability, respondents are asked questions regarding hardware, software, training, and funding threats and CMs.

See Figure 5.12 for the digital forensics risk diagram detailing vulnerabilities and threats. The responses are then used to generate a quantitative digital forensics risk index.

Using a game-theoretical mathematical approach, the calculated risk index is used to generate an optimization or lowering of risk to desired levels [56]. Further, in the same article cited, mitigation advice will be generated to show interested parties such as investigators, administrators, and officers of the court in what areas the risk can be reduced to optimized or desired levels such as from 45.8% to 35.8% as shown in the screenshot representing the median response from the study participants (Table 5.14).

See Figure 5.14 for a screenshot of the median digital forensics RM results displaying threat, CM, and residual risk indices; optimization options; and risk mitigation advice. For this study, a random sample of 27 respondents was taken and their residual risk results are tabulated and presented in Figure 5.14. The survey used in this section for the assessment showed the complexity of the field, as one realizes digital forensics encompasses tools, procedures, specific training, budget, and trial. Digital forensics has two crucial phases. The first phase involves all the forensics involved with the collection of data, while the second phase involves defending the data collected, the means by which it was collected, and chain of custody applied from the original collection until court. The initial goal was to obtain survey input from local city leaders. Although individuals from the governor's office, Montgomery Police Department, and district attorney's office were willing to assist, their busy schedule prevented their office from providing input to the digital forensics survey. Fortunately, a co-author had contacts at some law enforcement offices, and they agreed to make personnel available for the survey and eventual follow-up [96, 100].

TABLE 5.14 Companies' (AFIT, AUPD, ECSO, OPD) No-Names Disclosed Survey Results for the Risk-Meter Study, Ranked Within and Overall, Where Median is 45.83 (ECSO8) and Average is 44.73% (AUPD5: 44.59% is the Result that Comes the Closest)

AFIT1	52.47	6th	2nd out of 4 within AFIT
			(*group median for AFIT*)
AFIT2	49.90	9th	3rd out of 4 within AFIT
AFIT3	52.71	5th	1st out of 4 within AFIT
AFIT4	47.64	10th	4th out of 4 within AFIT
AUPD1	31.15	26th	7th out of 7 within AUPD
AUPD2	39.67	20th	5th out of 7 within AUPD
AUPD3	50.02	8th	1st out of 7 within AUPD
AUPD4	36.98	21st	6th out of 7 within AUPD
AUPD5	44.59	16th ~ *overall*	4th out of 7 within AUPD
		average	(*group median for AUPD*)
AUPD6	46.06	13th	3rd out of 7 within AUPD
AUPD7	47.06	11th	2nd out of 7 within AUPD
ECSO1	51.80	7th	5th out of 9 within ECSO
			(*group median for ECSO*)
ECSO2	46.66	12th	6th out of 9 within ECSO
ECSO3	56.94	2nd	2nd out of 9 within ECSO
ECSO4	57.67	1st	1st out of 9 within ECSO
ECSO5	54.87	3rd	3rd out of 9 within ECSO
ECSO6	41.36	19th	9th out of 9 within ECSO
ECSO7	54.84	4th	4th out of 9 within ECSO
ECSO8	45.83	14th *overall*	7th out of 9 within ECSO
		median	
ECSO9	45.01	15th	8th out of 9 within ECSO
OPD1	35.00	23rd	4th out of 7 within OPD
			(*group median for OPD*)
OPD2	42.56	18th	2nd out of 7 within OPD
OPD3	44.35	17th	1st out of 7 within OPD
OPD4	33.39	25th	6th out of 7 within OPD
OPD5	28.23	27th	7th out of 7 within OPD
OPD6	34.39	24th	5th out of 7 within OPD
OPD7	36.41	22nd	3rd out of 7 within OPD

Survey taker residual risk % ranked overall out of 27.

Ultimately, three law enforcement offices and one special investigation/training organization participated and provided valuable input. At each location, participants ranged from investigators, initial responders, digital forensics specialists, to legal experts, that is, district attorney's office personnel. The range of expertise of the participants was invaluable, as each provided insight into an aspect of the survey that is often unique to a position within a department. Because of this range of expertise, the author believes they were able to capture the three main components of the survey portion of the RM. Perspectives from collection of evidence, packaging of evidence for trial, and presentation of evidence at trial activities were all given. Although the special investigation/training organization had much less participants, they offered a unique perspective, as they had an organization that focuses on training digital forensics experts for the military.

The results were then run for each participant, determining the initial repair cost to mitigate. This was determined by using a criticality of 1.0 and a production cost of $1000. The median of all results was determined and then optimized through the RM to determine the best "bang for the buck" that would reduce the participant's total residual risk by 10%. The initial total residual risk for the median participant was 45.8% with an ECL of $458.34. Once optimized, the total risk was reduced to 35.8%, and the ECL was reduced by $100 to a total ECL of $358.34 as seen in Figure 5.14. The first optimized managerial advice was to increase the CM capacity for the threat "Examiner Notes" for the vulnerability "Documentation and Reporting" from 45.00% to 72.17% for an improvement of 27.17%. The second optimized managerial advice was to increase the CM capacity for the threat "Victim Rights and Support" for the vulnerability "Victim Relations" from 72.50% to 99.92% for an improvement of 27.42%.

In addition to determining the overall median and optimizing it, the median for each organization was determined. The optimization for each organization (except organization 4 with an even number of participants) was run and the results discussed with the point of contact for that organization. In each case, the representative seemed impressed with the results and noted the results for possible future implementation. One organization actually commented that they had already begun looking into increases in at least one CM that was identified by the optimization. Clearly, this validated the tool and its usefulness in their eyes. The digital forensics RM breaks new ground in that it provides a quantitative assessment of risk to the user as well as recommendations for mitigating that risk.

As such, it will be a highly useful tool to interested parties such as investigators, administrators, and officers of the court seeking to minimize/mitigate digital forensics risk. Future work will involve the addition of CLOUD computing concerns such as service provider cooperation and data accessibility as well as the incorporation of new questions so as to better refine user responses and subsequent calculation of risk and mitigation recommendations.

Mitigation of digital forensics risk, given the budgetary figures, will greatly facilitate the success of digital forensics investigations, ensuring that legal standards of proof and admissibility are ultimately met. The digital forensics RM tool and its future refinement provide the means to identify areas where risk can be minimized as well as provide the objective, dollar-based mitigation advice to analysts to take cautionary measures.

5.12 APPLICATION TO BUSINESS CONTRACTING RISK

The risk factors that affect business operations are many. Identifying and managing those vulnerabilities and threats scientifically is a key to conducting successful business operations extending to software risk operations [71]. Failure to identify and manage these sources of risk will have very real consequences ranging from poor financial performance to business collapse. In this section, a software tool to facilitate assessment and management of business risk is examined. The business RM provides this critical tool for management and high-level decision makers. Using game theory and statistically driven methodologies, it provides objective, quantitative risk assessment and, unlike any other tool available today, guidance for allocating resources for risk mitigation. As such, management and decision makers in commerce and industry will be greatly aided in their efforts to achieve optimal business operations by the use of this rational and objective tool for assessing and mitigating risk. The sources of business operation vulnerabilities and threats can range from the quality of personnel to macroeconomic factors and software applications [72]. The consequences to those corporations and organizations that fail to identify and manage vulnerabilities and risks result in diminished financial performance if not business failure. Indeed, the Census Bureau puts the survival rate of new firms founded in 2005 through 2010 at only 43% [73]. To minimize and avoid such threats and potential business failures, a rational, scientific approach that identifies, assesses, and manages business risk is required.

The identification and management of risk is a key aspect of successful business operations. The business RM tool proposed here provides a unique and objective methodology that is critically needed. This pioneering work represents a paradigm shift in risk assessment. The business RM provides a quantitative risk assessment, unlike the subjective high–medium–low or red–yellow–green scales commonly seen in other assessment methodologies. While there are other approaches to identifying and managing risk as detailed in the Institute of Management Accountants' Enterprise Risk Management: Tools and Techniques for Effective Implementation [75], none provide a means of allocating risk mitigation expenditures. In contrast, the business RM provides objective and scientific guidance in allocating monetary resources for managing risk in accordance with budgetary constraints. Additionally, the business RM provides a means to shift from often subjective and crude risk evaluation mechanisms to a verifiable, quantitative approach to risk management, resulting in an optimized expenditure of risk remediation dollars.

In this section, a model of business risk that quantifies the respondent's experience with ten crucial aspects of business risk is adopted. Those responses are subsequently used to calculate the business risk index through a designed algorithm by the principal author. To accomplish this task, numerical and/or cognitive data was collected from 40 respondents to supply the input parameters to calculate the quantitative business risk index. This section will not only present a quantitative model but also provide a remedial cost-optimized game-theoretic analysis about how to bring an undesirable risk down to a user-determined "tolerable level." Lastly, it is an adaptable framework that can be customized and configured by the analyst with no custom coding (XML inputs).

This applied section material implements a methodology on how to reduce business risk. A software-centered holistic approach is proposed to aid management and decision makers in identifying, assessing, and managing business risk. Ten vulnerabilities are assessed: Personnel Quality, Cost Factors and Delivery Time, Client Perceptions, Local Service Reps Missing, Communication Problems, Hardware Deficiency, Software Deficiency, Management Quality, and Macroeconomic Factors. Within each vulnerability category, questions pertain to specific threats and CMs. For example, within the Delivery Time vulnerability, respondents are asked questions regarding logistics, delivery companies, adverse events, and alternate delivery methods as threats, and pertaining CMs. Within the Communication Problems vulnerability, respondents are asked questions regarding language barriers, customs barriers, legal system differences, and technology threats and related CMs. See Figure 5.15 for the business risk diagram detailing

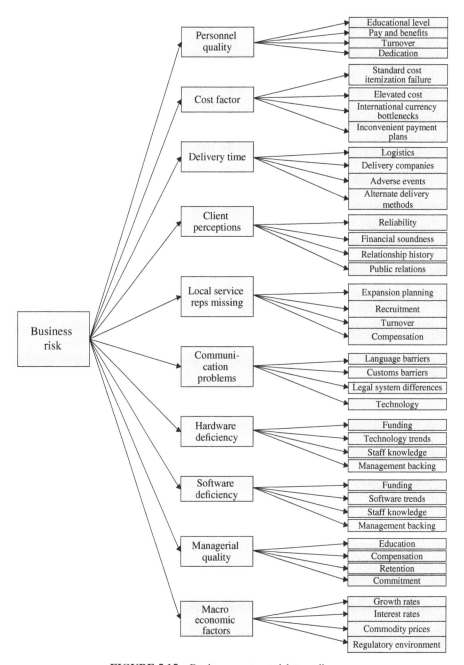

FIGURE 5.15 Business contract risk tree diagram.

vulnerabilities and threats. The respondents' answers are then used to generate a quantitative business risk index. While the business RM can be utilized on virtually any business process, this particular implementation focuses on ten key areas critical in ensuring optimal business operations [93].

- Personnel Quality: Fundamental to daily operations as well as long-term success, the need to employ the highest quality personnel is critical. This key area focuses on educational level, pay and benefits, turnover, and dedication. Each of these areas must be addressed to ensure the selection and retention of the highest quality personnel.
- Cost Factor: This area focuses on the costs and revenue streams integral to doing business, that is, standard cost itemization failure, elevated cost, international currency bottlenecks, and inconvenient payment plans.
- Delivery Time: Critical to modern commerce, this key component must be optimized to prevent delays and customer dissatisfaction. This key area focuses on logistics, delivery companies, adverse events, and alternate deliveries.
- Client Perceptions: Assuring positive perceptions by the public and the goodwill of clients is critical to continued business success. This key area focuses on reliability, financial soundness, relationship history, and public relations.
- Local Service Reps Missing: Critical because of potential market share loss, the need to have a business presence should be ensured. This key area focuses on expansion planning, recruitment, turnover, and compensation.
- Communication Problems: Critical to international business, this key component is a must in today's global economy. This key area focuses on language barriers, customs barriers, legal system differences, and technology.
- Hardware Deficiency: Essential for keeping up in today's tech-driven economy, this key area focuses on funding, technology trends, staff knowledge, and management backing.
- Software Deficiency: Also essential for keeping up in today's tech-driven economy, this key area focuses on funding, software trends, staff knowledge, and management backing.
- Managerial Quality: The quality of a company's leadership often makes or breaks it. This key area focuses on education, compensation, retention, and commitment.
- Macroeconomic Factors: This key area provides the environment in which businesses must operate and focuses on growth rates, interest rates, commodity prices, and the regulatory environment.

While these ten areas are not exhaustive, they are relatively comprehensive of and critical to business risk. This applied section material focuses on the areas vital to business operations and provides management and decision makers with an analytical framework they can use to more efficiently structure their business operations [95]. Questions are designed to elicit the user's response regarding the perceived business risk from particular threats and CMs which the users may employ to counteract those threats. For example, in the Communication Problems vulnerability, questions regarding legal system differences include both threat and CM questions.

Threat questions would include:

- Does the country lack a well-established legal system?
- Is the legal system based on something other than English or U.S common law?
- Are judicial decisions based on other than the rule of law?
- Does litigation take several years if not a decade?
- Do you lack a clear sense of what the legal system is in a particular country?

While CM questions would include:

- Did the parties agree to outside arbitration or adjudication in a third country?
- Has the company hired local legal representation?
- Did the company purchase political risk insurance?
- Did the company require prior payment?

Essentially, the users are responding yes or no to these questions. These responses are then used to calculate a residual risk index. Using a game-theoretical mathematical approach, the calculated risk index is then used to generate an optimization or lowering of risk to desired levels. Further, mitigation guidance will be generated to aid management and decision makers in resource allocation decisions for lowering risk. That is, in what areas can the risk be reduced to optimized or desired levels such as from 47.6% to 37.6% in the screenshot representing the median response from the survey participants or respondents? See Figure 5.16 for a screenshot of the median business RM results displaying threat, CM, and residual risk indices; optimization options, and risk mitigation advice.

For this study, a random sample of 40 respondents was taken, and their residual risk results are tabulated and presented at the end of this section [71]. See Table 5.15 and Figure 5.17. Respondents' familiarity with business risk was composed of corporate experience. The business RM breaks new ground in that it provides a quantitative assessment of risk to the user as well as recommendations for mitigating that risk [98].

As such, it will be a highly useful tool for management and decision makers seeking to minimize and mitigate business risk in an objective, quantitatively based manner. Future work will involve the incorporation of new vulnerabilities and additional questions so as to better refine user responses and subsequent calculation of risk and mitigation recommendations. Minimization and mitigation of business risk such as in Figure 5.16 will greatly benefit not only the companies deploying the tool but also the society at large through greater prosperity and economic stability. The business RM tool provides the means to do so [99].

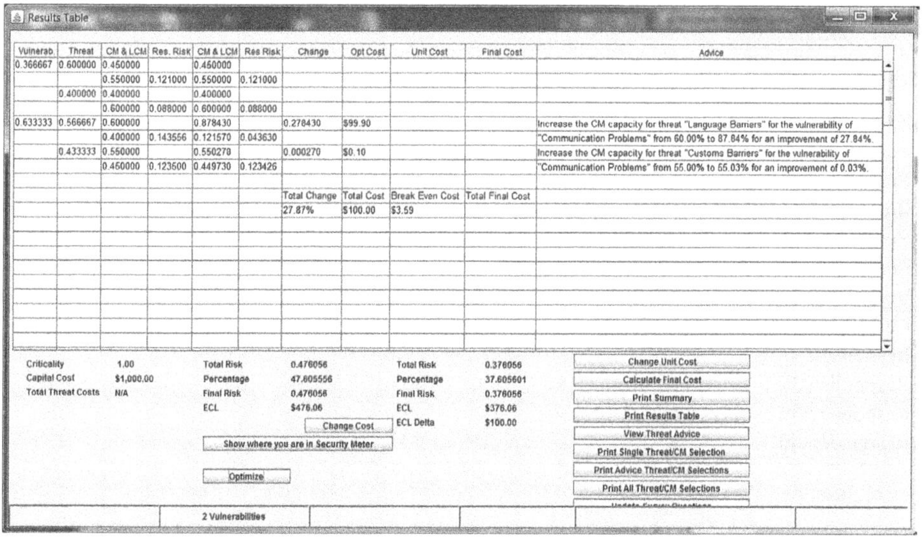

FIGURE 5.16   Median business contracting risk-meter results to represent 40 respondents.

TABLE 5.15 Respondent Residual Risk Results Survey Results For the Business Risk-O-Meter Study (rounded To Two Decimal Places), Ranked Overall, Where Median: 47.61% (Respondent20) and Average: 48.14% (Respondent21: 48.22% Is the Result That Comes the Closest)

Survey Taker	Residual Risk %	Ranked from Least to Greatest Risk (Out of 40)	Remarks
Respondent1	28.92	1st	
Respondent2	33.65	2nd	
Respondent3	34.36	3rd	
Respondent4	36.19	4th	
Respondent5	39.15	5th	
Respondent6	40.35	6th	
Respondent7	42.08	7th	
Respondent8	42.86	8th	
Respondent9	44.61	9th	
Respondent10	44.94	10th	
Respondent11	45.21	11th	
Respondent12	45.63	12th	
Respondent13	45.69	13th	
Respondent14	46.63	14th	
Respondent15	46.75	15th	
Respondent16	47.08	16th	
Respondent17	47.13	17th	
Respondent18	47.23	18th	
Respondent19	47.57	19th	
Respondent20	47.61	20th	*OVERALL MEDIAN*
Respondent21	48.22	21st	*OVERALL AVERAGE*
Respondent22	49.03	22nd	
Respondent23	49.10	23rd	
Respondent24	50.22	24th	
Respondent25	50.24	25th	
Respondent26	50.34	26th	
Respondent27	50.78	27th	
Respondent28	50.78	28th	
Respondent29	50.82	29th	
Respondent30	51.27	30th	
Respondent31	51.40	31st	
Respondent32	55.08	32nd	
Respondent33	56.13	33rd	
Respondent34	56.75	34th	
Respondent35	57.45	35th	
Respondent36	60.22	36th	
Respondent37	60.22	37th	
Respondent38	62.46	38th	
Respondent39	63.39	39th	
Respondent40	83.24	40th	

Business Risk Survey

This survey has 10 main categories of vulnerabilities. Please identify the areas below where you have observed vulnerabilities while involved with Software Development Lifecycle activities within your organization.

* A minimum of 2 categories must be chosen:

Vulnerability Area	Reference Page
☐ Personal Quality	3
☐ Cost Factor	5
☐ Delivery Time	7
☐ Client Perceptions	9
☐ Local Service Reps Missing	11
☐ Communication Problems	13
☐ Hardware Deficiency	15
☐ Software Deficiency	17
☐ Managerial Quality	19
☐ Macro Economics Factors	21

Directions:

This Page:
- Select all vulnerability areas that apply
- Proceed to appropriate pages to complete survey for each vulnerability area.

Survey Page(s):
Vulnerability
- Rate **Vulnerability** (0.1-10) with 10 being *most* vulnerable and 0.1 being *least* vulnerable
- Select all vulnerability statements that apply (*must choose at least one*)
Threat
- Rate **Threat** (0.1-10) with 10 being *greatest* threat and 0.1 being the *least* threat.
- Using square check box, select all threat statements that apply to each threat category chosen. (*must choose at least one*)
Countermeasure
- Rate associated **Countermeasure** for each threat category chosen above (0.1-10) with 0.1 being *least* effective and 10 being the *most* effective countermeasure.
- Using square check box, select all countermeasure statements that apply (*must choose at least one*)

FIGURE 5.17 A List of Vulnerability, Threat and Countermeasure Questions.

5.13 APPLICATION TO NATIONAL CYBERSECURITY RISK

One of the most severe threats facing the United States or all free nations today is the national (federal and state) cyber-security in the new cyberspace era [74]. The astronomically high malicious attacks, reminiscent of the 1950s cold war, has triggered a cyber-cold war among the world's once peaceful nations. The increasing number of attempted and actual cyber-security breaches, originating from both criminal organizations and state-sponsored ones, and the very real and potential consequences ranging from financial to catastrophic losses make this threat undeniably and urgently addressed. In this chapter, a software tool to facilitate assessment and management of this unprecedented global threat is proposed. The national cyber security RM provides this critical tool for policy makers. But beyond mere economic impact, the potential damage could be globally catastrophic as in the nightmare scenario of multiple nuclear facilities' supervisory control and data acquisition (SCADA) systems being taken over simultaneously and causing uncontrolled meltdowns that could blanket entire continents in radioactivity. Such an event would make Chernobyl pale in comparison. To minimize and avoid such threats and potential damage, a rational, scientific approach that identifies, assesses, and manages national cyber security threats is required.

The identification and management of risk is the essence of cyber-security. The national cyber-security RM tool proposed here provides a unique and objective methodology that is critically needed.

The pioneering analysis represents a paradigm shift in risk assessment. The national cyber-security RM provides a quantitative risk assessment, unlike the subjective quantitative risk assessment and unlike any other tool available today, guidance for allocating resources for risk mitigation. As such, decision and policy makers in government and industry will be greatly aided in their efforts to achieve greater cyber-security by the use of this rational and objective tool for assessing and mitigating risk [76].

Current national threats can range from mischievous lone hackers up the scale, to organized cybercriminal gangs, to state-sponsored cyber-espionage and cyberterrorism. The economic damage inflicted to individuals, corporations, and the national infrastructure is put high–medium–low or red–yellow–green scales commonly seen in other assessment methodologies. While there are other approaches to identifying and managing risk such as the National Institute of Standards and Technology's Common Vulnerability Scoring System (CVSS), none provide a means of allocating risk mitigation expenditures. In contrast, the national cyber-security RM provides objective and scientific guidance in allocating monetary resources for managing risk in accordance with budgetary constraints. Additionally, the national cyber-security RM provides a means to shift from often subjective and crude risk evaluation mechanisms to a verifiable, quantitative approach to risk management, resulting in an optimized expenditure of security remediation dollars.

In this section, a model of national cyber security risk that quantifies the respondent's experience with eight crucial aspects of national cyber security is adopted. Those responses are subsequently used to calculate the national cyber security risk index through a designed algorithm by the principal author. To accomplish this task, numerical and/or cognitive data was collected from 34 respondents to supply the input parameters to calculate the quantitative security risk index for national cyber security.

This section will not only present a quantitative model but also provide a remedial cost-optimized game-theoretic analysis about how to bring an undesirable risk down to a user-determined "tolerable level." Lastly, it is an adaptable framework that can be customized and configured by the analyst with no custom coding (XML inputs). This application implements a methodology on how to reduce national cyber security risk. A software-centered holistic approach is proposed to aid computer security personnel, facility managers, and decision and policy makers in identifying, assessing, and managing cyber-security risk. Eight vulnerabilities are assessed: Energy Facilities, Transport Hubs, the Internet, Government Net, Military Installations, Financial Net, Health Institutions, and Water Supply/Food Chain. Within each vulnerability category, questions pertain to specific threats

Vulnerab.	Threat	CM & LCM	Res. Risk	CM & LCM	Res Risk	Change	Opt Cost	Unit Cost	Final Cost	Advice
0.208333	1.000000	0.650000		0.650266		0.000266	$0.08			Increase the CM capacity for threat "Control Facilities" for the vulnerability of
		0.360000	0.072917	0.349734	0.072861					"Energy Facilities" from 65.00% to 65.03% for an improvement of 0.03%.
0.312500	1.000000	0.350000		0.678934		0.328934	$102.76			Increase the CM capacity for threat "Weapons Theft/Tampering" for the vulnerability of
		0.650000	0.203125	0.321066	0.100333					"Military Installations" from 35.00% to 67.89% for an improvement of 32.89%.
0.479167	0.2777	0.650000		0.650000						
		0.350000	0.046586	0.350000	0.046586					
	0.300000	0.450000		0.450000						
		0.550000	0.079062	0.550000	0.079063					
	0.422222	0.500000		0.500000						
		0.500000	0.101157	0.500000	0.101157					

Total Change	Total Cost	Break Even Cost	Total Final Cost
32.92%	$102.85	$3.12	

Criticality	1.00	Total Risk	0.502847	Total Risk	0.400000
Capital Cost	$1,000.00	Percentage	50.284722	Percentage	39.999997
Total Threat Costs	N/A	Final Risk	0.502847	Final Risk	0.400000
		ECL	$502.85	ECL	$400.00
				ECL Delta	$102.85

Change Cost
Show where you are in Security Meter
Optimize

Change Unit Cost
Calculate Final Cost
Print Summary
Print Results Table
View Threat Advice
Print Single Threat/CM Selection
Print Advice Threat/CM Selections
Print All Threat/CM Selections
Update Survey Questions

3 Vulnerabilities

FIGURE 5.18 Median national cyber security risk-meter results from the survey.

and CMs. For example, within the Energy Facilities vulnerability, respondents are asked questions regarding power lines, control facilities, hydroelectric power plants, fossil fuels, and nuclear power threats and CMs. Within the Internet vulnerability, respondents are asked questions regarding physical network, domain name servers, other servers, hacking, denial of service, other cyber-attacks, and virus threats and CMs. See Figure 5.18 for survey outcomes and Figure 5.19 for sample survey instructions. The respondents' answers are then used to generate a quantitative national cyber security risk index after the RM software.

The author's innovation, that is, the national cyber-security RM (an automated software tool), will provide computer security personnel, facility managers, and decision and policy makers a measurable assessment of their current cyber-security risk as well as detailed associated cost and risk mitigation suggestions for identified vulnerabilities and threats. The national cyber-security RM will be demonstrated to provide such assessment and guidance for the allocation of resources for mitigating that risk. The cyber-security metric out of 100% will be assessed and a remedial cost-optimized game-theoretic analysis provided to bring an undesirable risk down to a user-determined "tolerable level." The approach the author proposes here is a game-theoretical-based approach that emphasizes the quantitative analysis of vulnerabilities, threats, and CMs.

While the national cyber security RM can be utilized on virtually any aspect of infrastructure or type of facility, this particular implementation focuses on eight key areas critical in ensuring national cyber security:

- Energy Facilities: Fundamental to daily life as well as security, the need to secure these facilities is critical given the potential damage should something go awry. This key area focuses on power lines, control facilities, hydroelectric, fossil fuels, and nuclear power. Each of these areas must be addressed to ensure continued and undisrupted national operations.

National Cybersecurity Risk Survey

This survey has 8 main categories of vulnerabilities. Please identify the areas below where you have observed vulnerabilities while involved with digital forensics activities within your organization

* A minimum of 2 categories must be chosen:

Vulnerability Area	Reference Page
☐ Energy Facilities	Pages 1, 2
☐ Transport Hubs	Pages 3, 4
☐ Internet	Pages 5, 6, 7
☐ Government Net	Page 8
☐ Military Installations	Pages 9, 10
☐ Financial Net	Pages 11, 12
☐ Health Institutions	Pages 13, 14
☐ Water Supply/Food Chains	Pages 15, 16

Directions:

This Page:
- Select all vulnerability areas that apply
- Proceed to appropriate pages to complete survey for each vulnerability area.

Survey Page(s):
Vulnerability
- Rate **Vulnerability** (1-10) with 10 being *most* vulnerable and 1 being *least* vulnerable
- Select all vulnerability statements that apply (*must choose at least one*)
Threat
- Rate **Threat** (1-10) with 10 being *greatest* threat and 1 being the *least* threat.
- Using square check box, select all threat statements that apply to each threat category chosen. (*must choose at least one*)
Countermeasure
- Rate associated **Countermeasure** for each threat category chosen above (1-10) with 1 being *least* effective and 10 being the *most* effective countermeasure.
- Using square check box, select all countermeasure statements that apply (*must choose at least one*)

FIGURE 5.19   The national cyber security risk-meter survey instructions.

- Transport Hubs: This area focuses on the facilities integral to transporting people as well as goods and services nationally, that is, airports, harbors, railway systems, highway systems, and distribution logistics.
- The Internet: Critical to not only modern commerce but also control and communications, this key infrastructural component must be secured to prevent intellectual property, financial, and physical loss. This key area focuses on physical network, domain name servers, other servers, hacking, denial of service, other cyber-attacks, and viruses/malware.

- Government Net: Assuring the integrity, availability, and authenticity of governmental and associated contractors' networks is critical to national security. This key area focuses on federal, state, and local facilities.
- Military Installations: Critical because of the potential damage from misuse of weaponry and facilities, the need to keep unauthorized/unwanted individuals from gaining access to systems via electronic means as well as protecting the facilities that house these platforms must be ensured. This key area focuses on physical network, servers, weapons theft/tampering, and unconventional weapons.
- Financial Net: Critical to ensuring the daily life of citizens and the economy as a whole, this key infrastructural component must be secured to prevent financial loss and maintain a healthy economy. This key area focuses on physical network, servers, data and records, and power supply.
- Health Institutions: Essential for preserving the population's health and well-being as well as patient confidentiality, this key area focuses on physical network, servers, data and records, and nuclear/bio/chemical agents.
- Water Supply/Food Chain: Also essential for a nation's health and well-being, contamination of water and food supplies must be prevented. This key area focuses on data and records, inspection and testing facilities, physical access, and nuclear/bio/chemical agents.

While these eight areas are not exhaustive, they are relatively comprehensive of and critical to national cyber security. This applied section material focuses on the areas vital to national cyber security and provides computer security personnel, facility managers, and decision and policy makers with an analytical framework they can use to more efficiently secure their resources and facilities. Questions are designed to elicit the user's response regarding the perceived risk to national cyber security from particular threats and the CMs the users may employ to counteract those threats. For example, in the energy facilities vulnerability, questions regarding control facilities include both threat and CM questions. Threat questions include:

- Does your utility use an Ethernet-based substation automation system (SAS)?
- Does your utility fail to adhere to industry standards for reducing the risks from compromise of cyber assets?
- Does your utility use an SCADA?
- Can relay settings be accessed through the SAS user interface?
- Can the SAS server be remotely accessed over the Internet?

While CM questions would include:

- Is your utility's SAS firewall and password protected?
- Has your utility implemented NERC CIP standards and policies to reduce the risks to critical cyber assets?
- Has your utility implemented higher security levels for its SCADA?
- Is your utility SAS user interface for relay settings password protected using special character, uppercase/lowercase combinations, etc.?

- Is your utility's SAS server password protected using special characters, uppercase/lowercase combinations, etc.?

Essentially, the users are responding yes or no to these questions. These responses are used to calculate residual risk. Using a game-theoretical mathematical approach, the calculated risk index is used to generate an optimization or lowering of risk to desired levels. Further, mitigation advice will be generated to aid computer security personnel, facility managers, decision and policy makers, and other interested parties in mitigation and resource allocation decisions. That is, in what areas can the risk be reduced to desired levels such as from 50% to 40% in the screenshot representing the median respondents from the study below presented.

See Figure 5.18 for a screenshot of the median national cyber-security RM results displaying threat, CM, and residual risk indices; optimization options, and risk mitigation advice. See Figure 5.19 for the survey example and Figure 5.20 for the tree diagram. For this study, a random sample of 34 respondents was taken, and their residual risk results are tabulated and presented at the end of this section. Respondents' familiarity with national cyber security risk included corporate, governmental, and military experience. Cyberspace has quickly become the primary domain for current national security concerns in all industrialized nations.

Following the tragic 9/11 events, emerging terrorist threats against food and water supplies, electricity, and national networking capability sparked a review of the US critical infrastructure. The national cyber security RM breaks new ground in that it provides a quantitative assessment of risk to the user as well as recommendations for mitigating that risk. As such, it will be a highly useful tool for computer security personnel, facility managers, decision and policy makers, and other interested parties seeking to minimize and mitigate national cyber security risk in an objective, quantitatively based manner. Future work will involve the incorporation of new vulnerabilities and additional questions so as to better refine user responses and subsequent calculation of risk and mitigation recommendations. Minimization and mitigation of national cyber security risk will greatly benefit not only the organizations deploying the tool but also the society at large through the minimization of security breaches leading to intellectual property, financial, and physical loss. The national cyber security RM tool, and its future refinement provide the means to do so. The results for the median and mean of these surveys indicate that control facilities and weapons storage/protection are vulnerabilities that require the most attention.

Military installations have rules and regulations on the protection of weapons and critical infrastructure. Since most of these rules and regulations were not in place when certain facilities, to include armories, were constructed, it may not be possible to implement the rules. This could be due to environmental impacts, overall facility construction, or adjacent facilities. Sometimes implementing the new rules and regulations is extremely cost-prohibitive. Military installations will typically conduct a vulnerability assessment and make a decision to either implement compensatory measure or just waive the requirement for a specific facility. Respondents to this survey were aware of waivers and compensatory measures but still indicated a vulnerability to those areas.

Respondents seemed to believe the survey served a valuable purpose [19a, b] in Table 5.16. Most were a bit apprehensive about answering questions about vulnerabilities to a military installation. Military installations undergo multiple vulnerability assessments and evaluations. All military installations have their own in-house expertise on such matters;

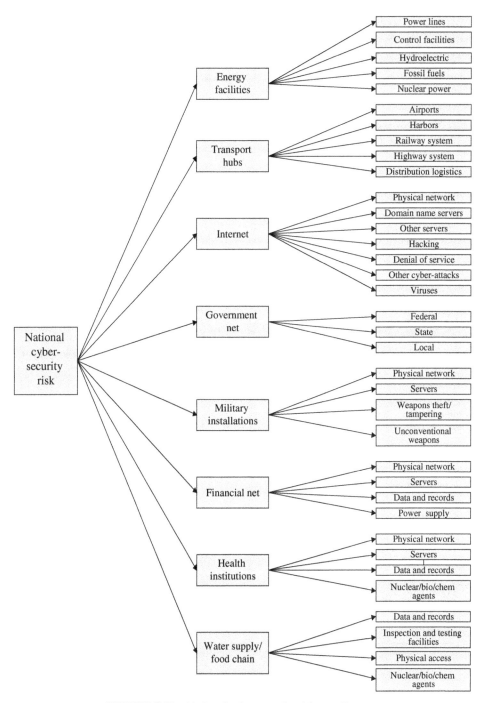

FIGURE 5.20 National cyber security risk tree diagram.

TABLE 5.16 Respondent (Companies A, B, C) Survey Residual Risk Results for the National Cyber Security Risk-Meter Study Ranked, Where Median is 50.28% (B10) and Average is 48.86% (B6: 48.6% Is the Result that Comes the Closest Out of 34 Subjects)

Company A1	51.98	8th	1st out of 13 within Company A
Company A2	44.41	29th	8th out of 13 within Company A
Company A3	48.23	21st	4th out of 13 within Company A
Company A4	50.34	17th	3rd out of 13 within Company A
Company A5	46.57	27th	7th out of 13 within Company A
			(group median for Company A)
Company A6	42.67	31st	10th out of 13 within Company A
Company A7	47.14	24th	5th out of 13 within Company A
Company A8	42.94	30th	9th out of 13 within Company A
Company A9	39.01	34th	12th out of 13 within Company A
Company A10	42.25	32nd	13th out of 13 within Company A
Company A11	51.07	11th	2nd out of 13 within Company A
Company A12	40.21	33rd	11th out of 13 within Company A
Company A13	46.59	26th	6th out of 13 within Company A
Company B1	50.83	13th	6th out of 14 within Company B
Company B2	51.06	12th	5th out of 14 within Company B
Company B3	54.55	2nd	2nd out of 14 within Company B
Company B4	47.45	22nd	13th out of 14 within Company B
Company B5	52.69	7th	4th out of 14 within Company B
Company B6	48.58	19th ~ *overall average*	11th out of 14 within Company B
Company B7	54.17	4th	3rd out of 14 within Company B
Company B8	55.03	1st	1st out of 14 within Company B
Company B9	50.66	14th	7th out of 14 within Company B
Company B10	50.28	18th = *overall median*	10th out of 14 within Company B
Company B11	29.77	20th	12th out of 14 within Company B
Company B12	50.38	16th	9th out of 14 within Company B
Company B13	50.64	15th	8th out of 14 within Company B
			(group median for Company B)
Company B14	47.03	25th	14th out of 14 within Company B
Company C1	44.92	28th	7th out of 7 within Company C
Company C2	51.77	9th	4th out of 7 within Company C
			(group median for Company C)
Company C3	53.12	6th	3rd out of 7 within Company C
Company C4	54.43	3rd	1st out of 7 within Company C
Company C5	47.41	23rd	6th out of 7 within Company C
Company C6	51.38	10th	5th out of 7 within Company C
Company C7	53.28	5th	2nd out of 7 within Company C

moreover there is extensive guidance from the Joint Staff and Headquarters Air Force on how vulnerabilities will be addressed. In future studies using the national cyber-security survey, one should focus their efforts on federal agencies outside the military, as well as state and local government agencies.

5.14 APPLICATION TO AIRPORT SERVICE QUALITY RISK

The topic of airport satisfaction, as a vivid example of service informatics, deals with assessing a quantitative index for airport satisfaction risk using RM software. The topic is one that anyone who has flown recently is certainly familiar with. The new millennium's environment has altered air travel as we knew it with additional security, crowding, and costs for the traveler. Airport satisfaction risk is concerned primarily with how travelers rate their experience with the various aspects of airport-related travel including issues such as security, food, and baggage claim and on-time performance to name a few. In this applied section material, we will adopt a model of airport satisfaction risk that quantifies the traveler's experience with eight crucial facets of airport-related travel. However, we will add an original concept of quantification to the existing model through a designed algorithm by the author to calculate the airport satisfaction risk index. To accomplish this task, numerical and/or cognitive data was collected to supply the input parameters to calculate the quantitative risk index for airport satisfaction. This section will not only present a quantitative model but also generate a prototype numerical index study that breaks new ground in this field.

Airport satisfaction is a familiar topic to air travelers and the source of many conversations and complaints. In addition to the changes brought about by the new millennium (increased traveler scrutiny, crowding, costs, and restrictions), the prolonged airline financial crisis has added to the diminution of services and their increased costs. Airport satisfaction becomes an issue when the travel experience is negatively impacted as in the case of lost luggage or surprise fees. In large part, travelers are satisfied when they can travel without hindrance or frustration. Assessing the nature of airport satisfaction is the goal of this section. To do so, an airport satisfaction RM based on a series of questions designed to assess the traveler's perceptions of airport satisfaction will be utilized. Based on the traveler's responses, an airport satisfaction risk index will be calculated. Where this approach differs from others such as *J.D. Power and Associates 2010 North America Airport Satisfaction Study* [77] or *Skytrax's Airport Quality* website [78] is that those approaches merely measure airport satisfaction and do not provide tools (based on game theory) for risk management and mitigation. The airport satisfaction RM will provide objective, automated, dollar-based risk mitigation advice for interested parties such as airport managers, ground personnel, customs/immigration officials, and airlines to enhance the air travel experience. See Figure 5.20's advice column employing game theory for sample mitigation advice generated from the respondent's submitted inputs.

Vulnerabilities and Threats: Inspired by the authors' travel experiences, eight vulnerabilities are assessed: Security Checks, Food Service and Amenities, Immigration and Customs, Service Personnel, Waiting Areas and Baggage Claim, Appearance and Cleanliness, Airport Transport Services, and On-Time Performance. Within each vulnerability category, questions pertain to specific threats and CMs. For example, within Security Checks vulnerability, travelers are asked questions regarding curbside, baggage screening, security checkpoints, gate security, and general airport security threats and CMs. Within Waiting Areas and Baggage Claim vulnerability, travelers are asked questions regarding comfort, waiting time, loss and delay, cart availability, delivery options, and multifaith area threats and CMs. Within Airport Transport Services vulnerability, travelers are asked questions regarding accessibility, gate and parking distance, timeliness, cost, and availability threats and CMs. See Figure 5.22 for the airport satisfaction risk diagram detailing vulnerabilities and threats. The user's responses are then used to generate a practical, easy-to- interpret, quantitatively workable, and manageable airport satisfaction risk metric or index [97].

Questions are designed to elicit the traveler's response regarding the perceived risk to airport satisfaction from particular threats and the CMs the travelers may employ to counteract those threats. For example, in the security checks vulnerability, questions regarding security checkpoint include both threat and CM questions. Threat questions would include:

- Does it take more than 15 min on average to go through security checkpoint lines?
- Are you required to remove articles of clothing other than belts and shoes when going through security checkpoints?
- Do you feel demeaned or violated such as being touched inappropriately after going through a security checkpoint?
- Are items confiscated from your carry-on luggage other than indicated items such as liquids?
- When you are going through a security checkpoint with small children, the elderly, or the infirm, do the officials treat you with respect and dignity?

While CM questions would include:

- Are there multiple security checkpoint lines besides the ones for the prescreened?
- Do you wear easy to remove items such as slip-on shoes when going through security checkpoints weather allowing?
- Are security checkpoint agents trained to behave professionally and courteously?
- Are you familiar with what items cannot be brought aboard a commercial airliner?
- Are appropriate security checkpoint inspections at a separate location made for small children, the elderly, and the infirm?

Sample vulnerability (On-Time Performance) assessment questions employed in the airport satisfaction RM are sampled in the above paragraph.

Risk Assessment and Management: Essentially, the travelers are responding yes or no to these questions. These responses are used to calculate residual risk. Using a game-theoretical mathematical approach, the calculated risk metric or index is used to generate an optimization or lowering of risk to desired levels.

Further, mitigation advice will be generated to show travelers, airport managers, customs /immigration officials, and airlines in what areas the risk can be reduced to optimized or desired levels such as from 56% to 40% in the screenshot representing the median response from the study participants. See Figure 5.21 for a screenshot of the median airport satisfaction RM results in Table 5.17 inspired by Figure 5.22's tree diagram, which displays the vulnerability, threat, CM, and residual risk indices; resource optimization options; and risk mitigation advice. The airport facility is advised to increase the CM for "Bars and Restaurants" by 53%. Also slightly (1%) for CM on the "Invasiveness" issue for the Food Service and Amenities at the Immigration and Customs is a necessity. For this study, a random sample of 25 respondents was taken and their residual risk results are tabulated in Table 5.17 at the end of this section. Respondents are domestic and international travelers.

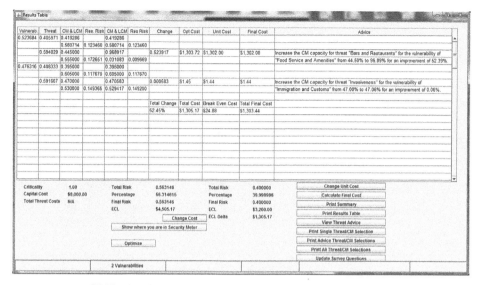

FIGURE 5.21 Median airport risk-meter management results.

TABLE 5.17   Respondents (25 Passengers) Survey Residual Risk Results for the Airport Service Risk-Meter Study, Ranked, Where Median is 56.31% (No. 17) Conducted in 2013

Respondent/DATE	Total Residual Risk (TRR)
Respondent1 Feb20	0.482224
Respondent2 Jun07	0.593035
Respondent3 Apr03	0.202892
Respondent4 Apr08	0.412031
Respondent5 Apr19	0.515245
Respondent6 Apr30	0.361296
Respondent7 May01	0.195347
Respondent8 Jun07	0.506403
Respondent9 Mar13	0.745874
Respondent10 Mar13	0.739829
Respondent11 Mar13	0.703571
Respondent12 Mar13	0.753439
Respondent13 Mar13	0.671285
Respondent14 Apr13	0.520104
Respondent15 Apr13	0.334549
Respondent16 Apr13	0.602795
Respondent17 Apr13	0.563146 Median (the middlemost of the survey)
Respondent18 Apr13	0.534278
Respondent19 Apr13	0.593769
Respondent20 Apr13	0.569956
Respondent21 Apr02	0.709571
Respondent22 Apr05	0.562413
Respondent23 Apr03	0.638719
Respondent24 Apr07	0.627699
Respondent25 Apr01	0.555374

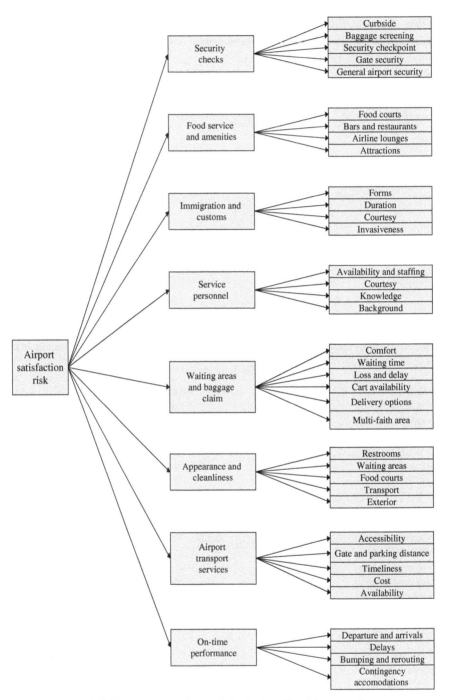

FIGURE 5.22 Airport service (satisfaction) quality risk-meter diagram.

The airport (service) satisfaction RM breaks new ground in that it provides a quantitative assessment of risk to the user as well as recommendations for mitigating that risk. As such, it will be a highly useful tool to travelers as well as airport managers, customs/immigration officials, and airlines seeking to enhance the air travel experience. Future work will involve the addition of information technology (IT) concerns such as the airport website and Wi-Fi availability as well as the incorporation of new questions so as to better refine user responses and subsequent calculation of risk and mitigation recommendations.

Enhancement of airport satisfaction specifically and air travel satisfaction generally will greatly benefit not only the comfort and pleasure of travelers but also the airports and airlines that serve those travelers profitability. The airport satisfaction RM tool and its future refinement provide the means to greatly enhance the air travel experience. As further, authors plan to incorporate more items such as language options, flight and shopping information, or leisure and disabled or children's needs to add to the XML file.

5.15   APPLICATION TO OFFSHORE OIL-DRILLING SPILL AND SECURITY RISK

This section addresses analytical (probabilistic and game-theoretic) treatments of risk assessment and management methodology using observational outcomes for unwanted oil spills and gas releases so as to study the goals of certain developments for improved response, mitigation, detection, characterization, and remediation associated with preventing catastrophes.

With the latest headlines of 2014 in US newspapers and overall electronic news media, US rises to No. 1 energy producer having recently surpassed Russia and Saudi Arabia in the amount of crude oil production and natural gas, thereby causing "a startling shift that is reshaping markets and eroding the clout of traditionally energy-rich nations," the article emphasizes [80]. US imports of natural gas and crude oil have fallen 32% and 15%, respectively, in the past 5 years, narrowing the US trade deficit. That is, US produced the equivalent of about 22 million barrels a day of oil, natural gas, and related fuels overtaking the 21.8 million barrels a day forecast of those of Russia's. The article further stresses that "U.S. Energy producers are drilling more efficiently and cutting costs in other ways." This is why analytical/statistical and simulation-based cost-effective risk forecasting methods have gained significance lately. Of recent interest to the petroleum engineers is the percentage of shale gas resources where fracturing is employed as the most innovative and newest form of manufacturing, which is on the rise and not seemingly dropping as fast as predicted. This newest groundbreaking manufacturing (fracturing) style is outside the scope of this chapter since no established analytical formulas are workable in effect as of yet. The traditional deep water drilling, pipeline operation, hydraulic fracturing, and well stimulation—oil and gas industry activities on beneath the sea, under the ground, and on the surface offer various combinations of high pressures, harsh environments, potential explosion, and possible environmental contamination that make engineering for safety increasingly important. Some hard and costly lessons have taught the oil and gas industry a lot about anticipating and controlling the risks that come with complex, high-energy system, and some in the industry think the effort has to go a lot farther.

There have been only a limited number of articles dealing with the mathematical modeling and algorithms for the problem of oil pollution proposing a novel method for the identification of the pollution source location and the accident time and transport and spreading of oil emission [81]. In the joint publication by Dang, Ehrhardt, Tran, and Le, numerical simulations have been employed to demonstrate the effectiveness of their proposed method [82]. Another article studying a comprehensive stochastic model is formulated to simulate the fate and transport of oil spills by AL-Rabeh, Cekirge, and Gunay, where their simulation modeling results also indicate that their proposed model can predict the fate and transport of oil slicks with reasonable accuracy [83]. J. Nihoul studies a nonlinear mathematical model for forecasting the transport and spreading oil slicks on the surface of the sea, where he claims that his proposed model differs from previous ones by its capability of taking simultaneously gravity, surface tension [84], friction, and weathering processes of the oil into account and by the introduction of a new parameterization of surface tension and friction, better adapted to real field conditions.

An offshore or similarly onshore land-based oil rig is a large complex structure, with many mechanical and electrical components that interact with and depend on each other. Accidents such as the recent explosion of the Deepwater Horizon on the Vermilion Block 380 platform in the Gulf of Mexico show that it is an enormous challenge to monitor and control critical events on an oil rig in a timely manner. From a geophysical perspective, sensor networks are the natural choice for monitoring oil rigs [85–87]. Additionally, forecasting such hazards is an enormous task with considerable hardships and challenges.

We will solely focus on the offshore maritime oil rigs to study the variations, including risk assessment and cost-effective management. An oil platform (offshore platform or colloquially oil rig) is a large structure with facilities to drill wells, to extract and process

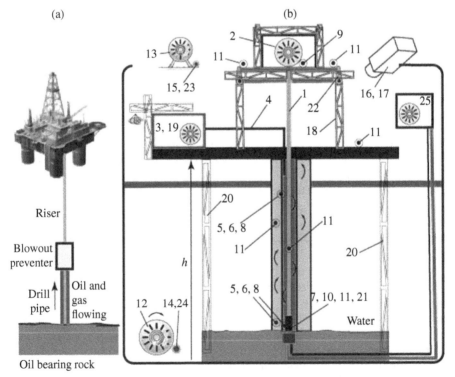

FIGURE 5.23   Oceanic submerged oil rig. (a) Pictorial, (b) front-section experimental.

oil and/or natural gas, and to temporarily store product until it can be brought to shore for refining and marketing. In many cases, the platform contains facilities to house the workforce as well. A typical offshore oil production platform is self-sufficient in energy and water needs, housing electrical generation, water desalinators, and all of the equipment necessary to process oil and gas such that it can be either delivered directly onshore by pipeline or to a floating platform or tanker loading facility or both. Elements in the oil/gas production process include wellhead, production manifold, production separator, glycol process to dry gas, gas compressors, water injection pumps, oil/gas export metering, and main oil line pumps. Figure 5.23a depicts an offshore oil rig. Figure 5.23b is the front-section format and one designed experimental setup for an offshore oil rig prepared by the co-authors [88]. In a futuristic test lab that may be emulating an offshore oil rig, the following components are defined by the co-authors from component 1 to component 25:

Legend for Figure 5.23:

1 Drilling shaft	**2** Drilling motor
3 Drilling fluid reservoir	**4** Pipe manifold for drilling fluid
5 Pressure sensor for drilling fluid (hydrostatic pressure)	
6 Temperature sensors for the drilling fluid	
7 Temperature sensors for the drilling tool	
8 Sensors for the speed of fluid traveling up the well (annular velocity)	
9 Sensors for the speed of the drilling tool	
10 Sensors for the penetration force	
11 Motion sensors for the solid components	
12 Wave generator	**13** Wind generator
14 Water probe	**15** Atmospheric probe
16 Video system	**17** Infrared system for the thermal analysis
18 Truss structure	**19** Oil-drilling pump
20 Anchoring structure	**21** Drilling bitt
22 Forced vibration shaker	**23** Gas sensor
24 Salinity sensor	**25** Oil and gas supply

The experimental lab of Figure 5.23b is configured to primarily address the risk assessment in sensor networks regarding deep sea oil exploration. The lab can develop experiments for indirectly recalculating the physical properties of drilling fluid such as:

26 Mud weight (density test)	**27** Mud rheology (viscosity, gel strength, yield point)
28 Mud resistivity	**29** Drilling fluid contamination
30 Sand content determination	**31** Hydrogen ion concentration (ph)
32 Coefficient of friction	

We will also take into consideration:

33 Pump horsepower	**34** Pressure losses inside drill string
35 Maximum allowable surface pressures	**36** Optimum flow rates
37 Drill string pressures' loses	

We will be able collect data from items once the lab is structured, such as:

---

38 Weight-on-bit digital readout of actual weight on bit
39 Rotary torque gauge that measures rotary torque
40 Rotary speed (rpm) gauge that measures the rotary rpm
41 Return mud flow gauge that measures the return in the flow line from the well
42 Mud pump stroke (spm) gauge that measures the pump stroke per minute
43 Drill pipe pressure gauge that measures drill pipe pressure
44 Mud weight indicator, a digital indicator that measures return mud weight
45 Manifold pressure gauge that measures manifold pressure (psi)
46 Air pressure gauge that measures air pressure (psi)
47 Annular pressure gauge that measures annular pressure
48 The oil rig will have a depth adjustment, h (for height)

The experimental drilling lab in the future would be working as a multifunction emulator that provides simulation of mathematically correct models of rigs while the goal is to achieve quasi real-time monitoring to model the risk events. Note that the items 42 and 48 are very similar measurements to estimate the million barrels per day, this time in a maritime scenario, to the SPM = strokes per minute and S_p = plunger stroke (inches) regarding the onshore oil rig in Equation (5.9), where P = production (barrels per day), K = pump plunger constant, S_p = plunger stroke (inches), and SPM = strokes per minute by Penta Catalog [89]:

$$P = K \times S_p \times \text{SPM} \tag{5.9}$$

An algorithm for a specific case study is as follows:

1. Choose plunger constant $K = 1.231$ in Ref. [89] for a specific (for a case study as for different plunger sizes, refer to different K) 3-1/4″ plunger size for subsurface pump data.

2. Go to table for "III recommended stroke lengths and strokes/min at given depths" in Ref. [89]. Choose at will maximum SPM to be 8 (normality assumed with standard deviation = 0.333, therefore approx. mean = 7). This row has 192 in. = stroke length.

3. Now insert all values in the "P = production (barrels per day)" equation to get $P = 1.231 \times 192 \times 7 = 1654.46$ barrels/day approx. with some error variation. This is akin to having a little more than a barrel a minute since 24 h × 60 min/h = 1440 min.

The RM tool therefore will greatly facilitate conducting an accurate and thorough assessment of the potential risks and vulnerabilities of onshore or offshore oil-rig spill risk such as follows (not collectively exhaustive) with possible threats in bracket (see Fig. 5.24):

1. Energy source {generators, diesel supply, reliability/maintenance}
2. IT and network connectivity {connection type/bandwidth, security, robustness/redundancy}
3. stability {anchoring, trussing, wellbore}
4. drilling assembly {shat/bit, motor, pump, fluid reservoir}

5. drilling fluid {mud weight/resistivity, rheology, contamination, temperature/pressure}
6. sensors {pressure/temperature resistance, robustness, physical location, longevity}
7. maritime environment {wind, wave height, storms, atmospheric conditions}
8. human aspect {monitoring, preparedness/education, control and management, human errors/tampering}
9. formation {hardness/brittleness, depth, salinity}

Note that the following set of linear equations to facilitate the game-theoretic risk analysis will be covered (1) to (35) from Table 5.18 where the data are taken from Figure 5.24 with the median value obtained from the survey outcomes (Table 5.19).

TABLE 5.18 Set of Linear Equations to Attain A Risk Mitigated to 20% From an Undesirable 31.6% Inspired by Figure 5.23

Minimize (Min) column loss (COLLOSS), subject to (s.t.):

$CM_{11} < 1$ (1), $CM_{12} < 1$ (2), $CM_{13} < 1$ (3), $CM_{21} < 1$ (4), $CM_{22} < 1$ (5), $CM_{31} < 1$ (6), $CM_{32} < 1$ (7), $CM_{41} < 1$ (8), $CM_{42} < 1$ (9), $CM_{51} < 1$ (10), $CM_{52} < 1$ (11), COLLOSS < 1 (12)
$CM_{11} > 0.675$ (13), $CM_{12} > 0.475$ (14), $CM_{13} > 0.725$ (15),
$CM_{21} > 0.725$ (16), $CM_{22} > 0.725$ (17),
$CM_{31} > 0.675$ (18), $CM_{32} > 0.675$ (19),
$CM_{41} > 0.675$ (20), $CM_{42} > 0.725$ (21),
$CM_{51} > 0.675$ (22), $CM_{52} > 0.675$ (23),
$0.0626\,CM_{11} - 1COLLOSS < 0$ (24), $0.05855\,CM_{12} - 1COLLOSS < 0$ (25),
$0.07489\,CM_{13} - 1COLLOSS < 0$ (26), $0.1183\,CM_{21} - 1COLLOSS < 0$ (27),
$0.1232\,CM_{22} - 1COLLOSS < 0$ (28), $0.0844\,CM_{31} - 1COLLOSS < 0$ (29),
$0.1116\,CM_{32} - 1COLLOSS < 0$ (30), $0.08037\,CM_{41} - 1COLLOSS < 0$ (31),
$0.098\,CM_{42} - 1COLLOSS < 0$ (32), $0.08433\,CM_{51} - 1COLLOSS < 0$ (33),
$0.10307\,CM_{52} - 1COLLOSS < 0$ (34),
$0.0626\,CM_{11} + 0.05855\,CM_{12} + 0.07489\,CM_{13} + 0.1183\,CM_{21} + 0.1232\,CM_{22} + 0.0844$
$\quad CM_{31} + 0.1116\,CM_{32} + 0.08037\,CM_{41} + 0.098\,CM_{42} + 0.08433\,CM_{51} + 0.10307\,CM_{52} > 0.8$ (35)

Total # constraints: 3 * # threats + 2 = 3 * 11 + 2 = 33 + 2 = 35.

Vuln.	Threat	CM & LCM	Res. Risk	CM & LCM	Res Risk	Change	Opt Cost	Unit Cost	Final Cost	Advice
0.2416	0.4900	0.725000		1.000000		0.275000	$31.78			Increase the CM capacity for threat "Connection Type/Bandwidth" for the vulnerability of
		0.275000	0.0325	0.000000	0.0000					"Information Technology and Network Connectivity" from 72.50% to 100.00% for an improvement
	0.6100	0.725000		0.999605		0.274605	$31.74			Increase the CM capacity for threat "Security" for the vulnerability of
		0.275000	0.0338	0.000395	0.0000					"Information Technology and Network Connectivity" from 72.50% to 99.96% for an improvement of
0.1961	0.4307	0.675000		0.675000						
		0.325000	0.0274	0.325000	0.0274					
	0.5892	0.675000		1.000000		0.325000	$37.56			Increase the CM capacity for threat "Temperature and Pressure" for the vulnerability of
		0.325000	0.0362	0.000000	0.0000					"Drilling Fluid" from 67.50% to 100.00% for an improvement of 32.50%.
0.1786	0.4500	0.675000		0.675000						
		0.325000	0.0261	0.325000	0.0261					
	0.5500	0.725000		0.725000						
		0.275000	0.0270	0.275000	0.0270					
0.1874	0.4500	0.675000		0.675000						
		0.325000	0.0274	0.325000	0.0274					
	0.5500	0.675000		0.803895		0.128895	$14.90			Increase the CM capacity for threat "Human Errors and Tampering" for the vulnerability of
		0.325000	0.0334	0.196105	0.0202					"Human Aspect" from 67.50% to 80.39% for an improvement of 12.89%.
				Total Cha...	Total C...	Break Even C...	Total Final C...			
				100.35%	$115.98	$1.16				

Criticality	1.00		Total Risk	0.315976		Total Risk	0.200000	Change Unit Cost
Capital Cost	$1,000.00		Percentage	31.597588		Percentage	20.000006	Calculate Final Cost
Total Threat Costs	N/A		Final Risk	0.315976		Final Risk	0.200000	Print Summary
			ECL	$315.98		ECL	$200.00	Print Results Table
				Change Cost		ECL Delta	$115.98	View Threat Advice

FIGURE 5.24 Oil-rig risk assessment and mitigation example using RM algorithm.

Optimal Solution: See column 5 in Figure 5.24 on the right-hand side of the improved server for the newly obtained solution to mitigate the risk from a previous 31.6% to 20%. The game theory application software stabilized this lack of equilibrium into a desired two-player zero-sum game with mixed strategy. This provides a list of CM probabilities; $CM_{11} = 1.00$, $CM_{12} = 0.999$, $CM_{22} = 1.00$, and $CM_{42} = 0.84$. The others stay the same. For related actions to take, see advice column. This is the optimal mixed strategy for defense to minimize its expected loss while offense maximizes its gain. There is no better game plan at equilibrium by improving CM_{ij} as shown. Addressing risk assessment and cost-efficient risk management with a game theory solution will prove this effort worthwhile (Figs. 5.24, 5.25 and 5.26).

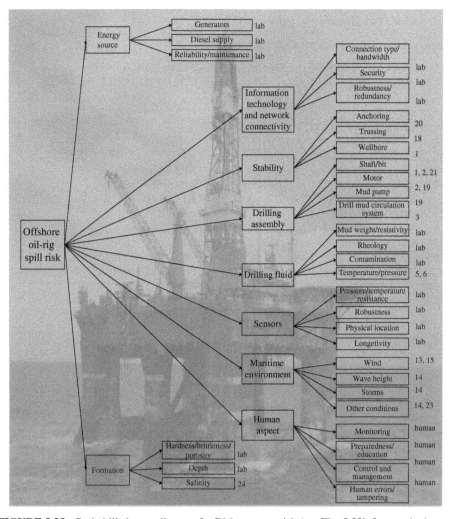

FIGURE 5.25 Probabilistic tree diagram for RM to assess risk (see Fig. 5.23b for attached numbers obtained by sensors in the lab environment; note that in the case of no data, the outcomes are sensed by the lab through human engineering).

Oil-Rig Spill Risk Survey

This survey has 9 main categories of vulnerabilities. Please identify the areas below where you have observed vulnerabilities while involved with oil rig activities within your organization

* A minimum of 2 categories must be chosen:

Vulnerability Area	Reference Page
☐ Energy Source	Page 1
☐ IT & Network Connectivity	Page 2
☐ Stability	Page 3
☐ Drilling Assembly	Page 4
☐ Drilling Fluid	Page 5
☐ Sensors	Page 6
☐ Formation	Page 7
☐ Human Aspect	Page 8
☐ Maritime Environment (if rig is not land-based)	Page 9

Directions:

This Page:
- Select all vulnerability areas that apply *(Must choose at least two)*
- Proceed to appropriate pages to complete survey for each vulnerability area.

Survey Page(s):

Vulnerability
- Rate **Vulnerability** (1-10) with 10 being *most* vulnerable and 1 being *least* vulnerable
- Select all vulnerability statements that apply (*must choose at least one*)

Threat
- Rate **Threat** (1-10) with 10 being *greatest* threat and 1 being the *least* threat. *(You must choose at least two threat categories for each vulnerability.)*
- Using round button, select all threat statements that apply to each threat category chosen. (*must choose at least one*)
- Using square Check Box, select a weight >1 if you feel this area deserves additional emphasis.

Countermeasure
- Rate associated **Countermeasure** for each threat category chosen above (1-10) with 1 being *least* effective and 10 being the *most* effective countermeasure.
- Using round button, select all countermeasure statements that apply (*must choose at least one*)
- Using square Check Box, select a weight >1 if you feel this area deserves additional emphasis.

FIGURE 5.26 The offshore oil-drilling spill and security risk-meter survey.

At the end of this algorithm, the managers and analysts of complex *wireless sensor networks* are expected to develop an awareness of what risk factors prevail by assessing and managing the risk content prematurely before preventable tragic events roll out of control, that is, in high-assurance systems such as oil rigs and hospital surgery wards or NASA projects using software-based event detection mechanisms in Table 5.18 [90].

TABLE 5.19 Respondents (23) Survey Residual Risk Results for the Offshore Oil-Rig Service Risk-Meter Study, Ranked, Where Median is 31.59% (12th Ranked Out of 23)

Respondent Total Residual Risk (TRR) Rank (Ascending Order)		
Respondent1/oilA1	0.331340	14
Respondent2/oilA2	0.329562	13
Respondent3/oilA3	0.284537	4
Respondent4/oilA4	0.313678	9
Respondent5/oilA5	0.295460	6
Respondent6/oilA6	0.284581	5
Respondent7/oilA7	0.315976 Median	12 (Middlemost outcome)
Respondent8/oilB1	0.300120	8
Respondent9/oilB2	0.315895	11
Respondent10/oilB3	0.354487	17
Respondent11/oilB4	0.333658	15
Respondent12/oilB5	0.378174	20
Respondent13/oilB6	0.315734	10
Respondent14/oilB7	0.469037	23
Respondent15/oilB8	0.367580	19
Respondent16/oilB9	0.337914	16
Respondent17/oilC1	0.296985	7
Respondent18/oilC2	0.380936	21
Respondent19/oilC3	0.254312	1
Respondent20/oilC4	0.416371	22
Respondent21/oilC5	0.267996	2
Respondent22/oilC6	0.284511	3
Respondent23/oilC7	0.365490	18

5.16 DISCUSSIONS AND CONCLUSION

Although game theory from its inception is almost 150 years old, it started gaining prevalence and worldwide recognition around the end of the Second World War (WW2) (1914–1918) precisely a century ago roughly 20 years before when decisions regarding newly introduced nuclear weapons were meant to signal possible life or death for mankind. Game theory-related computing began first in 1944 along with Dantzig's breakthrough on simplex method with Neumann and Morgenstern's pioneering book [3]. Nash brought a reconciliatory flavor to Neumann's WW2 era findings within an economic context in 1950 [5]. Since the advent of Internet connectivity in the 1990s and the exponential rise of correspondence and malicious malware without borders, game theory is viewed as a tool for protecting ubiquitous cybersystems and information security (CSIS) against enemies and adversaries, which operate in both rational and irrational modes. It is anticipated that cyber-armies will replace conventional forces with cyberspace command needing more resources than warplanes or submarines in the next decades. Scanning a history of 150 years, this chapter delves into computationally intensive methods to show why and how game-theoretic risk analysis works from statistical, business, and engineering viewpoints to name a few. Major thematic examples are illustrated to highlight the significance of these methods, that is, from Neumann's two-way zero-sum to those of mixed strategy, and moreover NE while citing computational and theoretical difficulties and solutions. An alternative approach, ARA, by certain scientists is also illustrated. Nowadays, game theory is not dichotomous as it used to be, such as Neumann versus Nash methods, but multifaceted. The new game theoreticians, for example, Aumann and Banks [16, 32], are exploring critiques in search of new techniques since the nature of players has changed from rational to irrational and erratic or terrorist. Moreover, Sahinoglu's RM technique is reviewed through pure and mixed strategy solutions from Neumann and NE viewpoints [24, 25, 50, 55].

This has led to a quantitative risk assessment and mitigation software tool, scalable and applicable into daily practice for diversely popular disciplines [57–61]. In summary, therefore, following an informative introduction to gaming and origins in Sections 5.1 and 5.2, a technical background with conceptual definitions supported by numerical examples is presented in Section 5.3. In Section 5.4, more in-depth Nash nomenclature and solutions are studied citing scenarios from the literature. Certain ARA models are reviewed in Section 5.5 with certain illustrations from their proponents. Regarding an alternative probabilistic risk assessment and cost-optimal game-theoretic management algorithm, that is, RM, various examples of Neumann's and NE solutions in Section 5.6 with respect to engineering realities and probabilistic laws are also reviewed. Nash solutions are shown to demonstrate a complete consensus between the elements of the defense (good) and offense (hostile). Whatever one player challenges, the rival player concurs with, leading to a complete agreement status in effect minimizing the damage or maximizes the gain from whatever angle one views it. This is evident from the identical equations (5.2) to (5.4) and (5.6) to (5.9) in Section 5.6. However, the reality is quite different from this idealistic scenario, since terrorists and defenders do not simply concur to be kind out of courtesy.

This chapter also examines only a nonexhaustive selection of predominant games, with recent alternative game solutions. There may be many solution genres of game theory as there are problems. Then other multidisciplinary applications of RM follow from Sections 5.8 to 5.14. Game-theoretic computing topics in risk analysis have recently become important elements of course syllabi taught at cyber-security degree programs such as in the CSIS graduate degree program at Auburn University at Montgomery, www.aum.edu/csis [56, 79].

The future of game-theoretic computing lies in not only deriving smart novel models but also articulating them for the layman or potential industrial user or risk analyst, by demonstrating how to apply them in an algorithmic order through crunching real-life data and obtaining meaningful solutions to interpret. The scope of future gaming research entails overriding some of the limitations of the status-quo game-theoretic practices, which include idealized scenarios [18]. One may go to http://gambit.sourceforge.net/gambit13/intro.html and http://gambit.sourceforge.net or http://www.gametheorysociety.org/resources.html among others. One may search regarding the "software tools for game theory" to collect more details. Gambit is a library of game theory software and tools for the construction and analysis of finite extensive and strategic games.

To download free, go to http://www.softpedia.com/get/Programming/Components-Libraries/Turocy-Gambit.shtml.

For pleasant reading, got to http://www.economist.com/node/21527025.

For computing NE, click the following link:

http://homepages.math.uic.edu/~jan/mcs563s09/mcs563p1.pdf. To download Ubuntu, click https://apps.ubuntu.com/cat/applications/precise/gambit software.

Last but not the least, the many themes that can be implemented by the aid of the SM or RM have been enumerated and listed in Section 5.7. These themes have been implemented to the extent they are already being considered [57–66, 88, 90–102].

5.17 EXERCISES

5.17.1 For the following themes, collect random data from your survey subjects and administer the survey by applying the RM software in Chapter 8 to the theme you selected to assess and manage risk:

1. Computer and network security RM
2. Computer and network (incl. social networks') privacy and security RM
3. Ecological RM
4. Electronic-voting RM
5. Business contract RM
6. Campus safety and security RM
7. Department of Public Health HIPAA (privacy/security) RM
8. Hospital-based nonambulatory patient-centered healthcare RM
9. Federal and state cyber-security RM
10. National healthcare (overall: ambulatory and nonambulatory) RM
11. Mining safety and security RM
12. Offshore oil-spill wireless sensory network (WSN) RM
13. Usability RM
14. CLOUD RM
15. Airport service RM
16. Bank customer service RM
17. Digital forensics RM
18. Home security RM
19. Software development RM
20. Software application RM

5.17.2 Consider the following model two-person zero-sum game. Payoffs are the winnings for player a. Identify the pure strategy solution. What is the value of the game?

		Player B		
		b1	b2	b3
Player A	a1	8	5	7
	a2	2	4	10

Solution

Player B

	b_1	b_2	b_3	Minimum
a_1	8	5	7	(5)
a_2	2	4	10	4
Maximum	8	(5)	7	

Player A

Minimum   Maximum

The game has a pure strategy: player A strategy a_1; player B strategy b_2; and value of game $= 5$.

5.17.3 Assume that a two-person zero-sum game has a pure strategy solution. If this game were solved using an LP formulation, how would you know from the LP solution that the game had a pure strategy solution?

5.17.4 Consider the payoff table below that shows the percentage increase in market share for Company A for each combination of Company A and Company B strategies. Assume that Company B implements a mixed strategy by using strategy $b2$ with probability 0.5 and strategy $b3$ with probability 0.5. Company B decides never to use strategy $b1$. What is the expected payoff to Company A under each of its three strategies? If Company B were to always use the stated mixed strategy probabilities, what is the optimal strategy for Company A?

		Company B		
		Increase advertising	Quantity discounts	Extend warranty
		b_1	b_2	b_3
Company A	Increase advertising a_1	4	3	2
	Quantity discounts a_2	-1	4	1
	Extend warranty a_3	5	-2	5

5.17.5 (i) Outline the difference between John von Neumann's and John Nash's interpretation of game theory through their own mixed strategy solution proposals by citing examples?

(ii) Two television stations compete with each other for viewing audience. Local programming options for the 5.00 p.m. weekday time slot include a sitcom rerun, an early news program, or a home improvement show. Each station has the same programming options and must make its preseason program selection before knowing what the order television station will do. The viewing audience gains in thousands of viewers for station A are shown in the payoff table.

		Station B		
		Sitcom rerun	News program	Home improvement
		b_1	b_2	b_3
Station A	Sitcom rerun a_1	10	−5	3
	News program a_2	8	7	6
	Home improvement a_3	4	8	7

5.17.6 Determine the optimal strategy for each station. What is the value of the game? Two Indiana state senate candidates must decide which city to visit the day before the November election. The same four cities, Indianapolis, Evansville, Fort Wayne, and South Bend, are available for both candidates. Travel plans must be made in advance, so the candidates must decide which city to visit prior to knowing the city the other candidate will visit. Values in the payoff table show thousands of voters gained by the Republican candidate based on the strategies selected by two candidates. Which city should each candidate visit and what is the value of the game?

		Democratic candidate			
		Indianapolis	Evansville	Fort Wayne	South Bend
		b_1	b_2	b_3	b_4
Republican candidate	Indianapolis a_1	0	−15	−8	20
	Evansville a_2	30	−5	5	−10
	Fort Wayne a_3	10	−25	0	20
	South Bend a_4	20	20	10	15

5.17.7 Consider a game in which each player selects one of three colored poker chips: red, white, or blue. The players must select a chip without knowing the color of the chip selected by the other player. The players then reveal their chips. Payoff to player A in dollars are as follows:

		Player B		
		Red	White	Blue
		b_1	b_2	b_3
Player A	Red a_1	0	−1	2
	White a_2	5	4	−3
	Blue a_3	2	3	−4

- What is the optimal strategy for each player?
- What is the value of the game?
- Would you prefer to be player A or player B? Why?

Solution

(a) The maximum of the row minimum is not equal to the minimum of the column maximum, so a mixed strategy exists.
Linear program for player A:
Max GAINA
s.t. player B strategy:
$5PA2 + 2PA3 - GAINA >= 0$ (red chip)
$-PA1 + 4PA2 + 3PA3 - GAINA >= 0$ (white chip)
$2PA1 - 3PA2 - 4PA3 - GAINA >= 0$ (blue print)
$PA1 + PA2 + PA3 = 1$
$PA1, PA2, PA3 >= 0$
Player A: P (red) = 0.7, P (white) = 0.3, p (blue) = 0.0
From dual prices:
Player B: P (red) = 0.0, p (white) = 0.5, p (blue) = 0.5

(b) The value of the game is a 50-cent expected gain for player A.

(c) Player A.

5.17.8 Two companies compete for a share of the soft drink market. Each has worked with an advertising agency in order to develop alternative advertising strategies for the coming year. A variety of television advertisements, newspaper advertisements, product promotions, and in-store displays have provided four different strategies for each company. The payoff table summarizes the gain in market share for Company A projected for the various combinations of Company A and Company B strategies. What is the optimal strategy for each company? What is the optimal strategy for each company? What is the value of the game?

		Company B			
		b_1	b_2	b_3	b_4
	a_1	3	0	2	4
Company A	a_2	2	-2	1	0
	a_3	4	2	5	6
	a_4	-2	6	-1	0

5.17.9 See Exercise 4.9.2. After an initial assessment solution, now enter your data in any LP software (EXCEL or others), and obtain your new CM solution vector in a game-theoretic risk management mitigating to 10% lower; for example, from your currently 25% risk down to 15% risk (mitigated to 10% lower)? Note that there are $U = 12$ unknowns, and one equation for max or min objective function, and one for final optimization constraint. Hence total number of equations is $3U + 2 = 38$, which are as follow:

1. $1X1 < 1$
2. $1X2 < 1$
3. $1X3 < 1$
4. $1X4 < 1$
5. $1X5 < 1$
6. $1X6 < 1$
7. $1X7 < 1$
8. $1X8 < 1$
9. $1X9 < 1$
10. $1X10 < 1$
11. $1X11 < 1$
12. $1X12 < 1$
13. $1X13 < 1$
14. $1X1 > 0.7$
15. $1X2 > 0.6$
16. $1X3 > 0.6$
17. $1X4 > 0.9$
18. $1X5 > 0.75$
19. $1X6 > 0.75$
20. $1X7 > 0.85$
21. $1X8 > 0.75$
22. $1X9 > 0.6$
23. $1X10 > 0.6$
24. $1X11 > 0.8$
25. $1X12 > 0.85$
26. $0.07X1 - 1X13 < 0$
27. $0.13X2 - 1X13 < 0$
28. $0.08X3 - 1X13 < 0$
29. $0.04X4 - 1X13 < 0$
30. $0.08X5 - 1X13 < 0$
31. $0.03X6 - 1X13 < 0$
32. $0.07X7 - 1X13 < 0$
33. $0.025X8 - 1X13 < 0$
34. $0.025X9 - 1X13 < 0$
35. $0.05X10 - 1X13 < 0$
36. $0.12X11 - 1X13 < 0$
37. $0.28X12 - 1X13 < 0$
38. $0.07X1 + 0.13X2 + 0.08X3 + 0.04X4 + 0.08X5 + 0.03X6 + 0.07X7 + 0.025X8 + 0.025X9 + 0.05X10 + 0.12X11 + 0.28X12 > 0.85$

REFERENCES

[1] Shubik, M., *Games for Society, Business and War: Towards a Theory of Gaming*, Elsevier, New York, 1975.

[2] Sahinoglu, M., Cueva-Parra, L., Ang, D. (2012). Game-theoretic computing in risk analysis, *WIREs Computational Statistics*, **4**, 227–248.

[3] Neumann, J. V., Morgenstern, O., *Theory of Games and Economic Behavior*, Princeton University Press, Princeton, 1944.

[4] Glicksman, A. M., *Linear Programming and the Theory of Games*, John Wiley & Sons Inc., New York/London, 1963.

[5] Nash, J. F. (1950). Equilibrium points in N-Person games, *Proceedings of the National Academy of Sciences of the United States of America*, **36**(1), 48–49.

[6] Cournot, A., *Recherché Sur Les Principles Mathematiques De La Theorie Des Richesses (Researches into the Mathematical Principles of the Theory of Wealth)*, The MacMillan Company, New York, 1897.

[7] Bertrand, J. (1883). Theorie Mathematique de la Richesse Social, *Journal des Savants*, **48**, 499–508.

[8] (a) Edgeworth, F. Y. (1897). La Teoria pura del monopolio, *Giornale degli Economisti*, 13–31; (b) Stigler, S. M. (1978). Francis Ysidro Edgeworth, statistician (with discussion), *Journal of the Royal Statistical Society Series A*, 287–322.

[9] (a) Selten, R. (1965). Spieltheoretishe behandlung eines oligopolmodels mit nachfragetragheit, *Zeitschrift fur die Gesamte Statswissenschaft*, **12**, 301–324; (b) Re-examination of the perfectness concept for equilibrium points in extensive games, *International Journal of Game Theory*, **4**(1), 25–55.

[10] Harsanyi, J. C. (1967). Games with incomplete information played by Bayesian players, parts I, II, III. *Management Science*, **14**(3): 159–182, 320–334, 486–502.

[11] Fudenberg, D., Tirole, J., *Game Theory*, MIT Press, Cambridge, 1991.

[12] (a) Osborne, M. J., Rubinstein, A., *A Course in Game Theory*, MIT Press, Cambridge, 1994; (b) Osborne, M. J., *An Introduction to Game Theory*, Oxford University Press, New York, 2004.

[13] Binmore, K. G., *Does Game Theory Work*, MIT Press, Cambridge, 2007.

[14] Morton, D. D., *Game Theory: A Nontechnical Introduction*, Basic Books Inc., New York, 1970.

[15] Jones, A. J., *Game Theory: Mathematical Models of Conflict*, Ellis Horwood Ltd., Chichester, 1980.

[16] Aumann, R., Dreze, J. (2008). Rational expectations in games. *American Economic Review*, **98**(1): 72–86.

[17] Kadane, J. B., Larkey, P. D. (1982). Subjective probability and the theory of games. *Management Science*, **28**(2), 113–120.

[18] Roy, S. E., Shiva, S., Dasgupta, D., Shandilya, V., Wu Q. (2010). A survey of game theory as applied to network security, in Proceedings 43rd Hawaii International Conference on System Sciences (HICSS), IEEE Press, Koloa, Kauai, Hawaii January 5 to January 8, 2010, 1–12.

[19] (a) Hamilton, S. N., Miller, W. L., Ott, A., Saydjari, O. S. (2002). Challenges in applying game theory to the domain of information warfare, in Proceedings of the 4th Information Survivability Workshop, ISW 2001/2002, Academic Press, Vancouver, BC; (b) The role of game theory in information warfare, in Proceedings of the 4th Information Survivability Workshop; ISW 2001/2002, Academic Press, Vancouver, BC.

[20] Lye, K. W., Wing, J. (2002). Game strategies in network security, in Proceedings of the Foundations of Computer Security, Defense Advanced Research Projects Agency (DARPA) and the Army Research Office (ARO), Copenhagen, Denmark; International Journal on Information Security, 4(1–2), 71–86, 2005.

[21] Cavusoglu, H., Mishra, B., Raghunatan, S. (2004). A model for evaluating IT security investments. *Communications of the ACM*, 47(7), 87–92.

[22] Patcha, A., Park, J. A. (2004). Game theoretic approach to modeling intrusion detection in mobile and ad hoc networks, in Proceedings of the 2004 IEEE Workshop on Information Assurance and Security, United States Military Academy, West Point, NY.

[23] Jormakka, J., Mölsä, J. V. E. (2005). Modeling information warfare as a game. *Journal of Information Warfare*, 4(2), 12–25.

[24] Sahinoglu, M. (2005). Security Meter: A practical decision tree model to quantify risk. *IEEE Security and Privacy*, 3(3), 18–24.

[25] Sahinoglu, M. (2008). An input–output measurable design for the security meter model to quantify and manage software security risk. *IEEE Transactions on Instrumentation and Measurement*, 57(6), 1251–1260.

[26] Sahinoglu, M. (2009). Can we quantitatively assess and manage risk of software privacy breaches?, *IJCITAE-International Journal of Computers, Information Technology and Engineering*, 3(2), 65–70.

[27] Sahinoglu, M., Yuan, Y. L., Banks, D. (2010). Validation of a security and privacy risk metric using triple uniform product rule. *International Journal of Computers, Information Technology and Engineering*, 4, 125–135.

[28] Sahinoglu, M. (2008). Generalized game theory applications to computer security risk, in Proceedings of the IEEE Symposium on Security and Privacy, May 18–21, Oakland, CA; Statistical and Applied Mathematical Sciences Institute (SAMSI) Symposium, Proceedings of Interface/SAMSI Risk Conference, May 22–24, Duke University, Durham, NC.

[29] Benini, M., Sicari, S. (2008). Risk assessment in practice: A real case study. *Computer Communications*, 31(15), 3691–3699.

[30] Fenz, S., Ekelhart, A. (2011). Verification, validation and evaluation in information security risk management. *IEEE Security and Privacy*, 58–65.

[31] Banks, D., Harris, B. (2009). Adversarial risk analysis in counterterrorism, in 57th Session of the International Statistical Institute (ISI09): Adversarial Risk Analysis—IPM 95, Durban.

[32] (a) Rios, J., Rios, D., Banks, D. (2009). Adversarial risk analysis, influence diagrams, and auctions, in 57th Session of the International Statistical Institute (ISI09): Adversarial Risk Analysis—IPM 95, Durban; (b) Adversarial risk analysis. *Journal of the American Statistical Association*, 104(486): 841–854.

[33] Singpurwalla, N. D. A. (2009). A framework for adversarial risk analysis, in 57th Session of the International Statistical Institute (ISI09): Adversarial Risk Analysis—IPM 95, Durban, South Africa.

[34] Kiekintveld, C., Jain, M., Tsai, J., Pita, J., Ordóñez, F., Tambe, M. (2009). Computing optimal randomized resource allocations for massive security games, in Proceedings of 8th International Conference on Autonomous Agents and Multiagent Systems (AAMAS 2009), May 10–15, Budapest, Hungary, 689–696.

[35] Herbert, J. P., Yao, J.. (2008). Game-theoretic risk analysis in decision-theoretic rough sets, in Proceedings of the 3rd International Conference on Rough Sets and Knowledge Technology, Springer-Verlag, Berlin, Heidelberg.

[36] He, W., Xia, C., Zhang, C., Ji, Y., Ma, X. (2008). A network security risk assessment framework based on game theory, in Second International Conference on Future Generation Communication and Networking, FGCN'08, Hainan Island, China, 249–253, 13–15.

[37] He, W., Xia, C., Wang, H., Zhang, C., Ji, Y. (2008). A game theoretical attack-defense model oriented to network security risk assessment, International Conference on Computer Science and Software Engineering, FGCN'08, Wuhan, China, 498–504, 12–14.

[38] Shiva, S., Simmons, C., Ellis, C., Dasgupta, D., Wu, Q. (2009). AVOIDIT: A Cyber Attack taxonomy. Technical Report: CS-09-003, University of Memphis, Memphis, TN.

[39] Roy, S., Ellis, C., Shiva, S., Dasgupta, D., Shandilya, V., Wu, Q. (2010). A survey of game theory as applied to network security, in Proceedings of the 43rd Hawaii International Conference on System Sciences (HICSS), IEEE Press, Koloa, Kauai, Hawaii January 5–8, 2010.

[40] Shiva, S., Roy, S., Bedi, H., Dasgupta, D., Wu, Q. (2010). A stochastic game with imperfect information for cyber security, in 5th International Conference on Warfare & Security (ICIW), April 8–9, Dayton, OH.

[41] Shiva, S., Roy, S., Ellis, C., Datla, V., Wu, Q. (2010). On modeling & simulation of game theory-based defense mechanisms against DoS and DDoS attacks, in Proceedings of the 43rd Annual Simulation, Symposium (ANSS'10) in the Spring Simulation Multi-Conference (SpringSim), Orlando, FL.

[42] Shiva, S., Roy, S., Dasgupta, D. (2010). Game theory for cyber security, in 6th Cyber Security and Information Intelligence Research Workshop, Oak Ridge National Laboratory, Oak Ridge, TN.

[43] Shiva, S., Bedi, H., Simmons, C., Fisher, M., Dharam, R. (2011). Holistic game inspired defense architecture, in International Conference on Data Engineering and Internet Technology, Bali Dynasty Resort, Bali.

[44] Bedi, H., Roy, S., Shiva, S. (2011). Game theory-based defense mechanisms against DDoS attacks on TCP/TCP-friendly flows, IEEE Symposium on Computational Intelligence in Cyber Security (CICS), part of (SSCI), Paris.

[45] Manshai, M. H., Zhu, Q., Alpcan, T., Basar, T., Hubaux, J. (2010). Game theory meets network security and privacy, *ACM Transactions on Computational Logic*, **10**, 1–35.

[46] Luo, Y., Szidarovzky, F., Nashif, Y., Hariri, S. (2010). Game theory based network security, *Journal of Information Security*, **1**, 41–44.

[47] Wang, S., Banks, D. (2011). Network routing for insurgency: an adversarial risk analysis framework. *Naval Research Logistics*, **58**(6), 595–607.

[48] Anderson, D. R., Sweeney, D. J., Williams, T. A., Martin, K. (2008). *An Introduction to Management Science—Quantitative Approaches to Decision Making*, Thompson/South-Western, Mason, 241–252.

[49] Colman, A. M. (1995), *Game Theory and Its Applications in the Social and Biological Sciences* (2nd edn.), Butterworth-Heinemann Ltd. and Routledge, Oxford and London, **1982**, xiv + 375.

[50] Sahinoglu, M. (2010). Method for cyber-security risk assessment and cost-efficient management in wireless sensor networks, in CRW'10: 3rd Cyberspace Research Workshop, Shreveport, LA. Proceedings of the 3rd Cyberspace Research Workshop, http://csc.test.latech.edu/crw10/proceedings.pdf, 8–13.

[51] Maille, P., Reichl, P., Tuffin, B. (2011). Of threats and costs: A game-theoretic approach to security risk management, in *Performance Models and Risk Management in Communications Systems, Springer Optimization and Its Application*, N. Gulpinar, P. Harrision, B. Rusterm (eds.), **46**, Springer Science + Business Media, LLC, New York.

[52] Papadopoulou, V., Gregoriades, A. (2010). Nonfunctional requirements validation using Nash equilibria, in *Management and Services (Open Access Book)*, M. Habib (ed.), InTech, Croatia.

[53] Banks, R., Rios I. (2015). *Adversarial Risk Analysis*, Chapman & Hall, Boca Raton.

[54] Rothkopf, M. (2007). Decision analysis, the right tool for auctions. *Decision Analysis*, **4**, 167–172.

[55] Singh, A., Lakhotia, A. (2010). Strategic methods in adversarial classifier combination, in CRW'10: 3rd Cyberspace Research Workshop, Shreveport, LA. Proceedings of the 3rd Cyberspace Research Workshop, http://csc.test.latech.edu/crw10/proceedings.pdf 1–7

[56] Sahinoglu, M. (2011). Cyber systems and information security: Master of Science program, at Auburn University Montgomery. *GSTF International Journal on Computing*, **1**(3), 71–76.

[57] Sahinoglu, M. (2011). Some interdisciplinary topics on game-theoretical solutions for quantitative cyber-risk estimation and management, in Computing Science and Statistics, Proceedings of the 42nd Symposium on the Interface, SAS Institute, Cary, NC.

[58] Sahinoglu, M. (2009). Quantitative risk assessment of software security and privacy, and risk management with game theory. Invited Speaker, CERIAS/Purdue University Annual Symposium Seminar, W. Lafayette, IN.

[59] Sahinoglu, M. (2009). World ecological risk assessment and management, in AFITC (Air Force Information Technology Conference), Montgomery, AL.

[60] Sahinoglu, M. (2011). National cyber-security risk assessment and management, in AFITC (Air Force Information Technology Conference) August 2010, Eisenhower Series Invited Speaker, Air War College, Maxwell AFB, Montgomery, AL.

[61] Akkaya, A. D., Sahinoglu, M., Morton, S., Phoha, V. A. (2011). Quantitative Security and Privacy risk assessment and management method for social networks, in IPS018 (Invited Session on Trustworthy Computing), ISI 2011, Dublin, 22–26.

[62] Sahinoglu, M., Wool, K. (2013). Risk assessment and management to estimate and improve hospital credibility score of a patient health care quality, *Book Chapter (Society of Design and Process Science) Cyber physical Systems of the Future: Transdisciplinary Convergence in the 21st Century*, S. Suh et al. (eds.), Springer Publishing contracted 'Applied Cyber Physical Systems', New York.

[63] Sahinoglu, M., Samelo, E., Morton S., (2013). Hospital healthcare satisfaction risk assessment and management using an automated Risk-O-Meter software with a game-theoretic algorithm—quantitative case study (2013) in Alabama USA, *Transactions of the SDPS, Journal of Integrated Design and Process Science*, **18**(2), 1–32.

[64] Sahinoglu, M. (2010). The applications of the quantitative security-meter algorithm to health-care cyber security and others, in Tutorial-Demo, SDPS'10, Dallas, TX.

[65] Sahinoglu, M., Simmons, S. J., Cahoon, L. (2012). Ecological Risk-O-Meter: A risk assessor and manager software for decision-making in ecosystems, *Environmetrics*, **23**, 729–737.

[66] Sahinoglu, M., Morton, S. (2013). An automated algorithm to assess and manage ecological risk, in ICOEST'2013, Nevsehir University Press, Urgup.

[67] US Department of Justice. (2004). Forensic examination of digital evidence: A guide for law enforcement. Available at https://www.ncjrs.gov/pdffiles1/nij/199408.pdf (accessed on September 21, 2015).

[68] Ahmad, A. R., Phan, R. C. W., Parish, D. J. (2009). Metrics for network forensics conviction evidence, *IEEE Transactions on Forensics and Security*.

[69] Sahinoglu, M., Akkaya Aysen, D. (2012). *Are Social Networks Risky? Assessing and Mitigating Risk*, in Significance the bimonthly magazine and website of the Royal Statistical Society (RSS), London.

[70] Sahinoglu, M., Akkaya, A., Ang, D. (2012). Can we assess and monitor privacy and security risk for social networks?, *Procedia Social and Behavioral Sciences*, **57**, 163–169.

[71] Sahinoglu, M., Morton, S., Ang, D., Vasudev, P., Kramer, W. (2015). Quantitative metrics to assess and manage business contracting risk using Risk-O-Meter software, in 2015 International Symposium on Business and Management (ISBM 2015), Kuala Lumpur, Malaysia, April 1–3, 2015. Available at http://www.tw-knowledge.org/isbm2015 (accessed on

October 31, 2015). Accepted by IJBI (International Journal of Business and Information), for publication, 2016.

[72] Sahinoglu, M., Stockton, S., Morton, S., Eryilmaz, M. (2014). Metrics to assess and manage software application security risk, Conference Proceedings, SAM'14, DOI: 10.13140/2.1.5151.9682 Conference: Int'l Conf. Security and Management | SAM'14 | World Com'14, At Las Vegas, NV, USA, pp. 275–282, July 20, 2014..

[73] Census Bureau, U.S. Dept. of Commerce, Business Dynamics Statistics. Available at http://www.census.gov/ces/dataproducts/bds/data_firm.html (accessed on May 16, 2014).

[74] Sahinoglu, M. (2010). National cyber-security risk assessment and management, in AFITC (Air Force Information Technology Conference), August 2010, Montgomery, AL and Eisenhower Series Invited Speaker, Air War College, Maxwell AFB, Montgomery, AL.

[75] Institute of Management Accountants. Enterprise risk management: Tools and techniques for effective implementation, www.imanet.org/PDFs/Public/Research/SMA/ERM_Tools%20 and%20Techniques (accessed on September 21, 2015).

[76] Sahinoglu, M., Kelsoe, C., Morton, S., and Eryilmaz, M. (2014). Quantitative metrics to assess and manage national cyber security risk using risk meter software, *International Journal of Computers, Information Technology and Engineering (IJCITAE)*, **8**(2), 83–98.

[77] J. D. Power and Associates. (2010). North America airport satisfaction study. Available at http://www.jdpower.com/content/detail.htm?jdpaArticleId=1320 (accessed on September 21, 2015).

[78] Skytrax, Airport customer reviews. Available at http://www.airlinequality.com/Airports/apt_ forum.htm (accessed on September 21, 2015).

[79] Sahinoglu, M., *Trustworthy Computing: Analytical and Quantitative Engineering Evaluation*, John Wiley & Sons Inc., Hoboken, NJ, 2007.

[80] Russell G., Daniel G.. (2013). U.S. rises to no. 1 energy producer, *The Wall Street Journal*, **CCXII #80**, 1, 8.

[81] Kaplan, D. (Presenter), Space and Energy: What NASA & Gas & Oil Industry Can Teach Other about Controlling Risk, IEEE Spectrum Tech Insider Webinar, Safety and Mission Assurance Partnership Development NASA, 30 September 2013.

[82] Dang, Q. A., Ehrhardt, M., Tran, G. L., Le, D. (2012), Mathematical Modeling and Numerical Algorithms for Simulation of Oil Pollution, Bergische Universitat, Wuppertal, Germany, *Environ Model Assess*, **17**(3), 275–288.

[83] Al-Rabeh, A. H.; Cekirge, H. M., Gunay, N. (1989). A stochastic simulation model of oil spill fate and transport, *Applied Mathematical Modeling*, **13**(6), 322–329.

[84] Nihoul, J. C. J. (1984). A non-linear mathematical model for the transport and spreading of oil slicks, *Developments in Environmental Modeling*, **6**, 325–339.

[85] Iyengar, S. S., Mukhopadhyaya, S., Steinmuller, C., Xin L. Preventing future oil spills with software-based event detection. *IEEE Computer*, **43**(8), 95–97, 2010.

[86] Ozdemir S., and Yang X. (2009). Secure data aggregation in wireless sensor networks: A comprehensive overview, *Computer Networks*, **53**(12), 2022–2037.

[87] Akkaya, K., Younis, M. (2005). A survey on routing protocols for wireless sensor networks, *Ad Hoc Networks*, **3**(3), 325–349.

[88] Sahinoglu M, Marghitu D. Phoha V., Cueva-Parra L., Stockton S., Morton S., Analytical and simulation studies of operational variations for onshore land and offshore oil drilling rigs to forecast, assess and manage security risk information, Working Research Paper for GOMRI, Informatics Institute, 2014.

[89] http://www.pentarods.com/Services.aspx (accessed on September 21, 2015).

[90] National Institute of Standards and Technology, National vulnerability database, common vulnerability scoring system. Available at http://nvd.nist.gov/cvss.cfm (accessed on April 25, 2014).

[91] Sahinoglu, M., Morton, S. (2012). CLOUD Risk-O-Meter: An algorithm for CLOUD risk assessment and management, in Conference of Society of Design and Process Science, Session X1 CLOUD Computing: Security and Reliability, Berlin, Germany.

[92] Center for Strategic and International Studies (CSIS), *The Economic Impact of Cybercrime and Cyber Espionage*, Washington, DC, 2013.

[93] Sahinoglu, M., Vasudev, P., Morton, S., and Eryilmaz, M. (2014). Bank customer service risk: quantitative risk assessment and management, *International Journal of Computers, Information Technology and Engineering (IJCITAE)*, **8**(2), 99–107.

[94] Sahinoglu, M. (2012). CLOUD Meter: A Risk Assessment and Mitigation Tool, in Cyber Security Training Conference (CSCT), Colorado Springs.

[95] Sahinoglu, M., Kramer, W., Ang, D. (2014). How to increase the ROI of software development lifecycle by managing the risk using Monte Carlo and discrete event simulation—A case study, in Proceedings of the International Conference on Business and Information (BAI2014), Osaka.

[96] Sahinoglu, M., Stockton, S., Morton, S., Barclay, R., Eryilmaz, M. (2014). Assessing digital forensics risk: A metric survey approach, in SDPS Conference Proceedings (Theme: Smart Innovative Societies), 19th International Conference on Transformative Science, Engineering Business and Social Innovation, Sarawak.

[97] Sahinoglu, M., Ang, D., Morton, S., and Vasudev, P. (2016). Quantitative Metrics for Airport Services Satisfaction Risk Assessment and Management with Risk-O-Meter Software, Proceedings of the 2016 Taiwan International Conference on Innovation and Management (ICIM), Taipei, Taiwan, January 13–15, 2016, pp. 68–75.

[98] Sahinoglu M, Marghitu D., Stockton S., Morton S., and Ang D. (2016). Analytical and Simulation Studies of Operational Variations for Onshore Land and Offshore Oil Drilling Rigs to Forecast, Assess and Manage Security Risk, Proceedings of the 2016 Taiwan International Conference on Innovation and Management (ICIM), Taipei, Taiwan, January 13–15, 2016.

[99] Sahinoglu, M., Morton, S., Venkatram, P., and Ozfirat K. (2016). Quantitative Metrics to Assess and Manage Mining Safety and Security Risk Using Risk-Meter Software, *International Journal of Computers, Information Technology and Engineering (IJCITAE)*, **10**(1), 88–96.

[100] Sahinoglu M, Stockton. S., Barclay, R. (2016). Morton, S., Metrics-Based Risk Assessment and Management of Digital Forensics, DAU (Defense Acquisition University) Hirsch Paper Competition 2nd Prize Winner, to be published in Defense ARJ, April 2016.

[101] Sahinoglu, M., Morton, S., and Ballamudi D. (2016). Quantitative Metrics to Assess and Campus Safety & Security Risk Using Risk-Meter Software, *International Journal of Computers, Information Technology and Engineering (IJCITAE)*, **10**(1), 106–114.

[102] Sahinoglu, M., Morton, S., and Kelum R. (2016). Quantitative Metrics to Assess and Manage E-Voting Security Risk Using Risk-Meter Software, *International Journal of Computers, Information Technology and Engineering (IJCITAE)*, **10**(1), 97–105.

6

MODELING AND SIMULATION IN CYBER-RISK

LEARNING OBJECTIVES

- Describe the concept of simulation with its static and dynamic components and its relevance to cyber-risk informatics and risk engineering.
- Explore the innovative and popular theme of engineering modeling and simulation, predominantly in the manufacturing industry and cyber-security world, citing severe challenges, advantages, and time- and budget saving solutions and its future.
- Study a cross section of engineering modeling and simulation practices illustrating a window of numerical examples with relevant and useful statistical data-scientific modeling.

6.1 INTRODUCTION AND A BRIEF HISTORY TO SIMULATION

The favorable computing outcomes since the advent of digital computers and software revolution could not have been achieved, especially without the multiple benefits of statistical simulation, which underlies the widespread use of modeling and simulation in engineering and sciences, stretching from A (anthropology) to Z (zoology). Modern computer simulation developed in parallel with the rapid growth of computer use during the development of the Manhattan Project in WWII to nondestructively model and simulate the nuclear detonation before it was destructively dropped on Hiroshima and Nagasaki in Japan in 1945. Therefore, the history of simulation is interesting and intriguing. Some earliest pioneers can be observed in [1]. Lord Rayleigh in 1899 showed that a one-dimensional random walk without absorbing barriers could provide an approximate solution to a parabolic differential equation.

Cyber-Risk Informatics: Engineering Evaluation with Data Science, First Edition. Mehmet Sahinoglu.
© 2016 John Wiley & Sons, Inc. Published 2016 by John Wiley & Sons, Inc.
Companion website: www.wiley.com/go/sahinoglu/informatics

In 1908 W. S. Gosset (with a nickname, Student) used experimental sampling to help him toward his discovery of the distribution of a correlation coefficient and to bolster his faith in his so-called t-distribution [2]. A. N. Kolmogorov in 1931 showed the relationship between Markov stochastic processes and certain integrodifferential equations. Stanislaw Ulam at Los Alamos labs performed simulation in 1945 during WWII in the bomb-building Manhattan Project before proposing the Teller–Ulam thermonuclear weapon design. Ulam suggested first the "Russian Roulette" and "splitting" methods for evaluating complicated mathematical integrals for nuclear chain reactions that later led to the systematic Monte Carlo (MC) methods by von Neumann, Metropolis, and others. John von Neumann explored the behavior of neutron chain reactions in fission devices using statistical sampling methods in 1948 (such as the acceptance–rejection method) employing the newly developed electronic computing techniques. Neumann proposed the agent-based von Neumann machine [3], a theoretical machine capable of reproduction following detailed instructions to copy itself. Ulam suggested a machine as a collection of cells on a grid. The idea intrigued von Neumann, who created the first of the devices later termed cellular automaton [4]. John Conway constructed the well-known Game of Life, operated in a virtual world in the form of a two-dimensional checkerboard [5]. A team headed by N. Metropolis using the ENIAC Computer in 1948 carried out what's contemporarily known as modern MC calculations.

Computer simulation has been widely used in engineering systems to validate the effectiveness of tentative decisions regarding a new plan or schedule, or its outcomes, without actually experiencing the actual conditions, which could in actuality cost more resources or partial to full destruction such as in the simulation of the nuclear bomb. Taxonomy-wise, simulated computer models may be stochastic or deterministic, and dynamic or static, and discrete or continuous. In a book entitled *Simulation Engineering*, by Jim Ledin in 2001 [6], the author outlines his twofold purpose as follows: (i) Simulation engineering (SE) is the application of engineering discipline to the development of good simulations. (ii) Similarly, SE occurs when simulations become part of an engineering process when applied as tools to develop better products and test processes with a greater efficiency for different types of complex embedded systems. The latter purpose (ii) is the subject matter of this review article. The IEEE June 2012 Spectrum issue emphasized that the modeling and simulation effect is a creative and timesaving topic of interest ranging from automotive engineering of hybrid vehicles to finding solutions to treating nuclear waste and upgrading the nuts and bolts of the Electrical Power (Smart) Grid and, moreover, supercomputing research [7].

6.2   GENERIC THEORY: CASE STUDIES ON GOODNESS OF FIT FOR UNIFORM NUMBERS

A formal scientific theory of simulation, to verify a validated model so as to mimic a physical or a social system does not exist in terms of conventional math-statistical theorems and their subsequent proofs. However, heuristic modeling formalisms at an advanced level for engineers through cellular automaton for MC and discrete event simulations (DES) are studied by Zeigler et al. [8, Ch. 4], although these formalisms do not lend themselves to easy algorithmic implementations for practicing engineers or scientists as this review article purports to. Moreover, the fundamental process of verifying sequences of uniform deviates from an associated generator where Ho: uniform random sequence is (quasi)random vs. Ha: sequence is nonrandom is an accepted technique. For instance, chi-square tests, such as those by Leven and Wolfowitz [9] and D. E. Knuth [10], are popularly well-accepted math-statistical scientific practices to theorize the verifiability of uniform random numbers essential to the realm of statistical simulation. In order to clarify the validation of the above-stated Ho: random sequence vs. Ha: nonrandom sequence, the commercial Java code's uniform number generator will be tested for randomness, as illustrated in a series of screenshots from Tables 6.A.1, 6.A.2, 6.A.3, 6.A.4, 6.A.5, 6.A.6, 6.A.7, 6.A.8, and 6.A.9 in Appendix A by using Stewart's JAVA program to implement Knuth's technique [11]. The results show that by law of large numbers for only $n \geq N \approx 50,000$; $E(\Theta) \rightarrow 0.5$ with probability 1, for $\Theta \sim$ uniform$(0,1)$ from the uniform number generator embedded in the Java code, "Ho: random sequence" cannot be rejected. Therefore, $n = 50,000$ runs is a new standard for attaining quasirandomness, not 5,000 anymore as practiced in the 1980s.

6.3 WHY CRUCIAL TO MANUFACTURING AND CYBER DEFENSE

The power of simulation is prevalent as the audio-visual reference [12] favorably explains certain topics related to production and manufacturing engineering. In "Modeling and Simulation in Manufacturing and Defense Systems Acquisition," the Board on Manufacturing and Engineering Design (BMED) emphasized the importance of modeling and simulation in not only making the right decisions but also incurring fewer expenses [13]. Similarly, the Wychavon (UK) council has adopted manufacturing industry's simulation model to reduce waste and improve performance [14]. Since the US manufacturing industry is challenged by increased global competition and price erosion, one can benefit from manufacturing simulation to eliminate bottlenecks, enhance lean manufacturing, optimize capacity planning, and optimize production output. In an annotated DES bibliography, there exist 325 articles on manufacturing simulation as cited in Ref. [15]. A certain bibliography displays 112 publications on "Load Models for Power Flow and Dynamic Performance Simulation" by the *IEEE Transactions on Electric Power Systems* [16].

On the contrary, there are fewer simulation studies in cyber-security-and-defense-related theoretical and applied research. In their 2007 article entitled "Cyber Attack Modeling and Simulation for Network Security Analysis," Kuhl et al. discuss a simulation modeling approach to represent computer networks and intrusion detection systems (IDS) to efficiently simulate cyber-attack scenarios in order to test and evaluate cyber-security systems [17]. YouTube-based audio-visual cyber-security simulation roundtable [18] underlines the power of simulation in cyber-security scenarios. Under "War game reveals U.S. lacks cyber-crisis skills" in a war game [19], sponsored by a nonprofit group and attended by former top-ranking national security officials, laid bare that the US government lacks answers to such key questions.

Former Clinton press secretary Joe Lockhart said that people would be scared by the simulation but he added, "...that's a good thing." Sahinoglu in his 2007 Wiley textbook, *Trustworthy Computing: Analytical and Quantitative Engineering Evaluation* [20], considers modeling and simulation of individual components and systems toward assessment of security risk, in addition to his publications where theoretical models have confirmed using MC and DES runs [21–24]. Further, certain manufacturing- and

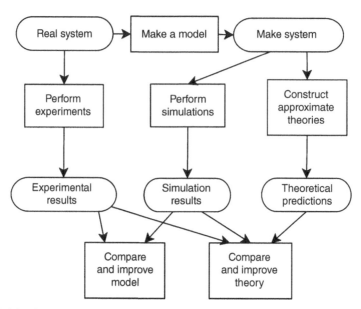

FIGURE 6.1   Computer modeling interplay between experiments, simulation, and theory [25].

cyber-security-themed examples will be reviewed through working details of how the modeling should be validating the physical model and the subsequent simulation computationally verifying the solutions accurately and cost effectively.

Figure 6.1 displays the interaction between the process of building a model by focusing on the interplay between (i) experimental results, (ii) simulation results, and (iii) theoretical predictions as displayed in [25, 26]. A favorable example of this interplay is presented in a recent WIREs article entitled "CLOUD Computing" [27, Figure 8 on p. 55], which displays an experimental scenario for a trivial Cyber CLOUD. On the other hand, whereas [27, Figure 9 on p. 57] outlines the Markovian theoretical predictions followed by the simulation results for the same scenario of two 1-gigabyte units serving a constant load of 1.5 GBYTE for 13 cycles. The resultant availability outcome of this small CLOUD: (i) 0.307 for experimental, (ii) 0.305 for simulation after one million runs, or trials, and (iii) 0.331 for Markov theoretical, allowing a negligible error content, which diminishes to less than 3% as the size of the experiment increases. In the event of large Cyber CLOUDS, the author showed that the experimental approach was infeasible. Theoretical result was not mathematically tractable. Supercomputer-driven programming worked for days regarding the basic two-state assumptions, crunching 2^{398} $(>>10^{100})$ Markov states to 93.8% reliability. DES result was comparable 90.5%.

6.4   A CROSS SECTION OF MODELING AND SIMULATION IN MANUFACTURING INDUSTRY

Simulation use in production is not new. For the sake of a few examples, various authors from 25 years ago published articles on simulating flexible manufacturing systems (FMS), machine utilizations and production rates, and modeling of automated manufacturing systems (AMS) [28, 29]. Given the advances in pervasive computing regarding communication networks, as well as recently popularized large-scale CLOUD Computing in cyber networks, quantitative risk assessment of a manufacturing unit and their network availability have become challenging tasks.

An often overlooked fact is that many real-life grid units such as routers or servers in cyber-physical systems to the manufacturing assemblies in automotive or avionics and the intricate telephony networks (wired or wireless), and water supply networks or hydro-electric dams, do not operate in an idealized simple setting of either full or zero capacity. This fact therefore necessitates the inclusion of degrees of derated (in-between the UP and DOWN states) capacity. Due to lack of closed-form solutions in the three-state model including DERATED as opposed to that of the conventional UP and DOWN dichotomous two-state model, a summary of three- or multistate system inferential analysis will be reviewed by using MC simulations, a method that was originally derived by [26].

This process will employ the empirical Bayesian principles to estimate the full and derated availability probability distributions. The historical failure and repair data, or operating (full or derated) and nonoperating hours, as the input data, will be used along with prior parameters for an empirical Bayesian analysis. The results satisfactorily lend themselves to statistical inference for multistates other than the traditional binary assumption (UP or DOWN), an outcome that can prove very useful to the manufacturing industry. In the past, various articles have studied a similar problem. For instance, "A hybrid Markov system dynamics approach for availability analysis of degraded systems" by M. S. Rao, A. Pradesh, and V. N. Naikan [30] is one. Similarly, I. D. Lins and E. L. Droguett study "Multiobjective optimization of availability and cost in repairable systems design via genetic algorithms and discrete event simulation" in [31] is another. Also, "Reliability and availability analysis of three-state device redundant systems with human errors and common-cause failures" by A. Shah and B. S. Dhillon studies somewhat similar but still different topics [32]. The primary difference between the above-listed three references and section 6.4 is the empirical Bayesian treatment of the three states to estimate their probability distributions by MC simulations based on the two-state version of the Sahinoglu–Libby (SL) probability density function (pdf), derived independently by both Sahinoglu and Libby in 1981 [33–37].

The closest among these three articles, that is, by Rao et al. [30], uses only four transition rates in a three-state Markov model, whereas Sahinoglu's model uses all six transitions [38, 39]. However, this section's simulation approach is even more powerful and flexible as the application can be extrapolated based on identical principles to four or more states, whereas reference by Rao et al. [30] deals solely with differential equations limited in scope. Others, by Lins et al. [31] and Shah et al. [32], are on slightly different but not identical topics, all of which do not employ modeling and simulation techniques or generate closed-form statistical pdf expressions and derivations.

6.4.1   Modeling and Simulation of Multistate Production Units and Systems in Manufacturing

Most research articles or books on reliability theory are devoted to traditional binary reliability models allowing for only two possible states for a system and its components: perfect functionality or complete failure. However, many real-world systems are composed of multistate components that have different performance levels and several failure modes with varying effects on the entire system performance. Such systems are called multistate systems (MSS) [40]. Examples of MSS are cyber systems where the unit performance is characterized by the data processing speed or server gigabyte capacity and similar to electric power systems, where the generating unit performance is depicted by its generating capacity. In the electric power supply system of generating facilities, each generator can function at different levels of capacity with a given probability.

This may result from the outages of several auxiliaries such as pulverizers, water pumps, fans, boilers, etc. Roy Billinton and Ron Allan [41] describe a three-state 50 MW (megawatt) generating unit. The performance rates (generating capacity) corresponding to these three states and probabilities of the three states that sum to unity are presented as follows: probability of state 1 (50 MW capacity) = 0.960, probability of state 2 (30 MW capacity) = 0.033, and probability of state 3 (0 MW capacity) = 0.007. Therefore, the reliability analysis of MSS is much more complex compared to binary systems. From the mid-1970s until now, numerous research articles focusing on MSS reliability were published [42, 43]. However, these works are deterministic, and not probabilistic, thus not lending themselves to probability distribution functions other than providing single summary measures. Therefore, statistical inference cannot be conducted. This section therefore reviews the methodology for the estimation of the probability distributions of three-state (now including a new derated or degraded state beyond the binary assumption of UP or DOWN) repairable hardware units or components by using MC simulations by employing the statistical random number generation techniques.

The power of simulation once again flexes its muscle as a favorable exit out of this theoretical impasse. The MC technique remains the only available feasible way to solve the proposed three-state problem, whose math-statistical closed-form solution does not actually exist. This is mainly because the three-state Markov model's random variables' (UP, DOWN, DER) probability distributions cannot be derived through math-statistical transformations due to mathematical intractability and lack of sufficient statistical theory. The pdf of the forced outage rate (FOR) was earlier analyzed in a textbook by the primary author, who designated that the Sahinoglu–Libby (SL) probability model can be used if certain underlying assumptions hold [20, 33–35]. Libby and Novick independently have studied multivariate generalized beta distributions for utility assessment; however, their analysis was for only two states similarly, not for multistate, hence the term generalized three-parameter beta (G3B) [36, 37] or SL (α, β, L), where $L = (\beta_1 / \beta_2)$ and $\beta_1 \neq \beta_2$.

The failure and repair rates were taken to be the generalized gamma random deviates where the corresponding gamma shape and scale parameters, respectively, were not equal. The two-state SL density was shown to default to that of a standard two-parameter beta density function when the shape parameters are identical, $\beta_1 = \beta_2$. The stochastic method proposed was superior to estimating availability by dividing total uptime by exposure time. Examples had shown the validity of this method to avoid over- or underestimation of availability when only small samples or insufficient data exist for the historical life cycles of units. In this article, however, additionally we shall also review, similar to the two-state SL, a computational three-state simulation model. Due to the infeasibility of closed-form solutions, the analysis will be carried out using MC simulations, obeying the Bayesian principles similar to Chapter 5 of the author's previous textbook [20] and [34]. In studying large-capacity production units, it is necessary to consider the probabilities associated with one or more forced derated states rather than accepting the unit being either available or unavailable, according to Billinton [44]. Following the

MC simulations, analytical pdfs of the multistates will be approximated to normal distributions, $N(\mu, \sigma)$, using their associated moments.

6.4.2 Two-State SL Probability Model of Units with Closed-Form Solution

In using the distribution function technique, the pdf of FOR $= q = [\lambda/(\lambda+\mu)]$ is obtained first by deriving its cumulative density function (cdf), that is, $GQ(q) = P(Q \leq q) = P[\lambda/(\lambda+\mu)] \leq q)$. Then, taking its derivative to obtain $g_Q(q)$ per equations on pp. 26–32 [20] and in reference to Sahinoglu et al., p. 1487 [33] and also p. 1293 in [34], $g_Q(q)$ is as follows:

$$g_Q(q) = \frac{\Gamma(a+b+c+d)}{\Gamma(a+c)\Gamma(b+d)} \frac{(\xi+x_T)^{a+c} (\eta+y_T)^{b+d} (1-q)^{b+d-1} q^{a+c-1}}{\left[\eta+y_T+q(\xi+x_T-\eta-y_T)\right]^{a+b+c+d}}$$

$$(\text{intermediate steps skipped}) \tag{6.1}$$

$$= \frac{\Gamma(\alpha+\beta)}{\Gamma(\alpha)\Gamma(\beta)}(1-q)^{\beta-1} q^{\alpha-1} \left[\frac{1}{1+q(L-1)}\right]^{\alpha+\beta} L^{\alpha}$$

Note that $g_Q(q)$ is the pdf of the random variable $Q = $ FOR, where $\alpha = a + c$, $\beta = b + d$, $\beta_1 = \xi + x_T$, and $\beta_2 = \eta + y_T$, and $0 \leq q \leq 1$. If $L = (\beta_1/\beta_2)$ for SL (α, β, L) or $\beta_1 = \beta_2$, the usual two-parameter beta pdf is obtained. An alternative original derivation of the same pdf termed under generalized multivariate beta distribution is given by Libby in 1981 and 1982 [36, 37]. The expression in Equation (6.1) can also be reformulated in terms of SL $(\alpha = a + c, \beta = b + d, L = (\beta_1/\beta_2))$ as follows:

$$g_Q(q) = \frac{L^{a+c} q^{a+c-1} (1-q)^{b+d-1}}{B(b+d,a+c)\left[1-(1-L)q\right]^{a+b+c+d}}, \text{where} \tag{6.2}$$

$$B(b+d,a+c) = \frac{\Gamma(a+c)\Gamma(b+d)}{\Gamma(a+b+c+d)}, \quad \text{and} \quad L = \frac{\xi+x_T}{\eta+y_T} \tag{6.3}$$

Note that if $L = 1$, SL pdf reduces to a standard beta (α, β) pdf. See Figure 6.2 for "$r = $ availability" and "$q = $ unavailability" confidence plots where $r = 1 - q$. Densities of SL (or G3B) distributions have been cited by [33–37] for a variety of L values. From a strictly mathematical point of view, the presence of the parameter L allows the SL pdf to take a variety of shapes besides the standard beta (α, β) where $L = 1$. For example, when $\alpha = \beta$, the standard beta (α, α) is symmetric with a mean at 0.5.

However, the SL (α, α, L) distribution is not necessarily symmetric and may be skewed positively or negatively, depending on $L > 1$ and $L < 1$, respectively, because the mode, skewness, and kurtosis of SL random variable now also depend on L. For $0 < L < 1$, the SL pdf stays below the plot of the related standard beta near zero but crosses the latter to become the greater of the two pdfs at a point:

$$y_0 = \left\{\frac{1}{1-L^{\alpha_1/(\alpha_1+\alpha_2)}}\right\} - (1-L)^{-1} \tag{6.4}$$

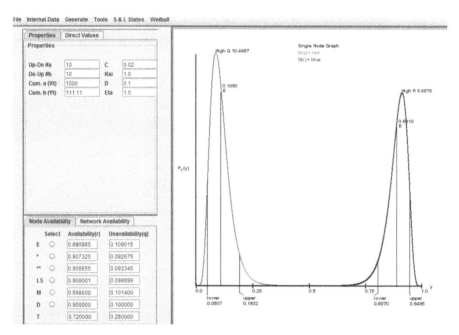

FIGURE 6.2 Given the input table, the pdf of the two-state SL is plotted for UP (r) and DOWN (q) for 90% confidence analytically showing mode (m) and mean (E) with upper and lower confidence bounds.

The reverse action holds true for $L > 1$ with the same crossing point, y_0. The major drawback to the distribution is that there is no closed form for finite estimates of the moments. The moment-generating function for the univariate SL distribution is an infinite series [36, 37].

6.4.3   Extended Three-State SL Probability Model of UP–DOWN–DERATED Units with MC Simulation

In studying large-capacity generation (power) or production (or cyber-physical) units, it may be necessary to consider the probabilities associated with one or more forced derated–outage states as in multistate, rather than considering the unit as being either available or unavailable [40–42, 44, 45]. In summary, there are gray areas or in-between capacities that are called derated or degraded states. However, in this review article, we will only consider a single derated state rather than multiple ones, which may well exist in practice such as in 50, 60, or 75% derated capacity. But now, we have not only full-FOR but also derated-FOR (or DFOR) that will be equal to the total derated operating time over the total exposure time. That is, DFOR = DER time/(UP time + DER time + DOWN time). It is also well documented that any calculated FOR or DFOR is not only a constant but also a specific single realization of its random variable [20]. The pdf of the FOR by empirical Bayesian analysis was identified in Section 6.4.2 to be SL probability density, where certain underlying assumptions hold. However, we shall review above and beyond a traditional closed-form two-state SL, namely, a three-state SL where

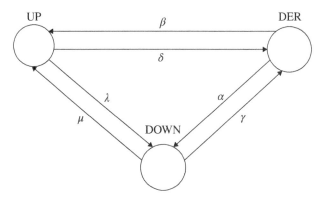

FIGURE 6.3   Three-state Markov diagram of a repairable hardware unit with UP, DOWN, and DER states.

the transition rates are gamma distributed (see derivations in Sections 4.3.1–4.3.6). Let us examine and review the following state space diagram in Figure 6.3 by Billinton from his textbook [44].

Let λ = transition rate from UP (fully operational) to DOWN (forced outage) state. Let μ = transition rate from DOWN to UP state; δ = transition rate from UP to DER (partially forced outage) state; β = transition rate from DER (partially forced outage) to UP state; α = transition rate from DER to DOWN state; and γ = transition rate from DOWN to DER state. Using Figure 6.3 given by changing to the Greek variables from the Latin originals (a to f) cited in the same reference [44, p. 156, Fig. 4.2], the time-dependent but steady-state probabilities of occupying one of the three states are given as follows from (6.5) to (6.7), assuming negative exponential densities for each state's sojourn time prevail, results of which will converge to

$$P(\text{UP}) = \text{FOR} = \frac{\mu\beta + \mu\gamma + \alpha\beta}{\text{DENOM}} \tag{6.5}$$

$$P(\text{DER}) = \text{DFOR} = \frac{\delta\mu + \delta\alpha + \lambda\mu}{\text{DENOM}} \tag{6.6}$$

$$P(\text{DOWN}) = 1 - P(\text{UP}) - P(\text{DER}) = \frac{\lambda\beta + \lambda\gamma + \delta\gamma}{\text{DENOM}} \tag{6.7}$$

$$\text{DENOMINATOR}(\text{DENOM}) = \mu\beta + \mu\gamma + \alpha\beta + \lambda\beta + \delta\mu + \delta\alpha + \lambda\mu + \delta\gamma \tag{6.8}$$

A closed-form pdf solution of the three-state SL is intractable and analytically impossible in this setting with six random variables, as compared solely to the two variables in Section 6.4.2. We will therefore have to simulate rvs $P(\text{UP})$, $P(\text{DER})$, and $P(\text{DOWN})$ from Equations (6.5)–(6.7) by generating multiple MC simulated deviates of the state transition rates recursively. Empirical Bayesian analysis will be pursued through deriving first the conditional posterior densities of the six transition rates through random uniforms for generating the transitions that constitute the probabilities in Equations (6.5) to (6.7). See Figure 6.4 for a sample draft scenario to illustrate transitions of Figure 6.3 in Sections 6.4.3.1–6.4.3.6.

6.4.3.1   UP-to-DOWN Failure Transition Rate (λ) from x_1 to w_1, or x_2 to w_2 in Figure 6.4

Let a = number of occurrences of UP (operating) times before DOWN (recovery)

$$X_i \sim \lambda e^{-\lambda X}$$

$x_T = \sum_1^a X_i$ = total UP (operating) times before DOWN (recovery) for "a" occurrences
λ = full UP-to-DOWN rate
c = shape parameter of gamma prior for the full UP-to-DOWN failure rate λ
ξ = inverse scale parameter of gamma prior for the full UP-to-DOWN failure rate λ

Now let the failure rate λ have a gamma prior distribution:

$$\theta_1(\lambda) = \frac{\xi^c}{\Gamma(c)} \lambda^{c-1} \exp(-\lambda\xi), \lambda > 0. \tag{6.9}$$

The joint likelihood of the UP-time random variables is

$$f(x_1, x_2, \ldots, x_a \mid \lambda) = \lambda^a \exp(-x_T\lambda), \tag{6.10}$$

The joint distribution of data and prior becomes

$$k(\underline{x},\lambda) = f(x_1, x_2, \ldots, x_a, \lambda) = \frac{\xi^c}{\Gamma(c)} \lambda^{a+c-1} \exp\left[-\lambda(x_T + \xi)\right] \tag{6.11}$$

Thus, the posterior distribution for the random variable λ is

$$\begin{aligned}
h_1(\lambda \mid \underline{x}) &= \frac{\xi^c}{\Gamma(c)} \lambda^{a+c-1} \exp\left[-\lambda(x_T + \xi)\right] \div \frac{\xi^c}{\Gamma(c)}(x_T + \xi)^{-1} \Gamma(a+c) \\
&= \frac{1}{\Gamma(a+c)}(x_T + \xi) \lambda^{a+c-1} \exp\left[-\lambda(x_T + \xi)\right]
\end{aligned} \tag{6.12}$$

which is also distributed as gamma $[a + c, x_T + \zeta - 1]$. Note that $\underline{x}$ is a vector.

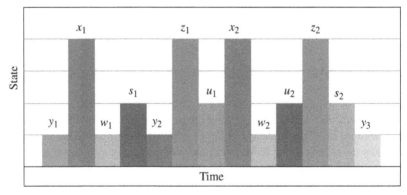

FIGURE 6.4   A sample illustration of feasible transitions from Figure 6.3 implemented to Sections 6.4.3.1 to 6.4.3.6.

6.4.3.2   DOWN-to-UP Recovery Transition Rate (μ) from y_1 to x_1, or y_2 to z_1 in Figure 6.4
Let b = number of occurrences of DOWN (recovery) times before UP (operating)

$$Y_i \sim \mu e^{-\mu Y}$$

$y_T = \sum_1^b Y_i$ = total DOWN (recovery) times before UP for "b" many such occurrences
μ = full recovery DOWN-to-UP rate
d = shape parameter of gamma prior for the full DOWN-to-UP recovery rate μ
η = inverse scale parameter of gamma prior for the full DOWN-to-UP recovery rate μ

Now let the full recovery rate μ have a gamma prior distribution:

$$\theta_2(\mu) = \frac{\eta^d}{\Gamma(d)} \mu^{d-1} \exp(-\mu\eta), \mu > 0 \tag{6.13}$$

The joint likelihood of the DOWN-time random variables is

$$f(y_1, y_2, \ldots, y_a \mid \mu) = \mu^b \exp[-y_T \mu]. \tag{6.14}$$

The joint distribution of data and prior becomes:

$$k(\underline{y}, \mu) = f(y_1, y_2, \ldots, y_b, \mu) = \frac{\eta^d}{\Gamma(d)} \mu^{b+d-1} \exp[-\mu(y_T + \eta)]. \tag{6.15}$$

Thus, similarly skipping two intermediate steps, the posterior distribution for μ is

$$h_2(\mu \mid \underline{y}) = \frac{1}{\Gamma(b+d)} (y_T + \eta) \mu^{b+d-1} \exp[-\mu(y_T + \eta)], \tag{6.16}$$

which is also distributed as gamma $[b + d, y_T + \eta - 1]$. Note that $\underline{y}$ is a vector.

6.4.3.3   UP-to-DER Failure Transition Rate (δ) from z_1 to μ_p, or z_2 to s_2 in Figure 6.4
Let o = number of occurrences of UP times before DER
$z_T = \sum_1^o Z_i$ = total UP times before DER for "o" many of such occurrences

$$Z_i \sim \delta e^{-\delta z}$$

δ = UP-to-DER failure rate
e = shape parameter of gamma prior for the UP-to-DER failure rate δ
Δ = inverse scale parameter of gamma prior for the UP-to-DER failure rate δ

Now let the UP-to-DER failure rate δ have a *gamma* prior distribution:

$$\theta_3(\delta) = \frac{\Delta^e}{\Gamma(e)} \delta^{e-1} \exp(-\delta\Delta), \ \delta > 0. \tag{6.17}$$

Similarly skipping two intermediate steps, the conditional posterior density of δ becomes

$$h_3\left(\delta \mid \underline{z}\right)=\frac{1}{\Gamma\left(o+e\right)}\left(z_T+\Delta\right)\delta^{o+e-1}\exp\left[-\delta\left(z_T+\Delta\right)\right],\tag{6.18}$$

which is also distributed as $\mathrm{gamma}\left[o+e,(z_T+\Delta)^{-1}\right]$. Note that $\underline{z}$ is a vector.

6.4.3.4   DER-to-UP Recovery Transition Rate (β) from u_1 to x_2, or u_2 to z_2, in Figure 6.4

Let k=number of occurrences of DER times before UP

$u_T=\sum_1^k U_i$ = total *DER* failure times before going UP for "k" many of such occurrences

$$U_i \sim \beta \ e^{-\beta U}$$

β = DER-to-UP recovery rate
ϕ = shape parameter of *gamma* prior for the DER-to-UP recovery rate β
f = inverse scale parameter of gamma prior for the DER-to-UP recovery rate

Now let the DER-to-UP recovery rate β have a *gamma* prior distribution:

$$\theta_4\left(\beta\right)=\frac{\phi^f}{\Gamma\left(f\right)}\beta^{f-1}\exp\left(-\beta\phi\right),\beta>0\tag{6.19}$$

Thus, similarly skipping two intermediate steps, the conditional posterior density of β becomes

$$h_4\left(\beta \mid \underline{u}\right)=\frac{1}{\Gamma\left(k+f\right)}\left(u_T+\phi\right)\beta^{k+f-1}\exp\left[-\beta\left(u_T+\phi\right)\right],\tag{6.20}$$

which is also distributed as $\mathrm{gamma}\left[k+f,(u_T+\phi)^{-1}\right]$. Note that $\underline{u}$ is a vector.

6.4.3.5   DER-to-DOWN Failure Transition Rate (α) from s_1 to y_2, or s_2 to y_3 in Figure 6.4

Let j=number of occurrences of DER failure times before DO

$s_T=\sum_1^j S_i$ = total *DER* failure times before going *DOWN* for "j" many such occurrences

$$S_i \sim \alpha e^{-\alpha s}$$

α = DER-to-DOWN failure rate
g = shape parameter of *gamma* prior for DER-to-DOWN failure rate α
ψ = inverse scale parameter of *gamma* prior for DER-to-DOWN failure rate α

Now let the DER-to-DOWN failure rate α have a *gamma* prior distribution:

$$\theta_5\left(\alpha\right)=\frac{\psi^g}{\Gamma\left(g\right)}\alpha^{g-1}\exp\left(-\alpha\psi\right),\quad \alpha>0.\tag{6.21}$$

Thus, similarly skipping two intermediate steps, the conditional posterior density of α becomes

$$h_5\left(\alpha \mid \underline{S}\right) = \frac{1}{\Gamma\left(j+g\right)}\left(s_T + \psi\right)\alpha^{j+g-1}\exp\left[-\alpha\left(s_T + \psi\right)\right], \qquad (6.22)$$

which is also a gamma$[\,j + g,(s_T + \psi)^{-1}\,]$. Note that $\underline{s}$ is a vector.

6.4.3.6 DOWN-to-DER Recovery Transition Rate (γ) from w_1 to s_p, or w_2 to u_2 in Figure 6.4

Let p = number of occurrences of DOWN times before DER

$w_T = \sum_1^p W_i$ = total DOWN times before going DER for "p" many such occurrences

$$W_i \sim \gamma e^{-\gamma w}$$

γ = DOWN-to-DER recovery rate
h = shape parameter of *gamma* prior for the DOWN-to-DER recovery rate γ
π = inverse scale parameter of *gamma* prior for the DOWN-to-DER recovery rate γ

Now let the DOWN-to-DER recovery rate γ have a *gamma* prior distribution:

$$\theta_6\left(\gamma\right) = \frac{\pi^h}{\Gamma\left(h\right)}\gamma^{h-1}\exp\left(-\gamma\pi\right), \quad \gamma > 0 \qquad (6.23)$$

Thus, similarly skipping two intermediate steps, the conditional posterior density of γ becomes

$$h_6\left(\gamma \mid \underline{w}\right) = \frac{1}{\Gamma\left(p+h\right)}\left(w_T + \pi\right)\gamma^{p+h-1}\exp\left[-\gamma\left(w_T + \pi\right)\right], \qquad (6.24)$$

which is also distributed as gamma$[\,p+h,(w_T + \pi)^{-1}\,]$. Note that $\underline{w}$ is a vector.

6.4.4 Statistical Simulation of Three-State Units to Estimate the Density of UP–DOWN–DER

Given the following example covering the first five episodes of six different sojourn times (see Figs. 6.3 and 6.4), we observe that Table 6.1 displays the input data as tabulated for an example analyzed below:

The cumulative probabilities of states are calculated by MC simulation method using input from Table 6.1 as follows in Tables 6.2, 6.3, and 6.4 for UP, DER, and DOWN states in 100, 1000, and 10,000 simulation runs, respectively. Figures 6.5, 6.6, and 6.7 using Equations (6.5)–(6.7) will convert these tabulations into cumulative frequency plots utilizing the six transitions of Figure 6.3 in Sections 6.4.3.1–6.4.3.6 covering Equations (6.9)–(6.24).

TABLE 6.1   Input Data Example for the Monte Carlo Simulations of UP, DOWN, and DER States for the First 5 Episodes; $a = 5$, $b = 5$, $o = 5$, $k = 5$, $j = 5$, and $p = 5$ from Figures 6.3 and 6.4

# Events	Exposure Time	Shape Parameter	Scale Parameter	Transition Rate
$a = 5$	$X_T = 25$	$c = 0.2$	$\xi = 1$	λ
$b = 5$	$Y_T = 5$	$d = 2$	$\eta = 0.5$	μ
$o = 5$	$Z_T = 10$	$e = 1$	$\Delta = 0.5$	δ
$k = 5$	$U_T = 20$	$f = 0.5$	$\varnothing = 1$	β
$j = 5$	$S_T = 10$	$g = 1$	$\psi = 0.5$	α
$p = 5$	$W_T = 15$	$h = 2$	$\pi = 1$	γ

TABLE 6.2   UP For 100, 1,000 and 10,000 Simulations

UP State EQ(5)

Cumulative Density	<0.1	<0.2	<0.3	<0.4	<0.5	<0.6	<0.7	<0.8
100 *simulation runs*								
Total count	0	2	19	62	92	100	100	100
Cumulative probability	0	0.02	0.19	0.62	0.92	1	1	1
1000 *simulation runs*								
Total count	0	21	185	597	885	978	998	1000
Cumulative probability	0	0.021	0.185	0.597	0.885	0.978	0.998	1
10,000 *simulation runs*								
Total count	0	187	2000	5874	8815	9816	9984	10,000
Cumulative probability	0	0.0187	0.2	0.5874	0.885	0.978	0.998	1

TABLE 6.3   DERATED For 100, 1,000 and 10,000 Simulations

DERATED State EQ(6)

Cumulative Density	<0.05	<0.1	<0.15	<0.2	<0.25	<0.3	<0.35	<0.4	<0.45
100 *simulation runs*									
Total count	0	10	43	80	97	100	100	100	100
Cumulative probability	0	0.1	0.43	0.8	0.97	1	1	1	1
1000 *simulation runs*									
Total count	0.34	181	552	829	954	984	995	998	999
Cumulative probability	0.034	0.181	0.552	0.829	0.954	0.984	0.995	0.998	0.999
10,000 *simulation runs*									
Total count	34	1893	5894	8543	9545	9882	9960	9989	9999
Cumulative probability	0.0034	0.1893	0.5894	0.8543	0.9545	0.9882	0.996	0.9989	0.9999

TABLE 6.4   DOWN For 100, 1,000 and 10,000 Simulations

DOWN State EQ(7)							
Cumulative Density	<0.1	<0.2	<0.3	<0.4	<0.5	<0.6	<0.7
100 *simulation runs*							
Total count	0	5	19	66	90	100	100
Cumulative probability	0	0.05	0.19	0.66	0.9	1	1
1000 *simulation runs*							
Total count	1	48	252	639	902	995	1000
Cumulative probability	0.001	0.048	0.252	0.639	0.902	0.995	1
10,000 *simulation runs*							
Total count	13	364	2435	6161	9032	9899	10,000
Cumulative probability	0.0013	0.0364	0.2435	0.6161	0.9032	0.9899	1

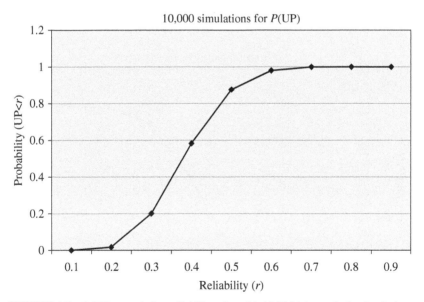

FIGURE 6.5 $P(\text{UP})$ cumulative reliability plot with 10,000 Monte Carlo simulations.

Figure 6.8's cdf plots are the extrapolated JAVA versions of the EXCEL applications in Section 6.4's Figures 6.5, 6.6, and 6.7 supported by Tables 6.2, 6.3, and 6.4. Consequently, a more detailed graphical JAVA version of the simulated probability density plots with $n = 100,000$ simulation runs is displayed in Figures 6.9 and 6.10 to illustrate statistical centrality and location measures. The input data covering the first $n = 5$ counts or episodes of each of six different sojourn times, as a hypothetical example in Table 6.1, with their due transitions are illustrated in Figure 6.4, as derived from Markov

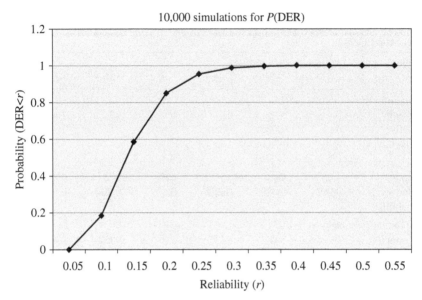

FIGURE 6.6 $P(DER)$ cumulative reliability plot with 10,000 Monte Carlo simulations.

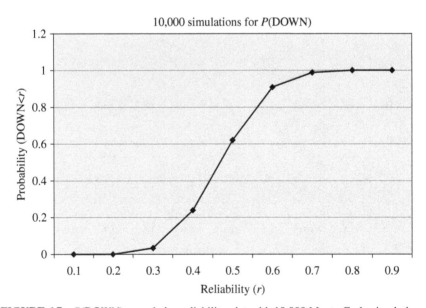

FIGURE 6.7 $P(DOWN)$ cumulative reliability plot with 10,000 Monte Carlo simulations.

state diagram in Figure 6.3. Consequently, calculated results of Tables 6.2, 6.3, and 6.4 and Figures 6.5, 6.6, and 6.7 are plotted for each of the three states (UP, DOWN, DER) cdf in Figure 6.8. Given the input tabulation in Table 6.1, the JAVA program will compute the popular statistical measures (mean, median, mode, variance, and standard deviation) of the three random variables (UP, DOWN, DER) as plotted in Figures 6.9 and 6.10.

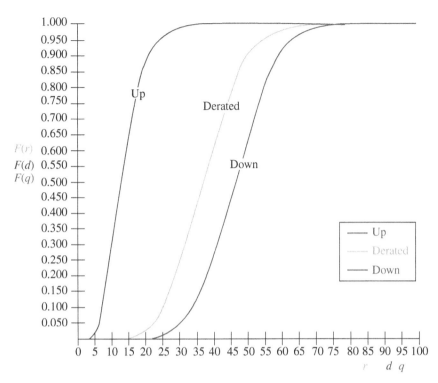

FIGURE 6.8   The input data in Table 6.1 and simulation results in Tables 6.2, 6.3, and 6.4 and Figures 6.5, 6.6, and 6.7 display the cumulative reliability plots of the three states for UP (r), DER (d), and DOWN (q).

The approximate Pdfs (probability density functions) of the three Markov states from Equations (6.5) to (6.7) with mean and standard deviation obtained by incremental piece-wise calculations in Figure 6.8 from the cdfs of Figures 6.5, 6.6, and 6.7, and 6.10 will follow as calculated in the format of $N(\mu, \sigma)$:

$$f(\text{UP}) \sim \text{normal}(0.267, 0.107), f(\text{DER}) \sim \text{normal}(0.433, 0.1),$$
$$\text{and } f(\text{DOWN}) \sim \text{normal}(0.299, 0.106).$$

Note that the 90% confidence limits for the three Markov states computed in Figure 6.9 are as follows:

$$\{\text{UP}_\text{u} = 0.12, \text{UP}_\text{L} = 0.46\}, \{\text{DER}_\text{u} = 0.27, \text{DER}_\text{L} = 0.60\}, \text{ and } \{\text{DOWNu} = 0.14,$$
$$\text{DOWN}_\text{L} = 0.49\}, \text{ respectively.}$$

Also note the first (Q1) and third (Q3) quartiles as location measures, computed in Figure 6.10, are as follows:

$$\{\text{UP}_{Q1} = 0.18, \text{UP}_{Q3} = 0.33\}, \{\text{DOWN}_{Q1} = 0.36, \text{DER}_{Q3} = 0.50\}, \text{ and}$$
$$\{\text{DOWN}_{Q1} = 0.22, \text{DOWN}_{Q3} = 0.37\}, \text{ respectively.}$$

Mean (E) $\approx$ median (M) $\approx >$ mode (m) for UP, DER, and DOWN are very close in a left-skewed shape. E:{0.267, 0.433, UP 0.299}, M:{0.25, 0.43, 0.29}, and m:{0.21, 0.38,

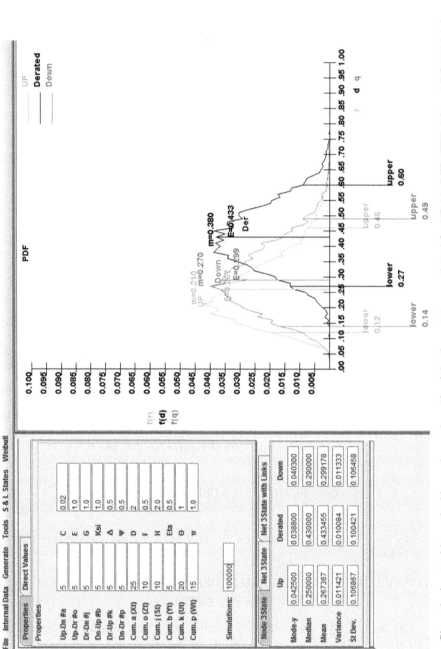

FIGURE 6.9 Given the input table on the l.h.s. column, the pdfs of the three states are plotted for UP (*r*), DERATED (*d*), and DOWN (*q*) for a 90% confidence level showing mode (*m*) and mean (*E*) with upper and lower confidence as centrality measures for *n* = 100,000.

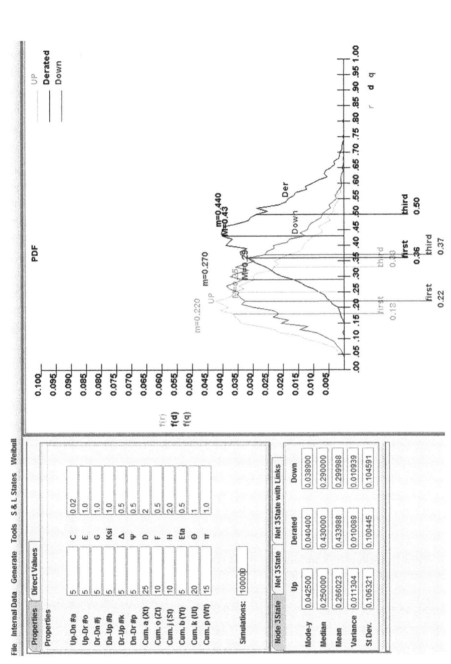

FIGURE 6.10 Similar to Figure 6.12 but with median (*M*), first and third quartiles as location measures for *n* = 100,000 runs plotted for UP (*r*), DERATED (*d*), and DOWN (*q*).

0.27} will result in a quasisymmetric plot. That is, mean $(E) \approx$ median (M) where a slight deviation for the mode (m) will not violate the symmetric appearance, as evident in Figures 6.9 and 6.10. These estimates may prove quite useful for network UP-DER-DOWN indices [45].

Note that mean $= E(q)$ and median $= q = 0.5$ if loss functions are assumed to be squared error and absolute error, respectively, where mode is the maximum likelihood estimator. This follows from the fact that $E(q - \hat{q})^2$, if it exists, is a minimum when $\hat{q} = E(q)$, that is, the mean of the conditional (posterior) distribution of q. Then $E(q)$ is the Bayes solution:

$$E(q) = \int_0^1 q g_Q(q) dq \tag{6.25}$$

Similarly according to Hogg and Craig [46, p. 262], the median of the random variable Q is the Bayes estimator using an informative prior when the loss function is given as $L(q, \hat{q}) = |q - \hat{q}|$. If $E(|q - \hat{q}|)$ exists, then $\hat{q} = q_{0.5}$ minimizes the loss function, that is, the median of the conditional posterior distribution of q. The median is resistant to changes. Then, $q_{0.5}$ or median of q, that is, q_M, is the Bayes solution as the 50th percentile or 0.5 quantile, or second quartile for q, as follows:

$$0.5 = \int_0^{q_{0.5}} g_Q(q) dq. \tag{6.26}$$

The main approaches to the selection of prior distributions may be summarized, also by [47]:

1. Physical reasoning (Bayes)—too restrictive for most practical purposes; thus, flat or uniform priors, including improper priors (Laplace and Jeffrey's), the most widely used.

2. Subjective priors (de Finetti and Savage)—used in certain specific situations such as weather forecasting and for certain kinds of business applications where prior information is very important and it is worthwhile to elicit the client's true subjective opinions, but hardly used at all.

3. Prior distributions for convenience and mathematical tractability, such as conjugate priors—in practice these are very often used just to simplify the calculations. This author will work with item 3 rather than 1 or 2.

6.4.5   How to Generate Random Numbers from SL pdf to Simulate Component and System Behavior

Assume the random variables, $y - \Gamma(\alpha_1 = a + c, \beta_1 = \zeta + x_T)$, and rv, $z \sim gamma\ (\alpha_2 = b + d, \beta_2 = \eta + y_T)$, where the random variable $q = y / (y + z)$ has the pdf and cdf as follows, respectively, where $\eta = $ eta and $\zeta = ksi$ from Equations (6.1)–(6.3) of Section 6.4.2:

$$g_Q(q) = \frac{\Gamma(m' + n')}{\Gamma(m')\Gamma(n')} a'^{m'} b'^{n'} \frac{(1-q)^{m'-1} q^{n'-1}}{\left[a' + q'(b' - a')\right]^{m'+n'}} \tag{6.27}$$

$$G_Q(q) = 1 - G_{F_{2m',2n'}}\left[\frac{a'n'}{b'm'}(q^{-1}-1)\right] = P\left[F2m',2n' > C_1 = \frac{a'n'}{b'm'}(q^{-1}-1)\right] \quad (6.28)$$

Resubstituting for $n' = a+c$, $m' = b+d$, $b' = \xi \mid x_T$, and $a' = \eta + y_T$, we obtain for (6.27)

$$g_Q(q) = \frac{\Gamma(a+b+c+d)}{\Gamma(a+c)\Gamma(b+d)}(\eta+y_T)^{b+d}(\xi+x_T)^{a+c}\frac{(1-q)^{b+d-1}q^{a+c-1}}{\left[\eta+y_T+q'(\xi+x_T-\eta-y_T)\right]^{a+b+c+d}}$$

$$(6.29)$$

where Snedecor's F distribution used in (6.28) can be found in Ref. [48]. By the inverse transform approach, find the constant $C_1 =$ inverse of $F2m',2n'_{(1-ui)}$ as in (6.28), by equating the cdf value $G_Q(q)$ to a random uniform number, u_i, for $i = 1,\dots,N$ (large), as follows:

$$C_1 = \frac{a'n'}{b'm'}(q^{-1}-1) \rightarrow q^* = \frac{a'n'}{a'n'+C_1 b'm'}, \quad 0 < q^* < 1 \quad (6.30)$$

where q^* is the $SL(\alpha,\beta,L) = SL(\alpha = a+c, \beta = b+d, L = \beta_1/\beta_2)$ random deviate for q (unavailability). Note that u_i are uniform (0,1) for $i = 1, \dots, N$ (large). Using pedagogues of Chapter 1, we refer to P44 (P for pedagogue) in Figure 6.11 to generate random deviates from the SL pdf. Figure 6.12 shows relationships between popular distributions for statistical simulations including SL [20, 26]. Refer to Table 1.15's and 1.16's item #5 in Chapter 1.

6.4.6 Example of SL Simulation for Modeling Network of 2-in-Simple-Series Two-State (UP–DN) Units

Given the following simplest series system of two identical components in Figure 6.13, whose default operational probability for each is $P(UP) = 0.9$ and hence $P(\text{system}) = 0.9^2 = 0.81$. We now force these units have their unavailability rv distributed with SL displayed as in Figure 6.2's l.h.s. column, where $g_Q(q)$ is formulated as follows: $SL(\alpha = a+c, \beta = b+d, L = \xi + x_T/\eta + y_T) = SL(\alpha = 10+0.02 = 10.02, \beta = 10+0.1 = 10.1; L = 1 + 1000/1 + 111.1/1001/112.1 = 9.7234)$. Use the SL random deviate simulator for q in Equation (6.30), where q_i are to be independently SL distributed. Historical failure and repair data are given in Figure 6.2. The flat deterministic outcome is $0.9^2 = 0.81$, whereas SL-distributional input–output relationship is unknown due to the closed-form derivation of the product of random variables being not available. Since Equations (6.25) and (6.26) are not closed-form solutions and tedious numerical integration is needed, MC simulation can be the only solution for much larger networks if analytical tools are not available [45, pp. 196–197, Figs. 6.4 and 6.5] where analytical integration becomes an impossible task. See Table 6.5.

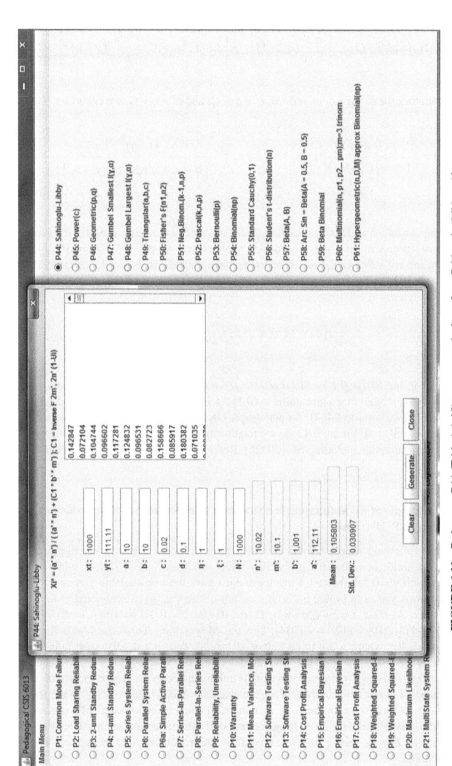

FIGURE 6.11 Pedagogue P44 (Table 1-1-18) to generate deviates from Sahinoglu–Libby pdf.

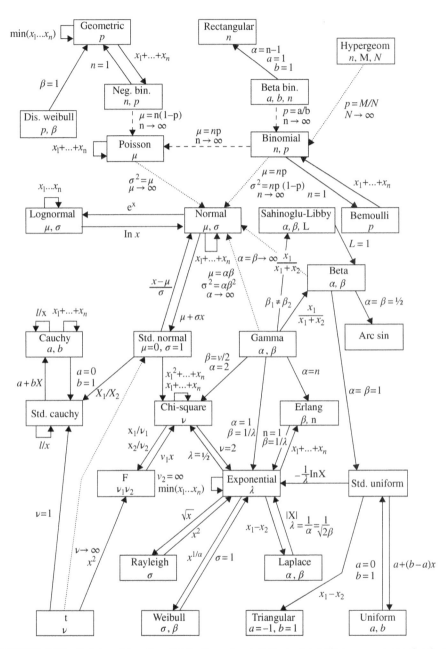

FIGURE 6.12 Relationships for distributions in statistical simulation, see where $\beta_1 \neq \beta_2$ or $L = (\beta_1/\beta_2) \neq 1 \rightarrow SL(\alpha, \beta, L)$ and $\beta_1 = \beta_2$ or $L = 1 \rightarrow$ beta; dashed arrows indicate $\rightarrow \infty$ [20, 26].

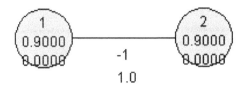

FIGURE 6.13   Simple series system of two units.

TABLE 6.5   Simulation of Simple Series Network Using SL-Distributed Unavailability

Using SL Simulation, Final Network: 79,617 successes out of 100,000 simulation runs
Network reliability = 0.79617
Network unreliability = 0.20383
Each of the 100 networks simulated 1000 times totaling to 100,000 runs in 65.444 s

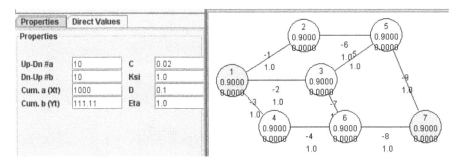

FIGURE 6.14   Complex network of seven units with input data, where source: $s = 1$ and target: $t = 7$.

6.4.7   Example of SL Simulation for Modeling a Network of 7-in-Complex-Topology Two-State (UP–DN) Units

For the sake of a convenient example, a feasible and probable 7-node complex architectural style is taken [20, p. 254] with failure and repair history including the prior parameters displayed on the l.h.s. with 10 each ups and downs lasting 1000 and 111.11 h, respectively, in Figure 6.14. The author assumes for the hypothetical control architecture an identical SL distribution for its unavailability as displayed in Table 6.6 employing historical data for its components simulated 1000 times in 100-tuples of networks. This means 100,000 simulation runs overall. The analytical result being unknown for a complex system as in the 7-node network depicted in Figure 6.14, the resulting simulation is 0.785 as in Table 6.6.

In the June 2012 issue of the IEEE Computer with "Computing in Asia" as the cover feature, an article entitled "Computing for the Next-Generation Automobile" displays three hybrid vehicle architectural styles—series, parallel, and series–parallel—and then the (Toyota) Prius integrated THS II control architecture. It is mentioned that most vehicles today come with more than 50 embedded computer components in a complex topology, called electronic control units (ECUs) [7, pp. 34–35].

TABLE 6.6   Simulation of a 7-Node Complex Production
Network Using SL-Distributed Unit Unavailability

Final Network: 0.78476 successes out of 100,000
Network reliability = 0.78476
Network unreliability = 0.21524
Each of the 100 networks simulated 1000 times in 148.36 s

6.5   A REVIEW OF MODELING AND SIMULATION IN CYBER-SECURITY

Modeling and simulation (M&S) is a vital tool that can be leveraged for process improvement and technology/capability development and evaluation. It is the process of designing a model of a system and conducting simulated experiments to preview and predict system behavior and evaluate optimal strategies for system operation. A short review of approaches will be covered in the world of cyber-security on MC or DES. With the cyber-security breaches rampant in the world, some of the most creative solutions to counteract these problems can be obtained by digital simulation faster, safer, and cheaper than they can be resolved in the physical labs. In his related article, Rinaldi highlights M&S as a crosscutting initiative to increase the security of critical infrastructures [49]. Their strategy states that modeling, simulation, and analysis must be employed to "develop creative approaches and enable complex decision support, risk management, and resource investment activities to combat terrorism at home." Rinaldi concludes that the multidisciplinary science of interdependent infrastructures is immature and requires M&S to mature it and adds that they are developing, among others, at Sandia Labs the following techniques. What-if analyses, dynamic simulations, and multiagent-based models (ABM), which at a macro level similar to cellular automata, are out of scope for this section. Some examples of M&S and DES in the cyber-security field will follow.

6.5.1   MC Value-at-Risk Approach by Kim et al. in CLOUD Computing

Based on today's volatile market conditions, the ability to generate accurate and timely risk measures has become critical to operating successfully and necessary for survival. Value at risk (VaR) is a market standard risk measure used by senior management and regulators to quantify the risk level of a firm's holdings. However, the time-critical nature and dynamic computational workloads of VaR applications make it essential for computing infrastructures to handle bursts in computing and storage resources needs. This requires on-demand scalability, dynamic provisioning, and the integration of distributed resources.

A VaR calculation will typically start after the end of the trading day, when market data and final positions have been verified. It must be complete, and updated risk numbers must be available, before the start of the next trading day. As the number and complexity of positions change, the computational requirements for the calculation can change significantly; however, the completion deadline of the beginning of the next trading day remains fixed. Furthermore, as market conditions change, a firm may want to vary the number of MC scenarios run (and thus the resolution of the calculation), which will add additional variability to the computation time. Specifically, the authors demonstrate how the Comet CLOUD autonomic computing engine can support online multiresolution VaR analytics, a candidate for CLOUD architecture by integrating of private and Internet CLOUD resources [50].

6.5.2 MC and DES in Security Meter (SM) Risk Model

Four examples will be studied regarding MC and digital event simulation in cyber-security.

6.5.2.1 Example for Security Meter Risk Modeling and Simulation   Assume two vulnerabilities and two threats in a $2 \times 2 \times 2$ setup as in Figure 6.15 [20, 22].

Let X (total number of cyber-attacks detected) $= 360/\text{year}$ and let $X_{11} = 98$, $X_{12} = 82$, $X_{21} = 82$, and $X_{22} = 98$.

Let Y (total number of attacks undetected) $= 10/\text{year}$ and let $Y_{11} = 2$, $Y_{12} = 3$, $Y_{21} = 3$, and $Y_{22} = 2$.

When we keep Figure 6.15 in sight, we obtain the risk ratios and expected cost of loss (ECL) as follows:

$$P_{11}\left(\text{threat 1 probability for vulnerability 1}\right) = \frac{\left(X_{11} + Y_{11}\right)}{\left(X_{11} + Y_{11} + X_{12} + Y_{12}\right)} \quad (6.31)$$

$$= \frac{100}{185} = 0.54$$

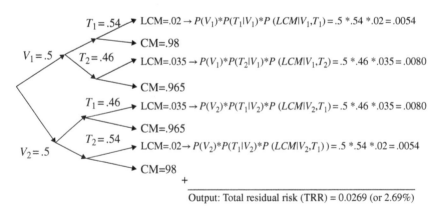

Output: Total residual risk (TRR) = 0.0269 (or 2.69%)

FIGURE 6.15 Simplest $2 \times 2 \times 2$ tree diagram for two threats and for two vulnerabilities in a cyber-risk scenario.

$$P_{12}\left(\text{threat 2 probability for vulnerability 1}\right) = \frac{X_{12} + Y_{12}}{X_{11} + Y_{11} + X_{12} + Y_{12}}$$
$$= \frac{85}{185} = 0.46$$
(6.32)

$$P_{21}\left(\text{threat 1 probability for vulnerability 2}\right) = \frac{X_{21} + Y_{21}}{X_{21} + Y_{21} + X_{22} + Y_{22}}$$
$$= \frac{85}{185} = 0.46$$
(6.33)

$$P_{22}\left(\text{threat 2 probability for vulnerability 2}\right) = \frac{X_{22} + Y_{22}}{X_{21} + Y_{21} + X_{22} + Y_{22}}$$
$$= \frac{100}{185} = 0.54$$
(6.34)

$$P_1\left(\text{vulnerability 1}\right) = \frac{X_{11} + Y_{11} + X_{12} + Y_{12}}{X_{11} + Y_{11} + X_{12} + Y_{12} + X_{21} + Y_{21} + X_{22} + Y_{22}}$$
$$= \frac{185}{370} = 0.5$$
(6.35)

$$P_2\left(\text{vulnerability 2}\right) = \frac{X_{21} + Y_{21} + X_{22} + Y_{22}}{X_{11} + Y_{11} + X_{12} + Y_{12} + X_{21} + Y_{21} + X_{22} + Y_{22}}$$
$$= \frac{185}{370} = 0.5.$$
(6.36)

The probabilities of lack of countermeasure (LCM) and countermeasure (CM) where CM+LCM=1 for the vulnerability–threat pairs demonstrated in Figure 6.15:

$$P\left(\text{LCM}_{11}\right) = \frac{Y_{11}}{X_{11} + Y_{11}} = \frac{2}{100} = 0.02, \quad \text{hence,} \quad P\left(\text{CM}_{11}\right) = 1 - 0.02 = 0.98 \quad (6.37)$$

$$P\left(\text{LCM}_{12}\right) = \frac{Y_{12}}{X_{12} + Y_{12}} = \frac{3}{85} = 0.035, \quad \text{hence,} \quad P\left(\text{CM}_{12}\right) = 1 - 0.035 = 0.965 \quad (6.38)$$

$$P\left(\text{LCM}_{21}\right) = \frac{Y_{21}}{X_{21} + Y_{21}} = \frac{3}{85} = 0.035, \quad \text{hence,} \, P\left(\text{CM}_{21}\right) = 1 - 0.035 = 0.965 \quad (6.39)$$

$$P\left(\text{LCM}_{22}\right) = \frac{Y_{22}}{X_{22} + Y_{22}} = \frac{2}{100} = 0.02, \quad \text{hence,} \, P\left(\text{CM}_{22}\right) = 1 - 0.02 = 0.98 \quad (6.40)$$

We place the estimated input values for the security meter in Figure 6.15 to calculate total residual risk.

Therefore, once you build the probabilistic model from the empirical data, as above, which should verify the final results, you can forecast or predict any "taxonomic" activity whether it is the number of vulnerabilities or threats or crashes as in Table 6.7. For the study above, the total number of crashes is 10 out of 370 total events, which gives a ratio of $10/370 = 0.0270$ to verify the final results as tabulated in Figure 6.14 using software.

Using this probabilistically accurate model, we can predict what will happen in a different setting or year for a newly given explanatory set of data as in Table 6.7. If a clue suggests to us a future 1000 total episodes and 500 episodes of vulnerabilities of V_1, then by the avalanche effect, we can fill in all the other blanks, such as for $V_2 = 500$. Then $(0.5405)(500) = 270.2$ of T_1 and $(0.4595)(500) = 229.7$ of T_2. Out of $270.2\,T_1$ episodes, $(0.02)(270.2) = 5.4054$ for LCM were yielding to 5.4 crashes. Therefore, antivirus devices or firewalls have led to 264.8 preventions or saves.

Again for T_2 of V_1, $(0.035)(229.7) = 8.1$ crashes and $(0.965)(229.7) = 221.6$ saves. The same holds for the V_2 due to symmetric data in this example depicted in Table 6.7. If the asset value is \$2500.00 and the criticality constant is 0.4, then the ECL as demonstrated in Figure 6.14 following calculations. As studied in earlier chapter on security meter,

$$\text{ECL} = \text{Residual risk} \times \text{criticality} \times \text{asset} = (0.0269)(0.4)(\$2500) = \$26.9. \quad (6.41)$$

6.5.2.2 Discrete Event (Dynamic Time-Dependent) Simulation Using Negative Exponential
The analyst is expected to simulate a cyber component's (such as a server) tree diagram 10 consecutive times from the beginning of the year (e.g., 1/1/2016) until the end of 1000 years (i.e., 12/31/3015) in an 8,760,000 h period, with a life cycle of crashes or saves for a total of $10 \times 1000 = 10,000$ simulation runs. The input data is tabulated in Table 6.7 to conduct the generation of random deviates. At the end of this planned time period, the analyst will fill in the elements of the tree diagram for a $2 \times 2 \times 2$ security meter's tree diagram model as in Figure 6.15.

Recall that the rates are the reciprocals of the means for the assumption of a negative exponential pdf to represent the distribution of time to crash. For example, if $\lambda = 98$ per 8760 h, the mean time to crash is $8760/98 = 89.38$ h. Use the input as in Table 6.16 of Section 5.2.1 [20, 22]. We observe a result of TRR $= 0.0269 \approx 0.027$ in Figure 6.16.

TABLE 6.7 The Deterministic Estimates of the SM Parameters in Figure 6.14
Given the Total Number of Attacks for Case Studies: (a) 370 and (b) 1000

Total Attacks	VB	Attacks	%	crashes	saves	Threat	events	%	crashes	saves	Risk	Post Pct	Post vb
370	v1	185	50.00	5	180	v1.t1	100.0	54.05	2.0	98.0	0.005405	20.00	
						v1.t2	85.0	45.95	3.0	82.0	0.008108	30.00	0.500000
	v2	185	50.00	5	180	v2.t1	100.0	54.05	2.0	98.0	0.005405	20.00	
						v2.t2	85.0	45.95	3.0	82.0	0.008108	30.00	0.500000
Total Attacks	VB	Attacks	%	crashes	saves	Threat	events	%	crashes	saves	Risk	Post Pct	Post vb
1000	v1	500	50.00	14	486	v1.t1	270.2...	54.05	5.4054...	264.8...	0.005405	20.00	
						v1.t2	229.7...	45.95	8.1081...	221.6...	0.008108	30.00	0.500000
	v2	500	50.00	14	486	v2.t1	270.2...	54.05	5.4054...	264.8...	0.005405	20.00	
						v2.t2	229.7...	45.95	8.1081...	221.6...	0.008108	30.00	0.500000

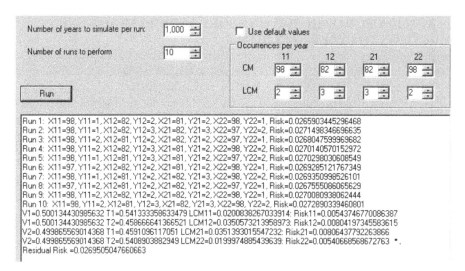

FIGURE 6.16   Discrete event simulation (DES) results of the $2 \times 2 \times 2$ security meter.

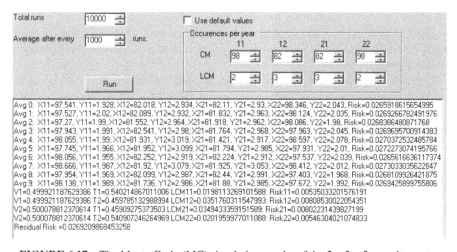

FIGURE 6.17   The Monte Carlo (MC) simulation results of the $2 \times 2 \times 2$ security meter.

6.5.2.3   MC (Static Time-Independent) Simulation Using Poisson pdf   Using the identical information in Section 6.5.2.1, the analyst is expected to use the principles of MC simulation to simulate the $2 \times 2 \times 2$ security meter as in Table 6.7 and Figure 6.15 for 10 repeated trials. One employs the Poisson distribution for generating failure and repair rates for each leg in the tree diagram of the $2 \times 2 \times 2$ model shown in Figure 6.15. The rates are given as the count of saves (repairs) or crashes (failures) annually. The necessary rates of occurrence for the Poisson distribution's random value generation were given in the empirical data in Figure 6.16. For each security meter realization, get a risk value and average it over $n = 10,000$ in 1,000 increments. When you average over $n = 1000$ runs, you should get the same DES value as in Figure 6.16. Using the same data, as projected, we get the same results in Figure 6.17 as in Figure 6.16. That is, TRR $= 0.0269 \approx 0.027$ [20, 24]. Therefore, DES and MC SIM results were identical to four decimals, as expected.

6.6 APPLICATION OF QUEUING THEORY AND MULTICHANNEL SIMULATION TO CYBER-SECURITY

Cyber-security risk analysis, in the most general sense, can be likened to a queuing scenario where malware events (arrivals) occur unexpectedly and then they are countermeasured (serviced) with respect to existing service facilities whether single or multichannel. In most queuing books, analytical formulas are presented to compute the steady-state characteristics of a waiting line. These usually are as follows: the average waiting time, the average number of units in the waiting line, the probability of waiting, and the utilization of servers among some more others. In many cases, the queuing (or waiting line) formulas are based on specific assumptions about the probability distributions for arrival times and for service times and the queue discipline such as M/M/1 or M/G/2 or G/G/∞.

Simulation, as a computational technique, poses a flexible alternative for studying queuing disciplines and waiting lines. In scenarios when the assumptions required by the waiting line formulas are not mathematically tractable or computationally reasonable, digital simulation may be the sole feasible approach to analyzing the queuing systems. In this section we will discuss the simulation of a waiting line, that is, process of a cyber system failing and being recovered, taking into account various statistical assumption regarding the arrivals and service times. Due to arising situations where the arrivals (malware events) and departures (recovery events) are episodes that occur at discrete points in time, the simulation model is referred to as a discrete event (dynamic) simulation model.

We develop a queuing system simulation model where the state of the system including the number of malware breaches or events waiting to be serviced (or recovered) and whether the service (recovery) facility is busy or idle and/or changing as time lapses. That is, over time, using a simulation clock, we record the times or epochs that each malware breach arrives for recovery (service) as well as the time each arrival is serviced successfully rendering the compromised unit to back to operation. Multichannel system is used for the purpose of receiving a large volume of requests by computer and/or telephone from customers. When a customer calls, the call must be serviced by an available channel. If there is no channel available, the customer must wait for the next available channel. Multichannel system wants to be able to simulate this process to determine how many channels are necessary to prevent the customers from having to wait over 10 min for instance. A multichannel system is operated through an extensive open workspace, with work stations that include a computer/telephone for each channel. Too many channels would be a waste of resources. It is of interest to optimize the number of channels.

6.6.1 Example 1: One Recovery-Crew Case for Cyber-Security Queuing Simulation

Imagine a computer network operated by a telephone call center-based enterprise, which is hacked and compromised by insider or outsider intruders with an interarrival rate of 0.7/h or 7 per 10 h. To counteract this, the company's IT recovery team and automated software by the customer service will react and recover with a speed of 1/h or 10 per 10 h. Both events are assumed to act with respect to a negative exponential time distribution. At the end of 1000 simulations and 1391 h nonstop (roughly 1400 h or approx. 57.95 days or almost 2 months of exposure time), the outcomes are listed below for one automatic technical maintenance (ATM) recovery crew, which are favorably compared to a theoretical queuing software [48, Management Scientist] accompanied (see Fig. 6.18).

Multi Channel Simulation

Inter-Arrival Time: Exponential A: 0.75
Service Time: Exponential A: 1
Waiting Cost per time period for each unit Cw in $: 10
Service Cost per time period for each channel Cs in $: 7
Trials: 5000
Channels: 1
Results#: 10
[Compute] [Help] [Simulate]

Customer	Inter-Arrival Time	Arrival Time	Service Start Time	Wait Time	Service Time	Completion Time	Time in System	Channel 1 Available
1	1.552901	1.552901	1.552901	0.0	0.207651	1.760552	0.207651	1.760552
2	2.107546	3.660449	3.660449	0.0	1.764125	5.424574	1.764125	5.424574
3	0.961974	4.622423	5.424574	0.802151	0.414763	5.839337	1.216914	5.839337
4	1.0911	5.713523	5.839337	0.125814	0.019566	5.858903	0.14538	5.858903
5	2.334179	8.047702	8.047702	0.0	1.636019	9.683721	1.636019	9.683721
6	1.261256	9.308957	9.683721	0.374764	0.585187	10.268908	0.959951	10.268908
7	0.03424	9.343197	10.268908	0.925711	0.052979	10.321887	0.97869	10.321887
8	4.000109	13.343306	13.343306	0.0	1.24635	14.589656	1.24635	14.589656
9	0.337286	13.680592	14.589656	0.909064	0.023345	14.613001	0.932409	14.613001
10	0.736214	14.416806	14.613001	0.196195	1.694702	16.307703	1.890897	16.307703
4990	0.735646	6606.089282	6608.086167	1.996885	1.354159	6609.450326	3.361044	6609.450326
4991	1.715256	6607.804538	6609.450326	1.645788	0.042774	6609.4931	1.688562	6609.4931
4992	1.042609	6608.847147	6609.4931	0.645953	0.882993	6610.376093	1.528946	6610.376093
4993	1.212185	6610.059332	6610.376093	0.316761	0.806678	6611.182771	1.123439	6611.182771
4994	2.310966	6612.370298	6612.370298	0.0	0.773475	6613.143773	0.773475	6613.143773
4995	1.726978	6614.097276	6614.097276	0.0	0.095386	6614.192662	0.095386	6614.192662
4996	0.474339	6614.571615	6614.571615	0.0	1.512748	6616.084363	1.512748	6616.084363
4997	0.288107	6614.859722	6616.084363	1.224641	0.257574	6616.341937	1.482215	6616.341937
4998	3.190076	6618.0498	6618.0498	0.0	0.198649	6618.248449	0.198649	6618.248449
4999	1.224129	6619.273929	6619.273929	0.0	2.768052	6622.041981	2.768052	6622.041981
5000	0.241421	6619.51535	6622.041981	2.526631	0.043448	6622.085429	2.570079	6622.085429

Summary Statistics

Number Waiting	3782
Probability of Waiting	0.7564
Average Wait Time	3.031973
Maximum Wait Time	28.369018
Average Utilization of Channel	0.760561
Number Waiting > 1 min	2934
Probability of Waiting > 1 min	0.5868
Average System Time	4.038984
Total Cost per time period	$37.29238

FIGURE 6.18 Solution for Example 6.6.1 for 5000 simulation where rates are entered.

Multi Channel Simulation

Inter-Arrival Time: Exponential A: 0.75
Service Time: Exponential A: 1
Waiting Cost per time period for each unit Cw in $: 10
Service Cost per time period for each channel Cs in $: 7
Trials: 5000
Channels: 2
Results#: 10
[Compute] [Help] [Simulate]

Customer	Inter-Arrival Time	Arrival Time	Service Start Time	Wait Time	Service Time	Completion Time	Time in System	Channel 1 Available	Channel 2 Available
1	1.151812	1.151812	1.151812	0.0	2.05551	3.207322	2.05551	3.207322	0.0
2	0.759982	1.911794	1.911794	0.0	0.152137	2.063931	0.152137	3.207322	2.063931
3	0.175233	2.087027	2.087027	0.0	1.899686	3.986713	1.899686	3.207322	3.986713
4	2.195856	4.282883	4.282883	0.0	0.220112	4.502995	0.220112	4.502995	3.986713
5	0.971268	5.254151	5.254151	0.0	2.21627	7.470421	2.21627	7.470421	3.986713
6	0.938779	6.19293	6.19293	0.0	1.189401	7.382331	1.189401	7.470421	7.382331
7	2.054137	8.247067	8.247067	0.0	0.575998	8.823065	0.575998	8.823065	7.382331
8	0.719832	8.966899	8.966899	0.0	0.010797	8.977696	0.010797	8.977696	7.382331
9	0.935338	9.902237	9.902237	0.0	5.310044	15.212281	5.310044	15.212281	7.382331
10	0.265829	10.168066	10.168066	0.0	0.391443	10.559509	0.391443	15.212281	10.559509
4990	0.229781	6642.646632	6642.646632	0.0	0.092655	6642.739287	0.092655	6642.739287	6642.543152
4991	0.743618	6643.39025	6643.39025	0.0	0.470076	6643.860326	0.470076	6643.860326	6642.543152
4992	0.334671	6643.724921	6643.724921	0.0	1.092594	6644.817515	1.092594	6643.860326	6644.817515
4993	4.743192	6648.468113	6648.468113	0.0	1.335283	6649.803396	1.335283	6649.803396	6644.817515
4994	0.183416	6648.651529	6648.651529	0.0	0.33189	6648.983419	0.33189	6649.803396	6648.983419
4995	6.155956	6654.807485	6654.807485	0.0	1.934488	6656.741973	1.934488	6656.741973	6648.983419
4996	1.612017	6656.419502	6656.419502	0.0	0.101463	6656.520965	0.101463	6656.741973	6656.520965
4997	0.129795	6656.549297	6656.549297	0.0	1.231739	6657.781036	1.231739	6656.741973	6657.781036
4998	1.082355	6657.631652	6657.631652	0.0	1.278331	6658.909983	1.278331	6658.909983	6657.781036
4999	0.957799	6658.589451	6658.589451	0.0	0.778835	6659.368086	0.778835	6658.909983	6659.368086
5000	0.109704	6658.699155	6658.909983	0.210828	0.421101	6659.331084	0.631929	6659.331084	6659.368086

Summary Statistics

Number Waiting	1024
Probability of Waiting	0.2048
Average Wait Time	0.166736
Maximum Wait Time	4.392033
Average Utilization of Channels	0.372406
Number Waiting > 1 min	313
Probability of Waiting > 1 min	0.0626
Average System Time	1.158249
Total Cost per time period	$22.686868

FIGURE 6.19 JAVA solution for Example 6.6.1 with one crew for 5000 simulation runs.

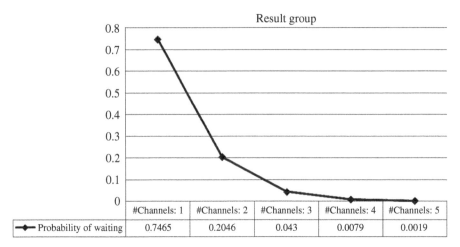

	#Channels: 1	#Channels: 2	#Channels: 3	#Channels: 4	#Channels: 5
◆ Probability of waiting	0.7465	0.2046	0.043	0.0079	0.0019

FIGURE 6.20 Probability of recovery waiting for $\lambda = 0.75$ and $\mu = 1$ per channel size.

Total cost in Java: TC $= (C_w * L) + (Cs * k)$

$L = \lambda W = 0.75 * 4.038984 = 3.029238$; total cost $= (10*3.029238) + (7*1) = \$37.29$

6.6.2 Example 2: Two Recovery-Crew Case for Cyber-Security Queuing Simulation

The same problem this time treated for a two ATM recovery crew is displayed below after 1434 h (59.75 days or almost 2 months of exposure time) and 1000 simulations, which are favorably compared to a theoretical queuing software accompanied. The improvement is noticeable from 1 to 2 malware-event recovery crew (see Figs. 6.19 and 6.20).

6.7 DISCUSSIONS AND CONCLUSION

The power of simulation is evident from countless number of contemporary research works in addition to industrial and military undertakings to save time and budget. Besides nondestructively "learning the truth" before "unexpected things happen" in the real-world sense at an incomparably cost-effective setting, the science and art of M&S crack the code for numerous challenging problems where analytical derivations or formulas prove inutile by reaching a dead end [51, 52]. The objective of applying simulation is to strengthen the advantages of the IT corporate circles and reduce the disadvantages, mainly because of the economic pressure and time constraints in the business world. A gamut of modeling and simulation practices in the Armed Forces flank can be advantageously utilized to plan saving time and resources so as to avoid wasting a tight budget for "the most bang for the buck" before new projects are hastily commissioned, only to see that they are not what to get the job done in a disappointing finale. Uses of simulation in medical oncology or else as well as its impact in the area of computational finance are only some of its virtually endless applications [52, 53].

Following a brief introduction and running a best-kept-secret historical perspective to the origins of simulation, the author first reviews the literature as to why the art and science of modeling and simulation are crucial to today's engineering world. This chapter further focuses on the currently popular manufacturing and cyber defense issues, to cite a few examples if not exhaustive, to set the stage for the rest of the plentiful engineering avenues.

On the manufacturing or production front, the author in response to then-in-2007-unsolved homework question 5.5 p. 256 from his Wiley textbook [20] reviews the set of techniques to generate the multistate probability distribution model of an important pillar of trustworthiness, that is, availability. Namely, when the availability or reliability (long-term availability) of a unit is at stake, and while the unit possesses the three operational states with a derated state added beyond the usual two-state, binary, or dichotomous assumption, habitual conventional applications do not suffice. Therefore, it is worth to review the fact that the primary difference between other related works [30–32] and author's empirical Bayesian treatment of the three states of a repairable hardware unit is to estimate the pdfs of these three states by using MC simulations [38, 39] with an extension of the SL pdf [33, 37]. The closest article to this one [30] uses only four transition rates in a three-state Markov model, whereas the reviewed MC model by the author uses all six transitions. The author's statistical simulation approach is powerful and flexible, whereas reference [30] deals with differential equations limited in scope. Other close references deal with different topics; however, none use any simulation techniques [31, 32].

It is currently infeasible to find closed-form solutions for the random variables of UP, DER, and DOWN expressed by Equations (6.5)–(6.8) due to a multiplicity of sums and products of gamma random variables expressed in the denominator term of Section 6.4.3. In the final analysis shown in Section 6.4.4, the resulting distributions for the three parameters (UP, DER, and DOWN) are approximated by quasisymmetric normal distributions. The outcome distributions in Section 6.4.4 are quasisymmetric with E (mean) and M (median) almost equal, although slightly right skewed because mean $\approx$ median > mode.

The reviewed Sahinoglu–Libby, a.k.a. SL (α, β, L), is the continuous pdf of the unavailability (or availability when duly reparameterized) of a two-state unit. For those units whose lifetime can be decomposed into operating (UP), derated (DER), and nonoperating (DOWN) states in a three-state setting, sojourn times are assumed to be distributed according to the generalized gamma pdf where both shape and scale parameters are nonidentical. The resultant density plots in Figures 6.9 and 6.10, following extensive statistical simulations in Section 6.4.4, are approximately symmetric normal distributed despite a spike for the mode. These plots definitely qualify to pass goodness of fit tested for normal pdf due to intractability of closed-form analytical solutions as for the explained three-state version; the MC simulation technique is rightfully selected as a mathematically tractable model to calculate the UP, DER, and DOWN probabilities for a three-state repairable hardware unit. These summary measures are all shown in the plots of the JAVA applications throughout Section 6.4. Network applications for medium and large networks are studied using MC simulations in Refs. [7, 20, 22]. After the analyses, the approximate closed-form pdfs can be derived as shown in Section 6.4 owing to the favorable results by normal probability plots. Researchers can utilize these simulated results for their related research when deriving the pdfs of their Markov states in other disciplines such as business, for example, banking [54]. Currently, only deterministic probabilities can be calculated through Markov algebra, but not their probability densities. For example, a credit card is either closed (if less than a critical credit score), open (more than), or only conditionally usable for urgent cases (between lower and upper). The bank actuaries may want to estimate the pdfs of these three states to conduct statistical inference using customer-based empirical data by employing empirical Bayesian analysis. Multistate systems such as in the case of four multiple derated states representing electric power turbines, as cited in [20, p. 280, Fig. 6.26] and [45, p. 201, Fig. 10], can be derived. These estimators for unit availability can further be propagated to simulate the source–target availability for troublesome complex networks.

Regarding the cyber-security science and engineering issues however, implementation of modeling and simulation compared to manufacturing industry is fairly new progressing at an experimental stage. This fact is not only due to involvement of human life and death situations in adversity, as compared to accidental casualties in the production world, but also due to lack of theoretical and experiential database dating back to only 1990s since the launch of public Internet. The author, by following examples in this area, proceeds with currently popular VaR technique by Kim et al. [50] and security meter and CLOUD simulation tools (CLOURAM) by Sahinoglu et al. [26]. MC VaR is costly to execute; it does not incorporate cost comparisons when taking measures. Consider a medium-size firm holding positions in 20,000 different financial instruments. Running a 100,000 simulation MC VaR calculation requires generating two billion simulated instrument prices. With a conservative estimate of 10 ms per pricing, this calculation requires more than 5500 h of processor time over an 8-h window. The capital cost of hardware plus the operational cost for data center space, power, cooling, and maintenance makes this cost prohibitive to all but the largest firms. However, scalable CLOURAM is a very fast algorithm, that is, it can simulate a CLOUD system with 430 servers for 1000 years in less than 4 min [26]. SM simulations as in Figures 6.16, 6.17, 6.18, 6.19, and 6.20 are relatively fast and accurately comparable to their analytical counterparts [20–22].

Overall M&S techniques abound, particularly face-saving in the case of theoretical impasses, and sometimes the only viable solutions in engineering and scientific applications in the business and academia [55]. The multiple cases of positive results render M&S methods among the most useful and practical as well as affordable algorithms of our time. If one day, humankind can make it to the surface of the red planet Mars, it will be possible because humans will have nondestructively traveled to Mars some trizillion times by riding on the cyberspace through digital simulation rather than riding a shuttle on the outer space.

The author contends that positive solutions will realize for cancer and currently incurable diseases by crunching computationally intensive and nonlethal M&S techniques. The application of M&S to engineering, cyberspace, and health informatics, however, is not an easy task with much progress remaining to be done. The late Distinguished Professor N. Johnson's support for SL pdf used in this chapter is invaluable (Personal Communications with the late Professor N. Johnson (see supplementary materials 1998–2003 of Ref. 26)) see [57–60] for more.

APPENDIX 6.A

Table 6.A.1 Uniform Numbers Testing; Ho: Random vs. Ha: Nonrandom for 500 runs. Ho is NOT rejected. See Section 2 for this table and the following tables.

Table 6.A.2 Uniform Numbers Testing; Ho: Random vs. Ha: Nonrandom for 500 runs. Ho is rejected. On the average, one out of 40 cycles of 500 runs = 20,000 simulations will end up rejecting Ho: Random.

Table 6.A.3 Uniform Numbers Testing; Ho: Random vs. Ha: Nonrandom for 5000 runs. Ho is NOT rejected.

Validating Sequences of Random Numbers

Random Numbers Testing

Number of Values: 5000

Degree of Freedom: 6

Significance Level: .05

Runs: r = 863 1012 460 125 33 11

Critical Value: 12.59

Chi-square: 7.47528

Press to Test

Assessment: ACCEPT

Trial	Random Number
0	.95162
1	.73773
2	.72635
3	.83132
4	.18739
5	.28005
6	.52069
7	.01491
8	.55777
9	.97447
10	.16006
11	.72681
12	.72906
13	.85314
14	.23105
15	.08898
16	.65905
17	.81807
18	.27867
19	.18883
20	.28774
21	.19498
22	.89793
23	.74370

Table 6.A.4 Uniform Numbers Testing; Ho: Random vs. Ha: Nonrandom for 5000 runs. Ho is rejected. On the average, one out of 10 cycles of 5,000 = 50,000 simulations will end up rejecting Ho: Random.

Validating Sequences of Random Numbers

Random Numbers Testing

Number of Values: 5000

Degree of Freedom: 6

Significance Level: .05

Runs: r = 833 1006 451 148 29 10

Critical Value: 12.59

Chi-square: 15.75656

Press to Test

Assessment: REJECT

Trial	Random Number
4975	.91774
4976	.52257
4977	.43453
4978	.83971
4979	.67841
4980	.42751
4981	.84492
4982	.32722
4983	.49055
4984	.04113
4985	.93558
4986	.78242
4987	.55336
4988	.00525
4989	.52498
4990	.16014
4991	.74509
4992	.14382
4993	.73198
4994	.95697
4995	.57639
4996	.32859
4997	.12994
4998	.83259
4999	.01971

Table 6.A.5 Uniform Numbers Testing; Ho: Random vs. Ha: Nonrandom for 10000 runs. Ho is NOT rejected.

Validating Sequences of Random Numbers		

Random Numbers Testing		9975	.81433
		9976	.80386
		9977	.13244
Number of Values:	10000	9978	.36301
		9979	.86845
		9980	.72018
Degree of Freedom:	6	9981	.08606
		9982	.10540
		9983	.08856
		9984	.60985
Significance Level:	.05	9985	.93867
		9986	.79729
Runs:	r = 1647 2103 908 279 48 11	9987	.62135
		9988	.03134
		9989	.05865
Critical Value:	12.59	9990	.77572
		9991	.14977
Chi-square:	3.45157	9992	.67842
		9993	.25260
		9994	.29307
Press to Test		9995	.49971
		9996	.00250
		9997	.52129
Assessment:	ACCEPT	9998	.91239
		9999	.26634

Table 6.A.6 Uniform Numbers Testing; Ho: Random vs. Ha: Nonrandom for 10,000 runs. Ho is rejected. On the average, one out of 25 cycles of 10,000 = 250,000 simulations will end up rejecting Ho: Random.

Validating Sequences of Random Numbers		

Random Numbers Testing		Trial	Random Number
		0	.82027
		1	.09444
Number of Values:	10000	2	.28535
		3	.80246
		4	.15350
Degree of Freedom:	6	5	.38225
		6	.37329
		7	.98910
Significance Level:	.05	8	.83817
		9	.53599
		10	.43865
Runs:	r = 1667 2022 914 271 67 20	11	.65546
		12	.35910
		13	.25590
Critical Value:	12.59	14	.47913
		15	.43641
Chi-square:	18.50944	16	.33185
		17	.31677
		18	.86309
Press to Test		19	.25959
		20	.07403
		21	.61763
Assessment:	REJECT	22	.69187

Table 6.A.7 Uniform Numbers Testing; Ho: Random vs. Ha: Nonrandom for 50,000 runs. Ho is NOT rejected. After 60 cycles × 50 K = 3,000 K = 3,000,000 simulations there is still no Reject Ho = Random Sequence. This may signal a cutoff point of no rejection of random sequence from this point on. Safe threshold may be 50 K for JAVA coding uniform random number generator.

Table 6.A.8 Uniform Numbers Testing; Ho: Random vs. Ha: Nonrandom for 100,000 runs. Ho is NOT rejected. After 50 cycles × 100 K = 5,000 K = 5,000,000 simulations, there is still no Reject Ho = Random Sequence. This may signal still no rejection of random sequence from the earlier safe threshold: 50 K for a JAVA coding uniform random number generator.

Table 6.A.9 Uniform Numbers Testing; Ho: Random vs. Ha: Nonrandom for 250,000 runs. Ho is not rejected. After 40 cycles × 250 K = 10,000 K = 10,000,000 simulations there is still no Reject Ho = Random Sequence. This may signal still no rejection of random sequence from the earlier safe threshold: 50 K simulations for JAVA coded uniform random number generator. Important Note; In Tables 6.A.1 to 6.A.9, buttons indicate: No of values = 250,000 (simulation runs), DF = 6 (Section 2, by Knuth's technique [10, 11]), Significance Level (Type I error) = 5%, Total Runs: 41606 × 1+ 51836 × 2 + 23059x3 × 6583 × 4 + 1482 × 5 + 290 × 6.093 (average for >6) = 250,000, where bold numbers from 1 to >6 are calculated run sizes by Knuth's method. Chi-square calculated = 7.57 < chi-square critical value = 12.59. Therefore, Do NOT Reject Ho.

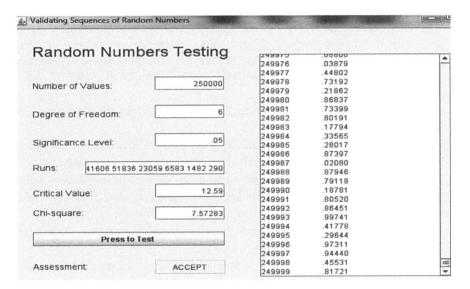

6.8   EXERCISES

6.8.1 How do you explain in 3–4 typed lines (3–4 short sentences) that you'd fare better if you worked at a cyber-security company and you knew M&S and your coworkers had no clue about what Monte Carlo or discrete event simulation. Would you use this notion in what sense and give a short example.

6.8.2 How do you explain (not more than a page) your solution proposal on the following? If your new boss or supervisor after you graduated from your college at your new corporate HQ that deals with cyber-security asked you to do the following: A client bank reported security breaches and pertinent statistics for each of the two main central servers for the past 5 years.

(a) (4 to 5 sentences) How would you simulate the next 5 years using static simulation (Monte Carlo) for each server, using, for example, what statistical distribution and what kind of software (EXCEL or JAVA approach would you draft)?

(b) (4 to 5 sentences) How would you simulate the next 5 years using dynamic simulation (discrete event) for each server, using, for example, what statistical distribution (EXCEL or JAVA approach would you draft)?

(c) (4 to 5 sentences) How would you use CLOUD simulation procedure you learned in this course to predict the banking operational cyber-security as a system, not separately, using, for example, what statistical distribution (EXCEL or JAVA approach would you draft)?

(d) (4 to 5 sentences) If I did not have a clue on simulation methodology, then I would have likely done what?

6.8.3 Multiple Choice on Simulation Concepts. Choose any of the following concepts to fill in the blanks once for each and twice the same for #4. Use the following choices:

(a) Controllable input, (b) best-case scenario, (c) most likely scenario, (d) worst-case scenario, (e) risk analysis, (f) simulation experiment, (g) validation, (h) event, (i) what-if analysis, (j) verification, (k) dynamic simulation model, (l) parameters, (m) probabilistic input, (n) simulation, (o) static simulation model, (p) discrete event simulation model

1. _____A method for learning about a real system by experimenting with a model that represents the system.

2. _____The generation of a sample of values for the probabilistic inputs of a simulation model and computing the resulting values of the model outputs.

3. _____Input to a simulation model that is selected by the decision maker.

4. _____ Input to a simulation model that is subject to uncertainty. A _____ is described by a probability distribution.

5. _____The process of predicting the outcome of a decision in the face of uncertainty.

6. _____ Numerical values that appear in the mathematical relationships of a model. Parameters are considered known and remain constant over all trials of a simulation.

7. _____ A trial-and-error approach to learning about the range of possible outputs for a model. Trail values are chosen for the model inputs (there are the what-ifs?) and the value of the output(s) is computed.

8. _____ Determining the output given the most likely values for the probabilistic inputs of a model.

9. _____ Determining the output given the worst values that can be expected for the probabilistic inputs of a model.

10. _____ Determining the output given the best values that can be expected for the probabilistic inputs of a model.

11. _____ A simulation model used in situations where the state of the system at one point does not affect the state of the system at future points in time. Each trial of the simulation is independent.

12. _____A simulation model used in situations where the state of the system affects how the system changes or evolves over time.

13. _____ An instantaneous occurrence that changes the state of the system in a simulation model.

14. _____ A simulation model that describes how a system evolves over time by using events that occur at discrete points in time.

15. _____ The process of determining that a computer program implements a simulation model as it is intended.

16. _____ The process of determining that a simulation model provides an accurate representation of a real system.

6.8.4 You're employed at a cyber-security-related firm once you graduate. B.B. Boss asks you to quantify the risk (percent) for a client company A's historical security-breach evidence as supplied by the company and/or after you execute the risk probes. Here are what you have complied for your security probes out of 1000 cyber-attacks:

800 vulnerability incidences exist on Internet domain (V1). With respect to hacking (V1-T1), 500 and w.r.t. virus (V1-T2), 300 were recorded. 200 vulnerability incidences on hardware domain (V2) w.r.t. power-outage (V2-T1), 180 and insider intrusion (V2-T2), 20 were recorded. Firewall (V1-T1-CM) countermeasured 95% of the hackers' attempts. Antivirus (V1-T2-CM) countermeasured 85% of the viruses BOTS. Uninterrupted power supply (UPS) (V2-T1-CM) countermeasured 80% storm caused outages. Motion-sensor V2-T2-CM countermeasured 90% of physical!

Show and apply a technical method by employing available software tools to quantify the residual risk for next year 2014 based on the past years' summary data. Use 1000 years of simulations for 10 rounds of security meter tree diagrams for each MC and DES. Also use sec meter in CyberRiskSolver to verify your simulation (MS and none DES) results with those of the analytical. Use Poisson from your EXCEL random generation for Monte Carlo SIM re: # failures and repairs.

Solution: EXCEL approach using sec meter diagram from above given inputs, total breaches are $800 + 200 = 1000$. Use ($X11 = 475$, $Y11 = 25$, $X12 = 255$, $Y12 = 45$, $X21 = 144$, $Y21 = 36$, $X22 = 18$, $Y22 = 2$) (see Fig. 6.21).

6.8.5 (A) For the salesman problem, transfer all you have experimentally done at home using primitive objects such as dice and coins (it is Monte Carlo time independent using random numbers; process is not deterministic) onto an EXCEL spreadsheet for 20 trials. CLASS members should have different outcomes (normally speaking with 1 or 2 exclusions) but the same theoretical results.

(B) Do the same as in (a) but this time using less primitive device, that is, random numbers listing obtained for uniform number generator (unbiased). Using the same rule as on page 56 unpublished notes, apply 5×20 trials (more than 20 U_i's will be needed since for some trials you may need to draw more than one U_i. You will have to proceed from left to right and up to down after the row ends to reach these random numbers. Due to same random numbers to be used, all 8 of you should have the same outcomes ($13,333 for the expected policy sale) and the same theoretical values as before. You should observe that as you approach 100, the results will converge.

(C) EXCEL applications to the same salesman problem as before. You will need to execute in 100 s and then sequential and get the results for the 100th, 200th, 500th, 900th, and 100th to see how the computations are proceeding to converge and concur with theoretical results…. Take \$10 K (not \$1 K) and 20 K(not \$2 K).

Trial	X11=475	Y11=25	X12=255	Y12=45	X21=144	Y21=36	X22=18	Y22=2	Sum_of_crashes	Risk
1	485	19	252	48	141	31	27	4	102	0.101290963
2	476	29	268	38	152	32	14	4	103	0.101678184
3	489	26	249	40	134	38	15	3	107	0.107645875
4	478	27	279	51	151	37	16	3	118	0.113243762
5	476	26	245	49	133	41	13	4	120	0.121580547
6	466	25	257	39	139	40	11	2	106	0.108273749
7	480	23	267	47	135	40	12	2	112	0.111332008
8	472	14	282	55	133	41	17	0	110	0.108481262
9	444	20	257	46	124	41	24	1	108	0.112852665
10	482	18	239	37	146	38	21	2	95	0.09664293
11	478	24	271	42	164	31	20	4	101	0.097678917
12	467	26	261	51	134	45	22	1	123	0.122144985
13	448	21	244	35	154	36	17	1	93	0.097280335
14	438	19	279	57	134	39	11	1	116	0.118609407
15	445	25	258	38	145	26	20	0	89	0.092998955
16	452	15	260	50	152	34	29	2	101	0.101609658
17	486	24	276	44	133	42	18	3	113	0.110136452
18	490	22	244	55	140	32	16	2	111	0.110889111
19	464	23	255	47	149	37	16	2	109	0.109768379
20	498	19	267	28	139	31	21	0	78	0.0777667
21	431	29	235	42	134	39	13	2	112	0.121081081
22	478	21	283	42	142	44	23	3	110	0.106177606
23	507	29	248	43	160	34	21	2	108	0.103448276
983	481	28	247	51	133	34	19	1	114	0.114688129
984	425	29	240	33	149	38	15	2	102	0.109559613
985	474	14	257	48	142	37	16	2	101	0.102020202
986	457	24	251	47	138	28	12	2	101	0.10531804
987	512	23	269	42	136	36	16	3	104	0.100289296
988	489	29	254	56	162	39	19	3	127	0.120837298
989	465	27	299	38	138	30	27	1	96	0.093658537
990	482	34	236	55	151	31	18	1	121	0.120039683
991	481	20	245	35	137	33	14	2	90	0.093071355
992	532	31	244	48	149	47	18	0	126	0.117867166
993	482	29	282	52	149	45	21	4	130	0.122180451
994	454	27	262	44	129	28	9	3	102	0.106694561
995	474	25	256	45	147	36	19	5	111	0.110228401
996	484	30	277	28	127	30	13	2	90	0.090817356
997	486	18	231	41	157	30	24	3	92	0.092929293
998	487	28	298	48	150	27	10	0	103	0.098282443
999	461	15	237	49	143	30	17	1	95	0.099685205
1000	467	17	252	42	148	30	16	2	91	0.093429158
									Average	0.108363521

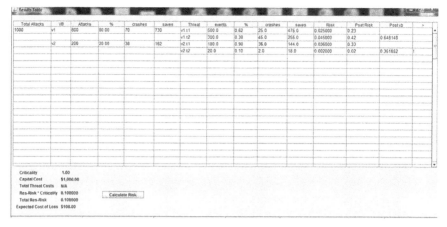

FIGURE 6.21a,b Compound Poisson approach using security meter technique.

6.8.6 Develop a worksheet simulation for the following problem. The Management of Madeline Manufacturing Company is considering the introduction of a brand-new product. The capital cost to begin the overall production is $30,000. The variable cost for the product is uniformly distributed between $16 and $24 per unit. The product will sell for $50 per unit. Demand for the product is best described by normal probability distribution with a mean $\mu = 1200$ units and a standard deviation $\sigma = 300$ units. Develop an EXCEL: spreadsheet simulation similar (not identical) to PORTA-COM project. Use 1000 simulation trials to answer these questions:

(a) What is the mean profit for the simulation? Standard deviation of the profit?

(b) What is the number of losses and the probability the project will result in a loss?

(c) What are the minimum and maximum profits? Do you recommend introducing this product, why or why not? What would you do (what-if?) if you wish to endorse this production line?
Carry on 2 trials longhand calculations by using the statistical simulators for the distributions in Q3. Use the Random Table attached and start from the 20th row as marked to utilize the random numbers from L (left) to R (right).

6.8.7 Use EXCEL MC SIM to solve the following problem. IQ scores are normally distributed with a mean of 100 and standard deviation of 15; N ($\mu = 100$, $\sigma = 15$). Use 10,000 simulation runs but summarize the first and last 10.

(a) What proportion of a society is "genius" with more than an IQ of 140?

(b) What proportion of the society will miss the genius category by 5 or less points?

(c) An IQ of 110 or more is required to make it through an accredited college; what is the proportion of a society that could be eliminated from completing a higher education?

6.8.8 The time to failure on an electronic subassembly can be modeled by Weibull distribution whose location parameter is zero, where alpha (α) scale parameter = 1000 h and beta (β) shape parameter = 1/2. After 1000 EXCEL simulations, display the first 10 and last 10 screenshots and summary statistics.

(a) What is the mean time to failure?

(b) What fraction of these subassemblies will fail by 3000 h?

6.8.9 Network Reliability Problem: Take the 6-node simple network attached with their specified reliabilities such as $R(1)=0.8$, $R(2)=0.9$, $R(3)=0.8$, $R(4)=0.9$, $R(5)=0.9$, and $R(6)=0.9$. Simulate the ingress–egress reliability by using EXCEL simulation and the given data for 1000 simulation runs where input (ingress) is UNIT 1 and output (egress) is UNIT 4. Need first 10 and last 10 screenshots. Verify 0.7115 or 71.15%. See Figure 6.1 on p. 260 Text [20] (Fig. 6.22).

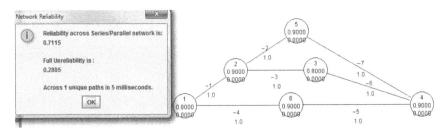

FIGURE 6.22 6-node simple network and network reliability solution.

6.8.10 Using the Monte Carlo technique and 1000 EXCEL random numbers, solve for the definite integral given as $I = \int_0^2 x^3 dx$?

6.8.11 How can you explain (a) distributed simulation practice, differing from (b) non-distributed simulation citing a short example? During the Chapter 6 text covered, do we practice in a normal Monte Carlo simulation course, (a) or (b), why?

6.8.12 Solve for the Examples 6.7.1 and 6.7.2 for a multichannel case where # channels >2 to 5 using JAVA multichannel queuing simulator. Take the combinations for interarrival (IAT) and service times (ST) as such:

(a) IAT: Neg. exponential vs. ST: negative exponential, chi-square, gamma, lognormal, normal, Erlang, Weibull

(b) IAT: gamma vs. ST: negative exponential, chi-square, gamma, lognormal, normal, Erlang, Weibull

(c) IAT: Uniform vs. ST: negative exponential, chi-square, gamma, lognormal, normal, Erlang, Weibull

(d) IAT: Erlang vs. ST: negative exponential, chi-square, gamma, lognormal, normal, Erlang, Weibull

(e) IAT: Weibull vs. ST: negative exponential, chi-square, gamma, lognormal, normal, Erlang, Weibull

NOTE: While selecting parameters, make sure you have a utilization factor of $0.75=$ arrival and service rate. Report the summary statistics:

(i) Number waiting, (ii) probability of waiting, (iii) average waiting time, (iv) max waiting time, (v) utilization of ATMs, (vi) number of waiting >1 min, (vii) probability of waiting >1 min

6.8.13 (a) Using the random uniform Table 1.17, proceeding row-wise from 20th row onward left-to right such as 0.6953, 0.5247, 01368, 0.9850, 0.7467, 0.3813, 0.5827, 0.7893, 0.7169, 0.8166, 0.0082, etc., for the first 11 uniform random numbers, work the computer center availability problem, where each of the two computers fails with respect to a negative exponential (Weibull with shape parameter beta = 1) with 1 failure in every 1 h (rate = λ = 1/year, mean time to failure = 1 year) and repaired again with respect to a negative exponential (Weibull with shape parameter beta = 1) at two repairs per year (rate = λ = 3/year, mean time to repair = 1/3 years). Simulate the computer center operation until all computers are failed and repaired exactly twice by hand calculations. Note that there is only one repair crew available. Use a graph paper for drawing historical data plot.

(b) Rank order the computers according to their availabilities, and propose which one to replace first? Don't ignore the waiting time for the repairman if need arises. Do you need a second repair person? Say yes, if there is a considerable waiting period involved (checking with the theoretical results in an M/M/1 problem from your formula sheet) as these servers cannot wait to be repaired and it is more economical to hire (say, $7/server and 5$/waiting time unit) someone than to have the servers not function. Hint: Use $x^* = \lambda\,[-\ln\,(1 - u)]1/\beta$ for Weibull random deviates where beta = shape, α = scale.

(c) Employing the CLOUD Java program, enter the two units one by one with the given failure and repair rates, say, each of which has 2-GBYTE capacity. Given a constant load of 3 GBYTE for 20 cycles (years), report the reliability of this operation conducting 1000 simulations with the same cycles in years (i.e., as you halted in Question 2A at the end of T when both failed and got repaired twice).

(d) You can compare parts (a) and (c) results, if you draw a 3-GBYTE straight line across the exposure period in part (a) hand calculations to see what the resultant reliability of the system is after taking into account the load information.

6.8.14 Using two-state and three-state input data examples in sections, use ERBDC to obtain the relevant plots for any selected input data of your choice from the ERBDC software.

6.8.15 You are expected to simulate a component, such as a server, from the beginning of the year (e.g., 1/1/08) to the end of the year (12/31/08) in a 8760-h period, with a life cycle of hits (crashes) or saves (e.g., by antimalware). The input data are supplied below for the simulation of random value, at the end of which you will fill in the elements of the security meter tree diagram. Recall that the rates are the reciprocals of the means for an assumption of negative exponential pdf to represent the distribution of time to crash. For example, if rate = 98/8760, the mean time to crash (MTTC) is 8760/98. Use the following data for a $2 \times 2 \times 2$ tree diagram. See the vulnerability–threat–countermeasure spreadsheet below.

Vulnerability	Threat	Countermeasure
Software Failure (Chance)	1. Design & Coding Error 2. System Down	1. Pre-release Testing 2. In-house generator
Software Failure (Intentional)	1. Virus 2. Hacking	1. Install antivirus software 2. Install firewall

Assume a security meter diagram of double vulnerability and double threat scenario such as in Tables 3.2 and 3.3. Let X (total number of crash preventions) be approx. 1/day. Assume 366/year. That is, let $X11 = 98$, $X12 = 85$, $X21 = 85$, and $X22 = 98$. Let Y (total number of crashes not prevented) = 10/year. That is, $Y11 = 3$, $Y12 = 4$, $Y21 = 5$, and $Y22 = 2$.

(a) Calculate the probabilities of all branches in the security meter tree diagram to calculate the risk and expected cost of loss if criticality = 0.5 and the capital cost = \$1000.

(b) Do the same as in (a) by applying a discrete event simulation technique using a negative exponential distribution to verify the results of (a) (Fig. 6.23).

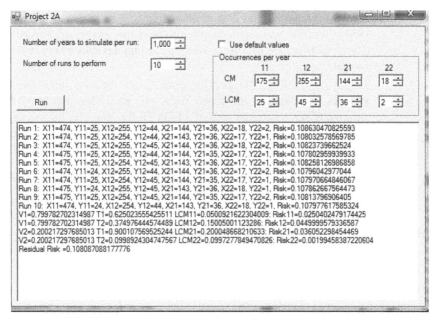

FIGURE 6.23   6-node simple network and network reliability solution.

6.8.16 Using all the information in Exercise 6.8.14, use the principles of Monte Carlo to simulate a $2 \times 2 \times 2$ security meter. Use the Poisson distribution for generating rates for each leg in the tree diagram of the $2 \times 2 \times 2$ setup in Exercise 6.8.14. The necessary rates of occurrence for the Poisson random value generation were given in the empirical data example above. For each security meter realization, get a risk value and then average it over $n = 1000$ to 5000 in increments of 1000. When you average over $n = 5000$ runs, you should get the same value. Calculate ECL for a criticality constant of 0.5 and a capital cost of \$1000.

6.8.17 The first priority in this chapter's exercises is to test the randomness of your uniform random number RAND () generator. For this purpose, you can use the chi-square test of randomness for uniform random numbers. See solution set for an example as follows:

6.8.18 (a) Using the random numbers Table 1.17 from 20th row attached, by hand perform the lunar-lander robot problem. If it lands on the moon where will it be {what coordinates if it lands initially at (0,0)} (i.e., X-axis=0, Y-axis=0 on the center of Mars) a certain time say 1000 simulation runs later? Start moving now. Generate random distances from uniform density with mean $U(a=-100$ ft, $b=100$ ft) for both X and Y coordinates. With 30% chance it will fall and not get up. After $n=5$ runs, doing this by hand, where is the Mars-lander robot landed by the Mars-shooter now in terms of X and Y coordinates with respect to (0,0) center of Mars. Then find the location and angle (0, 360 counterclockwise) as seen from the center of Mars (0,0) by using arctangent?

Solution:

(a) Given fall probability = 30%, X- and Y-axis movement is uniform distribution with $a=-100$ ft and $b=100$ ft. Assume robot landed safely at (0, 0). Rounding to nearest integers, Step 1

$$X1 = a+(b-a)u21 = -100+(100+100)(0.0785) = -84$$
$$Y1 = a+(b-a)u22 = -100+(100+100)(0.1467) = -71$$

Robot falls? $u23 < 0.3 = 0.388 < 0.3 = $ No

Continuing to step 2

$$X2 = X1+a+(b-a)u24 = -84-100+(100+100)(0.5274) = -79$$
$$Y2 = Y1+a+(b-a)u25 = -71-100+(100+100)(0.8723) = 3$$

Robot falls? $u26 < 0.3 = 0.7517 < 0.3 = $ No

Continuing to step 3

$$X3 = X2+a+(b-a)u27 = -79-100+(100+100)(0.9905) = 19$$
$$Y3 = Y2+a+(b-a)u28 = 3-100+(100+100)(0.8904) = 81$$

Robot falls? $u29 < 0.3 = 0.8177 < 0.3 = $ No

Continuing to step 4

$$X4 = X3 + a + (b-a)u30 = 19 - 100 + (100 + 100)(0.666) = 52$$
$$Y4 = Y3 + a + (b-a)u31 = 81 - 100 + (100 + 100)(0.1158) = 4$$
Robot falls? $u32 < 0.3 = 0.6635 < 0.3 =$ No

Continuing to step 5

$$X5 = X4 + a + (b-a)u33 = 52 - 100 + (100 + 100)(0.4992) = 52$$
$$Y5 = Y4 + a + (b-a)u34 = 4 - 100 + (100 + 100)(0.907) = 85$$
Robot falls? $u35 < 0.3 = 0.2975 < 0.3 =$ Yes

After 5 moves, robot falls at $(X5, Y5) = (52, 85)$. Angle = arc tan $(Y/X) = 58.5°$

(b) Repeat A with EXCEL for $n = 1000$ runs, now use 5% for falling and not getting up straight, so the project is doomed! When no more action, where is it (coordinates and angle w.r.t. 0,0) so that we can locate it and send repair crews from the base or space station?

Solution:
Taking X and Y as uniform random variables using $X = a + (b - a)$rand() and $Y = c + (d - c)$rand(). For a given iteration, robot is at point (Sum X, Sum Y). Fall probability as $z =$ rand(). If $z < 0.05$, robot falls. At this point angle is calculated using tan $- 1(Y/X)$.

MARS LANDER ROBOT MOVEMENT

Uniform Movement - X		Uniform Movement - Y			Fall Rate	
a	-100	c	-100		z	0.05
b	100	d	100			

Iteration	X	Sum X	Y	Sum Y	Fall Probability	Continue ?	Counter clockwise angle
0	0	0	0	0	0	TRUE	
1	-59.320041	-59	-30.3974798	-30	0.0545	TRUE	
2	-45.1464729	-104	18.8742673	-12	0.2375	TRUE	
3	-24.2329077	-129	23.95681272	12	0.4966	TRUE	
4	93.93535511	-35	-77.64369309	-65	0.9320	TRUE	
5	-76.9979504	-112	-80.62293015	-146	0.1831	TRUE	
6	89.12516585	-23	-26.3545215	-172	0.6544	TRUE	
7	-20.1128958	-43	24.45484339	-148	0.7345	TRUE	
8	-86.3682345	-129	74.41696812	-73	0.0251	FALSE	210
4995	-56.5433454	6820	72.6730417	-4955	0.5020	TRUE	
4996	94.10605005	6914	-84.70206782	-5039	0.0180	FALSE	324
4997	-72.8209287	6842	96.39673697	-4943	0.9031	TRUE	
4998	-34.7087716	6807	-97.83616121	-5041	0.0390	FALSE	323
4999	90.27778788	6897	-1.284334708	-5042	0.8644	TRUE	
5000	98.14255612	6995	48.44469717	-4994	0.4635	TRUE	

6.8.19 (a) On Security Meter Uniform-Distributed Simulation: Take the $2 \times 2 \times 2$ problem in 6.8.15 and by varying all uniform variables between 0.3 (lower) and 0.7 (upper), perform this routine $n = 4$ times by hand calculations, and take the average. Compare this with your TWC results when you enter the data in the software. Solution: Given $2 \times 2 \times 2$ problem, with all variables uniformly distributed between $a = 0.3$ and $b = 0.7$.

Vulnerability	Threat	Lack of Countermeasure
v1	t11	lcm11
	t12	lcm12
v2	t21	lcm21
	t22	lcm22

Equations are

$$v1 - a + (b-a)\text{rand}(\ ), v2 = 1 - v1$$
$$t11 = a + (b-a)\text{rand}(\ ), t12 = 1 - t11. \text{ Similarly, } t21 = a + (b-a)$$
$$\text{rand}(\ ), t22 = 1 - t21$$
$$lcm11 = lcm12 = lcm21 = lcm22 = a + (b-a)\text{rand}(\ )$$

Iteration 1:

$$v1 = 0.3 + (0.7 - 0.3) * 0.0785 = 0.3314$$
$$v2 = 1 - 0.3314 = 0.6686$$
$$t11 = 0.3 + (0.7 - 0.3) * 0.1467 = 0.3587$$
$$t12 = 1 - 0.3587 = 0.6413$$
$$t21 = 0.3 + (0.7 - 0.3) * 0.3880 = 0.4552$$
$$t22 = 1 - 0.1552 = 0.5448$$
$$lcm11 = 0.3 + (0.7 - 0.3) * 0.5274 = 0.5107$$
$$lcm12 = 0.3 + (0.7 - 0.3) * 0.8723 = 0.6489$$
$$lcm21 = 0.3 + (0.7 - 0.3) * 0.7517 = 0.6007$$
$$lcm22 = 0.3 + (0.7 - 0.3) * 0.9905 = 0.6962$$

Total risk = v1 * t11 * lcm11 + v1 * t12 * lcm12 + v2 * t21 * lcm21 + v2 * t22 *

lcm22 = 0.3314 * 0.3587 * 0.5107 + 0.3314 * 0.6413 * 0.6489
+ 0.6686 * 0.4552 * 0.6007 + 0.6686 * 0.5448 * 0.6962 = 0.6350

Final risk = 0.6350 * 1 = 0.6350; expected cost = $1000 * 0.635 = $635.0
Iteration 2:

$$v1 = 0.3 + (0.7 - 0.3) * 0.8904 = 0.6562$$
$$v2 = 1 - 0.6562 = 0.3438$$
$$t11 = 0.3 + (0.7 - 0.3) * 0.8177 = 0.6271$$
$$t12 = 1 - 0.6271 = 0.3729$$
$$t21 = 0.3 + (0.7 - 0.3) * 0.6660 = 0.5664$$
$$t22 = 1 - 0.5664 = 0.4336$$
$$lcm11 = 0.3 + (0.7 - 0.3) * 0.1158 = 0.3463$$
$$lcm12 = 0.3 + (0.7 - 0.3) * 0.6635 = 0.5654$$
$$lcm21 = 0.3 + (0.7 - 0.3) * 0.4992 = 0.4997$$
$$lcm22 = 0.3 + (0.7 - 0.3) * 0.9070 = 0.6628$$

Total risk $= v1 * t11 * lcm11 + v1 * t12 * lcm12 + v2 * t21 * lcm21 + v2 * t22 *$

$$lcm22 = 0.6562 * 0.6271 * 0.3463 + 0.6562 * 0.3729 * 0.5654 + 0.3438 *$$
$$0.5664 * 0.4997 + 0.3438 * 0.4336 * 0.6628 = 0.4767$$

Final risk $= 0.4767 * 1 = 0.4767$

Expected cost $= \$1000 * 0.4767 = \$476.7$

Average total risk $= (0.6350 + 0.4767) / 2 = 0.5559$

Average final risk $= (0.6350 + 0.4767) / 2 = 0.5559$

Average expected Cost $= (\$635.0 + \$476.7) / 2 = \$555.85$

This is comparable to security meter values as shown in screen capture as follows:

(b) Do the same with EXCEL spreadsheet and after $n = 1000$ simulation runs, what do you get? When simulated in excel, average expected cost of loss $= \$502.63$. This is comparable to security meter reading shown in pop-up.

6.8.20 On Numerical Integration: (a) Solve integral problem by $n = 1000$ runs for Example 16.1 on page 622, $I = \int_0^1 e^x \, dx$, in Ref. [11] by Stewart. See the solution presented for (a) where the area is 1.718. Also do (b) and (c):

(b) $I = \int_0^2 \frac{x}{\sqrt{2x^2+1}} \, dx$

(c) $I = \int_0^{\ln 2} \frac{e^{2x}}{\sqrt[4]{e^x+1}} \, dx$

NUMERICAL INTEGRATION

Variable	Value		Summary	
a	0		No. of Iterations	1000
b	1		Percentage of area	0.424
c1	1		**Value of Integral**	**1.7284**
c2	2.718			
y	a + (b-a) * rand()			
f(y)	e^y			
z	(c2-c1) * rand() + c1			

Iteration	Rand1()	y	f(y)	z	z <= f(y)
1	0.199435924	0.199435924	1.220713988	1.770663296	0
2	0.822871169	0.822871169	2.277028194	1.672160289	1
3	0.873424042	0.873424042	2.395097744	2.633633943	0
4	0.84879904	0.84879904	2.336838716	1.217878637	1
5	0.399019259	0.399019259	1.490362322	1.678747356	0
997	0.976755633	0.976755633	2.655825777	1.342457315	1
998	0.748509366	0.748509366	2.113846696	2.465572321	0
999	0.73865294	0.73865294	2.093114064	1.202815199	1
1000	0.665319888	0.665319888	1.94511264	2.29382521	0

6.8.21 *CSIS 6403 Assembly Line Maintenance Project*: Take the attached EXCEL 7-day × 24-h completed 5-LINE plant operation schedule with a single maintenance crew. You will continue independently of others with the operation of this factory until you stop after 3 weeks more days to complete to 30-day (month) period:

(i) Adapt for the 5 assembly lines by modeling and programming it with a 2-crew maintenance plan to see the difference for average performances on the assembly lines.

(ii) Do 6–10 assembly lines with 1- and 2- and up to 10-crew maintenance similarly.

(iii) Obtain a statistical distribution for the failure, repair, and wait times (use Weibull pdf to fit with the proper parameter after the first week, such as shape parameter=1 for the neg. exponential). Then continue until 360 days (52 weeks) with EXCEL to see the future performance of the plant.

(iv) Therefore, generalize the above process by EXCEL coding the above items for a general treatment with n = 10 (max) many assembly lines and m = 5 (max) many crews up to 45 scenarios. Your data in EXCEL you randomly entered will be your input data this time (Figs. 6.24, 6.25 and 6.26). Continue after both Figure 6.24 and Figure 6.25.

Here are the six graphs depicting the reduction of waiting time as we add the crew members for all the six cases of production lines mentioned above. The Y-axis shows the total waiting time and the X-axis shows the addition of the repair crew members. As we notice, the waiting time decreases as the crew members increase in each of these cases shown. The last diagram shows the project plan designed and executed. Continue from page 332, Exercise 6.8.21 (continued) for Figure 6.25.

6.8.22 *Hospital Patient Admissions and/or Cyber-Security Vulnerability Project*: Improve the patient arrival/treatment cycle further classified into 10 more hospital wards to start with (this can be treated as random variable treated as an input variable for your java coding however many you want then number of ward to be such as it can be generalized in completion of the project as to how many to be given as an input (like Ward 1,2,3,4,5,6,…,*k*) the following 10 wards at full service hospital: cardiology, (1) ENT, (2) x-ray, (3) orthopedics, (4) gynecology, (5) urology, (6) pediatrics, (7) geriatrics, (8) oncology, (9) psychiatry, and (10) cardiology. Then assigning no of doctors with the proper statistical pdfs obtain the performance metrics performing discrete event simulation (DES) after n-many simulation runs. Note that programmers will add three more distributions (TBA by the instructor) on top of the existing two on each arrival and service pattern. Also do the same this time converting to cyber-security nomenclature. See below screenshots for clarification (Figs. 6.27 and 6.28).

6.8.23 Using the input data, verify or correct the results in Table 6.8 using software for SL pdf below:

TABLE 6.8   Table for Application of Two-State SL Component Data to Various Networks

Input/Output Data	Component 1	Component 2	Component 3	Component 4
a (failure events)	10	5	10	100
b (repair events)	10	5	10	100
x_T (failure time)	1000	25	1000	10000
y_T (repair time)	111.11	5	111.11	1111.11
c (shape for λ)	0.02	0.2	0.5	0.5
ξ (inverse scale)	1	1	1	1
d (shape for μ)	0.1	2	2	2
η (inverse scale)	1	0.5	0.25	0.25
R *	0.907325	0.882397	0.917648	0.902028
R **	0.906655	0.849515	0.906655	0.900714
$E(r) =$ Mean	0.890985	0.758064	0.879164	0.89792
7-node =0.9, (0.7999)	0.7818	0.524	0.7587	0.7956
8-node, 0.9 (0.8082)	0.7915	0.5551	0.7702	0.8043
10-node, 0.9 (0.7986)	0.7802	0.5112	0.7566	0.7944
19-node: 0.9 (0.7299) link =0.9	0.7017	0.6053	0.7339	0.7215

R*: System reliability with weighted square error loss with informative prior.
R**: System reliability with weighted square error loss with non-informative (flat) prior.

6.8.24 A banking corporation is experiencing mighty severe unexpected security breaches with a risk (probability) of $c_1 = 0.5$ (or 50% of the time). Once the malicious attack arrives from the external sources, the probability of the bank's firewall software intercepting hacking etc. attack is $c_2 = 0.5$ (or 50%). If not intercepted successfully,

TABLE IN EXCEL 7 DAYS OF DISCRETE EVENT SIMULATION ON 5-PRODUCTION LINES with 1-CREW						
Time Change hr-min	Event Status	Line 1	Line 2	Line 3	Line 4	Line 5
0.00 Midnight	None					
3:08:00	Line 4 fails				Dn(service)	
3:23:00	Line 1 fails	Dn(waiting)			Dn(service)	
3:25:00	Line 4 repd.	Dn(service)			Operational	
4:05:00	Line 3 fails	Dn(service)		Dn(waiting)		
4:06:00	Line 1 repd.	Operational		Dn(service)		
4:25:00	Line 5 fails			Dn(service)		Dn(waiting)
5:00:00	Line 3 repd.			Operational		Dn(service)
5:23:00	Line 1 fails	Dn(waiting)				Dn(service)
6:40:00	Line 5 repd.	Dn(service)				Operational
14:00:00	Line 2 fails	Dn(service)	Dn(waiting)			
14:30:00	Line 1 repd.	Operational	Dn(service)			
15:00:00	Line 2 repd.		Operational			
15:30:00	Line 5 fails					Dn(service)
17:00:00	Line 5 repd.					Operational
18:30:00	Line 4 fails				Dn(service)	
19:00:00	Line 2 fails		Dn(waiting)		Dn(service)	
20:30:00	Line 1 fails	Dn(waiting)	Dn(waiting)		Dn(service)	
23:10:00	Line 4 repd.	Dn(waiting)	Dn(service)		Operational	
23:30:00	Line 2 repd.	Dn(service)	Operational			
24:00:00	Line 1 repd.	Operational				
0:50:00	Line 3 fails			Dn(service)		
1:00:00	Line 4 fails			Dn(service)	Dn(waiting)	
3:00:00	Line 3 repd.			Operational	Dn(service)	
3:05:00	Line 5 fails				Dn(service)	Dn(waiting)
6:00:00	Line 4 repd.				Operational	Dn(service)
8:30:00	Line 2 fails		Dn(waiting)			Dn(service)
11:00:00	Input line 5 repd.		Dn(service)			Operational
12:00:00	Line 1 fails	Dn(waiting)	Dn(service)			
16:00:00	Line 2 repd.	Dn(service)	Operational			
19:15:00	Line 2 fails	Dn(service)	Dn(waiting)			
20:30:00	Line 1 repd.	Operational	Dn(service)			
22:15:00	Line 2 repd.		Operational			
3:08:00	Line 4 fails				Dn(service)	
3:23:00	Line 1 fails	Dn(waiting)			Dn(service)	
3:25:00	Line 4 repd.	Dn(service)			Operational	
4:05:00	Line 3 fails	Dn(service)		Dn(waiting)		
4:06:00	Line 1 repd.	Operational		Dn(service)		

FIGURE 6.24 Input screenshots table for 7 days on 5 production lines with 1 crew.

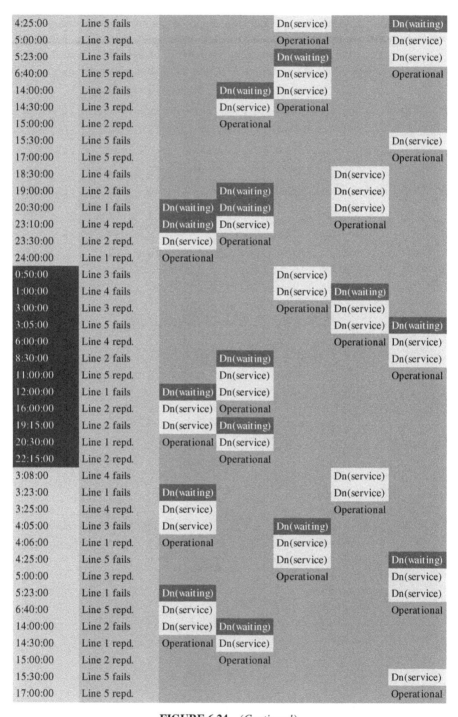

FIGURE 6.24 (*Continued*)

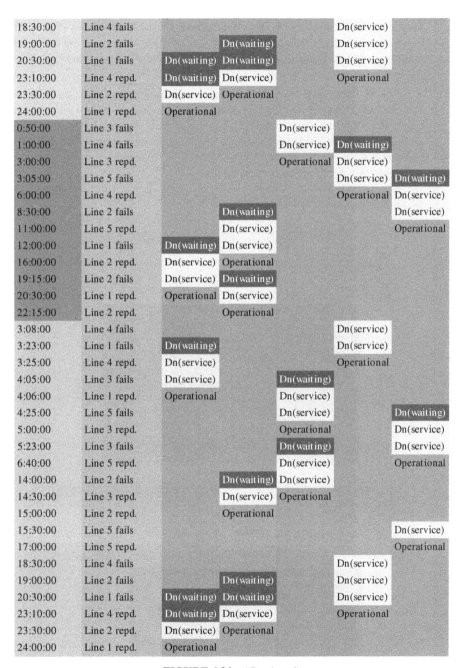

18:30:00	Line 4 fails			Dn(service)	
19:00:00	Line 2 fails		Dn(waiting)	Dn(service)	
20:30:00	Line 1 fails	Dn(waiting)	Dn(waiting)	Dn(service)	
23:10:00	Line 4 repd.	Dn(waiting)	Dn(service)	Operational	
23:30:00	Line 2 repd.	Dn(service)	Operational		
24:00:00	Line 1 repd.	Operational			
0:50:00	Line 3 fails			Dn(service)	
1:00:00	Line 4 fails			Dn(service)	Dn(waiting)
3:00:00	Line 3 repd.			Operational	Dn(service)
3:05:00	Line 5 fails			Dn(service)	Dn(waiting)
6:00:00	Line 4 repd.			Operational	Dn(service)
8:30:00	Line 2 fails		Dn(waiting)		Dn(service)
11:00:00	Line 5 repd.		Dn(service)		Operational
12:00:00	Line 1 fails	Dn(waiting)	Dn(service)		
16:00:00	Line 2 repd.	Dn(service)	Operational		
19:15:00	Line 2 fails	Dn(service)	Dn(waiting)		
20:30:00	Line 1 repd.	Operational	Dn(service)		
22:15:00	Line 2 repd.		Operational		
3:08:00	Line 4 fails			Dn(service)	
3:23:00	Line 1 fails	Dn(waiting)		Dn(service)	
3:25:00	Line 4 repd.	Dn(service)		Operational	
4:05:00	Line 3 fails	Dn(service)		Dn(waiting)	
4:06:00	Line 1 repd.	Operational		Dn(service)	
4:25:00	Line 5 fails			Dn(service)	Dn(waiting)
5:00:00	Line 3 repd.			Operational	Dn(service)
5:23:00	Line 3 fails			Dn(waiting)	Dn(service)
6:40:00	Line 5 repd.			Dn(service)	Operational
14:00:00	Line 2 fails		Dn(waiting)	Dn(service)	
14:30:00	Line 3 repd.		Dn(service)	Operational	
15:00:00	Line 2 repd.		Operational		
15:30:00	Line 5 fails				Dn(service)
17:00:00	Line 5 repd.				Operational
18:30:00	Line 4 fails			Dn(service)	
19:00:00	Line 2 fails		Dn(waiting)	Dn(service)	
20:30:00	Line 1 fails	Dn(waiting)	Dn(waiting)	Dn(service)	
23:10:00	Line 4 repd.	Dn(waiting)	Dn(service)	Operational	
23:30:00	Line 2 repd.	Dn(service)	Operational		
24:00:00	Line 1 repd.	Operational			

FIGURE 6.24 (*Continued*)

the damage it causes for $c_3 = 70\%$ of the time is a system shut-down of the entire company's ITS (Info Tech Services) with a $c_4 = \$10$ Million price-tag due to customer loss. Otherwise with a $c_5 = 30\%$ risk, the damage can be compensated with a $c_6 = \$5$million.

Using all these six C constants from c_1 to c_6, design a tree diagram first, then calculate the theoretical values for sale or no-sale, and the approximately same outcomes given that there is an interest; all tabulated. Of course, it is next time to do the EXCEL for 1000 runs to get close to these numbers. Show your EXCEL in CD and in your word summary file to report first 10 and last 10 results, showing how close you are to the theoretical table.

Exercise 6.8.21 (continued from page 328):

Waiting(hrs)	LINE 1	LINE 2	LINE 3	LINE 4	LINE 5	Total
1 CREW	114:29:00	126:15:00	10:31:00	30:00:00	52:30:00	333:45:00
2 CREW	131:00:00	64:00:00	8:45:00	39:00:00	15:30:00	258:15:00
3 CREW	7:14:00	7:42:00	0:42:00	2:48:00	4:26:00	22:52:00
4 CREW	0:00:00	0:00:00	0:00:00	2:00:00	3:45:00	5:45:00
5 CREW	0:00:00	0:00:00	0:00:00	0:00:00	0:00:00	0:00:00

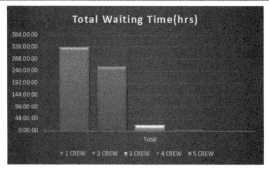

Waiting(hrs)	LINE 1	LINE 2	LINE 3	LINE 4	LINE 5	LINE 6	Total
1 CREW	162:27:00	115:10:00	10:30:00	30:00:00	51:15:00	8:32:00	377:54:00
2 CREW	129:43:00	63:59:00	8:00:00	105:17:00	15:15:00	3:48:00	326:02:00
3 CREW	7:14:00	7:06:00	0:51:00	2:48:00	4:35:00	35:48:00	58:22:00
4 CREW	0:00:00	0:00:00	0:00:00	1:52:00	3:34:00	23:31:00	28:57:00
5 CREW	0:00:00	0:00:00	0:00:00	0:00:00	0:00:00	0:15:00	0:15:00
6 CREW	0:00:00	0:00:00	0:00:00	0:00:00	0:00:00	0:00:00	0:00:00

FIGURE 6.25 The six graphs depicting the reduction of waiting time as we add the crew members for all the six cases of production lines.

Waiting(hrs)	Total
1 CREW	642:03:00
2 CREW	537:27:00
3 CREW	377:52:00
4 CREW	253:44:00
5 CREW	132:50:00
6 CREW	61:27:00
7 CREW	0:00:00

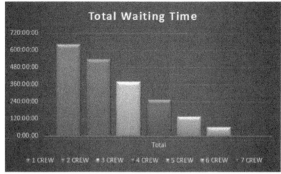

Waiting(hrs)	Total
1 CREW	842:04:00
2 CREW	704:08:00
3 CREW	590:12:00
4 CREW	371:12:00
5 CREW	261:22:00
6 CREW	175:32:00
7 CREW	124:34:00
8 CREW	0:00:00

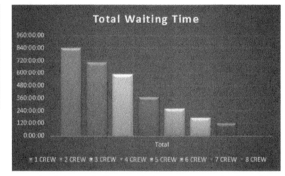

Waiting(hrs)	Total waiting
1 CREW	901:02:00
2 CREW	832:35:00
3 CREW	637:40:00
4 CREW	590:35:00
5 CREW	442:17:00
6 CREW	348:06:00
7 CREW	141:24:00
8 CREW	91:39:00
9 CREW	0:00:00

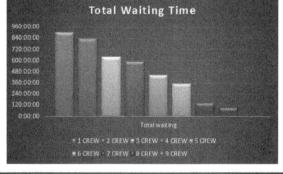

Waiting(hrs)	Total
1 CREW	960:46:00
2 CREW	896:26:00
3 CREW	651:05:00
4 CREW	620:54:00
5 CREW	280:54:00
6 CREW	166:09:00
7 CREW	142:09:00
8 CREW	114:11:00
9 CREW	52:49:00
10 CREW	0:00:00

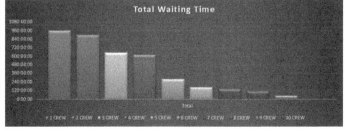

FIGURE 6.25 (*Continued*)

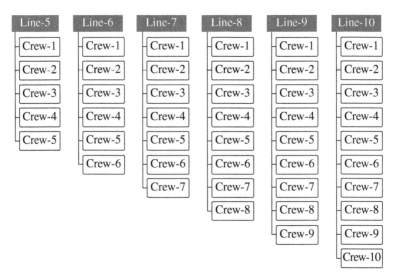

FIGURE 6.26 The last figure regarding the project design for Exercise 6.8.21.

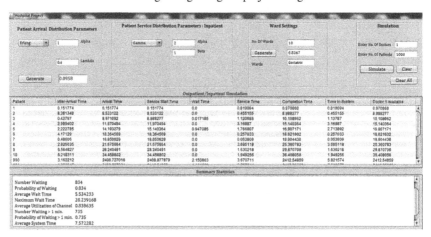

FIGURE 6.27 Hospital Project output of Exercise 6.8.22.

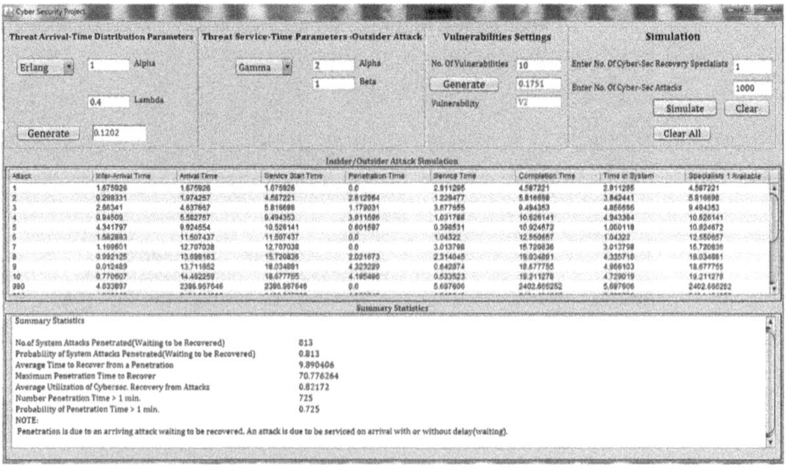

FIGURE 6.28 Cyber-security Project version of Exercise 6.8.22.

REFERENCES

[1] http://www.nucleonica.net/wiki/images/d/df/EMC_2008_short.pdf (accessed January 5, 2013).

[2] http://web.student.tuwien.ac.at/~e9527412/history.html (accessed January 5, 2013).

[3] http://www.britannica.com/EBchecked/topic/1252440/von-Neumann-machine (accessed January 5, 2013).

[4] http://mathworld.wolfram.com/CellularAutomaton.html (accessed January 5, 2013).

[5] http://www.math.com/students/wonders/life/life.html (accessed January 5, 2013).

[6] Ledin, J., *Simulation Engineering: Build Better Embedded Systems Faster'*, Taylor & Francis, 2001, http://books.google.com/books/about/Simulation_Engineering.html?id=GMRjR2shh XAC (accessed January 5, 2013).

[7] Aoyama, M. (June 2012). Computing for the next-generation automobile, *IEEE Computer*, 45(6), 32–37.

[8] Zeigler, B. P., Praehofer, H., Kim, T. G., *Theory of Modeling and Simulation*, 2nd Ed., Academic Press, San Diego, 2000.

[9] Levene, H., Wolfowitz, J. (1944). The covariance matrix of runs up and down, *Annals of Mathematical Statistics (AMS)* 15(1), 58–69.

[10] Knuth, D. E., *The Art of Computer Programming, Vol. 2, Seminumerical Algorithms*, 3rd Ed., Addison-Wesley, Reading, 1998.

[11] Stewart, W. J., *Probability, Markov Chains, Queues and Simulation*, Princeton University Press, Princeton, 2009.

[12] http://www.youtube.com/watch?v=_RBH0PeLhOk (accessed January 5, 2013).

[13] http://www.nap.edu/openbook.php?record_id=10425&page=77 (accessed January 5, 2013).

[14] http://www.guardian.co.uk/public-leaders-network/2011/may/20/local-councils-software-hard-cuts (accessed January 5, 2013).

[15] http://www.albrechts.com/mike/DES/Annotated%20Bibliography%20.pdf (accessed January 5, 2013).

[16] http://ieeexplore.ieee.org/stamp/stamp.jsp?tp=&arnumber=373979 (accessed January 5, 2013).

[17] Kuhl, E., Kistner, J., Costantini, K., Sudit, M., Cyber attack modeling and simulation for network security analysis, ACM digital library, in Proceedings of the 39th Conference on Winter Simulation Conference (WSC'07), Washington, DC, December 9–12, 2007, IEEE Press, Piscataway, NJ.

[18] http://www.youtube.com/watch?v=du6g__lgS3Q (accessed January 5, 2013).

[19] http://www.washingtonpost.com/wp-dyn/content/article/2010/02/16/AR2010021605762.html (accessed January 5, 2013).

[20] Sahinoglu, M., *Trustworthy Computing: Analytical and Quantitative Engineering Evaluation* (CD ROM included), John Wiley & Sons Inc., Hoboken, 2007.

[21] Sahinoglu, M. (April/May 2005). Security meter—a practical decision tree model to quantify risk, *IEEE Security and Privacy*, 3(3), 18–24.

[22] Sahinoglu M., (June 2008). An Input-Output Measurable Design for the Security Meter Model to Quantify and Manage Software Security Risk, *IEEE Trans on Instrumentation and Measurement*, 57(6), 1251–1260.

[23] Sahinoglu, M. (2009). Can we quantitatively assess and manage risk of software privacy breaches?, *International Journal of Computers, Information Technology and Engineering*, 3(2), 65–70.

[24] Sahinoglu, M., Yuan, Y.-L., Banks, D. (2010). Validation of a security and privacy risk metric using triple uniform product rule, *International Journal of Computers, Information Technology and Engineering*, 4(2), 125–135.

[25] http://en.wikipedia.org/wiki/File:Molecular_simulation_process.svg (accessed January 5, 2013) "This file appeared originally in the Wikipedia article entitled Computer Simulation. It is licensed under the Creative Commons Attribution-Share Alike 3.0 Unported License. Commons is a freely licensed media file repository."

[26] Sahinoglu, M. (2013). The modeling and simulation in engineering, Invitational Overview article for WIREs (Wiley Interdisciplinary Review Series), *WIREs Computational Statistics*, 239–266. http://www.aum.edu/UR_Media/NandH/13nandh/130429/Sahinoglu_WICS1254_article.pdf (accessed October 23, 2015).

[27] Sahinoglu, M., Cueva-Parra, L. (March 2011). CLOUD Computing, *Wiley Interdisciplinary Reviews Computational Statistics*, 3(1), 47–68.

[28] Schriber, T., Stecke, K. (1986). Machine utilizations and production rates achieved by using balanced aggregate FMS production ratios in a simulated setting, in Proceedings of the Second ORSA/TIMS Conference on Flexible Manufacturing Systems: Operations Research Models and Applications, Elsevier Science Publishers B. V., Amsterdam, 405–416.

[29] Dee, Z., Co, H., Wyek, R. (1986). SIM-Q: a simplified approach to simulation modeling of automated manufacturing systems, in Proceedings of the Second ORSA/TIMS Conference on Flexible Manufacturing Systems: Operations Research Models and Applications, Elsevier Science Publishers B.V., Amsterdam, 417–430.

[30] Rao, M., Naikan, V., Pradesh, A. (2011). A hybrid Markov system dynamics approach for availability analysis of degraded systems, in Proceedings of the 2011 International Conference on Industrial Engineering and Operations Management, Kula Lumpur, Malaysia, January 22–24, 2011.

[31] Lins, I. D., Droguett, E. L. (January/April 2009). Multiobjective optimization of availability and cost in repairable systems design via genetic algorithms and discrete event simulation, *Pesquisa Operacional*, 29(1), 43–66.

[32] Shah, A., Dhillon, B. (2007). Reliability and availability analysis of three-state device redundant systems with human errors and common-cause failures, 3 (4), *International Journal of Performability Engineering* 3(4, paper 2), 411–441.

[33] Sahinoglu, M., Longnecker. M., Ringer, L., Singh, C., Ayoub, A. (June 1983). Probability distribution function for generation reliability indices-analytical approach, *IEEE Transactions on Power, Apparatus, and Systems (PAS)*, 104, 1486–1493.

[34] Sahinoglu, M., Libby, D., Das, S. (2005). Measuring availability indices with small samples for component and network reliability using the Sahinoglu-Libby Probability Model, *IEEE Transactions on Instrumentation and Measurement*, 54(3), 1283–1295.

[35] Sahinoglu, M. (1981). Statistical inference on reliability performance index for electric power generation systems, Ph.D. dissertation, The Institute of Statistics jointly with Electrical and Computer Eng., Texas A&M University, College Station, December 11, 1981.

[36] Libby, D. (1981). Multivariate fixed state utility assessment, Ph.D. dissertation, University of Iowa, Iowa City.

[37] Libby, D., Novick, M. (1982). Multivariate generalized beta distributions with applications to utility assessment, *Journal of Educational Statistics*, 7(4, winter), 271–294.

[38] Sahinoglu, M., Yuan, Y.-L., Capar, S., Statistical inference on the two- and three-state availability of the repairable units with the Sahinoglu-Libby Model, IPS018 (Invited Paper Session): Statistical risk assessment in trustworthy computing, in Proceedings (CD ROM) of International Statistical Institute, 58th Congress, Dublin, August 21–26, 2011.

[39] Sahinoglu, M., Yuan, Y.-L. (July 2010), Multivariate statistical modeling on the 3-state (UP, DERATED, DOWN) availability of repairable hardware unit and their systems with the Sahinoglu-Libby Probability Distribution using Monte Carlo Simulation, in Proceedings of GCMS'10, Ottawa, Canada, vol. 12(14), 253–260.

[40] Lisniansky, A., Levitin, G., *Multi-State System Reliability: Assessment, Optimization and Applications*, World Scientific, Singapore, 2003.

[41] Billinton, R., Allan, R., *Reliability Evaluation of Power Systems*, Plenum Press, New York, 1996.

[42] Murchland, J. (1975). Fundamental concepts and relations for reliability analysis of multistate systems, reliability and fault tree analysis, in *Theoretical and Applied Aspects of System Reliability*, R. Barlow, S. Fussell, N. Singpurwalla (eds.), SIAM, Philadelphia, 81–618.

[43] Barlow, R. E., Wu, A. S. (1978). Coherent systems with multi-state components, *Math Operations Research*, 3(4), 275–281.

[44] R., Billinton, *Power System Reliability Evaluation*, Gordon and Breach Science Publishers Inc., New York, 1970.

[45] Sahinoglu, M., Rice, B. (March 2010). Network reliability evaluation, *Advanced Review Wiley Interdisciplinary Reviews: Computational Statistics*, 2(1), 189–211.

[46] Hogg, R., Craig, A., *Introduction to Mathematical Statistics*, 3rd Ed., MacMillan, New York, 1970.

[47] Young, G. A., Smith, R. L., *Essentials of Statistical Inference, Cambridge Series in Statistical and Probabilistic Mathematics*, Cambridge University Press, New York, 2005.

[48] Snedecor, G., Cochran, W., *Statistical Methods*, Iowa State University Press, Ames, 1989.

[49] Rinaldi, S., Modeling and simulating critical infrastructures and their interdependencies, in IEEE Proceedings of the 37th Hawaii International Conference on System Sciences, Hawaii, 1–8, 2004.

[50] Kim, H., Chaudhuri, S., Parashar, M., Marty, C. (2009), Online Risk Analytics on the Cloud, IEEE Computer Society Washington, DC, CCGRID'09, in Proceedings of the 2009 9th IEEE/ACM International Symposium on Cluster Computing and the Grid, IEEE Computer Society, Washington, DC, 484–489.

[51] Sahinoglu, M., Cueva-Parra, L., Ang, D. (2012). Game-theoretic computing in risk analysis, *WIREs Computational Statistics*, 4, 227–248.

[52] Thompson, J. (January/February 2010). Forward simulation models, *Advanced Review, Wiley Interdisciplinary, Reviews: Computational Statistics*, 2(1), 61–68.

[53] Kroese, D., Rubinstein, R. (2012). Monte Carlo methods, overview, *WIREs Computational Statistics*, 4, 48.

[54] Sahinoglu, M., Vasudev, P., Morton, S., Eryilmaz, M. (2014). Bank customer service risk: quantitative risk assessment and management, *International Journal of Computers, Information Technology and Engineering (IJCITAE)*, 8(2), 99–107.

[55] www.aum.edu/csis (accessed January 5, 2013).

[56] Johnson, N., Kotz, S., *Distributions in Statistics: Continuous Univariate Distributions*, Wiley Interscience, New York, 1970.

[57] Kramer, W., Sahinoglu, M., Ang, D. Increase Return on Investment of Software Development Life Cycle by Managing The Risk – A Case Study, Defense ARJ, April 2015, Vol. 22, No.2, 174–191; http://www.dau.mil (The Silver Medal for the 2015 Hirsch Paper Competiton).

[58] Sahinoglu, M., Ashokan, S., Vasudev, P. (2015). Cost-Efficient Risk Management with Reserve Repair Crew Planning in CLOUD Computing, The 2015 International Conference on Soft Computing and Software Engineering at Berkeley, Ca., (SCSE 2015), Procedia Computer Science, ELSEVIER, Vol. 62, pp. 335–342.

[59] Sahinoglu, M., Ashokan, S., Vasudev, P. (2015). CLOUD Computing: Cost-effective Risk Management with Additional Product Deployment, The 2015 International Conference on Soft Computing and Software Engineering at Berkeley, Ca., (SCSE 2015), Procedia Computer Science, ELSEVIER, Vol. 62, pp. 319–325.

[60] Sahinoglu, M., Vasudev, P. (2015). Stochastic simulation of cyber CLOUD and power grid, Proceedings of the International Conference on Information Technology and Science (ICITS), p. 45, Pattaya, Thailand. *IJCTE (International Journal of Computer Theory and Engineering)*, 9(1). Available at www.ijcte.org (accessed on October 31, 2015).; IJCTE (International Journal of Computer Theory and Engineering), Vol. 9, No.1, February 2017, 43–47.

7

CLOUD COMPUTING IN CYBER-RISK

LEARNING OBJECTIVES

- Describe the concept of CLOUD Computing with its advantages and disadvantages and its relevance to Cyber-Risk Informatics and related risk engineering/sciences.
- Explore the innovative and popular theme of CLOUD Computing modeling and its simulation in the cybersecurity arena citing challenges and risk management.
- Study a cross section of CLOUD Computing implementation other than physical as in the social world with the First Responder Groups of firefighters, rescue workers, law enforcement officers, etc. as it applies to Human Resources at large.
- Examine reserve recovery crew and extra product deployment planning to manage risk.

7.1 INTRODUCTION AND MOTIVATION

CLOUD computing, a relatively new form of computing using services provided through the largest network (Internet), has become a promising and lucrative alternative to traditional in-house IT computing services and provides computing resources (software and hardware) on-demand. All of these resources are connected to the Internet (and through CLOUD) and are provided dynamically to users as requested (see Fig. 7.1). Some companies envision this form of computing as the major type of service that will be demanded extensively in the next several decades. Companies like Apple, Google, IBM, Microsoft, HP, Amazon, and Yahoo among many others have already made investments not only in research but also in establishing CLOUD computing services. CLOUD computing, sometimes called the fifth utility (after electric power, gas, water, and telephony), could change the way individuals and companies operate.

However, as often apparent from the news media describing outages as simple glitches (usually downplayed by the CLOUD hosting companies and their providers or

Cyber-Risk Informatics: Engineering Evaluation with Data Science, First Edition. Mehmet Sahinoglu.
© 2016 John Wiley & Sons, Inc. Published 2016 by John Wiley & Sons, Inc.
Companion website: www.wiley.com/go/sahinoglu/informatics

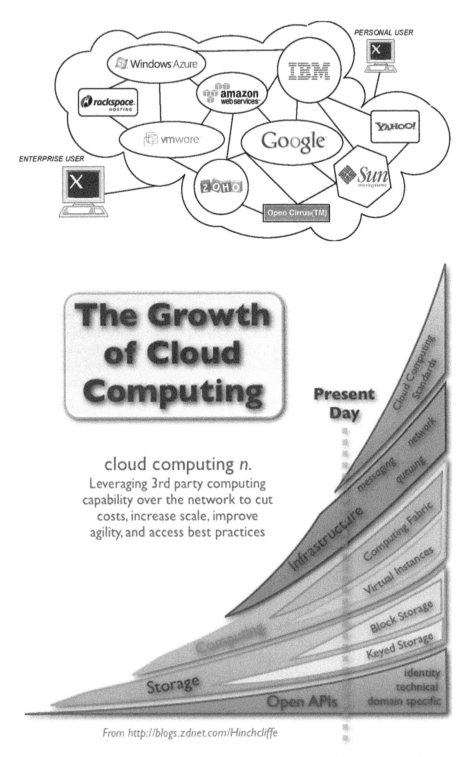

FIGURE 7.1 Various schematic representations and growth of CLOUD computing.

assigned responsible managers who cling to their 99.99% reliability slogan), the crucial problem with CLOUD computing is its occasional though dramatic lack of desired reliability and security and recently privacy. Why do those big firms delay using CLOUD? The response lies in the common belief that companies are hesitant to switch to CLOUD for applications that manage key parts of their businesses due to lack of trust as they believe there is still too much risk associated with potentially unreliable Internet connections and dependence on third parties to manage computer servers (see *Wall Street Journal*, July 17, 2014; Marketplace: "Why Big Firms Delay Using Cloud" by S. Norton and C. Boulton). Consequently, a quantitative assessment of the Quality of Service (QoS) in such enterprises is critically needed. The quality of CLOUD computing services can be difficult to measure, not only qualitatively but most importantly quantitatively.

An algorithmic discrete event simulation (DES) accompanied by related statistical inference is conducted to estimate the reliability indices in a CLOUD computing environment of small or large service-based systems to mimic real-life operations. The major advantages of CLOUD computing are scalability, flexibility, resilience, and affordability. However, as users (companies, organizations, and individual persons) turn to CLOUD computing services for their businesses and commercial operations, there is a growing concern from the security, privacy, and reliability perspectives as to how those services actually rate. Moreover, the federal government has approved commercial products to operate on a defense CLOUD, marking the industry's first online offerings with this level of security accessible to the military via such an environment [1].

As more clients migrate to the CLOUD and employ the technology, the cost of use will drop. Nevertheless, both CLOUD computing providers and users need a way to measure the quality of this service, mainly in the area of reliability and security. These metrics can provide the end users a better sense of what they are getting in terms of security correlated with their return on investment (ROI). As a result of the impact of the web, CLOUD computing, and mobility, technology companies must radically rethink how they build, package, deploy, market, and sell their solutions. Large physical systems such as commercial Cyber systems or Internet are depicted as in Figure 7.1's various CLOUD representations. Table 7.1 displays the three distinct groups of CLOUD usage with practical comparisons [2].

TABLE 7.1   Three Different Groups of Current CLOUD Structures Described and Compared

Groups	Definition	Clients Are Offered	Advantages
IaaS	Infrastructure as a service	Virtualized servers, storage, and networks	Delivers a full computer infrastructure via the Internet
SaaS	Software as a service	Software applications through web-based interfaces	Increased uptime, no need to maintain network; complete turnkey application with complex programs
PaaS	Platform as a service	Operating system maintenance, load balancing, scaling	Full and partial application development environment that users can access and utilize online in collaboration with others

7.2 CLOUD COMPUTING RISK ASSESSMENT

In recent decades, grid technology has emerged as an important tool for solving data-intensive problems within the scientific community and in major service industries. The CLOUD Risk Assessor and Manager' (CLOURAM) software examined later in this chapter provides the means to assess and mitigate the unreliability or insecurity of a cyber grid or any CLOUD (remember the five utilities) and depending on the nature of the input data, whether the unwanted risk is occurring by chance or maliciously implanted. It is an objective, and probabilistic assessment using digital simulation that mimics real-life operations and not a subjective guesswork or qualitative categorization such as high, medium, or low. The CLOURAM (a Java applet), as an expert system, will prove useful for an Internet Service Provider (ISP) or a CLOUD Administrator's grid planning and implementation purposes. The goal is to avoid estimations through quantification and subsequent management of bottlenecks with the right "What-If?" questions in a most efficient way to emulate the entire operation of a CLOUD prematurely on time before procuring or managing in the way of taking remedies, after the harm is incurred. This technique takes care of the reliability or quality assessment, and consequently risk mitigation by representing the entire grid operation with tangible and practical metrics, or indices. This scientifically sound practice provides timely management rather than working with routine intangibles and subjective attributes that the companies are wasting time with. CLOURAM is data driven and computationally intensive. A qualitative measure of security, for example, in terms of colors or any other arbitrary nonnumerical classification such as high, medium, or low, or yet another with severe, high, elevated, guarded, and low, for instance is inadequate. See Figure 7.2, which does not provide much other than a crude approximation. If one needs to implement an adequate risk management regime, it is necessary to have a numerical value for the level of security. It is imperative also to have a reliability and/or security metric for monetary comparison purposes since descriptive attributes do not lend themselves to budgetary implications as precisely as the quantitative metrics can.

It is difficult to improve something that is not measured or quantified. The next step is to describe what and how to measure. In order to provide a software assessment tool for calculating an index of security or lack thereof, we propose statistical inference on Loss of Service (LoS) in the event of security breaches as a metric for security or reliability, whether breaches are benign or malign, respectively. In terms of security, this clearly is focused on a single significant security principle: Availability [2, 3].

Therefore, in this chapter we will study how to mimic the operation of a CLOUD using digital simulation techniques preceded by an analytical math–statistical methodology. The purpose of conducting statistical inference is to estimate the probability density function (pdf) of LoS hours, contrary to a large-sample asymptotic or limiting probability distribution function earlier studied [2, 5]. We suggest an exact nonasymptotic estimation procedure through the Poisson^logarithmic series probability model. Therefore our goal is to estimate the Loss of Load (LoL) or synonymously Loss of Service (LoS) of an isolated cyber CLOUD computing system. We will employ the statistical counting

| Severe | High | Elevated | Guarded | Low |

FIGURE 7.2   Qualitative or descriptive security or reliability metrics.

Poisson process, for the purposes of enumerating number of deficiencies throughout a year, to be compounded by a discrete logarithmic series distribution (LSD). The parameters of Poisson^LSD, namely, the mean and q-ratio (variance/mean), are provided by utilizing the well-known frequency and duration method [6, 7]. This method will facilitate a closed-form discrete probability distribution function, thus reducing the error of estimation, for the total number of loss of load occurrences in terms of hours. This closed-form analytical approach is more credible than the former approximating asymptotic or limiting distributions [5, 8]. This is facilitated by using a nonapproximate but an exact closed-form probability distribution function, that is, Poisson^LSD [9].

We assert that this probabilistic model provides a more realistic modeling of the operation of a grid computing system, henceforth reducing the error of estimation by utilizing the advantages of the well-recognized frequency–duration method, which is deterministic. Additionally, a DES code will simulate the hour-to-hour operation so as to mimic the real-life CLOUD computing with assets, outages, demands, and other operational details. The statistical simulation results will then be compared favorably to a deterministic Markov steady-state solution at the final stage. A conclusive index of performance is therefore calculated for the purpose of quantitative risk assessment to plan ahead so as to minimize the hazards of outages that service-seeking and complaining customers are exposed to.

7.3   MOTIVATION AND METHODOLOGY

7.3.1   History of Theoretical Developments on CLOUD Modeling

In a 1990 publication, the distribution of the sum of negative-margin (loss of load) hours in an isolated power system—another form of CLOUD, one of five utilities—was approximated to be a limiting compound Poisson^geometric process as the sum of Markov Bernoulli random variables [4]. This publication by the principal author as referenced [5] was designed for a Binomial assumption rather than a nonidentical Bernoulli model, which varies from hour to hour. Eight years earlier in 1982, the loss of load was approximated by an asymptotic normal probability distribution function by the author [5]. In this chapter however, in addition to the digital DES method and contrary to an asymptotic or limiting probability distribution function, we will suggest an exact estimation procedure through the Poisson^LSD, where the Poisson process is compounded by a discrete LSD [9–12]. Note that LSD recognizes the true contagion property of the occurrences in a clump; such as a breakdown at a given time adversely affects and engenders more failures in the forthcoming hours until the failures are repaired [3, 5, 9, 13]. The parameters of Poisson^LSD, the mean and q-ratio (variance/mean), are calculated by utilizing the well-known frequency and duration method as in an electric power generation's system reliability evaluation. These necessary parameters of compound Poisson distribution are obtained from the popular frequency and duration method pioneered by Hall, Ringlee, and Wood in 1968, later to be followed by Ayoub and Patton in 1970 and 1976 [6, 9] and documented by Billinton et al. [14–17].

The proposed method will facilitate a closed-form discrete probability distribution function for the total number of loss of load events, usually assumed to be in terms of hours. The LoS events are assumed to occur in terms of clusters or multiple happenings [7, 11, 12].

The proposed closed-form analytical approach is facilitated by using a nonapproximate but exact closed-form probability distribution function, that is, Poisson^LSD model, generally called negative binomial (NB) pdf for convenience [3, 4, 5, 8, 18]. The author maintains that this new probabilistic model provides better accuracy toward a more realistic modeling of the operation of a power generation (or cyber CLOUD) system in utilizing the advantages of the well-recognized frequency–duration method.

7.3.2 Notation

rv	Random variable
LSD	Logarithmic series distribution
pdf	Probability density function
cdf	Cumulative probability density function
GB	Gigabyte (hardware storage capacity equal to $1\,GB = 1000$ million bytes)
MW	Megawatt (electric power capacity measure of a generator equal to 1 million watts)
Poisson^LSD	Poisson compounded by logarithmic series distribution
Poisson^geometric	Poisson compounded by geometric distribution
x_i	LSD rv
θ	Correlation-like unknown parameter of the LSD rv, $0 < \theta < 1$
α	Parameter of the LSD, as a function of θ
X	Poisson^LSD rv., that is, sum of x_i's that are LSD. Negative binomial rv for a given assumption of k as a function of Poisson parameter
k	Parameter of the Poisson^LSD
q	Variance to mean ratio, a parameter of the Poisson^LSD
λ	Parameter of the Poisson
f	Frequency
d	Average deficiency duration time
NHRS	Number of hours studied in a year (usually 365 days $= 8760\,h$)
LoL	Loss of load or service event, when capacity cannot meet load (service) demand plus outages at a given hour or cycle, whichever is used
LoLP	Loss of load (service) probability
LoLE	Loss of service expected $=$ LoLP $\times$ NHRS.
TOTCAP	Installed total capacity for the isolated CLOUD computing enterprise
L_i	Service demand forecast rv at each discrete ith hour for the isolated network
O_i	Unplanned forced capacity outage rv at the ith hour
m_i	Capacity margin rv at the ith hour, where $m_i < 0$ signifies a loss of load hour; where $m_i = \text{TOTCAP} - O_i - L_i$ with all variables in GB (Gigabyte) or MW (Megawatt).

7.3.3 Objectives

Therefore, the primary objectives of this chapter are (i) to study an analytical closed-form probability distribution function [3, 4, 5, 9] and (ii) to mimic the chronological events using the analytical DES techniques so as to estimate the widely used operational system's LoS (or Loss of Load) index for CLOUD systems in general [3, 19]. Although the conventional reliability indices such as Loss of Load Probability (LoLP) and Loss of Load Expected (LoLE) through deterministic methods such as frequency–duration technique provide some useful averaging information, it is very important that a statistical distribution function should be derived [6, 9, 10, 13, 20]. The purpose is to completely characterize the behavior of the loss of load hours in a year of operation so as to be able to conduct statistical tests of hypotheses concerning the unknown (statistical population built on samples) value of these indices [3, 5, 13, 21]. The author believes that a statistical approach in developing a closed-form and exact (nonasymptotic) pdf for the random variable of interest, LoS, is novel and more accurate. Additionally, the proposed compound Poisson model (i.e., negative binomial distribution (NBD)) respects the correlation of power failures in each occurrence of a clump or cluster, which adversely influences each other by engendering more failures, for example, once a power interruption occurs in an electric power system. The author believes that this probabilistic approach offers a more realistic alternative to the traditional reliability evaluation in electric power or service-based CLOUD systems, where the reliability index calculated is quoted solely as a single average number that bears no uncertainty clearly generated by the varying input data.

The Poisson counting process is compounded by a contagious LSD (Logarithmic Series Distribution), which develops to, Poisson^log series, or Poisson^LSD hereafter. Poisson^LSD is the governing probability distribution for the negative-margin or loss of load hours, a popular static capacity reserve index, i.e. loss of load or service expected (LoLE) [14–18, 22]. It is cited that the sum of LSD random variables governed by a Poisson counting process yields to a compound Poisson equivalent to an NBD when a certain simple mathematical assumption holds [9, 11, 12, 23]. Both CLOUD computing providers and users need a way to measure the quality of this service. This metric can provide users a better sense of what they are getting in terms of service quality correlated with their investment. Also, it gives CLOUD service providers a concrete numerical reference so that they can improve their service quality.

7.3.4 Frequency and Duration Method for the Loss of Load or Service

Numerous works have been published on methods to compute (power) system reliability indices, specifically LoLE [12, 14–18, 20, 22]. Consider an electric power supply or service-based system with operating (i.e., positive power margin) and nonoperating (i.e., negative power margin) states throughout a yearly long period of operational discrete hours [5, 24]. The quantities $m_1, m_2, ..., m_N$ are the margin values at hourly steps where a positive margin denotes a nondeficient state and negative margin denotes a deficient state. Margin at a discrete hour is the difference between the total generating capacity (TOTCAP) and the service demand (hourly peak load forecast, L_i) plus unplanned forced capacity outages, O_i. Hence $m_i = \text{TOTCAP} - O_i - L_i$, which indicates the capacity (MW for power CLOUD or GB for Cyber CLOUD) balance at each discrete step i, where the realization $\{m_i\}$ assumes either a positive margin or negative margin. Thus the count of negative-margin hours within a year is the LoLE as in section 7.3.2. Hence, LoLE when divided by total number of hours (NHRS) yields the Loss of Load (Service) Probability. Once the system is in a negative-margin state, it should usually cluster to a downtime of several hours before the overall system recuperation fully happens following a repair (or recovery) process. This section assumes that the arrival count to a negative-margin state is governed by a Poisson counting process, while interarrival times are exponentially distributed. However, at the final stage, the clump size of the negative-margin hours will be governed by the compounding LSD, which assumes the interdependence effect between the elements of the clump.

A few select papers have treated the issue in a stochastic sense where the number of loss of load or service expected hours in a year (LoLE = LoLP × NHRS) was expressed in terms of a pdf. Among those works, the asymptotic normal and limiting Poisson^geometric were published in 1983 and 1990, respectively [2, 5]. As for the power system reliability methods that compute the loss of load or service index as an expected value through the frequency and duration approach, all methods consist basically of two parts: a capacity model and a load model [6, 7, 22, 24]. The usual approach is to compute the required parameters of the capacity model from the parameters of individual generating units and then to combine the capacity model with the load model to compute the desired reliability indices. The parameters of the load model are determined in one way or another from the load cycle of the system being studied. As a result, frequency times average duration yields the loss of load hours in a time period usually taken as a year, that is, f (number of outages per year) × d (number of hours per outage) = LoLE (loss of load or service hours per year). In this research, one obtains the parameters of the Poisson (λ) and Logarithmic Series, LSD (θ), from the frequency–duration method [3, 7, 9, 13] as follows in the next sections.

7.3.5 NBD as a Compound Poisson Model

Any pure Poisson process with no specific compounding distribution in mind has interarrival times (e.g., between customer arrivals in a shopping mall) as negative exponentially distributed with a rate λ. That is, the pdf of interarrival times is independent of earlier arrival epochs with forgetfulness property. Suppose arrivals or incidents of power breakdown occur in a power generation system according to a Poisson counting process. Each arrival can demand or endure a positive integer amount "x" deficient hours, which are independently and identically distributed as $\{f_x\}$. When we consider any fixed time interval t, the number of demands (in batches or clumps) in that time interval is said to have a compound Poisson distribution. If the mean breakdown arrival rate is given as λ, then the compound Poisson probability of $X = x_1 + x_2 + x_3 + \cdots$ demands within a time interval or period t over total arrivals is given by

$$P(X) = \sum_{Y=0}^{X} \frac{(\lambda t)^Y e^{-\lambda t} f^{Y^*}(X)}{Y!}; \quad X = 0,1,2,\ldots; \quad Y = 0,1,2,\ldots,X; \quad \lambda > 0 \quad (7.1)$$

where $f^{Y^*}(X)$ is the Y-fold convolution of $\{f_x\}$, which denotes the probability that "Y interruptions cause a total of X failures." Of course, in the case where each interruption places exactly one failure (hence, the orderliness property of Poisson), Equation (7.1) reduces to a purely Poisson density function. It now remains to find the parameters of the compound Poisson process, "mean" and "q = variance/mean," where q is equal to the second moment divided by the first moment of the compounding distribution of $f\{x\}$:

$$q = E(x^2)/E(x) \quad (7.2)$$

NBD has been utilized in many disciplines involving count data, such as accident statistics, biological sciences, ecology, market research, computer software, and psychology.

NBD was originally formulated as the distribution of the number of tosses of a fair coin necessary to achieve a fixed number of heads [10–12]. Later on analyzing the effects of various departures from the conditions that lead to the Poisson distribution for the occurrence of individuals in divisions of time (and space), Gosset concluded that if different divisions have different chances of containing individuals, the NBD provides a better fit than does the Poisson [23]. This is why there is a strong similarity of this expression with the negative-margin hours adversely affecting each other in power or cyber system operations. Hence, NBD can also be defined to be the Poisson sum of a logarithmic series distributed rv. Now let $X = x_1 + x_2 + \cdots + x_N$, where x_i are independent identically distributed (iid) logarithmic series (LSD) rv with its probability density function and corresponding moments as follows:

$$f(x) = p(x;\theta) = \frac{\alpha\theta^x}{x}; \quad x = 1,2,3,\ldots,\infty; \quad \alpha = -\frac{1}{\ln(1-\theta)}; \quad 0 < \theta < 1 \qquad (7.3)$$

$$E(x) = \mu = \frac{\alpha\theta}{(1-\theta)} \qquad (7.4)$$

$$\mathrm{Var}(x) = \mu\left[\frac{1}{1-\theta} - \mu\right] \qquad (7.5)$$

Then, randomly stopped sum of x_i, which are LSD rv with parameter q, will possess an NBD with parameters k and $1-\theta = q^{-1}$ if the governing counting process is a Poisson, provided that its rate parameter is equal to

$$\lambda = -k\ln(1-\theta) = k\ln(1-\theta)^{-1} = k\ln q, \quad k < 0 \qquad (7.6)$$

Now let LSD pdf in (7.3) be reorganized and reparameterized as follows:

$$\theta = \left(\frac{p}{q}\right), \quad q = p+1 = (1-\theta)^{-1}, \quad \text{where } p = \theta(1-\theta)^{-1}.$$

$$\alpha = -\frac{1}{\ln(1-\theta)} = \frac{1}{\ln(1-\theta)^{-1}} = \frac{1}{\ln q} \qquad (7.7)$$

$$f(x) = \left\{\frac{1}{x\ln q}\right\}\left(\frac{p}{q}\right)^x; \quad x = 1,2,3,\ldots \quad \text{and} \quad q = p+1 > 1 \qquad (7.8)$$

$$E(x) = -\frac{\theta}{\left[(1-\theta)\ln(1-\theta)\right]} = \frac{p}{\ln q} = \frac{(q-1)}{\ln q} \qquad (7.9)$$

$$\mathrm{Var}(x) = \left\{\frac{q-1}{\ln q}\right\}\left\{q - \left[\frac{q-1}{\ln q}\right]\right\} \qquad (7.10)$$

$$q = \frac{\text{variance}}{\text{mean}} = \frac{F''(0)}{F'(0)} = \frac{E(x^2)}{E(x)} = \frac{1}{1-\theta} \tag{7.11}$$

where "ln" denotes natural logarithm. Then q can be either estimated as a root of moment in Equation (7.9) or (7.11), where $E(x)$ is the total number of failures divided by the number of arrivals. The Poisson^LSD, which has a mean, kp, and variance to mean ratio, q (variance/mean), can be expressed as follows:

$$E(x) = kp \tag{7.12}$$

$$P(X) = \left[\frac{(k+X-1)!}{(k-1)!X!}\right]\left(\frac{p^X}{q^{k+X}}\right) \tag{7.13}$$

The NBD is particularly convenient because of the simple recursion formula easily derived from (7.14) as follows [3, 9, 10, 12]:

$$P(X+1) = \left\{\frac{X+k}{X+1}\right\}\left(\frac{p}{q}\right)P(X) \tag{7.14}$$

Hence, for a given q = variance/mean ratio and $k = \lambda t / \ln q$ or given the mean "m" of the Poisson process, k = mean/p = mean/$(q-1)$, the discrete state probabilities can be computed through a simple coding. On the other hand, there are other noncompound Poisson probabilities that also yield NBD state probabilities by other chance mechanisms. However, these mechanisms are out of the scope of this study due to incompatibility with the existing physical modeling realities of this chapter.

7.3.6   NBD for the Loss of Load or Loss of CLOUD Service Expected

The objective of this subsection is to characterize the distribution function for the sum of negative-margin hours or Loss of Load Expected (LoLE) in an isolated power generating or CLOUD computing system. The Poisson arrivals of system breakdown are assumed to create clumps of failure hours, due to either the increase of the capacity outage or the rise of the load level. The size of the clump or the duration length of deficiency is assumed to be distributed according to logarithmic series (LSD), where the presence of one individual falling into a clump increases the chance of other individuals. This, in fact, is called the true contagion. This property inherently may exist in the operation of an electric power generation or cyber system by which deficient (or negative-margin) hours prevail until the system is recuperated following the repair activities of the capacity outages or the shedding activity of load levels. It is likely that the negative margin persists for some hours.

The proposed model makes use of the frequency–duration method to deduce information on the average length of a deficient state and its frequency of occurrence. A deficient hour is likely to invite a following deficient activity as a consequence of a true contagion. Hence, the Poisson compounded by LSD is called Poisson^LSD or equivalently an NBD given the mathematical expression that holds as in Equation (7.6). In a recent study, the Poisson was compounded by the limiting geometric distribution for the number of clumped failures. This present probabilistic approach estimates the number of loss of load hours within a planned target year through the frequency–duration method [22]. In the Poisson^LSD, the parameter λ of the Poisson is taken as the value of the frequency of loss of load within a year. The average outage duration is taken as $d=E(x)$ of the LSD where θ or q can be extracted from (7.9). Thus frequency (f) represents the number of times that the system is in negative margin within a year. Average duration (d) represents the average number of hours that the system stays in a negative margin at each system breakdown. Finally LoLE = $f \times d$. Using Equation (7.9) where x is from LSD and letting $E(x)=d=(q-1)/\ln(q)$, one obtains the q value through a nonlinear solution algorithm as in a nonlinear Newton–Raphson solution technique [9, 13]. Let $\lambda = f$, where the Poisson parameter λ is equal to the frequency of loss of load:

$$f = k \ln(q) \tag{7.15}$$

$$\text{LoLE} = f \times d = [k\ \ln(q)][(q-1))/\ln(q)] = k(q-1) \tag{7.16}$$

7.4 VARIOUS APPLICATIONS TO CYBER SYSTEMS

We will consider two different sizes for our model: a single small size or experimental cyber system with only two groups and a total of two units (one unit per group), and subsequently two large size cyber systems composed of (i) 24 groups with a total of 348 units and (ii) 103 groups with a total of 443 units. Let's take them one at a time. First an experimental analysis is presented to cover the theory yielding to the following large systems.

7.4.1 Small Sample Experimental Systems

For our small experimental cyber system model in Figure 7.3, we consider a basic operational case similar to which is shown in Equations (7.17)–(7.20). In this figure, we represent the operation of each unit (Units 1 and 2 for Capacity vs. Time) during the entire time period of the study, which is 13 h or cycles. We represent the operation of the entire system via the addition of the two one gigabyte units, with units (or components) described as 1 and 2 where 1 = UP (available) and 0 = DOWN (unavailable):

$$U_3(t) = U_1(t) + U_2(t), \quad 0 \le t \le 13, \tag{7.17}$$

$$\begin{aligned} U_1(t) &= 1, \quad 0 \le t < 4 \text{ and } 7 < t \le 10 \\ &= 0, \quad \text{elsewhere;} \end{aligned} \tag{7.18}$$

$$\begin{aligned} U_2(t) &= 1, \quad 0 \le t < 2;\ 3 \le t < 6 \text{ and } 9 \le t < 12 \\ &= 0, \quad \text{elsewhere;} \end{aligned} \tag{7.19}$$

$$\begin{aligned} U_3(t) &= 2, \quad 0 \le t < 2;\ 3 \le t < 4 \text{ and } 9 \le t < 10 \\ &= 1, \quad 2 \le t < 3;\ 5 \le t < 6;\ 7 \le t < 9 \text{ and } 10 \le t < 12 \\ &= 0, \quad \text{elsewhere.} \end{aligned} \tag{7.20}$$

In this sample graph of Figure 7.3, unit 1 is available during the initial 4 h servicing at its entire capacity of 1 GB. However at the end of the 4th hour, a disruption occurred, which caused unit 1 to be down.

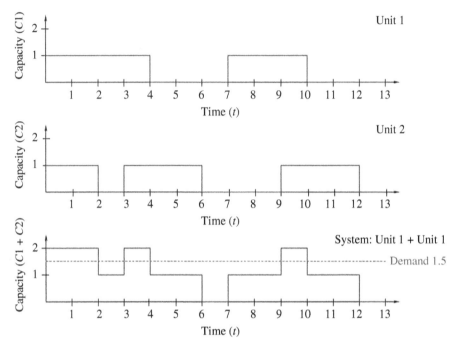

FIGURE 7.3 Equations (7.17)–(7.20) plotted versus time for units 1 and 2 all in GB units, and their sum with a constant load (demand) = 1.5 GB.

It takes 3 h for unit 1 to recover and back to operation, it fails after 3 h. Unit 2 operates other than between 2nd and 3rd and between 6th and 9th hours. So, we can see when each unit, U_1 and U_2, of the entire cyber system, U_3, is up (available) or down (nonavailable) in an additive and independent setting. Our model is a simplified CLOUD environment with additive resources. It is a conglomerate of computers (units) distributed in different locations but working or servicing in parallel (simultaneously) to an external clientele of customers on a relatively large scale. This cluster of computers is arranged in groups, comprising sets of computers with similar specifications. The parameters involved in our simple experimental model are given as follows:

- Disruption rate caused by security breaches: γ.
- Mean time to disruption: $m = 1 / \gamma$.
- Recovery rate: μ. The frequency with which a system recovers from a security breach.
- Mean recovery time: $r = 1/\mu$.
- Availability: $P = \mu / (\mu + \gamma)$.
- Unit capacity: C. It refers to maximum unit generation or production capacity.
- Demand of service: D. Total service demand or load for the entire system during the life cycle.

An initial study is designed for a constant demand (or service), but a more realistic, variable demand will be considered for larger-scale systems. Here unit capacity and service (or demand) is measured in terms of computing seconds (e.g., Flops) with the Gigabytes (GB) representing the capacity or storage, where a Gigaflop = Billion floating-point operations per second (Fig. 7.4).

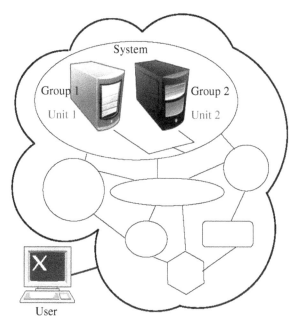

FIGURE 7.4   Two-component CLOUD system topology example.

How to estimate failure and repair rates from unit's historical failure in Figure 7.3

Unit 1 Availability (see uppermost plot for Unit 1 in Fig. 7.3):

$P_1 = 7/13 = 0.538461538 = \mu_1 / (\mu_1 + \gamma_1)$

Mean time to disruption: Average service hours before disruption, $m_1 = 7/2 = 3.5 = 1/\gamma_1$

Failure or disruption rate: $\gamma_1 = 1/3.5 = 0.285714286$

Mean recovery time: $r_1 = 6/2 = 3.0 = 1/\mu_1$

Repair or recovery rate: $\mu_1 = 1/3.0 = 0.333333333$

Unit 2 Availability (see middle plot for Unit 2 in Fig. 7.3):

$P_2 = 8/13 = 0.615384615 = \gamma_2 / (\mu_2 + \gamma_2)$

Mean time to disruption: Average service hours before disruption, $m_2 = 8/3 = 2.66 = 1/\gamma_2$

Disruption rate: $\gamma_2 = 1/2.66666667 = 0.375$

Mean recovery time: $r_2 = 5/3 = 1.66666667 = 1/\mu_2$

Recovery rate: $\mu_2 = 1/1.66666667 = 0.6$

The service demand is assumed to be constant and equal to 1.5 GB. The results for the small-scale experimental system availability from Figure 7.3 for UP state: $U_3(t)=2$ (larger than 1.5 GB) is $4/13=\mathbf{0.307}$. Markov chain's exact result by substituting the input values above into the Markov down state in Figure 7.3, where $P_1\left(\text{system UP}\right)=\mu_1\mu_2\,/\,(\gamma_1+\mu_1)(\gamma_2+\mu_2)$ inspired from Figure 7.5, is $P_1=(0.3333)(0.6)/[(0.2857+0.3333)\ (0.3750+0.6)]=\mathbf{0.331}$. DES's Load Surplus Probability (LSP) is **0.303** after 100,000 simulation runs where each simulation run: 13 h or cycles, also as shown in [25, Figure 7, p. 57]. LSP is a system reliability index, whereas LoLP is a system unreliability index.

With 1,000,000 simulation runs, the DES result will converge to **0.305**. All three solutions (experimental = **0.307**, DES = **0.3028** from Figure 7.6, Markov theoretical solution = **0.331**) obtained by three different methods are very satisfactorily close.

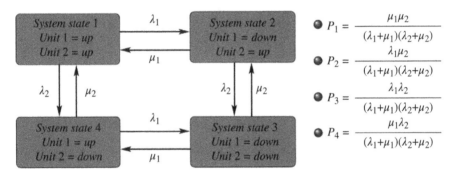

FIGURE 7.5 Markov states for a small cyber system and Markov chain state space analytical equations.

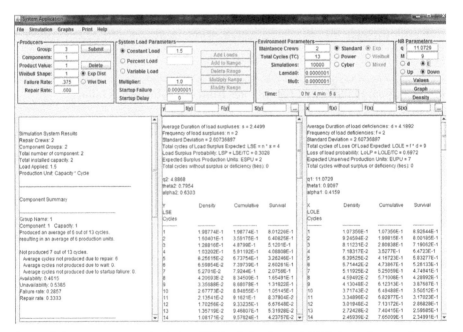

FIGURE 7.6 Discrete event simulation (DES) solution for $n=10,000$ simulation runs (or simulation years) for a simple two-component independent additive system.

The experimental operation lasts 13 cycles only. The experimental case denotes only a single realization of the DES because one can realize the simulation input data in many more than a single scenario among which realization of (7.17)–(7.20) is only one of them. This comparison duly demonstrates the validity of the DES of additive units under a constant or varying service demand, a feature that will prove very useful.

7.4.2 Large Cyber Systems

Assume now that there is a very large system to examine like those in Refs. [19, 25, 26] such as an interconnected power generation system or a cyber system (CLOUD) in a server farm with 103 production groups, each of which has a given number of components, totaling 443 servers, and each with its own distinct repair crew, one per server. Total installed capacity is 26,237 GB. A Java coded CLOURAM simulates the cyber grid for 10,000 runs covering 8760 cycles or h (for hours) resulting in LoLP = 13.71%.

The service demand as a varying load for an annual period of 8760 h is available and given in Figure 7.7 in Gigabytes. In a what-if study, one can choose less than a perfect

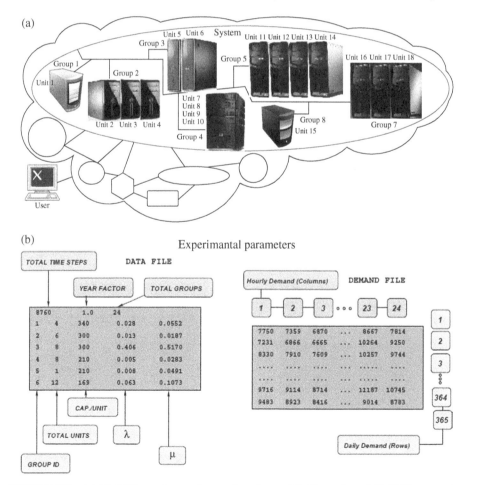

FIGURE 7.7 (a) CLOUD topology to be continued next. (b) Illustration of CLOUD computing infrastructure with multiple groups.

number (=443) of crews, such as 143 as in one stopping-rule study, where less than 143 will result promptly in an LoLP overriding 0.3 or 30% rise, so as to see what an adverse effect it plays if it ever does or when does it first need to be curtailed. See later sections on maintenance crew and product planning. This is a leverage for CLOUD managers to judge the extent of repair crews to employ (or not to) for mitigating the risk of reliability to a desirable value to render the ROI effective.

On the l.h.s. outcome column, simulation system results are presented on component-by-component basis. On the middle column, reliability (surplus) outcomes are presented. On the r.h.s column, the unreliability results are presented.

As Figure 7.8 shows, at the end of 41 min of computation time for 10,000 simulation runs, CLOURAM calculates that the system was interrupted for $f=384$ times, each of which lasted on the average $d=3.13$ h (or cycles). Overall outages led to LoLE (or Mean Number of Loss of Service Hours)$=f \times d=1201$ h of Loss of Load or Service or LoLP$=$LoLE/8760$=0.1371$ or $\approx 14\%$. The standard deviation is 178.3 h. However the LoL hours is not a symmetric normal distribution, but it is a right-skewed compound Poisson, rather NB with M (mean)$=1201$ and $q_1=7.15$ indicating the extent of cluster or clump. No ties are recorded where reserve margin$=0$. A dynamic index, Expected Unserved Production (EUP) units, in terms of gigabyte cycles, or Gigaflops, was 2,055,607. Figure 7.9 illustrates a multiple server group CLOUD and the equilibrium counts of the entire study where RHS (right hand side) and LHS (left hand side) values validate each other.

Further, in the middle column of Figure 7.8, a static index LSP $= 7559/8760=0.86$ or 86%. A dynamic index Expected Surplus Production Units or ESPU$=35,365,601$ GB-h or Gigaflops$\times 60$ since 1 h$=60$ s is valid. Also the program is sound when the entire system summary has an equilibrium that translates as TDCU + ESPU $-$ EUPU$=$EPU. The l.h.s.'s positive difference resulting from the sum of the total demanded consumption

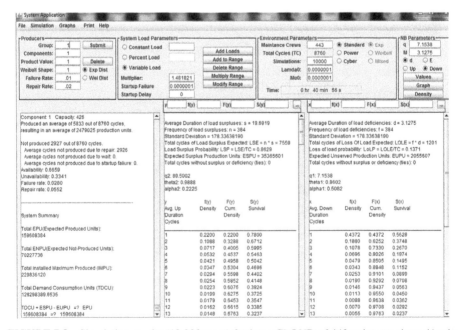

FIGURE 7.8 Simulation results (10,000 years) for large CLOUD of 443 units; run time: 41 min.

System Summary

Total EPU(Expected Produced Units):
159608384

Total ENPU(Expected Not-Produced Units):
70227736

Total Installed Maximum Produced (IMPU):
229836120

Total Demand Consumption Units (TDCU):
126,298,389.6535

TDCU + ESPU - EUPU =? EPU
159608384 =? 159608384

FIGURE 7.9 Equilibrium screenshot for CLOUD simulation from Figure 7.8.

units (TDCU) by adding up all load values and ESPU available for service now subtracted by the expected unserved production units (EUPU) should be equivalent to the r.h.s.'s expected production units (EPU) from the production assets. Therefore, in Figure 7.9, it checks 159,608,384 (l.h.s) = 159,608,384 (r.h.s) in gigabyte-hours.

Equivalently, $ESPU - EUPU = EPU - TDCU = 35,365,601 - 2,055,607 = 159,608,384 - 126,298,390 = 33,309,994$ from Figure 7.9. We run another large system with 398 units in Figure 7.10, which we compare with Markov solutions using the Alabama supercomputer (Fig. 7.11). Another large system with 348 units will follow.

The subtle difference between two very different assessment techniques (Markov and DES) is due to the dependencies that exist between the Markov states that idealistically assume complete independence. Therefore the analytical Markov probability for the up states becomes somewhat slightly inflated due to added correlations. To further increase the number of Markov states by including dependence scenarios would astronomically prolong the computing time, where $2^{398} > 6.45 \times 10^{109}$, which is an extremely large value. However, beyond discounting inter-correlation effects, the 3.332% deviation ($|90.47\%-93.8\%|$) is also partially due to randomness that results from DES employing quasirandom numbers.

The result obtained by the Markov chains similar to the small size system of Section 6.4.1 is because the steady-state probabilities are added for the operational units satisfying the demand. Therefore in summary, the experimental solution for large systems is impossible because it is intractable. The next large cyber system examined comprises 24 groups of units totaling to 348 units. Results are not shown here due to limited space. Therefore, the total number of Markov system's up and down states are $2^{348} = 5.73 \times 10^{104}$, which is also indescribably enormous. The failure (disruption) rate λ_k, repair (recovery)

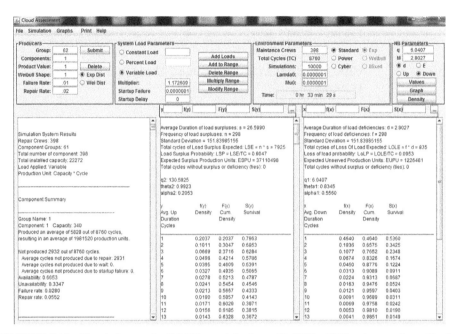

FIGURE 7.10 Simulation results (10,000 years) for large CLOUD of 398 units; run time: 33 min.

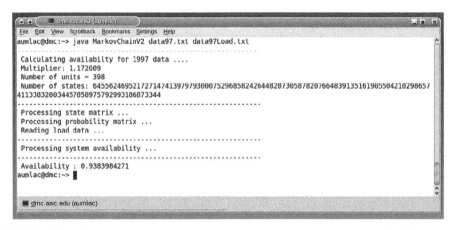

FIGURE 7.11 Alabama supercomputer (www.asc.edu) results regarding a large CLOUD system with 398 units for Figure 7.10 with 2^{398} Markov states (Monte Carlo Simulation took 1 full day of CPU: Central Processing Units)

rate μ_k, and capacity (storage or generation) C_k for each kth unit are supplied by the analyst. The demand (load) cycle is varying from hour to hour for the entire year (8760 h) of operations. Experimentally, it is very tedious and not practical, if not infeasible, to add the existing unit availabilities hour by hour for 348 units, a process that may take years. This simply signals that there is no way to use state space diagrams for such large number of Markov states when a complicated CLOUD simulation is at stake.

7.5   LARGE CYBER SYSTEMS USING STATISTICAL METHODS

The pdf, cumulative density function (cdf), and survival density function (sdf) columns are given in Figures 7.8 and 7.10 where any of the statistical plots can be extracted at will to facilitate statistical inference on the average duration (=d) and LoLE. The total hours or cycles of expected LoS are a compound Poisson, that is, NB, given that a special mathematical relationship holds true (Eq. 7.6). Then LoLE, distributed with respect to a Poisson^LSD, i.e. NBD ($M=835$, $q=6.04$) function, can be obtained from the NBD software as in Figure 7.12. The feature in Figures 7.7 and 7.10 has flexibilities to add a desired amount to all loads or modify a certain selected load or delete a selected load or add single selected load as well as add a desirable amount to a range of selected loads like from 8000th and 8760th or scaling a range like multiplying by 3/2 or 1/2.

These are necessary for load (service) maintenance or shedding or load appending. Surplus and deficiency productions (gigaflops) are not additive as in the case of LoLE and LSP to complement each other, and not related exhaustively other than the fact that if one increases, the other decreases. In the middle column of Figures 7.7 and 7.10 this time, surpluses instead of deficiencies are studied to estimate availability instead of unavailability. Figure 7.12 shows the plotting of NBD ($M=835$, $q=6.04$) using the earlier research by the author [3, 10]. Figures 7.13 and 7.14 show "Available Capacity" and "Reserve Margin=Installed Capacity – Load – Outage," respectively, at any given cycle. Figure 7.15 shows Group 1's Component 1 up–down fluctuations in a year with no waiting time due to maintenance crew's adequate reserve.

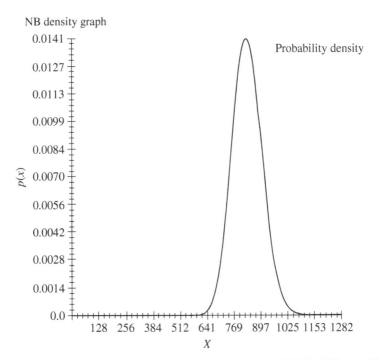

FIGURE 7.12   The frequency distribution function of the LoLE ($M=835$, $q=6.04$) from Figure 7.1's 398 units.

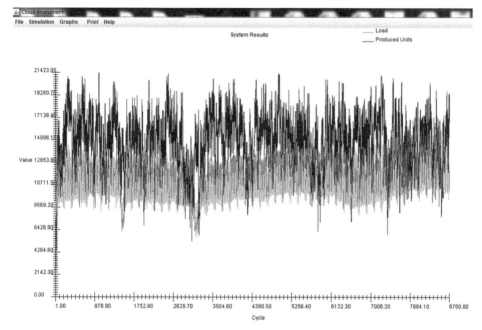

FIGURE 7.13   Available capacity = installed capacity – outages from Figure 7.10.

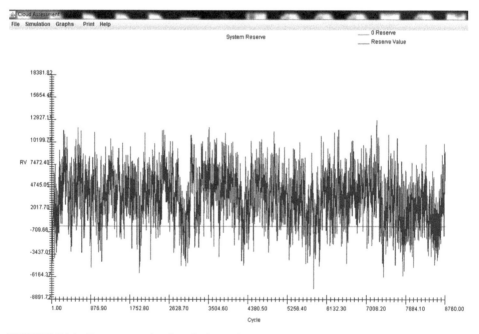

FIGURE 7.14   Reserve margin = installed capacity – outages – demand (load). Below zero: loss of load or service (LoLE). Above zero: surplus load (LSP).

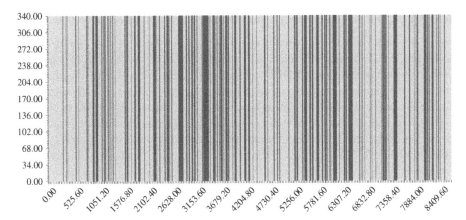

FIGURE 7.15 The sequences of up and down for the Group1 Unit 1's failure history. Note, white: operating and gray: not operating

7.6 REPAIR CREW AND PRODUCT RESERVE PLANNING TO MANAGE RISK COST EFFECTIVELY USING CYBERRISKSOLVER CLOUD MANAGEMENT JAVA TOOL

What does CLOURAM achieve uniquely that no other software tool does? [51–54] What CLOURAM (CLOUD Risk Assessment and Management Tool) achieves is the following: CLOURAM is both a simulation tool and an expert system. As a *simulator*, it will mimic real-life operation of the system in question to calculate critical reliability and/or security indices. As an *expert* system, it will help to quantify and manage the LoS index with the rightful and timely responses to certain useful cost-conscious "What-If?" questions. It will assist in taking care of the reliability assessment function so as to manage risk cost effectively by quantifying the entire CLOUD operation with tangible and practical metrics. Following the deterministic input data such as the number of servers or generators (or producers) with their failure (or disruption) and repair (or recovery) rates and number of repair crews and hourly (or cyclical) service demand that can be modified to reflect service maintenance or changes as implemented in hourly demand (load data), the operation starts at the first hour (or cycle) by randomly generating the negative exponentially or Weibull distributed operating (up) and nonoperating (down) times where the goal is to study the random evolution of a memoryless system. Then the available total capacity at each cycle is contrasted against the outages to calculate the available capacity, which is also compared to the service demand at that hour to determine the reserve capacity whether adequately meeting the load or not.

If the reserve capacity/(or margin) is less than a zero margin, then we have an undesired deficiency or LoS. Once these hours (or cycles) of negative margin are added, it will constitute the expected number of hours of loss of load or service (LoLE). Divided by the total number of exposure units, 8760h (NHRS) for a year, it will give the LoLP=LoLE/NHRS. Once the LoLE is known, as well as its frequency (f= number of such occurrences of deficiencies per annum), then the average duration, d=LoLE/f, will indicate how long on the average an LoS is expected to last. What are some of most significant scenarios regarding "What If?"

7.6.1 CLOUD Resource Management Planning for Employment of Repair Crews

A most popular example to a what-if query as frequently executed in simulation engineering practices is the resource allocation, which is one of the most vulnerable and softest (weakest) points of the entire CLOUD computing process. We will study the effect of the number of maintenance crews from full to lower. Figure 7.16 has originally displayed an unreliability index of 5.44% for 348 units with a perfect count of 348 repair crews.

Therefore, initially the total number of available production units is 348. In a new analysis, we will simulate (1000 runs or years) for a reduced resource of 100 crews to see the impact in Figure 7.17. That is how much less reliability we will have to suffice with if we save money by eliminating 248 repair (recovery) crews. This time we are expecting wait times and more unreliability from our CLOUD operation. Now see Figure 7.17. The unreliability index is unfavorably upped to 7.36%, a negligible difference when you take into account the savings you will accrue from employing 248 less repair crews. We now will reduce even further 50 more repair crews, 298 less than originally assumed. Finally so, we will employ solely 50 crews to see if it is economically profitable to do so in Figure 7.18. This time we hit the rock! Outcomes are disastrous. We saw the catastrophic results of a skyrocketing unreliability of 85.71% (while employing only 50 repair crews) from merely 7.46% when we had only 50 more crews. The difference is the breaking point. The CLOUD manager will halt at 100 crews before reaching disastrous results [53].

Therefore this CLOUD should not lower their repair crews to less [53] than around 100. More detailed studies can be conducted by trying 99…90…70…60… to see the drastic jump. This cost–benefit portfolio of crew planning analysis as one of the most crucial "What-If" scenarios could save millions of dollars for a CLOUD Resource Management to plan ahead wisely.

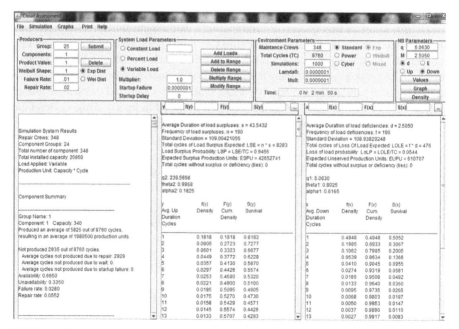

FIGURE 7.16 Simulation results (1000 years) for a CLOUD of 348 units and 348 repair crews.

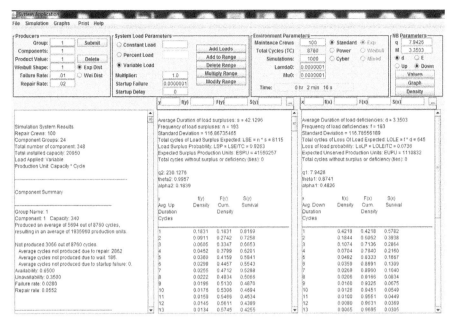

FIGURE 7.17 Simulation results (1000 years) for a CLOUD of 348 units for 100 repair crews.

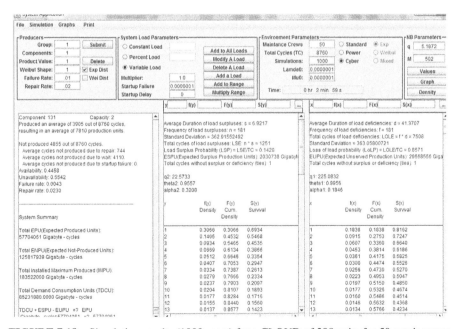

FIGURE 7.18 Simulation results (1000 years) for a CLOUD of 398 units for 50 repair crews.

7.6.1.1 Step-by-Step Algorithm CLOUD Management Planning for Repair Crew Employment The following software program (CLOUD Management for the manager part of the CLOURAM to follow up with the assessment part) will show you how to do this in a systematic and algorithmic order.

Here we will study how to implement the effect of maintenance crews on the LoLP = unreliability index. In this analysis we will simulate for a reduced resource of Crew Intervals (e.g., *50*, *100*, *150*, etc.).

Consider a larger-size example this time where the total number of production units available is 443. Now let us simulate for the reduced resource of 50 crews as in Figures 7.17 and 7.18 from 100 down to 50 for the 398 unit example. Initially the unreliability varies slightly; at one point it increases in a drastic manner, which is called breaking point. The CLOUD should not lower the repair crews to less than the breaking point.

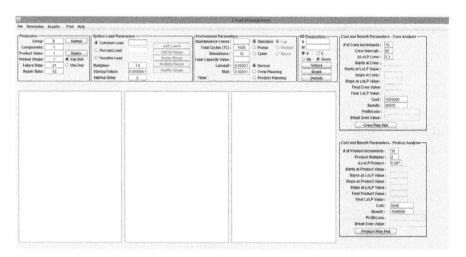

FIGURE 7.19   The overall dialogue box for both crew and product reserve planning.

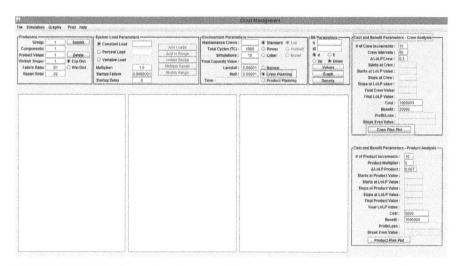

FIGURE 7.20   The dialogue box input data for only crew reserve planning in CLOURAM.

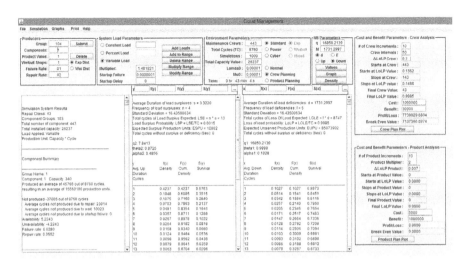

FIGURE 7.21 Output dialogue box for input data in Figure 7.20 for 1000 simulation runs with 443 repair crews.

Figures 7.19 and 7.20 are dialogue boxes for input. We can observe, as in Figure 7.21, the crew break-even point is 143. This cost–benefit portfolio of Reserve Crew Planning analysis can save millions through CLOUD Resource Management.

In Environment Parameters Section, three buttons are added, which indicates the type of execution, that is, Normal (only risk assessment without management), Crew Planning, and Product Planning, in subsequent sections.

First begin with selecting one among the three types of execution. Normal button is selected to implement a normal execution of CLOUD. Crew planning button is selected to implement Reserve Crew Planning and to obtain Crew Plan Plot so as to estimate the optimal crew value to halt at for ensuring certain reliability (lack of risk). Product planning button is further selected to implement Reserve Product Planning and to obtain Product Plan Plot so as to find the optimal capacity value to halt at so to ensure a desired reliability.

Follow the below algorithmic steps to implement Crew Reserve Planning:

Step 1: Radio button *Crew Planning* must be selected as shown in Figure 7.21.

Step 2: *# of Crew Increments* in default is given as 10, which indicates the number of crew intervals required to plot a graph.

Step 3: *Crew Intervals* in default is given as 50, which indicates the difference between two crew (working personnel employed) values.

Step 4: *ΔLoLP Crew* in default is given as 0.3, which indicates that if the difference between the two consecutive LoLP values is greater than 0.3, then the crew addition stops at the lowest LoLP value.

Step 5: *Starts at Crew* is the total number of maintenance crews initially, for 2000data. txt there are 443 crews.

Step 6: *Starts at LoLP Value* is the LoLP value for the initial number of maintenance crews.

Step 7: *Stops at Crew* is the optimal stopping crew value.

Step 8: *Stops at LoLP Value* is the optimal stopping LoLP value.

Step 9: *Final Crew Value* is the number of crews that are remaining at the end of the crew planning implementation.

Step 10: *Final LoLP Value* is the LoLP value for number of crews that are remaining at the end of the crew planning implementation.

Step 11: *Cost* in default given as $1,000,000.00 for a placeholder, which indicates the dollar amount loss to the entire CLOUD operation annually as accrued by 1% increase in Loss of Load resulting from sparing the determined number of extra crew members.

Step 12: *Benefit* in default given as $30,000.00, which indicates the dollar amount of investment spent for each new crew member employed per year, hence amount saved when a crew is released.

Now let us see how to implement the effect of maintenance crews on unreliability index. In this analysis we will simulate for a reduced resource of Crew Intervals (e.g., *50, 100, 150, 200, …*). Consider a large cyber CLOUD example where the total number of available units served by the same number of serving crew units available is 443. Now let us simulate for the reduced resource of 50 crews as in Figure 7.21 to see the impact that how unreliability will vary with the reduction of crew. Initially the unreliability varies slightly; at one point it increases in a drastic manner,which is called break-even point. The CLOUD should not lower the repair crews to less than the break-even point. Figure 7.21 shows the output for the above input. For the above input, with 2000data.txt, the stopping crew value is 143.

Profit/Loss: This indicates whether there is profit or loss by stopping at the optimal point. If cost of the LoLP increasing is greater than the benefit of sparing (saving) repair crew members, then it is Loss (negative value). If cost is less than benefit, then it is Profit (positive value).

Break-Even Value: This indicates the cost per percent for LoLP index required to have neither profit nor loss.

Step 13: *Solution* is as follows. Now $300 \times \$30K = \$9,000,000$ gained. $\Delta LoLP = 0.0126$ lost, that is, $0.0126 \times 100\% \times \$1M = \$1,260,000$. $\$9M - \$1.26M = \$7.74M$ or (+) $\$7,739,029$ exact benefit.

The Figure 7.21's cost–benefit portfolio of Reserve Crew Planning analysis will show how to save or lose millions of dollars' worth for a CLOUD Resource Management. Figure 7.22 plots the Crew Plan outcome. It also indicates what the break-even value would be if RHS = LHS in terms of cost and benefit such that the difference (profit or loss) is zero at balance. Further, as expected, Figure 7.23 depicts the triplet of operating modes (up, down, and waiting) where additionally waiting time is now a reality due to imperfect number of repair crews.

7.6.1.2 *Some Further Validations on Crew Planning* When stopping crew value and stopping LoLP value are zero, a message indicates to simulate again with different $\Delta LoLP$ crew constraint as red-flagged in Figure 7.24. This message that the analyst needs to enter a new set of feasible input values is also shown in Figure 7.25.

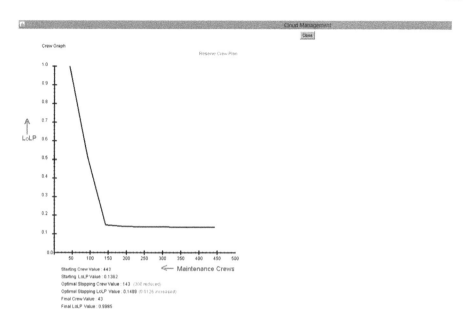

FIGURE 7.22   Output graph in response to input in Figure 7.21 for 1000 runs with 443 repair crews.

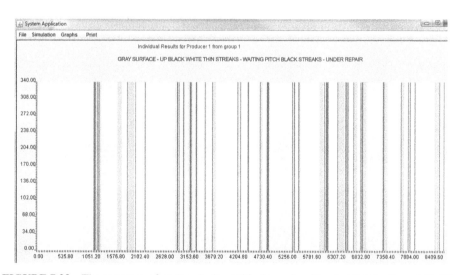

FIGURE 7.23   The sequence of up (gray), down (black), and waiting (white) for Group1 Unit1.

7.6.2   CLOUD Resource Management Planning by Production Deployment

One may want to add or discard certain cyber servers (or producers in general such as power plants at a power CLOUD scenario) by reorganizing the list of groups' units [54]. One can experiment with more or less number of servers at selected capacities to see how reliability may be affected. When, as in Figure 7.22, the reliability is drastically reduced by

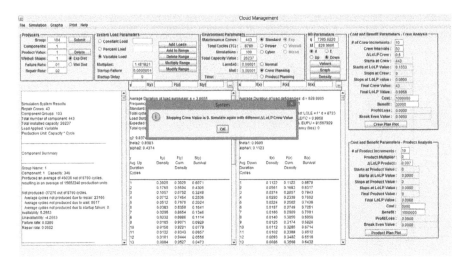

FIGURE 7.24 Output dialogue box for Figure 7.20's input for 100 runs when a new set of input is required.

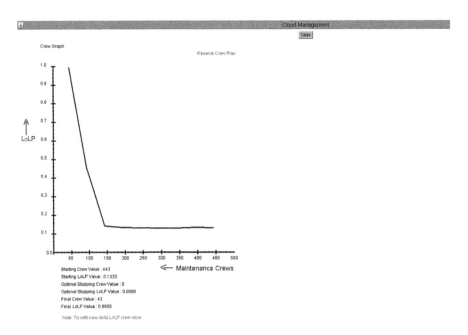

FIGURE 7.25 Plot of the LoLP (risk) versus # maintenance crews requiring a new set of input.

deploying only 50 in place of an original 348, then one may also want to see the operating/wait/repair times to see how a particular unit behaves due to appended capacity to handle more demand. If compared to Figure 7.15, one may see the change from all operating and repair times to the one showing the operating, repair and wait times for every unit in the system as in Figure 7.23. That way all units can be traced and tracked to take timely remedial measures to plan ahead.

7.6.2.1   Step-by-Step Algorithm CLOUD Management Planning for Additional Product Deployment   Follow the below steps to implement Product Reserve Planning:

Step 1: Radio button *Product Planning* must be selected as shown in Figure 7.26.

Step 2: *# of Product Increments* in default is given as 10, which indicates the number of product intervals required to plot a graph.

Step 3: *Product Multiplier* in default is given as 1–4, which indicates the number of components multiplied for the horizontal axis, such as 1×100 MW or 4×100 MW or GB.

Step 4: *Δ%LoLP Product* in default is given as 20%, which indicates that if the difference between two (start and end) LoLP values is greater than 20% of the starting LoLP, then the capacity value stops at the lower LoLP value. The case study is for 2000data.txt

Step 5: *Starts at Product Value* is the initial total capacity value, which is 26,237.

Step 6: *Starts at LoLP Value* (0.1386) is the LoLP value for the initial total capacity value.

Step 7: *Stops at Product Value* (30,487) is the optimal stopping product value.

Step 8: *Stops at LoLP Value* (0.1099) is the optimal stopping LoLP with at least 20% of $0.1386 = 0.0277$ less.

Step 9: *Final Product Value* (30,487) is the total capacity at the end of the product planning.

Step 10: *Final LoLP Value* (0.0574) is the LoLP value for the total capacity at the end of the product planning, i.e. 30,487.

Step 11: *Cost* in default given as $5000, which indicates the dollar amount investment expense to the entire CLOUD operation for adding one MW or GB of extra production capacity.

Step 12: *Benefit* in default given as $1,500,000, which indicates the dollar amount gain to the entire CLOUD operation annually, as accrued by 1% increase in Loss of Load related, for one or more products to increase production.

Consider an example where the total number of producer groups available is 103 with 443 units, and starting total installed capacity is 26,237, as in Figure 7.27. *Add a new group, Group Name 104 with 0 component and product value 100* for 2000data.txt as shown in Figure 7.26. We will examine how any additional 100 MW or 100 GB units we will add to stop at the ΔLoLP is satisfied. For the above input, with 2000data.txt, the stopping product value is plotted in Figure 7.27.

Total Capacity Value: This is the total capacity value before incrementing product values.

Profit/Loss: This indicates whether there is profit or loss by stopping at breaking point.

Break-Even Value: This indicates the $ amount for 1% gain required to have resulted in neither profit nor loss. This cost–benefit portfolio of Reserve Product Planning analysis will save (+) or lose (−) millions of dollars' worth for a CLOUD Resource Management. The LoLP value displayed is truncated to round off after four digits following the decimal; this is why hand calculations and software outcomes may vary slightly, also due to #simulation runs.

Step 13: *Solution* is as follows. We can also observe stopping LoLP value, that is, the LoLP value for stopping product addition value, which is at 26,637 for above input, that is, with 200 MW or GB added. This denotes $850 \times \$5,000 = 4,250,000$ for investments. Also, the final LoLP value to stop at is 27,087 for the above input of Figure 7.26 as depicted in Figure 7.27. "ΔLoLP=0.0313" is the decrease in LoLP value. This denotes $0.0313 \times 100\% \times \$1.5M = \$4,695,000$ gain. The result is $\$4,695,000 - \$850 \times 5,000 = \$445,000$ (profit approximately). Figure 7.27 indicates the final solution to +$446,575.34 with exact pennies (Figs. 7.28, 7.29, 7.30, and 7.31).

7.6.2.2 Some Further Validations on Product Reserve Planning   When stopping product value and stopping LoLP value are output to be 0, a message indicates to simulate again with a different $\Delta\%$LoLP constraint, red-flagged in Figure 7.32.

Therefore, we can observe that unreliability decreases as the product value is increased. The CLOUD simulation should stop at a point, where there is no more return for increasing the percentage change on the LoLP.

If we happen to have "Stop at Product# is 0" as an output, one may decrease the $\Delta\%$LoLP Reduced Value, for instance, from 65 to 40% and simulate again with the new set of input constraint values. As we see in Figure 7.32, a dialogue box shows message to simulate again.

7.7   REMARKS FOR "PHYSICAL CLOUD" EMPLOYING PHYSICAL PRODUCTS (SERVERS, GENERATORS, COMMUNICATION TOWERS, ETC.)

Following the deterministic input data such as the number of servers or generators (or producers) with their failure and repair rates and number of repair crews and hourly (or cyclical) service demand that can be modified to reflect service maintenance or changes as explained earlier, all in gigabyte units as in Figure 7.30 and 7.31 for 1995data.tx for

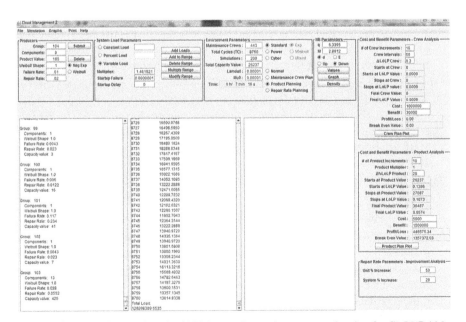

FIGURE 7.26   The dialogue box for 2000data.txt for product reserve planning for CLOURAM.

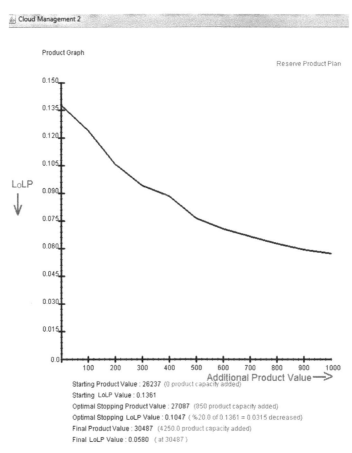

Starting Product Value : 26237 (0 product capacity added)
Starting LoLP Value : 0.1361
Optimal Stopping Product Value : 27087 (850 product capacity added)
Optimal Stopping LoLP Value : 0.1047 (%20.0 of 0.1361 = 0.0315 decreased)
Final Product Value : 30487 (4250.0 product capacity added)
Final LoLP Value : 0.0580 (at 30487)

FIGURE 7.27 Product Plot shows LoLP at 10.47% from 13.61% for 850+ capacity for 100 simulations.

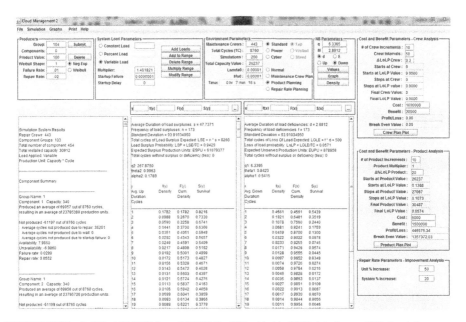

FIGURE 7.28 LoLP at 10.73% from 13.86% for 850 added in 2000 data for n = 200 simulation runs.

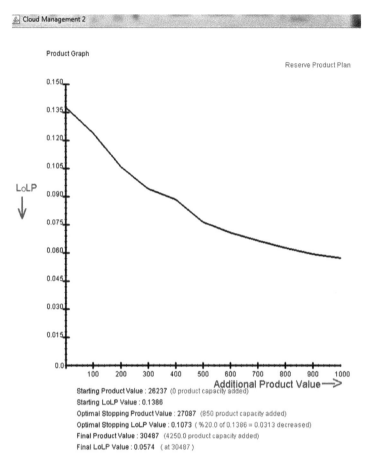

Product Graph

Reserve Product Plan

LoLP

Starting Product Value : 26237 (0 product capacity added)
Starting LoLP Value : 0.1386
Optimal Stopping Product Value : 27087 (850 product capacity added)
Optimal Stopping LoLP Value : 0.1073 (%20.0 of 0.1386 = 0.0313 decreased)
Final Product Value : 30487 (4250.0 product capacity added)
Final LoLP Value : 0.0574 (at 30487)

FIGURE 7.29 Product plot shows LoLP at 10.73% from 13.86% for 850+ capacity for 200 simulations.

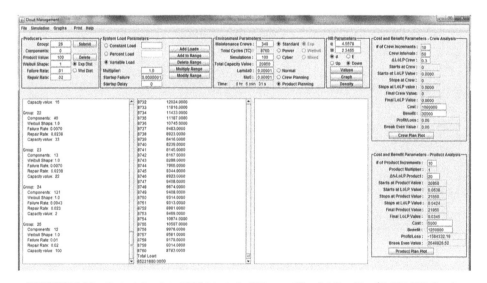

FIGURE 7.30 Output for data 1995data.tx in 100 runs (Fig. 7.16) with −$1,584,332 (loss).

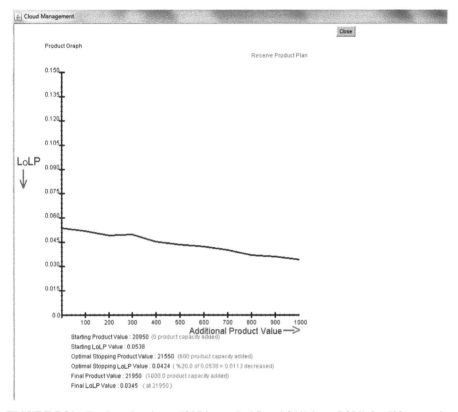

FIGURE 7.31 Product plot shows 1995data.tx LoLP at 4.24% from 5.38% for 600+ capacity.

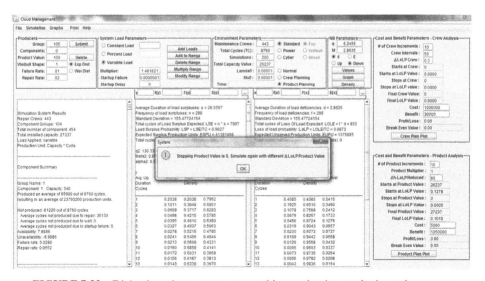

FIGURE 7.32 Dialog box shows up message asking to simulate again due to input error.

one example, the operation starts at the first hour (or cycle) by randomly generating the negative exponentially distributed operating (up) and repair (down) times where the goal is to study the random evolution of a memoryless system [3, 4]. Then the available total capacity at each cycle is contrasted against the outages to calculate the available capacity, which is also compared to the service demand at that hour to finally determine the reserve capacity.

If the reserve capacity (or margin) is less than a zero margin, then we have an undesired deficiency or LoL (Loss of Load). Once these hours (or cycles) of negative margin are added, it will constitute the expected number of hours of loss of load or service (LoLE). Divided by the total number of exposure units such as 8760 h (NHRS) for a year, it will give the LoLP = LoLE/NHRS. Once the LoLE is known, as well as its frequency (f = number of such occurrences of deficiencies per annum), then the average duration, d = LoLE/f, will indicate how long on the average an LoS is expected to last. If d stands for duration, as in Equation (7.10), $E(x) = d = (q-1)/\ln(q)$, one can best estimate the value of q using a Newton–Raphson nonlinear estimation technique, which later leads to the estimation of θ as in (7.11) and α as in (7.4). Then using (7.3), $f(x)$ for $x = 1$, 2, ... can be estimated to characterize the distribution of x. Further these probability values can be plotted. The similar can be duplicated for the operating cycles in the middle column of Figure 7.27 or similar. The plot for the LoLE, which is NBD, can be seen plotted in Figure 7.12 inspired from Figure 7.10. One may use Input Wizard in the Java software tool Help Desk to enter data both in physical and social in a step-by-step dialogue. Input Wizard uses are demoed in Figure 7.33.

7.8   APPLICATIONS TO "SOCIAL (HUMAN RESOURCES) CLOUD"

This modified implementation of CLOURAM simulates by mimicking the future Human Resources (HR) (such as Human Resources Group (HRG) in county or city police/fire department or hospital service) personnel activities if the proper "personnel input" and "customer service demand" are fed into the program. Input data about personnel with their daily working habits of how often they fail to come to work (rate of absence for whatever reasons) or how long it takes to recover (rate of recovery) from their expected absence and their daily working hourly capacities in a merit order will be entered. Also load (or service) demand hours expected to perform from the existing personnel will be entered as input. Outcomes will appear as percentage (or unreliability) of supply for not satisfying the demand (service) hourly or daily curve and also how many work hours lost. Graphical diagrams will illustrate at what stage of the work exposure period we are experiencing these unfavorable lost hours of workforce. This is after, for example, we run 1000 times a period of 100 days or 6 months or a year of HRG (a generic term to be used from now on) activity ahead. Also for each responder in each group, we can see on the average where First Responder Groups (FRG) personnel are failing to contribute so that we can work on remedial countermeasures regarding those weak spots. Last but not least, we can also execute backup or reserve personnel contingencies. Say, we have 20% backup reserve in the payroll, or we have only maybe 5% or less, so that we can count on the expenses. This tool proves useful for planning manpower to schedule or economize workforce. It is based on logical principles rather than haphazard guesswork, which can vary from one supervisor to another [52].

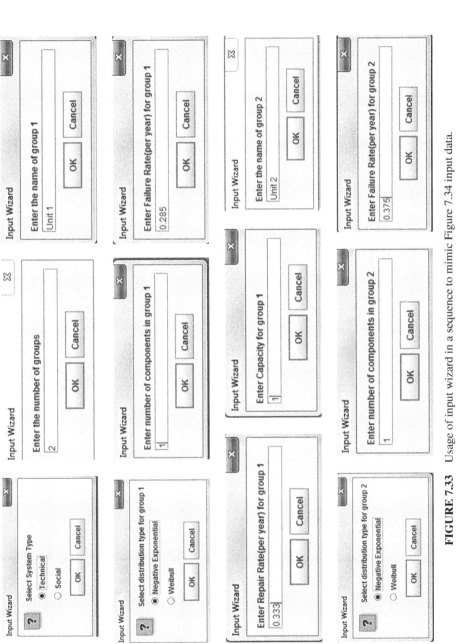

FIGURE 7.33 Usage of input wizard in a sequence to mimic Figure 7.34 input data.

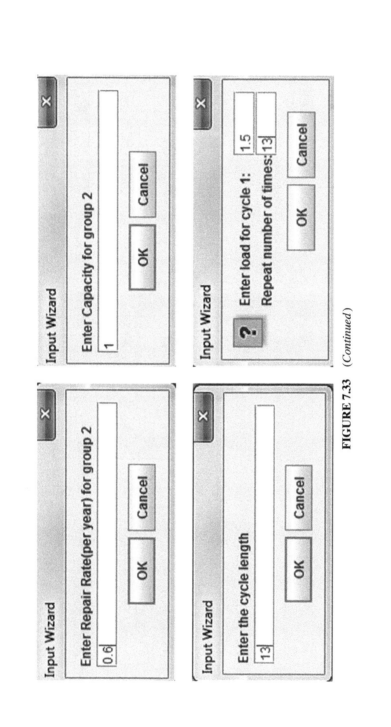

FIGURE 7.33 (*Continued*)

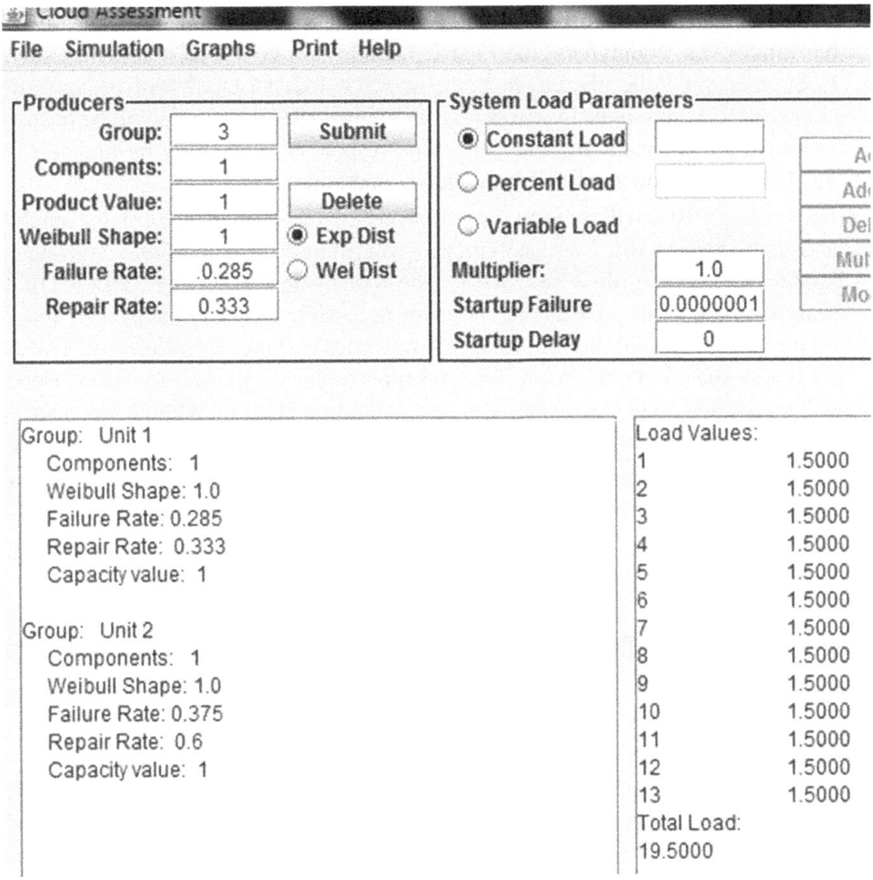

FIGURE 7.34 The input entered by Wizard in Figure 7.33 transformed to dialogue box.

What is the Motivation behind the Social CLOUD?

- Current lack of digital simulators for future HR availability planning.
- Incident commanders need to monitor HRG availability.
- Emergency response situations require efficient coordination and allocation of available resources that need to be controlled.
- Recent natural and man-made disasters have reinforced the need for stronger HRG response knowledge using objective IT solutions.

What does Social CLOUD implementation bring new to the table?

- A tested, peer-reviewed, accurate, and scalable algorithm.
- An insightful and meaningful system availability prediction model combined with historical resource and service data.
- Easy-to-implement, user-defined, and user-friendly easy-to-explain tool.
- This topic will be vital to HRG leaders monitoring availability.

- The topic team is proposing to model the daily operational realities of a defined but limited e.g. county/city, the First Responder Group's (FRG) activities such as Firefighters or Police Force. In doing so, SOCIAL CLOUD will be applied by collecting city/county historical data. City/county FRG operations will be positively impacted by assessing and managing first-responder availability by implementing this topic in the course of daily emergency operations.

- US regional HRGs will perform simulation tasks and assess an index of unavailability and then manage risk by responding to what-if remedial questions, conveniently applicable by using the CLOURAM (the tool name for SOCIAL CLOUD). The scalable and flexible program will be easily accessible for government FRG agencies with real-time availability improvement practices and preventive measures so as to act timely and efficiently. What-if queries offer usable projections for HRG reservists or backups and other operations with ease and minimal effort, without having to wait for a lengthy data collection to act.

- Finally, the development and implementation of the proposed application will significantly improve the area's emergency response capability. This tool not only assesses availability shortfalls but also enables emergency response planning in terms of staffing and maintenance.

7.8.1   Numerical Example for Social CLOUD (200 Employees Performing)

In a hypothetical HRG serving in a county's first responder or similar department, or a private banking or any small- or large-scale agency or corporation, there exist 8 groups, each of which contain 25 servers, a total of 200 employees. As in Figure 7.34, the first ranking (in merit order) Group 1 with 25 servers who perform with a capacity of 10 h/day have an absence (sickness or else) of 1 in 100 days (0.01/day) and recovery (return) of 1/day. This indicates that absentees, once in 100 days, return after a day of absence from the work on the average.

Assuming the times to absence and recovery are negative exponentially distributed, for the sake of example, with mean time to absence (1/absence rate = 1/0.01 = 100 days) and mean time to recovery (1/return rate = 1/1 = 1 day). If other distributions are desired, then one can utilize the Weibull option (Weibull = 1 means default case of negative exponential) other than Weibull Shape Parameter = 1. This continues until eight groups are completed as captured in two separate screenshots in Figure 7.35. Load (or service demand) values are displayed for 1000 days of service each at a constant 1200 required hours of service/day as a constant example. Disregard the variable load button as this was for a new scenario.

However, varying load values can be also entered at will as well as vacation time. A maintenance or backup reservist cadre of ideal 200 employees is set aside. The unreliability (probability) of not meeting the demand is 6.21% using the input data in Figure 7.34 evident from output in Figure 7.36 after 1000 simulations covering 1000 h of demanded service. It takes 30 s to perform 1000 times 1000 h of exposure time. In Figure 7.37, this time only 2 backups are used to cover a base of 2000 employees. The probability of not meeting the demand (unreliability) increases to 23.3% from an earlier 6.21%. In fact, there is no improvement of reliability all the way from 200 down to 4. This means that there is no need to keep a reservist cadre more than 5 backup employees so as not to waste money by overinvesting (Fig. 7.37). One can then implement the reserve crew planning to determine an optimal crew size as done in Section 7.6.1.

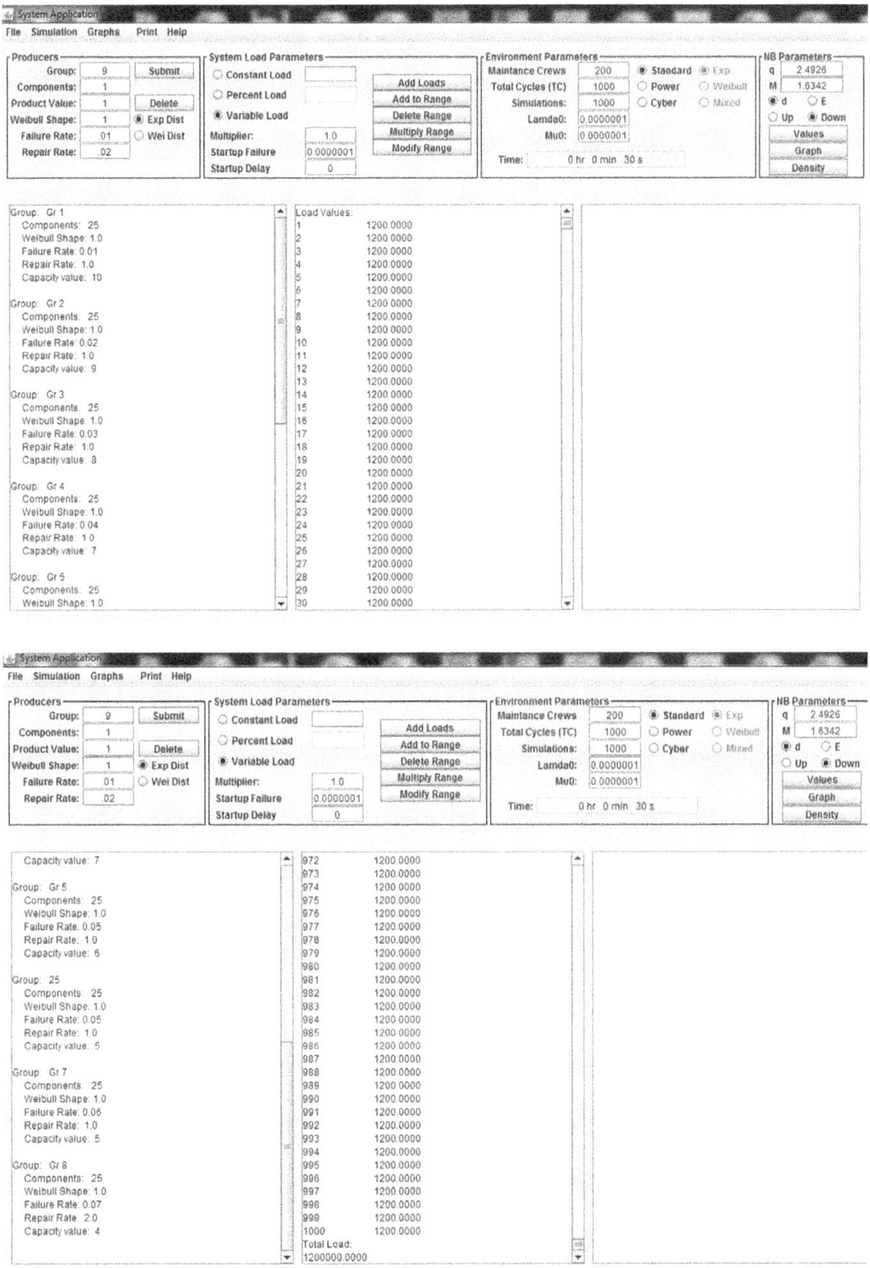

FIGURE 7.35 Input data in two separate dialogues for 200 personnel and 1000 load cycles.

New what-if scenarios, other than backups, such as modifying the load values and # of employees in the workforce can be simulated to see how much can be saved. This way of digitally simulating saves money and time by mimicking the future HR operations rather than waiting for year to observe what happens by trial and error. This practice by simulating

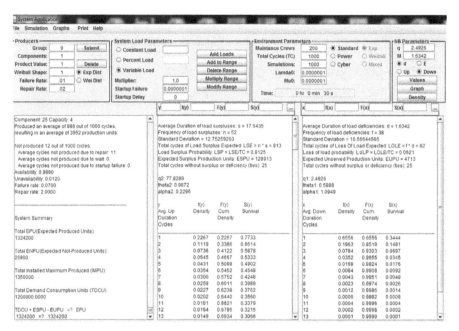

FIGURE 7.36   The CLOURAM output for the input in Figure 7.34 for 200 repair crews.

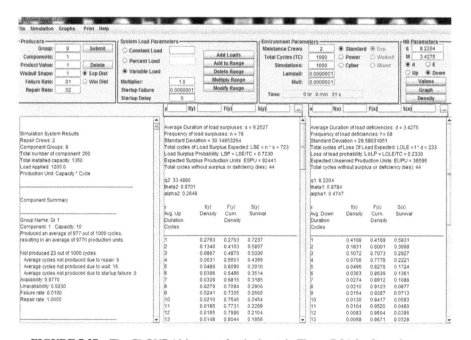

FIGURE 7.37   The CLOURAM output for the input in Figure 7.34 for 2 repair crews.

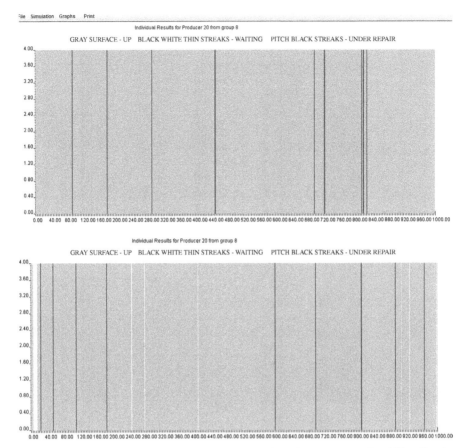

FIGURE 7.38   The individual (e.g., Group 8 server 20) for 1000 cycles regarding 200 and backups. Above: no black white thin streaks time windows appear for waiting due to perfectly sufficient backup personnel. Below: black white thin streaks windows due to backups to arrive before servers return to work, gray surface after absent, pitch black streaks.

the future operations is wiser and cheaper. Figure 7.38 shows one individual unit's performance cycle, whether red (off), green (on), or yellow (waiting to return to work).

7.8.2   Input Wizard Example for Social CLOUD (200 Employees Performing)

The following screenshots in Figure 7.39 illustrate how Input Wizard in the CLOUD Assessment Java tool enters the data for Figure 7.35 through a sequence of dialogue boxes, from left to right and top to bottom for the load data (Fig. 7.40).

7.9   STOCHASTIC CLOUD SYSTEM SIMULATION

Generally in cyber or power grid modeling and simulations, the failure rate, repair rate, and capacity of servers or generators and transmission lines or links, load (demand) on grid, and count of repair crew are collected as deterministic constants from external

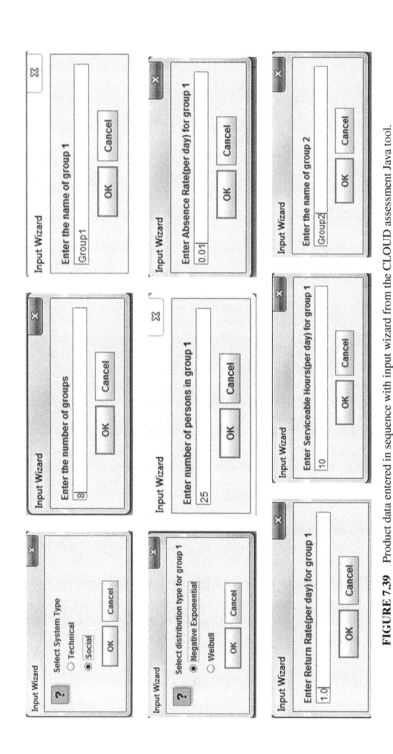

FIGURE 7.39 Product data entered in sequence with input wizard from the CLOUD assessment Java tool.

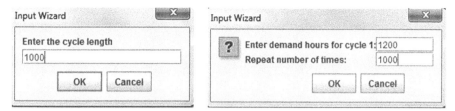

FIGURE 7.40 Load data entered in sequence with input wizard from the CLOUD Java tool for Fig. 7.35.

sources. CLOURAM is a risk assessment and management application that has been used to emulate a grid, where simulation is applied using failure and repair rates for a given group whose assigned failure and repair rate data and load remain constant across iterations. In this modified version of CLOURAM through Stochastic Simulation, randomizing CLOUD parameters such as failure and repair rates and the load cycle, the CLOUD metrics are compared favorably to those employing deterministic data to verify and validate [51]. Due to Cyber CLOUD air-medium's link data missing, only Power Systems' grid scenarios as examples will be studied.

First, we verify the conventional results through test runs by conducting Stochastic Simulation (SS). Once the verification process is carried out successfully, that is, the CLOUD non-SS metrics are compared favorably to those employing deterministic data; grid producer and link scenarios will be studied such as in the event of the links no more being perfectly reliable, but operating with specified values through uniform, or negative exponential input data assumptions. These will be executed in the examples of Sections 7.9.3–7.9.6. This innovative section illustrates that we can include lump-sum grid transmission (link) data as an averaging effect in the simulation of cyber or power CLOUD performance. Additionally, this algorithm can be used for any other stochastic (random) data entry for the producers as well as the links. The versatility of the algorithm stems from a wide area of usage by leveraging the Weibull distribution (whose default is negative exponential and used extensively for failures). In the event of the nonexistence of sophisticated data such as Weibull or similar, the analyst may use uniform deviations with percentages as shown in the examples of Sections 7.9.3–7.9.6. For further depth in this area, the author will seek the power grid data from electric power industry to compare practical results [51].

7.9.1 Introduction and Methodology

For a power or cyber grid scenario, the following tasks are vital. Thus one is expected to:

- Specify the generator or server (both producers) and transmission line (or link) failure and repair rates separately.
- Study the effect of different load distributions using SS. Load probability distributions supported are normal probability densities.
- Study the effect of different failure distributions using SS. Failure probability distributions supported are posterior gamma (empirical Bayesian) and uniform alternatively upon choice.
- Study the effect of different repair distributions using SS. Repair probability distributions supported are similarly posterior gamma and uniform.

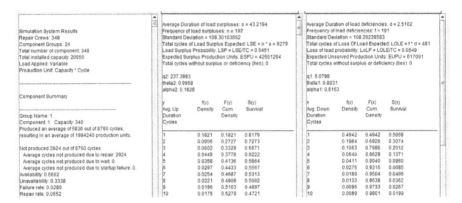

FIGURE 7.41 The LoLP = 5.49% outcome for the 348 units system with full maintenance, not applying stochastic simulation (SS).

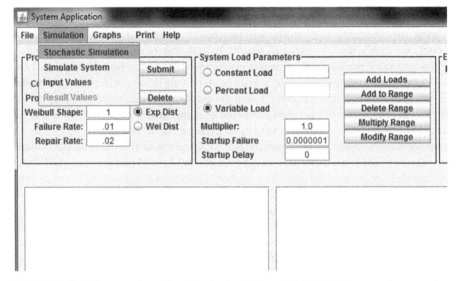

FIGURE 7.42 The appending of stochastic simulation to CLOURAM as a new icon to select.

In the following, the large power or cyber CLOUD system of 348 units (95data.txt) will be taken as an example as in Figure 7.41 to follow and compare to the earlier result of ≈5.5% LoLP.

User inputs normally collected grid data in one of the following ways:

1. Input wizard
2. Manual entry for each group
3. Import data that was saved earlier in CLOURAM required format

A new menu item "Stochastic Simulation" (SS) is added to "Simulation" menu in CLOURAM (CLOUD Risk Assessment and Management) studied in detail as follows in Figure 7.42. NS will denote non-SS. The following displays initial screen when user clicks Stochastic Simulation after importing data.

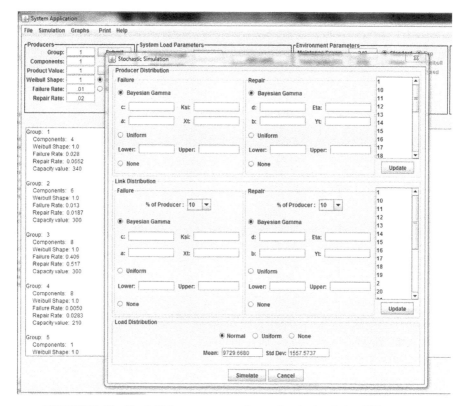

FIGURE 7.43 The initial screen to start the stochastic simulation (SS) process.

FIGURE 7.44 Dialogue box when producer probability distribution is negative exponential.

Figure 7.43 displays the initial screen when the user clicks Stochastic Simulation after importing the data.

7.9.1.1 Product Distributions (When Product Data Is in Negative Exponential)

Posterior (empirical Bayesian) gamma distribution is used [3, Chapter 5] (see Fig. 7.44). For Producer Group 1 with failure rate = 0.028 and repair rate = 0.0552, flat (noninformative) parameters are $c = ksi = d = eta = 0$, $a = 28$, $X_t = 1000$, $b = 552$, and $Y_t = 10,000$. This data is inspired from large CLOUD input (95data.txt) in Ref. [25, Fig. 17]. To generate random failure and repair rates, the empirical Bayesian posterior gamma distribution is used.

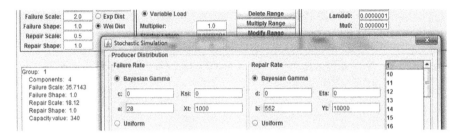

FIGURE 7.45 Dialogue box when product probability distribution is in Weibull.

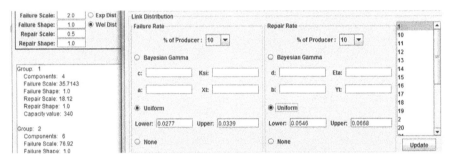

FIGURE 7.46 Dialogue box when producer probability distribution is in Weibull and link probability distribution is in uniform.

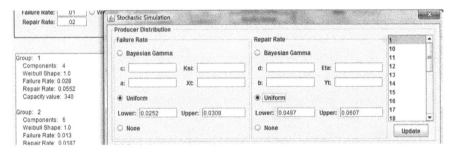

FIGURE 7.47 If uniform is used, default values are +10% of corresponding rates for lower and upper with producer probability distribution in negative exponential.

7.9.1.2 Product Distributions (When Product Data Is in Weibull) For the Product Group 1 with failure scale = 35.7143 and repair scale = 18.12, parameters are $c = ksi = d = eta = 0$, $a = 28$, $X_t = 1000$, $b = 552$, and $Y_t = 10,000$ (see Fig. 7.45).

7.9.1.3 Link Distributions (When Data Is Negative Exponential or Weibull) with Uniform and Bayesian Gamma Applied First, transmission failures and repair rates are computed by applying rules when the producer data is in Weibull or negative exponential. Then link failure rate = +10% of the producer failure rate and repair rate = +10% of the producer repair rate as an initiating example. Other parameters follow the same rules as above (see Figs. 7.46, 7.47, and 7.48).

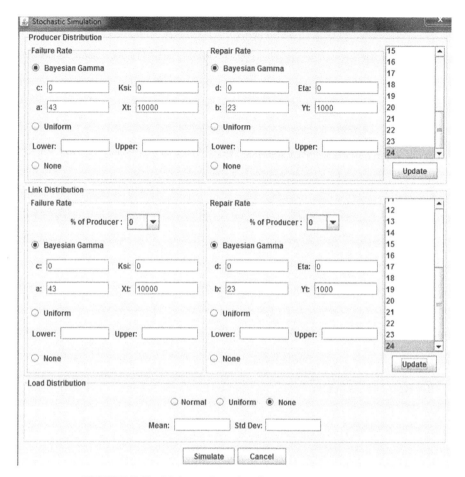

FIGURE 7.48 Links are Bayesian Gamma same as producers.

7.9.2 Numerical Applications for SS to Verify Non-SS

7.9.2.1 SS with Bayesian Gamma Input for Producers and Normal for Load with Perfect Links
Taking the same example as in Section 7.9.1, the first step is to express the rate as a ratio; for example, failure rate 0.028 is identical to 28/1000. Now, a numerator is assigned to "a" and a denominator is assigned to "X_t" and also the prior parameters "c" and "ksi" are set to zero. Along the same line, the repair rate 0.0552 is $552/10{,}000 \Rightarrow {}'b' = 552$; "$Y_t$" = 10,000. "$d$" and "$\eta$" (eta) are set to zero. See Figure 7.49 for input data. Figure 7.50 has outputs nearly same.

7.9.2.2 SS with Equal Failure and Repair Uniform Variation for Links and Normal for Load When Producer Data Is in Negative Exponential
Let's see the effect of varying link (transmission line in case of a power or cyber grid) failure and repair rates using the negative exponential. So, taking link failure and repair rates identical as +10% and LOAD mean = 9729.67 and LOAD standard deviation = 1557.5, we get

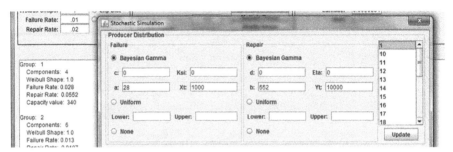

FIGURE 7.49   Bayesian Gamma probability distribution input template for stochastic simulation.

FIGURE 7.50   SS LoLP = 5.66%; NSS-LoLP = 5.49% for 348 units with load random.

FIGURE 7.51   If uniform is used, default values are +10% of corresponding rates for lower and upper.

an output not much changed due to 10% increases in failure and repair rates offsetting each other (see Figs. 7.51 and 7.52).

LoLP as in Figure 7.51 revolves around the same: 5.75% as in the original nonstochastic (NS) result of 5.49% since increased failure rate of links has been offset by an equal increase in their repair rates.

7.9.2.3   SS with Unequal Failure and Repair Rates Uniform Variation for Links with All Else the Same   LoLP as expected decreases to 4.24% from 5.49 due to 20% increase in the repair rates (better maintenance) compared to 10% in the failure rates (see Fig. 7.53).

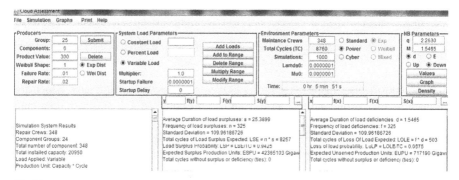

FIGURE 7.52 LoLP = 5.75% similar to LoLP = %5.49 when Figure 7.51 SS data for links.

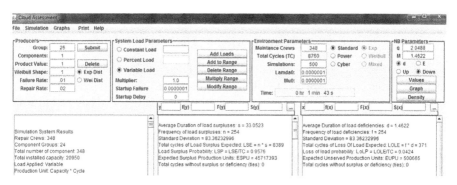

FIGURE 7.53 LoLP = 4.24%, that is, around 20% improved from 5.49% when both changes are identical = 10%.

7.9.3 Details of Probability Distributions Used in Stochastic Simulation

More details will be presented later in terms of statistical distributions used in the SS.

7.9.3.1 Empirical Bayesian Gamma Probability Distribution The gamma distribution is widely used as a conjugate prior in Bayesian statistics.

The results shown in many textbooks indicate that the residence times in the down state prior to the up state, or vice versa, are roughly exponentially distributed for most electronic hardware equipment. Let X_i and Y_j be the up and down times, respectively. The derivation of the Sahinoglu–Libby pdf is as follows [21]:

$$f(x_i) = \lambda \exp(-\lambda x_i), \quad i = 1, 2, \ldots, a, \quad \lambda > 0, \quad x_i > 0 \tag{7.21}$$

$$f(y_i) = \mu \exp(-\mu y_i), \quad j = 1, 2, \ldots, b, \quad \lambda > 0; \quad y_j > 0, \tag{7.22}$$

where a is the number of up times sampled and b is the number of down times sampled. Now let the generator failure rate, λ, and the repair rate μ, have independent prior distributions from the gamma family:

$$\theta_1(\lambda) = \frac{\xi^c}{\Gamma(c)} \lambda^{c-1} \exp(-\lambda \xi), \quad \lambda > 0 \tag{7.23}$$

where, for λ prior, c is a shape parameter and ξ is an inverse scale parameter and

$$\theta_2(\mu) = \frac{\eta^d}{\Gamma(d)} \mu^{d-1} \exp(-\mu\eta), \quad \mu > 0, \tag{7.24}$$

Note, for μ prior, d is a shape parameter, and η is an inverse scale parameter, which are all estimated by means of a suitable prior estimation technique. The posterior distributions of λ and μ will be obtained by mixing their priors with the data. See Sections 6.4.3.1 and 6.4.3.2.

Thus, the posterior distribution for λ was earlier derived to be

$$h_1(\lambda \mid \underline{x}) = \frac{k(x,\lambda)}{\int_\lambda f(\underline{x},\lambda)d\lambda} = \frac{\xi^c}{\Gamma(c)} \lambda^{a+c-1} \exp\left[-\lambda(x_T + \xi)\right] \div \frac{\xi^c}{\Gamma(c)} (x_T + \xi)^{-1} \Gamma(a+c)$$

$$= \frac{1}{\Gamma(a+c)} (x_T + \xi) \lambda^{a+c-1} \exp\left[-\lambda(x_T + \xi)\right], \tag{7.25}$$

which is Gamma$[a+c,(x_T + \xi)^{-1}]$ or Gamma $(n', 1/b')$ as earlier suggested due to the mathematical conjugacy property. The same arguments hold for the repair rate μ. That is,

$$h_2(\mu \mid \underline{y}) = \frac{1}{\Gamma(b+d)} (y_T + \eta) \mu^{a+c-1} \exp\left[-\mu(y_T + \eta)\right] \tag{7.26}$$

is the Gamma$[b+d,(y_T + \eta)^{-1}]$ or Gamma $(m', 1/a')$ posterior distribution for μ where b is the number of occurrences of down times sampled and y_T is the total sampled down times for b number of occurrences, usually $a=b$ or $a \approx b$.

Let Q be the random variable for the forced outage rate, FOR (unavailability) $= q = \lambda / (\lambda + \mu)$. Then derive its cdf where

$$G_Q(q) = P(Q \le q) = P\left(\frac{\lambda}{\lambda + \mu} \le q\right) = \text{Area}_1 \quad \text{where } 0 < q < 1 \tag{7.27}$$

Now, use the property that Gamma$(n', 1/b')$ has the moment generating function to be $\left(1 - \frac{t}{b}\right)^{n'}$. This is the m.g.f. of the Chi-square distribution with $2n'$ degrees of freedom. Then it follows

$$\frac{(2a'/2m')\mu \sim \chi_{2m'}^2 / 2m'}{(2b'/2n')\lambda \sim \chi_{2n'}^2 / 2n'} = F_{2m',2n'}, \tag{7.28}$$

which is the F_{df_1,df_2} distribution with numerator $df_1 = 2m'$ and denominator $df_2 = 2n'$.

From earlier $G_Q(q)$ in (7.9) by taking reciprocals of both sides and switching the inequality sign, we obtain

$$G_Q(q) = P\left(\frac{\lambda + \mu}{\lambda} \ge \frac{1}{q}\right) = P\left(1 + \frac{\mu}{\lambda} \ge \frac{1}{q}\right) = P\left(\frac{\mu}{\lambda} \ge \frac{1}{q} - 1\right) \tag{7.29}$$

Multiplying both sides of the inequality of (7.31) above by $a'n'/b'm'$, one obtains

$$G_Q(q) = P\left[\frac{(2a'/2m')\mu}{(2b'/2n')\lambda} > \frac{a'n'}{b'm'}(q^{-1}-1)\right] = P\left[F_{2m',2n'} > C_1 = \frac{a'n'}{b'm'}(q^{-1}-1)\right] \quad (7.30)$$

$$= \text{Area}_2$$

In other words, we obtain an equivalent Area$_2$ for the solution of $P(F_{2m',2n'} > C_1)$ in (7.28), instead of attempting to calculate the unknown Area$_1$ for Equation (7.29) whose distributional form is not known or not even recognized. That is, Area$_1$ = Area$_2$. Now that we have an accurate representation of the cdf of Q [i.e., $G_Q(q)$], let's find its mathematical expression by equating Area$_1$ to Area$_2$ [18] (Fig. 7.54):

$$G_Q(q) = 1 - G_{F_{2m',2n'}}\left[\frac{a'n'}{b'm'}(q^{-1}-1)\right] \quad (7.31)$$

Note that Snedecor's F density is given by [15, p. 23]

$$f(F) = \frac{\Gamma\left[(m+n)/2\right]}{\Gamma(m/2)\Gamma(n/2)}\left(\frac{m}{n}\right)^{m/2}\frac{F^{(m-2)/2}}{\left[1+(m/n)F\right]^{(m+n)/2}}, \quad 0 < F < \infty \quad (7.32)$$

where

$$\mu = E(F) = \frac{n}{n-2}, \quad \text{for } n > 2, \quad (7.33)$$

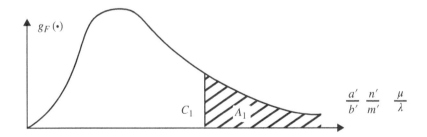

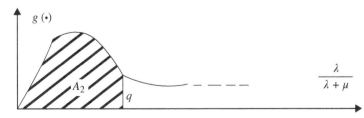

FIGURE 7.54 A_1=Area$_1$ (known "F" distribution) and A_2=Area$_2$ (unknown "q" distribution) illustrated.

$$\sigma^2 = \text{Var}(F) = \frac{2n^2(m+n-2)}{m(n-2)^2(n-4)} \quad \text{for } n > 4 \text{ and } F > 0 \tag{7.34}$$

Since (7.31) is differentiable, using (7.32) and differentiating with respect to q through obeying the differential chain rule leads to (note that $m' = m/2$ and $n' = n/2$)

$$
\begin{aligned}
g_Q(q) &= -g_{F_{2m',2n'}}\left[\frac{a'n'}{b'm'}\left(q^{-1}-1\right)\right]\left[-\frac{a'n'}{b'm'}\left(\frac{1}{q^2}\right)\right] \\
&= \frac{a'n'}{b'm'}\left[\frac{1}{q^2}\left(\frac{m'}{n'}\right)^{m'}\right]\frac{\Gamma(m'+n')}{\Gamma(m')\Gamma(n')}\frac{\left\{\left[(a'n'/b'm')\left(\frac{1}{q}-1\right)\right]^{m'-1}\right\}}{\left\{\left[1+\frac{m'a'n'}{n'b'm'}\left(\frac{1}{q}-1\right)\right]^{m'-n'}\right\}}
\end{aligned}
\tag{7.35}
$$

Simplifying and rearranging through a number of intermediate steps yields

$$
\begin{aligned}
g_Q(q) &= \frac{\Gamma(m'+n')}{\Gamma(m')\Gamma(n')}\frac{a'^{m'}}{b'^{m'}}\frac{(1-q)^{m'-1}}{\left\{\left[1+(a'/b')(1/q-1)\right]^{m'+n'}\right\}}\frac{1}{q^2q^{m'-1}} \\
&= \frac{\Gamma(m'+n')}{\Gamma(m')\Gamma(n')}\frac{(1-q)^{m'-1}}{qq^{m'}}\left\{\frac{\left[(b'q+a'(1-q))\right]^{m'}\left[b'q+a'(1-q)\right]^{n'}}{\left[b'q\frac{a'}{b'}\right]^{m'}\left[b'q'\right]^{n'}}\right\}^{-1}
\end{aligned}
\tag{7.36}
$$

$$g_Q(q) = \frac{\Gamma(m'+n')}{\Gamma(m')\Gamma(n')}a'^{m'}b'^{n'}\frac{(1-q)^{m'-1}q^{n'-1}}{\left[a'+q'(b'-a')\right]^{m'+n'}} \tag{7.37}$$

Resubstituting for $n' = a+c$, $m' = b+d$, $b' = \xi + x_T$ and $a' = \eta + y_T$, we obtain

$$
g_Q(q) = \frac{\Gamma(a+b+c+d)}{\Gamma(a+c)\Gamma(b+d)}(\eta+y_T)^{b+d}(\xi+x_T)^{a+c} \\
\frac{(1-q)^{b+d-1}q^{a+c-1}}{\left[\eta+y_T+q'(\xi+x_T-\eta-y_T)\right]^{a+b+c+d}}
\tag{7.38}
$$

which is the pdf of the random variable $0 < Q < 1$ as defined earlier for the underlying distributional assumptions. Similarly one can summarize as in a nutshell taken from Equations (7.23) and (7.24) both posterior gamma pdf as in reference [18].

Taking the same example as in Section 7.9.2, the first step is to express the rate as a ratio; for example, the failure rate 0.028 is identical to 28/1000. Now, a numerator is assigned to "a" and a denominator is assigned to "X_t" and also the prior parameters "c" and "ksi" are set to zero. Along the same argument, the repair rate 0.0552 is $552/10,000 \Rightarrow 'b' = 552$; "$Y_t$" = 10,000. "$d$" and "$\eta$" (eta) are set to zero (Fig. 7.55).

When the product data is in Weibull, first take the inverse of scale (failure or repair) and then proceed with expressing it as a ratio as demoed earlier. Finally, for a given group, default values for Stochastic Simulation's gamma distribution input variables are taken to be the same, irrespective of whether failure and repair rates or the shape and scale parameters of failure and repair are known. See Section 7.9.3 for further details.

7.9.3.2 Uniform (Rectangular) Distribution
Uniform distribution treats that all values have the same likelihood over interval (a, b):

$$f(x) = \begin{cases} \dfrac{1}{\beta - \alpha}, & \alpha \le x \le \beta \\ 0, & \text{otherwise} \end{cases} \tag{7.39}$$

To generate random number from uniform distribution, we use the below formula:

$$x^* = \alpha + (\beta - \alpha)u_i \tag{7.40}$$

where $u_i = U(0,1)$ is generated through software and α and β are the lower and upper values, respectively. Default values are +10% of the corresponding rates. For example, for Group 1 with failure rate = 0.028 and repair rate = 0.0552, the lower and upper values are set to 0.0252, 0.0308 and 0.0497, 0.0607, respectively (Fig. 7.56).

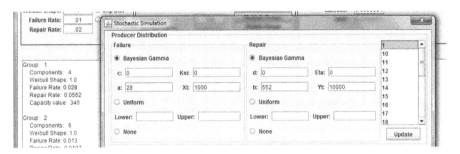

FIGURE 7.55 Bayesian Gamma probability distribution template for stochastic simulation.

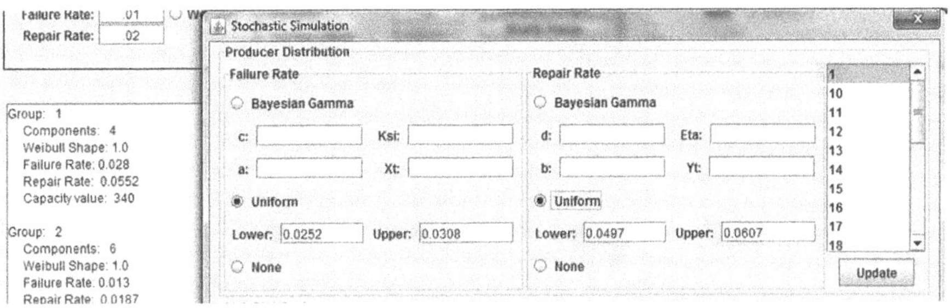

FIGURE 7.56 If uniform is used, default values are +10% of corresponding rates for lower and upper.

7.9.3.3 *Normal (Gaussian) Distribution* To generate random deviate from normal distribution, we use the below formula:

$$x^* = \mu + X_i\sigma$$

$$\text{where } X_1 = \sqrt{\left(-2\ln u_2\right)}\sin 2\pi u_1 ,$$ (7.41)

$$X_2 = \sqrt{\left(-2\ln u_2\right)}\cos 2\pi u_1$$

For load values from 95data.txt [25], number of load values = 8760, sum of load values = 85,231,880, mean = 9729.67, and standard deviation = 1557.57 (Fig. 7.57).

7.9.3.4 *Stochastic Simulation Results* Let's consider actual data taken in 1995 from a power or cyber CLOUD system to run an SS example. LSP and LoLP for 348 units and 348 maintenance crews for 1000 simulations are as follows. The deviation from the original LoLP = 5.44% in Figure 7.16 is minuscule since the new LoLP = 5.49%. Take load constant for now.

Let's now examine by varying load as a random deviate using normal distribution by taking mean and standard deviation of given input as in Figure 7.55. LSP and LoLP = 5.76% of this Stochastic Simulation are almost the same as that is in Figure 7.16 with an original LoLP = 5.44%. This is to verify the validity of the SS (Figs. 7.58 and 7.59).

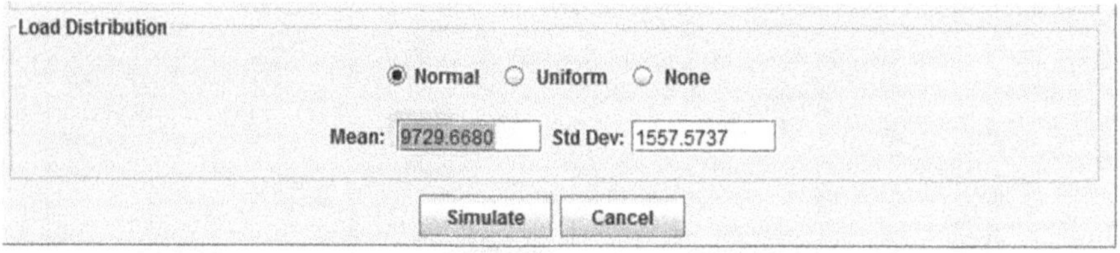

FIGURE 7.57   Load (demand) probability distribution; hourly load cycle to vary randomly.

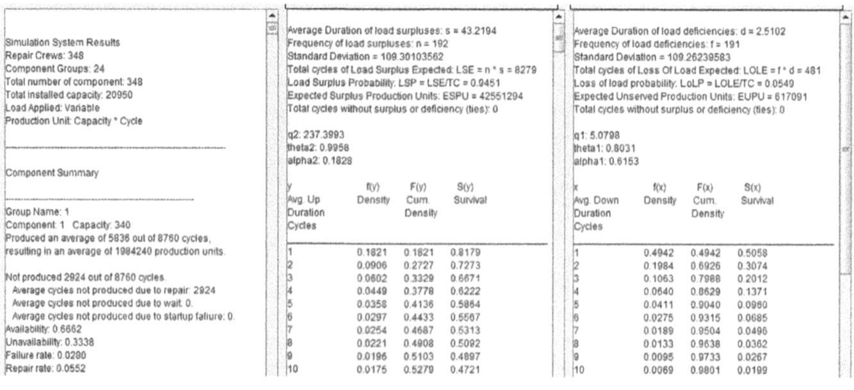

FIGURE 7.58   The LoLP = 5.49% outcomes for the 348 units system with full maintenance (=348 units).

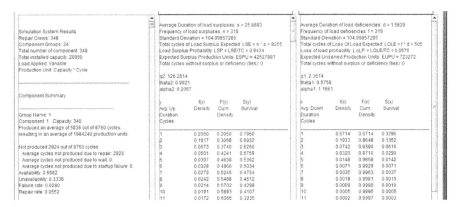

FIGURE 7.59 The LoLP = 5.76% for the 348 units 1995 system when load is treated as random.

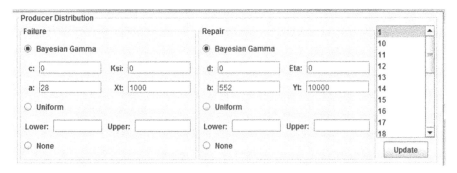

FIGURE 7.60 The 348 unit system outcomes when the failure and repair rates are random, not constant.

7.9.4 Varying Product Repair and Failure Date with Empirical Bayesian Posterior Gamma Approach

Let's see the effect of varying producer (a generator in case of power grid) failure and repair rates using Bayesian Gamma Distribution. For Producer Group 1 with failure rate = 0.028 and repair rate = 0.0552, parameters are $c = \xi$ (ksi) $= d = \eta$ (eta) $= 0$, and $a = 28$, $X_t = 1000$, $b = 552$ and $Y_t = 10{,}000$ (Fig. 7.60).

LSP = 94.32% and LoLP = 5.68% are as follows, which have negligible difference from the original LSP = 94.56% and LoLP = 5.44% copied from Figures 7.16 and 7.61.

7.9.5 Varying Link Repair and Failure Using Gamma Distribution

Let's see the effect of varying link (transmission line in case of a power grid) failure and repair rates using gamma distribution. Usually transmission (link) medium has a larger failure rate than a generator (producer). So, taking link failure rate as +10% of the generator failure rate and repair rate +10% of generator repair rate, other parameters follow the same rule as above (Fig. 7.62).

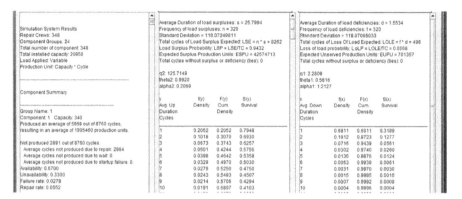

FIGURE 7.61   LoLP = 5.68% not much changed from 5.49% when Figure 7.52 random input data applied.

FIGURE 7.62   Link failure and repair rate as +10% of the generator failure and repair rate, respectively.

We observe that LSP and LoLP revolve around same values as in the original Figure 7.16 since increased failure rate of transmission lines has been offset by an increase in repair rate of transmission lines (Fig. 7.63).

7.9.6   SS Applied to a Power or Cyber Grid

7.9.6.1   With Negative Exponential Input for Failure and Repair Rates   After the verification processes in earlier sections where the Stochastic and NS (nonstochastic) outputs lead to almost identical results, we need to work on power grid scenarios this time for the estimation of system performance other than verification purpose (Fig. 7.64).

Let's suppose an electric power generation grid (1996data.txt) comprising 364 generating units of 28 groups composed of different variety of power plants [25]. See Figure 7.16 outputs for 1000 years of simulation if for 364 units, prompt maintenance attention with 364 repair crews is available. The unavailability or LoLP is 0.0812 or 8.12% for an average year over 1000 years.

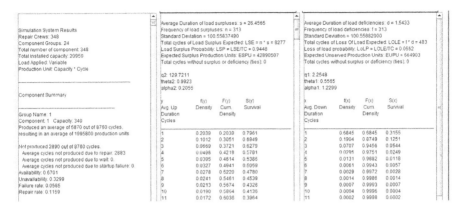

FIGURE 7.63 LoLP = 5.52% not much changed from 5.49% when Figure 7.53 random input data applied.

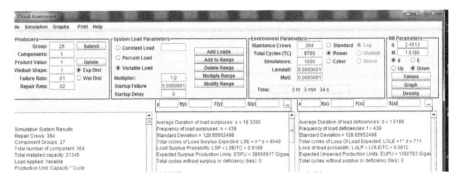

FIGURE 7.64 The 1996data.txt LoLP (0.0812 = 8.12%) for 1000 years without stochastic simulation (only non-SS).

We have earlier substantiated that when we randomize the producer parameters as well as that of the load, we verify to obtain the original results in a controlled experimental status (except for the unparalleled scenario that repair rates were 10% higher than those of failure rates). Therefore now with more changes, otherwise to reflect the grid input data, we will reach a stochastically (purely random) scenario. The output of Figures 7.43 or 7.44 is not a grid analysis but only that of production, that is, without any transmission lines (or links) and from purely generation-based data. However in power grid scenarios, each generating unit is attached to links to transmit the power generated by the units—hence the composite link.

Let's assume then that each power generating unit has failure and repair rates as identical inspired by the producer's data given for each group. Also assume that each unit is linked to its entire perimeter in supplying the generated energy specified by the identical failure and repair rates of the generating unit on the average. This is different than assuming 10% increase on the failure rates or 10% on the repair rates for an alternative "uniform distribution" study we presented in Figure 7.62. It has dropped to 7.08 from 8.12% due to now link in effect, that is, links not being perfectly reliable, thus averaging 1000 years of non-SS (Fig. 7.65).

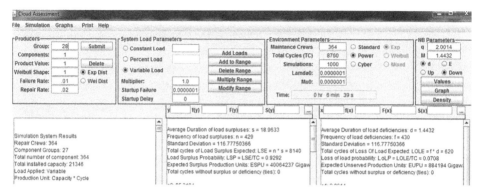

FIGURE 7.65   The LoLP increased to 7.08% from 5.49 with links activated having the same failure and repair rates as the generating units.

7.9.6.2   With the Weibull Input for Failure and Repair Rates   This time, the product failure and repair rate distributions are Weibull rather than negative exponential where the input dialogue box is as follows for a different 1995data.txt. The output for LoLP is approximately the same (=0.057) as the usual negative exponential assumption (=0.055) since shape parameters for both failure and repair are 1.0 for Weibull (Fig. 7.66).

Let's imagine a sample power grid with links connected to the entire set of generating units to possess the same lump-sum failure and repair rates as the units did assuming Weibull distributed failure and repair rates such as follows in a simulated sample topology (Fig. 7.67).

As a result of 1000 years of SS, while we assumed 348 generating units with the Weibull distributed failure and repair rates and the identical data for the links connected to each unit as a lump sum, we obtained an unavailability metric of LoLP (=0.0582) or 5.82%, that is, worse than the expected 5.49% in Figure 7.16. See now Figure 7.68. This was expected since the links worked with no more perfect availability, but carried certain failure and repair rates (Fig. 7.68).

7.9.7   Error Checking or Flagging

Error checks are made at every stage of SS. Error condition could be one such that user clicks Stochastic Distribution before loading group production and load data or one clicks update button without inputting both values required for given distribution or selecting group from right-hand list first and similar.

7.9.7.1   When and If Groups and Load Are Not Defined   See Figure 7.69.

7.9.7.2   When User Tries to Update Product Distribution without Selecting Its Group   See Figure 7.70.

7.9.7.3   When User Forgets to Input Required Values for a Given Distribution Updating   See Figure 7.71.

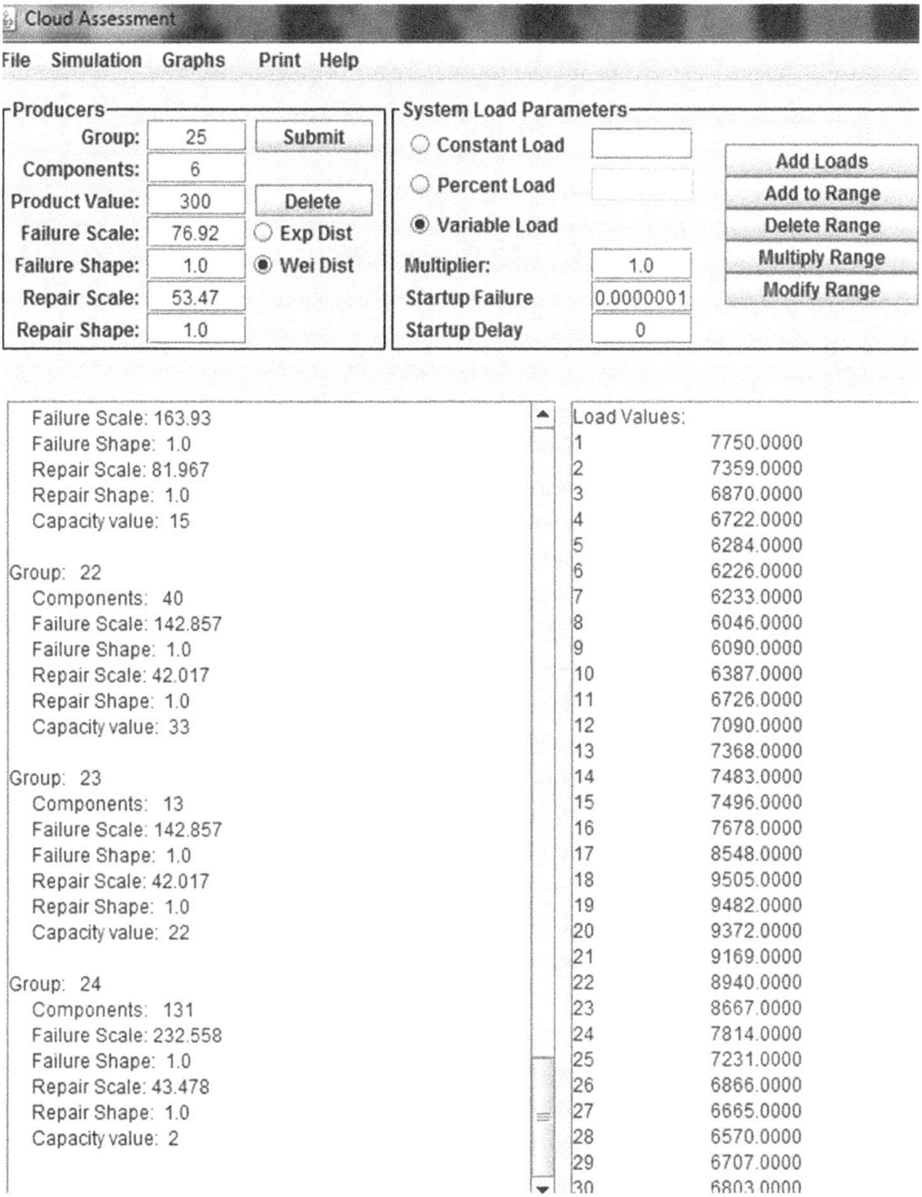

FIGURE 7.66 Weibull input failure and repair rates for 1995data.txt.

7.10 CLOUD RISK METER ANALYSIS

Many times, the management will not know how the receiving end or the CLOUD end user evaluates the network, in addition to the numerous self-assessment efforts executed by the CLOUD owners and managers who want to deliver a good product

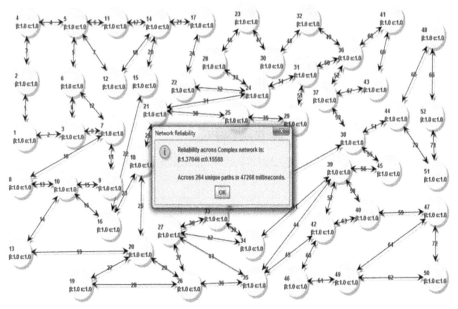

FIGURE 7.67   A sample complex telecom grid with 52 Weibull ($\alpha=1$, $\beta=1$) units and perfectly reliable links; output: Weibull$_{1-52}$ ($\alpha=1.37$, $\beta=0.16$).

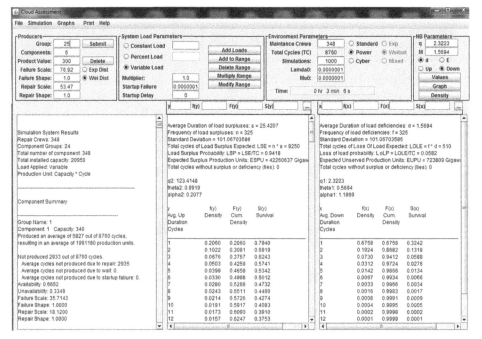

FIGURE 7.68   LoLP (=0.0582 = 5.82%) for 1995data.txt for power grid with Weibull parameters applied to both generating units and links.

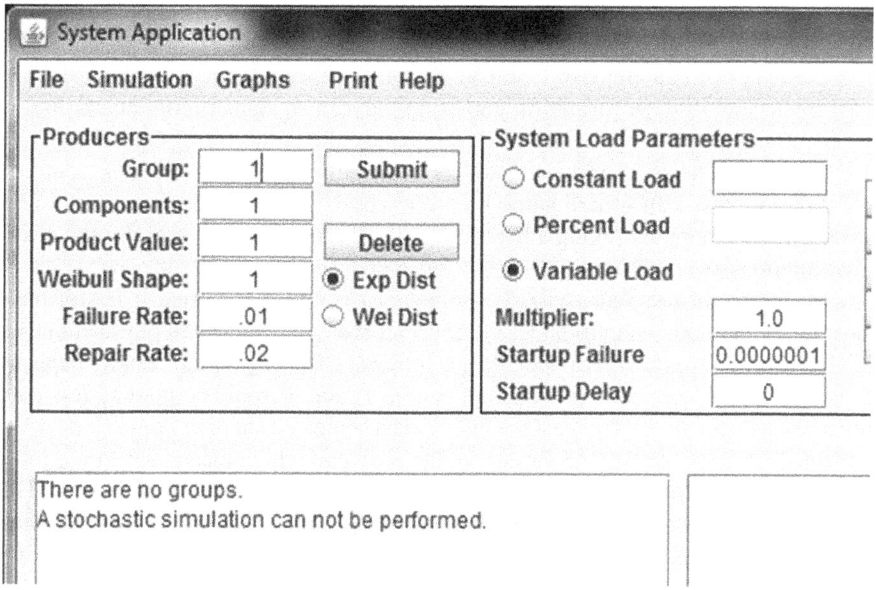

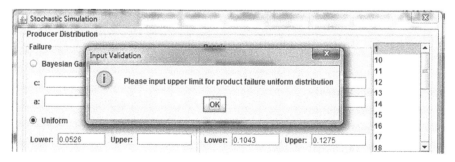

FIGURE 7.69 Red-flag warnings if groups are not defined properly.

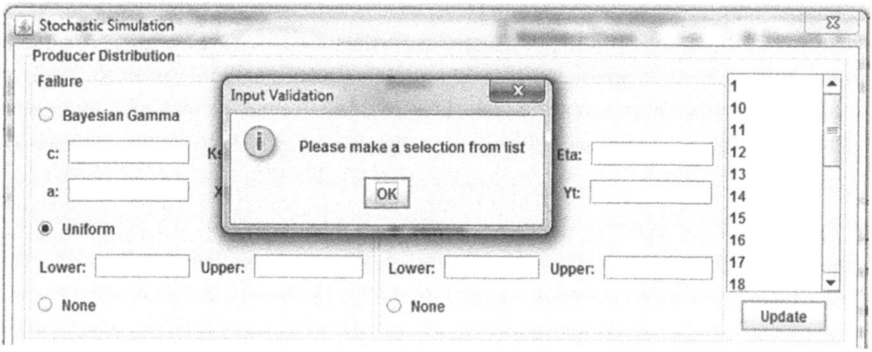

FIGURE 7.70 Red-flag warnings when user fails to update the group whose data is being modified.

FIGURE 7.71 Red-flag warnings when user forgets to input required data for a given distribution.

with minimal glitches. The hosting side will need to know what the customer base thinks so that the management (or host) can take countermeasures for the vulnerabilities that are threatened causing risk factor to increase without control. To that effect, the management has to do information gathering surveys of dynamic nature to find out what is missing. One such algorithm developed by the author is CLOUD Risk Meter (CLOUD RM). The proposed software tool not only can assess the risk content in percentage but also can utilize game-theoretic approaches that execute cost-minimal recovery management by taking a list of prioritized precautions to monitor the desired mitigation process [27, 28].

Even with all of the data centers' assurance of complete security, it is still unsafe to host important data on a virtual CLOUD server than on a dedicated physical machine [29, 30]. Some strong voices include as follows: "Imagine what would happen if the hackers gained access to thousands of people's data. It would be nothing less than a catastrophe (especially for businesses) and the data center would pretty much have to stop all or some outgoing data while they solve the problem, which means downtime for not only one, but a lot of clients and their sites and data" [31]. Boland studies Private CLOUD [32]. See Srinivasan and Getov for more details [33]. The CLOUD RM is an automated tool for information gathering, quantifying, assessing, and cost-effective managing risk. It further provides objective dollar-based mitigation advice, allowing the user to see where their funds will be best allocated to lower risk to an acceptable level. This section will examine CLOUD computing risk in the context of vulnerability categories (threats) presented and specific countermeasures [34, 35]. Threat countermeasures are used to mitigate risk and lower it to a desirable level.

Using game-theoretic optimization techniques, the user will see how his/her budgetary resource can be at best spent toward an optimal allocation plan, so as to lower the undesirable risk to a more tolerable level [27, 28]. In summary, innovative quantitative risk measurements are needed to objectively compare risk alternatives and manage risks as compared to conventional guesswork using hand calculators. The CLOUD RM has two versions imbedded. The CLOUD RM provider version is geared toward service providers and corporate users. The CLOUD RM client version is geared toward individual and smaller corporate end users, for whom a new vulnerability titled Client Perception (PR) and Transparency is included. Let's begin with a relevant comprehensive tree diagram as follows. Detailed list of vulnerabilities for CLOUD RM with related threats [27] is presented below.

Accessibility and Privacy Threats
- Insufficient Network-Based Controls
- Insider/Outsider Intrusion
- Poor Key Management and Inadequate Cryptography
- Lack of Availability

Software Capacity Threats
- Software Incompatibility
- Unsecure Code
- Lack of User-Friendly Software
- Inadequate CLOUD Applications

Internet Protocol Threats
- Web Applications and Services
- Lack of Security and Privacy
- Virtualization
- Inadequate Cryptography

Server Capacity and Scalability Threats
- Lack of Sufficient Hardware
- Lack of Existing Hardware Scalability
- Server Farm Incapacity to Meet Customer Demand
- Incorrect Configuration

Physical Infrastructure Threats
- Power Outages
- Unreliable Network Connections
- Inadequate Facilities
- Inadequate Repair Crews

Data and Disaster Recovery Threats
- Lack of a Contingency Plan
- Lack of Multiple Sites
- Inadequate Software and Hardware
- Recovery Time

Managerial Quality Threats
- Lack of Quality Crisis Response Personnel
- Inadequate Technical Education
- Insufficient Load Demand Management
- Lack of Service Monitoring

Macroeconomic and Cost Factor Threats
- Inadequate Payment Plans
- Low Growth Rates
- High Interest Rates
- Adverse Regulatory Environment

Client Perceptions (PR) and Transparency Threats
- Lack of PR Promotion
- Adverse Company News
- Unresponsiveness to Client Complaints
- Lack of Openness

Questions are designed to elicit the user's response regarding the perceived risk from particular threats and the countermeasures the users may employ to counteract those threats. For example, regarding Internet Protocols' vulnerability, questions regarding Virtualization include both threat and countermeasure questions.

Threat questions would include the following:

- Do your provider's virtualization appliances have packet inspection settings set on default?
- Is escape to the hypervisor likely in the case of a breach of the virtualization platform?
- Does your provider use Microsoft's Virtual PC hypervisor?
- Does your provider fail to scan the correct customer system?
- Does your provider fail to monitor its virtual machines?

Countermeasure questions would include the following:

- Did the provider's virtualization appliances inspect all packets?
- Did the provider extend their vulnerability and configuration management process to the virtualization platform?
- Did the provider patch the vulnerability or switch to another platform?
- Did the provider read-in current asset or deployment information from the CLOUD and then dynamically update the IP address information before scans commence?
- Did the provider utilize Network Access Control-based enforcement for continuous monitoring of its virtual machine population and virtual machine sprawl prevention?

Risk calculation and mitigation would include the following:

- Essentially, the users are responding yes or no to these questions. These responses are used to calculate residual risk.
- Using a game-theoretical optimization approach, the calculated risk index is used further to generate a cost-optimal plan to lower the risk to tolerable levels from those unwanted or unacceptable.
- Mitigation advice will be generated to show the user in what areas the risk can be reduced to optimize or desired levels such as from 50 to 45% in the screenshot (displaying threat, countermeasure, and residual risk indices; optimization options; as well as risk mitigation advice).

7.10.1 Risk Assessment and Management Clarifications for Figures 7.72 and 7.73

Using the RM results for the risk assessment step from Figure 7.73 inspired form Figure 7.72, so as to mitigate the base risk by mitigating from 50.32% down to 40%, we implement the prioritized four RM recommended actions. (i) Increase the CM capacity for the vulnerability of "Accessibility and Privacy" and its threat "Lack of Availability" from the current 32 to 99.97%. (ii) Increase the CM capacity for the vulnerability of "Data and Disaster Recovery" and its threat "Recovery Time" from the current 48 to 82.44%.

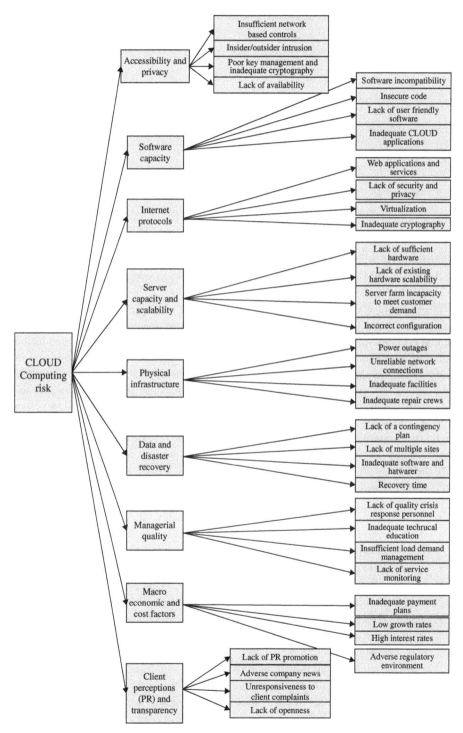

FIGURE 7.72 Tree diagram for CLOUD Risk Meter: Comprehensive (both client and host inclusive).

Vulnerab.	Threat	CM & LCM	Res. Risk	CM & LCM	Res Risk	Change	Opt Cost	Unit Cost	Final Cost	Advice
0.350000	0.480000	0.760000		1.000000		0.900000	$170.13	$170.00	$170.00	Increase the CM capacity against the threat of "v1 t1" for the vulnerability of
		0.300000	0.050400	0.000000	0.000000					"v1" from the current 70.00% to suggested 100.00% for an improvement of 30.00%.
	0.160000	0.420000		0.420000						
		0.580000	0.032480	0.580000	0.032480					
	0.320000	0.970000		0.970000						
		0.030000	0.003360	0.030000	0.003360					
	0.040000	0.800000		0.800000						
		0.200000	0.002800	0.200000	0.002800					
0.260000	0.220000	0.360000		0.360000						
		0.650000	0.037180	0.650000	0.037180					
	0.020000	0.360000		0.360000						
		0.650000	0.003380	0.650000	0.003380					
	0.760000	0.980000		1.000000		0.040000	$22.68	$20.00	$20.00	Increase the CM capacity against the threat of "v2 t3" for the vulnerability of
		0.040000	0.007904	0.000000	0.000000					"v2" from the current 96.00% to suggested 100.00% for an improvement of 4.00%.
0.390000	0.320000	0.720000		0.985410		0.265410	$150.51	$150.00	$150.00	Increase the CM capacity against the threat of "v3 t1" for the vulnerability of
		0.280000	0.034944	0.014590	0.001821					"v3" from the current 72.00% to suggested 98.54% for an improvement of 26.54%.
	0.590000	0.700000		0.999890		0.299890	$170.06	$170.00	$170.00	Increase the CM capacity against the threat of "v3 t2" for the vulnerability of
		0.300000	0.069030	0.000110	0.000025					"v3" from the current 70.00% to suggested 99.99% for an improvement of 29.99%.
	0.090000	0.460000		0.460000						
		0.640000	0.018954	0.640000	0.018954					

	Total Change	Total Cost	Break Even Cost	Total Final Cost
	90.53%	$513.38	$5.67	$510.00

Criticality	0.40	Total Risk	0.260432	Total Risk	0.100000
Capital Cost	$8000.00	Percentage	26.043200	Percentage	10.000004
		Final Risk	0.104173	Final Risk	0.040000
		ECL	$833.38	ECL	$320.00
		Optimize / Change Cost		ECL Delta	$513.38

Enter Unit Cost for Each Advice
Print Summary
Print Single Selection
Print All Selections
Print Results Table

Show where you are in Security Meter

3 Vulnerabilities

FIGURE 7.73 RM Risk Assessment and Management Results applying Figure 7.72's Tree Diagram.

(iii) Increase the CM capacity for the vulnerability of "Managerial Quality" and its threat "Insufficient Load Demand Management" from the current 52.50 to 100%. (iv) Increase the CM capacity for the vulnerability of "Macroeconomic and Cost Factors" and its threat "Adverse Regulatory Market" from the current 55 to 100.00%. In taking these actions, a total positive change of 194.91% is the possible minimized total change for guaranteeing the improvement percentage (from 50.32 to 40%). Under the given circumstances using the game-theoretic principles for the risk management step, out of total CLOUD investment of $1M, a total amount of $101,000 is dispensed (<$103,222.73 as advised), each within the limits of optimal costs annotated, staying below the break-even cost of $5.29 per 1% improvement. The next step proceeds with optimization to a next desirable percentage once these acquisitions or services are provided, such as mitigated to 35% from 45% if the budget still exists. See Figure 7.73 for the mitigation step. In summary:

- CLOUD computing, also viewed as a fifth utility after water, electric power, telephony, and gas, is set to expand dramatically if issues of availability and security can be trustfully resolved.
- The CLOUD simulator tool (CLOURAM) by the author and its further refinement will aid in that expansion. Also Monte Carlo VaR is an alternative method for day-to-day monitoring of the CLOUD [36].
- The CLOUD RM breaks new ground in that it provides a quantitative assessment of risk to the user as well as recommendations to mitigate that risk. A cross section of draft questions (subject to change as required by the CLOUD management organization) are listed before the References.
- As such, it will be a highly useful tool to both the end user and IT professionals involved in CLOUD service provision due to mounting customer complaints on the breach of reliability [37].
- Both CLOURAM and Monte Carlo VaR (as SIMULATION METHODS) only cited here and CLOUD RM (as an INFORMATION-GATHERING CUSTOMER SURVEY

METHOD) will provide quantitative risk assessment and management solutions if the correctly collected data needed for both approaches can be justified. Besides Markov chain method is only useful for small-scale problems, utilized as a theoretical comparison alternative, mainly because large-scale problems with excessive Markov states are intractable to compute even with supercomputers exceeding 500 servers.

- Further research commands reliable random data collection practices to render these two recommended methods by the author, that is, DES and RM, useful and applicable "most bang for the buck" to aid managers with assessing and managing CLOUD risk, conventionally left to chance or haphazard saving the day.

7.11 DISCUSSIONS AND CONCLUSION

CLOUD computing has become such a powerful entity for cyber users as well as large commercial companies that someday users will not need to buy other than a terminal connectivity with all security aspects provided, such as in the case we only provide for electric bulbs at our homes to light up our homes from the power grid as currently practiced [38, 39]. However, these cyber CLOUDs at the turn of the twenty-first century, just as the electric power companies at the turn of the twentieth century did, will need to sell reliable (not just any) and secure service that is free of hacking and virus malware to their new breed clients. This is only possible if the service-based system managers can quantify and manage their risks of not meeting the service demand as planned. In many ways, electric power utilities' challenges will be revisited as they once were eminent in the latter half of the twentieth century.

In this extensive theoretical and applied chapter material, the author has shown the statistical estimation of the sum of loss of load or service events in hours or cycles by modeling through a compound Poisson process, particularly one such NBD ,where the compounding distribution is assumed to be an LSD. NBD is math-statistically a reasonable approximation for two essential reasons. The first one is the taking into account of the phenomenon of interdependence or true contagion property of the system failures that constitute a cluster at each breakdown in concert with the electric power utility or cyber system engineering practices as two prominent examples.

Secondly, the underlying distribution to estimate the probability distribution function for the number of power or cyber system failures in this research chapter is no more an asymptotical or an approximate expression, whereas it is a closed-form and nonasymptotic rather an exact probability distribution function using statistical jargon [3, 4, 13]. When the system is in a negative margin at any hour, the contagious condition affects the forthcoming hours until full system recuperation. Due to this truly contagion property, the usage of Poisson^LSD gives mathematically sound results where the failures are interdependent. The parameters of the Poisson^LSD are obtained by the well-known method, namely, frequency and duration method, as in a power generation system reliability evaluation. Contrary to limiting Poisson^geometric process, the proposed Poisson^LSD gives a closed-form distribution for loss of load hours in a power generating or cyber CLOUD computing system or similar CLOUD utility. In the event of a cyber system, the process is simulated hour by hour based on the additive property of the distributed server farms with their adequate or inadequate number of repair crews to handle the service outages, therefore meeting the demand of service (load) such as in the case of an electric power generation system. The ratio of unsuccessful interception of the load(service) cycles or hours, Loss of Load or Service Expected = LoLE, by the supply side is calculated in addition to the frequency of LoS (f) and average duration of LoS (d). Further, the pdf of "LoLE" and "d" as random variables are estimated for statistical inference. Load management is also available, and desired maintenance planning can be incorporated. In the cyber world, an ISP will benefit by first assessing the reliability of CLOUD computing systems rising in popularity. There are other cyber networks where source–target (s–t) is sought where the topology is directional [40–42], not regional as in this study. Then, the CLOUD managers will use this expert system (CLOURAM to avoid bottlenecks by preliminary planning through emulating the operations and checking where one can improve. The bottom-line impact is that an ISP or CLOUD planning department will know in advance through examining and responding to what-if questions to plan to assess its physical resources before actually taking remedies or buying the equipment or hiring new personnel to beef up repair. The physical glitches and monetary losses (excluding the erosion of customer trust) could have been many times avoided if the operations centers knew the actual reliability status of the supply/demand system and what to do to raise the QoS (as opposite index to LoS) by taking the necessary precautions to plan ahead. Of course, not to forget, input data to be used carries a very important responsibility for the success of this software tool, that is, CLOURAM as a versatile tool or expert system for the job of risk assessment and risk management. It can apply dependence between the units (components) by using the necessary features as in Figure 7.15. The much neglected reliability or security assessment will continue to be a liability if otherwise with media coverage of glitches becoming everyday news. This is why the CLOUD reliability and/or security index has to be computed and CLOUD operations ought to be simulated to circumvent any potential problems in advance before undesirable glitches happen and consequently commercial customers lose trust [37]. However, if the growth of CLOUD technology is to continue, it will be important that grid systems also provide high reliability. In particular, it will be critical to ensure that grid systems are reliable as they continue to grow in scale, exhibit greater dynamism, and become more heterogeneous in composition [43].

As for the SS subtopic, we verify the conventional results through test runs by conducting SS. Once the verification process is carried out successfully, that is, the CLOUD non-SS metrics are compared favorably to those employing deterministic data; grid producer and link scenarios will be studied such as in the event of the links no more being perfectly reliable, but operating with specified values through uniform, or negative exponential input data assumptions. These were executed in the examples presented earlier. This innovative research illustrates that we can include lump-sum composite grid transmission (link) data as an averaging effect in the simulation of cyber or power CLOUD performance. Additionally, this algorithm can be used for any other stochastic (random) data entry for the producers as well as the links. The versatility of the algorithm stems from a wide area of usage by leveraging the Weibull distribution (whose default with shape parameter $\beta = 1$ is negative exponential and used extensively for failures). In the event of the nonexistence of sophisticated data such as Weibull or similar, the analyst may use uniform deviations with percentages as shown in the examples regarding the power grid for further research, the authors will seek the power grid data from industry to compare results.

Regarding Social CLOUD in this subsection, this tool proves useful for planning manpower to schedule or economize workforce. It is based on logical principles rather than haphazard guesswork, which can vary from one supervisor to another. Social CLOUDs can be effective like physical ones. Observing our example in the subsection, we run 1000 times a period of 100 days or 6 months or a year of FRG or HRG activity ahead. Also for each responder in each group, we can see on the average where FRG or HRG personnel are failing to contribute so that we can work on remedial countermeasures regarding those weak spots. Last but not least, we can also execute backup or reserve personnel contingencies. Say, we have 20% backup reserve in the payroll, or we have only maybe 5% or less, so that we can save on the expenses. Overall for market planning in terms of substitute crew or new employees to employ, the "Social CLOUD" is necessary [52].

In brief, ensuring CLOUD system reliability in turn requires that the specifications used to build these systems fully support reliable support services [44–46]. This information may also lead to providing the failure (disruption or breach) and repair (recovery) data of many critical network components in data-intensive computing [25]. High reliability and high security as the two primary characteristics of data-intensive computing systems can be achieved through a careful planning in conducting such reliability and security evaluations employing digital simulation as an optimization tool [47, 48]. Last but not the least, reference [49] published by the author in a book chapter and journal article [50] would help recap it all along with the most recent publications on this topic regarding CLOUD risk assessment and management using simulation techniques as studied in Section 7.6 [51–57].

7.12 EXERCISES

7.12.1 The company HQ you will have been employed at, say, has 2 client servers. They operate (and fail) with respect to a negative exponential density with lambda = 1/year due to an unknown security breach and get repaired w.r.t. Mu = 2/year, that is, $\lambda = 1$; $\mu = 2$. Thus, the mean time to failure is 1 year and mean time to repair is 1/2 year (6 months). Namely, they can be repaired 2 times faster than they fail if the standby repair crews suffice. Simulate the HQ server system and terminate the analysis until both fail and recuperate at least twice. Use the random numbers (Table 1.17) from the very first row, left to right. Accuracy is very important in this analysis, and severe deviations from true calculations by the company HQ will not be tolerated. Doing hand calculations, use 4 decimal points by rounding off. Take into account the waiting times for each server during the process and report the % operation (UP status) for Server 1 and Server 2, respectively. You need to report total waiting times for each server at the termination of the analysis when both fail and get repaired twice at stopping time = T. Report to your supervisor if recruiting a second server will eliminate the waiting problem completely or partially. Each server has 2 GB and constant load is 3 GB.

7.12.2 (A) Employing the CLOUD Java program in your book website titled CyberRiskSolver, enter the two units one by one with the given failure and repair rates, say, each of which has 2 GB capacity. Given a constant load of 3 GB for 20 cycles (years), report the reliability of this operation conducting 1000 simulations with the same cycles or years. (B) You can compare parts 7.12.1 and 7.12.2 results if you draw a 3 GB straight line across the exposure period in 7.12.1 hand calculations to see what the resultant reliability of the system is after taking into account the load information. See the hints on a similar problem attached from a recent journal paper. See Figure 7.3 for similar data.

Sample solution of 7.12.1 and 7.12.2a (for Uniform random numbers, $u_i \rightarrow$ Table 1.17):

Use $X_i = -\dfrac{\ln(1-u_1)}{\lambda}$ and $Y_i = -\dfrac{\ln(1-u_1)}{\mu}$.

Let $\lambda = 1$; $\mu = 2$

$$u_1 = 0.6953, x_1 = -\frac{\ln(1-0.6953)}{1} = 1.188$$

$$u_2 = 0.5247, x_2 = -\frac{\ln(1-0.5247)}{1} = 0.7438$$

$$u_3 = 0.1368, y_3 = -\frac{\ln(1-0.1368)}{2} = 0.0735$$

$$u_4 = 0.985, x_4 = -\ln(1-0.985) = 4.199$$

$$u_5 = 0.7467, y_5 = -\frac{\ln(1-0.7467)}{2} = 0.6866$$

$$u_6 = 0.3813, x_6 = -\ln(1-0.3813) = 0.4801$$

$$u_7 = 0.5827, y_7 = -\frac{\ln(1-0.5827)}{2} = 0.437$$

$$u_8 = 0.7893, x_8 = -\ln(1-0.7893) = 1.557$$

$$u_9 = 0.7169, y_9 = -\frac{\ln(1-0.7169)}{2} = 0.631$$

$$u_{10} = 0.8166, x_{10} = -\ln(1-0.8166) = 1.696$$

$$u_{11} = 0.0082, y_{11} = -\frac{\ln(1-0.0082)}{2} = 0.00$$

Note: 7.12.2a's analytical will converge to 7.12.2a's CLOUD simulation result if 1000 simulation runs executed, such as running the RANDOM TABLE (Table 1.17) given in Chapter 1 for many multiple times nonstop (Figs. 7.74, 7.75, and 7.76).

$$\frac{\text{Operational good times}}{\text{Total exposure}} = \frac{1.188+0.48+1.557+0.037}{5.11} = \frac{3.262}{5.017} = 65\% \text{ for unit 1,}$$

$$\frac{\text{Operational good times}}{\text{Total exposure}} = \frac{0.744+4.199}{5.017} = \frac{4.943}{5.017} = 98.5\% \text{ for unit 2,}$$

$$\% \text{ system up (for 3 Gigabyte load)} = \frac{\text{operational good times (both operative)}}{\text{total exposure}}$$

$$= \frac{3.197}{5.017} = 63.7\%$$

Markov Chain theoretical for $P_{1,1(\text{up\&up})} = \dfrac{\mu 1 \mu 2}{(\mu 1+\lambda 1)(\mu 2+\lambda 2)}$

$$= \frac{2*2}{(2+1)(2+1)} = \frac{4}{9} = 0.444 = 44.4\%$$

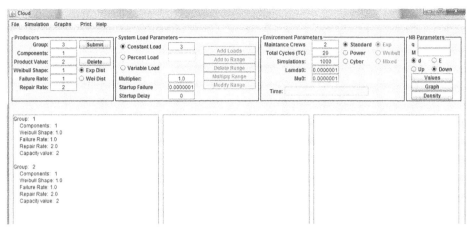

FIGURE 7.74 1000 simulation runs (20 cycles as in the hand calculations where the process terminates).

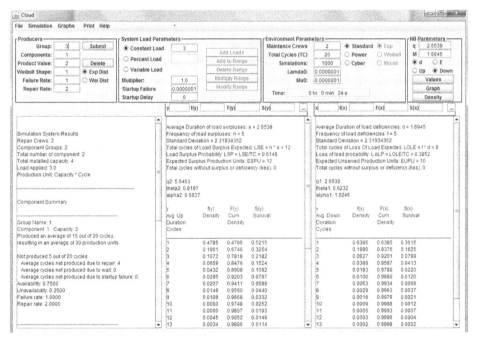

FIGURE 7.75 System input data for 20 cycles as in the hand calculations where the process terminates.

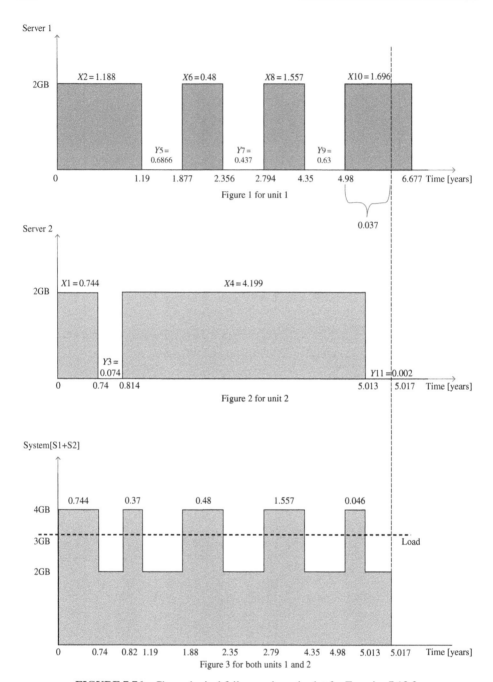

FIGURE 7.76   Chronological failure and repair plot for Exercise 7.12.2.

7.12.3   Using the random numbers (Table 1.17) in Chapter 1, proceeding row-wise from 20th row onward left to right such as 0.6953, 0.5247, 0.1368, 0.9850, 0.7467, 0.3813, 0.5827, 0.7893, 0.7169, 0.8166, 0.0082, etc. (a) For the first 11 uniform random numbers, work the computer center availability problem, where each of the two computers fails with respect to a negative exponential (Weibull with shape parameter Beta=1) with 1 failure in every 1 h (rate $= \lambda = 1/$ year; mean time to failure$=1$ year) and repaired again with respect to a negative exponential (Weibull with shape parameter Beta=1) at four repairs per year (rate $= \mu = 4/$ year, mean time to repair $= 1/4$ year). Simulate the computer center operation until all computers are failed and repaired exactly twice by hand calculations. Note that there is only one repair crew available. Use a graph paper to draw a plot for easy historical data recording. (b) Rank-order the computers according to their availabilities, and propose which one to replace first. Don't ignore the waiting time for the repairman if need arises. Do you need a second repair person? Say yes, if there is a considerable waiting period involved (checking with the theoretical results in an $M/M/1$ problem) as these servers cannot wait to be repaired and it is more economical to hire. Hint: Use $x^* = \theta[-\ln(1-u)]^{1/\beta}$ for Weibull random deviates where Beta$=$shape, $\theta =$ scale.

7.12.4 (a) Employing the CLOUD Java program, enter the two units one by one with the given failure and repair rates, say, each of which has 2 GB capacity. Given a constant load of 3 GB for 20 cycles (years), report the reliability of this operation conducting 1000 simulations with the same cycles in years. (b) You can compare parts 7.12.3's (a) and 7.12.4's (a) results if you draw a 3 GB straight line across the exposure period in part 7.12.3's (a) hand calculations to see what the resultant reliability of the system is after taking into account the load information (Figs. 7.77, 7.78, and 7.79).

Sample solution 7.12.3a and 7.12.4a (use different uniform numbers, u_i for 1 to n):

Use $X_i = -\ln(1-u_i)/\lambda$ and $Y_i = -\ln(1-u_i)/\mu$.

Let $\lambda = 1/$year; $\mu = 4/$year.

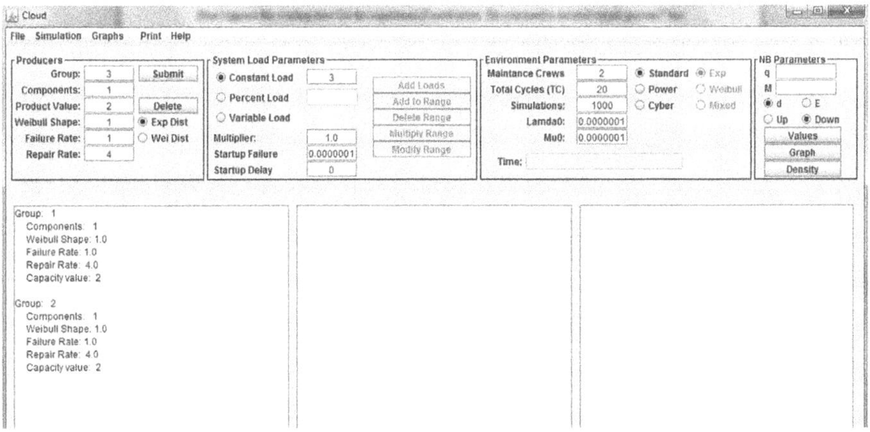

FIGURE 7.77   Input data for Exercise 7.12.4.

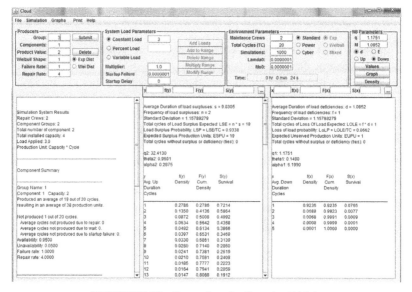

FIGURE 7.78 Output box for Exercise 7.12.4.

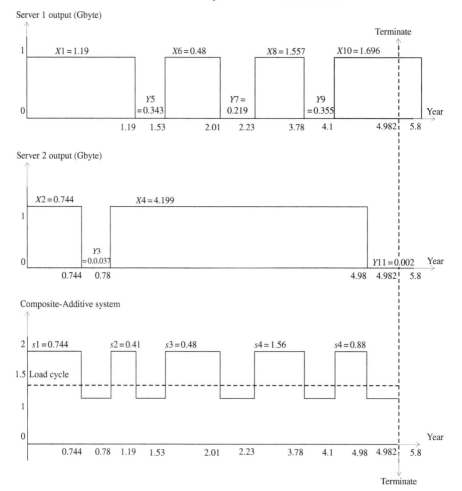

FIGURE 7.79 Chronological failure and repair plot for Exercise 7.12.4.

$$u_1 = 0.6953, x_1 = -\ln(1-0.6953)/1 = 1.188$$
$$u_2 = 0.5247, x_2 = -\ln(1-0.5247)/1 = 0.7438$$
$$u_3 = 0.1368, y_3 = -\ln(1-0.1368)/4 = 0.037$$
$$u_4 = 0.985, x_4 = -\ln(1-0.985)/1 = 4.199$$
$$u_5 = 0.9467, y_5 = -\ln(1-0.7461)/4 = 0.3433$$
$$u_6 = 0.3813, y_6 = -\ln(1-0.3813)/1 = 0.4801$$
$$u_7 = 0.5827, x_7 = -\ln(1-0.5827)/4 = 0.2185$$
$$u_8 = 0.7893, x_8 = -\ln(1-0.7893)/1 = 1.557$$
$$u_9 = 0.7169, y_9 = -\ln(1-0.7169)/4 = 0.3155$$
$$u_{10} = 0.8166, x_{10} = -\ln(1-0.8166)/1 = 1.696$$
$$u_{11} = 0.0082, y_{11} = -\ln(1-0.0082)/4 = 0.002$$

Server 1:

$$\%\text{reliability} = \frac{X1+X6+X8+(4.982-4.10)}{4.982} = \frac{1.188+0.48+1.557+0.882}{4.92}$$
$$= \frac{4.107}{4.982} = 82.4\%$$

Server 2:

$$\%\text{reliability} = \frac{X2+X4}{4.982} = \frac{0.744+4.199}{4.982} = \frac{4.983}{4.982} = 92.2\%$$

System Composite

$$\%\text{reliability} = \frac{S1+S2+S3+S4+S5}{\text{exposure time}} = \frac{0.744+0.41+0.48+1.56+0.88}{4.982} = 81.8\%$$

7.12.5   (a) Using the random numbers (Table 1.17) of Chapter 1, proceeding row-wise from 20th row onward left to right such as 0.6953, 0.5247, 0.1368, 0.9850, 0.7467, 0.3813, 0.5827, 0.7893, 0.7169, 0.8166, 0.0082, etc., for the first 11 uniform random numbers, work the computer center availability problem, where each of the two computers fails w.r.t. a negative exponential (Weibull with shape parameter $\beta=1$) with 1 failure in every 10 h (rate $=\lambda=0.1$/h; mean $= 10$ h) and repaired again 10 times faster w.r.t. a negative exponential (Weibull with shape parameter $\beta=1$) at 1 repair per hour (rate $=\lambda=1$/h, mean $= 1$ h). Simulate the computer center operation until all computers are failed and repaired exactly twice. Note that there is only one repair crew available. Use a graph paper to draw for easy historical data recording. (b) Rank-order the computers according to their availabilities, and propose which one to replace first. Don't ignore the waiting time for the repairman if need arises. Do you need a second repair person? Say yes, if there is a considerable waiting period involved, and it is more economical to hire (say $7/ server and 5$/waiting time unit) someone than to have the servers not

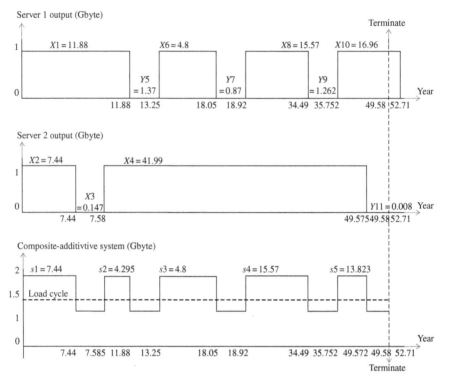

FIGURE 7.80   Chronological failure and repair plot for Exercise 7.12.5.

function. Hint: Use $x^* = \alpha[-\ln(1-u)]^{1/\beta}$ for Weibull random deviates where $m =$ shape, $\alpha = (\text{rate} = \lambda)^{-1} =$ scale. See solution hints as follows (Fig. 7.80):

$$\text{Prob. }\left(\text{Unit}_1\text{Up}\right) = \frac{\Sigma X_i}{\text{total exposure}} = \frac{11.88 + 4.8 + 15.57 + \left(49.575 - 35.752\right)}{49.583}$$

$$= \frac{46.073}{49.583} = 92.687\%$$

$$\text{Prob. }\left(\text{Unit}_2\text{Up}\right) = \frac{\Sigma X_i}{\text{total exposure}} = \frac{7.438 + 41.99}{49.583}$$

$$= \frac{49.42}{49.59} = 99.687\%$$

$$\text{Prob. of system up} = \frac{S_i}{\text{total exposure}} = \frac{7.438 + 4.295 + 4.8 + 15.57 + 13.823}{49.583}$$

$$= \frac{45.926}{49.583} = 92.62\%$$

No we do not need a second repair crew since waiting time = 0. We must stop at the epoch (49.58) when both units at least will have failed and been repaired twice. Total exposure = 49.58 (~50 years).

Time to failure rv, $X_i = \dfrac{\ln(1-U_i)}{\lambda}$, where $\lambda = 0.1 /$ year, for individual up times

Time to repair rv, $Y_i = \dfrac{\ln(1-Ui)}{\mu}$, where $\mu = 1/\text{year}$, for individual down times:

$$X_1 = -\ln(1-0.6953)/0.1 = 11.88$$
$$X_2 = -\ln(1-0.5247)/0.1 = 7.44$$
$$Y_3 = -\ln(1-0.1368)/1 = 0.147$$
$$X_4 = -\ln(1-0.985)/0.1 = 41.99$$
$$Y_5 = -\ln(1-0.7461)/1 = 1.37$$
$$X_6 = -\ln(1-0.3813)/0.1 = 4.8$$
$$Y_7 = -\ln(1-0.5827)/1 = 0.87$$
$$X_8 = -\ln(1-0.7893)/0.1 = 15.57$$
$$Y_9 = -\ln(1-0.7169)/1 = 1.262$$
$$X_{10} = -\ln((1-0.8166)/0.1 = 16.96$$
$$Y_{11} = -\ln(1-0.0082)/1 = 0.008$$

7.12.6 Use 1996, 1998, and 1999 data from data files in the CLOUD simulator with 1000 runs to obtain the screen captures. Apply reserve crew and additional product planning for 1995, 1997 and 2000 data sets to compare with the usual CLOUD outcomes without reserve planning as described in Section 7.6. Also use 1995 to 2000 data sets to perform Stochastic Simulation as described in Section 7.9.

7.12.7 Use the FRG (Frequent Responder Group) data files FRG1 to FRG5 for Social CLOUD computing (see Section 7.8).

7.12.8 What famous romantic poet (WW) and what particular famous poem (an alternative title for his 1809 pastoral poem was "Daffodils") has this book's author been inspired by in writing an alternative satirical poem on a Cyber-CLOUD on the current topic of CLOUD risk management and continued on the next page? (A: http://www.poetryfoundation.org/poem/174790).

I AUTHORED LONELY ABOUT A CLOUD

I wandered lonely around a Computing CLOUD
That floats nowadays on high risks and breaches,
When all at once I saw a tailed virus.
A host of worms, logic bombs and ankle biters,
Beside the hardware and beneath the software,
Hideous, heinous, frustrating, and hiding in the rear.

Continuous as the STUXNET and zombies move
And I twittered HELP on my way to office,
They, the hackers, stirred in never-ending chaos,
Along the million confusions of terror and vice:
Thousands of service denials a day I saw at a glance,
Tossing their heads mockingly in utter defiance.

The Trojans inside the horse danced, while they
Outdid the antivirus software and firewall:
The insecurity analyst and intruder could not but be delighted,
In such an uncertain malware call;
I gaz'd -and gaz'd- but little understood,
What for the Cyberspace and Internet to me had stood.

For oft on my laptop while I write, I doze off
In undefended or in pensive lunacy,
Hackers prey upon targeting banks rough and tough.
Which is the blissful and solid end of privacy?
And then my heart fills with anguish and hope,
Dances in sympathy with our younger script kiddies!

REFERENCES

[1] Viega, J. (2009). Cloud computing and the common man, *Computer*, 42(8), 106–108.

[2] Sahinoglu, M., Cueva-Parra, L., Das, S., Tyson, D. (2009). Statistical inference and simulation of security metrics in CLOUD computing for large cyber systems, Invited Session 204120: Quantitative Security and Cyber Systems, JSM Risk Section, Washington, DC, August 1–6, 2009, and 12th SDPS Transdisciplinary Conference on Integrated Systems, Design and Process Science, Montgomery, AL.

[3] Sahinoglu, M., *Trustworthy Computing: Analytical and Quantitative Engineering Evaluation*, John Wiley & Sons Inc., Hoboken, NJ, 2007.

[4] Sahinoglu, M., (1990). The limit of sum of Markov Bernoulli variables in system reliability evaluation, *IEEE Transactions on Reliability*, 39, 46–50.

[5] Sahinoglu, M., Longnecker, M., Ringer, L., Singh, C., Ayoub, A. (1983). Probability distribution function for generation reliability indices—Analytical approach, Publication 82JPGC 603–9, IEEE/PES/ASME/ASCE Joint Power Generation Conference, 1982, and *IEEE Transactions on Power Apparatus & Systems*, 102, 486–1493.

[6] Hall, J. D., Ringlee, R. J., Wood, A. J. (1968). Frequency and duration methods for power system reliability calculations: Part I—Generation system model, *IEEE* PAS-87, (9), 1787–1796.

[7] Ayoub, A. K., Patton, A. D. (1976). A frequency and duration method for generating system reliability evaluation, *IEEE Transactions on Power Apparatus and Systems*, PAS-95(6), 1929–1933.

[8] Serfozo, R. F. (1986). Compound Poisson approximations for sums of random variables, *Annals of Probability*, 14, 1391–1398.

[9] Sahinoglu, M. (1992). Compound Poisson software reliability model, *IEEE Transactions on Software Engineering*, 18, 624–630.

[10] Sahinoglu, M. (1990). Negative binomial (Poisson^Logarithmic) density estimation of the software failure count, in Proceedings of the 5th International Symposium on Computer and Information Sciences (ISCIS), Goreme (Cappadocia), Turkey, vol. 1, 231–240.

[11] Brown, B., *Some Tables of the Negative Binomial Distribution and Their Use*, Memorandum RM-4577-PR, The Rand Corporation, Santa Monica, CA, 1965.

[12] Sherbrooke, C. C., *Discrete Compound Poisson Processes and Tables of the Geometric Poisson Distribution*, Memorandum RM-4831-PR, The Rand Corporation, Santa Monica, CA, 1966.

[13] Gokmen, M. (1996). An exact compound Poisson probability density function for loss of load in electric power generation reliability evaluation, M.S. thesis (Supervised by: Dr. M. Sahinoglu), Dokuz Eylul University, Izmir.

[14] Billinton, R., *Power System Reliability Evaluation*, Gordon & Breach Science Publishers, New York, 1974.

[15] Singh, C., Billinton, R., *System Reliability Modeling and Evaluation*, Hutchinson Educational, London, 1977.

[16] Billinton, R. (1972). Bibliography on the application of probability methods in power system reliability evaluation, in IEEE Trans on PAS, vol. 91, no. 2, pp. 649–660, March/April 1972.

[17] Allan, R. N., Billinton, R., Lee, S. H. (1984). Bibliography on the application of probability methods in power system reliability, *IEEE Transactions on Power Apparatus and Systems*, PAS-103(2), 275–282.

[18] Sahinoglu, M. (1981). Statistical inference of reliability performance index for electric power generation systems, Ph.D. dissertation, Institute of Statistics, Texas A&M University, College Station, TX.

[19] Sahinoglu, M., Selcuk, A. S. (1993). Application of Monte Carlo simulation method for the estimation of reliability indices in electric power generation systems, Doga-Tr, *Journal of Engineering and Environmental Science*, 17, 157–163.

[20] Ayoub, A. K., Guy, J. D., Patton, A. D. (1970). Evaluation and comparison of some methods for calculating generation system reliability, *IEEE Transactions on Power Apparatus and Systems*, PAS-89(4), 514–521.

[21] Sahinoglu, M., Libby, D., Das, S. R. (2005). Measuring availability indices with small samples for component and network reliability using the Sahinoglu-Libby probability model, *IEEE Transactions on Instrumentation and Measurement*, 54(3), 1283–1295.

[22] Patton, A. D., Singh, C., Sahinoglu, M. (1980). Operating considerations in generation reliability modeling—Analytical approach, IEEE Winter Power Meeting, Publication A80-082-8, *IEEE Transactions on Power Apparatus and Systems*, 100, 2656–2663.

[23] Student. (1919). *Biometrika*, 12, 211–215.

[24] Sahinoglu, M., Gebizlioglu, O. (1986). Exact PMF estimation of system reliability indices in a boundary crossing problem, *First World Congress of the Bernoulli Society, Tashkent, Uzbekistan and Communications Faculty of Sciences, University of Ankara, 1987; Series A1*, 36(2), 115–121.

[25] Sahinoglu, M., Cueva-Parra, L. (2011). CLOUD Computing, *Invited Author (Advanced Review) for Wiley Interdisciplinary Reviews: Computational Statistics, New Jersey*, 3(1), 47–68.

[26] Sahinoglu, M. (1988). Global benefits of interconnection among Balkan power systems (1990), Final Report, Coordinating Committee of Development of Interconnection of the Electric Power Systems of Balkan Countries, Geneva-Switzerland, Project No:06.3.1.3.-EP/ GE.2/R.70.3.

[27] Sahinoglu, M., Morton, S. (2012). CLOUD Risk-O-Meter: An algorithm for cloud risk assessment and management, in Conference of Society of Design and Process Science (SDPS), Session X1 CLOUD Computing: Security and Reliability, Berlin.

[28] Sahinoglu, M. (2012). CLOUD meter: A risk assessment and mitigation tool, in Cyber Security Training Conference (CSCT), Colorado Springs, CO.

[29] Anthes, G. (2010). Security in the cloud, *Communications of the ACM*, 53(11), 16–18.

[30] Benini, M., Sicari, S. (2008). Risk assessment in practice: A real case study, *Computer Communications*, 31(15), 3691–3699.

[31] Greengard, S. (2010). Cloud computing and developing nations, *Communications of the ACM*, 53(5), 18–20.

[32] Boland, R. (2011). Approval granted for private software to run in secure cloud, *SIGNAL, Information Security*, 48, 35–38.

[33] Srinivasan, S., Getov, V. (2011). Navigating the cloud computing landscape—Technologies, services, and adopters, *IEEE Computer*, 44(3), 22–28.

[34] Grobauer, B., Walloschek, S. (2011). Understanding cloud computing vulnerabilities, *IEEE Security & Privacy*, 9(2), 50–57.

[35] Khalidi, Y. (2011). Building a cloud computing platform for new possibilities, *IEEE Computer*, 44(3), 29–34.

[36] Kim, H., Chaudhuri, S., Parashar, M., Marty, C. (2009). Online risk analytics on the cloud, in Proceedings of the 2009 9th IEEE/ACM International Symposium on Cluster Computing and the Grid (CCGRID'09), IEEE Computer Society, Washington, DC.

[37] Worthen, G., Vascellaro, J. (2009). E Mail glitch shows pitfalls of online software—Photo: Services like Gmail run on vast computer farms. A Google center in Lenoir, NC, *Media and Marketing, Wall Street Journal*, B4–5.

[38] Gruman, G. (2008). What Cloud computing really means, *InfoWorld*. Available at http://www.infoworld.com/article/08/04/07/15FE-Cloud-computing-reality_1.html (accessed on January 13, 2009).

[39] Rajkumar, B., Shin Yeo, C., Venugopal, S. (July 18, 2008), *Market-Oriented Cloud Computing: Vision, Hype, and Reality for Delivering IT Services as Computing Utilities*. University of Melbourne, Parkville, VIC.

[40] Sahinoglu, M., Ramamoorthy, C. V. (2005). RBD tools using compression and hybrid techniques to code, decode and compute s-t reliability in simple and complex networks, *IEEE Transactions on Instrumentation and Measurement*, Special Guest Edition on Testing, 54(3), 1789–1799.

[41] Sahinoglu, M., Rice, B. (2010). Network Reliability Evaluation, *Invited Author for Wiley Interdisciplinary Reviews: Computational Statistics, New Jersey*, 2(2), 189–211.

[42] Sahinoglu, M., Rice, B., Tyson, D. (2008). An analytical exact RBD method to calculate s-t reliability in complex networks, *IJCITAE—International Journal of Computers, Information Technology and Engineering*, 2(2), 95–104.

[43] Dabrowski, C. (2009). Reliability in Grid Computing Systems, *US Government Work, Concurrency and Computation: Practice and Experience*, 21(8), 927–959.

[44] Jha, S., Merzky, A., Fox, G. (2009). Using clouds to provide grids with higher levels of abstraction and explicit support for usage modes, *Concurrency and Computation: Practice and Experience*, 21, 1087–1108.

[45] Liu, G., Orban Gridbatch, D. (2008). Cloud computing for large-scale data-intensive batch applications, in 8th IEEE International Symposium on Cluster Computing and the Grid, Curran Associates Inc. 2009, IEEE, 1–818.

[46] Buyya, R., Yeo, C. S., Venugopal, S. (2008). *Market-oriented cloud computing: Vision, hype, and reality for delivering it services as computing utilities*, in Proceedings of the 10th IEEE International Conference on High Performance Computing and Communications (HPCC-08, IEEE CS Press, Los Alamitos, CA), September 25–27, 2008, Dalian, China.

[47] Leavitt, N. (2009). Is cloud computing really ready for prime time, *IEEE Computer*, 42(1), 15–20.

[48] Vasan, R. A. (2011). Venture perspective on cloud computing, *IEEE Computer*, 44(3), 60–70.

[49] Sahinoglu, M., *CLOUD Computing Risk Assessment and Management, Book Chapter, (Risk Assessment and Management*, Academy Publish.org, Cheyenne, 2012.

[50] Sahinoglu, M. (2013). The modeling and simulation in engineering, Invitational overview article for WIREs (Wiley Interdisciplinary Review Series), *WIREs Computational Statistics*, 239–266. Doi:10.1002/wics 1254, April 2013. http://www.aum.edu/UR_Media/NandH/

[51] Sahinoglu, M., Vasudev, P. (2017). Stochastic simulation of cyber CLOUD and power grid, Proceedings of the International Conference on Information Technology and Science (ICITS), p. 45, Pattaya, Thailand. *IJCTE (International Journal of Computer Theory and Engineering)*, 9(1), 43–47. Available at www.ijcte.org (accessed on October 31, 2015).

[52] Sahinoglu, M., Vasudev, P. (2015) Social CLOUD Computing for Human Resources Performance Risk Assessment and Management, ICRA 6/ RISK 2015, International Conference on Risk Assessment and Risk Analysis in Engineering, Barcelona, Spain, May 26–29, 2015.

[53] Sahinoglu, M., Ashokan, S, and Vasudev P. (2015), Cost-Efficient Risk Management with Reserve Repair Crew Planning in CLOUD Computing, The 2015 International Conference on Soft Computing and Software Engineering at Berkeley, Ca., (SCSE 2015), Procedia Computer Science, ELSEVIER, 62, 335–342.

[54] Sahinoglu, M., Ashokan, S, and Vasudev P. (2015), CLOUD Computing: Cost-effective Risk Management with Additional Product Deployment, The 2015 International Conference on Soft Computing and Software Engineering at Berkeley, Ca., (SCSE 2015), Procedia Computer Science, ELSEVIER, 62, 319–325.

[55] Sahinoglu, M., Summer School Keynote Lecture on Cyber-Risk Informatics, July 7–9, 2015, PUPR (Polytechnical University of Puerto Rico), San Juan, Puerto Rico.

[56] Sahinoglu, M., CLOURA: CLOUD Risk Assessor (with Stochastic & Non-Stochastic Simulations), Tutorial (Invited) presented at the 2015 International Conference on Soft Computing and Software Engineering (SCSE'15), University of California, Berkeley, Sutardjai Dai Hall, Berkeley, Calif., USA, March 5–6, 2015; URL: SoftEngConf.org.

[57] Sahinoglu, M. (2015), What Can Be the Extent of Contributions of Statistical Sciences to Cyber-Risk and CLOUD Computing Domain in a Security and Privacy Conscious World?, Organizer and Moderator of the Round Table at JSM 2015, Risk Section, Seattle, August 8–13.

8

SOFTWARE RELIABILITY MODELING AND METRICS IN CYBER-RISK

> **LEARNING OBJECTIVES**
>
> - Present an overview of the state of the art and science in software reliability.
> - Review historically traditional models and recently discovered advances in modeling and form a basis of comparison with analytical techniques studied in hardware reliability.
> - Categorize reliability models: (i) time-between-failures (Poisson and binomial types), (ii) failure count, (iii) Bayesian, (iv) static (nondynamic), and (v) others.
> - Study the "reliability growth models" decomposed into (i) negative exponential class of failure times, (ii) Gamma, Weibull, and (iii) other classes of failure times.
> - Study Musa–Okumoto, Goel–Okumoto, and Sahinoglu's compound Poisson failure-count models with examples, as well as the parametric and nonparametric models.

8.1 INTRODUCTION, MOTIVATION, AND METHODOLOGY

Software reliability models do not consider the same statistical techniques as those used in hardware reliability models described earlier [1–3]. Software reliability is defined as the quality measure of a piece of software. It is generally defined as the probability of failure-free performance of computer logic within a specified period of time (mission time) under the predefined conditions and environment (operational profile) encountered. Simplicity and practicality are two key factors in bridging the gap between the state of the art and that of applied software reliability modeling. The assumptions must be realistic and testable as well as applicable and accurate and valid from a predictive viewpoint. One should perform goodness-of-fit tests to assess how reasonably the suggested model fits the data. Software reliability model is an essentially mathematical–statistical technique used to model an engineering phenomenon: Specifically, obtain a quantitative measure of

Cyber-Risk Informatics: Engineering Evaluation with Data Science, First Edition. Mehmet Sahinoglu.
© 2016 John Wiley & Sons, Inc. Published 2016 by John Wiley & Sons, Inc.
Companion website: www.wiley.com/go/sahinoglu/informatics

reliability such as the expected number of failures within a given or residual time interval, the failure intensity while in operation, or the mean time between failures. These models are not derived by simply a cookbook approach but require academic expertise in statistics and mathematics and overall data sciences [4]. Some of these modeling concepts are outside the discipline of computer science and cannot easily be appreciated by software developers.

The definition of reliability is no different from that of its hardware counterpart when hardware is replaced by software. However, as the reader will observe, software models are treated considerably different from hardware models. Hardware (due to material defects and tear and wear) reliability tends to diminish with mission time, whereas software (human-caused logical error) reliability may or may not be perfect all the time during the mission. Faults (or bugs due to an old story that in 50 s, a system analyst actually spotted a physical bug or cockroach stuck idling to look for food perhaps, in an old computer's machinery pipeline) may or may not cause computer failures. Again, there have been many books and thousands of journal and conference proceeding papers on this broad topic since the inception of software reliability science and engineering in early 1970s [5–10]. Leading software reliability taxonomists have broken down the multiplicity of research papers into several general areas [2, 5, 11]. In a pioneering software reliability study in 1967, Hudson modeled software development as a Markovian birth (fault generation during the design or debugging stages) and death (failures resulting from the triggering of faults) process with transition probabilities from one to another [12]. He showed that the number of faults detected, which increased with time, displayed a binomial distribution whose mean value function had the form of a Weibull pdf. Other studies followed with the advances in software in the late 1970s. Failure rates, as rates at which errors are detected in the software, are considered to be important parameters for software reliability growth models only in the sense of perfect debugging models developed in the early years. The reason was that after each failure, the software can be debugged with the premise of correcting more faults not to cause any more faults that we call "reliability growth" over time. Conversely, other software models that may introduce more faults and failures after the debugging process are called imperfect debugging models [3].

8.2 HISTORY AND CLASSIFICATION OF SOFTWARE RELIABILITY MODELS

8.2.1 Time-between-Failures Models

Some of the earliest examples of research on times between failures are studied by Jelinski and Moranda [13, 14], Shooman [15], and Shick and Wolverton [16].

8.2.2 Failure-Counting Models

A representative group of failure-counting models is that of nonhomogeneous Poisson processes (NHHP), where predictions can be made for future epochs. The earlier leading models in this category are the popularly used model of Goel and Okumoto of 1979 [17] and the Musa–Okumoto logarithmic Poisson in 1984 [18]. Discrete versions of this type model have been studied by Ohba [19], Duane [20], and Littlewood [21] all in 1984; Yamada et al. in 1986 [22]; Knafl and Sacks in 1991 [23]; and Sahinoglu through his compound Poisson modeling (CPM) techniques [24–27] and Zhao and Xie [28] both in 1992. Musa's basic execution model of 1975 is also in this category [29].

8.2.3 Bayesian Model

This type of model, a Bayesian estimation technique for models already studied, uses a prior distribution to represent the view from past behavior and thus a posterior distribution to integrate current data with the past judgment. By way of posterior distributions, after deciding on the choice of the loss functions and minimizing the expected loss, estimates for the unknown parameter are substituted in the reliability or hazard functions. For example, for a squared error loss function, the best estimate is the mean of the posterior distribution; and for an absolute-value loss function, the median of the posterior is the best estimate. However, if the empirical Bayesian approach is used to derive more appropriate models, they can be classified as another modeling technique. The most popular model in this category is the Littlewood–Verrall (L–V) empirical Bayes model [30]. There are many other papers on Bayesian treatment of the Jelinski–Moranda (J–M) model, for example, those of Jewell [31] in 1985. These models are difficult to apply without parameter estimation solutions. Empirical Bayesian failure-count models using compound Poisson (CP) by Sahinoglu [24], Sahinoglu and Can [25], are worth noting respectively, as well as by Sahinoglu [26] and Randolph and Sahinoglu [27].

8.2.4 Static (Nondynamic) Models

These models, which include complexity measures, failure injection, and fault seeding, do not deal with time. One of the first models was that of Nelson in 1978 [32]. An excellent must-read review paper for all interested beginners is that of Ramamoorthy and Bastani, published in 1982 [33]. Bastani and Ramamoorthy later (1986) emphasized correctness estimation of software failures rather than using time-dependent probability approach [34]. This latter publication describes a detailed study of correctness probability, which is estimated using a type of continuity assumption. Also discussed is a fuzzy set-based input domain model that is focused on aiming developing more theoretical models. The earlier model of Nelson was a special case of an input domain-based model, extended by Munson and Khosgoftaar in 1981 [6]; Hamlet [35] and Scott et al. [36] both in 1987; and Weiss and Weyuker in 1988 [37] in the area of software fault tolerance. The same was studied by Littlewood and Miller in 1989 [38] and by Butler and Finelli in 1993 [39]. Software fault trees used as a conventional reliability engineering method were studied by Stalhane in 1989 [40], and Wohlin and Korner proposed a fault-spreading model [41]. The original seeding model discussed by Mills [42] has never been formally published other than an IBM report, although Huang in 1984 [43], Duran and Wiorkowski in 1981 [44], and Schick and Wolverton in 1978 [45] have written on the topic.

8.2.5 Others

This group combines all the other topics, such as papers on the optimal release time (ORT) of software after testing by Xie in 1991 [1, 2] and by Randolph and Sahinoglu in 1995, and Sahinoglu in 2003, to name a few [26, 27]. Model comparison papers have also been published such as those by Keiller and Miller in 1991 [46] and Lyu and Nikora in 1991 [47], in addition to Bendell and Mellor in 1986 [48] and Littlewood in 1987 [49]. A complete stochastic treatment of comparison of predictive accuracy between competing reliability models using Bayesian principles was published by Sahinoglu, Deely, and Capar in 2001 [50]. Non- or semiparametric models surface when parametric assumptions are relaxed to achieve robustness; however, those models have not found any degree of popular use in software reliability modeling. Among most known was the one introduced by El-Aroui and Soler [51] where the authors proposed negative exponentially distributed conditionally independent times between failures, classified under the Bayesian exponential Markov assumption.

8.3 SOFTWARE RELIABILITY MODELS IN TIME DOMAIN

Next we study the time-domain (non-dynamic) models in which time is either continuous non-stop or discrete, in distinct time units such as days, weeks, or years. The basic goal is to model the past failure data to predict behavior in the future (i.e., reliability projection) before the software is released to the customer at the end of the development cycle. Reliability models are also useful to model failure patterns and provide input to maintain software before faults (defects) are triggered to cause failures.

The data consist of *failures per time period*, meaning the number of failures discovered in a time period, or *time between failures*, denoting the calendar or central processing unit (CPU) time actually observed between software failures. We take up nontime- or effort-based models where the efforts are made at equal intervals (e.g., days or weeks or months) or simply effort by effort, where the effort can be a test case or any input in a calendar time period. This approach can be likened to a time domain if efforts are made at equal intervals.

Any model used for prediction has to be tested for goodness of fit. We do distinguish in this book between failures and faults (or bugs), but recorded failures are actually triggered faults inherent in the software. There is another classification with respect to the type of statistical distribution that underlies the finite failure count within a given period. We consider the Poisson process over time for the countable finite quantity of failures, the binomial model, or other types. In the Poisson model, we have a Poisson process over time where the total number of failures is not known in advance.

Poisson-type models assume that the number of failures detected within distinct time intervals is independent with separate means: (i) with the same rate of failure, the homogeneous Poisson process; (ii) with a varying rate of failure, the NHPP; or (iii) comprising a compound Poisson process (CPP) beyond the HPP and NHPP, if the failures occur in sizes or clusters rather than in terms of the conventional assumption of a single failure at a time.

Binomial-type models are based on similar assumptions: a binomial setting in which (i) a software defect will be removed whenever a failure occurs, (ii) there is a known quantity of embedded defects or faults independent in the program in advance, and (iii) the hazard rates are identical for all defects. Models that differ from these two types of count processes are what we call "other types."

8.4 SOFTWARE RELIABILITY GROWTH MODELS

Again, for failure distribution over time, whether the distribution is negative exponential, Weibull, or other, the models differ from one another. Let's first study the negative exponential class of failure time models in Poisson and binomial and other types. In software reliability, we employ the mean value function, $\mu(t) = E[M(t)]$, to represent the expectation of failures with respect to time, where $M(t)$ is a random process to denote the number of failures achieved until time t. On the other hand, the failure intensity function, $\lambda(t) = \mu'(t)$, is the first derivative of $\mu(t)$ with respect to (w.r.t.) time. $\lambda(t)$ denotes the instantaneous rate of change of the expectation of failures w.r.t. time t. Note that the hazard rate $h(t) = f(t)[R(t)]^{-1}$ is the conditional failure density given that no failures up to time t. Equations (1.22)–(1.35) as illustrated in Figure 1.13 showed these facts earlier.

8.4.1 Negative Exponential Class of Failure Times

In this class, the failure intensity $\lambda(t)$ is in the form of a negative exponential. The binomial types for this class have per failure constant hazard rate $h(t) = c$ and $\lambda(t) = Nc\exp(-ct)$. The Poisson types in this class also have a constant hazard rate of $h(t) = c$, but with a negative exponential time to failure $f(t) = c\exp(-ct)$. However, the number of failures that occur over a given period of time for either a HPP or an NHPP is Poisson. Next, let's look at models contained in this class.

8.4.2 J–M De-eutrophication Model (Binomial Type)

A very early model proposed is the J–M time-between-failures (~negative exponential) model in 1972 by Jelinski and Moranda [13]. The model assumes N faults (or potential failures) triggered randomly with equal probability. One also assumes that the failure fix ("as good as new") time is negligible, and this leads to the software's improvement by the same amount at each fix. Now, the hazard function during the time $x_i = t_i - t_{i-1}$ between the $(i-1)^{st}$ and i^{th} failures is given by

$$h(x_i) = C[N - i + 1] \tag{8.1}$$

where N is the total count of software faults at the very beginning, with C proportionality constant. The hazard function remains a constant between the failures but decreases in steps of after the removal of each fault, a fact that results in the improvement of the time between failures. Now, let's study the mathematical–statistical model in which $x_i = t_i - t_{i-1}$ are i.i.d. with a negative exponential pdf with mean $\theta = \{\phi[N - i + 1]\}^{-1}; f(x_i) = (1/\theta)\exp(-x_i/\theta)$ being the pdf of interarrival times.

$\mu(t) = N[1 - \exp(-\phi t)]$ is the finite mean value function, since $\lim_{t \to \infty} \mu(t) = N\lambda(t) = N\phi \exp(-\phi t)$ is the failure intensity function. For the model above, the estimates of the parameters and reliability prediction are given by

$$\sum_{i=1}^{n} \frac{1}{\hat{N} - i + 1} = \frac{n}{\hat{N} - \left(1 / \sum_{i=1}^{n} x_i\right)\left[\sum_{i=1}^{n}(i-1)x_i\right]} \tag{8.2}$$

$$\hat{\phi} = \frac{n}{N\left(\sum_{i=1}^{n} x_i\right) - \left(\sum_{i=1}^{n}(i-1)x_i\right)} \tag{8.3}$$

First, N is estimated from the first nonlinear equation and then installed in the second nonlinear equation to estimate ϕ. Then, after $n = i - 1$ faults have been observed, the estimate of the MTBF for the $(n+1)^{st}$ fault is $\{z(t)\}^{-1} = 1 / \hat{\phi}(\hat{N} - n)$. Shooman's safeguard reliability model (1972) is very similar to the J–M model [9, 13]. These pioneering models have inspired other authors in sequence and have since been replaced by more modern methods.

8.4.3 Moranda's Geometric Model (Poisson Type)

The geometric model proposed by Moranda is a variation of the original J–M model [14]. The interarrival time for failures is also a negative exponential, $f(x_i) = D\phi^{i-1} \exp(-D\phi^{i-1} x_i)$, whose mean decreases with respect to a *geometric* trend (i.e., $h(t) = D\phi^{i-1}$, $i = 1,2,\dots,n$; $0 < \phi < 1$ at the $(i-1)^{st}$ failure). The expected time between failures is $E(X_i) = h^{-1}(t_{i-1})$. The hazard rate decreases in a geometric progression as each failure occurs. The functional form of the failure intensity (in terms of the expected number of failures) is geometric. The mean value and failure intensity functions are given below, where $\beta = -\ln\phi$, $0 < \phi < 1$ in an infinite failure model:

$$\mu(t) = \frac{1}{\beta}\ln\left\{\left[D\beta \exp(\beta)\right]t + 1\right\} \quad \text{and} \quad \lim_{t \to \infty} \mu(t) = \infty \tag{8.4}$$

$$\lambda(t) = \frac{D\exp(\beta)}{\left[D\beta \exp(\beta)\right]t + 1} \tag{8.5}$$

To estimate the parameters, we take the natural logarithm of the likelihood function $\prod_{i=1}^{n} f(X_i)$ and the partial derivatives with respect to C and D. The maximum likelihood estimators (MLEs) are then solutions of the following pair:

$$\hat{D} = \frac{\hat{\phi} n}{\sum_{i=1}^{n} \hat{\phi}^i X_i} \quad \text{and} \quad \frac{\sum_{i=1}^{n} i\hat{\phi}^i X_i}{\sum_{i=1}^{n} \hat{\phi}^i X_i} = \frac{n+1}{2} \tag{8.6}$$

Using these MLEs for D and ϕ, and their invariance property, the MLE of the failure intensity and mean value function can be estimated by inserting these MLEs in the equations for $\mu(t)$ and $\lambda(t)$.

8.4.4 Goel–Okumoto Nonhomogeneous Poisson Process (Poisson Type)

This Poisson-type model was proposed by Goel and Okumoto in 1979 using the number of failures observed per unit time in groups. See Goel's 1985 paper [52] for a well-done overview. They suggested that the cumulative count of failures, $N(t)$, observed at time t can be modeled as an NHPP, a Poisson process with time-varying failure rate, which follows a negative exponential distribution:

$$P\{N(t)=y\} = \frac{\left[\mu(t)\right]^y}{y!} e^{-\mu(t)}, \quad y = 0,1,2,\ldots \tag{8.7}$$

where $\mu(t) = N(1-e^{-bt})$ is the mean value function for b, the per-fault detection rate. N, the expected number of faults, is not known (hence not of binomial type) and has to be estimated. The failure intensity function

$$\lambda(t) = \mu'(t) = Nbe^{-bt} \tag{8.8}$$

is strictly decreasing for $t>0$. It is not difficult to see that $\mu(t)$ and $\lambda(t)$ are the cumulative function, $F(t)$, and probability density function, $f(t)$, of the negative exponential, respectively. The MLEs of N and b can be estimated as solutions for the following pair of equations:

$$\hat{N} = \frac{\displaystyle\sum_{i=1}^{n} f_i}{1-e^{-\hat{b}t_n}} \tag{8.9}$$

$$\frac{t_n e^{-\hat{b}t_n} \displaystyle\sum_{i=1}^{n} f_i}{1-e^{-\hat{b}t_n}} = \frac{f_i \left(t_i e^{-\hat{b}t_i} - t_{i-1} e^{-\hat{b}t_{i-1}} \right)}{e^{-\hat{b}t_{i-1}} - e^{-\hat{b}t_i}} \tag{8.10}$$

The second equation is solved for $\hat{b}$ by numerical (nonlinear) techniques. Then it is substituted into the first equation to calculate $\hat{N}$. One can then substitute these MLEs to find others such as

$$\hat{\mu}(t) = \hat{N}\left(1-e^{\hat{b}t}\right) \quad \text{and} \quad \hat{\lambda}(t) = \mu'(t) = \hat{N}\hat{b}e^{\hat{b}t} \tag{8.11}$$

and hence, the estimated expected number of faults to be detected in the $(n+1)^{\text{th}}$ observation period is given by

$$\hat{N}\left(e^{-\hat{b}t_n} - e^{-\hat{b}t_{n+1}}\right) \tag{8.12}$$

Okumoto and Goel also determined an ORT of observation for a software product if the reliability desired is R for a specified operational period of T_o [53]:

$$\text{ORT} = \left(\frac{1}{b}\right)\left\{\ln\left[a\left(1-e^{-bT_o}\right)\right]-\left[\ln\left(\ln\frac{1}{R}\right)\right]\right\} \tag{8.13}$$

There is a trend toward diminishing defect rates or failures with the negative exponential assumption. However, in real life, there have been cases where the failure rate first increases (due to adding code) and then decreases (due to fixes) or sometimes cruises at a constant rate (adding code and at the same time equal effect of fixes). Goel's 1985 paper generalized the Goel–Okumoto NHPP model using a three-parameter Weibull model [52]:

$$\mu(t) = N\left(1-e^{-bt^d}\right) \tag{8.14}$$

$$\lambda(t) = \mu'(t) = Nbde^{-bt^d}t^{d-1} \tag{8.15}$$

where the shape parameter $d=1$ gives negative exponential with a constant hazard rate and $d=2$ for the Rayleigh model. The shape parameter $d<1$ denotes infancy, $d=1$ denotes useful life, and $d>1$ denotes the wear-out period in the traditional bathtub curve of the hazard function for most electronic components.

Example 1
For a generalized Goel–Okumoto NHPP model, given the following input data—N (the number of failures expected at the end of mission time)$=100$, b (the fault detection rate per fault)$=0.02$—calculate the mean value of failures at 80 h. Take $d=1$ and $d=2$, respectively.

$$\mu(t) = N\left(1-e^{-bt^d}\right) = 100\left(1-e^{-0.02(80)}\right) = 100\left(1-e^{-1.6}\right) = 78.8 \text{ failures;} \quad d=1 \tag{8.16}$$

$$\mu(t) = N\left(1-e^{-bt^d}\right) = 100\left(1-e^{-0.02(80)(80)}\right) \approx 100 \text{ failures;} \quad d=2 \tag{8.17}$$

8.4.5   Musa's Basic Execution Time Model (Poisson Type)

John D. Musa's model was one of the earliest to use the actual CPU execution time rather than the clock or calendar time, which is actually irrelevant to the operating stress of the software environment [29]. The fundamental assumptions are as follows:

1. The cumulative number of failures, $M(t)$, follows an NHPP, where the probability distribution functions of the random process, with mean value function $\mu(t) = \beta_0[1-\exp(-\beta_1 t)]$, vary with time. It is a finite failure model: $\lim_{t\to\infty}\mu(t) = \beta_0$.

2. The interfailure times are piecewise negative exponentially distributed, implying that the hazard rate for a single fault is a constant:

$$\lambda(t) = \mu'(t) = \beta_0 \beta_1 \left[1 - \exp(-\beta_1 t)\right] \tag{8.18}$$

The conditional reliability and hazard functions after $(i-1)$ failures have occurred are

$$R(t \mid t_{i-1}) = \exp\left\{-\left[\beta_0 \exp(\beta_1 t_{i-1})\right]\left[1 - \exp(-\beta_1 t)\right]\right\} \tag{8.19}$$

$$h(t \mid t_{i-1}) = \beta_0 \beta_1 \exp(\beta_1 t_{i-1})\left[\exp(-\beta_1 t)\right] \tag{8.20}$$

Assume that n failures have occurred and that t_n is the last failure time and $t_n + x$ is the stopping time. The MLEs of β_0 and β_1, which possess the invariance property needed to estimate other functions, such as reliability, hazard, and failure intensity, are given by

$$\hat{\beta}_0 = \frac{n}{1 - \exp\left[-\hat{\beta}_1\left(t_n + x\right)\right]} \tag{8.21}$$

$$\frac{n}{\hat{\beta}_1} - \frac{n\left(t_n + x\right)}{\exp\left(\hat{\beta}_1\left(t_n + x\right)\right) + 1} - \sum_{i=1}^{n} t_i = 0 \tag{8.22}$$

Example 2
Let us consider a software program with an initial failure density of 10 failures/h and 100 total failures to be experienced in infinite time. Determine the failure intensity, $\lambda(t)$, and the number of failures predicted, $\mu(t)$, at $t = 10$ and 100 h. Use basic execution model.

Solution: At $t = 10$, $\lambda(t) = \lambda_0 \exp(-\lambda_0 / v_0)t = 10\exp(-(10/100)(10)] = 10\exp(-1) = 3.68$ failures/CPU hour. Note that $\lambda_0 = \beta_0 \beta_1 = 10$ and $\beta_1 = 0.1$ and the initial # failures $\beta_0 = 100$. Hence, $\mu(t) = \beta_0[1 - \exp(-\beta_1 t)] = 100(1 - e^{-0.1 \times 10}) = 100(1 - e^{-1}) = 100(1 - 0.368) = 63$ failures.
At $t = 100$, $\lambda(t) = \lambda_0 \exp(-(\lambda_0 / v_0)t) = 10\exp(-(10/100)(100)] = 10\exp(-10) = 0.454 \times 10^{-6}$ failures / CPU h. $\mu(t) = \beta_0[1 - \exp(-\beta_1 t)] = 100(1 - e^{-0.1 \times 100}) = 100(1 - e^{-10}) \approx 100$ failures.

8.4.6 Musa–Okumoto Logarithmic Poisson Execution Time Model (Poisson Type)

This is similar to the Goel–Okumoto (G–O) NHPP model in which the number of failures experienced by a certain time t, $M(t)$, also follows an NHPP with a negative exponentially decreasing intensity function, $\lambda(t) = \lambda_0 \exp[\theta\mu(t)]$, where $\mu(t) = (1/\theta)\ln(\lambda_0 \theta t + 1)$ is the mean value function, $\theta > 0$ is the failure decay parameter (or rate of reduction in the normalized failure intensity per failure), and λ_0 is the initial failure rate [47]. Hence, when

$\mu(t)$ is substituted, we obtain $\lambda(t) = \lambda_0 / (\lambda_0 \theta t + 1)$, since $\lim_{t \to \infty} \lambda(t) \to \infty$. This is an infinite failure model compared to the basic execution model's finite behavior. The rate of decrease explains the fact that earlier fixes of the failures detected reduced the failure rate of the latter part, thus causing fewer fixes by the end. The difference from the G–O NHPP is that its mean value function is different. It is defined to be logarithmic Poisson since the number of failures expected over time is a logarithmic function. The logarithmic Poisson process is thought to be superior for highly nonuniform distributions. The data needed are actual times, t_i, $i = 1, 2, \ldots$ or interfailure times, $x_i = t_i - t_{i-1}$.

If we let $\beta_0 = \theta^{-1}$ and $\beta_1 = \lambda_0 \theta$, which is same as $\lambda_0 = \beta_0 \beta_1$ in the basic execution model, the failure intensity and mean value functions become

$$\lambda(t) = \frac{\lambda_0}{\lambda_0 \theta t + 1} = \frac{\beta_0 \beta_1}{\beta_1 t + 1} \tag{8.23}$$

$$\mu(t) = \beta_0 \ln(\beta_1 t + 1) \tag{8.24}$$

The conditional reliability and hazard rate functions at time t after the $(i-1)^{\text{th}}$ failure are

$$R(t \mid t_{i-1}) = \left[\frac{\beta_1 t_{i-1} + 1}{\beta_1(t_{i-1} + t) + 1} \right]^{\beta_0} \tag{8.25}$$

$$h(t \mid t_{i-1}) = \frac{\beta_0 \beta_1}{\beta_1(t_{i-1} + t) + 1} \tag{8.26}$$

Note that "|" denotes "given that" or "conditional upon." Use the reparameterized model to find the MLEs from the failure intensity and mean functions:

$$\hat{\beta}_0 = \frac{n}{\ln\left(1 + \hat{\beta}_1 t_n\right)} \tag{8.27}$$

$$\frac{1}{\hat{\beta}_1} \sum_{i=1}^{n} \frac{1}{1 + \hat{\beta}_1 t_i} = \frac{n(t_n)}{\left(1 + \hat{\beta}_1 t_n\right)\ln\left(1 + \hat{\beta}_1 t_n\right)} \tag{8.28}$$

As in the basic execution model, these MLEs calculated using their invariance property can be substituted in the failure intensity and mean value functions to estimate $\lambda(t)$ and $\mu(t)$.

Example 3

Let us consider a software program with an initial failure density of 10 failures/h and 100 total failures to be experienced in infinite time. Find failure intensity, $\hat{\lambda}(t)$, and number of failures predicted, $\mu(t)$, at $t = 10$ and 100 execution hours. Also, $\theta = 0.02$, that is, two defects per $100\,\text{h}$ will decrease with time. Use the logarithmic Poisson model.

Solution: At $t = 10$, $\lambda(t = 10) = \dfrac{\lambda_0}{\lambda_0 \theta t + 1} = \dfrac{10}{10(0.02)(10) + 1} = 0.476$ failures / CPU h.

Note that $\lambda_0 = \beta_0 \beta_1 = 10$ and $\beta_1 = 10/50 = 0.2$, since $\beta_0 = \theta^{-1} = 50$. Then

$\lambda(t = 10) = \dfrac{\beta_0 \beta_1}{\beta_1 t + 1} = \dfrac{50(0.2)}{0.2(10) + 1} = 10/3 = 3.33$ failures / CPU h.

Also, $\mu(t = 10) = \theta^{-1} \ln(\lambda_0 \theta t + 1) 50 \ln[(10)(0.02)(10) + 1] = 50 \ln(3) = 55$ failures, or $\mu(t = 10) = \beta_0 \ln(\beta_1 t + 1) = 50 \ln[0.2(10) + 1] = 50 \ln(3) = 55$ failures.

At $t = 100$, $\lambda(t = 100) = \dfrac{\lambda_0}{\lambda_0 \theta t + 1} = \dfrac{10}{10(0.02)(100) + 1} = 10/21 = 0.476$ failure / CPU h.

Also, $\lambda_0 = \beta_0 \beta_1 = 10$, and $\beta_1 = 10/50 = 0.2$, since $\beta_0 = \theta^{-1} = 50$. Then,

$\lambda(t = 100) = \dfrac{\beta_0 \beta_1}{\beta_1 t + 1} = \dfrac{50(0.2)}{0.2(100) + 1} = 10/21 = 3.33$ failures / CPU h.

Also, $\mu(t = 100) = \theta^{-1} \ln(\lambda_0 \theta t + 1) = 50 \ln[(10)(0.02)(100) + 1] = 50 \ln 21 = 152$ failures, or $\mu(t = 100) = \beta_0 \ln(\beta_1 t + 1) = 50 \ln[0.2(100) + 1] = 50 \ln(21) = 152$ failures.

8.4.7 L–V Bayesian Model

This others' category model is a result of a Bayesian approach, also by Littlewood and Verrall in which they regarded software reliability measures as representing the strength of belief that a program is operating successfully [30]. This opposed the classical view taken by the majority of the models in which the reliability is a measure of goodness or success in a given number of random trials. While the hazard rate is a function of the number of defects remaining, the L–V model assumed it was a random variable, a fact that has caused uncertainty in the effectiveness of the fault correction or failure prevention process. Therefore, even though failure time distributions are negative exponential (assumed in earlier classical models to behave with a certain failure rate), that rate is a random variable under the principles of Bayesian prior and posterior analysis. The distribution of this random failure rate powered by a gamma prior is also a gamma posterior distribution.

A similar Bayesian approach was adopted independently by Sahinoglu for the failure and repair rates of electric power generators [54] and in later research through a textbook [55] to estimate their forced outage rate (FOR) in the estimation of the electric power system reliability index, loss of load expected (LOLE). Littlewood's differential fault model (1981), a variant of the original L–V model that uses the hazard rate as a random variable in a Bayesian framework, was a binomial model using a Pareto class of interfailure time distributions [56]. However, the reliability growth is modeled in a process of two mechanisms, such as fault detection and fault correction, similar to some earlier models that adopted the same approach of differing stages. Later Keiller et al. proposed a variation of the model very similar to their initial model using the same randomness of hazard rate but employing a different parameter (the shape parameter, α, rather than the scale parameter, ξ) of that prior distribution to explain the effect of change on reliability [57]. Although their model used a negative exponential class of failure time distributions, it was neither Poisson nor binomial type, but "others." There are many other Bayesian approaches such as Liu's Bayesian geometric model, and Thompson and Chelson's Bayesian model, to name but two [58, 59]. Formulation of the L–V model can be summarized as follows. The sequential failure times are assumed to be independent exponential random variables with parameter λ_i:

$$f(x_i) = \lambda \exp(-\lambda x_i), \quad i = 1, 2, \ldots, \ a, \lambda > 0, \ x_i > 0 \tag{8.29}$$

Now let the software failure rate λ have a prior distribution from the gamma family:

$$\theta_1(\lambda) = \frac{\xi^c}{\Gamma(c)} \lambda^{c-1} \exp(-\lambda\xi), \quad \lambda > 0 \tag{8.30}$$

The joint distribution of data and prior, assuming that all shape and scale parameters are identical, is given by

$$k(x, \lambda) = f(x_1, x_2, \ldots, x_n; \lambda) = \frac{\xi^a}{\Gamma(a)} \lambda^{n+a-1} \exp\left[-\lambda(x_T + \xi)\right] \tag{8.31}$$

where n is the number of occurrences and $x_T = \sum_{i=1}^{n} x_i$ represents the total sampled failure times for n occurrences. Thus, the posterior distribution for λ can be derived as

$$h(\lambda \mid \underline{x}) = \frac{k(\underline{x}, \lambda)}{\int_{\lambda} f(\underline{x}, \lambda) d\lambda} = \frac{1}{\Gamma(n+a)} (x_T + \xi) \lambda^{n+a-1} \exp\{-\lambda(x_T + \xi)\} \tag{8.32}$$

which is the Gamma $\{n + a, (x_T + \xi)^{-1}\}$.

For $h(\lambda \mid x_i) \sim \text{Gamma}(\alpha + 1, (x_i + \xi_i)^{-1})$, $E(\lambda) = (\alpha + 1 / x_i + 1)$ using a quadratic loss function. Recall $\underline{x}$ denotes a vector of x_i. Then, the marginal distribution of the random variable, $x_i > 0$, $i = 1, 2, \ldots, n$ given the gamma prior can be derived as

$$f(x_i \mid \alpha, \xi_i) = \frac{\alpha(\xi_i)^a}{(x_i + \xi_i)^{\alpha+1}} \tag{8.33}$$

(8.33) is a Pareto distribution with joint density

$$f(x_1, x_2, \ldots, x_n) = \frac{\alpha^n \prod_{i=1}^{n} (\xi_i)^a}{\prod_{i=1}^{n} (x_i + \xi_i)^{\alpha+1}} \tag{8.34}$$

For model and reliability estimation, if one assumes that $\xi_i = \beta_0 + \beta_1 i$ (the linear form) or $\xi_i = \beta_0 + \beta_1 i^2$ (the quadratic form), then by using the foregoing marginal distribution for the x_i's, we calculate the MLEs for α, β_0 and β_1 as the solutions to the following system of equations:

$$\frac{n}{\hat{\alpha}} + \sum_{i=1}^{n} \ln \hat{\xi}_i - \sum_{i=1}^{n} \ln\left(x_i + \hat{\xi}_i\right) = 0 \tag{8.35}$$

$$\hat{\alpha} \sum_{i=1}^{n} \frac{i'}{\hat{\xi}_i} - (\hat{\alpha} + 1) \sum_{i=1}^{n} \frac{i'}{x_i + \hat{\xi}_i} \tag{8.36}$$

where $\xi_i = \beta_0 + \beta_1 i'$ and $i' = i$, or $i' = i^2$. Using a uniform prior, $U(a,b)$, for the shape parameter α, Littlewood and Verrall derived the marginal distribution of the x_i's as a function of β_0 and β_1 only. Once the three unknowns α, β_0, and β_1 are estimated, the linear intensity function is, for an example,

$$\lambda_{\text{linear}}(t) = \frac{\alpha - 1}{\sqrt{\beta_0^2 + 2\beta_1 t(\alpha - 1)}} \tag{8.37}$$

A final procedure is to estimate the least squares estimates using the fact that for a Pareto pdf, $E(X_i) = \xi_i / (\alpha - 1)$. Once the parameters are estimated, reliability measures such as reliability and failure intensity functions can be estimated. Additionally, the mean time to failure for the ith failure can be estimated as $E(X_i) = \text{MTTF} = \xi_{i'} / (\alpha - 1)$, where i' is the linear or quadratic assumed term for i. Again, recall that $\xi_i = \beta_0 + \beta_1 i'$; $i' = i$, or i^2.

Musa and Okumoto in 1984 proposed that ξ_i be a function related inversely to the number of failures remaining, inspired by an efficient debugging process: $\xi_i = N(\alpha + 1) / \lambda_0 (N - i)$, where N is the number of defects expected as time goes large, λ_0 is the initial failure intensity function, i is the failure index, and α is the shape parameter of the gamma prior for the rate λ [60]. It shows that the scale parameter increases as the number of remaining failures decreases with diminishing i.

8.4.8 Sahinoglu's Compound Poisson^Geometric and Poisson^Logarithmic Series Models

A generalized CPP (or a CP model) is proposed for estimation of the residual count of software failures in References [24–27]. It is observed that conventional NHPP models do not allow for the possibility of multiple counts and the CP model is superior when clumping of failures at any given epoch exists [61]. Specifically a model called *Poisson^geometric* (or stuttering Poisson) is studied in which the underlying failure process is assumed to be Poisson, whereas a geometrically distributed number of failures may be detected at each failure epoch. The model proposed is validated using a few of Musa's data sets. Further, the Poisson^logarithmic series (equivalent to negative binomial given certain assumptions) is studied similarly where the compounding pdf is logarithmic series, while the counting process is the same as before, NHPP [26, 55]. The results obtained from software programs can easily be used to obtain the CP plots [61].

8.4.8.1 Generalizations of the Poisson Model The Poisson theorem asserts that a counting process is a Poisson process if the jumps in all intervals of the same length are identically distributed and independent of past jumps (an assumption of stationary and independent increments) and the events singly occur at each epoch (an assumption of orderliness) [62]. Failure interarrival times may be negative exponentially distributed, but this is not sufficient to prove that the counting process is Poisson [63, p. 434]. Let us observe two generalizations (sometimes called *degenerations*) of the Poisson process [64, 65]: The first is the well-known NHPP, obtained by dropping the "stationary increments" property in the Poisson theorem and replacing it with the "time-dependent increments" property, where the Poisson failure-arrival rate β varies with time t (e.g., in software testing or unexpected ambulance calls on an ordinary day). The second is the less popularly known CPP, which is the process obtained if the orderliness property is dropped from the conventional Poisson theorem and replaced with that of stationary jumps. Let Z_n be the size of the nth jump, where $\{Z_n, n=1,2,...\}$ are i.i.d. random variables. Let $J(t)$ be the size of jumps that occur during $(0,t]$; then $N(t)$ is a CPP with $N(T)=Z_1+Z_2+\cdots+Z_{J(t)}, t \ge 0$ [62].

The discrete CP pdf in this section is one of two types. It may be of geometric density type with its forgetfulness property to govern the failure size $(x>1)$ distribution, where the conventional Poisson is a special case when $q(=\text{variance/mean})=1$. The symbol $\wedge$ designates that the parent Poisson distribution to the left of $\wedge$ is compounded by the compounding distribution to the right of $\wedge$ [55]. A similar publication by Sahinoglu on the Poisson^geometric pdf has studied the limiting sum of Markov Bernoulli variables [66]. Or, if the forgetfulness property does not exist, there is a positive correlation between the failures in a clump upon arrival. The author uses a logarithmic series distribution (LSD) for jump sizes with a true contagion property (positive correlation). The sum of LSD random variables governed by a Poisson counting process results in Poisson^logarithmic series, which simply defaults to a negative binomial distribution (NBD) given a certain mathematical assumption holds [67–73].

8.4.8.2 Truncated Poisson^Geometric (Stuttering Poisson)

A CP with a specific compounding distribution has negative exponentially distributed failure interarrival times with rate β [74]. This implies that the pdf of negative exponential interarrival times is independent of or not influenced by the earlier arrival epochs—hence the forgetfulness property of the Poisson process. Suppose that each Poisson arrival dictates a positive discrete amount x of failures, which are i.i.d. as $\{f_x\}$. P^G was covered in Chapter 7:

$$P(X) = \sum_{Y=0}^{\infty} \frac{(\beta t)^Y e^{-\beta t}}{Y!} f^{Y^*}(X); \quad X = 0,1,2,..., \quad \beta > 0 \tag{8.38}$$

where $f^{Y^*}(x)$ is the Y-fold convolution of $\{f_x\}$ when $f_x=1$ for $x=1$ and $f_x=0$ for $x=0$ for a conventional Poisson process. Therefore, this equation reduces to a Poisson distribution in the case of a single failure per arrival. On the other hand, the geometric distribution is given as

$$f_x(x) = (1-r)r^{x-1}, \quad x = 1,2,3,... \tag{8.39}$$

Thus, a special case of CP distribution is the Poisson^geometric. The rate β of the Poisson process is the average number of arrivals per unit time, and r is the probability of finding the next independent failure in the batch or clump within each arrival. Then $p=1-r$ is the probability of starting the Poisson process for the next arrival. In summary, the total count of failures $X = \sum x_i$ within time interval t is a Poisson^geometric distribution [24], where $P(X = 0 \mid Y = 0) = e^{-\beta t}$, or $e^{-\beta}$ if $t=1$ [55]. Each term in the summation in Table 8.1 is the product of Poisson pdf and geometric p.m.f. values that add up to $E(X) = \beta / (1-r)$ of the Poisson^geometric:

$$P(X \mid Y) = \sum_{Y=1}^{X} \frac{(\beta t)^Y e^{-\beta t}}{Y!} \binom{X-1}{Y-1} r^{X-Y} (1-r)^Y, \quad X = 1,2,3... \; 0 < r < 1, \; \beta > 0 \tag{8.40}$$

From equation (8.38), the joint distribution of $P\{X(t),Y(t)\}$ for unit time $t=1$ is given in Table 8.1. The expected value of the CP random variable for the marginal distribution of X is obtained by multiplying the first row by 0, the second row by 1, the third row by 2, and so on and adding the columns. Summing over X rows of 1 to Y columns, we get

$$E(X) = \frac{\beta}{1-r} = \frac{\beta}{p} \tag{8.41}$$

$$\text{Var}(X) = E(X^2) - [E(X)]^2 = \frac{\beta(1+r)}{(1-r)^2} = \frac{\beta(1+r)}{(1-r)(1+r)} = \frac{\beta}{1-r} \tag{8.42}$$

This is identical to $E(X)$. Therefore, $E(X^2) = (\beta/p) + (\beta^2/p^2)$. Similarly $E(Y) = \text{Var}(Y) = \beta$ in the Poisson process. Note that geometric p.m.f. is a discrete analog of the continuous negative exponential pdf and has a similar nonaging Markov forgetfulness property. Hence, for the $X \sim$ Poisson^geometric (β), and $x \sim$ geometric(r) processes, see Table 8.1:

$$\begin{aligned}
Q = (\text{variance/mean}) &= \frac{E(x^2)}{E(x)} = \frac{(q+q^2)p^{-2}}{qp^{-1}} = \frac{q+q^2}{qp}. \\
&= \frac{1+q}{p} = \frac{1+1-p}{p} = (2-p)p^{-1}
\end{aligned} \tag{8.43}$$

The probabilities and moments of the zero-truncated Poisson^geometric $P \wedge G(\mu, Q)$ are $(1 - e^{-\beta t})^{-1}$ times the nontruncated:

$$\mu = E(X) = \beta t \left[(1-r)(1 - e^{-\beta t}) \right]^{-1} \tag{8.44}$$

8.4.8.3 *Truncated Poisson^Logarithmic Series (NBD)*   Of a number of chance mechanisms generating the NBD, it can also be defined to be a Poisson sum of logarithmic series distributed random variables [75, 76]. NBD was covered in Chapter 7. See Table 8.2 for analysis of $T1$–$T5$.

8.4.9 Gamma, Weibull, and Other Classes of Failure Times

In the classes in which the failure intensity $\lambda(t)$ is not in the form of a negative exponential, but in gamma, Weibull, or other distributions, the number of failures to occur over a given period of time is either homogeneous or nonhomogeneous Poisson, binomial, or other. Next we look at the models that fall in these classes.

8.4.9.1 *Yamada's Delayed and Ohba's Inflection S and Hyperexponential Models (Poisson Type)*   The interfailure distribution is *gamma* pdf, but the failure count per unit time is a Poisson type of model, not binomial. Ohba, Yamada, and joint authors proposed a software reliability growth model based on the assumption that there exist two types of defects, one of which is easier to detect [19, 22]. Yamada and Osaki [22] claimed that a testing process is a combination of both a defect detection process and a defect isolation process. They indicated that their model is more reasonable and useful when defects can be classified into two such categories. Since the model employs more parameters than those of the simple G–O model, it becomes more complicated to apply this technique in practice.

TABLE 8.1 Joint Distribution of Poisson^Geometric X and Poisson Y

X	Y				Expected, $E(X)=\sum X\,P(X)$
	0	1	2	3···	
0	$e^{-\beta t}$	—	—	—	0
1	—	$\beta e^{-\beta}(1-r)$	—	—	$\beta e^{-\beta}(1-r)$
2	—	$\beta e^{-\beta}r(1-r)$	$\dfrac{\beta^2 e^{-\beta}}{2!}\dbinom{1}{1}(1-r)^2$	—	$2\beta e^{-\beta}r(1-r)+\beta e^{-\beta}(1-r)^2$
3	—	$\beta e^{-\beta}r^2(1-r)$	$\dfrac{\beta^2 e^{-\beta}}{2!}\dbinom{2}{1}r(1-r)^2$	$\dfrac{\beta^3 e^{-\beta}}{3!}\dbinom{2}{2}(1-r)^3$	$3\beta e^{-\beta}r^2(1-r)+3\beta^2 e^{-\beta}(1-r)^2+\dfrac{\beta^3 e^{-\beta}}{2}(1-r)^3$
4	—	$\beta e^{-\beta}r^3(1-r)$	$\dfrac{\beta^2 e^{-\beta}}{2!}\dbinom{3}{1}r^2(1-r)^2$	$\dfrac{\beta^3 e^{-\beta}}{3!}\dbinom{3}{2}r(1-r)^3$	$\cdots$
5	—	$\beta e^{-\beta}r^4(1-r)$	$\dfrac{\beta^2 e^{-\beta}}{2!}\dbinom{4}{1}r^3(1-r)^2$	$\dfrac{\beta^3 e^{-\beta}}{3!}\dbinom{4}{2}r^2(1-r)^3$	$\cdots$
···		—	—	—	$\cdots$
Sum[a]	0	$\beta e^{-\beta}[(1-r)]$ $(1+2r+3r^2+4r^3+\cdots)$	$\beta^2 e^{-\beta}(1-r)^2$ $(1+3r+6r^2+10r^3+\cdots)$	$\cdots$	$E(X)=\dfrac{\beta}{1-r}$ by math series expansion

[a]Each term in the summation is the product of the Poisson pmf and geometric pmf values that add up to $E(x)=\beta/(1-r)$ of the Poisson^geometric.

With this method, there can be a significant delay between the time of the first failure observation and the time of reporting it. The authors proposed a delayed S-shaped reliability model where the experienced growth curve of the cumulative count of detected defects becomes S-shaped. Their model is based on an NHPP to govern the failure-count process, but their mean value function (similar to the G–O) whose limit is finite [i.e., $\lim_{t \to \infty} \mu(t) = \kappa$ (= total count of defects) $< \infty$] reflects the delay in reporting the defects, as the team members become familiar with the software; usually followed by growth and then decay as the residual defects get more difficult to discover. This results in an S-shaped curve unlike the exponential growth of the G–O model:

$$\mu(t) = \left[1 - (1 + \lambda t)e^{-\lambda t}\right]\kappa \tag{8.45}$$

and the interfailure time distribution is gamma:

$$f(t) = \lambda^2 t e^{-\lambda t} \tag{8.46}$$

where t is the time of occurrence, λ is the error detection rate, and κ is the total count of defects. Ohba later (1984) proposed another S-shaped reliability model, also an NHPP, which he called the *inflection S model* [19]. The new model explains a software failure detection process, where the defects detected are mutually dependent. This implies that the more failures that one detects, the more undetected failures become easily recognizable. This proposal introduces a more practical approach than that of earlier models that invariably adopt the independence assumption of defects in a software program by default. The mean value function for this approach on the other hand is

$$\mu(t) = \kappa \frac{1 - e^{-\lambda t}}{1 + ie^{-\lambda t}} \tag{8.47}$$

where t is the time, λ is the error detection rate, i is the infection factor, and κ is also the total cumulative defect rate (count per unit time). On the other hand, the failure intensity function can be found to be $\lambda(t) = \mu'(t)$, the first derivative of $\mu(t)$ w.r.t. time. Yamada's delayed S and Ohba's inflection S models are both considered to account for the learning or training period (reflected as delayed or inflection patterns of the respective methods) that analysts experience at the infancy level of the software testing process. The mean value function (cdf) and failure intensity function (pdf) curves of both models are different from the negative exponential model. The exponential model assumes that the peak defect arrival is time zero (beginning) of the test phase and decays afterward. The delayed S model assumes a slightly delayed peak, and the inflection S model assumes a sharper peak later in a symmetrical shape.

The hyperexponential model is an extended exponential model. That is, the different sections of the software experience varying rates of failure, as when differing groups of people do too many different things in different languages under different circumstances. In mathematical–statistical analysis, the sum of these varying exponential curves can best be formulated by a hyperexponential. The cumulative count of failures by time t, $M(t)$, follows a Poisson process with a mean value function $\mu(t) = N$:

$$\sum_{i=1}^{k} p_i \left[1 - \exp(-\beta_i t)\right], \quad \text{where } 0 < \beta_i < 1, \sum_{i=1}^{k} p_i = 1, \text{ and } 0 < p_i < 1 \tag{8.48}$$

TABLE 8.2 Statistical Analysis of Data T1–T5 For Poisson^Geometric and Poisson^Logarithmic

Data set	No. of Failures	No of Stops	First Moment	Second Moment		Empirical	q(Poisson^ Geometric)	q (NBD) from Nonlinear $E(x)$
	X	Y	$E(x)=X/Y$	$E(x^2)$	$p=1-r$	$q=$Var/Mean		
					$p=Y/X$	$q=E(x^2)/E(x)$	$q=(2-p)/p$	$E(x)=(q-1)/\ln q$
T1	136	133	1.0226	1.0677	0.9779	1.0441	1.0451	1.0219
T2	54	52	1.0385	1.1539	0.9630	1.1111	1.0769	1.0546
T3	38	37	1.0270	1.0841	0.9737	1.0555	1.0541	1.0275
T4	53	50	1.06	1.18	0.9434	1.1132	1.12	1.0556
T5	831	810	1.0259	1.0975	0.9747	1.0698	1.0523	1.0345

N is finite in a finite failure model. The defect counts in each testing interval, the f_i's, are given as input data, as well as the completion time of each period of software observation, t_i's. If $k=1$, it is an NHPP. Since $\lambda(t) = \mu'(t)$ and Np_i is the expected number of faults for the ith class,

$$\lambda(t) = N\sum_{i=1}^{k} p_i \beta_i \left[1 - \exp(-\beta_i t)\right] \tag{8.49}$$

is strictly decreasing for $t>0$. For model estimation and reliability prediction, estimate N_i as the number of defects in each class from the MLE equations presented in the NHPP model. The MLE of N is then the sum of the MLEs over the k classes. If the practice suggests that there exist only two classes, such as new versus old or easy versus difficult, the new model is called the *modified exponential software reliability growth model* [51]. Also, Laprie and Kanoun designed a hyperexponential model for $k=2$ with an equivalent failure rate function [77]:

$$\lambda(t) = \frac{p_1 \beta_1 e^{-\beta_1 t} + p_2 \beta_2 e^{-\beta_2 t}}{p_1 e^{-\beta_1 t} + p_2 e^{-\beta_2 t}} \tag{8.50}$$

and then they derived a system availability model to integrate the two classes, $k=1$ for hardware and $k=2$ for software.

8.4.9.2 Schick–Wolverton Model (Binomial Type) Schick and Wolverton modified the J–M model by assuming that the failure rate is not only proportional to the number of operating errors but also increases linearly with operating time t, where the hazard function is [13]

$$h(t) = k(N - i + 1)t \tag{8.51}$$

The interfailure times are assumed to be w.r.t. the *Weibull* pdf with the negative exponential being a special case. Later, they proposed a more general model [16] in which the per-fault hazard rate is parabolic instead of a linear function as in their original model:

$$h(t) = k(N - i + 1)\left(-b_1 t^2 + b_2 t + b_3\right) \tag{8.52}$$

Critics have pointed out that the model is no longer valid since $h(t)$ should decrease over time. The main reason is that the latter errors are hidden and difficult to encounter in operation in modern software operations.

8.4.10 Duane Model (Poisson Type)

This model was originally proposed as a hardware design by Duane who discovered that the cumulative failure rate or cumulative hazard function $H(t)$ versus the cumulated testing time resulted in a straight line on log-log plotting paper [20]. It is also an NHPP where the fact that the failure intensity function has the same rate for a *Weibull* pdf has been used for some software systems. It is a reliability growth model later adopted by Army Materiel

Systems Analysis Activity (AMSAA) that uses a relationship between a cumulative test time and cumulative failures. It is an infinite failure model, since $\lim_{t \to \infty} \mu(t) = \infty$. The reason it is also referred to as a *power model* (see item 15 in Tables 1.15 and 1.16) is because the mean value function for the cumulative number of failures by time t is taken as a power of t:

$$\mu(t) = at^b, \quad \text{for } a > 0, \; b > 0 \quad (b = 1 \text{ implies a homogeneous Poisson process})$$
(8.53)

The actual times to failure need to be given or the elapsed time between the failures, where $t_0 = 0$. The cumulative count of failures, $M(t)$, follows a Poisson process with a mean value function $\mu(t) = at^b$. If we divide the right- and left-hand sides by total testing time T and take the natural log of both sides, we obtain

$$Y = \ln \frac{\mu(t)}{T} = \ln \frac{at^b}{T} = \ln(a) + (b - 1) \ln T$$
(8.54)

One plots this equation versus T on ln–ln plotting paper to get a straight line. On the other hand, $\lambda(t) = abt^{b-1}$ is the failure intensity function strictly increasing for $b > 1$ (no reliability growth recorded), strictly decreasing for $0 < b < 1$ (reliability growth recorded), and constant for $b = 1$ (HPP with a constant rate). MLEs later derived for a and b are

$$\hat{a} = \frac{n}{T^{\hat{b}}}$$
(8.55)

$$\hat{b} = \frac{n - 1}{\sum_{i=1}^{n} \ln(T / t_i)}$$
(8.56)

where $t_n = T$, which when inserted in $\hat{\mu}(t) = \hat{a}t^{\hat{b}}$ and $\hat{\lambda}(t) = \hat{a}\hat{b}t^{\hat{b}-1}$ give the MLEs for their respective functions. Reference [78] also derived the MLE for MTTF $= \hat{\mu} = t_{(n)} / n\hat{b}$ for the $t_{(n)} =$ time to the $(n+1)^{\text{st}}$ failure, and constructed confidence intervals for the MTTF reliability measure for unrepairable systems.

8.5 NUMERICAL EXAMPLES USING PEDAGOGUES

8.5.1 Example 1

Given the following input data, calculate and compare the mean values of the number of failures expected to be predicted by the end of a time "t" for each NHPP model, that is, t (time at which to predict) $= 80$ CPU h; b (the fault detection rate per fault) $= 0.02$; d (shape) $= 1$ for negative exponential, a special case of Weibull; and N (the number of failures expected at the end of the mission) $= 100$; then the mean value of failures at $t = 80$h is given by $\mu(80) = 79.8$. Similarly for $d = 2$, regarding Rayleigh distribution, a special case of Weibull, $\mu(80) = 100$. This is the Goel–Okumoto failure-count prediction model [17]. See Table 1.18 for a list of Pedagogues and Figure 8.1.

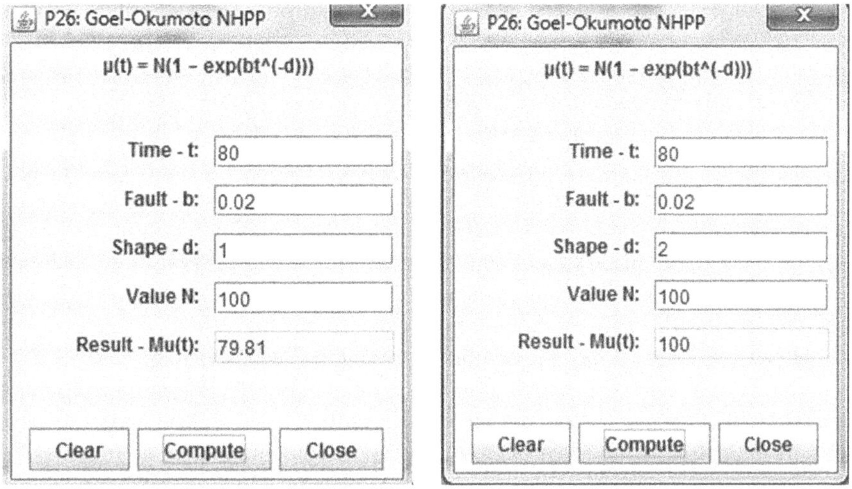

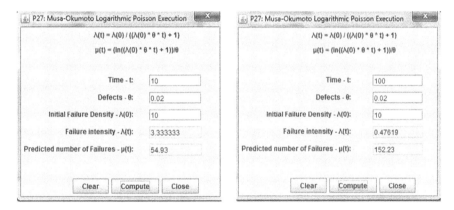

FIGURE 8.1 Pedagogue P26 for Goel–Okumoto's two different input data.

FIGURE 8.2 Pedagogue P27 for Musa–Okumoto's two different input data.

8.5.2 Example 2

Let us consider a software program with an initial failure density of 10 failures/h and 100 total failures to be experienced in infinite time with $\theta = 0.02$ (2 defects per 100 h will decrease with time) using logarithmic Poisson model. Find the failure intensity, $\lambda(t)$, and # failures predicted, $\mu(t)$, at $t = 10$ and $t = 100$ execution hours. This is Musa–Okumoto prediction model [18]. See Figure 8.2, which is detailed in Example 3 of Section 8.4.6.

8.6 RECENT TRENDS IN SOFTWARE RELIABILITY

In 2012, a new article was proposed, titled "Parameter Estimation for the Compound Poisson Software Reliability Model," where the CPM was compounded by a Poisson truncated at zero [79]. It compared new findings with those of the author's 1992 and 1997 publications [24, 25]. The newly proposed article suggests a Poisson truncated at zero as the compounding distribution instead of a geometric and then use a Poisson^Poisson truncated at zero instead of a

Poisson^Geometric. Then, it models the failure cluster sizes as a Poisson truncated at zero, where the clusters' arrivals follow a Poisson in the same as Sahinoglu's. As a result, favorably comparable results are obtained. On the other hand, Poisson truncated at zero is more suitable to employ several estimation methods such as those of Tate and Goen [80].

The CP models have not been fully treated the way it deserves in the bibliography conversely as the nonhomogeneous Poisson models have been recognized although CP Models have more flexibility and practicality. CP Models are easier to implement and their parameters can be rapidly obtained through simple equations from the beginning of the testing phase in addition to its being suitable for applying several biased estimators. This characteristic allows it to adapt faster to changes in the project. Additionally, the CP process model can adjust better to data whose cluster size of maximum occurrence moves from high to low values along the testing time. The main disadvantage of the CP is the constantly varying failure rate prediction that is not so good for a long-range prediction cycles. More effort needs to be spent on adjusting software reliability models toward CP Models to be applied in the event of agile software development methodology.

In 2013, another recently new topic was published under the title of "Software Reliability Testing Using Monte Carlo Methods" where Monte Carlo (MC) and multi-level MC are used for the fault tolerance of multilevel MC methods [81]. The testing process comprises feature test, load test, and regression test. Results were obtained and analyzed using MATLAB. Among hundreds of many, "Lognormal Process Software Reliability Modeling with Testing-Effort" was published in 2013 where the authors proposed a software reliability growth model with testing effort based on a continuous-state space stochastic process, such as a lognormal process, and conducts its goodness of fit evaluation. They also discussed a parameter estimation method of the same model. Then, they derived several software reliability assessment measures by the probability distribution of its solution process and compared their model with existing continuous-state space software reliability growth models in terms of the mean squared error and the Akaike's information criterion by using actual fault-count data [82].

Yet another article worth mentioning published in 2013 is the "Reliability Modeling and Analysis for Open Source Cloud Computing" [83]. The authors express that CLOUD computing is attracting attention as a network service to share the computing resources, such as networks, servers, storage, applications, and services. Also, the article adds that many open source softwares are developed in all parts of the world, for example, Firefox, Apache HTTP server, Linux, Android, etc. This article focuses on a CLOUD computing environment by using open source software such as OpenStack and Eucalyptus because of the unify management of data and low cost. This article also proposes a new approach to software reliability assessment based on the stochastic differential equations and hierarchical Bayesian modeling in order to consider the interesting aspect of the network status of a CLOUD computing environment. Also, actual software fault-count data to show numerical examples of software reliability assessment considering the characteristics of network environment is analyzed.

8.7 DISCUSSIONS AND CONCLUSION

In this chapter, the author has presented an overview of software reliability modeling, a process that can be also utilized and inspired by the security modeling concerns in so far as the underlying fundamental math–statistical assumptions hold. The groundwork concepts of software reliability's taxonomy as related to classification of these models with respect to their usage of statistical time-domain models are examined. Failure-count models related to discrete effort domain are deferred to Chapter 9 for a more thorough coverage. Musa–Okumoto, G–O, and Sahinoglu's CP failure-count models with examples, as well as parametric and nonparametric models, are examined. Lastly, a sample of newest trends is studied citing a few of the most recent articles from the CLOUD computing, simulation, and statistical modeling aspects of software reliability to CP treatment of failure counts. There is not much progress on data collection of software failures.

Software reliability and security modeling is a more in-depth issue than simple computational mechanics of plugging failure data in the meticulously derived formulas of plentiful abundance. It is an endless struggle of fitting your models to real-life, at times high-assurance, life-and-death practices such as those currently used in space programs. There are newer sour episodes indicating that Pentagon is reporting faults with their F-35 programs on software reliability. http://www.reuters.com/article/2014/01/23/us-usa-lockheed-fighter-idUSBREA0M1L920140123 writes: "A new U.S. Defense Department report warns that ongoing software, maintenance and reliability problems with Lockheed Martin Corp's F-35 stealth fighter could delay the Marine Corps' plans to start using its F-35 jets by mid-2015. The latest report by the Pentagon's chief weapons tester, Michael Gilmore, provides a detailed critique of the F-35's technical challenges, and focuses heavily on what it calls the 'unacceptable' performance of the plane's software, according to a 25-page draft obtained by Reuters. The report forecast a possible 13-month delay in completing testing of the Block 2B software needed for the Marine Corps to clear the jets for initial combat use next year, a priority given the high cost of maintaining current aging warplanes."

The modeling technique for software reliability is reaching its pinnacle after five decades or more. However, before using the techniques, we must carefully select the appropriate model that can best suit our case. Measurement in software is still in its infancy after so many years. No flawless quantitative methods have been developed to represent software reliability without extensive limitations. Various approaches can be used to improve the reliability of software; however, it is hard to leverage development time and budget with software reliability. Although crucial to software quality and widely deployed by programmers and testers, software testing still remains an art, due to limited understanding of the principles of software. The difficulty in software testing stems from the complexity of software. Testing as a remedy is more than just debugging. The purpose of testing can be quality assurance, verification and validation, or reliability estimation, and to judge when to stop testing before releasing the product. Testing results can be used as generic metrics as treated in Chapter 3. Software testing is a trade-off between budget, time, and quality, and since up to 80% of software costs are testing related, it is an integral part of software reliability modeling. Especially when we are on the brink of a new era of CLOUD Computing and Big Data and their security-related software challenges, as compared to existing repository or applied to Reliability Engineering as well [84, 85, 86].

To recap, from the early days of Software Reliability Engineering's kick-off conference in April 1990 at Washington D.C. where the author was one of the select invited speakers up to date, much progress has been achieved, and more to arrive in the decades to come [87].

8.8 EXERCISES

8.8.1 (a) Let us consider a software program with an initial failure intensity of 10 failures/h and 100 total failures to be experienced in infinite time. What is the failure intensity $\lambda(\tau)$ going to be at $\tau = 10$ and $\tau = 100$ execution hours for (1) for Musa's basic execution model and (2) for the Musa–Okumoto logarithmic Poisson model?

     (b) Having calculated those, estimate the predicted number of failures, $\mu(\tau)$, at $\tau = 10$ and $\tau = 100$ execution hours for (1) and (2) as above. You may use Pedagogues as in Chapter Exercise 1.7.49 referring to Table 1.17.

8.8.2 For the grouped (clustered) failure data formulated in Table 8.3 and presented in Table 8.4 on system $T38$ [85], use Goel–Okumoto and Musa–Okumoto to estimate the number of failures to be expected by the end of the mission time (at the end of eleventh interval) at step 7 by applying (1) Goel–Okumoto model and (2) Musa–Okumoto model, and (3) Sahinoglu CPMLE model.

8.8.3 Given the grouped data of WD1, WD2, WD3, WD4, and WD5 in the data bank of this book's website, use a software reliability model of your choice to predict expected value and hazard functions at the end of the mission.

8.8.4 Repeat 8.8.3 for DR1, DR2, DR3, DR4, and DR5 data.

TABLE 8.3 Grouped Failure Data Format

Interval Number	Total Test Time after the Interval	Duration of the Interval	Number of Failures in the Interval	Cumulative Number of Failures
1	x_1	x_1	y'_1	y_1
2	x_2	$x_2 - x_1$	y'_2	y_2
$\vdots$	$\vdots$	$\vdots$	$\vdots$	$\vdots$
P	x_p	$x_p - x_{p-1}$	y'_p	y_p

TABLE 8.4 Grouped Failure Data For System T38

Interval Number	Total Test Time at the End of Interval (CPU h)	Duration of Test Interval (CPU h)	No. of Failures in Interval	Cumulative # Failures
1	5	5	1	1
2	15	10	0	1
3	25	10	16	17
4	35	10	1	18
5	45	10	1	19
6	50	5	0	19
7	65	15	1	20
8	75	10	3	23
9	95	20	2	25
10	120	25	7	32
11	125	5	0	32

8.8.5 Utilizing the principles of software reliability modeling, how can you adapt the metrics you learned in Chapter 3 on security to software reliability modeling?

8.8.6 Given compound Poisson^geometric with $M = 10$ and 50 with $q = 1, 3, 5, \ldots$, draw the plot using the book's Java software for PG (for Poisson^geometric). See Figure 7.13 for a similar example in Chapter 7.

8.8.7 Given compound Poisson^LSD with $M = 10$ and 50 with $q = 1, 3, 5$, draw the plot using the book's Java software NB (for NBD = Poisson^LSD). Note the difference if any major when compared with Exercise 8.8.6.
See Figure 7.13 for a similar example in Chapter 7.

REFERENCES

[1] Xie, M., *Software Reliability Modeling*, World Scientific Publishing, Singapore, 1991.

[2] Xie, M. (1993). Software reliability models—Selected annotated bibliography, *Software Testing, Verification, and Reliability*, **3**, 3–28.

[3] Lyu, M. (1996). Software reliability modeling survey, in *Handbook of Software Reliability Engineering*, W. Farr (ed.), IEEE Computer Society Press/McGraw Hill, Los Alamitos.

[4] Kan, S. H., *Metrics and Models in Software Quality Engineering*, Addison-Wesley, Reading, MA, 1995.

[5] Musa, J. D., Iannino, I., Okumoto, K. *Software Reliability—Measurement, Prediction, Application*, Mc-Graw Hill International, 1987.

[6] Munson, J. C., *Software Engineering Measurement*, Auerbach Publications, CRC Press Company, Boca Raton, 2003.

[7] Friedman, J., Voas, M., *Software Assessment—Reliability, Safety, Testability*, John Wiley & Sons Inc., New York, 1995.

[8] Shooman, M. L., *Software Engineering: Design, Reliability and Management*, McGraw Hill, New York, 1983.

[9] Shooman, M. L., *Reliability of Computer Systems and Networks, Fault Tolerance, Analysis, and Design*, John Wiley & Sons Inc., Hoboken, 2002.

[10] Bastani, F. B., *Software reliability, Special Issue of IEEE Transactions on Software Engineering*, IEEE Computer Society, Washington, DC, 1993.

[11] Bernstein, L., Yuhas, M., *Trustworthy Systems through Quantitative Software Engineering*, IEEE Computer Society, Los Alamitos, 2005.

[12] Hudson, G. R., Program errors as a birth and death process, System Development Corporation, Report SP-3011, Santa Monica, CA, 1967.

[13] Jelinski, Z., Moranda, P. B. (1972). Software reliability research, in W. Freiberger (ed.), *Statistical Computer Performance Evaluation*, Academic Press, New York, 465–497.

[14] Moranda, P. B. (1975). Prediction of software reliability during debugging, in Proceedings of the Annual Reliability and Maintainability Symposium, Washington, DC, IEEE Reliability Society, 327–333.

[15] Shooman, M. L., Probabilistic models for software reliability prediction, in W. Freiberger (ed.), *Statistical Computer Performance Evaluation*, Academic Press, New York, 1972, 485–502.

[16] Schick, G. J., Wolverton, R. W. (1978). An analysis of competing software reliability models, *IEEE Transactions on Software Engineering*, **4**(2), 104–120.

[17] Goel, A. L., Okumoto, K. (1979). Time-dependent error-detection rate model for software reliability and other performance measures, *IEEE Transactions on Reliability*, **28**(3), 206–211.

[18] Musa, J. D., Okumoto, K. (1984). A logarithmic Poisson execution time model for software reliability measurement, in Proceedings of the 6th International Conference on Software Engineering, Orlando, FL, IEEE Computer Society, 230–238.

[19] Ohba, M. (1984). Software reliability analysis models, *IBM Journal of Research and development*, **28**(4), 428–443.

[20] Duane, J. T. (1964). Learning curve approach to reliability monitoring, *IEEE Transactions on Aerospace*, **AS-2**(2), 563–566.

[21] Littlewood, B. (1984). Rationale for a modified Duane model, *IEEE Transactions on Reliability*, **33**(2), 157–159.

[22] Yamada, S., Osaki, S., Narihisa, H. (1986). Discrete models for software reliability, in *Reliability and Quality Control*, Elsevier, New York, 401–412.

[23] Knafl, G. J., Sacks J. (1991). Poisson process with nearly constant failure intensity, in Proceedings of the International Symposium on Software Reliability Engineering, Austin, TX, IEEE Computer Society, 60–66.

[24] Sahinoglu, M. (1992). Compound-Poisson software reliability model, *IEEE Transactions on Software Engineering*, **18**(7), 624–630.

[25] Sahinoglu, M., Can, U. (1997). Alternative parameter estimation methods for the compound Poisson software reliability model with clustered failure data. *Software Testing, Verification and Reliability*, **7**(1), 35–57.

[26] Sahinoglu, M. (2003). An empirical Bayesian stopping rule in testing and verification of behavioral models, *IEEE Transactions on Instrumentation and Measurement*, **52**, 1428–1443.

[27] Randolph, P., Sahinoglu, M. (1995). A stopping-rule for a compound Poisson random variable, *Applied Stochastic Models and Data Analysis*, **11**, 135–143.

[28] Zhao, M. and Xie, M. (1992). On the log-power model and its applications, in Proceedings of the International Symposium on Software Reliability Engineering, Research Triangle Park, NC, IEEE Computer Society, 14–22.

[29] Musa, J. D. (1975). A theory of software reliability and its application, *IEEE Transactions on Software Engineering*, **1**(3), 312–327.

[30] Littlewood, B., Verrall, J. L. (1973). A Bayesian reliability growth model for computer software, *Applied Statistics*, **22**(3), 332–346.

[31] Jewell, W. S. (1985). Bayesian extensions to a basic model of software reliability, *IEEE Transactions on Software Engineering*, **11**(12), 1465–1471.

[32] Nelson, E. (1978). Estimating software reliability from test data, *Microelectronics and Reliability*, **17**(1), 67–74.

[33] Ramamoorthy, C. V., Bastani, F. B. (1982). Software reliability—Status and perspectives, *IEEE Transactions on Software Engineering*, **8**(4), 354–371.

[34] Bastani, F. B., Ramamoorthy, C. V. (1986). Input-domain-based models for estimating the correctness of process control programs, in A. Serra and R. E. Barlow (eds.), *Reliability Theory*, North Holland, Amsterdam, 321–378.

[35] Hamlet, R. G. (1987). Probable correctness theory, *Information Processing Letters*, **25**(1), 17–25.

[36] Scott, R. K., Gault, J. W., McAllister, D. F. (1987). Fault-tolerant software reliability modeling, *IEEE Transactions on Software Engineering*, **13**(5), 582–592.

[37] Weiss, S. N., Weyuker, E. J. (1988). An extended domain-based model of software reliability, *IEEE Transactions on Software Engineering*, **14**(12), 1512–1524.

[38] Littlewood, B., Miller, D. R. (1989). Conceptual modeling of coincident failures in multi version software, *IEEE Transactions on Software Engineering*, **15**(12), 1596–1614.

[39] Butler, R. W., Finelli, G. B., (1993). The infeasibility of quantifying the reliability of life-critical real-time software, *IEEE Transactions on Software Engineering*, **19**(1), 3–12.

[40] Stalhane, T. (1989). Fault tree analysis applied to software, in T. Aven (ed.) *Reliability Achievement—The Commercial Incentive*, Elsevier, London, 166–178.

[41] Wohlin, C., Korner, U. (1990). Software faults: Spreading, detection and costs, *Software Engineering Journal*, **5**(1), 33–42.

[42] Mills, H. D. (1972). On the statistical validation of computer programs, IBM Federal Systems Division, Report FSC-72-6015, Gaithersburg, MD.

[43] Huang, X. Z. (1984). The hypergeometric distribution model for predicting the reliability of software, *Microelectronics and Reliability*, **24**(1), 11–20.

[44] Duran, J. W., Wiorkowski, J. J. (1981). Capture-recapture sampling for estimating software error content, *IEEE Transactions on Software Engineering*, **7**(1), 147–148.

[45] Schick, G. J., Wolverton, R. W. (1978). An analysis of competing software reliability models, *IEEE Transactions on Software Engineering*, **SE-4**(2), 104–120.

[46] Keiller, P. A., Miller, D. R. (1991). On the use and the performance of software reliability growth models, *Reliability Engineering and System Safety*, **32**(2), 95–117.

[47] Lyu, M. R., Nikora, A. (1991). A heuristic approach for software reliability prediction, the equally-weighted linear combination model, in Proceedings of the International Symposium on Software Reliability Engineering, Austin, TX, IEEE Computer Society, 172–181.

[48] Bendell, T., Mellor, P., *Software Reliability: State of the Art Report*, Pergamon Info-tech Ltd., London, 1986.

[49] Littlewood, B., *Software Reliability: Achievement and Assessment*, Blackwell, Oxford, 1987.

[50] Sahinoglu, M., Deely, J., Capar, S. (2001). Stochastic Bayesian procedures to compare forecast accuracy of software reliability models, *IEEE Transactions on Reliability*, **50**, 92–97.

[51] El-Aroui, M. A., Soler, J. L. (1996). A Bayes non-parametric framework for software reliability analysis, *IEEE Transactions on Reliability*, **R-45**, 652–660.

[52] Goel, A. L. (1985). Software reliability models: Assumptions, limitations, and applicability, *IEEE Transactions on Software Engineering*, **11**(12), 1411–1423.

[53] Okumoto, K., Goel, A. L. (1980). Optimum release time for software systems based on reliability and other performance measures, *Journal of Systems and Software*, **1**(4), 315–318.

[54] Sahinoglu, M., Longnecker, M. T., Ringer, L. J., Singh, C., Ayoub, A. K. (1983). Probability distribution function for generation reliability indices-analytical approach, *IEEE Transactions on Power, Apparatus, and Systems (PAS)*, **104**, 1486–1493.

[55] Sahinoglu, M., *Trustworthy Computing: Analytical and Quantitative Engineering Evaluation*, John Wiley & Sons, Inc., Hoboken, 2007.

[56] Littlewood, B. (1980). Stochastic reliability growth: A model for fault-removal in computer programs and hardware designs, *IEEE Transactions on Reliability*, **30**(4), 313–320.

[57] Keiller, P. A., Littlewood, B., Miller, D. R. Sofer, A. (1983). Comparison of software reliability predictions, in Proceedings of the 13th IEEE International Symposium on Fault Tolerant Computing, ITCS-13, Milano, Italy, 128–134.

[58] Liu, G. (1987). A Bayesian assessing method of software reliability growth, in *Reliability Theory and Applications*, S. Osaki and J. Cao (eds.), World Scientific Publishing, Singapore, 237–244.

[59] Thompson, W. E., Chelson, P. O. (1980). On the specification of testing of software reliability, in Proceedings of the 1980 Annual Reliability and Maintainability Symposium, IEEE, New York, 379–383.

[60] Musa, J. D., Okumoto, K. (1984). A comparison of time domains for software reliability models, *Journal of Systems and Software*, **4**(4), 277–287.

[61] Sherbrooke, C. C., *Discrete Compound Poisson Processes and Tables of the Geometric Poisson Distribution, Memorandum RM-4831-PR*, The Rand Corporation, Santa Monica, 1966.

[62] Cinlar, E., *Introduction to Stochastic Processes*, Prentice-Hall, Englewood Cliffs, 1975.

[63] D'Agostino, R. B., Stephens, M. A., *Goodness of Fit Techniques*, Marcel Dekker, New York, 1986.

[64] Consul, P. C., *Generalized Poisson Distributions*, Marcel Dekker, New York, 1989.

[65] Adelson, R. M. (1966). Compound Poisson distributions, *Operational Research Quarterly*, **17**, 73–74.

[66] Sahinoglu, M. (1990). The limit of sum of Markov Bernoulli variables in system reliability estimation, *IEEE Transactions on Reliability*, **39**, 46–50.

[67] Serfozo, R. F. (1986). Compound Poisson approximations for sums of random variables, *The Annals of Probability*, **14**, 1391–1398.

[68] Fisher, R. A. (1950). The significance of deviations from expectation in a Poisson series, *Biometrics*, **6**, 17–24.

[69] Feller, W., *An Introduction to Probability Theory and Its Applications*, John Wiley & Sons, Inc., New York, 288–292, 1968.

[70] Sahinoglu, M. (1990). Geometric Poisson density estimation of the number of software failures, in IEEE Proceedings of the 28th Annual Reliability, Spring Seminar of the Central New England Council IEEE, The Boston Chapter Reliability Society, RAYTHEON Company, Boston, MA, 149–174.

[71] Student (1919). *Biometrical*, **12**, 211–215.

[72] Greenwood, M., Yule, G. U. (1920). An inquiry into the nature of frequency distributions representative of multiple happenings, *Journal of the Royal Statistical Society*, **83**, 255–279.

[73] Brown, B., *Some Tables of the Negative Binomial Distribution and Their Use, Memorandum RM-4577-PR*, The Rand Corporation, Santa Monica, 1965.

[74] David, F. N., Johnson, N. L. (1952). The truncated Poisson, *Biometrics*, **8**, 275–285.

[75] Kotz, S. (1988). *Encyclopedia of Statistical Sciences*, **5**, Wiley-Interscience, New York, 92–93 and 111–113.

[76] Kotz, S. (1988). *Encyclopedia of Statistical Sciences*, vol. **6**, Wiley-Interscience, New York, 169–176.

[77] Laprie, J. C., Kanoun, K. (1992). X-ware reliability and availability modeling, *IEEE Transactions on Software Engineering*, **18**(2), 130–147.

[78] Crow, L. H. (1974). Reliability analysis for complex, repairable systems, in *Reliability and Biometry*, F. Proshan and R.J. Serfling (eds.), SIAM, Philadelphia, 379–410.

[79] Barazza, N. (2013). Parameter estimation for the compound Poisson software reliability model, *International Journal of Software Engineering and its Applications*, **7**(1), 137–148.

[80] Tate, R. F., Goen, R. L. (1958). Minimum variance unbiased estimation for the truncated Poisson distribution, *Annals of Mathematical Statistics*, **29**, 755–765.

[81] Singh, H., Pal, P. (2013). Software reliability using Monte Carlo methods, *International Journal of Computer Applications*, **69**(4), 41–44.

[82] Inoue, S., Yamada, S. (2013). Lognormal process software reliability modeling with testing-effort, *Journal of Software Engineering and Applications*, **6**, 8–14.

[83] Tamura, Y., Kawakami, M., Yamada S. (2013). Reliability modeling and analysis for open source cloud computing, *Proceedings of the Institution of Mechanical Engineers, Part O: Journal of Risk and Reliability*, **227**, 179–186.

[84] Krishnan, K., *Data Warehousing in the Age of Big Data*, Elsevier (Morgan Kaufman), Burlington, 2011.

[85] Musa, J. D., *Software Reliability Data*, Bell Telephone Labs, Murray Hill, 1979.

[86] Sahinoglu M. (1985). Probability Distributions for reliability indices – analytical approach II, abstracts book (IS Statistics Subject Classification 14:130), III International Meeting of Statistics in the Basque Country, p. 117, Bilbao, Printed by Statistical Office, Basque Government and The British Council of Spain.

[87] Sahinoglu, M. (1990) Compound Poisson estimation of the number of software failures, (invited at) Software Reliability Workshop (kick-off) by IEEE Tech. Comm. on Software Reliability Eng., Subcomm. on Software Reliability Eng, Washington D.C., USA.

9

METRICS FOR SOFTWARE RELIABILITY FAILURE-COUNT MODELS IN CYBER-RISK

LEARNING OBJECTIVES

- Present an overview of failure-count models and the state of the art and science of their predictive accuracy for comparison purposes.
- Review traditional models and recently discovered advances in Bayesian modeling to form a basis of comparison through metrics.
- Show examples to illustrate how these methods work through a software program.

9.1 INTRODUCTION AND METHODOLOGY ON FAILURE-COUNT ESTIMATION IN SOFTWARE RELIABILITY

This chapter is related to the general problem of ranking usual means discussed in the literature and others as a background to the 2001 publication by Sahinoglu et al. focusing on statistical measures for comparing the predictive merits of software reliability models [1–7]. There is increasing pressure to develop and quantify measures of computer software reliability. With the ascent of software reliability models as detailed previously in Chapter 8, there is now even more pressure on assessment of the predictive quality of these measures, both in the sense of their goodness of fit and their pairwise comparisons [8, 9]. However, current methods used to compare these models use deterministic measures, and hence their results do not reflect the uncertainty inherent in these observations. In particular, the predictive accuracy of various methods is compared through measures such as average absolute (to avoid a zero average) relative error (ARE) and mean squared error (MSE), both of which are constant measures and thus do not consider the effect of stochastic (random) variability. The author also suggests designing and analyzing more precise methods for choosing the best predictive procedure through frequentist methods such as one- and two-sample *t*-tests of hypotheses, which do consider this inherent variability. In this section, we propose to

Cyber-Risk Informatics: Engineering Evaluation with Data Science, First Edition. Mehmet Sahinoglu.
© 2016 John Wiley & Sons, Inc. Published 2016 by John Wiley & Sons, Inc.
Companion website: www.wiley.com/go/sahinoglu/informatics

study several data-supported Bayesian methods of comparative assessment, which acknowledge the stochastic variation in the observed sequence of failure data. In addition to assessing the quality of fit of an individual estimation technique such as through ARE, it was desirable to obtain comparisons between competing techniques by two-sample t-tests and further calculating the probability of one method scoring better than another. Such research was necessary in order to choose between the many new and old reliability models.

Pairs of certain reliability models' predictive accuracy have already been compared employing statistical hypothesis tests in the frequentist sense. It was observed that a constant difference between the means of random variable, ARE (for AvRE), of any two methods did not necessarily prove statistically significant as to which of two competing estimation procedures was better. An alternative way of measurement through a more severe squared penalty reflected in random variable SRE (for SqRE) is also considered. This chapter brings a new dimension to a comparative assessment of the predictive accuracy of a pair of competing failure-count methods. In developing Bayesian methods otherwise as a valid alternative, an innovative approach is proposed to not only allow for determining which method is better but additionally to describe quantitatively how much better one is than the other. This is done by experimenting with prior noninformative distribution for the unknown parameters in the light of a priori software engineering field experience. Informative prior analyses, except for one easy case, are left out of the context of this chapter due to their theoretical complexity beyond scope. Results show the trend in comparisons beginning from a purely arithmetic approach by comparing absolute values to those using statistical t-tests and finally to a probability-based Bayesian approach using noninformative priors. However, prior to this predictive accuracy subject matter, the software reliability failure-count methods under observation will be studied at length.

9.1.1 Statistical Estimation Models, Computational Formulas, and Examples

We are interested in comparing one method of predicting software reliability against another method based on the data observed and on predictions obtained from these methods. The five discrete-effort weekly data sets will be briefly described [10–12]. WD1 has 131 failures in 64 weeks. WD2 has 213 failures in 224 weeks. WD3 has 340 failures in 41 weeks. WD4 has 197 failures in 114 weeks. WD5 has 366 failures in 50 weeks, as the data can be observed in book's Java-coded software website. WD1, WD3, and WD5 are tabulated in Appendix 9.A. It is well accepted that the MLE method is computationally quite straightforward, having many desired properties, such as asymptotic normality, admissibility, robustness, and consistency in Kendall and Stuart's classic textbook [13]. The main idea behind MLE is the use of an n-tuple joint likelihood function of the random vector X to estimate the parameters of the (compound) Poisson^geometric,

$$f_X(X_i, \theta) = P(X) = \sum_{Y=1}^{X} \frac{(\beta t)^Y e^{-\beta t}}{Y!} C_{Y-1}^{X-1} r^{X-Y} (1-r)^Y, \quad \theta = (\beta, r), \quad \beta > 0, \quad 0 < r < 1$$

(9.1)

Let $X_1, X_2, \ldots, X_n$ be a vector of random samples from $f_X(X_i, \theta)$ and let L be its joint likelihood function whose logarithm is to be maximized to find the maximum likelihood estimates of parameters b and r,

$$L = L(\theta) = \prod_{i=1}^{n} f_X(X_i, u) \tag{9.2}$$

$$L^* = \ln(L) \tag{9.3}$$

$$\frac{\partial L^*}{\partial \beta} = 0 \tag{9.4}$$

$$\frac{\partial L^*}{\partial r} = 0 \tag{9.5}$$

where the ∂ operator denotes partial derivative of. Hence, by two nonlinear equations for β and r, and two unknowns,

$$\beta = \frac{\sum y_i}{\sum t_i} = \frac{Y_{past}}{t_{past}}, \quad i = 1, \ldots, n \tag{9.6}$$

$$r = 1 - \frac{\sum y_i}{\sum x_i} = 1 - \frac{Y_{past}}{X_{past}} \tag{9.7}$$

are the maximum likelihood estimators of the unknown parameters β and r. Consequently, the expected value of X, the Poisson^geometric random variable, within the next unit time interval $\{t, t+1\}$ is β/p, where $p = 1 - r$. The proposed CP (Compound Poisson) reliability model suggested that the number of remaining software failures expected to occur within the next time interval $\{t, t_{rem}\}$ was [14–16]

$$E[X(t_{rem})] = \beta/(1-r)t_{rem} + e \tag{9.8}$$

In other words, the estimate of the quotient $\beta/(1-r)$ multiplied by the remaining unexecuted time units (i.e., t_{rem} in CPU seconds or calendar weeks) will estimate the expected number of future failures remaining. Thus, X_{rem}, which is the remaining number of failures from the end of the initial testing phase until the prescribed stopping time, is a function of the past information and remaining (residual) time, t_{rem}. The total number of unknown failures is X_{tot} and the sum of all single or multiple failures already discovered is X_{past}. Note that β of the Poisson process is the average number of (failure) arrivals per unit time and r is the probability of finding the next failure in the batch or clump (e.g., week) following that arrival. Then $p = 1 - r$ is the probability of starting the Poisson process for the next failure arrival. Recall that $X_{tot} = X_{past} + \frac{\beta \ t_{rem}}{1 - r} + \varepsilon$ for a total count.

It is appropriate to describe briefly the weekly recorded software failure weekly data (hence named WD) sets WD1 to WD5, which were time-based simulated. The absolute average relative error is the mean of the absolute relative errors calculated at each point:

$$\text{ARE} = \left(\frac{1}{n}\right) \sum_{i=1}^{n} \frac{|\text{estimate}_i - \text{true}|}{\text{true}} \tag{9.9}$$

MSE is the squared error version of ARE. Therefore, another compact measure for assessing the prediction is a mean squared error as the average of the deviation squares:

$$\text{MSE} = \frac{1}{n-1}\sum_{i=1}^{n}\left(\text{true} - \text{estimate}_i\right)^2 \tag{9.10}$$

Recall that for K–S (Kolmogorov-Smirnov) statistics, the proposed estimation model's $G_n(x)$ is compared for goodness of fit to the empirical distribution $G(x)$, where $D_n = \sup_i |G_n(x) - G(x)|$ for H_0: $G_n(x) = G(x)$, where $i = 1, \ldots, n$, for an n retrospective prediction points. Hence, the nonparametric K–S test statistics at each epoch of estimation can be summed and divided by n to give the K–S:

$$\text{K–S average } D_n = \frac{1}{n}\sum_{i=1}^{n}\left(\sup_i |G(x) - F(x)|\right) \tag{9.11}$$

Table 9.1 generally indicates that in the CPNLR (Compound Poisson Non-Linear Regression) method, the ARE and MSE results are more favorable for WD1 (Fig. 9.1), WD2, and WD4. For WD5, the CPMLE (Compound Poisson Maximum Likelihood Estimation) results are best in terms of ARE and MSE. For WD3, however, M–O (Musa-Okumoto) performs better. The K–S statistics (i.e., average D_n) produced identical results for both of the CPMLE and CPNLR parameter estimation methods due to their inherently close performance. Unlike ARE and MSE, the K–S statistic is not sensitive enough to detect differences between these two parameter estimation techniques (CPMLE and CPNLR), but it is sensitive enough to tell the difference between the CP and M–O methods of parameter estimation. However, the nonparametric K–S statistics are the least favorable, uniformly, for all the data sets, WD1 to WD5 as for the competing M–O model. Using the principles noted above, Table 9.2 summarizes the CPMLE parameter estimation results, for the example data set WD1 illustrated in Figure 9.2a. The results of Table 9.2 are plotted in Figure 9.2b and c. Similarly, they are plotted in Figure 9.3b and c, Figure 9.4b and c, Figure 9.5b and c, and Figure 9.6b and c for WD2, WD3, WD4, and WD5, respectively. Table 9.3, following Figures 9.2, 9.3, 9.4, 9.5, and 9.6, respectively summarizes the CPNLR parameter estimation results.

Table 9.3 for WD1 can be obtained by applying an SPSS algorithm as illustrated in the following screens, Figures 9.7, 9.6, 9.8, 9.9, and 9.10. The Levenberg–Marquardt (L–M) algorithm is employed to solve for the unknown parameter vector (β, r) in this nonlinear regression equation by means of least squares estimation [17–19]. The method developed by Marquardt and Levenberg appears to minimize considerably the number of practical

TABLE 9.1   ARE, MSE, and K–S Average D_n for Selected Methods: M–O, CPNLR, CPMLE

	M–O			CPNLR			CPMLE		
	ARE	MSE	Av.D_n	ARE	MSE	Av.D_n	ARE	MSE	Av.D_n
WD1	0.3201	3,247	0.428	0.0689	160	0.128	0.0885	257	0.128
WD2	0.5386	18,902	0.792	0.3164	6,465	0.209	0.3183	7,389	0.209
WD3	0.2127	13,289	0.337	0.4543	31,869	0.151	0.3265	16,906	0.151
WD4	0.4489	11,906	0.737	0.1439	1,795	0.195	0.1623	2,501	0.195
WD5	0.2759	27,245	0.275	0.1599	6,200	0.097	0.0675	1,813	0.097

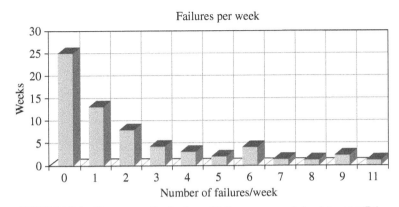

FIGURE 9.1   Frequency distribution of failures per week for data set WD1.

TABLE 9.2   CPMLE Parameter Estimation Results for Data WD1

Time (%)	X_{past}	Y_{past}	t_{past}	t_{rem}	$1-r$	β	X_{tot}	Rel. Error (%)
10	13	4	6	54	0.30769	0.66667	130.0	−0.76
15	22	5	9	51	0.22727	0.55556	146.7	11.98
20	25	7	12	48	0.28000	0.58333	125.0	−4.58
25	43	10	15	45	0.23256	0.66667	172	31.29
30	49	11	18	42	0.22449	0.61111	163.3	24.65
38·3	51	12	23	37	0.23529	0.52174	133	1.52
43·3	52	13	26	34	0.25000	0.50000	120	−8.39
45	55	14	27	33	0.25455	0.51852	122.2	−6.72
50	74	17	30	30	0.22973	0.56667	148	12.98
55	81	20	33	27	0.24691	0.60606	147.3	12.44
60	85	23	36	24	0.27059	0.63889	141.7	8.17
65	89	24	39	21	0.26966	0.61538	136.9	4.50
70	92	26	42	18	0.28261	0.61905	131.4	0.31
75	104	28	45	15	0.26923	0.62222	138.7	5.87
80	119	31	48	12	0.26050	0.64583	148.8	13.59
86·7	126	34	52	8	0.26984	0.65385	145.4	10.99
00	128	36	54	6	0.28125	0.66667	142.2	8.55
98·3	130	38	59	1	0.29231	0·64407	132.2	0.929
100	131	39	60	0	0.29771	0.65000	131	0.00

problems that can be tackled by nonlinear estimation. The L–M method is one that appears to work well in many circumstances and is thus a sensible practical choice [20]. However, no method can be called the "best" for all nonlinear problems [18]. The Jacobian matrix, $J(u)$, is an important step within nonlinear regression calculations, and if it is rank deficient or nearly so in Gauss–Newton iterations, this may admit multiple solutions. Therefore, the L–M modification transforms $J(u)$ to a better-conditioned full-rank matrix.

The L–M method is the technique most often used for nonlinear least squares estimation problems. The modified Levenberg–Marquardt algorithm is used and the required iteration terminates to reach a convergence; the parameter estimates and standard errors are listed. Table 9.3 summarizes the results for data set WD1 by CPNLR using L–M.

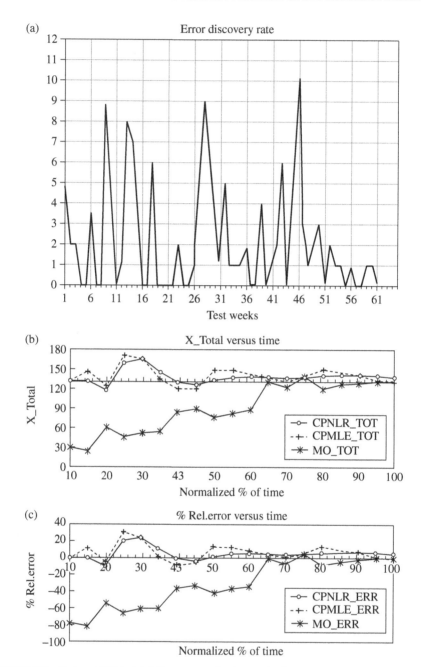

FIGURE 9.2   Data set WD1: (a) failures per calendar week; (b) X_{tot} versus time; (c) percentage relative error versus time.

The results are plotted along with the CPMLE results in Figure 9.2b and c. Similarly, the CPNLR results for WD2 to WD5 along with the CPMLE results are plotted in Figures 9.3b to c and 9.6b to c, and Figures 9.12, 9.13, and 9.14 for WD3, WD4, and WD5 respectively. Note, M–O results accompany for comparison sake.

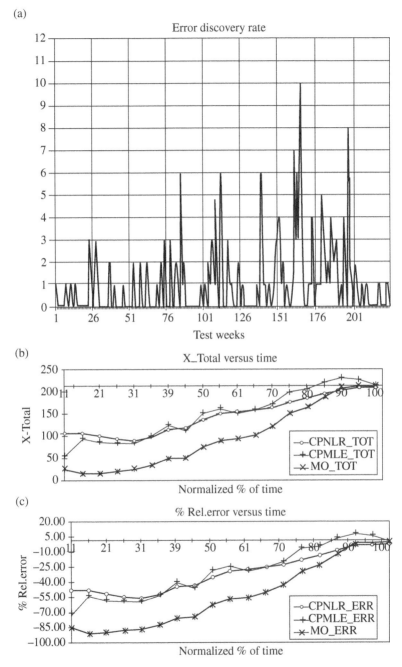

FIGURE 9.3 Data set WD2: (a) failures per calendar week; (b) X_{tot} versus time; (c) percentage relative error versus time.

(a)

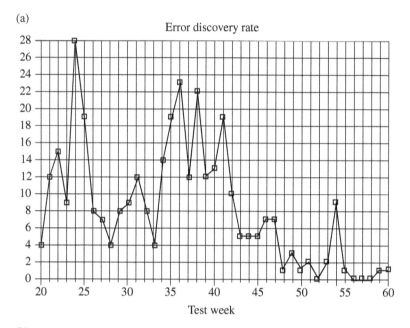

(b)

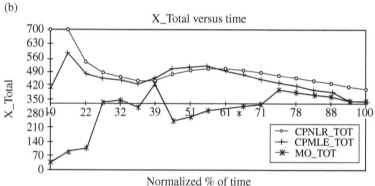

(c)

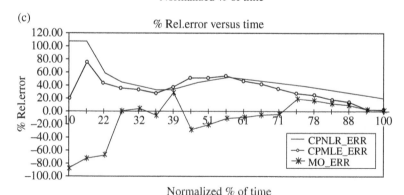

FIGURE 9.4   Data set WD3: (a) failures per calendar week; (b) X_{tot} versus time; (c) percentage relative error versus time.

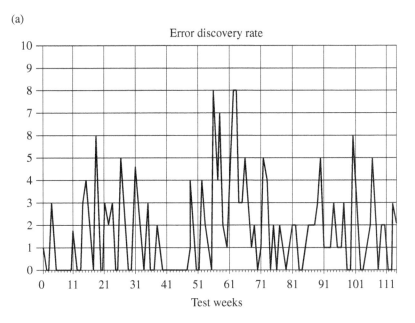

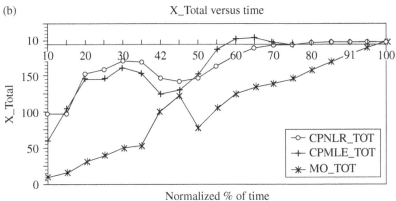

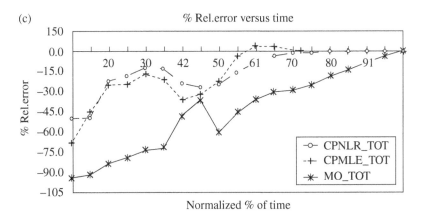

FIGURE 9.5 Data set WD4: (a) failures per calendar week; (b) X_{tot} versus time; (c) percentage relative error versus time.

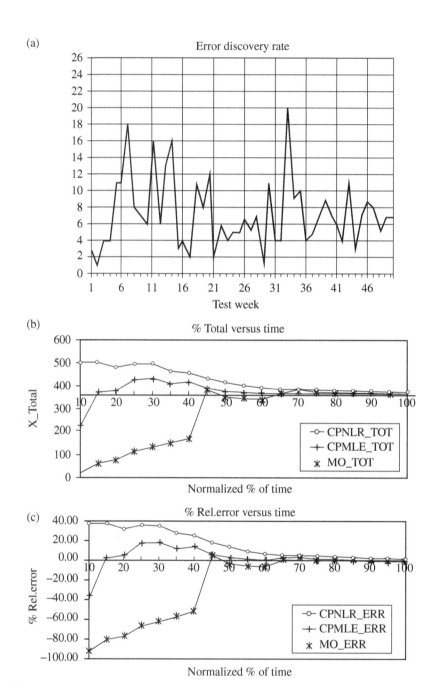

FIGURE 9.6   Data set WD5: (a) failures per calendar week; (b) X_{tot} versus time; (c) percentage relative error versus time.

TABLE 9.3 CPNLR Parameter Estimation Results for Data WD1

Time (%)	X_{past}	Y_{past}	t_{past}	t_{rem}	$1-r$	β	X_{tot}	Rel. Error (%)
10	13	4	6	54	0.03880	0.08408	131.7	0.53
15	22	5	9	51	0.03880	0.08408	131.7	0.53
20	25	7	12	48	0.00419	0.00796	117.	−10.69
25	43	10	15	45	0.00236	0.00630	158.4	20.92
30	49	11	18	42	0.00010	0.00028	165.0	25.95
38.3	51	12	23	37	0.00028	0.00067	144.6	10.38
43.3	52	13	26	34	0.03050	0.06416	129.7	−0.99
45	55	14	27	33	0.11346	0.22707	124.6	−4.88
50	74	17	30	30	0.00005	0.00010	132.2	0.92
55	81	20	33	27	0.08637	0.19479	137.0	4.50
60	85	23	36	24	0.00413	0.00943	138.2	5.49
65	89	24	39	21	0.04978	0.11287	137.6	4.96
70	92	26	42	18	0.15697	0.34892	135.6	3.51
75	104	28	45	15	0.04810	0.10763	136.2	3.97
80	119	31	48	12	0.00271	0.00626	139.2	6.26
86.7	126	34	52	8	0.00131	0.00307	140.7	7.32
90	128	36	54	6	0.00852	0.02003	141.0	7.64
98.3	130	38	59	1	0.00001	0.00003	139.1	6.18
100	131	39	60	0	0.00282	0.00640	137.7	5.11

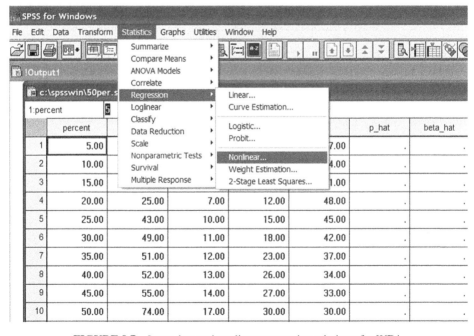

FIGURE 9.7 Input data and nonlinear regression windows for WD1.

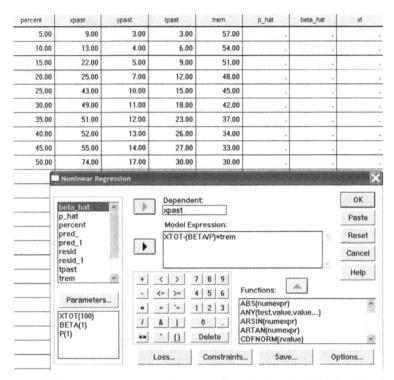

FIGURE 9.8   Input data and nonlinear equations windows for WD1 (continued).

Iteration	Residual SS	XTOT	BETA	P
1	4428.000000	100.000000	1.00000000	1.00000000
1.1	25891.57103	132.233289	190.811079	189.654857
1.2	24272.06066	132.233497	28.0226085	26.8663792
2	2132.121747	132.233530	1.94456559	.788335187
2.1	418.2751429	132.233530	2.48055763	1.10484457
3	418.2751429	132.233530	2.48055763	1.10484457
3.1	413.4601078	132.233531	1.15192006	.556831485
4	413.4601078	132.233531	1.15192006	.556831485
4.1	350.7329532	132.233529	.703300207	.316412110
5	350.7329532	132.233529	.703300207	.316412110
5.1	293.8995230	132.233530	.424009478	.200227337
6	293.8995230	132.233530	.424009478	.200227337
6.1	267.3373187	132.233529	.597951596	.278718161
7	267.3373187	132.233529	.597951596	.278718161
7.1	265.3509934	132.233530	.941894713	.437625614
8	265.3509934	132.233530	.941894713	.437625614
8.1	265.1028084	132.233529	1.62873530	.755944939
9	265.1028084	132.233529	1.62873530	.755944939
9.1	266.5961492	132.233530	.256653447	.118537539
9.2	265.0497739	132.233530	1.49208261	.691937305
10	265.0497739	132.233530	1.49208261	.691937305
10.1	265.0493272	132.233530	1.76668667	.819331318
11	265.0493272	132.233530	1.76668667	.819331318
11.1	265.0493183	132.233530	1.21738072	.564590321
12	265.0493183	132.233530	1.21738072	.564590321
12.1	265.0493176	132.233530	.668091710	.309841182
13	265.0493176	132.233530	.668091710	.309841182
13.1	265.0493168	132.233531	.393443146	.182468563
14	265.0493168	132.233531	.393443146	.182468563
14.1	265.0493182	132.233530	.145385871	.067425618

Run stopped after 32 model evaluations and 14 derivative evaluations.
Iterations have been stopped because the relative reduction between successive
residual sums of squares is at most SSCON = 1.000E-08

FIGURE 9.9   Output data and convergence at X_{tot} = 132.23. See Table 9.3 for 50%.

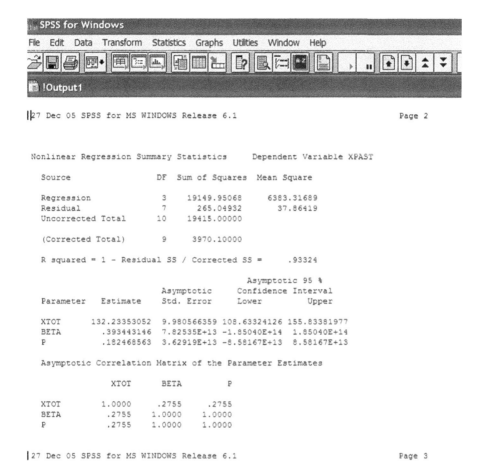

```
Nonlinear Regression Summary Statistics      Dependent Variable XPAST

   Source                DF   Sum of Squares  Mean Square

   Regression             3     19149.95068    6383.31689
   Residual               7       265.04932      37.86419
   Uncorrected Total     10     19415.00000

   (Corrected Total)      9      3970.10000

   R squared = 1 - Residual SS / Corrected SS =     .93324

                                          Asymptotic 95 %
                            Asymptotic    Confidence Interval
   Parameter    Estimate    Std. Error    Lower         Upper

   XTOT      132.23353052  9.980566359 108.63324126 155.83381977
   BETA        .393443146  7.82535E+13 -1.85040E+14  1.85040E+14
   P           .182468563  3.62919E+13 -8.58167E+13  8.58167E+13

   Asymptotic Correlation Matrix of the Parameter Estimates

                  XTOT       BETA         P

   XTOT         1.0000      .2755      .2755
   BETA          .2755     1.0000     1.0000
   P             .2755     1.0000     1.0000
```

FIGURE 9.10   ANOVA table for the nonlinear regression. R-Sq = 0.93 and 95% confidence interval for X_{tot} is (108.63→109, 155.83→156).

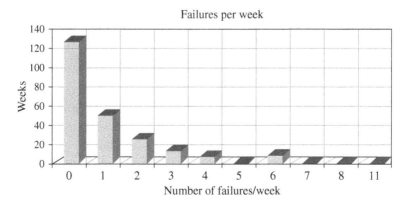

FIGURE 9.11   Weekly frequency distribution of failures for data set WD2.

FIGURE 9.12   Weekly frequency distribution of failures for data set WD3.

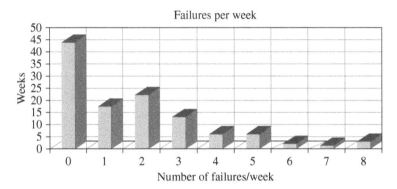

FIGURE 9.13   Weekly frequency distribution of failures for data set WD4.

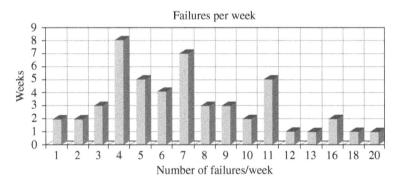

FIGURE 9.14   Weekly frequency distribution of failures for data set WD5.

9.1.2   Interpretations of Numerical Examples and Discussions

In terms of the ARE, MSE, and K–S Av. *Dn*, the newly proposed parameter estimation methods—compound Poisson nonlinear regression (CPNLR) and compound Poisson maximum likelihood estimation (CPMLE)—are generally superior to the Musa–Okumoto logarithmic Poisson model in predicting the outcomes for the grouped or clustered software failure data sets described in this chapter. The basic reason is that the CP models proposed evaluate clumping or clustering effects of software failures not evaluated by the usual Poisson or logarithmic Poisson processes for certain data structures. For weekly recorded software failure data sets WD1 to WD5, this phenomenon occurred in four out of five cases: For WD1 (Fig. 9.1), WD2 (Fig. 9.11), and WD4 (Fig. 9.13), CPNLR performed better, with CPMLE a better choice for WD5 (Fig. 9.14). The M–O Poisson interval estimation model did better only for WD3 (Fig. 9.12). This result was not a surprise, because an exploratory data analysis showed that WD3 has a nonexponential or quasiuniform frequency distribution for the random variable of "clump size" per week as a result of the logarithmic effect. On the other hand, the frequency plots for WD1, WD2, WD4, and WD5 displayed an exponential nature.

As outlined in the *Software Reliability Handbook* [21], the M–O logarithmic Poisson model is a better fit for a nonexponential class of failure counts, whereas for the exponential class, the generalized exponential models such as the generalized Poisson in this work are sound. One way to associate with this fact is that the natural logarithm of Poisson function's equation yields to a constant value. No single summary measure alone is adequate to determine the best parameter estimation method for a given data set. Sometimes an estimation method can generate more favorable predictive results at, or after, a certain percentage of the normalized time as observed in a plot. However, the three performance measures given in Equations (9.9)–(9.11) and cited in the literature serve to summarize the situation compactly for the entire range covering all prediction points [1, 10, 11].

As a matter of fact, one would prefer gradually to see smaller predictive error percentage values, because the further advanced the testing process is, the more expensive it becomes. Recall that of the two prospective (forward) performance measures, ARE recognizes the absolute value penalty, whereas MSE penalizes the deviations more severely by squaring them. Consequently, the K–S statistics are different in the retrospective (backward) sense where the actual empirical distribution is compared to the cumulative distribution function estimated.

This suggests that one should consider at least a pair or triplets of measures of goodness of fit—ARE, MSE, and K–S Av. D_n—instead of a single summary measure. Predictions and corresponding relative error percentages can be observed in Figures 9.2, 9.3, 9.4, 9.5, and 9.6 for the weekly recorded failure data sets, WD1 to WD5. Table 9.1 provides an overall comparison of the estimation results due to different models and their parameter estimation techniques in terms of popular measures of forecast quality of fit. It has been observed that the average relative error and mean squared error outputs for the CPNLR and CPMLE methods are more favorable than the competing M–O method. This is also validated by the trends in parts (*b*) and (*c*) of Figures 9.2, 9.3, 9.4, 9.5, and 9.6 where the CP (CPMLE and CPNLR) methods produce predictions and related errors closer to the target (or true) count and zero percent relative error line, respectively, except for Figure 9.4b and c for WD3, where the predictions of the M–O model results are clearly closer. Another striking difference in these graphs is that the M–O model mostly underestimates the target value, whereas CP models alternate in over—or underestimating the target, depending on the given data set.

The CPMLE method is very straightforward to apply, with negligible algebra involved, whereas CPNLR may occasionally require extensive computational time to reach convergence through the nonlinear iterative process involved in the L–M method. It is also more secure to use NLR estimates, due to the nonlinear and especially nonnormal nature of the expressions observed in Equations (9.6)–(9.8). However, first-guess easy-to-obtain MLE results are also useful for obtaining an initial value during the L–M nonlinear solution process. Despite all the advantages of the nonlinear regression method, MLE—due to its generally accepted statistical advantages of admissibility, consistency, and asymptotic normality—can still provide more favorable results, as in WD5.

For further research to follow up on the deterministic measures such as ARE and MSE, stochastic performance measures in the form of statistical tests are sought to assess the forecast quality of parameter estimation methods. Thus, if closed-form probability distribution functions can be derived for what used to be deterministic measures such as ARE and MSE, any two competing parameter estimation methods would be fully comparable in terms of statistical hypothesis tests. Further, Bayesian methods using informative and noninformative priors will be studied in Section 9.2 to assess the probability of one method's predictive accuracy scoring better than its alternative. Finally, not all software reliability models and related parameter estimation methods are best for all software failure data types. Exploratory data and goodness of fit analyses are necessary to judge the behavior of the software failure data before deciding on the type of prediction model to be used.

9.2 PREDICTIVE ACCURACY TO COMPARE FAILURE-COUNT MODELS

Let $y_1, \ldots, y_n$ denote the true failures observed over n time intervals, called checkpoints. For some given estimation procedure, let $X_{est}(k)$ denote the estimate of the total number of software failures to be observed over the n time intervals. The true number of failures over the n intervals is given by $X_{true} = \Sigma y_k$, where $k = 1, \ldots, n$.

To summarize and review:

| RE |	absolute relative error
k	checkpoint between 1 and n observations
$\mathbf{y_k}$	true number of software failures over $k = 1, \ldots, n$
$\mathbf{X_j}$	error random variable $j = 1, 2$ for the two competing methods to be compared
$\mathbf{X_{est}(k)}$	forecast value of the number of software failures estimated at time point, $1 < k < n$
$\mathbf{X_{true}}$	$\sum_{k=1}^{n} y_k$
ARE	arithmetic average of | RE | of sample observations
SqRE	squared | RE | of sample observations
AvSqRE	arithmetic average of SqRE (or SRE short for AvSqRE)
CPNLR	compound Poisson nonlinear regression method of estimation
CPMLE	compound Poisson MLE method of estimation
MO	Musa–Okumoto logarithmic Poisson method of estimation, or M–O
WD	weekly data
X	ARE random variable for CPNLR
Y	ARE random variables for CPMLE
Z	ARE random variables for MO
U	SRE random variable for CPNLR
V	SRE random variable for CPMLE
W	SRE random variable for MO

Define the random variables ARE (average relative error) as in (9.9), and then, | RE | (absolute relative error) and SqRE (squared relative error), respectively, as follows [10]:

$$\left|\mathrm{RE}(k)\right| = \frac{\left|X_{\mathrm{est}}(k) - X_{\mathrm{true}}\right|}{X_{\mathrm{true}}} \tag{9.12}$$

$$\left|\mathrm{SqRE}(k)\right| = \frac{\left[X_{\mathrm{est}}(k) - X_{\mathrm{true}}\right]^2}{X_{\mathrm{true}}} \tag{9.13}$$

Then, the popularly used ARE is the arithmetic average of | RE | as in (9.10). AvSqRE is the arithmetic average of the | SqRE | over n checkpoints. See below ARE and SRE (short for SqRE) of WD1 plotted versus proportion sampled (Figs. 9.15 and 9.16):

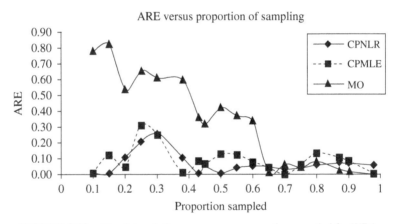

FIGURE 9.15   Absolute relative error versus proportion sampled for WD1.

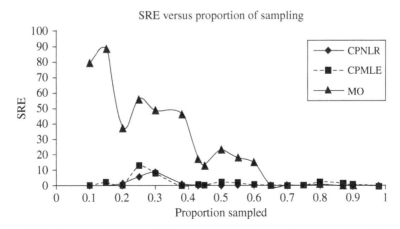

FIGURE 9.16   AvSqRE (or SRE) versus proportion sampled obtained for WD1.

9.2.1 Classical Distribution Approach

Detailed explanations of the competing methods CPMLE, CPNLR, and MO are given in references [1, 10, 11]. An arithmetic difference in the mean values of the ARE or SqRE may not necessarily be statistically significant. In this study, however, we search for the probability that one method's mean is higher (worse) or lower (better) than another's by a specific margin in proportion to the difference between them. We approach this problem using Bayesian noninformative prior distributions and their posterior distributions computationally [1–6]. Note that t-values are calculated for testing $H_{01} : \mu_{ARE_1} = \mu_{ARE_2}$ and $H_{02} : \mu_{SRE_1} = \mu_{SRE_2}$ with the decision on their right whether to accept or reject if α (Type I error probability) = 0.05 as in Tables 9.4 and 9.5. The { . } are simple arithmetical differences of the respective means (ARE) with n =18. Then the [.] are Bayesian probabilities of comparisons of one method scoring worse (more difference) or better (less difference) for which see Section 9.2.2. Note that minor ARE deviations between Tables 9.1 and 9.4 are due to alternate vantage points (%) to predict the true value. Tables 9.4 and 9.5 will utilize the results displayed in Tables 9.6, 9.7, 9.8, 9.9, and 9.10 using $\gamma = 0$.

TABLE 9.4 t-Tests with Decision, Arithmetic Difference, and Probabilistic Results to Compare the Means of |RE|

Data Set	CPMLE versus CPNLR	MO versus CPNLR	MO versus CPMLE
WD1	$t = 0.97$ Accept H_0 {0.024} [0.7799]	$t = 3.89$ Reject H_0 {0.264} [0.9998]	$t = 3.49$ Reject H_0 {0.237} [0.9991]
WD2	$t = 0.043$ Accept H_0 {0.003} [0.5136]	$t = 2.78$ Reject H_0 {0.236} [0.9916]	$t = 2.56$ Reject H_0 {0.233} [0.9856]
WD3	$t = 1.29$ Accept H_0 {0.06} [0.8527]	$t = |-1.63|$ Accept H_0 {−0.12} [0.9101]	$t = |-2.74|$ Reject H_0 {−0.18} [0.9913]
WD4	$t = 0.34$ Accept H_0 {0.0197} [0.6044]	$t = 4.09$ Reject H_0 {0.322} [0.9999]	$t = 3.64$ Reject H_0 {0.303} [0.9995]
WD5	$t = |-0.95|$ Accept H_0 {−0.1234} [0.7761]	$t = 3.3$ Reject H_0 {0.421} [0.9983]	$t = 13.77$ Reject H_0 {0.5441} [0.9999]

Accept: Fail to reject equality of means; $H_{01ij} : \mu_{ARE_i} = \mu_{ARE_j}$.

TABLE 9.5 t-Tests with Decision, Arithmetic Difference, and Probabilistic Results to Compare the SqRE Means

Data Set	CPMLE versus CPNLR	MO versus CPNLR	MO versus CPMLE
WD1	$t = 0.8$ Accept H_0 {0.76} [0.7389]	$t = 3.51$ Reject H_0 {23.6} [0.9992]	$t = 3.39$ Reject H_0 {22.84} [0.9988]
WD2	$t = 0.43$ Accept H_0 {4.35} [0.6321]	$t = 3.45$ Reject H_0 {58.4} [0.9993]	$t = 3.01$ Reject H_0 {54.05} [0.9988]
WD3	$t = 0.083$ Accept H_0 {8.87} [0.7152]	$t = |-1.03|$ Accept H_0 {−19.5} [0.6563]	$t = |-0.51|$ Accept H_0 {−10.63} [0.7945]
WD4	$t = 0.56$ Accept H_0 {3.59} [0.6693]	$t = 3.53$ Reject H_0 {51.33} [0.9992]	$t = 3.16$ Reject H_0 {47.74} [0.9973]
WD5	$t = |-2.19|$ Reject H_0 {−11.98} [0.9674]	$t = 2.27$ Reject H_0 {57.51} [0.9729]	$t = 2.77$ Reject H_0 {69.49} [0.9919]

Accept: Fail to reject equality of means; that is, $H_{02ij} : \mu_{SRE_i} = \mu_{SRE_j}$.

From Tables 9.4 and 9.5, we can conclude that those t-test results with Accept (=FTR) H_0 show that the ARE or SRE predictive error indices for the competing methods are not significantly different at a 0.05 Type I error probability level. For WD3's and WD5's MO versus CPNLR hypothesis decisions to reject or accept ARE and AvSqRE (SRE) tables do not always concur due to different loss definitions, but in majority of the cases, they score very close. We may agree with Table 9.5 of SRE that supports the square penalty definition to be on the conservative side of rejecting slightly more than the ARE comparisons that use absolute penalty.

With a method and its prediction we associate an "error" random variable which we will denote by X_j where $j = 1,2$ for the two methods being compared. In this work, the error random variable will be the means: ARE_1 and ARE_2 (or SRE_1 and SRE_2) as defined. We assume:

1. X_j is normally distributed with unknown mean μ_j and standard deviation σ_j, which will be taken as known.

2. The n (sample size) is large enough to facilitate a large-sample approach to the problem to utilize normal theory.

3. Even though μ_1 and μ_2 are unknown, method one is better than method two if $\mu_1 < \mu_2$ in probability.

4. The quantitative measure of *how much better* method 1 is than method 2 is obtained by assessing the difference $\mu_1 - \mu_2$. This difference is unknown and can only be estimated, but the Bayesian model here produces a probability assessment of the *magnitude* of this difference.

5. In particular as a *comparison criterion*, we compute the posterior probability that μ_1 is smaller than μ_2 by a tolerance b; that is, compute the quantity

$$P = P\left(\mu_1 \leq \mu_2 - b \mid X_1, X_2\right), \quad b \geq 0 \tag{9.14}$$

where $b = \gamma = $ [greater mean of ARE (or SRE) of X_2] – [smaller mean of ARE (or SRE) of X_1].

A casual perusal of *comparison criterion* in Equation (9.22) should indicate why it can be used to make realistic and quantitative comparisons between any two methods being studied. It should also be pointed out here that if comparisons among a group of three or more methods were desired, then Equation (9.22) could be suitably modified to give the desired comparison; that is, the posterior probability that *any one* of several methods is sufficiently smaller than *all* of the others could be computed. These details are discussed extensively for the general problem of ranking normal means, where we restrict the problem to comparing only two methods at a time [2]. We now introduce the Bayesian model with the relevant formulas necessary to compute the criterion function in Equation (9.19).

9.2.2 Prior Distribution Approach

For development of the prior distribution on μ_1 and μ_2, we use a hierarchical Bayesian model, which assumes, a priori, that the unknown means are exchangeable. This has the desirable property that knowledge of one mean gives some information about the other. For a fuller discussion of this general model, see Berger [2, 3] and Sahinoglu et al. [1].

Let μ_1 and μ_2 have a normal distribution, say, $\pi(\mu_1,\mu_2 \mid \beta,\tau^2)$ with mean β and variance τ^2, where β and τ^2 are called hyperparameters and have hyperprior distributions denoted by h_1 and h_2, respectively. Thus, the prior distribution on μ_1 and μ_2 is given by a mixture,

$$\pi(\mu_1,\mu_2)=\int \pi(\mu_1,\mu_2 \mid \beta,\tau^2)h_1(\beta)h_2(\tau^2)d\beta d\tau^2 \qquad (9.15)$$

Choices for h_1 and h_2 depend on the type of prior information available in the given problem. It is also true that a choice for π other than normal may also be indicated by the prior information. Even so when π is normal, the closed form of this prior is not available, but this will not be necessary in order to compute the value of the criterion function in (9.19). Rather, only the conditional distributions will be used, as we show next. We can now derive the computational formulas required to obtain the value for P given in the criterion function. Using the conditional probability rules for densities, we can write

$$\begin{aligned}P &= P(\mu_1 \le \mu_2 - b \mid X_1,X_2) \\ &= \iint P(\mu_1 \le \mu_2 - b \mid X_1,X_2,\beta,\tau^2)h_1(\beta \mid X_1,X_2,\tau^2)h_2(\tau^2 \mid X_1,X_2)d\beta \ d\tau^2 \end{aligned} \qquad (9.16)$$

and then note that the conditional distribution of $\mu_1 - \mu_2$ is normal with mean and variance given by

$$m = \left(\frac{\sigma_1^2}{\sigma_1^2+\tau^2}-\frac{\sigma_2^2}{\sigma_2^2+\tau^2}\right)\beta +\left(\frac{X_1}{\sigma_1^2+\tau^2}-\frac{X_2}{\sigma_2^2+\tau^2}\right)\tau^2 \qquad (9.17)$$

$$\text{var} = \left(\frac{\sigma_1^2}{\sigma_1^2+\tau^2}+\frac{\sigma_2^2}{\sigma_2^2+\tau^2}\right)\tau^2 \qquad (9.18)$$

Thus, we can write the first term in the integral above as

$$P(\mu_1 \le \mu_2 - b \mid X_1,X_2,\beta,\tau^2)=\Phi\left(\frac{-b-m}{\sqrt{\text{var}}}\right) \qquad (9.19)$$

where $b = \gamma = $ [greater mean of $X_2 - $ smaller mean of X_1]; $\gamma \ge 0$, is given as in (9.19).

This equation allows numerical calculation of P quite easily for various choices for h_1 and h_2 but would not be true if $\pi(\mu_1,\mu_2 \mid \beta,\tau^2)$ were not chosen as normal. Even so, in that case the Monte Carlo evaluation for P is straightforward. We now give details for the noninformative case. The informative case is beyond the scope of this book although it will be mentioned in comparison. For this case we assume that only vague opinions of the values for μ_1 and μ_2 are available. This knowledge is reflected by taking h_1 as a normal distribution, whose variance approaches infinity and h_2 as follows:

$$h_2(\tau^2)=\left(\sigma_1^2+\sigma_2^2+2\tau^2\right)^{-1} \qquad (9.20)$$

A truly noninformative case for this variance type of random variable τ^2 would have been the improper choice $1/\tau^2$. However, this does not lead to a proper posterior, and hence the foregoing choice was used. It is also the case that we can approach the same situation by taking the limit of uniform distributions on larger and larger intervals for τ^2. The details of the choices above can be found in the work of Sahinoglu et al. [1] and Berger and Deely [2], and given this same model, the following formula can be derived:

$$P = \int_0^{\Delta^2} \Phi\left(\sqrt{\Delta^2 - t} - \frac{\gamma\Delta^2}{\sqrt{\Delta^2 - t}}\right) \frac{e^{-t/2}t^{-1/2}}{f(X_1,X_2)} dt \tag{9.21}$$

$e^{-t/2}t^{-1/2}dt/f(X_1,X_2)$ integrates to 1.0 where $f(X_1,X_2)$ is the normalizing factor. Φ denotes c.d.f. of the standard normal. To solve this integral by using Monte Carlo simulation, simulate

$$P\left[Z \leq \left(\sqrt{\Delta^2 - Z_1^2} - \frac{\gamma\Delta^2}{\sqrt{\Delta^2 - Z_1^2}}\right) \cap Z_1^2 \leq \Delta^2\right] \tag{9.22}$$

a large N number of times for a given $\gamma > 0$, where Z_1 is a standard normal variable. See book Software for applications. That is, draw a standard normal variable Z_1 that satisfies $Z_1^2 \leq \Delta^2$; otherwise, draw another standard normal variable that does. Among feasible such choices, $m = 1, \ldots, M$ that satisfy this criterion, calculate the expression

$$\Phi\left(\sqrt{\Delta^2 - Z_1^2} - \frac{\gamma\Delta^2}{\sqrt{\Delta^2 - Z_1^2}}\right) \tag{9.23}$$

that is, the quantity

$$q_m = P\left[Z \leq \left(\sqrt{\Delta^2 - Z_1^2} - \frac{\gamma\Delta^2}{\sqrt{\Delta^2 - Z_1^2}}\right)\right] \tag{9.24}$$

from standard normal tables. Divide the value of sum $= \sum_1^M q_m$ by N simulation runs. The final result becomes $P = $ sum$/N$. Note that

$$\Delta = \frac{\text{Greater mean of } X_2 - \text{Smaller mean of } X_1}{\sqrt{s_1^2/n_1 + s_2^2/n_2}} \tag{9.25}$$

However, for noninformative or flat priors when $\gamma = 0$, for example, calculating for WD1, we obtain

$$P = \frac{\Phi(\Delta) - 0.5e^{-0.5\Delta^2}}{2\Phi(\Delta) - 1} \tag{9.26}$$

$$P = \frac{\Phi(0.9662) - 0.5e^{-0.5(0.9662)^2}}{2\Phi(\Delta) - 1} = \frac{0.83303 - 0.31351}{1.66652 - 1} = 0.779 \tag{9.27}$$

as on the top left for $\gamma = 0$ in Table 9.6 in Section 9.2.3, where $\Delta = 0.966$. See Cyber-Risk Solver software menu and click on the "Flat" program for software applications.

9.2.3   Applications to Data Sets and Comparisons

Tables 9.6, 9.7, 9.8, 9.9, and 9.10 cover data set WD1–WD5 where γ constant is varied between 0 and 1. X denotes ARE for CPNLR, Y denotes ARE for CPMLE, and Z denotes ARE for MO. Similarly, U denotes SRE for CPNLR, V denotes SRE for CPMLE, and W denotes SRE for MO. Each table contains the probability that $\mu_i > \mu_j$ where $i, j = X, Y, Z$ for ARE and $i, j = U, V, W$ for SRE, for $i \neq j$. The means, m_i; standard errors, σ_{m_i}; and standard deviations, σ_i, of each data set WD1–WD5 ($n = 18$ checkpoints between 10th and 95th percentiles (such as in Tables 9.2 and 9.3) are listed in Tables 9.6, 9.7, 9.8, 9.9, and 9.10, and Figures 9.17, 9.18, 9.19, and Tables 9.11 and 9.12 regarding WD1 only for informative priors of Bayesian comparative probabilities as follows [1]:

TABLE 9.6   Bayesian Noninformative Prior Analysis for Data WD1 with 0 To 1.0 Tolerance

	$\gamma = 0.0$	$\gamma = 0.25$	$\gamma = 0.5$	$\gamma = 0.75$	$\gamma = 1.0$	m_1	σ_{m_1}	σ_1	m_2	σ_{m_2}	σ_2
ARE											
$P(Y > X)$	0.7797	0.6634	0.5390	0.4048	0.2803	0.094	0.019	0.08	0.070	0.016	0.0678
$P(Z > X)$	0.9997	0.9945	0.9479	0.7537	0.3882	0.334	0.066	0.28	0.070	0.016	0.0678
$P(Z > Y)$	0.9991	0.9867	0.9174	0.7090	0.3684	0.334	0.066	0.28	0.094	0.019	0.0806
AvSqRE											
$P(V > U)$	0.7389	0.6351	0.5250	0.4077	0.2978	1.96	0.773	3.28	1.20	0.544	2.31
$P(W > U)$	0.9992	0.9874	0.9194	0.7198	0.3789	24.8	6.70	28.42	1.20	0.544	2.31
$P(W > V)$	0.9988	0.9835	0.9073	0.6970	0.3606	24.8	6.70	28.42	1.96	0.773	3.28

TABLE 9.7   Bayesian Noninformative Prior Analysis for Data WD2 with 0 To 1.0 Tolerance

	$\gamma = 0.0$	$\gamma = 0.25$	$\gamma = 0.5$	$\gamma = 0.75$	$\gamma = 1.0$	m_1	σ_{m_1}	σ_1	m_2	σ_{m_2}	σ_2
ARE											
$P(Y > X)$	0.5136	0.5067	0.5005	0.4937	0.4868	0.3357	0.054	0.23	0.3327	0.043	0.1833
$P(Z > X)$	0.9916	0.9455	0.8278	0.6078	0.3232	0.5685	0.074	0.31	0.3327	0.043	0.1833
$P(Z > Y)$	0.9856	0.9283	0.7932	0.5723	0.2982	0.5685	0.074	0.31	0.3357	0.054	0.2300
AvSqRE											
$P(V > U)$	0.6321	0.5699	0.5105	0.4399	0.3862	34.69	8.324	35.32	30.34	5.877	24.93
$P(W > U)$	0.9993	0.9868	0.9120	0.7069	0.3645	88.74	15.87	67.33	30.34	5.877	24.93
$P(W > V)$	0.9988	0.9631	0.8656	0.6432	0.3327	88.74	15.87	67.33	34.69	8.324	35.32

TABLE 9.8   Bayesian Noninformative Prior Analysis for Data WD3 with 0 to 1.0 Tolerance

	$\gamma = 0.0$	$\gamma = 0.25$	$\gamma = 0.5$	$\gamma = 0.75$	$\gamma = 1.0$	m_1	σ_{m_1}	σ_1	m_2	σ_{m_2}	σ_2
ARE											
$P(Y > X)$	0.8527	0.7231	0.5747	0.4138	0.2478	0.4044	0.0227	0.096	0.3446	0.0402	0.171
$P(X > Z)$	0.9101	0.7868	0.6252	0.4356	0.2427	0.3446	0.0402	0.171	0.2247	0.0616	0.261
$P(Y > Z)$	0.9913	0.9463	0.8255	0.6018	0.3197	0.4044	0.0227	0.096	0.2247	0.0616	0.261
AvSqRE											
$P(V > U)$	0.7152	0.6196	0.5205	0.4174	0.3114	58.59	6.231	26.44	49.72	10.70	45.40
$P(V > W)$	0.7945	0.6766	0.5382	0.4018	0.2671	58.59	6.231	26.44	39.09	17.91	75.99
$P(U > W)$	0.6563	0.5815	0.5149	0.4438	0.3569	49.72	10.70	45.40	39.09	17.91	75.99

TABLE 9.9 Bayesian Noninformative Prior Analysis for Data WD4 with 0 To 1.0 Tolerance

	$\gamma=0.0$	$\gamma=0.25$	$\gamma=0.5$	$\gamma=0.75$	$\gamma=1.0$	m_1	σ_{m_1}	σ_1	m_2	σ_{m_2}	σ_2
ARE											
$P(Y>X)$	0.6044	0.5544	0.5053	0.4546	0.3973	0.1713	0.0454	0.193	0.1516	0.037	0.1567
$P(Z>X)$	0.9999	0.9966	0.9591	0.7748	0.3929	0.4739	0.0695	0.295	0.1516	0.037	0.1567
$P(Z>Y)$	0.9995	0.9905	0.9302	0.7269	0.3787	0.4739	0.0695	0.295	0.1713	0.045	0.1926
AvSqRE											
$P(V>U)$	0.6693	0.5938	0.5076	0.4255	0.3497	12.70	5.386	22.85	9.112	3.564	15.12
$P(W>U)$	0.9992	0.9873	0.9169	0.7152	0.3761	60.44	14.12	59.91	9.112	3.564	15.12
$P(W>V)$	0.9973	0.9731	0.8853	0.6530	0.3559	60.44	14.12	59.91	12.70	5.386	22.85

TABLE 9.10 Bayesian Noninformative Prior Analysis for Data WD5 with 0 To 1.0 Tolerance

	$\gamma=0.0$	$\gamma=0.25$	$\gamma=0.5$	$\gamma=0.75$	$\gamma=1.0$	m_1	σ_{m_1}	σ_1	m_2	σ_{m_2}	σ_2
ARE											
$P(X>Y)$	0.7761	0.6599	0.5368	0.4044	0.2811	0.2913	0.1256	0.533	0.1679	0.0326	0.138
$P(Z>X)$	0.9983	0.9797	0.8985	0.6841	0.3604	0.7120	0.0223	0.095	0.2913	0.1256	0.533
$P(Z>Y)$	0.9999	0.9999	0.9999	0.9996	0.4712	0.7120	0.0223	0.095	0.1679	0.0326	0.138
AvSqRE											
$P(U>V)$	0.9674	0.8826	0.7246	0.5149	0.2719	16.93	4.695	19.92	4.953	2.828	12.0
$P(W>U)$	0.9729	0.8935	0.7435	0.5263	0.2783	74.44	24.92	105.73	16.93	4.695	19.92
$P(W>V)$	0.9919	0.9484	0.8299	0.6036	0.3165	74.44	24.92	105.73	4.953	2.828	12.0

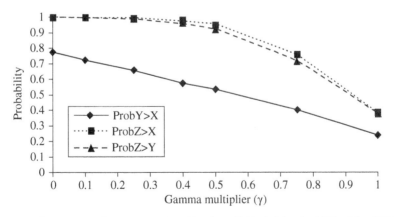

FIGURE 9.17 Noninformative probabilities from Table 9.6 for the ARE of data WD1.

9.3 DISCUSSIONS AND CONCLUSION

Tables 9.4 and 9.5 for (i.e., supported by simple arithmetic differences and two sample *t*-tests as well as bracketed Bayesian probabilities of one scoring how much better or worse than another with $\gamma=0$) are plotted in Figures 9.17 and 9.18 for WD1 only.

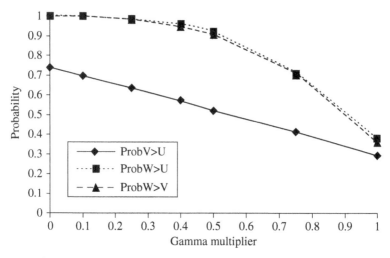

FIGURE 9.18   Noninformative probabilities from Table 9.6 for AvSqRE (or SRE) of WD1.

TABLE 9.11   Informative Prior Results of Comparing $P(Y>X)$ for the ARE in WD1 from Table 9.6[a]

$\tau^2 (0, C)$	$\gamma = 0.0$	$\gamma = 0.1$	$\gamma = 0.25$
$(0,\infty)$	0.79705	0.72499	0.66167
$(0, 0.001468)$	0.70375	0.68742	0.61351
$(0, 0.001101)$	0.69223	0.70382	0.59847
$(0, 0.000734)$	0.68632	0.67054	0.57585
$(0, 0.000367)$	0.64455	0.64581	0.56924

[a] $\tau^2 = (0, C = \infty) \Rightarrow$ Noninformative range where C is the constant for upper boundary of τ^2.

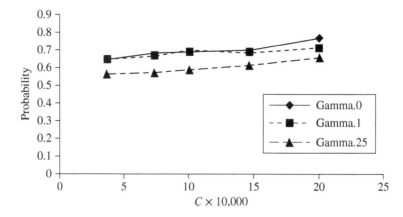

FIGURE 9.19   Informative probabilities from Table 9.11 for the ARE of WD1.

TABLE 9.12   Informative Prior Results of $P(V > U)$ for AvSqRE in WD1 from Table 9.6[a]

$\tau^2 (0, C)$	$\gamma = 0.0$	$\gamma = 0.1$	$\gamma = 0.25$
$(0,\infty)$	0.73861	0.69524	0.63301
$(0, 2.4)$	0.67962	0.66515	0.52232
$(0, 1.8)$	0.65597	0.64137	0.50739
$(0, 1.2)$	0.62332	0.60757	0.47465
$(0, 0.6)$	0.55602	0.59866	0.45853

[a] $\tau^2 = (0, C = \infty) \Rightarrow$ Noninformative range where C is the constant for upper boundary of τ^2.

Table 9.6 for WD1 in detail shows that as γ tolerance constant increases from $\gamma = 0$ or $b = 0$, which is purely the hypothesis of testing means such as $H_{01} : \mu_{ARE_i} = \mu_{ARE_j}, i \neq j$ to $\gamma = 1$ or $b = \overline{X}_2 - \overline{X}_1$, in the criterion equation (9.19), a competing method's predictive accuracy proving a worse (more difference) or better (less difference) in probability decreases in support of the t-tests given in Tables 9.4 and 9.5. With the increase of γ, the difference between the two sample means is decreased in the hypothesis setting. Thus, the probability that one mean is greater than the other is decreased consequently. Note that one can also conduct two sample t-tests of equality of means by indicating a tolerance or threshold in the null hypothesis as shown in the book software applets. Empirically from the examples studied, a noninformative Bayesian probability of exceeding 0.9 for ARE comparisons (note that lower probabilities recorded for SRE with the squared penalty) using criterion function (9.19) concurs strongly with the rejection of the equality of means at a significance of $\alpha = 0.05$.

For example, the Bayesian noninformative (or flat where anything goes with no restraint on the prior information of variance) probabilities of CPNLR predicting more accurately than CPMLE for ARE and SRE are 0.7797 and 0.7389, respectively, for the special case $\gamma = 0$ in Table 9.6 of WD1. Recall that this probability was not adequate to reject the equality of ARE. Further, Tables 9.11 and 9.12 clearly show that these probabilities fall to 0.65 and 0.56 for ARE and SRE, respectively, when upper boundary C for τ^2 is no more at infinity (anything goes) but restrained by reasonable values. A trend is illustrated in Figure 9.19 where $C \gg 0.002$ for ARE is too large already to call for noninformative approach in WD1. Similarly, $C \gg 2.4$ for SRE in Table 9.12 is too large, and hence we quickly approach infinity.

Therefore, the informative treatment of the problem may be only too productive in the case of borderline decisions because we are using more informative priors than none (or flat) in order to produce more secure results. Such as the cubicle of Table 9.4 presents for MO versus CPMLE in WD3 with an arithmetic difference of -0.18 and a t-test statistic of -2.74 and Bayesian noninformative comparative probability of 0.9913. If an informative approach were taken up here with restraints placed on the upper values of prior variance τ^2, then MO scoring better than CPMLE would be contested due to a lower (<0.9913) informative probability than that of flat prior. In such contested comparisons, it is useful to test using the SRE (average square penalty) in addition to ARE (average absolute penalty) as conducted in Table 9.5 resulting in the FTR: failure to reject (or acceptance) of the hypothesis of equality of SRE between MO and CPMLE from an earlier rejection. The Bayesian noninformative comparative probability of rejection went down to a weaker 0.7945 in Table 9.5 from an earlier 0.9913 in Table 9.4 while contrasting MO vs CPMLE for WD1. Note that stronger Bayesian comparative probabilities signal for rejection of equality of predictive accuracies between two competing models. This way of quantifying whether one method is better (lower ARE or SRE) or worse (higher ARE or SRE) than another is far more realistic than deciding deterministically that one method is better merely by comparing the ARE or SRE arithmetic values or deciding stochastically by performing statistical hypothesis tests of pairwise means, although an approach more realistic than simply comparing sample mean values [1, 10]. This way, one can place a measure of quantification on how much better or worse one method is in predictive accuracy than another. However, this quantification cannot be tested yet, so statistical hypothesis tests may then be used to assist decision makers to reject the equality of means or fail to reject. They usually will agree at last.

More in-depth study concerning informative priors is required. In this chapter, half-normal distribution is used for informative prior distribution of the means, ARE and SRE, to obtain Table 9.11 or 9.12. However, the formulation is beyond the scope of this chapter. This is because ARE and SRE are positive quantities whose ideal values peak around zero. Recall that an absolute penalty of deviation of prediction from the true value can be attributed to alpha testing (before the release of software) in the case of ARE. However, the more severe squared penalty deviation of prediction from the true value may well be attributed to beta testing (after the release of software) as errors are more dollar costly to redeem after software has been released to the end user. The impact of this methodology on software reliability measurement employing a variety of models is rather significant. It opens a new avenue for comparing and contrasting the predictive accuracy of competing methods ARE (due to absolute penalty) and SRE (due to squared penalty) in terms of how much better or worse they are rather than whether they are good or bad approaches through a qualitative comparison, as performed earlier [1, 10]. Newly proposed quantitative ways of comparisons are far superior to arithmetical comparisons of AREs performed conventionally by software analysts. Finally, with the rising number of software reliability estimation models, it is equally important to assess the predictive accuracy and forecast quality of these modeling techniques [1, 10, 22–24]. The material presented in this chapter is an attempt to quantify the probability of how much better one method's prediction ability is than another, rather than simply to qualify that one is superior to another. The statistical Bayesian technique proposed is superior scientifically to those that mention one competing method has less ARE or AvSqRE (= SRE) than another. In security testing, rather than an insufficient comparison of two prediction techniques being better or worse, how much better or worse quantitatively in probability tells us how much to invest for the less favorable method to reach the predictive quality of the more favorable having a numerical quality target in mind.

APPENDIX 9.A

TABLE 9.A.1 Grouped Failure Weekly Data Set: WD1

Week	No. of Failures	Cumul.	Week	No. of Failures	Cumul.	Week	No. of Failures	Cumul.
1	5	**5**	21	0	**43**	41	1	**80**
2	2	**7**	22	0	**43**	42	2	**82**
3	2	**9**	23	2	**45**	43	6	**88**
4	0	**9**	24	0	**45**	44	0	**88**
5	0	**9**	25	0	**45**	45	6	**94**
6	4	**13**	26	1	**46**	46	11	**105**
7	0	**13**	27	3	**49**	47	3	**108**
8	0	**13**	28	9	**58**	48	1	**109**
9	9	**22**	29	6	**64**	49	2	**111**
10	2	**24**	30	4	**68**	50	3	**114**
11	0	**24**	31	1	**69**	51	0	**114**
12	1	**25**	32	5	**74**	52	2	**116**
13	8	**33**	33	1	**75**	53	1	**117**
14	7	**40**	34	1	**76**	54	1	**118**
15	3	**43**	35	1	**77**	55	0	**118**
16	0	**43**	36	2	**79**	56	1	**119**
17	0	**43**	37	0	**79**	57	0	**119**
18	6	**125**	38	0	**125**	58	0	**129**
19	0	**125**	39	4	**129**	59	1	**130**
20	0	**125**	40	0	**129**	60	1	**131**

$n = 60$, sample mean = 2.18, sample standard deviation = 2.71, sample variance = 7.34, and sum = 131.

TABLE 9.A.2 Grouped Failure Weekly Data Set WD3

Week	No. of Failures	Cumul.	Week	No. of Failures	Cumul.	Week	No. of Failures	Cumul.
1	4	4	15	14	**161**	29	1	**321**
2	12	16	16	19	**180**	30	3	**324**
3	15	31	17	23	**203**	31	1	**325**
4	9	40	18	12	**215**	32	2	**327**
5	28	68	19	22	**237**	33	0	**327**
6	19	87	20	12	**249**	34	1	**328**
7	8	95	21	13	**262**	35	9	**337**
8	7	102	22	19	**281**	36	1	**338**
9	4	106	23	10	**291**	37	0	**338**
10	8	114	24	5	**296**	38	0	**338**
11	9	123	25	5	**301**	39	0	**338**
12	12	135	26	5	**306**	40	1	**339**
13	8	143	27	7	**313**	41	1	**340**
14	4	147	28	7	**320**			

$n = 41$, sample mean = 8.29, sample standard deviation = 7.16, sample variance = 51.26, and sum = 340.

TABLE 9.A.3   Grouped Failure Weekly Data Set WD5

Week	No. of Failures	Cumul.	Week	No. of Failures	Cumul.	Week	No. of Failures	Cumul.
1	3	**3**	18	11	**147**	35	10	**267**
2	1	**4**	19	8	**155**	36	4	**271**
3	4	**8**	20	12	**167**	37	5	**276**
4	4	**12**	21	2	**169**	38	7	**283**
5	11	**23**	22	6	**175**	39	9	**292**
6	11	**34**	23	4	**179**	40	7	**299**
7	18	**52**	24	5	**184**	41	6	**305**
8	8	**60**	25	5	**189**	42	4	**309**
9	6	**66**	26	7	**196**	43	11	**320**
10	10	**76**	27	5	**201**	44	3	**323**
11	16	**92**	28	7	**208**	45	7	**330**
12	6	**98**	29	1	**209**	46	9	**339**
13	13	**111**	30	11	**220**	47	8	**347**
14	16	**127**	31	4	**224**	48	5	**352**
15	3	**130**	32	4	**228**	49	7	**359**
16	4	**134**	33	20	**248**	50	7	**366**
17	2	**136**	34	9	**257**			

$n = 50$, sample mean = 7.32, sample standard deviation = 4.25, *sample* variance = 18.1 and sum = 366.

9.4   EXERCISES

9.4.1 Let us now consider Sahinoglu's CPMLE: Compound Poisson Maximum Likelihood Estimation, using Poisson^geometric (Poisson compounded by geometric) method to predict the no of remaining failures following a set of testing results, where X_{past} = failures experience in the past, t_{past}, where $t_{past} + t_{remaining} = t_{total}$, Y_{past} = at how many distinct stoppages up to X_{past}, β(Poisson parameter) = Y_{past}/t_{past}, r (geometric parameter) =

P28: Sahinoglu Poisson^Geometric Model

Xrem = Xtot - Xpast = (β/1-r)*Trem

Xtot' = Xpast + Xrem

e ≈ ((Xtot' - Xtot)/Xtot)*100

Xrem' = (β/1-r)*Trem + e

Exact Total Failures - Xtot :	131
Xpast :	92
Ypast :	26
Tpast :	42
Remaining Time - Trem :	18
Beta - β :	0.619048
Value - r :	0.717391
Remaining Failures without rel.error - Xrem :	39.428571
Estimated Total Failures - Xtot' :	131.43
Rel.Error(%) - e :	0.33
Remaining Failures with rel.error - Xrem' :	39.76

Clear   Compute   Close

$1 - Y_{past}/X_{past}$. Hence, $E[X(t_{rem})] = \beta / (1-r)t_{rem}$, or $X_{rem} = X_{tot} - X_{past} = \left\{ \dfrac{\beta}{1-r} \right\} t_{rem} + \varepsilon$.

Take $X_{past} = 92$, $Y_{past} = 26$, $t_{past} = 42$ (wk), $t_{rem} = 18$(wks); find β, r, X_{rem}, X_{tot}, and e. Repeat for $X_{past} = 74$, $Y_{past} = 17$, $t_{past} = 30$(wks), $t_{rem} = 30$(wks) for Sahinoglu failure-count prediction model. Solution Hint: Using Pedagogue P28:

9.4.2 Using the input data for WD1 in Table 9.2 by applying the straightforward analytical CPMLE method as in Equations (9.6)–(9.8), verify for the X_{tot} calculations for 20, 50, and 70%. You should get $X_{tot} = 125$, $X_{tot} = 148$ and $X_{tot} = 131.4$ using a hand calculator.

9.4.3 Do the same for WD1 as in Table 9.3 by applying the SPSS (Statistical Package) implementing the CPNLR technique, which follows the L–M algorithm, and use Equations (9.6) and (9.8). Stop at 50% of the observations and then estimate as follows:

1. Click on the SPSS windows version available for PCs.

2. Go to "files" and ask for the "50PER.SAV" input data file that contains input data up to and including 50% of the measurements as in Figure 9.11. If not available, prepare your own Figure 9.11.

3. Click on "Statistics" in the menu bar, and then click "Regression" and "Nonlinear." Stay in Figure 9.8.

4. Click on the nonlinear regression frame, and enter "XPAST" for the "Dependent" window.

5. For the "Model Expression" window, enter XTOT–(BETA/P)*TREM.

6. For "Nonlinear Regression: Parameters" window, enter the unknown initial values:

   Name: XTOT, Starting (initial) Value: 100, then click ADD.

   Name: BETA, Starting (initial) Value: 1, then click ADD.

   Name: P, Starting (initial) Value: 1, then click ADD. Now click CONTINUE.

7. For the Loss-Function submenu, choose "Sum of Squared Residuals" about L–M.

8. For the Constraints submenu, choose "Unconstrained."

9. Click OK to finalize the calculations and receive the convergence in Figure 9.9.

10. Read R-Square = 0.93(very good) and XTOT=132.23 with 95% upper and lower confidence estimates.

9.4.4 Repeat Exercise 9.4.2 for 70% cumulated data.

9.4.5 Download data WD2 from the website to do as in Exercises 9.4.2, 9.4.3, and 9.4.4.

9.4.6 Download data WD3 from the website (or Appendix) to do as in Exercise 9.4.5.

9.4.7 Download data WD4 from the website and do as in Exercise 9.4.6.

9.4.8 Download data WD5 from the website (or Appendix) to do as in Exercise 9.4.7.

9.4.9 Verify Tables 9.4 and 9.5 using the two sample t-test software in the website for **WD1**.

9.4.10 (Noninformative Bayes) Using Tables 9.6, 9.7, 9.8, 9.9, and 9.10, and FLAT program in the website as given in Figures 9.20 and 9.21 for WD1 to show as examples, verify Tables 9.6, 9.7, 9.8, 9.9, and 9.10 by using FLAT software. Note that there may be differences due to round-off errors.

9.4.11 Using any other competing software reliability prediction techniques, compare any pair of those methods by using the t-test and noninformative approaches as in Tables 9.4 and 9.5, provided that at least a sample of 15–18 predictive measurements are calculated.

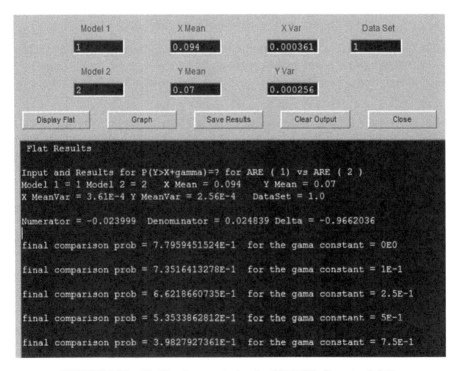

FIGURE 9.20 FLAT software solution for CPMLE in Exercise 9.4.10.

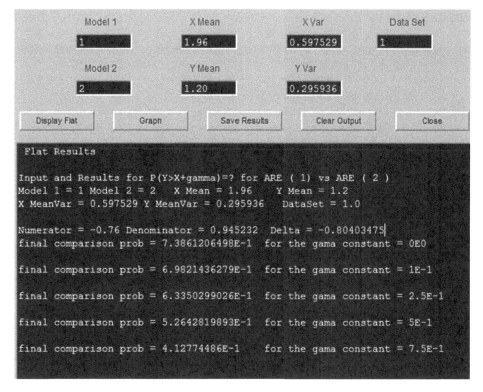

FIGURE 9.21 FLAT software solution for CPMLE Exercise 9.4.10.

9.4.12 In Tables 9.4 and 9.5, verify the $5 \times 3 = 15$ cubicles' contents in each, that is, difference, t-test and P value using (9.25–9.27) and by supporting by FLAT software for the metric: ARE (average absolute relative error) and SRE (squared error relative error). Use Tables 9.6, 9.7, 9.8, 9.9, and 9.10 input data to compare the prediction methods of CPMLE (by Sahinoglu), CPNLR (by Sahinoglu), and MO (by Musa–Okumoto). Use the two-sample t-test software from the menu. Note that $t = 0.97$, for example, is the t-test statistic to reject or accept the H_0:(null hypothesis of equality of the two means). Also, $\{.\} = \{0.024\}$, for example, is the arithmetic difference and $[.] = [0.779]$ is the FLAT software (to be used in this question) outcome probability of how much better the larger mean is scoring versus the smaller mean observing only tolerance γ (Gama) = 0.0.

9.4.13 Write a paragraph of 8–10 sentences discussing that why the FLAT software verified by (9.25–9.27) bring a new dimension to conventionally comparing the two prediction techniques pairwise by traditional t-tests for equality. Explain the contrasts and/or similarities between t-tests and FLAT Bayesian approach. Which one is more superior and why? How you justify your response at a security testing site?

REFERENCES

[1] Sahinoglu, M., Deely, J., Capar, S. (2001). Stochastic Bayesian measures to compare forecast accuracy of software reliability models, *IEEE Transactions on Reliability*, **50**, 92–97.

[2] Berger, J. O., Deely, J. (1988). A Bayesian approach to ranking and selection of related means and alternatives to AOV methodology, *JASA*, **83**, 364–373.

[3] Berger, J. O., *Statistical Decision Theory and Bayesian Analysis*, Springer, New York, 1985.

[4] Deely, J. J., Keats, J. B. (1994). Bayes stopping rules for reliability testing with the exponential distribution, *IEEE Transactions on Reliability*, **43**(2), 288–293.

[5] Deely, J. J., Smith, A. F. M. (1998). Quantitative refinements for comparisons of *Institutional Performance*, *Journal of Royal Statistical Society A*, **161**(1), 5–12.

[6] Deely, J. J., Zimmer, W. J. (1988). Choosing a quality supplier—a Bayesian approach, *in Bayesian Statistics 3*, *Oxford Press*, London, 585–592.

[7] Gelfand, A. E., Smith, A. F. M. (1992). Bayesian statistics without tears: A sampling-resampling perspective, *The American Statistician*, **46** (2), 84–88.

[8] Downs, T., Scott, A. (1992). Evaluating the performance of software-reliability models, *IEEE Transactions on Reliability*, **41**(4), 533–538.

[9] Abdel-Ghaly, A. A., Chan, P. Y., Littlewood, B. (1986). Evaluation of competing software reliability predictions, *IEEE Transactions on Software Engineering*, **2**(9), 950–967.

[10] Sahinoglu, M., *Trustworthy Computing: Analytical and Quantitative Engineering Evaluation*, John Wiley & Sons, Inc., Hoboken, 2007.

[11] Sahinoglu, M., Capar, S. (1997). Statistical Measures to Evaluate and Compare Predictive Quality of Software Reliability Estimation Methods, *Proceedings of the International Statistical Institute* (ISI'97), **IP-46**, 525–528, August 18–26, DIE Press (State Institute of Statistics, Ankara), Istanbul, Turkey.

[12] Romeu, J. L. (1997). Discussion of Invited Paper: Statistical Measures to Evaluate and Compare Predictive Quality of Software Reliability Estimation Methods, *Proceedings of the International Statistical Institute* (ISI'97), **IP-46**, 529–530. August 18–26, DIE Press (State Institute of Statistics, Ankara), Istanbul, Turkey.

[13] Kendall, M. G., Stuart, A., *The Advanced Theory of Statistics*, Vol. **2**, Hafner Pub., New York, 1961.

[14] Sahinoglu, M. (1992). Compound-Poisson Software Reliability Model. *IEEE Transactions on Software Engineering* **18** (7), 624–630.

[15] Sahinoglu, M., Can, U. (1997). Alternative parameter estimation methods for the compound poisson software reliability model with clustered failure data, *Software Testing, Verification and Reliability*, **7**(1), 35–57.

[16] Randolph, P., Sahinoglu, M. (1995). A stopping-rule for a compound Poisson random variable. *Applied Stochastic Models and Data Analysis*, **11**, 135–143.

[17] SPSS reference guide, SPSS Inc., Chicago, IL, 475–488, 1990.

[18] Draper, N. R., Smith, H., *Applied Regression Analysis*, John Wiley & Sons, New York, 1966.

[19] Bard, Y., *Nonlinear Parameter Estimation*, Academic Press, New York, 1974.

[20] More, J. J. (1977). The Levenberg-Marquardt Algorithm: Implementation & Theory, in *Numerical Analysis*, G. A. Watson (Ed.), Lecture Notes in Mathematics, vol. 630, pp. 105–116, Springer-Verlag, Berlin.

[21] Siefert, D. M., Stark, G. E. (1992). *Software Reliability Handbook: Achieving Reliable Software*, American Institute of Astronautics and Aeronautics, Reston.

[22] Sahinoglu, M. (2003). An empirical Bayesian stopping rule in testing and verification of behavioral models. *IEEE Transactions on Instrumentation and Measurement*, **52**, 1428–1443.

[23] Schneidewind, N. F. (1992). Method for validating software metrics, *IEEE-TSE*, **18**, 410–422.

[24] Zimmer, W. J. Deeply, J. J. (1996). A Bayesian ranking of survival distributions using accelerated or correlated data, *IEEE Transactions on Reliability*, **45**(3), 499–504.

10

PRACTICAL HANDS-ON LAB TOPICS IN CYBER-RISK

LEARNING OBJECTIVES

- Given a cybersystems lab, perform hardening procedures on Windows-based servers, switches, routers, and a wireless network.
- Given a series of emails, determine which are valid and which are spam/phishing emails, and utilizing tools and commands, determine the originating IP address.
- Utilize MS-DOS commands to perform or explore a Windows-based network.
- Identify and utilize various logging mechanisms to monitor a network and threats.
- Given a firewall, create access rules permitting or denying traffic based upon organizational requirements.

10.1 SYSTEM HARDENING

System hardening is a process in which *Every Device* on the network is locked down (hardened), where all services and protocols not necessary are denied or prohibited from running or accessing the network or device. Too many administrators ignore this step or only harden servers and firewalls and in due process ignore everything else. System hardening is required on servers, computers, mobile devices, routers, switches, and *Every Device* that touches the network. It is unacceptable when devices run on an operational network with default passwords and configurations. When patches and updates are not applied, the threat is amplified. Though this chapter focuses on Windows-based systems, the theory remains the same regardless of the operating system or setup.

10.1.1 General

1. Inventory: Without an accurate inventory of devices and operating systems, you are not aware of your system resources.
2. Create policies, checklists, and procedures.

Cyber-Risk Informatics: Engineering Evaluation with Data Science, First Edition. Mehmet Sahinoglu.
© 2016 John Wiley & Sons, Inc. Published 2016 by John Wiley & Sons, Inc.
Companion website: www.wiley.com/go/sahinoglu/informatics

3. Enable logging on all devices and off-load the logs to a central server(s) with access restricted to authorized personnel only.

4. Set a patching schedule and implement on a regular basis.

5. Enforce separation of duties/access to those who have a need to know.

6. Implement a change management policy and enforce it.

7. Follow RFC/FIPS/STIG/regulatory requirements (DNS, IIS, PCI, and HIPPA). This should go without saying although it always seems to be an afterthought.

8. Do not install unnecessary software/programs on servers/PCs.

9. Install an endpoint protection service, since antivirus only is not sufficient any more.

10. Install a vulnerability scanner or utilize a network-based vulnerability scanner.

11. Change default passwords and implement password controls such as complexity requirements, age, lockout durations, and unlock procedures.

12. Disable all accounts when someone leaves or is terminated.

10.1.2 Windows Servers

1. Use NTFS file system on Windows-based machines.

2. Change the default administrators account name. This should match the format of your standard network named accounts. Logs should be monitored to see if there are any attempts to logon with "Admin" or "Administrator," this should be a red flag.

3. Disable the guest account and change the default guest account name (see requirements in #2). Set a password that is very long and complex just in case the account is enabled again.

4. Remove all unnecessary file shares and place Access Control Lists (ACL) on those shares that are required.

5. Utilize dual-factor authentication for server administrators.

6. Create and display a "Logon Warning Banner." Though this may seem trivial, this becomes a major legal hurdle when prosecuting illegal activity. Consult with law enforcement or an attorney on proper wording and requirements.

7. Restrict domain administrator and power user accounts to those who require them. Far too many users have admin privileges because it is easier.

8. Turn off all unnecessary services and protocols and centralize uncommon or high-threat protocols. For example, FTP should be prohibited from a user PC and only authorized accounts established on a central FTP server (Fig. 10.1).

10.1.3 Wireless

1. Change the default service set identifier (SSID) and hide the SSID broadcast when feasible.

2. When manageable (small networks), utilize media access control (MAC) filtering.

3. Utilize an encryption protocol such as WPA2 (Wi-Fi Protected Access).

4. Manage wireless access point (WAP) and controllers through Secure Sockets Layer (SSL) or SSH. Ensure that HyperText Transmission Protocol (HTTP) and telnet are turned off.

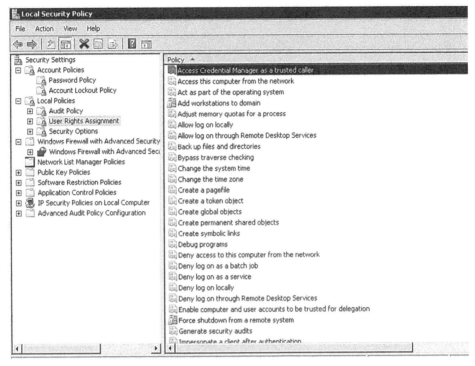

FIGURE 10.1 A screenshot of Windows Server Security Policy tabs.

5. Secure or harden mobile device and laptops when not attached to the network.

6. Minimize the Dynamic Host Configuration Protocol (DHCP) pool when feasible.

10.1.4 Firewalls, Routers, and Switches

1. Disable unsecure remote management access and implement secure remote administrative procedures and protocols.
   - Utilize Secure Shell (SSH) or HyperText Transmission Protocol Secure (HTTPS).
   - Create ACL by username and IP address where possible.
   - Restrict access to the "Enable Password" to those with a valid need to know.

2. Disable remote access for devices outside the firewall.

3. Shut down unused ports to prevent unauthorized devices from connecting to the network.

4. Physically secure firewalls, routers, and switches in locked cabinets or closets.

5. Block ICMP requests on the network, particularly on the boundary device.

6. Disable IP directed broadcasts on routers.

7. Create a logon and warning banner stating that access is restricted and that it is a secure device.

10.2 EMAIL SECURITY

Email continues to be a major security threat. This is for the following reasons:

1. Once past a filter, it relies on the human element (in author's opinion the weakest security link).
2. The cost to the malicious actor is minimal.
3. Very easy to target hundreds or thousands of individuals within an organization.
4. Repeated attempts can go unnoticed by administrators.

TrendMicro in their 2012 Advanced Persistent Threat (APT) Research Report called Spear Phishing the most favored of attacks to infiltrate targeted networks [1].

10.2.1 Identifying Fake Emails

In the following example, there are many indicators that this is a fake email; however, many of these go unnoticed by the typical user. This is why it is important for administrators to train users on phishing email detection. It is also imperative that organizations have a reporting mechanism for users to report suspected or known phishing emails. It is also critical for administrators to follow up on these emails to determine how they got through the filters and how to prevent further reoccurrence. It is also necessary to check and ensure that other users did not receive the phishing email and verify that they did not fall prey by getting tricked and clicked or responded to the email:

1. The email from the header is from paypall.com rather than paypal.com.
2. The URLs in the embedded emails are associated with the domain 01877hsvx7t-cyx1.com.
3. Improper sentence structure.
4. Requiring the user to login and submitting information.
5. Invalid case ID.
6. The IP address contained in the header is not associated with Paypal.com.

10.2.2 Emotion Responses

Phishing emails usually play upon a recipient's emotions in which the malicious attacker is trying to get an immediate response from the recipient. The most common emotional vectors are:

1. The threatening email attempts to force the recipient into acting to avoid huge penalties, jail time, or other undesirable consequence. Many threatening email scams appear to come from government agencies, law enforcement, or some type of court/legal action.
2. Fear is another emotion that can get people to respond quickly without thinking twice. This type of email invokes fear or helplessness into the recipient. The email usually plays upon a medical diagnosis or safety issue.
3. Another common email is one that promises a reward, usually monetary in nature but not always. They usually ask for help transferring large sums of money, unclaimed funds, lottery winnings, or free devices. This type of email plays upon an individual's greed.

FIGURE 10.2   A screenshot of spear phishing incidence.

4. After a major disaster or catastrophe, a huge spike of phishing emails appear asking for donations to assist the victims of the disaster. Another common technique is to ask assistance for a stranded traveler or crime victim. These types of emails appeal to an individual's compassion and pity.

5. A targeted email campaign is called spear phishing and is intended for a small group of individuals or even a single individual. These emails are usually crafted very convincingly and formatted in a way that would seem normal. These emails usually have attachments and contain subjects such as: "Here is the report that you requested!" (Fig. 10.2).

10.3   MS-DOS COMMANDS

Many organizations establish their network security utilizing what is called the "Raw Egg Security Principle." They protect the boundary very hard but implement little if any security on the inside. The downside to this hard perimeter defense strategy is that once a hacker infiltrates the boundary, they can move freely and advance undetected on the inside. When performing security assessments, system administrators far too often state that internal controls are not necessary because it is blocked on the boundary. However, upon scanning the boundary it is discovered that these so-called holes were open. The truth is defense in depth needs to play a role and the raw egg needs to become a hard-boiled egg.

The MS-DOS prompt is usually not locked down due to three reasons:

1. Administrators like to utilize these tools internally without the hassle of utilizing administrative privileges.
2. It is surprising how many administrators didn't realize the MS-DOS prompt exist or still available with the newer versions of Windows.
3. Administrators do not realize the security implications of leaving the MS-DOS prompt widely available for use.

The truth is, the MS-DOS prompt should be disabled to all standard users and only available to network administrators. In addition, commands for telnet, SSH, RDP, and so on should be blocked at the network boundary.

10.3.1 Mapping Intel

In the initial stages, a malicious actor wants to map or fingerprint the target network. This coincides with SANS' number one control in their Top 20 Security Controls, which is hardware inventory [2]. During the footprint process the malicious actor is trying to identify the following:

1. IP Address(es)
2. Host names
3. Operating systems
4. Patch state/known vulnerabilities
5. Applications/Programs

Once an actor has the above information, they have the information needed to plan their attack. Many of these parameters are easily gotten thru the MS-DOS command prompts.

The top 11 (in author's opinion) of the most dangerous MS-DOS commands are:

1. IPCONFIG/all/displaydns is a DOS command that shows the IP address (IPV4 and IPV6), default gateway, and MAC address for all adaptors. It also shows the default mask; since most networks utilize subnet masks to segregate similar network resources, this can be particularly useful to a malicious actor (Fig. 10.3).
2. NSLOOKUP & type=mx is a DOS command that shows the DNS records for a particular device. This can translate the IP address obtained with the IPCONFIG to the actual device name. NSLOOKUP can also be set to MX to display the IP address/name of a domains email server(s) (Fig. 10.4).

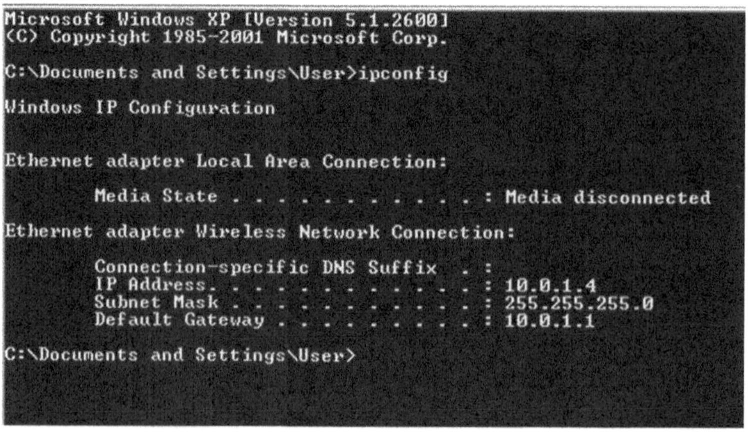

```
Microsoft Windows XP [Version 5.1.2600]
(C) Copyright 1985-2001 Microsoft Corp.

C:\Documents and Settings\User>ipconfig

Windows IP Configuration

Ethernet adapter Local Area Connection:

        Media State . . . . . . . . . . . : Media disconnected

Ethernet adapter Wireless Network Connection:

        Connection-specific DNS Suffix  . :
        IP Address. . . . . . . . . . . . : 10.0.1.4
        Subnet Mask . . . . . . . . . . . : 255.255.255.0
        Default Gateway . . . . . . . . . : 10.0.1.1

C:\Documents and Settings\User>
```

FIGURE 10.3   A screenshot of IPCONFIG command.

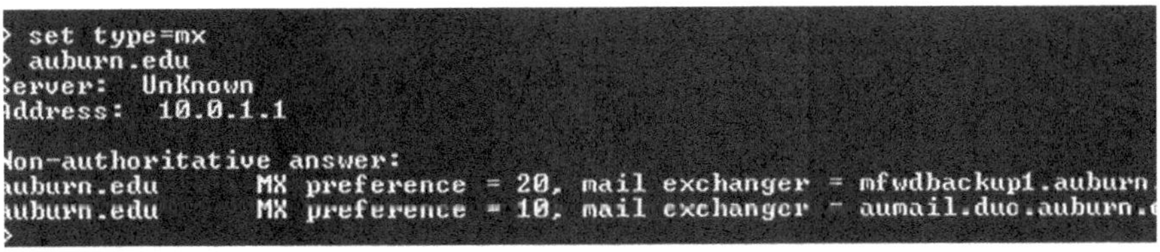

> set type=mx
> auburn.edu
Server: UnKnown
Address: 10.0.1.1

Non-authoritative answer:
auburn.edu   MX preference = 20, mail exchanger = mfwdbackup1.auburn
auburn.edu   MX preference = 10, mail exchanger = aumail.duc.auburn.
>

FIGURE 10.4   A screenshot of NSLOOKUP & type=mx DOS command.

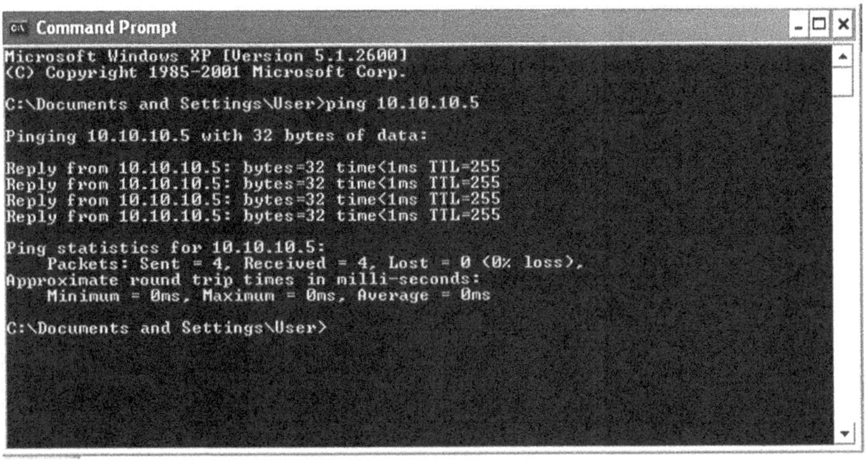

```
Command Prompt                                                          _ □ ×

Microsoft Windows XP [Version 5.1.2600]
(C) Copyright 1985-2001 Microsoft Corp.

C:\Documents and Settings\User>ping 10.10.10.5

Pinging 10.10.10.5 with 32 bytes of data:

Reply from 10.10.10.5: bytes=32 time<1ms TTL=255
Reply from 10.10.10.5: bytes=32 time<1ms TTL=255
Reply from 10.10.10.5: bytes=32 time<1ms TTL=255
Reply from 10.10.10.5: bytes=32 time<1ms TTL=255

Ping statistics for 10.10.10.5:
    Packets: Sent = 4, Received = 4, Lost = 0 (0% loss),
Approximate round trip times in milli-seconds:
    Minimum = 0ms, Maximum = 0ms, Average = 0ms

C:\Documents and Settings\User>
```

FIGURE 10.5   A screenshot of PING DOS command.

3. PING is a DOS command that when left open allows a malicious actor the ability to explore a device or network. Ping in itself may not seem dangerous; however, when utilized with other tools, a malicious actor can get a very accurate picture of the target network (Fig. 10.5).

4. TRACERT is a DOS command that performs a trace between two devices that displays "hops" or other known devices between the two target devices. TRACERT is significant to a malicious actor for two reasons: First, it shows devices that are between the actor and the target. It should be stated that not all devices may display during a TRACERT such as a transparent firewall. Second, it helps provide a picture or map of the target network possibly giving the malicious actor a means to bypass or work around devices so as to reach his or her malicious goal.

5. NETSTAT -a -b -r is a DOS command that displays target PCs open connections. This is also a great tool to explore a target network. If a network is using Communicator, Active Directory, etc., it also displays what browser (IExplorer, Firefox, etc.) the PC is using. The -a flag displays all open TCP/UDP open connections. The -b flag displays active applications listening and the -r flag displays the contents of the routing table (Fig. 10.6).

6. SYSTEMINFO is a DOS command that displays a plethora of information. It shows which hotfixes, and security updates have been applied, the domain name, BIOS version, and other pertinent data (Figs. 10.7 and 10.8).

```
C:\>netstat -b

Active Connections

  Proto   Local Address              Foreign Address            State          PID
  TCP     informaticslab:2727        50.31.164.186:https        ESTABLISHED    2036
  [iexplore.exe]

  TCP     informaticslab:2734        a23-4-43-27.deploy.static.akamaitechnologies.c
:http  ESTABLISHED    2908
  [firefox.exe]

  TCP     informaticslab:2736        l1.ycs.vip.dcb.yahoo.com:https  ESTABLISHED
2908
  [firefox.exe]
```

FIGURE 10.6   A screenshot of NETSTAT -a -b -r DOS command.

```
Interface List
0x1 ............................ MS TCP Loopback interface
0x2 ...00 21 70 74 44 96 ...... Broadcom NetXtreme 57xx Gigabit Controller - P
ket Scheduler Miniport
0x3 ...00 16 44 f7 50 02 ...... Dell Wireless 1395 WLAN Mini-Card - Packet Sche
uler Miniport
=============================================================================
=============================================================================
Active Routes:
Network Destination        Netmask          Gateway       Interface  Metric
          0.0.0.0          0.0.0.0          10.0.1.1       10.0.1.4      25
         10.0.1.0    255.255.255.0          10.0.1.4       10.0.1.4      25
         10.0.1.4  255.255.255.255          127.0.0.1      127.0.0.1     25
    10.255.255.255  255.255.255.255          10.0.1.4       10.0.1.4      25
        127.0.0.0        255.0.0.0          127.0.0.1      127.0.0.1      1
        224.0.0.0        240.0.0.0          10.0.1.4       10.0.1.4      25
  255.255.255.255  255.255.255.255          10.0.1.4          2           1
  255.255.255.255  255.255.255.255          10.0.1.4       10.0.1.4       1
Default Gateway:          10.0.1.1
=============================================================================
Persistent Routes:
  None
```

FIGURE 10.7   A screenshot of Interface List.

```
C:\>systeminfo

Host Name:                   INFORMATICSLAB
OS Name:                     Microsoft Windows XP Professional
OS Version:                  5.1.2600 Service Pack 3 Build 2600
OS Manufacturer:             Microsoft Corporation
OS Configuration:            Standalone Workstation
OS Build Type:               Multiprocessor Free
Registered Owner:            Registered User
Registered Organization:     Auburn University at Montgomery
Product ID:                  76487-640-7045946-23993
Original Install Date:       9/27/2013, 3:58:57 PM
System Up Time:              6 Days, 12 Hours, 7 Minutes, 12 Seconds
System Manufacturer:         Dell Inc.
System Model:                Latitude D830
System type:                 X86-based PC
Processor(s):                1 Processor(s) Installed.
                             [01]: x86 Family 6 Model 15 Stepping 13 GenuineIntel
~777 Mhz
BIOS Version:                DELL    - 27d80514
Windows Directory:           C:\WINDOWS
System Directory:            C:\WINDOWS\system32
Boot Device:                 \Device\HarddiskVolume1
System Locale:               en-us;English (United States)
Input Locale:                en-us;English (United States)
```

FIGURE 10.8   A screenshot of SYSTEMINFO DOS command.

7. GPRESULT is a DOS command that displays Group Policy on the machine. It also displays the security groups on the machine.

8. TASKLIST is a DOS command that displays the tasks and applications running on the target machine.

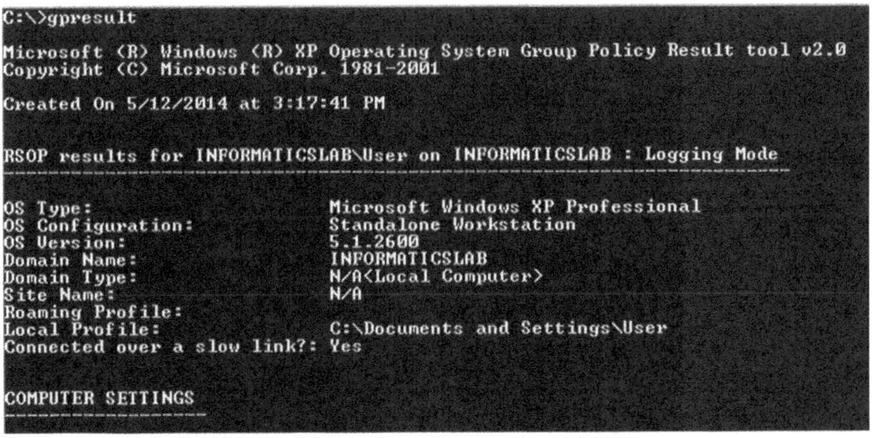

```
C:\>gpresult

Microsoft (R) Windows (R) XP Operating System Group Policy Result tool v2.0
Copyright (C) Microsoft Corp. 1981-2001

Created On 5/12/2014 at 3:17:41 PM


RSOP results for INFORMATICSLAB\User on INFORMATICSLAB : Logging Mode


OS Type:                        Microsoft Windows XP Professional
OS Configuration:               Standalone Workstation
OS Version:                     5.1.2600
Domain Name:                    INFORMATICSLAB
Domain Type:                    N/A<Local Computer>
Site Name:                      N/A
Roaming Profile:
Local Profile:                  C:\Documents and Settings\User
Connected over a slow link?:    Yes


COMPUTER SETTINGS
```

FIGURE 10.9   A screenshot of GPRESULT DOS command.

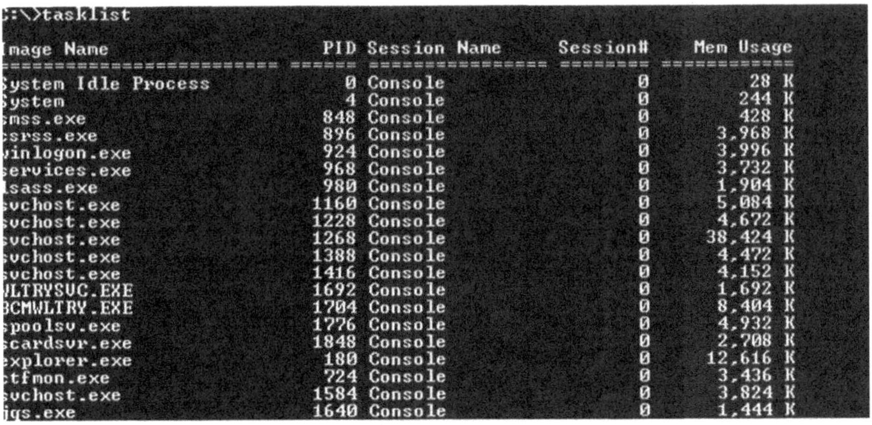

```
C:\>tasklist

Image Name                    PID Session Name      Session#     Mem Usage
========================= ======= ================ ========== ============
System Idle Process             0 Console                   0          28 K
System                          4 Console                   0         244 K
smss.exe                      848 Console                   0         428 K
csrss.exe                     896 Console                   0       3,968 K
winlogon.exe                  924 Console                   0       3,996 K
services.exe                  968 Console                   0       3,732 K
lsass.exe                     980 Console                   0       1,904 K
svchost.exe                  1160 Console                   0       5,084 K
svchost.exe                  1228 Console                   0       4,672 K
svchost.exe                  1268 Console                   0      38,424 K
svchost.exe                  1388 Console                   0       4,472 K
svchost.exe                  1416 Console                   0       4,152 K
ULTRYSUC.EXE                 1692 Console                   0       1,692 K
BCMWLTRY.EXE                 1704 Console                   0       8,404 K
spoolsv.exe                  1776 Console                   0       4,932 K
scardsvr.exe                 1848 Console                   0       2,708 K
explorer.exe                  180 Console                   0      12,616 K
tfmon.exe                     724 Console                   0       3,436 K
svchost.exe                  1584 Console                   0       3,824 K
igs.exe                      1640 Console                   0       1,444 K
```

FIGURE 10.10   A screenshot of TASKLIST DOS command.

9. TASKKILL is a DOS command in which the actor can kill a process on the target machine thus causing a denial of service attack (Figs. 10.9, 10.10, and 10.11).

10. TYPE is a DOS command that allows a malicious actor to read text files on a computer. What makes this significant is that many individuals copy and paste significant data to Notepad and forget to delete it thus allowing a malicious actor to read the files and possibly to read sensitive data. In particular many system administrators copy system configurations such as routers and switches to Notepad as a backup copy and store them on systems. Once found, a malicious actor now has complete configuration lists (Fig. 10.12).

11. NETSH allows a malicious actor to turn particular systems functionality on or off. According to Microsoft [3] you can use the Netsh.exe tool to perform the following tasks:
   • Configure interfaces
   • Configure routing protocols

```
C:\>
C:\>
C:\>taskkill /pid 3844
SUCCESS: The process with PID 3844 has been terminated.
C:\>
```

FIGURE 10.11   A screenshot of TASKKILL DOS command.

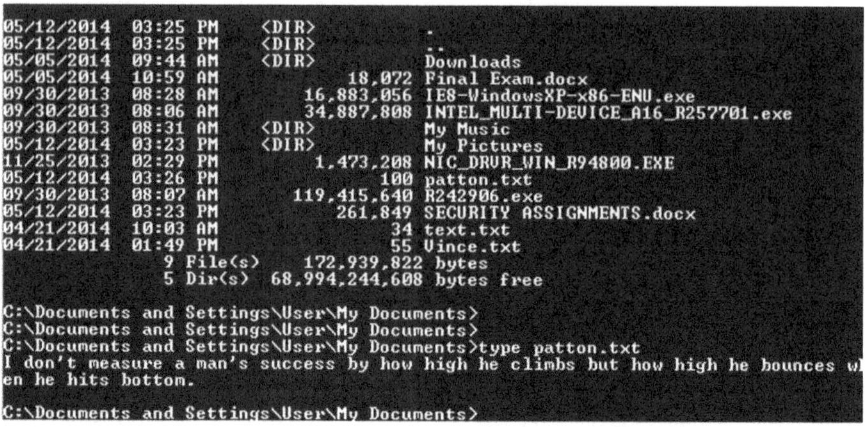

```
05/12/2014  03:25 PM    <DIR>          .
05/12/2014  03:25 PM    <DIR>          ..
05/05/2014  09:44 AM    <DIR>          Downloads
05/05/2014  10:59 AM            18,072 Final Exam.docx
09/30/2013  08:28 AM        16,883,056 IE8-WindowsXP-x86-ENU.exe
09/30/2013  08:06 AM        34,887,808 INTEL_MULTI-DEVICE_A16_R257701.exe
09/30/2013  08:31 AM    <DIR>          My Music
05/12/2014  03:23 PM    <DIR>          My Pictures
11/25/2013  02:29 PM         1,473,208 NIC_DRVR_WIN_R94800.EXE
05/12/2014  03:26 PM               100 patton.txt
09/30/2013  08:07 AM       119,415,640 R242906.exe
05/12/2014  03:23 PM           261,849 SECURITY ASSIGNMENTS.docx
04/21/2014  10:03 AM                34 text.txt
04/21/2014  01:49 PM                55 Vince.txt
               9 File(s)    172,939,822 bytes
               5 Dir(s)  68,994,244,608 bytes free

C:\Documents and Settings\User\My Documents>
C:\Documents and Settings\User\My Documents>
C:\Documents and Settings\User\My Documents>type patton.txt
I don't measure a man's success by how high he climbs but how high he bounces wh
en he hits bottom.

C:\Documents and Settings\User\My Documents>
```

FIGURE 10.12   A screenshot of TYPE DOS command.

- Configure filters
- Configure routes
- Configure remote access behavior for Windows-based remote access routers that are running the Routing and Remote Access Server (RRAS) Service
  - Display the configuration of a currently running router on any computer
  - Use the scripting feature to run a collection of commands in batch mode against a specified router

In the above illustration, the NETSH command was utilized to get the RAS IP configuration (Fig. 10.13).

10.4   LOGGING

Logging has been already mentioned, despite casually throughout this chapter. Now let us take an in-depth look into logging and the benefits it offers to network security. Logging is often overlooked and underrated by system administrators. Granted at times, logs can get overwhelming and daunting; however, logs provide insight into what is happening on your network and devices. One important fact about logs should be mentioned here and, that is, the right time and the right place.

For log correlation and to properly track down network events, system times need to be accurate. Therefore, it is absolutely critical that network devices update their time regularly and from the same time source.

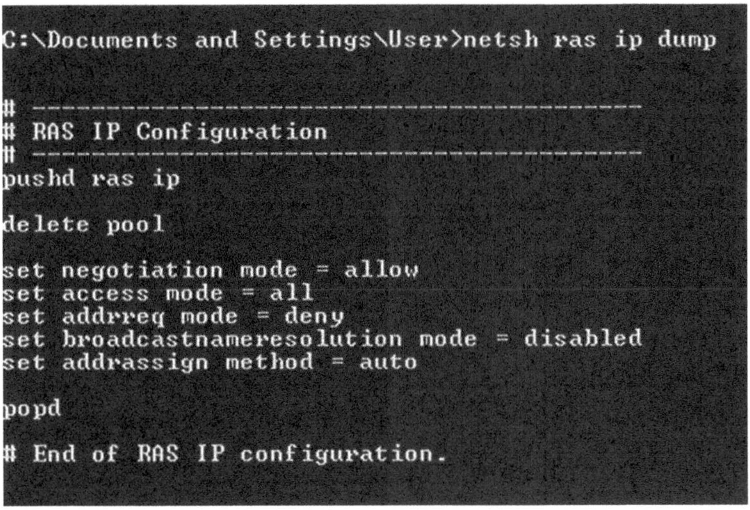

```
C:\Documents and Settings\User>netsh ras ip dump

#  ------------------------------------------------------------
#  RAS IP Configuration
#  ------------------------------------------------------------
pushd ras ip

delete pool

set negotiation mode = allow
set access mode = all
set addrreq mode = deny
set broadcastnameresolution mode = disabled
set addrassign method = auto

popd

# End of RAS IP configuration.
```

FIGURE 10.13   A screenshot of NETSH DOS command.

10.4.1   Policy

Logging policies need to include the following:

1. Identify—There are three parts to the "Identify" requirement: (i) Identify the devices and the types of logs they provide. (ii) Identify the types of logs that require support such as Windows Event Logs, syslogs, etc. (iii) Identify regulatory and policy requirements such as HIPPA, PCI, HR Policies, etc. The "Identify" questions above need to be answered prior to any logging policy or system established. If the network consists of a "hodgepodge" of different supported equipment, the logging system may become complex.

2. Review—Establish who can review log data. Review requirements may need to include individuals outside of the IT department, such as compliance officers, project managers, etc. If there is a possibility of legal action or law enforcement investigations, a "chain of custody" may be required. Reviewing log data is critical to network security and health.

3. Access—Determine who requires access to the logs (locally and centralized) and determine what is their purpose. Establish procedures to prevent alteration and deletion of the logs and ensure that all log access is logged. Creating a centralized server (sometimes more than one maybe required) where all devices off-load their logs. Access to the central servers can be restricted and reports can be generated and given to reviewers, thus restricting access further.

4. Investigations (Policy and Law Enforcement)—Policies need to state specifically who can initiate an investigation, notification, and how it is conducted. Policy violations may need different procedures than law enforcement investigation. Work with local law enforcement to establish procedures and safeguards, and create policies that conform to local, state, and federal laws. It is too late to comply once an investigation has started.

5. Retention—Retention policy needs to include local logs and centralized logs. If logs are to be backed up, the policy needs to include how and where the backups stored. Do not forget to establish and who can access and restore the backups.

10.4.2 Understanding Logs

There are no log standards per se and thus there are many different log formats. Each log type may also include different information, date formats, etc. It is very important for administrators to become familiar with the various log types contained within their network and to properly read and understand them.

Many systems are Syslog compatible and utilize the Syslog Daemon to off-load the logs to a centralized server. Syslog is the closest to a standard log; however, there are no requirements for vendors to utilize a particular format. Syslog uses a severity system to classify entries to assist administrators. The priorities are 0: emergency; 1: alert; 2: critical; 3: error; 4: warning; 5: notice; 6: information; and 7: debug.

The first example is a log excerpt from a Fortigate 800F Firewall. The log is neat and easily readable to what actions took place (Fig. 10.14).

The next two examples are logs from a Windows XP machine. The first log contains an overview of the log. If the administrator double clicks on an entry, then a more detailed window pops up (Fig. 10.15).

This next log is a more detailed look into a Microsoft Windows Event ID with a description of the event provided (Fig. 10.16).

#	Date	Time	Level	User Interface	Action	Message
1	2014-05-12	14:44:12	information	GUI(10.10.10.6)	login	User admin login successfully from GUI(10.10.10.6)
2	2014-05-12	11:29:22	notice	GUI(10.10.10.6)		User admin deleted a firewall policy from GUI(10.10.10.6)
3	2014-05-12	11:29:14	notice	GUI(10.10.10.6)		User admin deleted a firewall policy from GUI(10.10.10.6)
4	2014-05-12	11:29:05	notice	GUI(10.10.10.6)		User admin changed a firewall policy from GUI(10.10.10.6)
5	2014-05-12	11:28:43	notice	GUI(10.10.10.6)		User admin changed a firewall policy from GUI(10.10.10.6)
6	2014-05-12	11:28:00	notice	GUI(10.10.10.6)		User admin changed the setting of an interface from GUI(10.10.10.6)
7	2014-05-12	11:27:10	notice	GUI(10.10.10.6)		User admin added a new static routing entry from GUI(10.10.10.6)
8	2014-05-12	11:26:56	information	console	logout	User admin Logs out from console
9	2014-05-12	11:23:47	information	GUI(10.10.10.6)	login	User admin login successfully from GUI(10.10.10.6)
10	2014-05-12	11:21:50	information	console	login	User admin login accepted from console

FIGURE 10.14   A screenshot of Fortigate 800F Firewall.

Type	Date	Time	Source	Category	Event	User
Information	5/27/2014	8:38:45 AM	Tcpip	None	4201	N/A
Information	5/27/2014	8:38:30 AM	Tcpip	None	4201	N/A
Information	5/27/2014	8:34:37 AM	Windows Update Agent	Installation	19	N/A
Error	5/27/2014	8:33:08 AM	W32Time	None	29	N/A
Error	5/27/2014	8:33:08 AM	W32Time	None	17	N/A
Information	5/27/2014	8:32:50 AM	Tcpip	None	4201	N/A
Information	5/27/2014	8:32:40 AM	Tcpip	None	4202	N/A
Information	5/27/2014	8:32:40 AM	Service Control Manager	None	7036	N/A
Error	5/27/2014	8:32:35 AM	Dhcp	None	1000	N/A
Warning	5/27/2014	8:32:35 AM	Dhcp	None	1003	N/A
Information	5/19/2014	3:04:53 PM	Tcpip	None	4201	N/A
Information	5/19/2014	3:04:48 PM	Tcpip	None	4202	N/A
Information	5/19/2014	3:04:48 PM	Service Control Manager	None	7036	N/A
Information	5/19/2014	3:03:09 PM	Tcpip	None	4201	N/A

FIGURE 10.15   A screenshot of logs from a Windows XP machine.

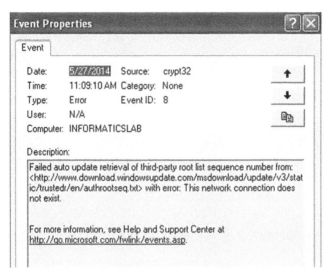

FIGURE 10.16 A screenshot of Microsoft Windows Event ID.

10.5 FIREWALL

Firewalls provide security by allowing or denying traffic based on a set of rules. Organizations typically place firewalls on the network perimeter. However, in theory firewalls should be placed throughout the network to provide the hardened security discussed at the beginning of the chapter. There are many types and flavors of firewalls, and the included features are endless. Many firewalls may include intrusion prevention detection prevention modules, provide VPN services, network address translations (NAT) or port address translations (PAT), etc. However, for our purpose we are going to strictly work with the typical firewall rule sets.

Many firewalls have a default rule of "Any More Secure" to a "Less Secure" to be automatically permitted. This is typically not a good practice, and administrators need to limit traffic that goes out of a network just as much as traffic that comes into a network. This has added benefits such as data loss prevention, and bot and spambot mitigation. There are two main types of firewalls; traditional and next generation.

Firewall administrators must have extensive "maintenance" knowledge of ports (services), NAT, PAT, and how communications work in general such as the "three-way handshake." Without a thorough compression of these topics, a firewall technician may in fact block required network traffic causing a costly denial of service or permit unnecessary traffic potentially opening a network to unwanted risk.

10.5.1 Traditional Firewalls

Traditional firewalls operate on layer 3 and 4 of the OSI model. The OSI or Open Systems Interconnection model is a conceptual model that characterizes and standardizes the internal functions of a communication system by partitioning it into seven abstraction layers. Administrators can allow and deny access based upon the IP address and the port number (services) required. Though some argue that traditional firewalls in today's

FortiGate 800F
WEB CONFIG

System
Firewall
  Policy
  Address
  Service
  Schedule
  Protection Profile
User
VPN
IPS
Anti-Virus
Web Filter
Spam Filter
Log&Report

Policy

Create New

ID	Source	Dest	Schedule	Service	Action
▼ external -> server (2)					
5	all	Monty	always	PING	DENY
1	all	Monty	always	ANY	ACCEPT
▼ external -> Server2 (12)					
14	all	Monty	always	HTTP	ACCEPT
18	all	Monty	always	FTP	DENY
20	all	Monty	always	SMTP	DENY
22	partner1	Monty	always	TELNET	ACCEPT
23	all	Monty	always	TELNET	DENY
33	bpartner1	Monty	always	bgroup	DENY
34	bpartner2	Monty	always	bgroup	ACCEPT
35	bpartner3	Monty	always	bgroup	DENY
36	bpartner4	Monty	always	FTP	ACCEPT
37	bpartner3	Monty	always	FTP	DENY
39	all	Monty	always	PING	ACCEPT
16	all	Monty	always	HTTPS	ACCEPT

FIGURE 10.17   A screenshot of Next-Generation Firewalls (NGF).

landscape are obsolete, this book maintains that they still have their uses and provide essential security especially when a large organization requires multiple firewalls and cannot afford the more costly "Next-Generation Firewalls" (NGF).

10.5.2 NGFs

NGFs not only operate on the layer 3 and layer 4 of the OSI model but operate all the way to layer 7. NGFs provide a much deeper packet inspection and thus can allow and deny traffic with much more granularity. For example, NGFs can inspect an HTTP request and allow a GET but deny a POST. This is far greater capability than a traditional firewall. However, this capability comes at a far greater price tag (Fig. 10.17).

10.5.3 Host-Based Firewalls

Host-based or built-in firewalls such as Windows Firewall are a critical component to network and PC security. Network-based firewalls are not a substitute for a PC-based firewall. Many endpoint protection systems offer a firewall that is more granular and better suited for security than the local built-in firewall. Just like a network firewall, host-based firewalls need to be properly configured. Very seldom is the default firewall setting adequate. Located in the Exceptions Tab in the Windows Firewall is the list of standard exceptions. Unless specifically required all options should be unchecked.

The security logging and ICMP settings are located in the Advanced Tab, and administrators should configure both to meet network requirements (Figs. 10.18 and 10.19).

10.6 WIRELESS NETWORKS

There are two primary types of wireless networks. Most users are familiar with their home wireless network, which usually consists of a wireless router. In this configuration, users typically utilize a WEP key to connect to the wireless network. Any management of the wireless network must be done on the wireless router itself. Typically enterprises

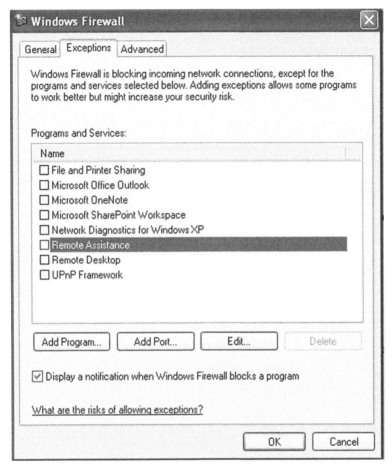

FIGURE 10.18 A screenshot of host-based Firewalls.

utilize WAPs that are controlled via a wireless controller. This allows an administrator to control multiple wireless points via a single console, even if the WAPs are remotely located. Typically wireless access is granted via Active Directory or radius or some other enterprise credential service.

Wireless networks have several advantages over traditional wired networks. These advantages include mobility, flexibility, and costs. However, wireless networks also have their own unique vulnerabilities and security concerns.

Mobility and flexibility are the two greatest advantages of wireless networks. Instead of being locked down where the "cable goes," users can now locate anywhere, wherever a wireless signal can be reached. This allows a business to grow, shrink, and renovate upon demand without the hassle of relocating wires.

Another advantage to wireless is costs. Wireless systems typically cost less than having to run wires to all workstations, installing additional switches, etc.

Wireless systems however come with their own unique security concerns. Typically wireless systems are less secure than wired systems. One main reason is that wireless

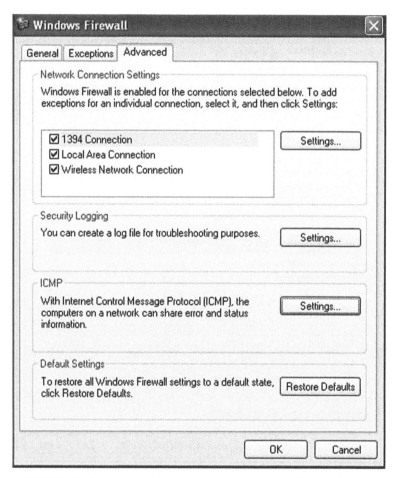

FIGURE 10.19   A screenshot of the Windows Advanced Firewall Settings.

footprint can extend beyond the physical control of the facility. "War driving" is one threat takes advantage of this overextended footprint. Malicious actors can sit in a parking lot, in a coffee shop across the street, or any other inconspicuous location and perform active attacks on the targeted network. If proper encryption is not utilized, the malicious actors can intercept and read all data across the wireless network.

Another attack is the installation of a rogue access point or router. In this scenario an attacker installs the WAP or router on the network behind the firewall and thus giving them access to the network from a safe distance, for example, an automobile in the parking lot. Many enterprise solutions scan for rogue WAPs and alert administrators when one is detected. However, if there are no detection mechanisms in place, this attack can be very successful.

A third attack is installing a WAP with the same or similar SSID and creating an "Evil Twin." In this scenario, an attacker tries to lure unsuspecting employees by connecting to the bogus WAP in hopes of capturing credentials or other sensitive information.

A fourth attack is a simple "denial of service" attack. By creating interference of the wireless signal, an attacker can cause the network to "shutdown," thereby preventing the organization from fulfilling its day to day transactions.

10.7   DISCUSSIONS AND CONCLUSION

Far too often, some students may find it difficult to apply academically gained knowledge to real-world mitigation techniques or understand how the threat factor really works. The objective of this final chapter of the textbook titled "Cyber-Risk Informatics" is to provide the student with challenging real-world scenarios in a hands-on lab environment to identify, mitigate, and monitor a system/network and so much more beyond the fundamentals he or she has digested in so far as the topic commands. Hands-on lab practice is a must-have addition for students to understand the concepts of today's threats and thus to train them in mitigating the dangers facing information security and system-based vulnerabilities. This chapter poses the questions and answers them: What is it to really patch a system? How to identify and mitigate vulnerabilities? How to monitor a network for threats? What is a firewall beyond turning the firewall on within the Windows Control Panel?

Though this chapter is relatively short, it goes beyond the pages and explores the intricacies of network security. That is, the lab environment can be daunting to many students, especially when a student has not touched any equipment beyond their personal PC. Overall the goal is to give the student an understanding of what it really means to secure a network and mitigate the insecure environment inherent under the conditions encountered.

A few comments about the "Penetration Awareness" are worth spending. A PC or server connected to the Internet on the average is attacked every 5 min [4]. A penetration test is the best way to tell what services are in fact executing on your system. Normally you prefer to test a system on the Internet and attempt to break in or at least get accesses to services running on the system from a malicious attacker's perspective. Akin to, but somewhat short of penetration testing, is vulnerability testing, where you normally run a software program that contains the database of known vulnerabilities versus your system to identify weaknesses. Two of the most popular vulnerability scanners are www.nessus.org/nessus and http://nmap.org. To facilitate an even further understanding of the threats and mitigation strategies, the author recommends that discussions and real-world exercises should be incorporated into the program. See Figures 10.A.1, 10.A.2, and 10.A.3.

This can be partially accomplished by visiting the following sites for current events, threats, and news related to cyber-security:

SANS Internet Storm Center: https://isc.sans.edu

Homeland Security News Wire: http://www.homelandsecuritynewswire.com/topics/cybersecurity

National Vulnerability Database: http://web.nvd.nist.gov/ncas/alerts

US Computer Emergency Readiness Team: http://www.us-cert.gov

APPENDIX 10.A

FIGURE 10.A.1   AUM CSIS 6952 Cybersecurity Seminar Internship graduating class students (Spring 2014) in the AUM Cyber Security Lab (www.aum.edu/csis).

FIGURE 10.A.2   AUM CySecLab main rack composed of switch, router, firewalls, KVM, and servers in order.

10.8 EXERCISES

10.8.1 System Hardening

1 Perform the following on a network-based router:
   (A) Shutdown telnet and implement SSH remote management access.
   (B) Create standard IP access control list 1350 and implement the following:
   - Permit class A 2.x.x.x
   - Permit class A 5.x.x.x
   - Permit class A 74.x.x.x
   - Deny class B 74.10.x.x
   - Deny Class C 5.6.7.x

2 Perform the following on a switch:
   (A) Shutdown unused ports.
   (B) Enable logging and forward to central server.

3 Perform the following on a firewall:
   (A) Restrict management access to management VLAN/Port with a secure protocol.
   (B) Block ICMP on the outside interface to prevent ICMP from the Internet.

4 Perform the following on a Windows Server:
   (A) Account management
   - Set complex passwords for the Guest Account.
   - Set complex password for the Administrator Account.
   - Disable the Guest Account.
   - Rename the Administrator Account.
   - Set password lockout threshold.
   - Set password expiration policy.
   (B) Set Access Control List only allowing domain admins remote access.
   (C) Enable IIS services and disable all other non-IIS-related services.
   (D) Create and display a "Warning Banner."

5 Configure the following on the labs wireless controller:
   (A) Set the DHCP pool to 15 IP addresses.
   (B) Set encryption to WPA2.
   (C) Change the SSID to Lab and hide the SSID.
   (D) Set management interface to HTTPS or SSH and turn off telnet and http access.
   (E) Set the time to a central time source.

10.8.2 Email

1 What is the IP address of the domain FBI.org?

2 What county is FBI.org hosted in?

3 Provide a sample phishing email and have the student provide the following:

(A) Provide the originating IP address from the header.

(B) Provide the domain, IP address, and country of origin of the embedded URL.

(C) Describe in detail three "red flags" that identify the email as phishing.

(D) Provide a training plan to teach users on how to identify and to report phishing emails.

(E) Describe what they believe is the most effective type of phishing email (have the student back up their findings with facts):

- The email that threatens the recipient with action.
- The email that utilizes fear in the recipient.
- The email that plays upon the recipient's greed.
- The email that plays upon compassion and pity.
- The spear phishing email.

10.8.3 MS-DOS

1 With minimal programs opened, perform a NETSTAT -b command

(A) Open a webpage to Yahoo and perform another NETSTAT -b.

(B) Describe the differences between the two results.

2 Using Notepad, create a text file and name it homework. Copy and paste the bullets below that contain famous quotes from General George S. Patton [5] into the text file. Afterward read the file thru the MS-DOS prompt and provide a screenshot.

(A) I do not measure a man's success by how high he climbs but how high he bounces when he hits the bottom.

(B) If everyone is thinking alike, then somebody isn't thinking.

3 Display the task list thru task manager and thru MS-DOS command prompt; compare the two and discuss any differences.

4 Using MS-DOS command(s) display the following (screenshot your results):

(A) NIC cards in use

(B) Operating system

(C) Updates/service packs

(D) System manufacturer/model/type

(E) Domain

(F) Open connections

(G) System IP address

(H) The next device beyond the gateway

(I) The web browser(s) installed on the system

5 Perform an IPConfig command and provide screenshot.

6 How many "hops" does it take to get from your computer (network) to Yahoo.com?

7 What is the primary IP address for the domain aum.edu?

8 What is the exchange server IP address for the domain aum.edu?

9 Within the command prompt, display group policy and screenshot the results.

10.8.4 Logging

1 In depth, explain three advantages for having central logging services such as syslog?

2 In depth, explain three disadvantages to centralized syslogs?

3 Explain three vulnerabilities to syslogs and methods to eliminate and reduce those vulnerabilities.

4 As the CISO of a corporation, develop a logging policy that includes local host logs and central logs for your organization. The policy should include retention requirements, access, review, policy investigations, and law enforcement investigations. Justify each requirement in depth to ensure that the Board of Directors and the CEO will approve of the policy.

10.8.5 Firewall

Configure the lab firewall to the following requirements. The following is provided:

PIPA is where the instructor provides the students with a valid public IP address.

The DMZ network utilizes the 172.10.10.0/24 network and contains the following services for the general public to access:

- Email
- DNS
- FTP
- HTTP
- HTTPS

The Business Partner network (WAN) utilizes the 172.20.20.0/24 network and contains the following services. This network supports three business partners:

- All three have access to the WAN email server.
- All three have access to an HTTPS application contained in the WAN network.
- One partner has access to secure FTP in the WAN network.

The private network utilizes the 10.100.0.0/16 network and only allows the following services thru the firewall:

- The 192.168.1.0/24 network is reserved for employee VPN services and is permitted from the outside.

TABLE 10.1   Tabulation for Exercise 10.8.5

DMZ Network

SOURCE	Ext to DMZ DESTINATION	SERVICE	ACTION
Any	172.10.10.50	DNS	Permit
Any	172.10.10.25	SMTP	Permit
Any	172.10.10.10	FTP	Permit
Any	172.10.10.0/24	HTTP	Permit
Any	172.10.10.0/24	HTTPS	Permit
Any	172.10.10.0/24	Any	Deny
	DMZ to Ext		
172.10.10.50	Any	DNS	Permit
172.10.10.25	Any	SMTP	permit
172.10.10.10	Any	FTP	Permit
172.10.10.0/24	Any	HTTP	Permit
172.10.10.0/24	Any	HTTPS	Permit
172.10.10.0/24	Any	Any	Deny

Business Partner Network

SOURCE	EXT to PARTNER DESTINATION	SERVICE	ACTION
PIPA	172.20.20.25	SMTP	Permit
PIPA	172.20.20.25	SMTP	Permit
PIPA	172.20.20.25	SMTP	Permit
PIPA	172.20.20.10	FTPS	Permit
PIPA	172.20.20.100	HTTPS	Permit
PIPA	172.20.20.100	HTTPS	Permit
PIPA	172.20.20.100	HTTPS	Permit
any	172.20.20.0/24	Any	Deny

SOURCE	Partner to Ext DESTINATION	SERVICE	ACTION
172.20.20.25	PIPA	SMTP	Permit
172.20.20.25	PIPA	SMTP	Permit
172.20.20.25	PIPA	SMTP	Permit
172.20.20.10	PIPA	FTPS	Permit
172.20.20.100	PIPA	HTTPS	Permit
172.20.20.100	PIPA	HTTPS	Permit
172.20.20.100	PIPA	HTTPS	Permit
172.20.20.0/24	Any	Any	Deny

Private Network

SOURCE	Ext to private DESTINATION	SERVICE	ACTION
192.168.1.0/24	10.100.100.0/24	Any	Permit
Any	Any	Any	Deny

SOURCE	Private to Ext DESTINATION	SERVICE	ACTION
10.100.50.0/24	172.20.20.0/24	Any	deny
10.100.50.0/24	Any	Any	Permit
10.100.100.0/24	Any	Any	Permit
Any	Any	Any	Deny

- General users on the private network utilize the 10.100.50.0/24 network.
- Users that interact with the business partners utilize the 10.100.100.0/24 network and require access to the WAN (Table 10.1).

10.8.6 Wireless

1 Using an available wireless network such as the local campus perform the following:

(A) Identify the wireless footprint.

(B) Provide solutions to reduce the footprint to cover only "authorized areas."

(C) Identify physical security vulnerabilities in which an attacker could "war drive" or place "evil twin" access points.

(Answers will vary depending on the network used and the students' findings.)

2 Configure a wireless router with the following settings:

(A) SSID: INFOSEC

(B) Encryption: WPA2

(C) WEP: S3ku!tyL@bT3$t

(D) DNS Pool: 192.168.1.xxx

10.8.7 Comprehensive Exercises

Email Security

****

From: Stephanie Carpers [mailto:carper983@mail.aol.com]

Sent: Thursday, May 4, 2014 8:31 AM

Subject: Notice of Failed Logon Attempts

We at RMB support have discovered that multiple failed logon attempts with your account. The IP addresses associated with these attempts do not match an IP range normally associated with RMB associates. As part of our security procedures, please login to your account by clicking on the link below and verify all account information to ensure that it remains secure. We shall continuously keep you informed of these changes to any account attempts.

http://logon.rmbsupport.net

Sincerely,

RMB Support

1. Identify five suspicious items with the email above that identify it as fake.

2. Write the command(s) (command line) to find the MX Records for rmbsupport.net.

3. List two security measures to minimize/prevent spambots from generating traffic on your network.

4. If your exchange server's IP address is 10.50.50.10 and your network is 10.0.0.0/8, write a firewall matrix chart that blocks all outbound emails from the network except from the exchange server.

Firewall Security

Write a firewall matrix chart that performs the following (must demonstrate knowledge of port numbers within the chart):

Assume the following: Private network is 10.0.0.0/8

DMZ network is 172.17.1.0/24

Users' subnet is 10.10.100.0./24

Inbound Rules (Outside Interface)

(A) Permit web traffic to 172.17.1.20 and to 172.17.1.21

(B) Permit secure web traffic to 172.17.1.25 and to 172.17.1.26

(C) Block all web and secure web traffic to other IP address

(D) Permit FTP to 172.17.1.30

(E) Deny FTP to all other IP address

(F) Permit DNS traffic to 172.17.1.50

(G) Deny DNS traffic to all other IP addresses

(H) Permit email traffic to 172.17.1.60

(I) Deny email traffic to all other IP addresses

(J) Deny all inbound SSH

Outbound Rules (Inside Interface)

(A) Permit users to browse all web and secure web

(B) Permit outbound FTP traffic from 10.10.30.1 to 172.17.1.30

(C) Deny all other FTP traffic

(D) Permit DNS traffic from 10.10.50.1 to 172.17.1.50

(E) Deny all other outbound DNS

(F) Permit email from 10.10.60.1 to 172.17.1.60

(G) Deny all other email traffic

(H) Permit SSH traffic from 10.10.80.1 to 172.17.1.0/24

(I) Block all other outbound SSH traffic

Outbound Rules (DMZ Interface)

(A) Permit DNS traffic 172.17.1. 50 to 10.10.50.1

(B) Deny all other DNS traffic

(C) Permit email traffic from 172.17.1.60 to 10.10.60.1

(D) Deny all email traffic to 10.0.0.0/8

(E) Permit all email traffic outbound

(F) Permit FTP traffic from 172.17.1.30 to 10.10.30.1

(G) Deny all FTP traffic to 10.0.0.0/8

(H) Permit all other FTP traffic

(I) Block all outbound SSH traffic

Command Line

1. Explain in detail the purpose of the following command lines:

(A) IPCONFIG

(B) NETSTAT -b

(C) System Info

(D) NSLOOKUP

(E) TYPE

(F) TASKLIST

(G) TASKKILL

(H) TRACERT

(I) GPRESULT

System Hardening

1. In a Windows system, when would it be appropriate to have the "Windows" firewall turned off?

2. Describe two actions that should be done to secure the built-in administrator account.

3. Describe two actions that should be done to secure a wireless network.

4. Describe in detail the top five ways from 1 to 5 to secure a Windows web server (justify your answers).

5. Instruction Lab: (See Fig. 10.A.3)

(A) Identify the components in the instruction rack in the Appendix from top to toe.

(B) How many servers, firewalls and KVM, and routers are there? What is each component's function?

10.8.8 Cryptology Projects

1 Write a Java program to implement password-based cryptography, covering the following aspects, such as encryption schemes and message authentication schemes. This cryptographic technique should be based on passwords, such as password-based key entity authentication. Encrypt and decrypt a document (for example, any MS Word doc), that is, saved on desktop or flash drive, using a password. For encryption and decryption processes, the same key/password can be used.

Hints to follow:

(A) From the main dialogue box, as shown in the following figure, the user should be able to select either encrypt or decrypt (Fig. 10.20).

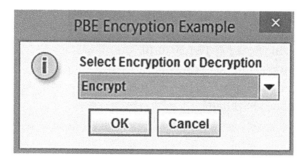

FIGURE 10.20   Exercise 10.8.8: Project algorithmic step 1.

FIGURE 10.21   Exercise 10.8.8: Project algorithmic step 2.

(B) Now, the user should be allowed to select a document from either desktop or flash drive.

(C) Once document is selected, the user should be able to encrypt it with a password (Fig. 10.21).

(D) The encrypted document should be decrypted again by following the same steps (from A to C), but now decrypt should be selected from main dialogue and same password should be entered to decrypt that particular document.

2   Write a Java program to serve as a "digital signature." You can write two programs. One program is to generate the signature, and another is to verify the same signature.

In the Generate program, you should generate the keys like private key and digital signature key. Also you can use the document with authorizing people's original signature to generate keys. Using the private key will generate the digital signature for the document. Finally, the program will export the public key and the signature to any file. The program will create separate functions to generate the public and the private Key and get a signature object to initialize it for signing and saving the signature and public key in the same file, as well as functioning to join above-mentioned function.

Hint 1: You can use private key for generating signature key. In the verification program you can use the signature and public key from the receiver's document file. The program will import the public key from the receiver's document and verify the authenticity of the signature. Use those two keys for the same purpose. To verify the

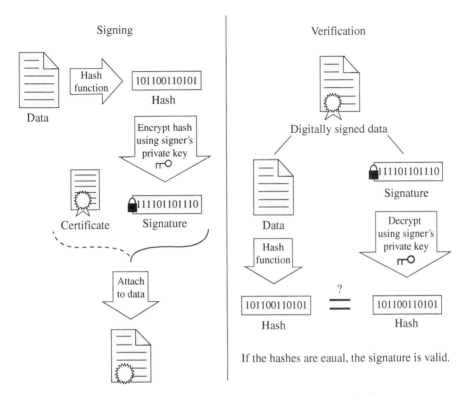

FIGURE 10.22 Exercise 10.8.8: Algorithm signing and verification steps.

signature, the program needs the data, the signature, and the public key associated with the private key used to sign the data.

Hint 2: The program includes function to input and convert the encoded public key bytes, input the signature bytes, and verify the signature. Here, you can use symmetric cryptography concept, and keys are created using RSA algorithm (Fig. 10.22).

REFERENCES

[1] Trend Micro Research Paper 2012, Spear-Phishing Email: Most Favored APT Attack Bait, TrendLabs[SM] APT Research Team, http://www.trendmicro.com/cloud-content/us/pdfs/security-intelligence/white-papers/wp-spear-phishing-email-most-favored-apt-attack-bait.pdf (accessed on September 12, 2015).

[2] Sans Institute—SANS Review SIEM—Critical Security Controls (2014). http://www.sans.org/critical-security-controls (accessed on September 12, 2015).

[3] Microsoft (2010) How to Use the Netsh.Exe" tool and Command-Line Switches. http://support.microsoft.com/?kbid=242468 (accessed on September 12, 2015).

[4] Whitman, M. E., Mattord, H. J., Schackleford, D. M., *Hands-On Information Security Lab Manual*, Thompson Course Technology, Boston, MA, 2006.

[5] Patton, S.http://www.brainyquote.com/quotes/authors/g/george_s_patton.html (accessed on September 12, 2015).

WHAT THE CYBER-RISK INFORMATICS TEXTBOOK AND THE AUTHOR ARE ABOUT?

This book contains innovative information in the area of quantitative risk assessment that simply does not appear in other books that may display none other than scant touches of metrics. Since the topics covered are relatively new, there is much originality in this vivid and dynamic text. Many of the seemingly perpendicular chapters however are intertwined horizontally with conceptually interfacing bridges and represent cutting-edge research whose applications are currently being developed. There are many advanced areas discussed, requiring more than a hand calculator, such as Java software as in most college programs. The programming aspect should rather be regarded a strength to capture many new emerging concepts. Therefore, the book provides an author-facilitated web access to implement these ideas. The author believes in a well-rounded theoretical and applied cybersecurity curriculum, in the brink of the global *cyberwars*, *as* the fastest-growing strategic area with much new advancement. This text utilizes a data analytical approach rather than heuristical and ad hoc approach that many current authors may employ through individual case studies solely without positive scientific modeling. This creative text fills a significant void in current books by providing "one-stop mall" with "neighboring-related shops" when evaluating strengths and weaknesses for risk assessment and management. The book offers practical ways toward quantitative evaluation with class-room- and internship-tested methods and proven hands-on lab practices. The following concepts are vital for theoreticians and practitioners.

1. METRICS, STATISTICAL QUALITY CONTROL, AND BASIC RELIABILITY IN CYBER-RISK
2. COMPLEX NETWORK RELIABILITY EVALUATION AND ESTIMATION IN CYBER-RISK

Cyber-Risk Informatics: Engineering Evaluation with Data Science, First Edition. Mehmet Sahinoglu.
© 2016 John Wiley & Sons, Inc. Published 2016 by John Wiley & Sons, Inc.
Companion website: www.wiley.com/go/sahinoglu/informatics

3. STOPPING RULES FOR RELIABILITY AND SECURITY TESTS IN CYBER-RISK
4. SECURITY ASSESSMENT AND MANAGEMENT IN CYBER-RISK
5. GAME-THEORETIC COMPUTING IN CYBER-RISK
6. MODELING AND SIMULATION IN CYBER-RISK
7. CLOUD COMPUTING IN CYBER-RISK
8. SOFTWARE RELIABILITY MODELING AND METRICS IN CYBER-RISK
9. METRICS FOR SOFTWARE RELIABILITY FAILURE-COUNT MODELS IN CYBER-RISK
10. PRACTICAL HANDS-ON LAB TOPICS IN CYBER-RISK

Dr. M. Sahinoglu, a tenured Professor of ECE since 1990 and Professor Emeritus from Turkey since 2000, is the founder of the Informatics Institute (2009) and its SACS-accredited (2010) and NSA-certified (2013) flagship Cybersystems and Information Security (CSIS) graduate program (the first such full degree in-class program in Southeastern United States) at AUM, Auburn University's metropolitan campus in Montgomery, Alabama. He is formerly the founder Dean of Arts and Sciences, Head of the Department of Applied Statistics at DEU/Izmir (1992–1997), the visiting Fulbright and NATO Scholar at Purdue University (1989–1990, 1997–1998) and Case Western Reserve University (1998–1999), and the Eminent Scholar and Chair-Professor of the Troy University Montgomery campus (1999–2008). Dr. Sahinoglu has a BSEE from METU/Ankara (1973), MSEE from the University of Manchester (1975), and Ph.D. in ECE and Statistics from Texas A&M University (1981). Dr. Sahinoglu taught at Texas A&M University (1978–1981), METU/Ankara (1976–1992) and DEU/Izmir (1992–1997), Purdue University (1998–1999, 1997–1998), CWRU (1998–1999), Troy University at Montgomery (1999–2008), and AUM (2008–). He is a recipient of Microsoft's global Trustworthy Computing Curriculum award (2006), a fellow member of SDPS Society since 2002, a senior member of IEEE since 1993, and an elected member of ISI since 1995; Dr. Sahinoglu's journal articles titled "Network Reliability Evaluation" and "CLOUD Computing" appearing in Wiley's WIREs stayed atop as the most accessed for three consecutive years in 2010 and 2011–2012, respectively. Dr. Sahinoglu published *Trustworthy Computing* by Wiley & Sons in 2007. He has authored around 170 peer-reviewed articles and managed over 20 grants. He is a polyglott and a former simultaneous interpreter and has authored four memoirs-based social style books: *Wrist-Fight of the Giants: Japan & USA* (1992); *Made in China/Made in Japan* (1993); *Dreaming America* (2004), all three in Turkish; and recently *Raindrops on My Life's Umbrella* (2016) in English. He has been invited by Turkish TV in the 1990s and 2000s and by NPR locally on educational topics since 1999. He is married since 1983 and has three boys.

INDEX

Cyber-Risk Informatics: Engineering Evaluation with Data Science, First Edition. Mehmet Sahinoglu.
© 2016 John Wiley & Sons, Inc. Published 2016 by John Wiley & Sons, Inc.
Companion website: www.wiley.com/go/sahinoglu/informatics